The Family Experience
A Reader in Cultural Diversity

Second Edition

*Edited, and with
Introductions by*

Mark Hutter
Rowan College of New Jersey

Allyn and Bacon
Boston • London • Toronto • Sydney • Tokyo • Singapore

Editor in Chief: *Karen Hanson*
Editorial Assistant: *Jennifer Jacobson*
Marketing Manager: *Joyce Nilsen*
Editorial Production Service: *Chestnut Hill Enterprises, Inc.*
Composition Buyer: *Linda Cox*
Manufacturing Buyer: *Megan Cochran*
Cover Administrator: *Suzanne Harbison*

Copyright © 1997 by Allyn & Bacon
A Viacom Company
Needham Heights, MA 02194

Library of Congress Cataloging-in-Publication Data
The family experience: a reader in cultural diversity / edited, and
   with introductions by Mark Hutter. — 2nd ed.
      p. cm.
   Includes bibliographical references and index.
   ISBN 0-205-19532-6
    1. Family—United States—Cross-cultural studies.   2. Sex—United
States—Cross-cultural studies.   3. Intergenerational relations—
United States—Cross-cultural studies.   4. Problem families—United
States—Cross-cultural studies.   I. Hutter, Mark, (date)   .
HQ536.F3655   1996
306.85—dc20   96-3286
                                                     CIP

Printed in the United States of America

10 9 8 7 6 5 4 3 2 1   01 00 99 98 97 96

To the memory
of my parents

Contents

Preface

In the first edition of this book, I referred to the great debate in higher education regarding the nature and quality of the college curriculum and what, if any, place "outsiders"—women, people of color, and ethnic groups—should have in it. This debate continues. In many ways it is a continuation of the major redirection of historical study that began about thirty years ago. The "new social history" stressed day-to-day experiences of ordinary people. It sensitized us to the importance of studying women, the poor, working people, and racial and ethnic minorities in order to have a better understanding of our past. No longer would history be restricted to the study of great men and of epochal events that emphasized the powerful and neglected the rest of us.

For the last fifteen years, colleges and universities have become concerned with the integration of issues regarding gender, race, class, and ethnicity. Often the resolution of this concern tries to achieve a balance between the traditional core curriculum, which emphasized white, male-dominated Western culture, and the more recent diversified curriculum that reflects global concerns, the study of non-Western cultures, and the inclusion of women, minorities, and persons of color.

Sociology formally recognizes the importance of internationalizing the curriculum and integrating issues of gender, race, class, and ethnicity. What sociology has actually attained, however, is the "ghettoization" of that curriculum. In terms of internationalization, sociology has developed separate and distinct courses under the general rubric "Comparative Sociology"; more specifically courses with such titles as "Sociology of the Middle East," or "Sociology of India." Regarding gender, race, class, and ethnicity, we often find separate and distinct courses with such titles as Gender Roles, Sociology of Women, Ethnic Studies, and African-American Studies. For the introductory sociology course, a welcome change has been the recent introduction of a number of books and course syllabi reflecting this new sensitivity for curriculum integration. However, for most first- and second-year sociology courses, including the sociology of the family, they continue to devote their attention to what often proves to be white middle-class concerns. When cross-cultural materials are introduced into institutional courses such as the family, they are often perceived as upper-level courses.

The undergraduate sociology of the family course has begun to incorporate a greater awareness of gender. Matters of ethnicity, race, and class are now being given greater recognition, but for the most part, they are separated from the curriculum and are either not discussed or relegated to peripheral study topics. The result is that a major characteristic of the American family—its class and cultural diversity—is omitted from discussion.

The second edition of this anthology continues to provide the student with materials integrating gender, class, race, and ethnicity into the introductory sociology of the family curriculum. In this edition, fourteen readings are new, reflecting current concerns that include family and community involvements, kinship interaction patterns, teenage pregnancy, homeless families, family violence, generational relationships, and gender roles and economic matters. Many of the readings reflect a social-policy orientation to looking at family continuity and change. Taken together, this book reveals both historical trends and unique variations that widen our understanding of the diversity of the family. The readings inform and increase understanding of the patterns and dynamics of the American family.

The selected readings reflect my continued concern for materials that get at the "guts" of the family experience. They are biased toward an ethnographic, qualitative orientation. A conscious attempt has been made to avoid using articles that are overly quantitative and "number crunching." The goal is to provide the reader with scholarly materials that are interesting and free of unnecessary jargon.

The organizational structure follows the standard format of sociology of family courses. Each part of the book contains an introductory essay that outlines major issues and concerns. For each reading, a brief overview is provided to orient the reader and highlight its sociological significance. The goal is an anthology that can be used with or without an accompanying textbook in sociology of the family courses.

Acknowledgments

Rowan College of New Jersey (formerly Glassboro State College) and its students, faculty, and administration have fostered the viewpoint expressed in this book. Since the publication of the first edition, I have had the wonderful opportunity to participate in National Endowment of the Humanities programs at the University of Virginia; University of North Carolina, Chapel Hill; and in Moscow, Russia. The respective directors, Olivier Zunz, Townsend Ludington, Joy Kasson, John Kasson, and William Brumfield and James Curtis, and fellow participants broadened my appreciation of interdisciplinary study. Through the National Endowment of the Humanities and through professional involvements in a number of associations including the Society for the Study of Symbolic Interaction; Alpha Kappa Delta, the International Sociology Honors Society; and the National Collegiate Honors Council, I have been able to extend my understanding of curriculum matters and pedagogical concerns. I am most grateful.

The sociology editor at Allyn and Bacon, Karen Hanson, and the entire Allyn and Bacon production staff provided the support necessary to ensure the completion of this project. Much thanks is expressed to the reviewers, who include Judy Aulette, University of North Carolina; Carol Chenault, Calhoun Community College; and Kristi L. Hoffman, Virginia Polytechnic Institute and State University.

The authors and publishers of these articles are thankfully acknowledged for granting permission to reprint their work. My wife, Lorraine, and my children, Daniel and Elizabeth, continue to provide an emotional and intellectual haven and I am most appreciative. My parents and my parents-in-law have taught me to value and understand the immigrant family experience, and by so doing, have enriched my life.

Mark Hutter

General Introduction

The average man—or woman—of fifty years or more ago had the greatest respect for the institution called the family, and wished to learn nothing about it. According to the Victorian ideology, all husbands and wives lived together in perfect amity; all children loved the parents to whom they were indebted for the gift of life; and if these things were not true, they should be, and even if one knew that these things were not true, he ought not to mention it. Everything that concerned the life of men and women and their children was shrouded, like a dark deed, from the light.

Today all that is changed. Gone is the concealment of the way in which life begins, gone the irrational sanctity of the home. The pathos which once protected the family from discussion clings to it no more. Now we do not want to be ignorant about the family; we want to learn as much about it as we can and to understand it as completely as possible. We are engaged in the process of reconstructing our family institutions through criticism and discussion (Waller 1938, p. 13).

Willard Waller was one of the most prominent American family sociologists of the mid-twentieth century. These words, written more than fifty years ago in his seminal work, *The Family: A Dynamic Interpretation,* are reflective of his gadfly status in American sociology. His contemporaries did not agree with his critical—some would say scathing—look at the middle-class American family. Most had a much more sanguine view of the American family system that reflected their own middle-class biases. They saw harmony and concord, not tension and discord. Their perspective was shared by the popular media, which typified the American family as exclusively Caucasian, affluent, and residing in suburban and rural areas in peaceful harmony.

Indeed, American sociology was so uncritical of the family that it failed to foresee the revolution that swept across the United States beginning in the early 1960s and continues to the present. Social protest movements called for equality and civil rights for all those "forgotten" in affluent America. These movements, led by "outsiders"—people of color, ethnic groups, feminists, and gays—ushered in a wave of new thought in the study of the family that stressed the diversity of the American experience. These outsiders led American sociology to at last follow the call made by Willard Waller to engage "in the process of reconstructing our family institutions through criticism and discussion."

1

New conceptual frameworks allowed us to "see" family phenomena formerly hidden from view. We began to understand patterns and dynamics of family violence that we once did not even know existed. Further, new family structures—including dual-career families, single-parent families, and families reconstituted by divorce and remarriage—increases in the rates of desertion and divorce, teenage pregnancy, abortion, singlehood, voluntary child-lessness, and the feminization of poverty underwent sociological scrutiny and analysis.

The nature of marriage, family, and kinship systems in American society has under-gone a new examination. Conventional assumptions about the necessity of maintaining kin-ship relations and the role of the nuclear family in today's world are being questioned: What are the proper gender roles for women and men? Is parenthood an inevitable and desirable consequence of maturation? A new, more permissive sexual morality led to the re-examination of previously held beliefs and attitudes regarding premarital and extramarital sexual relations, out-of-wedlock pregnancies, and abortions.

Family structures have fluctuated considerably in the last thirty years. More couples than ever before have voluntarily chosen to have fewer children. Many have voluntarily chosen childlessness. Still others have reconsidered that decision and opted to have chil-dren in later years. Divorce rates that were accelerating in the 1970s have leveled off and stabilized but remain at a higher rate than ever before in U.S. history.

New family patterns have emerged. That cohabitation has, for many, become an Amer-ican way of life comments not only on premarital or nonmarital relationships but has impli-cation for marital relationships as well. For those who eventually marry, the full implication of cohabitation as a facilitator for, or a hindrance to, marital adjustment and happiness is still unknown. Singlehood is accepted by many. Media discussion of the "marriage squeeze" raises questions on whether singlehood is a voluntary permanent option, or a state caused principally by the relatively low number of eligible men for "career" women. Regardless, singlehood involves a different series of life commitments than marriage and family.

Women have been particularly affected by and have affected family life. The number of single-parent families headed by women has been steadily growing. Much of this increase was caused by the rising divorce rate, but another major factor was the rising ille-gitimacy rate, especially among poor teenage females. These trends have led to the femini-zation of poverty. Women's labor force participation has been constantly rising in the last fifty years. Further, a significant number of working wives have children, especially young children. Because mothers are generally the primary caretakers, women have had to juggle their career aspirations and family responsibilities. This has led to the demand for increased day-care facilities and to talk of a "mommy-track" career ladder depending on the ages of children and the husband's occupational and familial career patterns.

The legitimacy of abortion has become the crystallizing issue in reaction to changes in family behavior. Passions ignite over the issue. A polarization has developed between "pro-choice" and "pro-life" advocates that has as its fundamental basis the nature of family val-ues and individual options. Homosexuality is yet another area that has become a debating ground for issues regarding changes in the family. The debate on the acceptability of homo-sexuality as a legitimate alternative family lifestyle has been exacerbated by the deadly dis-ease AIDS. Fear of AIDS has been used to incite the expression of homophobia and the rejection of gay rights.

The controversy surrounding sexuality, marriage, and the family has entered the world of politics and public policy more than ever before. Laws regarding abortion and homosexuality are continually argued, challenged, and changed. Laws regarding illegitimacy, and regulations regarding welfare for single-parent households, are being written, argued, rewritten, and reargued. Politics continues to intrude on the government's responsibility to provide public support for child-care facilities. Arguments and counterarguments continue on this issue between traditionalists, who seek to preserve "natural" family values, and proponents of individual options in a family system more amicable to family diversity. The divorce revolution brought about by no-fault legislation has had the unintended consequence of dramatically improving the economic situation of divorcing husbands/fathers while at the same time leading to the povertization of wives/mothers and children. Economic discrimination of women justified by a traditional belief in women's "natural" role in the family and the inappropriateness of their participating in the workplace still exists. Although increased attention has recently been given to parallel concerns regarding men's roles, this has not generated nearly the same attention and controversy as women's commitments and options.

As a result of all these changes, debates, and controversies, there has been great discussion about the future of the family. A widespread view declares that the family is a dying institution and expresses much concern about the implications for the "American way of life." A counter view holds that the "family" itself is not dying, but rather that one form of the family is declining and being replaced by new types of families that are supportive of individuals of both sexes and of all ages. These new family forms will usher in emancipatory and egalitarian transformations in sexual relations that include, but are not limited to, marital and family relations.

To understand the contemporary status of the American family, and to be able to predict its future, is vital. Unfortunately, American sociology has only recently recognized the importance of studying the historical and cultural diversity of family systems. In the last fifteen years, American sociology has increasingly realized that comparative and multicultural analysis can frequently help in understanding things that are so near to us they are difficult to see. Ignoring such diversity, in fact, distorts analysis of the American family; diversity in American families is the very essence of the American family.

The aim here is to develop understanding of the causes, conditions, consequences, and implications of American family diversity for individual, family, and society. This book looks at the diversity of the family experience through time. A multicultural approach is the best way to answer questions about family processes and structures and their relationship to other societal institutions. The family is a prime reflector of the major societal changes experienced in the twentieth century. The study of the family experience allows us to see the impact of broader patterns of societal change on individuals and their everyday lives. The rapid economic, political, and social changes characteristic of present times make such a comparative perspective crucial.

Reference

Waller, Willard. 1938. *The Family: A Dynamic Interpretation.* New York: Dryden.

Part I

Multicultural Perspectives

In this the last decade of the twentieth century, we can look back at more than two centuries of continual economic, religious, political, and social upheavals throughout the world. Massive modifications and breakdowns of social structures and cultural values have been associated with social and individual crises in which everyday experiences could no longer be taken for granted. Conventional assumptions regarding gender role relationships, marriage, and the family have been under scrutiny and challenge. The sociological perspective is vital to understand these social forces that have affected people's lives.

Throughout history, the family has been the social institution that has stood at the very center of society. For most people, the family is the most important group to which they belong throughout their lives. The family provides intimate and enduring relationships and acts as a mediator between its members and the larger society. It transmits the traditional ways of a culture to each new generation. It is the primary socializing agent and a continuing force in shaping people's lives. Through the family women and men satisfy most of their interpersonal, emotional, and sexual needs. Children are raised in families, providing a tangible link among past, present, and future generations. The family provides the setting in which individuals are socialized and motivated for integration into occupational, religious, political, and social positions that ensure the continuation of societal institutions and structures.

These prefatory remarks suggest why the family is vital to the society and to the individual. It should, therefore, be apparent that changes in the family will have serious ramifications for a given society and its people. Sociology as a discipline developed in the early nineteenth century as a response to the major changes that occurred first in Western Europe and the United States and then rapidly spread through the rest of the world as a consequence of Western colonization. The sociological perspective on marriage and the family was to view it in terms of the social forces that affect people's lives.

Prior to the nineteenth century, Western thought generally held to a biblical belief in the origins of the family stemming from God's creation of the world, including Adam and Eve. Although there was a recognition of relatively minor familial changes over time, the biblical family form and its underlying patriarchal ideological precepts were seen as

5

continuing intact into the nineteenth century. Western thought clung to uniformity through-out the world in terms of family structures, processes, and underlying familial beliefs and values. These governed the behavior of men, women, and children in families.

This belief in the worldwide uniformity of the family underwent severe challenge and was finally discarded as a result of a number of important factors. Western societies were industrializing and urbanizing at a rapid rate, destroying the old societal class systems as a new social class structure developed. Individual rights, duties, and obligations were rede-fined, and the relationships of the individual to the family and the family to the larger com-munity were reworked. Western colonial expansionism and imperialism fostered a new eco-nomic system that had global implications for all cultures. Contacts were being made with people whose systems of family life were markedly different from each other. The recogni-tion of worldwide family diversity led to the overthrow of the belief that there was a single family form. What was needed was an alternative theoretical perspective to reevaluate the origins of the family. This alternative perspective took the form of evolutionary theory.

The theory of evolutionary change developed by Charles Darwin in his *Origin of Spe-cies* in 1859 was the culmination of an intellectual revolution begun much earlier that pro-moted the idea of progressive development. As the theory of evolution became the domi-nant form in explaining biological principles, social scientists of the nineteenth century developed belief that there was a link between biological and cultural evolution. These social scientists were called Social Darwinists. Their basic tenet was that since biological evolution proceeded through a series of stages (from the simple to the complex), the same process would hold for cultures.

Henry Sumner Maine, Lewis Henry Morgan, J. J. Bachofen, and Herbert Spencer were among those who applied evolutionary theories to the study of the human family. Social Darwinists seemingly dealt with such nonimmediate concerns as the origins and historical development of the family, yet their theories had social and political implications. Social Darwinism provided "scientific" legitimation for Western colonization and exploitation of "primitive" peoples through the erroneous belief that Western culture represented "civiliza-tion" and non-Western cultures, particularly among nonliterate, low-technology societies, represented a primeval state of savagery or barbarity. And through its advocacy of evolu-tionary progress, Social Darwinism provided laissez-faire guidelines that supported neglect of the poorer classes of American and Western European societies. It also had implications for the roles of men and women in nineteenth-century family systems. By arguing for a patriarchal evolutionary theory of male supremacy and dominance over females, Social Darwinists gave implicit support to the Victorian notions of male supremacy and female dependency.

An important rebuttal to Social Darwinism that in part also developed out of evolution-ary theory was made by Friedrich Engels ([1884]1972) in *The Origins of the Family, Pri-vate Property, and the State*. Concerns for gender role egalitarianism, as opposed to patri-archy and male sexual dominance, achieved their fullest evolutionary theory expression in this work. Engels' evolutionary theory saw economic factors as the primary determinants of social change and linked particular technological forms with particular family forms. Echoing Lewis Henry Morgan, Engels depicted the stage of savagery as one with no economic inequalities and no private ownership of property. The family form was group marriage based on matriarchy. During the stage of barbarism, men gained economic control over the means of production. In civilization, the last stage, women became subjugated to the male-dominated economic system and monogamy. This stage, in Engels' view, rather than representing the apex of marital and familial forms, represented the victory of private property over common ownership and group marriage. Engels speculated that the coming of socialist revolution would usher in a new evolutionary stage marked by gender equality and by common ownership of property.

Engels' main achievement was in defining the family as an economic unit. This has become a major focus in much of the subsequent historical research on the family and is of great theoretical importance in the sociology of the family. But, insofar as Engels' Marxist view constituted a branch of evolutionary thought, it was subject to many of the same objections (see below) raised against other evolutionary theories.

By the end of the nineteenth century, the popularity of Social Darwinism was rapidly declining. Contributing to the decline were the methodological weaknesses of the approach (data obtained by nontrained, impressionistic, and biased travelers and missionaries) and growing rejection of both its explicit value assumptions on the superiority of Western family forms and its belief in unilinear evolutionary development of the family. More importantly, the shift in the focus of the sociology of the family was at least in part precipitated by the sweeping changes in U.S. and European societies during the nineteenth century. There was a dramatic increase of awareness to such conditions as poverty, child labor, desertions, prostitution, illegitimacy, and abuse of women and children. Social scientists were appalled by the excesses of industrial urban society and the calamitous changes in the family system.

The Industrial Revolution dramatically changed the nature of economic and social life. The factory system developed, and with its development there was a transformation from home industries in rural areas to factories. Rural people were lured by the greater economic opportunities that the city promised. The domestic economy of the preindustrial family disappeared. The rural- and village-based family system no longer served as a productive unit. The domestic economy had enabled the family to combine economic activities with the supervision and training of its children; the development of the factory system led to a major change in the the division of labor in family roles.

Patriarchal authority was weakened with urbanization. Previously, in rural and village settings, fathers reigned supreme; they were knowledgeable in economic skills and were able to train their children. The great diversity of city life rendered this socialization function relatively useless. The rapid change of industrial technology and the innumerable forms of work necessitated a more formal institutional setting—the school—to help raise the children. Laws came into existence to regulate the amount of time children were allowed to work and their work conditions. Laws also required that children attend school. These legal changes reflected the change in the family situation of the urban setting; families were no longer available or able to watch constantly over their children.

The separation of work from the home had important implications for family members. Increasingly, men became the sole provider for the family and the women and children developed a life centered around the family, the home, and the school. Their contacts with the outside world diminished, and they were removed from community involvements. The family's withdrawal from the community was characterized by its hostile attitude toward the surrounding city. The city was thought of as a sprawling and planless development bereft of meaningful community and neighborhood relationships. The tremendous movement of a large population into the industrial centers provided little opportunity for the family to form deep or lasting ties with neighbors. Instead, the family viewed neighbors with suspicion and wariness. Exaggerated beliefs developed on the prevalence of urban poverty, crime, and disorganization.

Social scientists began to see the decline in the importance of kinship and community involvements and the changes in the makeup of the nuclear family as more important areas of investigation than the study of the evolutionary transformations of the family. Their research and theories focused on the causal connections relating family change to the larger industrial and urban developments occurring in the last two centuries. Much attention has also been given to theoretical analyses of the effects these changes have had on the individual, on women, men, and children, on the family, on kinship structures, and on the larger community and the society.

For almost 200 years sociologists have wrestled with these concerns. The readings in the first part of this book focus on the relationship between societal change and the family. Chapter One, "The Changing Family: History and Politics," opens with Steven Mintz's social historical examination of the American family since 1955. Mintz argues that during this time period there has been a dramatic transformation of the American family. He attributes this change, which includes the sharp increase in divorce and single parenting and in working mothers and two-career families, to a broad-based shift in values made possible by an era of economic prosperity for many. A movement toward individualistic values became articulated in family law. Mintz then turns his attention to the sources of anxiety regarding the changing family. These include the changing world of children, working mothers, single-parent households, teenage pregnancy, domestic violence, African American families in poverty, and artificial reproduction. The essay concludes with a discussion of the role of public policy and the family.

Reading 2, "The War over the Family Is Not over the Family," by Susan Cohen and Mary Fainsod Katzenstein, extends the discussion on the politics of the family. The authors approach this subject by analyzing the diversity within feminism and within right-wing conservatism, which advocates traditional familial roles. Although the battle is presumably fought over the needs of children, Cohen and Katzenstein view the nature of gender roles and values as the underlying issue. Further, they treat the different views regarding female autonomy, individualism, and community involvement as the heart of the debate.

The history of the African American family in the United States reflects to a large degree many of the historical turning points and changes experienced by the American family of European origin. However, the African American family experience also has unique characteristics that stem from its African origins as well as from the extraordinary historical experience it has had in the United States. The study of the African American family's historical experience has been influenced by a discussion on the relative importance of the African cultural heritage on African American family organization. Niara Sudarkasa (Reading 3) provides an overview of African family and Black American family structure as it developed in the political and economic context of U.S. history. The cultural and historical importance placed on the extended consanguineal kinship relationship over the importance of the marital or conjugal relationship is seen to distinguish the African American family from the American family of European origin.

The readings in Chapter Two, "The Family, Kinship, and the Community," focus on the relationship of the nuclear family to both the extended family and the larger community. Family historians have emphasized that changes in Western society resulted in the gradual separation of the public institution of work and the community from the private sphere of the family. Middle-class family life since the nineteenth century has been distinguished by this removal from the community setting. And the American suburb has continued to foster this privatizing process. Kenneth T. Jackson (Reading 4) in the opening selection of this chapter provides an historical overview of the interrelatedness of the private family ideology and the suburbanization of the United States.

Many sociologists see the privatization of the middle-class family as antithetical to women's independence. More specifically, the spatial segregation of residence from home and the development of the single-family house led to the increased dependence of women on income-earning husbands. In addition, and most significantly, the house became the setting that required the full involvement of women. As Ruth Schwartz Cowan (1983) and Susan Strasser (1982) have demonstrated, women's domestic labor paradoxically increased with the development of mechanized techniques, e.g., vacuum cleaners and sewing, washing, and dishwashing machines that were designed supposedly for efficiency's sake but in fact have set new housekeeping standards. In addition, the automobile fostered the end of home delivery services for all kinds of goods and services, thus requiring that families own an automobile to perform these services. These new tasks included driving spouses to commuter transportation stations, picking up and delivering children to school and after-school activities, and taking sick family members to doctors, who no longer made house calls.

One technological advance that ran counter to the prevailing "more work for mother" pattern was the residential telephone (Fischer, 1988). Historically, the residential telephone has been used by women to foster gender-linked social relationships and involvements. Often, women used the telephone for what Micaela di Leonardo (Reading 5) calls "kin-work." Kin-work involves kinship contact across households and is as much a part of domestic labor as housework. It includes maintaining kinship ties, organizing holiday gatherings, and the creation and sustaining of kinship relationships. Kin-work is seen to fuse both the labor perspective and the domestic network categories of female work. The concern of di Leonardo's article is examining kin-work in the context of the interrelationships between women's kinship and economic lives of Italian American women who work in the labor market and at home.

In contrast to the relative separation of the nuclear family from extended kinship ties and community involvement as described by Kenneth T. Jackson (Reading 4) of middle-class suburbia, is the family life of working class and ethnic groups. Di Leonardo's article provides one such illustrative example. So does Reading 6, "Mexican American Women

Grassroots Community Activists: 'Mothers of East Los Angeles.'" In this article, Mary Pardo discusses the community activities of a group called the Mothers of East Los Angeles (MELA). It demonstrates how women use their family networks and family roles as the basis for political action that includes the building of new schools and safe work sites.

Pardo's work, as well as the readings in Chapter Three, "Immigrant and Ethnic Families," demonstrate that the family structures of many immigrant and ethnic family groups in the United States are characterized by a developed social network comprising extended kin and neighbors. This social support structure is often an important mediating factor in a given family's involvement with the larger community.

The rise of American suburbia in the late nineteenth century can also be seen as a response to mass immigration and the massive industrial growth of U.S. cities. Underlying these responses was the desire for class segregation. In particular, the middle and upper classes were frightened of the immigration from southern and eastern Europe into the United States during the period from 1880 to 1924. In Reading 7, written by the editor of this anthology, Mark Hutter, there is an examination of the urban ways of life of some of these immigrant family groups.

Immigrants from these areas concentrated in the industrial cities of the Northeast and the Midwest, where job opportunities were plentiful and chances of success were greatest. The ultimate success of an immigrant group depended in large part on its ability to re-establish a normal pattern of family life in the United States. However, popular as well as sociological opinion saw the emerging immigrant ghettos as settings of social disorganization, with alienation, anomie, social isolation, juvenile delinquency, crime, mental illness, suicide, child abuse, separation, and divorce as inherent characteristics of urban life. The social reform movement that developed during this time period saw family disorganization as pervasive and as a consequence arising from governmental nonsupervision of industrial and urban institutions. In Reading 7, the nature of the social organizational patterns that were developing among these immigrant groups is examined.

The next two articles also center on the immigration experience and its impact on families. However, they both have a contemporary time frame and are concerned with recent events. Reading 8, by Robert J. Young, discusses the complexity of factors that ultimately affect immigrants in their assimilation into American society. Young studied the Asian American immigrant experience in the Philadelphia, Pennsylvania, metropolitan area (the Delaware Valley); he examines the interplay of family and economic involvements in the context of community life.

The concluding article (Reading 9) in Chapter Three, by Ruth Horowitz, examines contemporary patterns of family life that occur among people living in a Chicano community in Chicago. She provides a vivid portrayal of how the important symbols of Mexican family life—solidarity, male domination, virginity, motherhood, and respect—are articulated in the context of an American industrial and urban community. The reading provides a dramatic illustration of the difficulties that a juxtaposition of different cultures imposes on family dynamics that include people of different ages and sexes.

Chapter Four, "Social Policy and Families," which concludes Part I, continues the examination of the diversity of the family experience by presenting three articles that deal with social policy concerns relating to different aspects of the American family experience. Reading 10, by William Julius Wilson (with Kathryn Neckerman), is an investigation and discussion of social policy implications for poor African American families.

There is great social class diversity of African American families. The majority of black families have both parents present, and the vast majority of adult black males work and provide family support. Yet there are significant differences between black families and white families in the United States. For example, a larger proportion of black families than families of other races have children within the household. A large and continually growing number of single-parent households are maintained by women. Further, blacks marry later and are more likely to remarry after divorce. These prevailing variations in black family dynamics have been interpreted, in part, as adaptations to the special circumstances in which blacks find themselves and, in part, as the result of certain values attributable to these circumstantial variations. The growing diversity within the black community has been explained by two somewhat contradictory theories put forth by Wilson and Charles V. Willie.

Charles V. Willie is an important social scientist who has extensively studied the black family. Willie (1988), in the third edition of his influential book, *A New Look at Black Families,* puts forth the opinion that economic factors in themselves can provide only partial explanation for black poverty. He argues that racism still permeates American society, affects all social institutions, and controls entry to all desirable positions in education, employment, housing, and social status. Wilson, on the other hand, makes the argument that racial distinction is not as important a factor in determining the economic opportunities of blacks as is their social class. Wilson does not claim that racism has completely vanished, but he does contend that economic and class differences have become more important than race for determining access to positions of power and privilege and for entering middle-class and upper-class social groups. Wilson critically examines public policy approaches to the ghetto underclass and calls for comprehensive public policy attention to the connection between the poverty status of female-headed families and black male prospects for stable employment.

The theme of Cohen and Katzenstein's work on the politics of the family is continued by next presenting the conservative position on the necessity to restore "traditional family values" to the family. In essence this position calls for the re-separation of family roles with men primarily, if not exclusively, involved with paid employment and women primarily, if not exclusively, involved with child-care and domestic involvements. David Popenoe (Reading 11) has been a leading advocate of the conservative viewpoint that sees the contemporary family in severe decline. Popenoe argues that four major social trends have emerged which call into question both the "ideal and the reality" of the traditional nuclear family. These are the decline in fertility, the sexual revolution, working married mothers, and the increased divorce rate.

The decline or "breakdown of the family" is seen as a primary factor for the rise of a host of social ills including the extensive use of drugs, startling increases in teenage pregnancies, family violence and child neglect, the decline in educational standards, and the overall decline in societal morality and ethics. The debate is closely linked with "decline of community" and "self-centered" or "self-development" arguments. This perspective argues that close-knit bonds of moral reciprocity have declined and have been replaced in its stead with a vocabulary of individualism. As a consequence, the middle class finds itself without a language of commitment in which to create its moral discourse (Bellah et al., 1985).

Robert Bellah and his associates (1985) emphasize that one theme has been of central concern to sociologists since the nineteenth century: the debate about individualism versus social commitment and individual rights versus civic responsibility. America's moral dilemma is seen to revolve around the conflict between the desire for fierce individualism on the one hand and the need for community and commitment on the other. Bellah and his colleagues find that the failure of contemporary Americans is in their weakening of motivational commitments to collective purposes of families, communities, and the nation. The unchecked growth of individualism, "inside the family as well as outside it," is the cause of the society's general decline (Bellah et al., 1985:90). An all-powerful market economy is seen to have fostered individualism and achieved its first manifestation in the family by allowing its members to freely choose love matches. More recently, individualism appears in the form of the quest for personal growth that is not necessarily associated with commitment and emotional bonds. As a consequence, the security of lasting relationships and of stable marriages is in jeopardy as individuals seek self-knowledge and self-realization. The meaning of one's life is no longer seen to be anchored or derived from one's relationships with one's parents or children.

David Popenoe builds on Bellah's assessment of the decline of American character by seeing its counterpart in the decline of the American family. Popenoe concludes by suggesting the forms that social policy should take to restore the traditional family.

The counter-argument to the conservative position is that the changes in the American family that have occurred in the last thirty years do not represent a decline of the family but rather the opportunity for the empowerment of women. The decline is not of the family, but rather of a particular form of family life based on traditional nineteenth-century notions of father as the good provider and mother as the moral guardian of the home. Critics of the conservative viewpoint believe that increased attention to underlying family processes, particularly in terms of how the family deals with new stresses, reaches out for assistance, adopts new roles, alters patterns of courtship and sexuality, and satisfactorily adapts to social change, is needed. Also, the difficulties for family members associated with family change must be investigated to better understand them and deal with them. This, in their view, is more constructive than bemoaning the loss of traditional gender roles in the family.

The next selection does examine one aspect of family change—the dramatic shifts in marriage and divorce practices during this contemporary time period to document its impact on family dynamics. Since the late 1960s, persistent patterns of gender inequality have resulted in the "feminization of poverty," or the growing impoverishment of women and their children. Sex discrimination in the workplace, a stratified job market that places women in lower-paying positions, and the high divorce rate associated with unanticipated negative consequences in divorce laws are all associated with the increased number of women and their children living at or under poverty levels. Lenore Weitzman (1985) referred to the demographic and social changes that have come about as the "divorce revolution." Weitzman's book, *The Divorce Revolution,* had as its subtitle "The Unexpected Social and Economic Consequences for Women and Children in America," and it indicates the major theme of her research project on the impact of no-fault divorce laws. No-fault divorce is a legal viewpoint on divorce that was designed to reduce accusation, acrimony, and artificial marital misconduct during divorce proceedings. In her book, Weitzman outlined the larger cultural themes of individualism, personal fulfillment, and self-sufficiency that are reflected in no-fault divorce laws. No-fault legislation resulted in unanticipated problems and had devastating economic effects on women and children.

This is the concern of Frank F. Furstenberg, Jr. (Reading 12). Furstenberg begins by comparing the United States to other industrial societies. He then identifies some of the key factors that have transformed marriage patterns and the impact of divorce upon the changing family experiences of children. The author concludes by suggesting future trends in family patterns and discusses various policy initiatives and their potential to influence the future of the family.

References

Bellah, Robert N., Richard Madsen, William M. Sullivan, Ann Swidler, and Steven M. Tipton. 1985. *Habits of the Heart: Individualism and Commitment in American Life.* New York: Perennial Library, Harper & Row.

Cowan, Ruth Schwartz. 1983. *More Work for Mother: The Ironies of Household Technology from the Open Hearth to the Microwave.* New York: Basic Books.

Engels, Friedrich. 1972. *The Origins of the Family, Private Property, and the State.* New York: Pathfinder Press. (Originally published in 1884.)

Fischer, Claude S. 1988. "Gender and the Residential Telephone: 1890–1940." *Sociological Forum* 3(2):211–233.

Strasser, Susan. 1982. *Never Done: A History of American Housework.* New York: Pantheon.

Weitzman, Lenore. 1985. *The Divorce Revolution: The Unexpected Social and Economic Consequences for Women and Children in America.* New York: The Free Press.

Willie, Charles Vert. 1988. *A New Look at Black Families.* 3rd ed. Dix Hills, NY: General Hall.

Chapter

1

The Changing Family: History and Politics

Reading 1   New Rules: Postwar Families (1955–Present)*

STEVEN MINTZ

To understand the changes that have taken place in American family life since the early 1950s, one would do well to start by looking at television. Television is not a mere pastime; it is also a powerful cultural medium that communicates values and conveys messages about how adults and children are expected to behave.

During the 1950s, the most popular television shows were family comedies such as "The Adventures of Ozzie and Harriet," "Father Knows Best," and "Leave It to Beaver" that gave expression to the prevailing American dream. Situated in neat tree-lined suburbs, in spacious homes featuring gleaming kitchens and carefully appointed living rooms, these shows depicted a world in which "Dad presided over the dinner table in a suit and tie; Mom—trim, prim and loyal—stood by in a well-starched apron; pesky sons like Bud and Beaver made mild stabs at independence; and daughters were 'Princess' and 'Kitten,' ever Daddy's little girls."[1]

Three decades later, domestic comedies remain a staple of prime-time television. Yet television's images of family life have radically shifted. Diversity—not uniformity—characterizes today's television families. They run the gamut from traditional families like "The Waltons" to two-career families like the Huxtables on "The Cosby Show" or the Keatons on "Family Ties"; "blended" families like the Bradys on "The Brady Bunch," with children from previous marriages; motherless families on "My Two Dads" and "Full House"; two single mothers and their children on "Kate and Allie"; a homosexual who serves as a surrogate father on "Love, Sidney"; an unmarried couple who cohabit in the same house on "Who's the Boss?"; and a circle of friends who think of themselves as a family, congregating at a Boston bar on "Cheers."[2]

Not only has family structure grown more diverse, but the emotional and psychological dynamics of television family life have also undergone profound changes. Family roles have been inverted. The children, on such current television shows as "Full House" or "My Two Dads" are portrayed as knowledgeable and independent, indeed as wiser and more sensible than their parents, who appear to be confused and guilt-ridden about how to rear their own children properly.[3]

The changes that have occurred in television's images of the family mirror a much broader transformation of American family patterns. Over

*Mintz, Steven. 1991. "New Rules: Postwar Families (1955–Present)." Pp. 183–220 in Joseph M. Hawes and Elizabeth I. Nybakken (eds.), *American Families: A Research Guide and Historical Notebook*. Westport, CT: Greenwood Press. Reprinted with permission of Greenwood Publishing Group, Inc., Westport, CT.

the past three decades, American family life has undergone a historical transformation as radical as any that has taken place in the last 150 years. As recently as 1960, 70 percent of all American households consisted of a breadwinner father, a housewife mother, and their children. Today, fewer than 15 percent of American households consist of a go-to-work dad, a stay-at-home wife, and the kids.[4]

In the space of a decade, divorce rates doubled from 2.5 divorces per thousand people in 1966 to 5 per thousand a decade later. The number of divorces today is twice as high as in 1966 and three times higher than in 1950. As the divorce rate climbed, the stigma attached to divorce declined. In the 1960s, a divorce shattered Nelson Rockefeller's presidential aspirations, but in 1980 when Ronald W. Reagan became the first divorced president, attitudes had clearly shifted.[5]

Climbing divorce rates contributed to the rapid growth of stepfamilies—or what are now called "reconstituted" or "blended" families. Today there are 11 million families in which at least one spouse has been married before, an increase from 8.9 million in 1970. About 5 million stepfamilies have children under the age of eighteen. Recent census statistics suggest that one child in four will become a stepchild before reaching age eighteen.[6]

The rapid upsurge in the divorce rate also contributed to a dramatic increase in the number of single-parent households, or what used to be known as "broken homes." The number of households consisting of a woman and her children has tripled since 1960. A shattering of traditional family norms was, in the eyes of many Americans, also evident in a declining marriage rate, delayed marriage, a falling birthrate, and a proliferation of individuals living alone or cohabiting outside of marriage. The marriage rate dropped sharply after 1970, reaching a low of ten marriages per thousand people in 1976,

and young people began to delay marriage and childbearing. By 1980, women married on average a year later than in 1975 and two years later than in the 1950s, and the number of women thirty-five or over who are giving birth for the first time quadrupled over the past decade. At the same time the birthrate fell sharply (from 18.4 per thousand in 1970 to just 14.8 per thousand in 1975), and the ratio of children per mother declined by 50 percent, from nearly 3.5 children during the 1950s to 1.8, which was below the natural population replacement level.[7]

Living arrangements changed drastically. The number of people living alone grew by 60 percent during the 1970s, and by 1980 nearly a quarter of all American households consisted of a single member. Although this was mainly the product of a growing elderly population, it also reflected a sharp increase in the number of "swinging singles"—single adults who had never married or who had once married and were now divorced. At the same time, the number of unmarried couples cohabiting climbed steeply. Since 1960, the number of unmarried couples living together has quadrupled.[8]

American sexual behavior has also changed radically. In 1960 nearly half of all women waited until marriage to become sexually active; today the proportion has declined to one in five. Meanwhile, the proportion of births among unmarried women has quadrupled. In 1965 just 5 percent of births took place out of wedlock; by 1986 the figure had climbed to 23 percent— suggesting that out-of-wedlock births would soon overtake divorce as the primary cause of families headed by single mothers. The female adultery rate has risen since the 1950s by about a third. At the same time, rates of abortion have also risen. Each year, for the past decade, 3 percent of women between the ages of fifteen and forty-four have an abortion. Perhaps the most dramatic change lies in the number of Americans who lived with someone of the opposite sex before marriage. Nearly half of all Americans who married between 1980 and 1984 cohabited with a member of the opposite sex while they were single, compared to just one in nine Americans married between 1965 and 1974.[9]

The old stereotype of the housewife mother and breadwinner father has broken down as millions of married women joined the paid labor force. In 1950, 25 percent of married women living with their husbands worked outside the home; in the late 1980s, the figure has climbed to nearly 60 percent. The increase in working mothers was particularly rapid among mothers of young children. Now more than half of all mothers of school-age children hold jobs. What Americans have witnessed since 1960 is a fundamental challenge to the forms, ideals, and role expectations that defined the family for the last century and a half.[10]

These dramatic changes have evoked anxiety, apprehension, and alarm. Pessimists fear that the structure of American family life has eroded as the divorce rate has soared, out-of-wedlock births have increased, rising numbers of children grow up in poverty, and the number of female-headed families has grown. They worry that falling birthrates mean that individuals have grown too self-centered to have children, that increasing numbers of working mothers mean that more and more children fail to get sufficient attention to their needs, that soaring rates of unmarried teenage mothers consign growing numbers of women and their offspring to lives of poverty, unemployment, and dependence, and that high divorce rates and the trend toward delayed marriage spell the impending demise of the family as an institution.[11]

Other more optimistic observers respond that these prophecies of doom are exaggerated, that commitment to marriage is still strong, that the proportion of young people marrying remains very high, and that most women want to have children. They note, for example, that high divorce rates simply indicate people will no longer tolerate loveless marriages that previous generations put up with, that declining birthrates mean parents are having fewer unwanted children, and that middle-class fathers are far more involved in childrearing than were their counterparts of a generation ago. Yet despite many upbeat commentaries, a majority of the public believes that the family is in worse shape today than it was a generation ago.[12]

THE POSTWAR FAMILY

During the 1950s, many American men and women reacted against the poverty of the Depression and the upheavals of World War II by placing renewed emphasis upon family life. The divorce rate slowed and young women married earlier than their mothers had, and had more children and bore them faster. The average marriage age of American women dropped to twenty, a record low. The fertility rate rose 50 percent between 1940 and 1950—producing a population growth rate approaching that of India. Growing numbers of women decided to forsake higher education or a full-time career and achieve emotional fulfillment as wives and mothers. A 1952 advertisement for Gimbel's department store expressed the prevailing point of view. "What's college?" the ad asked. "That's where girls who are above cooking and sewing go to meet a man so they can spend their lives cooking and sewing." By "marrying at an earlier age, rearing larger families," and purchasing a house in the suburbs, young Americans believed, in the words of *McCall's* magazine, that they could find their "deepest satisfaction."[13]

Politicians, educators, psychologists, and the mass media all echoed the view that women would find their highest fulfillment managing a house and caring for children. Many educators agreed with the president of Barnard College, who argued that women could not compete with men in the workplace because they "had less physical strength, a lower fatigue point, and a less stable nervous system." Women's magazines pictured housewives as happy with their tasks and depicted career women as neurotic, unhappy, and dissatisfied.[14]

THE GREAT EXCEPTION

Although many Americans think of the 1950s family as a kind of ideal, it was in fact an historical anomaly, unlike other families in this century. During the preceding decades, couples married in their mid- or late twenties, the birthrate was declining, and the divorce rate was steadily rising. During the 1950s, in contrast, the marriage age dropped to an historic low, the birthrate rose sharply, and the divorce rate stabilized. Since the 1950s, the marriage age returned to its historic norms, the birthrate resumed its downward drift, and the divorce rate resumed its upward climb.[15]

Yet even in the 1950s, a series of dramatic social changes was under way that would contribute to major transformations in American family life during the 1960s and 1970s. A dramatic upsurge took place during the 1950s in women's employment. More and more married women entered the labor force, and by 1960 the proportion of married women working outside the home was one in three. The number of women receiving college degrees also rose. The proportion of bachelor's and master's degrees received by women rose from just 24 percent in 1950 to over 35 percent a decade later. Meanwhile, beginning in 1957 the birthrate began to drop as women elected to have fewer children.[16]

At the same time that women were breaking away from a single identity as wife and mother, youths were becoming a group more separate and distinct from children and adults. For the first time in recent American history, a large proportion of young people from their teens into their twenties developed a separate existence, relatively free of the demands of adulthood and more independent of parental supervision than children, in a culture marked by distinctive dress, music, and life-styles. During the 1950s, youth culture evolved its own language, employing such terms as "cool," "with it," and "hip." It developed its own distinctive social roles, such as the "greaser," and "beatnik," the "frat rat," and the "hood." It created its own form of music, rock and roll. And in such figures as Holden Caulfield of *The Catcher in the Rye* and actor James Dean, it had its own heroes and archetypes.[17]

During the 1960s and 1970s, these dramatic social transformations in women's and young peoples' lives would undermine the patterns of early marriage, large families, and stable divorce rates characteristic of the early postwar era.

A SHIFT IN VALUES

What are the causes of the dramatic transformations that have taken place in American family life since the late 1950s, such as the sharp increase in divorce and single parenting, in working mothers and two-career families? The driving force behind these transformations lies in a far-reaching shift in values. Three decades ago, an overwhelming majority of Americans endorsed marriage as a prerequisite of well-being, social adjustment, and maturity. Men and women who failed to marry were denigrated as "sick," "neurotic," or "immoral," and couples who did not have children were deemed "selfish." A large majority of the public believed that an unhappily married couple should stay together for the sake of their children; that a woman should not work if she had a husband who could support her; that premarital sex was always wrong; and that an unmarried couple had to get married if they were expecting a baby.[18]

During the 1960s and 1970s, popular attitudes toward marriage, sex, and divorce underwent a dramatic change. Cultural biases against divorce, working mothers, premarital sex, and out-of-wedlock births eroded, encouraged by a sexual revolution, expanding job opportunities for women, women's liberation, and the growing popularity of psychological therapies stressing "growth," "self-realization," and "fulfillment."[19]

Economic affluence played a major role in the emergence of a new outlook. Individuals who came of age during the 1960s and 1970s spent their childhoods during an era of unprecedented affluence. Between 1950 and 1970, median family income tripled. Increased affluence increased opportunities for education, travel, and leisure, all of which helped to heighten expectations for fulfillment and personal happiness.[20]

In keeping with the mood of an era of increasing affluence, new philosophies and psychological therapies stressing individual self-realization flourished. Beginning in the 1950s, humanistic psychologies stressing growth and self-actualization triumphed over earlier theories that had emphasized adjustment as the solution to individual problems. The underlying assumptions of these new "third force" psychologies (a name chosen to distinguish them from the more pessimistic psychoanalytic and behaviorist psychologies) were that a person's spontaneous impulses were intrinsically good and that maturity is not a process of "settling down" and suppressing instinctual needs but of achieving one's potential. Unlike the earlier psychology of adjustment associated with Alfred Adler and Dale Carnegie that had counseled compromise, suppression of instinctual impulses, avoidance of confrontations, and the desirability of acceding to the wishes of others, the new humanistic psychologies of Abraham Maslow, Carl Rogers, and Erich Fromm advised individuals to "get in touch" with their feelings and freely voice their opinions, even if this generated feelings of guilt. A similar impulse toward self-fulfillment and liberation could also be found in the countercul-

ture and New Left, both of which strongly criticized repression of an individual's instinctual needs.[21]

Another far-reaching force for change in the family was the sexual revolution. Contemporary Americans are much more likely than their predecessors to postpone marriage, to live alone, and to engage in sexual intercourse outside of marriage. Today, over 80 percent of all women say they were not virgins when they married, compared to less than 20 percent a generation ago. Simultaneously, rates of adultery soared. Philip Blumstein and Pepper Schwartz, in their 1983 study *American Couples,* reported an adultery rate of 21 percent for women after two years of marriage; Morton Hunt in his *Sexual Behavior in the 1970s* cited a 1974 overall rate of 30 percent.[22]

The roots of these developments were planted in the early 1960s, when a new openness about sexuality swept the nation's literature, movies, theater, advertising, and fashion. In 1960, the birth control pill was introduced, offering a highly effective method of contraception. Two years later, Grossinger's resort in New York State's Catskill mountains introduced the first singles-only weekend, thereby acknowledging couples outside marriage. In 1964 the first singles bar opened in New York City; the musical "Hair" introduced nudity to the Broadway stage; California designer Rudi Gernreich created the first topless bathing suit; and bars began to feature topless waitresses and dancers. Sexually oriented magazines began to display full frontal nudity, and filmmakers began to show simulated sexual acts on the screen. A new era of public sexuality was ushered in, and as a result it became far easier and more acceptable to have an active social life and sex life outside of marriage.[23]

At the same time, the nation's courts and state legislatures liberalized laws governing sex and contraception. In 1957, the Supreme Court narrowed the legal definition of obscenity, ruling that the portrayal of sex in art, literature, and film was entitled to constitutional protections of free speech, unless the work was utterly without redeeming social value. In 1962, Illinois became the first state to decriminalize all forms of private sexual conduct between consenting adults. In succeeding years, the Supreme Court struck down a series of state statutes that prohibited the prescription or distribution of contraceptives, and in 1973, in the case of *Roe* v. *Wade,* the high court decriminalized abortion. Perhaps the most striking changes of all took place in a number of public schools that, beginning in the late 1970s, established birth control clinics and began to encourage unwed mothers to stay in school instead of expelling them. These decisions, to a large extent, took government out of the business of regulating private sexual behavior and defining the sexual norms according to which citizens were supposed to live.[24]

Another factor reshaping family life has been a massive influx of mothers into the work force. As late as 1940, less than 12 percent of white married women were in the work force; today the figure is nearly 60 percent, and over half of all mothers of preschoolers work outside the home. The major forces that have propelled women into the work force include: a rising cost of living, which spurred many families to seek a second source of income; increased control over fertility through contraception and abortion, which allowed women to work without interruption; and rising educational levels, which led many women to seek employment for intellectual stimulation and fulfillment.[25]

As wives assumed a larger role in their family's financial support, they felt justified in demanding that husbands perform more child care and housework. At the same time, fewer children had a full-time mother, and an increasing number were cared for during the day by adults other than their own mother. Today, over two-thirds of all three-to-five year olds take part in a day-care, nursery school, or prekindergarten program, compared to one-fifth in 1970.[26]

Feminism has been another major force that has transformed American family life. The women's liberation movement attacked the societal expectation that women defer to the needs of spouses and children as part of their roles as wives and mothers. Militant feminist activists like Ti-Grace Atkinson denounced marriage as "slavery" and "legalized rape." The larger mainstream of the women's movement articulated a powerful critique of the idea that child care and housework were the apex of a woman's accomplishments or her sole means of fulfillment. As a result of feminism, a substantial majority of women now believe that both husband and wife should have jobs, do housework, and take care of children.[27]

During the 1960s and 1970s, economic affluence, humanistic psychologies, the sexual revolution, the influx of married women into the labor force, and the women's liberation movement combined to produce a heightened spirit of individualism, a preoccupation with self, and a growing commitment to personal freedom, that, in the eyes of a number of recent social critics including Daniel Yankelovich, Peter and Brigitte Berger, Christopher Lasch, and Robert Bellah, is inconsistent with a strong commitment to the family. They fear that today's ideals of love and marital and family relationships, based on therapeutic ideals of openness, emotional honesty, and communication of intimate feelings have proven incapable, in many instances, of sustaining anything stronger than undemanding, short-term, narcissistic sexual relationships.[28]

A REVOLUTION IN FAMILY LAW

The triumph of extreme individualistic values and a therapeutic mindset has been especially evident in the realm of family law. Today, some

50 percent of all court business involves domestic relations. In addressing these cases, traditional views of morality and authority have been thrown into question, and jurists and legislators have become increasingly hesitant about discussing family issues in moral terms.[29]

Older legal definitions of what constitutes a family have been overturned. In cases involving zoning and public welfare, the courts have declared that local, state, and federal authorities cannot define family too restrictively, holding that common-law marriages, cohabitation outside of marriage, and large extended households occupying the same living quarters are entitled to protection against hostile regulation. The Supreme Court has held that government cannot discriminate against groups of nonrelated individuals living together (such as hippie communes), in providing food stamps (while upholding zoning ordinances that limit occupancy of homes to members of families related by blood, marriage, and adoption), and that state legislatures cannot designate one form of the family as a preferred form.[30]

Nineteenth-century legal presumptions about the proper roles of husband and wife have also been called into question. Until recently, the law considered the husband to be "head and master" of his family. His surname became his children's surname, his residence was the family's legal residence, he was immune from lawsuits initiated by his wife, and he was entitled to sexual relations with his spouse. Since the 1970s several state supreme courts have ruled that husbands and wives can sue each other, that a husband cannot give his children his surname without his wife's agreement, and that husbands can be prosecuted for raping their wives.[31]

In addressing questions of divorce or child custody, courts today tend to avoid issues of fault or moral fitness. State legislatures responded to the sharp upsurge in divorce rates in the late 1960s and 1970s by radically liberalizing divorce

statutes, making it possible to end a marriage without establishing specific grounds and, in many states, allowing one spouse to terminate a marriage without the consent of the other.[32]

Before California adopted the nation's first no-fault divorce law in 1970, a basic legal assumption was that marital relationships could only be ended for serious causes. California's no-fault divorce legislation abolished the need to demonstrate any moral wrongdoing on the part of one of the spouses in order to dissolve a marriage. Between 1970 and 1975, all but five states adopted the principle of no-fault divorce. Today, every state except South Dakota has enacted some kind of no-fault statute. Rather than sue the other partner, a husband or wife can obtain a divorce by mutual consent or on such grounds as "incompatibility," living apart for a specified period, or "irretrievable breakdown" of the marriage. In an effort to reduce the bitterness associated with divorce, many states changed the terminology used in divorce proceedings, substituting the term "dissolution" for the word "divorce" and eliminating any terms denoting fault or guilt.[33]

In recent years, courts have tended to abandon the so-called "tender years" doctrine that a young child is better off with the mother unless she is proved to be unfit. The current trend is for the courts not to presume in favor of mothers in custody disputes over young children. Most judges now only make custody awards after considering psychological reports and the wishes of the children. To spare children the trauma of custody conflict, a number of jurisdictions now allow judges to award divorced parents joint custody, in which both parents have equal legal rights and responsibilities in decisions affecting the child's welfare.[34]

Likewise, courts have moved away from the concept of alimony and replaced it with a new concept called "spousal support" or "maintenance." In the past, courts regarded marriage as a lifelong commitment and, in cases in which the husband was found guilty of marital misconduct, held that the wife was entitled to lifelong support. Now maintenance can be awarded for a limited period of time to either the husband or wife.[35]

Another dramatic change in the field of family law is the courts' tendency to grant legal rights to minor children. In the past, parents enjoyed wide discretionary authority over the details of their children's upbringing. More recently the nation's courts have held that minors do have independent rights that can override parental authority. The U.S. Supreme Court has struck down state laws that give parents an absolute veto over whether a minor girl can obtain an abortion (while upholding a Utah statute requiring doctors to notify parents before performing an abortion). Two states—Iowa and Utah—have enacted laws greatly expanding minors' rights. These states permit children to seek temporary placement in another home if serious conflict exists between them and their parents, even if the parents are not guilty of abuse or neglect. In one of the most important decisions involving juvenile offenders and the juvenile courts, the 1967 case *In re Gault,* the Supreme Court ruled that juveniles who are subject to commitment to a state institution are entitled to advance notice of the charges against them, as well as the right to legal counsel, the right to confront witnesses, and protections against self-incrimination.[36]

Recent transformations in family law have been characterized by two seemingly contradictory trends. On the one hand, courts have modified or struck down many traditional infringements on the right to privacy. On the other hand, courts have permitted government intrusion into areas traditionally regarded as bastions of family autonomy. Shocked by reports of abuse against children, wives, and the elderly, state legislatures have strengthened penalties for domestic

violence and sexual abuse. Courts have reversed traditional precedents and ruled that husbands can be prosecuted for raping their wives. A 1984 federal law gave states new authority to seize property, wages, dividends, and tax refunds from parents who fail to make court-ordered child support payments.[37]

What links these two apparently contradictory trends is a growing sensitivity on the part of the courts and state legislatures toward the individual even when family privacy is at stake. Thus, in recent cases, the courts have held that a husband cannot legally prevent his wife from having an abortion, since it is she who must bear the burden of pregnancy. Court decisions on marital rape reflect a growing recognition that a wife is not her husband's property.[38]

One ironic effect of these legal decisions has been a gradual erosion of the traditional conception of the family as a legal entity. In the collision between two sets of conflicting values—individualism and the family—the courts have tended to stress individual rights. Earlier in time the law was used to reinforce relationships between spouses and parents and children, but the current trend is to emphasize the separateness and autonomy of family members. The Supreme Court has repeatedly overturned state laws that require minor children to receive parental consent before obtaining contraceptive information or an abortion, and lower courts have been unwilling to grant parents immunity from testifying against their own children. Similarly, state legislatures have weakened or abolished earlier laws that made children legally responsible for the support of indigent parents, while laws in states that hold parents accountable for crimes committed by their minor children have been ruled unconstitutional.[39]

Ironically, a heightened judicial concern with protecting individual privacy has not meant a withdrawal from private affairs by the courts. Courts, in recent years, have become more willing to mediate disputes between family members. In the past, judges tended to subscribe to a tradition of noninterference in the family's internal functioning except in extreme circumstances, on the grounds that intervention would embroil the courts in endless disputes and that legal intervention would be futile or counterproductive. In recent years, this tradition of noninterference has broken down as courts have taken on the role of defining and enforcing the rights of wives and mothers, fathers of illegitimate children, grandparents, cohabiting couples, handicapped children, and surrogate mothers. As courts have reconceptualized family life in terms of individual rights, autonomy, and equality, judges have necessarily assumed the role of legal referee.[40]

State involvement in nonmarital relations has increased noticeably. Courts in many states have begun enforcing oral contracts and implied contracts between couples cohabiting outside of marriage, reversing the legal tradition of not enforcing a "contract founded upon an illegal or immoral consideration." Similarly, government has grown increasingly concerned about such issues as enforcement of child support duties, supervision of pre- and postnuptial agreements, and domestic violence.[41]

Judicial intervention in the lives of children has undergone certain important changes. While the legal system has surrendered some of its powers of *parens patriae,* it has gained the legal means to treat older juveniles as adults, fully responsible for their actions. Although it has grown more difficult to strip natural parents of their parental rights and remove children permanently from their custody, temporary foster care services have expanded. Today, approximately 500,000 children are in foster care. In cases of child abuse, legislatures have mandated reporting from professionals working with children and have attempted to abrogate professional-client privilege to make reporting more effective.[42]

To say that the drift in family law is away from explicit moral judgments is not to suggest that the law does not make implicit moral judgments. Prior to the adoption of no-fault divorce statutes, the law of marriage implicitly upheld a marital ideal involving lifelong support and marital fidelity. Since divorce was available only on fault grounds, the spouse who was opposed to a divorce had an advantage in negotiating a property settlement. The tendency now is to avoid questions of fault or responsibility in dividing marital assets. Among the messages conveyed by current divorce laws are that either spouse is free to terminate a marriage at will; that after a divorce each spouse is expected to be economically self-sufficient; and that termination of a marriage frees individuals from most economic responsibilities to their former dependents.[43]

In practice, the shift toward family laws emphasizing equality and individual rights has come at the expense of certain other values. Our current no-fault divorce system, for example, does a poor job of protecting the welfare of children, who are involved in about two-thirds of all divorces. Compared to the divorce laws in Western European countries, American divorce laws make it relatively easy for noncustodial divorced parents to shed financial responsibility to their ex-spouses and minor children. Child support payments are generally low (and are not adjusted for inflation), and spouses have great leeway in negotiating financial arrangements, including child support (in over 90 percent of all divorce cases, the parties themselves negotiate custody, child support, and division of marital property without court supervision). In addition, feminist legal scholars maintain that under present law, divorced women are deprived of the financial support they need. Under no-fault laws many older women, who would have been entitled to lifelong alimony or substantial child support payments under the old fault statutes, find it extremely difficult to support their families.

Courts, following the principle of equality, generally require ex-husbands to pay only half of what is needed to raise children, on the assumption that the wife will provide the remainder. Furthermore, the shift toward gender-blind custody standards has led courts to move away from standards that favored the mother—by stressing day-to-day caretaking responsibilities, such as feeding, bathing, dressing, and attending to the health-care needs of the child—and to attach more emphasis on standards that favor the father, such as emphasis on the child's economic well-being.[44]

Earlier in American history, one of the basic functions of family law was to articulate and reinforce certain standards and norms about the family. In recent years, jurists and legislators have tended to back away from using law to enunciate family standards. Yet value judgments remain implicit in the law, and the values that the law tends to emphasize today, such as the terminability of family relationships and obligations, tend to reinforce broader individualistic and therapeutic ideals, stressing self-fulfillment and individual happiness as ultimate values.[45]

SOURCES OF ANXIETY

As America's families have changed, public anxiety about the family's future has mounted. Many Americans fear that traditional norms about marriage, divorce, and illegitimacy have broken down, that unwed teenage motherhood has become epidemic, that black families are disintegrating, and that the well-being of the nation's children is declining. How justified are these fears? And what are the social consequences of the upheavals that have taken place in American family life?

The Changing World of Children

When Americans worry about the future of the family, much of their anxiety centers on chil-dren. For the past decade, over a million children have been involved annually in divorces. Today, one child in four lives with only one parent, and a higher proportion of children live in poverty today than in 1975. Educational achievement scores have fallen and today a quarter of all students drop out of high school before graduation. The teenage suicide rate has tripled since 1960, juvenile delinquency has jumped 130 percent, and childhood obesity, drug and alcohol use, eating disorders, and teenage pregnancy rates all are at alarming levels.[46]

Many Americans believe that the lot of children has declined sharply since 1960. They worry about the deleterious effects of divorce, day care, and overexposure—through television, movies, music, and advertisements—to drugs, violence, and sex. They are concerned that parents have absorbed a far too egalitarian view of their relationship with their children and have become incapable of exercising authority and discipline. Above all, they fear that recent social transformations have eroded an earlier conception of childhood as a special protected state—a carefree period of innocence—and that today's permissive culture encourages a "new precocity" that thrusts children into the adult world before they are mature enough to deal with it.[47]

What are the consequences for children, many Americans ask, of increasing divorce rates and single-parent households, of working mothers and day care?

The Impact of Television

Among the most potent forces that have altered relations between parents and children since 1960 is television. The single most important caretaker of children in the United States today is not a child's mother or a baby-sitter or even a day-care center but the television set in each child's home. Young children spend more time watching television than they do in any other activity besides sleep. The typical child between the ages of two and five spends about thirty hours a week viewing television, nearly a third of the child's waking time. Older children spend almost as much time in front of the television. Since 1960 the tendency has been for children to become heavier and heavier television viewers.[48]

The debate about television's impact on children has raged furiously since the early 1950s. Critics are worried about parents' use of the television set as a baby-sitter and pacifier and as a substitute for an active parental role in socialization. They argue that excessive television viewing is detrimental because it encourages passivity and inhibits communication among family members. They express concern that children who watch large amounts of television tend to develop poor language skills, an inability to concentrate, and a disinclination to read. Moreover, they feel that television viewing tends to replace hours previously devoted to playtime, either alone or with others. And, most worrisome, they believe that violence on television provokes children to emulate aggressive behavior and acquire distorted views of adult relationships and communication.[49]

Research into the impact of television on children has substantiated some of these concerns and invalidated others. Television does appear to be a cause of cognitive and behavioral disturbances. Heavy television viewing is associated with reduced reading skills, less verbal fluency, and lower academic effort. Exposure to violence on television tends to make children more willing to hurt people and more aggressive in their play and in their methods of resolving conflicts. Time spent in front of the television set does displace time previously spent on other activities, and as a result, many games and activities—marbles, jacks, and trading cards, for example—are rapidly disappearing from American childhood.[50]

However, television also introduces children to new experiences easily and painlessly and stimulates interest in issues to which they might not otherwise be exposed. For many disadvantaged children, it provides a form of intellectual enhancement that deprived homes lacking books and newspapers could not afford. And, for many children, television programs provide a semblance of extended kinship attachments and outlets for their fantasies and unexpressed emotions. On balance it seems clear, however, that television cannot adequately take the place of parental or adult involvement and supervision of children and that the tendency for it to do so is a justifiable reason for increased public concern.[51]

Working Mothers

The single most profound change that has taken place in children's lives since 1960 is the rapid movement of millions of their mothers into the paid labor force. Between 1975 and 1986, the proportion of mothers who are in the work force and have preschool children jumped by half, from 38 percent to 57 percent. One-quarter of these mothers work full time year-round; the remainder work part time, or full time for part of the year. As a result, half of all infants—and a higher proportion of older preschoolers—are regularly cared for by someone other than their parents.[52]

Who minds these children while their mothers work? Since licensed day-care centers have room for fewer than 3 million youngsters, most children have been cared for in less formal settings. The largest share—37 percent—were cared for in another mother's home. Another 31 percent of preschoolers were cared for in their own homes while their mothers worked, with nearly half watched by their father. Some 22.3 percent were cared for by a nonrelative, 10.2 percent by a grandparent, and 4.5 percent by some other relative. Altogether, there are around 60,000 professional day-care centers in the country, half nonprofit, the other half for profit.

Despite widespread demand for day care, relatively few businesses provide child care for their employees' children. Of the nation's 6 million employers in 1987, only about 3,000 provided child-care assistance, and just 150 provide on-site or near-site care.[53]

Although only about 22 percent of preschool children are cared for in organized day-care centers or preschools, this represents the fastest growing form of child care, and public debate has centered on the effects of these institutions on children's psychological well-being, children's social and psychological growth, their intellectual development, and their emotional bond with their mothers. The first shot in this debate was fired four decades ago, when English psychiatrist John Bowlby, who studied orphans in British institutions following World War II, argued that children deprived of an intense maternal relationship exhibited antisocial behavior and an inability to form intense relationships with significant others. Later commentators interpreted Bowlby's scholarship to mean that children needed a full-time mother in order to develop normally and that the family was superior to any other institution in raising well-adjusted young children.[54]

By the early 1970s, expert opinion had shifted. Studies of the federal government's Head Start early education program found that children enrolled in the program were more likely to finish high school, stay off welfare, and avoid crime and teenage pregnancy. Other research emphasized the psychologically beneficial effects of a stimulating peer environment and the fact that children could assimilate information earlier than previously thought.[55]

Today, debate rages anew over the effects of day care on children, particularly upon infants. One highly controversial 1987 review of the scholarly literature by Jay Belsky, a professor of human development at Pennsylvania State University, suggested that infants who are cared for more than twenty hours a week by a surrogate are at risk for future psychological and behavioral difficulties. Belsky argued that extensive infant care is associated with elevated rates of insecurity, less competent functioning at older ages, and heightened aggression and noncompliance—points hotly contested by Belsky's critics. The effects on extensive day care on older children are as yet unknown. Preliminary scholarship appears to suggest that quality day care has "neither salutary nor adverse effects on the intellectual development of most children"; that early entry into full-time care may interfere with "the formation of a close attachment to the parents"; and that children in group day care are somewhat more aggressive, more independent, more involved with other children, more physically active, and less cooperative with adults than mother-raised children.[56]

The most pressing problem for parents is an inadequate supply of quality day care. Child care in the United States today is costly (with high quality care costing upwards of $70 a week), often of low quality, and difficult to find, especially for infants, for older children who need care before or after school, and for children who are ill. Low-income children have a particularly difficult time enrolling in child-care programs, even though studies have suggested that such programs promote intellectual growth in children from underprivileged homes. Seventy-five percent of all children from families with incomes of more than $25,000 a year participate in day-care or preschool programs by the age of six, compared to just a third of children from families with incomes of less than $15,000.[57]

The quality of day-care centers varies widely. High-quality centers, which can charge more than $500 a month, usually enroll only a small group of children and provide a great deal of individual attention. Low-quality centers, in contrast, tend to have a high ratio of children to caretakers, a high level of staff turnover, inadequate supervision of children, a reliance on untrained, underpaid personnel, a low level of parental involvement, and a high noise level.[58]

Single-Parent Households

For a growing number of American children, especially for black children, the two-parent family is not a part of their everyday experience. Between 1970 and 1985, the proportion of white children living with one parent rose from 9 percent to 18 percent; for black children, from 32 percent to 54 percent. Three decades ago, 19 percent of white children and 48 percent of black children spent a portion of their childhood in a single-parent household. Demographers project that nearly 70 percent of white children and 94 percent of black children born in 1980 will live with only one parent for part of their childhood. Not only do more children spend a portion of their childhood with only one parent, they also spend an increasing proportion of their childhood in a one-parent home. White children born in the early 1950s spent on average about 8 percent of their childhood in a single-parent home; black children, about 22 percent. Demographers project that white children born in 1980 will spend an average of 31 percent of their childhood in a one-parent household, while black children will spend 59 percent of their childhood with one parent.[59]

The major reason for the growth of single-parent households is the rising rate of divorce and separation. Two-thirds of the children living in single-parent homes are in that situation because of divorce or separation; the remainder, because of the death of a parent or an out-of-wedlock birth.[60]

What are the effects of living with only one parent? And what are the emotional consequences of divorce for children? Back in the 1920s authorities on the family, using the case-study method, concluded that children experienced the divorce of their parents as a devastat-

ing blow that stunted their psychological and emotional growth and caused maladjustments that persisted for years. Beginning in the late 1950s and continuing into the early 1970s, a new generation of researchers argued that children were better off when their parents divorced than when they had an unstable marriage; that divorce disrupted children's lives no more painfully than the death of a parent, which used to break up families just as frequently; and that the adverse effects of divorce were generally of short duration.[61]

Recent research has thrown both points of view into question. On the one hand, it appears that conflict-laden, tension-filled marriages have more adverse effects on children than divorce. Children from discordant homes permeated by tension and instability are more likely to suffer psychosomatic illnesses, suicide attempts, delinquency, and other social maladjustments than are children whose parents divorce. There is no empirical evidence to suggest that children from "broken" homes suffer more health or mental problems, personality disorders, or lower school grades than children from "intact" homes.[62]

On the other hand, it is clear that divorce is severely disruptive, at least initially, for a majority of children and that a minority of children continue to suffer from the economic and psychological repercussions of divorce for many years after the breakup of their parents' marriage. It is also apparent that children respond very differently to a divorce than to a parent's death. When a father dies children are often moody and despairing; during a divorce many children, and especially sons, exhibit anger, hostility, and conflicting loyalties.[63]

Children's reaction to divorce varies enormously, depending on their age, sex, the amicability or the bitterness of their parents, custody arrangements, and above all, their perception of their parents' marriage. Preadolescent boys, who tend to be less emotionally mature and socially competent than girls of the same age, sometimes exhibit anger, hostility, sadness, withdrawal, and regressive behavior such as bed-wetting following a divorce. Some preadolescent girls grow subdued and depressed. In adolescence, a number of studies have suggested, girls from divorced families are somewhat more likely than girls from two-parent families to use illegal drugs and to become sexually active at an earlier age. Boys sometimes exhibit aggression and hostility.[64]

How well children deal with the stress of divorce appears to be related to the bitterness of the divorce and postdivorce custody arrangements. Children whose parents have gone though a bitter divorce tend to suffer more emotional turmoil than children whose parents remain on amicable terms, and children who are shifted between hostile parents tend to suffer more problems than children who remain in the custody of one parent. Children's perceptions of their parents' marriage also appear to influence how successfully children handle divorce. Children who viewed their parents' marriage as unhappy tend to adjust more easily to divorce than those who regarded their home life as basically happy.[65]

For many children, the most disruptive consequence of divorce is economic. In the immediate aftermath of a divorce, the income of the divorced woman and her children falls sharply by 73 percent in the year following divorce, while the father's income rises by 42 percent. Adding to the financial pressures facing children of divorce is the fact that a majority of divorced men evade court orders to support their children. Other sources of stress result from the mother's new financial responsibilities as her family's breadwinner, additional demands on her time as she tries to balance economic and child-rearing responsibilities, and frequently, adjustment to unfamiliar and less comfortable living arrangements.[66]

The emotional, economic, and psychological upheavals caused by divorce are often aggravated by a series of readjustments children must deal with, such as loss of contact with the noncustodial parent. More than nine of every ten children are placed in their mother's custody, and recent studies have found that two months following a divorce fewer than half the fathers see their children as often as once a week, and after three years, half the fathers do not visit their children at all.[67]

Further complicating children's adjustment to their parents' divorce is the impact of remarriage. Roughly half of all mothers remarry within approximately two years of their divorce. These reconstituted families often confront jealousies and conflicts of loyalty not found in families untouched by divorce; at the same time, a number of researchers have found that most children of divorce favored remarriage.[68]

Teenage Pregnancy

Few social issues generated a more profound sense of urgency and crisis during the 1970s and 1980s than teenage pregnancy. Between 1960 and 1977, the number of out-of-wedlock births among teenage women age fifteen to nineteen doubled and then rose another 13 percent between 1977 and 1983. Arousing particular concern was a sharp increase in the number of out-of-wedlock births among very young girls. Between 1966 and 1977, the birthrate among girls ten to fourteen rose by a third.[69]

The number of out-of-wedlock teenage births rose for two fundamental reasons: a sharp increase in premarital adolescent sexual activity and a decrease in the teenage marriage rate. Adolescent premarital sexual activity increased dramatically during the 1970s. The proportion of unmarried teenage women fifteen to nineteen who had experienced sexual intercourse climbed from 27.6 percent in 1971 to 46 percent in 1979 (it declined to 42.2 percent in 1982). Today, nearly a million teenagers become pregnant each year and almost half a million have babies. Altogether, 40 percent of all teenage girls become pregnant as adolescents.[70]

During the 1970s, teenagers who became pregnant grew increasingly unwilling to put the child up for adoption or to enter an unwanted marriage. In the early 1970s, as many as 50 percent of out-of-wedlock children were put up for adoption; today, the figure is around 10 percent. At the same time, the proportion of unwed pregnant teenagers who married before their child's birth declined from almost one-half in the early 1950s to less than a third by the early 1980s.[71]

Many Americans fear that these unmarried teenage mothers and their children are doomed to lives of welfare dependence and poverty. The findings of a recent study conducted by Frank Furstenberg, Jr., J. Brooks-Gunn, and S. Philip Morgan contradict the stereotype. After studying some three hundred predominantly black pregnant teenagers in Baltimore from the time of their pregnancy in the late 1960s until the mid-1980s, these researchers found that only about a quarter were still on welfare when they reached their early thirties and that just 13 percent of the women were continuously on the welfare rolls for the preceding five years. A striking number of the unwed adolescent mothers had succeeded in pulling themselves and their families out of poverty. A third of the mothers had received some postsecondary education, and a quarter of the women earned enough to place themselves in the middle class.[72]

Although teenage pregnancy remains a serious social problem, it is important not to exaggerate its severity. Neither the rate nor actual number of teenage births has increased markedly since 1960. Back in 1960, women ages fifteen to nineteen had 586,966 births; in 1977, the number was 559,154. One reason why the number of teenage pregnancies has not increased faster, despite an increase in sexually active

teenagers, is because use of contraceptives has increased. In 1971, just 45.4 percent of teenagers had used contraception the last time they had intercourse; by 1976, the figure was 63.5 percent; since then, contraception use has continued to rise.[73]

Domestic Violence

One source of anxiety about the family lies in the fear that changes in young peoples' lives have placed increasing stress on youth—evident in rising rates of suicide, drug use, teenage births, and a deterioration of educational achievement. Another major source of anxiety can be found in widely publicized reports of domestic violence, child abuse, and child abandonment.

In the mid-1950s, the television show "The Honeymooners" poked fun at the issue of domestic violence. Ralph Kramden would raise his fist and shout at his wife, "One of these days, Alice—Pow! Right in the kisser!" Twenty-five years later, domestic violence is not a laughing matter.[74]

As many as two million to four million women each year suffer serious injury at the hands of husbands or boyfriends, more than are hurt in auto accidents, rapes, or muggings. The FBI says that every four days a woman is beaten to death by a man she knows well. Abusive behavior also extends to children. According to the American Association for Protecting Children's data from child protective services around the nation, the number of reports of sexual abuse of children has risen from fewer than 1 in 10,000 children in 1976 to 18 in 10,000 in 1985. In three-quarters of the cases, the abuser was a close relative, most often a father or stepfather.[75]

Domestic violence can be found in homes of all races and social classes. Two of the most highly publicized recent cases involved Joel Steinberg, a New York lawyer, and Hedda Nussbaum, a New York editor, charged with beating to death six-year-old Elizabeth Steinberg; and

John Fedders, a former head of the Securities and Exchange Commission, accused of battering his wife. It does appear, however, that domestic violence ending in death is more common in poor and less educated households. New York City statistics for 1984 found that 67 percent of fatal child abuse cases occurred in black families; 21 percent in Hispanic families; and 6 percent in white families. Families on welfare accounted for 71 percent of fatal child abuse cases.[76]

Professional concern about child abuse and family violence first emerged during the mid-1950s. In 1954, the Children's Division of the American Humane Association conducted the first national survey of child neglect, abuse, and exploitation. Three years later the U.S. Children's Bureau launched the first major federal study of child neglect, abuse, and abandonment. By the early 1960s, child cruelty had captured the attention of a growing number of radiologists and pediatricians who found bone fractures and physical trauma in children, suggesting deliberate injury. After C. Henry Kempe, a pediatrician at the University of Colorado Medical School, published a famous essay on the "battered child syndrome" in the *Journal of the American Medical Association* in 1962, legal, medical, psychological, and educational journals began to focus attention on family violence. Growing professional concern about child abuse led to calls for greater state protection and services for abused and neglected children and their parents. At the end of the 1960s, women's groups established the first shelters for battered women and their children.[77]

Black Families in Poverty

Of all the issues that have aroused concern about the family, none has generated more heated controversy than the problems besetting black families living in poverty. The issue first came to public attention in 1965 when the federal government released a confidential report by an obscure assistant secretary of labor named Daniel Patrick Moynihan entitled *The Negro Family: The Case for National Action.* In his report, Moynihan argued that the major obstacle to black advancement was the breakdown of the black family. The black middle class had managed to create stable families, "but for the vast numbers of the unskilled, poorly educated city working class, the fabric of conventional social relationships has all but disintegrated."[78]

Moynihan supported his thesis with startling statistics. Nearly 25 percent of all black women were divorced, separated, or living apart from their husbands, three times the rate for whites. Illegitimacy among blacks had climbed from 16.8 percent in 1940 to 23.6 percent in 1963, while the white rate had only risen from 2 to 3 percent. The breakdown of the black family, Moynihan contended, had led to a sharp increase in welfare dependency, delinquency, unemployment, drug addiction, and failure in school.[79]

The Moynihan Report attributed the instability of the black family to the effects of slavery, Reconstruction, poor education, rapid urbanization, and three to five years of unemployment rates twice those of whites and wages half those of white Americans. The report concluded with a call for national action to strengthen the black family through programs of jobs, family allowances, and birth control.[80]

The Moynihan Report was greeted with a barrage of criticism. Critics charged Moynihan with ignoring the strengths of the black family, exaggerating the problems of illegitimacy and absent fathers, and overestimating the differences between black and white families. Contrary to the impression conveyed by the report, the overwhelming majority of black families during the 1960s, 1970s, and 1980s were composed of two spouses. In 1960, 75 percent of black children lived with two parents; a decade later, 67 percent did. The report's discussion of illegitimacy also distorted the facts. Far from increasing, the black illegitimacy rate was actually declining. In 1960, 98 out of every 1,000 single black women gave birth to a baby. In 1980, only 77 did. By focusing on instability, weakness, and pathology, critics charged, the Moynihan Report ignored the strength and durability of the lower-class black kinship system— an extensive network of kin and friends supporting and reinforcing the lower-class black family.[81]

Over the past quarter century, black Americans have made impressive social and economic gains. The percentage of blacks earning more than $35,000 a year, in constant dollars, nearly doubled between 1970 and 1988. Yet despite civil rights victories, enactment of Great Society programs, and establishment of affirmative action programs, many of the issues identified in the Moynihan Report have intensified. The income gap between black and white families has widened over the last fifteen years; three times as many blacks as whites live in poverty; fewer black Americans live in two-parent families today than in the 1950s; and the proportion of black children born to single women has grown. Today, most black children spend at least a portion of their childhood in a female-headed household, at or near the poverty level, having impermanent relationships with their father or father surrogates. In 1960, just 20 percent of all black children lived in fatherless families; by 1985, the figure was 51 percent. In 1960, 75 percent of all black children were born to a married black woman; in 1985, the figure was less than 40 percent. Why?[82]

Conservative social analysts such as Charles Murray have taken the position that state and federal social welfare policies encouraged family dissolution and out-of-wedlock births. President Ronald Reagan voiced a common conservative viewpoint when he declared, "There is no question that many well-intentioned Great Society-type programs contributed to family breakups, welfare dependency, and a large increase in births out of wedlock." Murray argued that government welfare policies provided poor women with more purchasing power than a minimum-wage job while encouraging nonmarriage, illegitimate births, and nonwork. The belief that government welfare expenditures caused family breakdown rests on close chronological correlations between rising welfare spending and dramatic increases in female-headed households and illegitimacy among the poor. Back in 1959, just 10 percent of low-income black Americans lived in a single parent household. By 1980 the figure had climbed to 44 percent. Had the number of single-parent families remained at the 1970 level, the number of poor families in 1980 would have been 32 percent lower than it was.[83]

Did the expansion of state services contribute to rising rates of illegitimacy and single-parent families? The answer appears to be no. Recent studies by David Ellwood and Mary Jo Bane have found no correlation between the level of welfare payments and the incidence of out-of-wedlock births (although states with higher welfare benefits do tend to have slightly higher divorce rates and lower rates of remarriage). Between 1972 and 1980, for example, the number of black children in single-parent families jumped 20 percent, even though the number of black children on welfare declined. And even though welfare benefits fell in real terms during the 1970s, the number of black female-headed families continued to climb.[84]

The influential sociologist William Julius Wilson has offered an alternate explanation emphasizing structural changes in the American economy. He argues that increases in joblessness among poor black men have made marriage a less attractive option for poor black women. He contends that the number of marriageable black men capable of supporting a family fell after

1970, as the number of jobs in central cities requiring less than a high school education, particularly in manufacturing, decreased. In 1960, there were 70 employed black men ages twenty to twenty-four for every 100 black women in the same age group. By the early 1980s, the number of employed men had fallen to less than 50. In New York City alone, 492,000 low-skill jobs disappeared between 1970 and 1984.[85]

Is male joblessness the primary cause of high rates of divorce and single parenthood in poor black communities? Apparently not. The ratio of marriageable nonwhite men to nonwhite women during the prime years of marriage (ages 25 to 44) did not change markedly between the 1950s and 1960s and the 1980s, dropping from 70 employed black men per 100 black women to 63 per 100 black women in 1982. In fact, the marriage rate among black men with steady jobs declined nearly as much as the rate among all black men, suggesting that noneconomic factors contributed significantly to the decline in black marriage rates.[86]

The fact that needs to be emphasized is that divorce rates, single parenthood, and out-of-wedlock births have increased throughout American society since the 1960s. The trend has affected affluent whites as well as poorer blacks, and middle-class suburbs as well as inner-city ghettos. Increases in single parenthood, divorce, and illegitimacy, however, have posed particular problems for poorer black communities, where rates of divorce, desertion, and single parenthood historically have been much higher than among other groups. In these neighborhoods, a majority of children now grow up without the support of an adult male's earnings.[87]

In an attempt to address problems of poverty, illegitimacy, and single parenthood, Congress in 1988 enacted the first major overhaul of federal welfare laws in half a century. The new law requires states to set up educational, train-ing, work, and child-care programs to help move welfare recipients into private jobs. It also requires absent fathers to contribute to the financial support of their children.

Artificial Reproduction

Of all the transformations that have taken place in the family in recent years, the most unprecedented development lies in the emergence of new reproductive technologies that enable people who could not otherwise have babies to have them. These artificial birth technologies include *in vitro* (literally "in glass") fertilization, artificial insemination, ovum donation (where a third-party female is fertilized with a husband's sperm and the embryo is implanted in the wife), embryo freezing for future use, embryo transfer, and surrogate mothering (in which a woman is artificially inseminated with the semen of another woman's husband or has the couple's embryo implanted in her uterus).[88]

The issue captured public attention in July 1979 when Lesley Brown, a thirty-year-old English woman, gave birth to the world's first "test-tube" baby. Since Mrs. Brown was unable to bear children naturally due to an obstruction in her fallopian tubes, surgeons removed an egg from her ovary, fertilized it in a culture dish in a suspension of sperm, and several days later, placed the fertilized egg in her uterus. A five-pound, twelve-ounce girl, Louise Brown, was born almost nine months later. Supporters of in vitro fertilization defend it as a way for infertile couples to have children, noting that one of every six couples of childbearing age is unable to conceive. Many critics expressed fear about the possibilities of discarding of spare embryos, experimentation on or genetic manipulation of the embryo, and growing fetuses on organ farms for transplant into adult patients suffering from such ailments as Alzheimer's or Parkinson's disease. Between 1981 and 1987, about eight hundred test-tube babies were born in the United States.[89]

Controversy erupted anew in 1986 and 1987, when a bitter New Jersey court battle broke out between a surrogate mother, Mary Beth Whitehead, and a biological father, William Stern, over custody of their infant daughter. Under a surrogacy agreement, Whitehead was artificially impregnated by Stern, and she carried their child to term. At issue in the court case was the legality and enforceability of surrogate motherhood contracts, whether such contracts violated state laws against baby selling, and whether a mother should have an opportunity to change her mind about surrendering the baby. The case also provoked debate over whether surrogate motherhood involved class exploitation, since such mothers tended to be less educated and poorer than the couples who hired them. Altogether, about six hundred children had been born to surrogate mothers by 1987, and five surrogate mothers had refused to surrender custody.[90]

With infertility increasing—as a result of venereal disease, exposure to dangerous chemicals, use of intrauterine birth control devices, and the growing number of couples waiting until their thirties or later to start a family—and adoption growing more difficult as the number of the most-desired babies has dropped, many prospective parents have turned to artificial techniques of reproduction. These techniques present a wide range of perplexing ethical and moral dilemmas, including the question of which individuals will be allowed to create children artificially (for example, should artificial reproduction be limited to married couples?); the right of children to know their biological parents; and the question of responsibility if a child is born with a handicap. Surrogate mothering has aroused particularly bitter controversy. Among the issues it has raised are the right of a surrogate

mother to change her mind about relinquishing a child and the question of whether women should be encouraged to carry a child for financial gain.[91]

PUBLIC POLICY AND THE FAMILY

Should the federal government help working parents take care of their children? Should parents have the right to take unpaid leave after the birth or adoption of a child? Should the federal government establish national standards governing staff qualifications, child-teacher ratios, and health and safety requirements in child-care centers? These are among the questions that the nation's legislatures have wrestled with as the nature of American family life has, in the course of a generation, been revolutionized.

The changes that have taken place in American family life since 1960 have been disruptive and troubling and have transformed the family into a major political battleground. Conservative activists, fearful that climbing rates of divorce, single parenthood, and working mothers represented a breakdown of family values, launched a politically influential "pro-family" movement during the 1970s. They sought to restrict access to abortion, block ratification of proposed Equal Rights Amendment to the Constitution, restrict eroticism on television, and limit teenagers' access to contraceptives. They have tended to take the position that government has a positive duty to define and enforce family norms and values.[92]

Liberals have approached family issues from a different tack. Unlike conservatives, they are more willing to use government social policies to try to help individual families. Some of the proposals they have made to assist families include expanded nutritional and health programs for pregnant women, federal subsidies for day-care services for low-income families, uniform national standards for child-care centers, and a requirement that employers give parents unpaid leave to take care of a newborn or seriously ill child.[93]

Today, the United States is a society deeply divided over the meaning of what constitutes a family and what role government should take in strengthening American families. Given this deep sense of division, it appears likely that the family will remain a major political battleground.

Reading 2   The War over the Family Is Not over the Family*

SUSAN COHEN AND MARY FAINSOD KATZENSTEIN

The War over the Family (Berger and Berger 1983), *In Defense of the Family* (Kramer 1983), and *Rethinking the Family* (Thorne and Yalom 1982) are but a few of the books produced over the last decade in the political encounters between feminists and traditionalists. Curiously, the battle is not fundamentally about the family, but rather a conflict over the roles and relationships of men and women. Moreover, the differences of opinion over the needs and interests of children constitute a skirmish more than a war. This essay advances an argument: Feminists and traditionalists disagree deeply about issues fundamental to the nature of society and the role of men and women within it. Finding a middle ground is neither easy nor perhaps even possible. But to say that the controversy is over who is pro- or antifamily obscures rather than illuminates the issue. The debate is fundamentally about the places in society of men and women. The discourse about what is good for children is simply not so polarized; to see it as such would be to misspecify the nature of the feminist–traditional division.

We recognize, of course, that there is a close connection between children's interests and the interests of adults. Suppositions about the roles and relationships of men and women have implications for the upbringing of children. How we raise our children depends on our conceptions of the adults we want them to become. At the same time, people who otherwise have widely varying world views may hold similar ideas about the kind of care children should receive and the persons from whom they should receive it.

In this essay, we will analyze the arguments about the family that have preoccupied the American public over the last decade or so. Our intention is threefold:

1. To convey an understanding of the multiplicity of views among both traditionalists and feminists that, while they do not deny the differences between the two ideological camps, do complicate the easy stereotypes to which popular debate so readily resorts;

2. To explore the idea that the rift between feminists and traditionalists revolves largely around issues of adult roles rather than children's needs;

3. To explicate the tensions that exist among both feminists and traditionalists in their

*Cohen, Susan and Mary Fainsod Katzenstein. 1988. "The War over the Family Is Not over the Family." Pp. 25–46 in *Feminism, Children, and the New Families,* edited by Sanford M. Dornbusch and Myra H. Strober. New York: The Guilford Press. Reprinted by permission of the Guilford Press.

attempts to reconcile the sometimes con-flicting values embodied within their writ-ings on the family.

Feminism and the traditionalist Right are terms that require definition if our discussion is to proceed. When we speak of feminism and the Right, we will be distinguishing between two theoretical perspectives that are themselves extraordinarily heterogeneous. By feminist views, we refer to arguments that start from the premise that society now and in the past has been arranged hierarchically by gender and that such arrangements must be challenged. Within this feminist perspective, however, we discuss a range of views: revisionist theories, such as those of Jean Elshtain (1982) that exhort femi-nists to return to "female-created and -sustained values" of mothering and nurturance, as well as the more radical views of such theorists as Adri-enne Rich (1976), that insist on a basic restruc-turing of family life.

By rightist, traditional, or conservative views (we use the terms interchangeably), we refer to writings of wide-ranging perspectives on the economic, social, and moral responsibility of the state to its citizens. What these writings share is a belief either in the different natures of men and women, or in the desirability of a continued division of labor by gender whatever might be the similarity or difference in men and women's nature (Christensen 1977). Thus the writings of the New Right speak of the religious and biolog-ically mandated differences in the life callings of men and women. Neoconservatives, by contrast, emphasize the desirability of gender-neutral, nonintrusive laws that afford equal educational and job opportunities for men and women even as they "prefer" that women elect different life priorities from those men choose (see Berger and Berger 1983). Absolutely central to both views is the assumption that the government has now done all it can do, that virtually all antidis-crimination laws that might provide guarantees of equal opportunity are now in place.[1]

THE REAL WAR OVER THE FAMILY: GENDER ROLES AND THE VIEW FROM THE RIGHT

Diverse as different components of the Right are, they are united around an idealization of the tra-ditional nuclear family. Contained in this ideali-zation is a particular view of men's and women's roles that is absolutely crucial to an understand-ing of the ideological divide between feminism and the Right.

The Right's view of gender roles is remark-ably invariant across neoconservative and New Right positions. A man's responsibility to his family is best met by his success in the market, his ability as a wage earner to support his wife and children; a woman's worth is measured by her dedication to her role as wife and mother. This case is made with evangelical conviction by Phyllis Schlafly in *The Power of the Positive Woman* (1978) and *The Power of the Christian Woman* (1981). Motherhood is a woman's call-ing. If a woman wants love, emotional, social, or financial security, or the satisfaction of achieve-ment, no career in the world can compete with motherhood. That is not to say that women can never find fulfillment outside the home. The rare woman (Mother Theresa is one example that Schlafly offers) may find fulfillment in life's other options, and some may successfully pursue both marriage and career. But this pursuit of dual responsibilities is possible only if two conditions are met: (1) if a woman relies on her own resourcefulness rather than expecting others, the government in particular, to come to her assis-tance; and (2) if she does not allow her primary role as wife and mother to be superseded by other interests or responsibilities. Here Schlafly offers the example of "Mrs." Thatcher, who managed both to become Prime Minister of

Great Britain and to cook breakfast every morning for her husband (in contrast to Mrs. Betty Ford "who stayed in bed while her husband cooked his own breakfast during the many years he was Congressman" (1978, p. 44).

Brigitte Berger and Peter Berger, who have written in defense of the bourgeois family from a neoconservative perspective, are less proselytizing but no less convinced:

> *Individual women will have to decide on their priorities. Our own hope is that many will come to understand that life is more than a career and that this "more" is above all to be found in the family. But however individual women decide, they should not expect public policy to underwrite and subsidize their life plans. (1983, p. 205)*

The emphasis on the primacy of motherhood and the secondary concession to women's other sources of identity and fulfillment (as long as women don't expect any special help) are common to New Right and neoconservative perspectives alike.

Greater differences do exist within the Right over the question of why this arrangement of gender roles is socially desirable. Schlafly and the evangelical Right accept a traditional sexual division of labor as natural—biologically destined and God-given. Schlafly (1978, pp. 17, 33, 49–50) and Falwell (1980, p. 150) both speak of an "innate maternal instinct," of a "natural maternal need," and of God-given roles. The Bergers are less sure. Whether or not there is a maternal instinct in the human species, it should still be evident, the Bergers argue, that the division of labor embodied in the bourgeois family is preferable to any other arrangement (Berger and Berger 1983, p. 152). The bourgeois family produced individuals whose traits made possible

both capitalism and a democratic order (1983, p. 157).[2] The more secular, supply-side exponents of the New Right, as evidenced in the writing of George Gilder (1981, pp. 69–71), make a similar argument, proposing that the heterosexual nuclear family is essential to an efficient and productive society. Married men form stable work patterns and contribute more productively to the economic well-being of the nation than do bachelors who have no family responsibilities and dissipate their energies in nonproductive sexual and economic concerns.

Gender Roles and Public Policy

According to the Right, the traditional bourgeois family as it is now constituted offers women and men nearly all the options they should want. In contrast to the feminist position, the Right seeks a roll-back of state initiatives, maintaining that there is little the state should do beyond what it has already done to lend support to women or men who might seek to alter the traditional gender arrangements both within and outside the family. The list of public policy measures that most feminists would see as essential to the enlargement of life options for men and women (legalized abortion . . . , expanded day-care services, programs to assist victims of domestic violence, insurance provisions for maternity/paternity leaves, protection of homosexual rights) are either actively opposed or simply ignored by virtually all sections of the Right. The New Right's position on these issues is well known: opposition to federal legislation on domestic violence, opposition to the legalization of abortion, and support for the Family Protection Act (barring governmental recognition of homosexual rights, and the use of educational materials that question traditional family roles). The New Right does not oppose an activist state. As feminist scholar Zillah Eisenstein (1982) explains, the New Right share the neoconservative opposition to the expansion of the welfare state but departs from the neoconservative position in its enthusiastic support of a state that seeks to assert its influence over the social and sexual mores of its citizens. The New Right encourages the state to engage in moral leadership but certainly in ways that would pressure or reestablish the breadwinner system. . . .

This is one important distinction between the New Right exponents such as Schlafly or Gilder, and neoconservatives, such as the Bergers, Nathan Glazer, and Irving Kristol. While the former exhort the state to actively exercise moral authority, the latter generally eschew such expectations. The Bergers, for example, go to some lengths to distinguish themselves from moral majority activists. They aver that they are not part of the chorus arguing for the dismantling of the welfare state, and they indict those who would use the state to "influence or control behavior within the family" (1983, p. 207). They thus do not share the New Right's enthusiasm for patrolling antifamily educational materials; they also do not display anything like the almost ecclesiastical tone of George Gilder's case for returning to the era of the male breadwinner. Nevertheless, the Bergers' search for the middle ground lands them closer to the New Right than to feminism. Although they support a (restricted) version of legalized abortion, they insist that abortion has nothing to do with family policy. They therefore refuse to make a case for abortion in their discussion of policies needed to "strengthen" the family; nor do they give even a mention to the desirability of legislation for programs to extend child care or reduce domestic violence. Homosexual rights, they argue, are in no way related to family policy. They write: "It is not a function of the state, at least in a democracy to regulate the arrangements by which 'consenting adults' arrange their private lives—AS LONG AS THEY ARE UNENCUMBERED BY CHILDREN" (1983, p. 206). Hence the neoconservative position, at least as espoused by the Bergers, appears to reject expanded day care, additional funding of services for victims of battering, abortion, or homosexual rights, as long as any of those claims are related to the needs of family members. The position is strongly suggestive of John Stuart Mill's 19th-century argument (progressive for its time) that women should have rights similar to men—except when they choose to marry and have children. In the course of his long essay otherwise decrying the subjection of women, Mill wrote:

> *Like a man when he chooses a profession, so, when a woman marries it may in general be understood that she makes choice of the management of a household and the upbringing of a family, as the first call upon her exertions . . . and that she renounces not all other objects and occupations, but all which are not consistent with the requirements of this. (Mill 1859/1970, p. 179)*

The policies that the Bergers say would help to strengthen the bourgeois family—redressing the heavier tax burden on married couples; providing child allowances; furnishing special allowances for the care of the sick, handicapped, and aged family members; offering vouchers that would empower families to make educational choices for their children—are also policies that the New Right would find easy to support because they in no way threaten the gender-based traditional division of labor. In their common belief that public policy has no place in facilitating the abilities of men and women to depart from their traditional roles within and outside the family, both neoconservative and New Right perspectives stand in direct opposition to the position of most feminists. It is to feminist views on the family—and the roles of men and women—that we now turn.

THE REAL DEBATE OVER THE FAMILY: FEMINISM AND THE AUTONOMY OF WOMEN WITHIN THE FAMILY

According to the Right, feminists are against the family. This antifamily charge is basically a slogan that muddles rather than clarifies the true political issue. The real debate is over women's autonomy within and outside the family.

While the Right idealizes the traditional nuclear family in which the man works for wages and the woman stays home to raise the children, feminists reject the claim that this particular version of family life is the only acceptable form. As Barrie Thorne says in her introduction to *Rethinking the Family,* "Feminists have challenged beliefs that any specific family arrangement is natural, biological, or 'functional' in a timeless way" (1982, p. 2). Thus if one is asking who is for the family and who against it, one must also ask, "Which family?"

A profound disagreement between the Right and feminists does exist—one that focuses on the relationship of women to the family. It is this, rather than the debate over the needs and interests of children, that has fueled the feminist–Right conflagrations. Feminism has been the source of serious criticisms of the traditional family. Yet, in exploring feminist critiques of the traditional family, it is at once apparent that feminist thought is anything but monolithic. At some level, all feminists have insisted that the traditional nuclear family has deprived women of autonomy and in so doing has been an oppressive force that must be altered. But the broad and widely divergent set of views within that position needs to be acknowledged.

A number of the early feminist writings of the late 1960s and early 1970s condemned the nuclear family as the institution centrally responsible for the denial of women's freedom. The writings of Shulamith Firestone (1970) and Kate Millet (1969) argue that the biological family is basic to women's oppression; thus for women to be free within a reconstituted nonbiological family, they must reject their biologically given childbearing role. A revolution in the technology of childbirth (test-tube babies) for Firestone and a separatist, lesbian politics for Millet were the necessary prerequisites of women's liberation from the traditional family.

Yet other feminists writing in the same period took a quite different view. Autonomy for women *could* occur within the biological/ heterosexual family provided certain changes in the traditional family could be realized. According to the politics of the National Organization for Women (NOW) in the early 1970s, the demand for autonomy meant, among other things, the right to define and express a woman's own sexuality, economic independence, and a sense of identity not wholly dependent on relationships to other people (Freeman 1975, p. 20). These views translated into demands for equal pay, equality of education and job opportunities, reproductive choice, and personal sexual choice. The thrust of NOW's politics was quite different, however, from the radicalism of Firestone and Millet. For the latter, autonomy was impossible without women divorcing themselves from the biological and heterosexual family. For many NOW members, gay sexuality was an option women might choose, but it was not the *sine qua non* of female autonomy. For some groups within NOW, the issue was how to realize greater autonomy for women within rather than apart from the heterosexual and biological family. For others it was how to constitute a family, but one not defined by traditional heterosexual/ biological norms.

The writings of other feminists made it clear that a critique of heterosexuality was not identical with the rejection of motherhood. Adrienne Rich, like Millet, protested the tyranny of traditional gender roles and the fact that heterosexuality occupied the exalted status of an "institution," instead of being one of many legitimate sexual choices. Yet Rich found much to celebrate in the mother-knot, unlike Firestone, whose negative view of motherhood suffuses the pages of her writings. There is a resonant image in *Of Women Born* (Rich 1976) of what the abolition of motherhood as an institution might mean: Rich and her three young sons, alone in a summer house in Vermont, living temporarily joyous and anarchic lives. "We were conspirators, outlaws from the institution of motherhood; I felt enormously in charge of my life" (p. 193). The picture is one of attentive love, but love freed of compulsion and the incessant guilt that comes of not being the perfect mother mythologized by the institution of motherhood. Clearly Rich believes that restructuring motherhood to be free of all vestiges of patriarchal control is both necessary and possible.

Nancy Chodorow explores the issue of autonomy at considerable depth in the *Reproduction of Mothering* (1978). She argues that the subordination of women derives from a pattern of upbringing in which women are the primary caregivers—a pattern that prohibits young girls from experiencing a necessary independence, just as it forces young boys into an excessive independence that deprives them of the capacity for nurturance. What is needed to break this cycle is a new mode of childrearing in which both parents play a substantial role. The fruits of such an arrangement would be more autonomy for mothers, as well as for their female children. Both male and female children would become more whole and ultimately more capable of satisfying relationships than their parents were.

More recent feminist writings (mistakenly characterized by some as feminist capitulation to the Right [Barber 1983]) echo the earlier sentiments of Chodorow and others that autonomy for women is ultimately possible within the bio-logical and heterosexual family. Betty Friedan's *The Second Stage* (1981) makes an argument that is hardly new to feminism, although it has been seen by the media as a redirection of contemporary feminist thinking. In the early years of the women's movement, she says (castigating herself along with others), feminists believed that work alone could make for a meaningful life. But this was a mistaken, unbalanced view since all people need love as well as work. Based on this insight, *The Second Stage* is above all a reaffirmation of the family. While Friedan tries to encourage the growth of new kinds of family ties, it is clear that she still sees the heterosexual biological family as the norm, the major change from old patterns being the sharing of child care and household tasks.

Friedan's argument is not explicitly an argument for autonomy, but it is highly individualistic in character, and it clearly rests on the assumption that the vision of family life presented is compatible with autonomy for both men and women. Demands such as flex-time (flexible working hours), reproductive rights, and quality day-care can be seen as mechanisms by which women's range of choices is expanded.

Like Friedan, Jean Elshtain believes that family life is extremely important and that women can be autonomous within the blood-tied family, or at least autonomous enough that one can say that they are not oppressed. At the same time, much of what Elshtain writes appears to echo the Right's view of the family: Her rejection of androgyny, her suggestion that women are particularly suited to mothering, her inattention to abortion and homosexuality, and her insistence on the separation of private and public spheres (see also Rossi 1977). And although she writes of the importance of parenting (close child–parent bonding) in gender-neutral terms, she caps her discussion by calling on not all men and women but rather the feminist thinker, to "ask at what price she would gain the world for herself or other women, utterly rejecting the victories that come at the cost of the bodies and spirits of human infants" (1981, p. 331).

How close is the affinity between Elshtain and the Right? Parallels with the Bergers, for example, are striking: Even as all three allow for variations on the traditional theme, their highest praise is reserved for families where women are responsible for the care of their children. And yet, there are serious differences. Elshtain's work is self-consciously feminist. It is interesting to contrast her concern with the political resonance of language, and the language she herself uses (e.g., her references to the "isolation and debasement of women under terms of male-dominated ideology and social structures" [1982, p. 333]) to the Bergers' sarcastic discussion of "Femspeak" (i.e., nonsexist language).

Elshtain can be seen as traditional in her stress on the private sphere (Stacey 1986). Yet, she wants to revitalize the private, not only for its own sake but also for its potential to change public values and structural arrangements. In this Elshtain is linked to 19th-century feminists, as well as to contemporary feminist thinkers like Carol Gilligan. The Bergers praise the traditional (bourgeois) family for producing the sort of people who do well in a liberal capitalist order; Elshtain sees the family as a place from which to challenge that order.

Finally, it is important to recognize that Elshtain is not without objections to the traditional family. She speaks of a need to "articulate a *particular ideal* of family life that does not repeat the earlier terms of female oppression and exploitation" (1982, p. 323). She repeatedly expresses a concern that women be viewed as autonomous subjects, and that the voices that relate women's experience of their lives not be silenced. Unlike the Right, she does not simply evoke the past; instead she asks people to forge links with it through traditions that do not oppress women. The point here is that even that

part of feminist thinking that is closest to the Right's view of the family and women's role within it rejects those conceptualizations of the family that give little attention to the value of women's autonomy.

The policy demands that stem from feminist conceptions of women's autonomy include quality day care, reproductive rights and rights of sexual preference, shelters for battered women, programs for displaced homemakers, incentives for industry to make available parental leaves and flex-time, and the Equal Rights Amendment (ERA). Various feminist writings reveal, of course, different emphases. Elshtain hardly talks about policy at all. Friedan says most women "do not want impersonal 'government day care'" (1981, p. 260); she urges the widespread adoption of flex-time and job sharing and speculates on new forms of domestic architecture that would be conducive to communal cooking, housework, and child care. Adrienne Rich warns against looking to public day care or communal living arrangements for an easy solution to the problem of women's oppression; what is needed, she says, is a transfiguration of society for which there is no exact blueprint. Firestone writes of the need for a technological revolution in reproductive biology. However diverse the policy issues addressed, the basic idea underlying feminist discourse is to give women greater autonomy than that provided by the family in which husband is breadwinner and wife homemaker.

THE DEBATE OVER CHILDREN'S INTERESTS

Feminist views do, then, stand in clear opposition to the perceptions of the Right about the relationship of women to the family and to society. These views of women in family roles are separated by a deep ideological chasm from those of the right. The argument of this section, however, is that there is no such vast divide between the views of feminism and the Right over the interests and needs of children.

The views of the Right are well known. Children's interests are met best in a heterosexual, two-parent family where the mother stays home to raise her children. This is the optimal situation, at least. If it were also the absolute requisite of decent childbearing, then the views of the Right and of feminism would be entirely uncongenial. But in fact the views of the Right and, as we shall see later, those of feminism are neither monolithic nor unbending.

Most conservative exponents are prepared to recognize the exigency of some variations on the theme of full-time mother's care. Phyllis Schlafly makes it as clear as anyone on the Right that a child is best brought up by the biological mother. Having recently become a grandmother, Schlafly says, she has been able to observe first hand that babies' needs "are the same now as they always have been."[3] Babies are constantly demanding and need the love, care, and attention of someone who will be a steadfast part of their lives. But as Schlafly recognizes, the presence of a biological mother as the chief caretaker is not always possible. She acknowledges the mothering capacities of the nonbiological mother who has adopted a child; and she observes that there are occasions when the mother may need to work outside the home, where families "must accommodate themselves to such situations." In that case, the person caring for the child may be, at best, "a grandmother, an aunt, a relative or some other person." What is harmful to a child, she says, is government-funded day care, because staff is constantly changing, as well as situations where "women, the feminists, argue for day care simply out of a desire to justify their own life styles."

Schlafly's arguments about the needs and interests of children insist on children being raised by a devoted and constant caretaker. Her emphatic view that a child suffers in the hands of government-funded day care or feminists out to justify their own life-styles may have at least as much to do with her antipathy towards government intrusion and feminist ideologies as it does with the needs and interests of children. If these needs and interests were her sole or even primary concern, she would presumably be more interested in whether the "bonding between mother and child" can occur alongside government day care settings or within feminist households. The argument here is as much about society and the place of men and women as it is about the needs and interests of children.

The Bergers' preference for the mother assuming the primary task of infant and child care is only somewhat less explicit. They write, however, that "the anthropological evidence suggests that the precise form [of the family] does not matter for the infant as long as the minimal imperatives are not violated—most important as long as the structure is stable and allows for the expression of love toward the infant" (1983, p. 152).

The Bergers then go on to note that the evidence leaves open the possibility that a female need not play the role of mother figure (they do not address the analogous possibility that the male need not play the role of father figure). But their speculation ends there. Because arrangements where males predominate as childrearers have not been known historically, they conclude that it is unlikely that alternate family forms would be equally viable. The Bergers' preference for the biological mother as childrearer[4] does at least leave open the possibility of a less than always-present mother, and even of some other gender-structured arrangement as long as it could be demonstrated to be stable and loving.

An enormous body of feminist writing on the family focuses on the importance of mothering, but from the primary perspective of its impact on women. Adrienne Rich's *Of Woman Born* (1976) is one such work whose principal concerns is the experience of mothering for women. But her description of children's needs, like Schlafly's comment about the unrelenting demands of her new grandchild, evokes the passion of small children for unconditional love ("from dawn to dark, and often in the middle of the night" [1976, p. 4]). Rich's book is largely about the way in which mothering in a patriarchal society imprisons women, and about the need to release mothering from patriarchal burdens, although not from children. This is closely connected to her argument about children's needs: Mothering, she argues, when it is imbedded in patriarchal society, cannot meet children's needs—daughters learn to resent the powerlessness of their mothers, sons grow to be sent either literally or figuratively into the fields of battle.

Throughout Rich's analysis of mothering, there is little discussion, however, of the needs of children apart from the adults they will become. What needs infants or children may have, independent of their gender socialization is hardly addressed.[5]

Chodorow's book on mothering is similarly structured to address the question of how sex roles get reproduced through the mothering process; children "mothered" within patriarchal society grow up less than whole. Girls emerge as dependent women; boys grow into adults who experience difficulty in their ability to relate to others. Children thus need the parenting of both male and female–parenting that provides "consistency of care and the ability to relate to a small number of people stably over time" (1978, p. 217).

More recent feminist writing critical of "first stage" feminism—allegedly preoccupied with the emancipation of women—makes an explicit case for the primacy of children's needs. And yet even this writing has little to say about what actually constitutes the needs and interests of children. This brand of feminism is represented by Jean Elshtain, who comes closer than most feminists to associating the traditional family structure with the capacity of the adult world to meet the needs of infant and child. Elshtain asserts (and there would be many feminists and conservatives who would agree) that children need "strong early attachment to specific adult others" (p. 320). She continues,

> *Not every neglected and abused child becomes a Charles Manson but every Charles Manson was an abused and neglected child. "The jailhouse was my father," Charles Manson cried. (1981, p. 329)*

In sketching a feminist theory that calls for a newly strengthened but nonoppressive family, Elshtain says, "Responsibilities for children are paramount . . . social feminist of the sort I propose places children in the center of its concern" (1982, p. 448). Elshtain's argument does not require women to take on the primary task of childrearing, nor does she explicitly, as do the Bergers, hail the success of the traditional bourgeois family. Rather abstractly, however, she insists on the preservation of the "[private] sphere that makes [such] a morality of responsibility possible" (1982, p. 336). Traditional feminine virtues of nurturance and compassion must be maintained, both for the sake of children and for the construction of a moral society. This restructuring of the private sphere (whatever it may look like—and Elshtain is less than clear on this) will have enormous ramifications. The rediscovery of "maternal" values will serve women because, by strengthening the private, the public life that has excluded and debased women (and the poor) will be challenged. Children will benefit from the love and compassion now surrounding them, and society will be altered in desirable ways by the infusion of feminine values.[6]

The isomorphism of children's, family's, women's, and societal needs in feminist writings—writings as different as those of Chodorow, Rich, and Elshtain—is extraordinary. Perhaps this coincidence of interests can be explained by the possibility that views concerning the interests of children are derivations of an idealization about the lives of the adults that these children are to become. Children's needs are not identified independent of the adult qualities (autonomy, sensitivity, compassion—all strikingly adult in sound) that these authors hope children will acquire. In most feminist writings, there is little concerned attempt to explore the needs of children apart from the models of adulthood it is hoped that children will later fulfill.

The failure of feminist theory to properly address ideas of children's needs and interests is recognized in an essay by Chodorow and Contratto. They exhort feminists to rethink ideas about mothering and the family based on a more fully elaborated exploration of child development. They call for theories that are:

interactive and that accord the infant and child agency and intentionality, rather than characterize it as a passive reactor to drives or environmental pressures. We need to build theories that recognize collaboration and compromise as well as conflict, theories in which needs do not equal wants; in which separation is not equivalent to deprivation and in which autonomy is different from abandonment. We must begin to look at times other than infancy in the developmental life span and relationships over time to people other than the mother to get a more accurate picture of what growing up is about. (1982, p. 71)

In an article titled "Re-visioning Women and Social Change: Where Are the Children?" (1986), Barrie Thorne undertakes the beginning of such an analysis. She observes that feminists have seen children largely as threats to an ordered society, as victims of a disordered society, or as learners of adult culture. She argues instead for a conceptualization that attributes agency to children.

Most feminists and conservatives would agree on a "bottom line" of childrearing—that infants and young children need constant, committed devotion from a stable cast of adults. Nor does there appear to be an irremediable polarization over how such basic children's needs are to be met. The Right prefers the full-time presence of the biological mother but is not implacably opposed to at least a limited array of alternative arrangements. Some feminists are deeply opposed to the institution of full-time motherhood under conditions of patriarchy (e.g., Rich and Chodorow). Others, such as Elshtain, celebrate the possibility of the reconsecration of mothering in a domestic setting that may or may not involve shared parenting (Elshtain is unclear). Some feminist theories appear to prefer dual, heterosexual parenting; others reject or do not require such arrangements.

Kristin Luker's (1983) fascinating study of pro-life and pro-choice activists lends support to the claim that the usual pro- and antifamily slogans applied to the Right and to feminism are not useful labels. Almost counterintuitively, pro-choice activists, Luker observes, are often *preoccupied* with planning for the care and education of their children. They insist that parenting must be purposeful, designed to give the child maximum parental guidance and every possible advantage. Pro-life activists, by contrast, tend to be laissez-faire individualists in their attitude towards child upbringing. Advocates of large families, pro-life activists assert that the individual qualities of the particular child, rather than parental planning, or material advantage, will determine the child's destiny.[7]

But the beliefs of such activists aside, what is most remarkable about the *writings* of both the Right and of feminism on the family is the scarcity of attention paid to the identification of children's needs. Common to both is the tendency to derive conceptions about children's needs from assumptions about desirable gender arrangements to which those children are expected later to conform. There appears to be a dual agenda for both feminists and conservative writings on the family. In the construction of this agenda, children's needs seem all too readily subsumed by the eagerness to win acceptance for a particular preferred arrangement of men's and women's place in adult society.

AUTONOMY, COMMUNITY, AND SOCIETY

In their writings about the kind of society in which children attain adulthood, both conservatives and feminists struggle to reconcile the often conflicting goals of autonomy and community. The fostering of individualism and the creation of community are themes that preoccupy both feminism and the Right, and the tensions between these dual goals are a constant source of problems for both theoretical perspectives.

The Bergers' *The War over the Family* (1983) treats these themes at some length. Their defense of the bourgeois family rests on what they believe to be the particular strength of that institution: its capacity to provide community and a sense of belonging while at the same time creating in its members the spirit of individualism. "Human beings," they write, "cannot live without community any more than they can live without institutions" (1983, p. 146). The family,

better than other institutions, can create sharing, trust, and identity. At the same time, they argue, the great contribution of the bourgeois family has been the promotion of individualism. The bourgeois family fosters self-assertion, the belief in the individual's ability to control the world through rational calculations. They write: "Put simply, the bourgeois family socialized individuals with personalities and values conducive to entrepreneurial capitalism on the one hand and democracy on the other" (1983, p. 157).

It would be surprising if a single institution that bred moral harmony and community on the one hand and individualism on the other were not to experience the tension that derives from reconciling these potentially conflicting values. And indeed, as the Bergers acknowledge, the family as the locale where both harmony and individualism are to be nurtured does find itself under siege. Although they accede explicitly to the importance of this problem, they do no more than acknowledge it:

> *Also the very values of the bourgeois family ethos from the beginning, had within them the seeds of their own destruction. Individualism brought forth within the family, would turn against it. (1983, p. 103)*

They acknowledge that individualism bred in the bourgeois family has led to educational institutions that can challenge the family and to a middle class that is far more skeptical than lower-income populations about reigning values. The efflorescence of individualism, by this argument, may be at the very root of feminist discontent with the family. They acknowledge this idea in a single flippant observation:

> *Perhaps it should not surprise us that some women become disenchanted*

*with this role [within the household]
quite apart from the feminist movement as such. Civilization building is
a weary-making task, with its own
psychic costs. In the (somewhat misleading) language of the critics; it
can become tiresome to be "on a
pedestal." (1983, p. 103)*

Beyond this passing acknowledgement,
there is little discussion by the Bergers of how
the inculcation of individualism in the family may
affect male and female members differently.
Self-assertion and rational calculation are mentioned as qualities that families breed in their
members, presumably without regard to gender.
There is absolutely no discussion of battering or
incest, experiences that curtail the "autonomy"
of male and female family members in quite different ways.

The potential tension between individualism spawned within the bourgeois family and the
sense of community that the family is also
expected to transmit is reconciled only when the
range of individualist aspirations is limited. Individualism that promotes, as the Bergers describe
it, "the ideal of the 'swinging single,' with no
ties on his or her project of endless self-
realization; the idealization of abortion, once
and for all eliminating the vestigial risk of pregnancy, the insistence that a 'gay life style' is as
socially legitimate as heterosexual marriage"
(1983, p. 135) is individualism that cannot be
reconciled with the harmony of the bourgeois
family. The possibility of reconciling community and autonomy within the bourgeois family
is, then, entirely dependent on the creation of
individualist values that conform to standards
that do not fundamentally undermine the traditional nuclear, heterosexual family.

A central motif in feminist discussion is,
likewise, the idea of autonomy. Most of the
changes sought by feminists can be understood

as means toward, or aspects of, this end. But the
idea of autonomy has some problematic implications in spite of its pivotal role in feminist theory.

Autonomy can take different shapes. One
involves "the right of all individuals to develop
their highest potential" (Gordon 1982, p. 50). A
classic presentation of this notion of autonomy
can be found in John Stuart Mill's 1859 essay,
On Liberty. Going further back in time, to the
philosophical origins of liberalism, one finds a
somewhat different version of autonomy: In
Hobbes and Locke the emphasis is on acquisi-
tions and competition. This egoistic and often
aggressive type of autonomy is a *modus oper-
andi* that many feminists explicitly reject, and
that they perceive as a serious threat to another
feminist goal—egalitarian communities.

Liberal feminists are prone to overlook the
issue of community and instead tend to portray
feminism in almost wholly individualistic terms.
Betty Friedan writes,

*feminism is threatening to despots
of fascism, communism, or religious fundamentalism, Third World
or American brand, because it is an
expression of individualism, human
autonomy, personal freedom, which
once freely experienced, can never
be erased or completely controlled.
(1981, p. 329)*

The primary concern of *The Second Stage* is the
needs of the individual. While it is true that
Friedan gives much attention to our needs for
connectedness, her focus remains on the individual. Moreover, she sees the need for connection
being met primarily within the nuclear family.
Friedan seems to attach little importance to the
notion of political community, or to communities of women.

Many feminists write about individualism
in a more guarded way than does Friedan. Linda

Gordon, in her essay in *Rethinking the Family,* expresses an "ambivalence between individualism and its critique" (1982, p. 50). The task of feminism, she says, is

> *to develop a feminist program and philosophy that defends individual rights and also builds constructive bonds between individuals to defend all the gains of bourgeois individualism and liberal feminism, while transcending the capitalist-competitive aspects of individualism with a vision of loving, egalitarian communities. (1982, pp. 51–52)*

Many feminist writers would find themselves in accord with this formulation of feminist goals. However, the uncomfortable question arises as to whether the transcendence that Gordon envisions can ever actually be achieved.

Jean Elshtain has written on this issue in a sobering if not pessimistic way. She makes a case for the primacy of community over individualism, arguing that much of feminism rejects the possibility of community within the bonds of traditional ethnic family life that provided a basic identity to women like her grandmother. She goes on to argue that, in this world at least, it is impossible to establish both individual autonomy and strong communal ties: "Feminism of the sort I propose recognizes that there is no final resolution to the twin goals of individual and social good" (1982, p. 448).

Many radical, Marxist, and social feminists would dispute Elshtain's claim, or grant that while it may be true now, it will not be so after the revolution (of whatever sort). Unfortunately this issue is addressed directly far too infrequently by feminists of the Left. Instead of explicit discussion, there is often an underlying assumption that once the revolution takes place, each person will have the freedom to realize

her- or himself fully and at the same time will naturally join others in creating egalitarian communities.

Among less revolutionary feminists there is a tendency to see the tension between individual freedom and social good as an inevitable, if unfortunate, aspect of the human condition. According to this view, political life is an arena in which compromises are always necessary. Decisions must be made as to how much freedom one is willing to give up for the sake of a strong community, and how far one is willing to weaken communal authority for the sake of individual freedom.

Elshtain's argument, though, is not merely that these two important ends are contradictory, but also that they are in a fundamental sense dependent on one another. In a discussion of Dostoyevsky's "Grand Inquisitor," she comments,

> *In the Inquisitor's world, there is neither freedom nor community. Dostoyevsky's mass are "pitiful" and "childlike" in the worse sense— hardly a community, hardly exemplars of mutuality. They have security but the price they pay is the loss of both community and liberty. (1983a, pp. 251–252)*

> *Freedom requires roots and roots involve communities and no community has ever existed without constraints of some kind. (1983a, p. 253)*

It is thus not just that perfect freedom and perfect community are impossible. Freedom paradoxically requires constraints, including the constraints that are inevitably an aspect of family life. While Elshtain clearly doesn't equate community with family—she stresses the importance of political participation and a sense of political purpose beyond the family—she does see strong families as an essential element of communal life: "There is no way to create real communities out of an aggregate of 'freely' choosing adults" (1982, p. 442). Not only is community impossible without families, freedom (paradoxically) is impossible without families; as she states above, "Freedom requires roots." Roots are composed of family, ethnic, and religious ties, ties that are largely involuntary.

One way in which families nourish freedom, says Elshtain, is by fulfilling our needs for intimacy, security, and a sense of purpose that, if unmet by the family, will be met elsewhere, in ways that may prove disastrous.

> *Cults moved into the vacuum created by the "thinning-out" of community and family ties, even as they further eroded those ties to preclude any outside locus for human relations. In an argument that eerily replicates radical claims that attachment to the family vitiates commitment to "the Cause," Jim Jones rejected a request by two members of his doomed cult for a Thanksgiving visit to the family of one of them in these words: "It's time for you to cut your family ties.... Blood ties are dangerous because they prevent people from being totally dedicated to the Cause." (1982, pp. 444–445)*

Yet many feminists would reject Elshtain's contention that freedom and community require the blood-tie of the family. Her argument about the threat from cults might well be met with the response that some families are cult-like in the way they treat individual members. Linda Gordon states:

> *Feminism has undermined the family as it once existed faster than it has*

> *been able to substitute more egalitarian communities. This is not a criticism of the women's movement. Perhaps families held together by domination, fear, violence, squelched talents, and resignation should not survive. (1982, p. 50)*

Elshtain recognizes that families have often restricted freedom for women and says this must be changed (1981, pp. 144, 323). However, she disagrees with many feminists on the extent to which "domination, fear, violence, squelched talents, and resignation" have marked family life.

Elshtain makes another argument as to why families are essential to freedom, and it rests on a particular conception of freedom. Her understanding of freedom is not the classical liberal one centering around an absence of restraint, nor is it freedom to fulfill one's potential, although it includes elements of both these ideas. Elshtain's conception of freedom includes the idea of moral responsibility. For her, to be free is above all to be free to act morally. Here the family is crucial; as a place where moral responsibility is taught to children, and is part of the experience of family members in their relations with one another.

> *My vision holds that if we are to learn to care for others, we must first learn to care for those we find ourselves joined to by accident of birth. Such commitments are essential to a social order grounded in the image of a social compact or covenant rather than in contract and self-interest. (1983b, p. 108)*

She says,

> *The social compact is a different notion from that of contract. It is*

inseparable from ideals of civic virtue and retains a hold on working-class, religious, and rural culture. A compact is no contingent agreement but a solemn commitment to create something "new" out of disparate elements—a family, a community, a polity—whose individual members do not remain "as before" once they become part of this social mode of existence. Within the social compact, community members, ideally, share values that are sustained by moral suasion, not enforced by coercion. (1982, p. 446)

This is a vision that involves both freedom and morality. "Morality" is a term rarely used by feminists of the Left, except in a negative way. Moral systems are frequently portrayed as part of the array of tools men have used to deprive women of their autonomy. There is little discussion of possibilities for creating a new morality to replace the codes that in the past have been so oppressive to women. Rather, there seems to be an underlying assumption that if people—especially women—are finally allowed the autonomy that is their right, moral behavior will somehow flow from that. Women allowed autonomy will bring into the public sphere values of caring and nurturance. What sanctions will be needed, which moral precepts will define the rules governing who is "cared for," how, by whom, and why, are less fully examined.[8] Thus we return to the view that individual autonomy and social good are not in tension, that genuine autonomy for all entails the social good.

Clearly, this debate over the relation between autonomy and community is of utmost importance for feminist theory. Further exploration of this issue—both for what it can tell us about how to view the family and for its overall implications for feminism—is essential.

It is of no less importance for the Right. Both perspectives are troubled by the problems of creating an institutional setting (the "family" or some alternative structure) in which children can be raised and that can foster the qualities of individualism within the supportive parameters of community.

CONCLUSION

In the struggle between feminists and the Right the family has been a battleground, but it is not, in fact, the real source of conflict. Feminism is not antifamily; the Right is not simply pro-family. To recognize that there has been a misnaming of the issue is, we hope, to introduce a note of calm into the conflict, a conflict that has frequently been tinged with hysteria. There *are* serious, deep differences between feminism and the Right. These cannot be minimized. However, there are differences not primarily over what children need or whether the family ought to be abolished, but over the place of men and women in society. Looking past the turmoil, one finds this common ground: an acceptance of the family as an arrangement that is, at least potentially, productive for the human spirit as well as the body, and a recognition that all children need stable affectionate care.

Where feminists and conservatives part ways, often bitterly, is over the traditional sexual division of labor. In a fundamental sense this question of gender roles is a question about autonomy.

"Autonomy" is a term often heard in liberal democracies, and in this country both feminism and the Right claim to value it highly. But it is a protean word. One finds widely varying notions about what it means, who has a right to it, in what ways, and what it has to do with public policy. Conservatives, many of whom are in reality laissez-faire liberals, tend to think in terms of "being left alone." Feminists, on the other hand, are far more likely to hold government responsible for giving people *tools* for autonomy; public policy is to increase life-options.

The central question today, of course, is autonomy for women. Recognizing that neither feminism nor the Right represents monolithic entities, we generalize in the following way: The New Right sees a natural sexual order outside the realm of autonomy; in it, biology determines how we live. What it mandates for women is not only the physical act of giving birth but a female essence, a female place in society, flowing almost entirely from that physical act (or the capacity for it) and from the rearing that follows childbirth. The neoconservative Right avoids the implication that biology is destiny. Women and men are said to choose their destiny, to affect through individual effort and talent the course of their own life careers. Yet both implicitly and explicitly, neoconservatives express their expectations that men and women will choose differently.

Feminists, with the exception of those such as Firestone, gracefully, often joyfully, accept the gift of biology, but respond to it so as to preserve women's autonomy as much as possible. The capacity to bear children is seen as a gift to be used when motherhood is genuinely desired; it should not mean an unwanted child. Most feminists are reluctant to draw neobiological conclusions from biological facts. That is to say, having the capacity for childbirth says little about who one is or how one is to find meaning in life or what sort of freedom one has or should have. Although feminists such as Elshtain are exceptions, most feminists assiduously avoid the advocacy of a social or moral division of labor lest it appear to evoke the traditional strictures of biological destiny.

With the exception of radical thinkers like Millet and Firestone, most feminists believe that a large measure of autonomy is possible for women, whether they are mothers or not, within the confines of the nuclear (not necessarily heterosexual or dual-parenting) family. The traditional family has to be rethought and refash-

ioned. Feminist visions of the family are far more varied than the vision of the family that is idealized by the Right (in which the woman meets her destiny by channeling all energy into motherhood). Feminism calls on people to give up such cherished but mistaken notions as: all women have a vocation in motherhood; a child needs constant care from her or his biological mother; lesbians are morally inferior mothers; men aren't suited to be the nurturers of small children. A sharing of child care and household tasks, and day care arrangements in which there is stable, affectionate attention, are two ways in which family life can be reshaped so as to make it possible to be both a woman and a person who is economically, politically, psychologically, and spiritually autonomous.

While insisting on autonomy as perhaps the most essential of feminist goals, most feminists recognize other important goals, including that of community. The family, in fact, represents one attempt to achieve both of these. But there is widespread criticism both external to and within feminism that denies the easy possibility of reconciling autonomy and community within a restructured family institution. Autonomy and community are in constant tension, this criticism claims, even as they might nourish each other in certain ways.

The Right also endorses the twin goals of individuality and community, though their definitions and arguments are quite different from those of feminists. Individualism, for the Right, is encouraged by the family even as it must be, in another sense, sacrificed to the family. The Right maintains that the family is uniquely qualified to instill norms of independence and freedom in its young. Yet the exercise of this individualism is to happen outside, not within, the family. Within the family, community supersedes individuality. The choices men and women make inside the family are to be curtailed by the parameters of biology and tradition. Outside the family, however, individualism may flourish— but an individualism (feminist critics charge) that embraces only men. The Right, then, seeks to reconcile the goals of community and autonomy by assigning community to the family and individuality to society; such an equation, its critics maintain, aggravates rather than reconciles the tension between individualist and community values.

Much more work needs to be done by feminists as well as conservatives about what individualism and community mean, about the complicated ways they relate to each other, and about how people try to realize them in daily life. In the meantime, we must recognize the debate over the family for what it is: true discordance about the roles and values of men and women—rather than a contest over the needs and interests of children.

ACKNOWLEDGMENTS

The authors thank Gretchen Ritter for her bibliographic help and ever insistent questioning, as well as Diana Meyers and Helene Silverberg for their comments on an earlier draft. Mary Katzenstein is grateful to the Jonathan Meigs Fund and to the Ford Foundation funding of the Stanford project which provided research support.

Reading 3   Interpreting the African Heritage in Afro-American Family Organization*

NIARA SUDARKASA

Many of the debates concerning explanations of Black family organization are waged around false dichotomies. The experience of slavery in America is juxtaposed to the heritage of Africa as *the* explanation of certain aspects of Black family structure. "Class" versus "culture" becomes the framework for discussing determinants of household structure and role relationships. Black families are characterized either as "alternative institutions" or as groups whose structures reflect their "adaptive strategies," as if the two viewpoints were mutually exclusive.

Just as surely as Black American family patterns are in part an outgrowth of the descent into slavery (Frazier, 1939 [1966]), so too are they partly a reflection of the archetypical African institutions and values that informed and influenced the behavior of those Africans who were enslaved in America (Herskovits, 1941 [1958]). With respect to "class" and "culture," it is indeed the case that the variations in historical and contemporary Black family organization cannot be explained without reference to the socioeconomic contexts in which they devel-

oped (Allen, 1979). But neither can they be explained without reference to the cultural contexts from which they derived (Nobles, 1974a, 1974b, 1978). Whereas Black families can be analyzed as groups with strategies for coping with wider societal forces (Stack, 1974), they must also be understood as institutions with historical traditions that set them apart as "alternative" formations that are not identical to (or pathological variants of) family structures found among other groups in America (Aschenbrenner, 1978).

After more than a decade of rethinking Black family structure (see, for example, Billingsley, 1968; Staples, 1971, 1978; Aschenbrenner, 1973; English, 1974; Sudarkasa, 1975a; Allen, 1978; Shimkin et al., 1978), it is still the case that a holistic theory of past and present Black family organization remains to be developed. Such a theory or explanation must rest on the premise that political-economic variables are *always* part of any explanation of family formation and functioning, but that the cultural historical derivation of the formations in question

Author's note: I wish to thank Tao-Lin Hwang for his assistance with the research for this chapter, and Bamidele Agbasegbe Demerson for his helpful comments.

helps to explain the nature of their adaptation to particular political-economic contexts.

Obviously, it is beyond the scope of this chapter to try to set forth such a holistic explanation of Black family organization. Its more modest aim is to take a step in this direction by laying to rest one of the false dichotomies that stand in the way of such an explanation. This review seeks to show how an understanding of African family structure sheds light on the form and functioning of Black American family structure as it developed in *the context of slavery* and later periods. It seeks to elucidate African institutional arrangements and values that were manifest in the family organization of Blacks enslaved in America, and suggests that some of these values and institutional arrangements continue to be recognizable in contemporary formations.

The relationships of causality, correlation, and constraint that exist between the political-economic sphere and that of the family cannot be dealt with here. What the chapter seeks to clarify is why Black familial institutions embrace certain alternatives of behavior and not others. It suggests a cultural historical basis for the fact that Black family organization differs from that of other groups even when political and economic factors are held relatively constant.

Thus, it is suggested that it cannot suffice to look to political and economic factors to explain, for example, the difference between lower-class Anglo- or Italian-American families and lower-class Afro-American families. One has to come to grips with the divergent culture histories of the groups concerned. In other words, one is led back to the institutional heritage stemming from Western Europe on the one hand and from West Africa on the other. Knowledge of the structure and functioning of kinship and the family in these areas helps to explain the structure and functioning of families formed among their descendants in America.

It might appear that this is too obvious a point to be belabored. However, when it comes to the study of Black American families, the scholarly community has historically taken a different view. Whereas it is generally agreed that the history of the family in Europe is pertinent to an understanding of European derived family organization in America (and throughout the world), many—if not most—scholars working on Black American families have argued or assumed that the African family heritage was all but obliterated by the institution of slavery. This view has retained credence, despite the accumulation of evidence to the contrary, in large measure because E. Franklin Frazier (1939), the most prestigious and prolific student of the Black American family, all but discounted the relevance of Africa in his analyses.

This chapter takes its departure from W.E.B. DuBois (1908[1969]), Carter G. Woodson (1936), and M. J. Herskovits (1958), all of whom looked to Africa as well as to the legacy of slavery for explanations of Afro-American social institutions. Herskovits is the best-known advocate of the concept of African survivals in Afro-American family life, but DuBois was the first scholar to stress the need to study the Black American family against the background of its African origins. In his 1908 study of the Black family, DuBois prefaced his discussions of marriage, household structure, and economic organization with observations concerning the African antecedents of the patterns developed in America.

In each case an attempt has been made to connect present conditions with the African past. This is not because Negro-Americans are Africans, or can trace an unbroken social history from Africa, but because there is a distinct nexus between Africa and America which,

though broken and perverted, is nev-
ertheless not to be neglected by the
careful student [DuBois, 1969: 9].

Having documented the persistence of African family patterns in the Caribbean, and of African derived wedding ceremonies in Alabama, DuBois noted:

Careful research would doubtless
reveal many other traces of the Afri-
can family in America. They would,
however, be traces only, for the
effectiveness of the slave system
meant the practically complete
crushing out of the African clan and
family life [p. 21].

With the evidence that has accumulated since DuBois wrote, it is possible to argue that even though the constraints of slavery did prohibit the replication of African lineage ("clan") and family life in America, the principles on which these kin groups were based, and the values underlying them, led to the emergence of variants of African family life in the form of the extended families which developed among the enslaved Blacks in America. Evidence of the Africanity to which DuBois alluded is to be found not only in the relatively few "traces" of direct *institutional transfer* from Africa to America, but also in the numerous examples of *institutional transformation* from Africa to America.

No discussion of the relevance of Africa for understanding Afro-American family organization can proceed without confronting the issue of the "diversity" of the backgrounds of "African slaves" (read "enslaved Africans") brought to America. Obviously for certain purposes, each African community or each ethnic group can be described in terms of the linguistic, cultural, and/or social structural features which distinguish it from others. At the same time, however, these communities or ethnic groups can be analyzed

from the point of view of their similarity to other groups.

It has long been established that the Africans enslaved in the United States and the rest of the Americas came from the Western part of the continent where there had been a long history of culture contact and widespread similarities in certain institutions (Herskovits, 1958: chs. 2 and 3). For example, some features of kinship organization were almost universal. Lineages, large co-resident domestic groups, and polygynous marriages are among the recurrent features found in groups speaking different languages, organized into states as well as "segmentary" societies, and living along the coast as well as in the interior (Radcliffe-Brown, 1950; Fortes, 1953; Onwuejeogwu, 1975).

When the concept of "African family structure" is used here, it refers to those organizational principles and patterns which are common to the different ethnic groups whose members were enslaved in America. These features of family organization are known to have existed for centuries on the African continent and are, therefore, legitimately termed a part of the African heritage.

AFRICAN FAMILY STRUCTURE: UNDERSTANDING THE DYNAMICS OF CONSANGUINITY AND CONJUGALITY

African families, like those in other parts of the world, embody two contrasting bases for membership: *consanguinity,* which refers to kinship that is commonly assumed or presumed to be biologically based and rooted in "blood ties," and *affinity,* which refers to kinship created by law and rooted "in-law." *Conjugality* refers specifically to the affinal kinship created between spouses (Marshall, 1968). Generally, all kinship entails a dynamic tension between the operation of the contrasting principles of consanguinity and affinity. The comparative study of family organization led Ralph Linton (1936: 159–163) to observe that in different societies families tend to be built either around a conjugal core or around a consanguineal core. In either case, the other principle is subordinate.

According to current historical research on the family in Europe, the principle of conjugality appears to have dominated family organization in the Western part of that continent (including Britain) at least since the Middle Ages, when a number of economic and political factors led to the predominancy of nuclear and/or stem families built around married couples. Certainly for the past three or four hundred years, the conjugally based family has been the ideal and the norm in Western Europe (Shorter, 1975; Stone, 1975; Tilly and Scott, 1978). Whether or not the European conjugal family was a structural isolate is not the issue here. The point is that European families, whether nuclear or extended (as in the case of stem families), tended to emphasize the conjugal relationship in matters of household formation, decision making, property transmission, and socialization of the young (Goody, 1976).

African families, on the other hand, have traditionally been organized around consanguineal cores formed by adult siblings of the same sex or by larger same-sex segments of patri- or matrilineages. The groups which formed around these consanguineally related core members included their spouses and children, and perhaps some of their divorced siblings of the opposite sex. This co-resident *extended family* occupied a group of adjoining or contiguous dwellings known as a compound. Upon marriage, Africans did not normally form new isolated households, but joined a compound in which the extended family of the groom, or that of the bride, was already domiciled (Sudarkasa, 1980: 38–49).

African extended families could be subdivided in two ways. From one perspective, there was the division between the nucleus formed by the consanguineal core group and their children and the "outer group" formed by the in-marrying spouses. In many African languages, in-marrying spouses are collectively referred to as "wives" or "husbands" by both females and males of the core group. Thus, for example, in any compound in a patrilineal society, the in-marrying women may be known as the "wives of the house." They are, of course, also the mothers of the children of the compound. Their collective designation as "wives of the house" stresses the fact that their membership in the compound is rooted in law and can be terminated by law, whereas that of the core group is rooted in descent and is presumed to exist in perpetuity.

African extended families may also be divided into their constituent conjugally based family units comprised of parents and children. In the traditional African family, these conjugal units did not have the characteristics of the typical "nuclear family" of the West. In the first place, African conjugal families normally involved polygynous marriages at some stage in their developmental cycle. A number of Western scholars have chosen to characterize the polygynous conjugal family as several distinct nuclear families with one husband/father in common (Rivers, 1924: 12; Murdock, 1949: 2; Colson, 1962). In the African conception, however, whether a man had one wife and children or many wives and children, his was *one* family. In the case of polygynous families, both the husband and the senior co-wife played important roles in integrating the entire group (Fortes, 1949: chs. III and IV; Sudarkasa, 1973: ch. V; Ware, 1979). The very existence of the extended family as an "umbrella" group for the conjugal family meant that the latter group differed from the Western nuclear family. Since, for many purposes and on many occasions, *all* the children of the same generation within the compound regarded themselves as brothers and sisters (rather than dividing into siblings versus "cousins"), and since the adults assumed certain responsibilities toward their "nephews" and "nieces" (whom they term sons and daughters) as well as toward their own offspring, African conjugal families did not have the rigid boundaries characteristic of nuclear families of the West.

The most far-reaching difference between African and European families stems from their differential emphasis on consanguinity and conjugality. This difference becomes clear when one considers extended family organization in the two contexts. The most common type of European extended family consisted of two or more nuclear families joined through the parent-child or sibling tie. It was this model of the stem family and the joint family that was put forth by George P. Murdock (1949: 23, 33, 39–40) as the generic form of the extended family. However, the African data show that on that continent, extended families were built around consanguineal cores and the conjugal components of these larger families differed significantly from the nuclear families of the West.

In Africa, unlike Europe, in many critical areas of family life the consanguineal core group rather than the conjugal pair was paramount. With respect to household formation, I have already indicated that married couples joined existing compounds. It was the lineage core that owned (or had the right of usufruct over) the land and the compound where families lived, farmed, and/or practiced their crafts. The most important properties in African societies—land, titles, and entitlements—were transmitted through the lineages, and spouses did not inherit from each other (Goody, 1976).

Within the extended family residing in a single compound, decision making centered in the consanguineal core group. The oldest male in the compound was usually its head, and all the men in his generation constituted the elders of the group. Together they were ultimately responsible for settling internal disputes, including those that could not be settled within the separate conjugal families or, in some cases, by the female elders among the wives (Sudarkasa, 1973, 1976). They also made decisions, such as those involving the allocation of land and other resources, which affected the functioning of the constituent conjugal families.

Given the presence of multiple spouses within the *conjugal* families, it is not surprising that decision making within them also differed from the model associated with nuclear family organization. Separate rather than joint decision making was common. In fact, husbands and wives normally had distinct purviews and responsibilities within the conjugal family (Sudarkasa, 1973; Oppong, 1974). Excepting those areas where Islamic traditions overshadowed indigenous African traditions, women had a good deal of control over the fruits of their own labor. Even though husbands typically had ultimate authority over wives, this authority did not extend to control over their wives' properties (Oppong, 1974; Robertson, 1976; Sudarkasa, 1976). Moreover, even though women were subordinate in their roles as wives, as mothers and sisters they wielded considerable authority, power, and influence. This distinction in the power attached to women's roles is symbolized by the fact that in the same society where wives knelt before their husbands, sons prostrated before their mothers and seniority as determined by age, rather than gender, governed relationships among siblings (Sudarkasa, 1973, 1976).

Socialization of the young involved the entire extended family, not just the separate conjugal families, even though each conjugal family had special responsibility for the children (theirs or their relatives') living with them. It is important to note that the concept of "living with" a conjugal family took on a different meaning in the context of the African compound. In the first place, husbands, wives, and children did not live in a bounded space, apart from other such units.

Wives had their own rooms or small dwellings, and husbands had theirs. These were not necessarily adjacent to one another. (In some matrilineal societies, husbands and wives resided in separate compounds). Children ordinarily slept in their mothers' rooms until they were of a certain age, after which they customarily slept in communal rooms allocated to boys or girls. Children usually ate their meals with their mothers but they might also eat some of these meals with their fathers' co-wives (assuming that no hostility existed between the women concerned) or with their grandmothers. Children of the same compound played together and shared many learning experiences. They were socialized by all the adults to identify themselves collectively as sons and daughters of a particular lineage and compound, which entailed a kinship, based on descent, with all the lineage ancestors and with generations unborn (Radcliffe-Brown and Forde, 1950; Uchendu, 1965; Sudarkasa, 1980).

The stability of the African extended family did not depend on the stability of the marriage(s) of the individual core group members. Although traditional African marriages (particularly those in patrilineal societies) were more stable than those of most contemporary societies, marital dissolution did not have the ramifications it has in nuclear family systems. When divorces did occur, they were usually followed by remarriage. Normally, all adults other than those who held certain ceremonial offices or who were severely mentally or physically handicapped lived in a marital union (though not necessarily the same one) throughout their lives (for example, Lloyd, 1968). The children of a divorced couple were usually brought up in their natal compound (or by members of their lineage residing elsewhere), even though the in-marrying parent had left that compound.

Several scholars have remarked on the relative ease of divorce in some traditional African societies, particularly those in which matrilineal descent was the rule (for example, Fortes, 1950: 283). Jack Goody (1976: 64) has even suggested that the rate of divorce in precolonial Africa was higher than in parts of Europe and Asia in comparable periods as a corollary of contrasting patterns of property transmission, contrasting attitudes toward the remarriage of women (especially widows), and contrasting implications of polygyny and monogamy. If indeed there was a higher incidence of divorce in precolonial Africa, this would not be inconsistent with the wide-ranging emphasis on consanguinity in Africa as opposed to conjugality in Europe.

Marriage in Africa was a contractual union which often involved long-lasting compassionate relationships, but it was not expected to be the all-encompassing, exclusive relationship of the Euro-American ideal type. Both men and women relied on their extended families and friends, as well as on their spouses, for emotionally gratifying relationships. Often, too, in the context of polygyny women as well as men had sexual liaisons with more than one partner. A woman's clandestine affairs did not necessarily lead to divorce because, in the absence of publicized information to the contrary, her husband was considered the father of all her children (Radcliffe-Brown, 1950). And in the context of the lineage (especially the patrilineage), all men aspired to have as many children as possible.

Interpersonal relationships within African families were governed by principles and values which I have elsewhere summarized under the concepts of respect, restraint, responsibility, and reciprocity. Common to all these principles was a notion of commitment to the collectivity. The family offered a network of security, but it also imposed a burden of obligations (Sudarkasa, 1980: 49–50). From the foregoing discussion, it should be understandable that, in their material form, these obligations extended first and foremost to consanguineal kin. Excepting the gifts that were exchanged at the time of marriage, the material obligations entailed in the conjugal relationship and the wider affinal relationships created by marriage were of a lesser magnitude than those associated with "blood" ties.

AFRO-AMERICAN FAMILY STRUCTURE: INTERPRETING THE AFRICAN CONNECTION

Rather than start with the question of what was *African* about the families established by those Africans who were enslaved in America, it would be more appropriate to ask what was *not* African about them. Most of the Africans who were captured and brought to America arrived without any members of their families, but they brought with them the societal codes they had learned regarding family life. To argue that the trans-Atlantic voyage and the trauma of enslavement made them forget, or rendered useless their memories of how they had been brought up or how they had lived before their capture, is to argue from premises laden with myths about the Black experience (Elkins, 1963: 101–102; see also Frazier, 1966: ch. 1).

Given the African tradition of multilingualism and the widespread use of lingua francas (Maquet, 1972: 18–25)—which in West Africa would include Hausa, Yoruba, Djoula, and Twi—it is probable that many more of the enslaved Africans could communicate among themselves than is implied by those who remark on the multiplicity of "tribes" represented among the slaves. As Landman (1978: 80) has pointed out:

> In many areas of the world, individuals are expected to learn only one language in the ordinary course of their lives. But many Africans have been enculturated in social systems where multiple language or dialect acquisition have been regarded as normal.

The fact that Africans typically spoke three to five languages also makes it understandable why they quickly adopted "pidginized" forms of European languages as lingua francas for communicating among themselves and with their captors.

The relationships which the Blacks in America established among themselves would have reflected their own backgrounds *and* the conditions in which they found themselves. It is as erroneous to try to attribute what developed among them solely to slavery as it is to attribute it solely to the African background. Writers such as Herbert Gutman (1976), who emphasize the "adaptive" nature of "slave culture" must ask what it was that was being adapted as well as in what context this adaptation took place. Moreover, they must realize that adaptation does not necessarily imply extensive modification of an institution, especially when its structure is already suited (or "preadapted") to survival in the new context. Such an institution was the African extended family, which had served on that continent, in various environments and different political contexts, as a unit of production and distribution; of socialization, education, and social control; and of emotional and material support for the aged and the infirm as well as the hale and hearty (Kerri, 1979; Okediji, 1975; Shimkin and Uchendu, 1978; Sudarkasa, 1975b).

The extended family networks that were formed during slavery by Africans *and their descendants* were based on the institutional heritage which the Africans had brought with them to this continent, and the specific forms they took reflected the influence of European-derived institutions as well as the political and economic circumstances in which the enslaved population found itself.

The picture of Black families during slavery has become clearer over the past decade, particularly as a result of the wealth of data in Gutman's justly heralded study. Individual households were normally comprised of a conjugal pair, their children, and sometimes their grandchildren, other relatives, or non-kin. Marriage was usually monogamous, but polygynous unions where the wives lived in separate households have also been reported (Gutman, 1976: 59, 158; Blassingame, 1979: 171; Perdue et al., 1980: 209).

Probably only in a few localities did female-headed households constitute as much as one-quarter of all households (Gutman, 1976: esp. chs. 1–3). The rarity of this household type was in keeping with the African tradition whereby women normally bore children within the context of marriage and lived in monogamous or polygynous conjugal families that were part of larger extended families. I have tried to show elsewhere why it is inappropriate to apply the term "nuclear family" to the mother-child dyads within African polygynous families (Sudarkasa, 1980: 43–46). In some African societies—especially in matrilineal ones—a small percentage of previously married women, or married women living apart from their husbands, might head households that were usually attached to larger compounds. However, in my view, on the question of the origin of female-headed households among Blacks in America, Herskovits was wrong, and Frazier was right in attributing this development to conditions that arose during slavery and in the context of urbanization in later periods (Frazier, 1966; Herskovits, 1958; Furstenberg et al., 1975).

Gutman's data suggest that enslaved women who had their first children out of wedlock did not normally set up independent households, but rather continued to live with their parents. Most of them subsequently married and set up neolocal residence with their husbands. The data also suggest that female-headed households developed mainly in two situations: (1) A woman whose husband died or was sold off the planta-

tion might head a household comprised of her children and perhaps her grandchildren born to an unmarried daughter; (2) a woman who did not marry after having one or two children out of wedlock but continued to have children (no doubt often for the "master") might have her own cabin built for her (Gutman, 1976: chs. 1–3).

It is very important to distinguish these two types of female-headed households, the first being only a phase in the developmental cycle of a conjugally headed household, and the second being a case of neolocal residence by an unmarried female. The pattern of households headed by widows was definitely not typical of family structure in Africa, where normally a widow married another member of her deceased husband's lineage. The pattern of neolocal residence by an unmarried woman with children would have been virtually unheard of in Africa. Indeed, it was also relatively rare among enslaved Blacks and in Black communities in later periods. Before the twentieth-century policy of public assistance for unwed mothers, virtually all young unmarried mothers in Black communities continued to live in households headed by other adults. If in later years they did establish their own households, these tended to be tied into transresidential family networks.

The existence during slavery of long-lasting conjugal unions among Blacks was not a departure from African family tradition. Even with the relative ease of divorce in matrilineal societies, most Africans lived in marital unions that ended only with the death of one of the spouses. In the patrilineal societies from which most American Blacks were taken, a number of factors, including the custom of returning bridewealth payments upon the dissolution of marriage, served to encourage marital stability (Radcliffe-Brown, 1950: 43–54). Given that the conditions of slavery did not permit the *replication* of African families, it might be expected that the husband and wife as elders in the household would assume even greater importance than they had in Africa, where the elders within the consanguineal core of the extended family and those among the wives would have had major leadership roles within the compound.

When the distinction is made between family and household—and, following Bender (1967), between the composition of the co-resident group and the domestic functions associated with both households and families—it becomes apparent that the question of who lived with whom during slavery (or later) must be subordinate to the questions of who was doing what for whom and what kin relationships were maintained over space and time. In any case, decisions concerning residence per se were not always in the hands of the enslaved Blacks themselves, and space alone served as a constraint on the size, and consequently to some extent on the composition, of the "slave" cabins.

That each conjugally based household formed a primary unit for food consumption and production among the enslaved Blacks is consistent with domestic organization within the African compound. However, Gutman's data, and those reported by enslaved Blacks themselves, on the strong bonds of obligation among kinsmen suggest that even within the constraints imposed by the slave regime, transresidential cooperation—including that between households in different localities—was the rule rather than the exception (Gutman, 1976: esp. 131–138; Perdue et al., 1980: esp. 26, 256, 323). One might hypothesize that on the larger plantations with a number of Black families related through consanguineal and affinal ties, the households of these families might have formed groupings similar to African compounds. Certainly we know that in later times such groupings were found in the South Carolina Sea Islands and other parts of the South (Agbasegbe, 1976, 1981; Gutman, 1976; Johnson, 1934: ch. 2; Powdermaker, 1939: ch. 8).

By focusing on extended families (rather than simply on households) among the enslaved Blacks, it becomes apparent that these kin networks had many of the features of continental African extended families. These Afro-American groupings were built around consanguineal kin whose spouses were related to or incorporated into the networks in different degrees. The significance of the consanguineal principle in these networks is indicated by Gutman's statement that "the pull between ties to an immediate family and to an enlarged kin network sometimes strained husbands and wives" (1976: 202; see also Frazier, 1966: pt. 2).

The literature on Black families during slavery provides a wealth of data on the way in which consanguineal kin assisted each other with child rearing, in life crisis events such as birth and death, in work groups, in efforts to obtain freedom, and so on. They maintained their networks against formidable odds and, after slavery, sought out those parents, siblings, aunts, and uncles from whom they had been torn (Blassingame, 1979; Genovese, 1974; Gutman, 1976; Owens, 1976). Relationships within these groups were governed by principles and values stemming from the African background. Respect for elders and reciprocity among kinsmen are noted in all discussions of Black families during slavery. The willingness to assume responsibility for relatives beyond the conjugal family and selflessness (a form of restraint) in the face of these responsibilities are also characteristics attributed to the enslaved population.

As would be expected, early Afro-American extended families differed from their African prototypes in ways that reflected the influence of slavery and of Euro-American values, especially their proscriptions and prescriptions regarding mating, marriage, and the family. No doubt, too, the Euro-American emphasis on the primacy of marriage within the family reinforced conjugality among the Afro-Americans even though the "legal" marriage of enslaved Blacks was prohibited. As DuBois noted at the turn of the century, African corporate lineages could not survive intact during slavery. Hence, the consanguineal core groups of Afro-American extended families differed in some ways from those of their African antecedents. It appears that in some of these Afro-American families membership in the core group was traced bilaterally, whereas in others there was a unilineal emphasis without full-fledged lineages.

Interestingly, after slavery, some of the corporate functions of African lineages reemerged in some extended families which became property-owning collectivities. I have suggested elsewhere that "the disappearance of the lineage principle or its absorption into the concept of extended family" is one of the aspects of the transformation of African family organization in America that requires research (Sudarkasa, 1980: 57). Among the various other issues that remain to be studied concerning these extended families are these: (1) Did members belong by virtue of bilateral or unilineal descent from a common ancestor or because of shared kinship with a living person? (2) How were group boundaries established and maintained? (3) What was the nature and extent of the authority of the elder(s)? (4) How long did the group last and what factors determined its span in time and space?

CONCLUSION

At the outset of this chapter it was suggested that a holistic explanation of Black family organization requires discarding or recasting some of the debates which have framed discussions in the past. I have tried to show why it is time to move beyond the debate over whether it was slavery *or* the African heritage which "determined" Black family organization to a synthesis which looks at institutional transformation as well as institu-

tional transfer for the interplay between Africa and America in shaping the family structures of Afro-Americans.

Obviously, Black families have changed over time, and today one would expect that the evidence for African "retentions" (Herskovits, 1958: xxii–xxiii) in them would be more controvertible than in the past. Nevertheless, the persistence of some features of African family organization among contemporary Black American families has been documented for both rural and urban areas. Although this study cannot attempt a full-scale analysis of these features and the changes they have undergone, it is important to make reference to one of them, precisely because it impacts upon so many other aspects of Black family organization, and because its connection to Africa has not been acknowledged by most contemporary scholars. I refer to the emphasis on consanguinity noted especially among lower-income Black families and those in the rural South. Some writers, including Shimkin and Uchendu (1978), Agbasegbe (1976; 1981), Aschenbrenner (1973; 1975; 1978; Aschenbrenner and Carr, 1980) and the present author (1975a, 1980, 1981) have dealt explicitly with this concept in their discussions of Black family organization. However, without labelling it as such, many other scholars have described some aspects of the operation of consanguinity within the Black family in their discussions of "matrifocality" and "female-headed households." Too often, the origin of this consanguineal emphasis in Black families, which can be manifest even in households with both husband and wife present, is left unexplained or is "explained" by labelling it an "adaptive" characteristic.

In my view, historical realities require that the derivation of this aspect of Black family organization be traced to its African antecedents. Such a view does not deny the adaptive significance of consanguineal networks. In fact, it helps to clarify why these networks had the flexibility they had and why they, rather than conjugal relationships, came to be the stabilizing factor in Black families. The significance of this principle of organization is indicated by the list of Black family characteristics derived from it. Scrutiny of the list of Black family characteristics given by Aschenbrenner (1978) shows that 12 of the 18 "separate" features she lists are manifestations of the overall strength and entailments of consanguineal relationships.

Some writers have viewed the consanguineally based extended family as a factor of *instability* in the Black family because it sometimes undermines the conjugal relationships in which its members are involved. I would suggest that historically among Black Americans the concept of "family" meant first and foremost relationships created by "blood" rather than by marriage. (R. T. Smith [1973] has made substantially the same point with respect to West Indian family organization.) Children were socialized to think in terms of obligations to parents (especially mothers), siblings, and others defined as "close kin." Obligations to "outsiders," who would include prospective spouses and in-laws, were definitely less compelling. Once a marriage took place, if the demands of the conjugal relationship came into irreconcilable conflict with consanguineal commitments, the former would often be sacrificed. Instead of interpreting instances of *marital* instability as prima facie evidence of family instability, it should be realized that the fragility of the conjugal relationship could be a consequence or corollary of the *stability* of the consanguineal family network. Historically, such groups survived by nurturing a strong sense of responsibility among members and by fostering a code of reciprocity which could strain relations with persons not bound by it.

Not all Black families exhibit the same emphasis on consanguinity relationships. Various factors, including education, occupational demands, aspirations toward upward mobility, and acceptance of American ideals concerning marriage and the family, have moved some (mainly middle- and upper-class) Black families toward conjugally focused households and conjugally centered extended family groupings. Even when such households include relatives other than the nuclear family, those relatives tend to be subordinated to the conjugal pair who form the core of the group. This contrasts with some older type Black families where a senior relative (especially the wife's or the husband's mother) could have a position of authority in the household equal to or greater than that of one or both of the spouses. Children in many contemporary Black homes are not socialized to think in terms of the parent-sibling group as the primary kin group, but rather in terms of their future spouses and families of procreation as the main source of their future emotional and material satisfaction and support. Among these Blacks, the nuclear household tends to be more isolated in terms of instrumental functions, and such extended family networks as exist tend to be clusters of nuclear families conforming to the model put forth by Murdock (1949: chs. 1 and 2).

For scholars interested in the heritage of Europe as well as the heritage of Africa in Afro-American family organization, a study of the operation of the principles of conjugality and consanguinity in these families would provide considerable insight into the ways in which these two institutional traditions have been interwoven. By looking at the differential impact of these principles in matters of household formation, delegation of authority, maintenance of solidarity and support, acquisition and transmission of property, financial management, and so on (Sudarkasa, 1981), and by examining the political and economic variables which favor the predominance of one or the other principle, we will emerge with questions and formulations that can move us beyond debates over "pathology" and "normalcy" in Black family life.

The Family, Kinship, and the Community

Reading 4   Home, Sweet Home: The House and the Yard*

KENNETH T. JACKSON

In 1840 suburbs had not yet developed into a recognizable entity, distinct from either the city or the farm. Peripheral towns were merely lesser versions of small cities. Outlying residents looked upon urban centers as agents of progress and culture. It was in the cities that the latest innovations developed: Philadelphia with a marvelous public waterworks in 1799, Boston with free public education in 1818, New York with public transportation in 1829. The eastern cities imported the elegant style of the Georgian London town house, they provided gas lamps and public health systems, and in every way they offered urban services superior to those of any suburb.[1]

William Dean Howells (1837–1920), America's foremost man of letters after the Civil War, experienced firsthand the relative advantages of city, small town, and suburb. An outlander from Martins Ferry and Hamilton, Ohio, Howells located in Boston as a young adult and rose with spectacular speed to become editor of the *Atlantic Monthly*. Moving successively to suburban Cambridge, to the Back Bay near the center of Boston, back to Cambridge, to suburban Belmont, back to an apartment hotel in Cambridge, to the old Beacon Hill neighborhood, and finally

and permanently in the 1890s to New York City, Howells knew better than most the problems caused by the lack of urban services in the suburbs. Writing in 1871 of residence just a few miles from Boston, he noted, "We had not before this thought it was a grave disadvantage that our street was unlighted. Our street was not drained nor graded; no municipal cart ever came to carry away our ashes; there was not a waterbutt within half a mile to save us from fire, nor more than a thousandth part of a policeman to protect us from theft."[2]

Peripheral towns patterned themselves after urban models and sought to project an image of dynamic growth; with the right combination of luck, grit, and leadership, any one of them could grow into a really big city. The example of Brooklyn, vigorously competing with mighty New York, was an inspiration. Although known by the sobriquet "City of Churches," the upstart community was not simply an "overgrown village" or a "bedroom" for Gotham. Brooklyn early developed the institutions that enabled it to become a leading metropolis in its own right— colleges, art museums, opera companies, music academies, libraries, and fire, police, and sanitation systems.

Even the nomenclature of outlying communities suggested connections with a metropolis or aspirations to urban greatness. Thus the nineteenth century produced in a single region a South Chicago, North Chicago, South Chicago Heights, and Chicago Heights. Meanwhile, a few miles distant from Detroit, founders of a new community took the name of Birmingham, after a smoky English industrial metropolis, even though in the next century it would become not a center of manufacture but a leafy residential retreat for wealthy executives. This predeliction for urbanism led some boosters to incorporate their dreams into town names—as in Oklahoma City, Carson City, and Kansas City—in the hope that the wish might father the fact.

By 1890, however, only half a century later, the suburban image was quite distinct from that of large cities. No longer mini-metropolises, peripheral communities, like Brookline outside of Boston, followed a different path. Moreover, the expectations about residential space shared by most Americans today had become firmly implanted in middle-class culture. This shift had many dimensions and sprang from many causes, but the suburban ideal of a detached dwelling in a semirural setting was related to an emerging distinction between *Gemeinschaft,* the primary, face-to-face relationships of home and family, and *Gesellschaft,* the impersonal and sometimes hostile outside society. In 1840 only New York and Philadelphia had as many as 125,000 residents, and the factory system was in its infancy. The typical urban worker toiled in an establishment employing fewer than a dozen persons. By 1890, when the Bureau of the Census announced that the Western frontier no longer existed, the United States had become the world's leading industrial nation. In that year the country was already one-third urban and the population of the Northeast was well over one-half urban (defined by the census as communities of 2,500 or more persons). New York was closing on London as

the world's largest city, while Chicago and Philadelphia each contained about one million inhabitants. Minneapolis, Denver, Seattle, San Francisco, and Atlanta, which hardly existed in 1840, had become major regional metropolises. Perhaps more important was the rise of heavily layered government bureaucracies and of factories employing hundreds and sometimes thousands of workers. As more people crowded together in public spaces, families sought to protect home life by building private spaces. Conviviality and group interaction, despite the massive growth of fraternal societies in the late nineteenth century, gave way to new ways of thinking about the family, the house, and the yard, and ultimately, to new ways of building cities.

FAMILY AND HOME

In both Christian and Jewish culture, the family has always occupied an exalted station. It represents the chosen instrument of God for the reproduction of the species, the nurturing of the young, and the propagation of moral principles. But as the French social historian Philippe Ariès has noted, the family as a tightly knit group of parents and children is a development only of the last two hundred years. Prior to the eighteenth century, the community was more important in determining an individual's fate than was his family. In pre-Napoleonic Europe, about 75 percent of the populace lived in squalid hovels, which were shared with unrelated individuals and with farm animals. Another 15 percent lived and worked in the castles and manor houses of the rich and powerful, where any notion of the nuclear family (father, mother, and children in isolation) was impossible. In cities the population was arrayed around production rather than biological units. Each household was a business—a bakery, hotel, livery stable, counting-house—and apprentices, journeymen, servants, and retainers lived there along with assorted spouses and children. Much of life was inescapably public; privacy hardly existed at all. In every case, the image of the home as the ideal domestic arrangement was missing. Even the word *home* referred to the town or region rather than to a particular dwelling.[3]

In the eighteenth century, however, the zone of private life began to expand, and the family came to be a personal bastion against society, a place of refuge, free from outside control. Ariès notes how the arrangement of the house and the development of individual rooms reflected this desire to keep the world at bay and made it possible, in theory at least, for people to eat, sleep, and relax in different spaces. The new social and psychological concept of privacy meant that both families and individuals increased their demand for personal rooms. In the United States, especially in the suburbs, intricate floor plans soon allowed for distinct zones for different activities, with formal social spaces and private sleeping areas.[4]

Although this attitudinal and behavioral shift characterized much of European and Oriental culture, the emerging values of domesticity, privacy, and isolation reached fullest development in the United States, especially in the middle third of the nineteenth century. In part, this was a function of American wealth. In Japan the family, and especially the household, has been the central socioeconomic unit since the fifteenth century, a notion that fits with the Buddhist ideal of suppressing individual desires if they are not in conformity with the best interests of the house. Social and economic conditions in Japan, however, imposed such severe restrictions on residential space that dwellings there were (and continue to be) dwarfishly small in comparison with the West. Houses there are regarded as little more than shells required to keep out the rain, for the focus is the business of living going on within the structure.[5]

Aside from America's greater wealth, an important cultural dimension to the shift should be noted. In countless sermons and articles, ministers glorified the family even more than their predecessors had done, and they cited its importance as a safeguard against the moral slide of society as a whole into sinfulness and greed. They made extravagant claims about the virtues of domestic life, insisting that the individual could find a degree of fulfillment, serenity, and satisfaction in the house that was possible nowhere else.[6] As the Reverend William G. Eliot, Jr., told a female audience in 1853: "The foundation of our free institutions is in our love, as a people, for our homes. The strength of our country is found, not in the declaration that all men are free and equal, but in the quiet influence of the fireside, the bonds which unite together in the family circle. The cornerstone of our republic is the hearth-stone."[7]

Such injunctions took place as industrial and commercial capitalism changed the rhythm of daily life. Between 1820 and 1850, work and men left the home. The growth of manufacturing meant that married couples became more isolated from each other during the working day, with the husband employed away from home, and the wife responsible for everything connected with the residence. The family became isolated and feminized, and this "woman's sphere" came to be regarded as superior to the nondomestic institutions of the world. Young ladies especially were encouraged to nurse extravagant hopes for their personal environment and for the tendering of husband and children. For example, Horace Bushnell's *Christian Nurture,* first published in 1847, described how the home and family life could foster "virtuous habits" and thereby help assure the blessed eternal peace of "home comforts" in heaven.[8]

Whether women regarded the family as a training ground for the real world or as an utter retreat from the compromises and unpleasantries of competitive life, they were told that the home ought to be perfect and could be made so. Through the religious training and moral behavior of its inhabitants and the careful design of the physical structure, a simple abode could actually be a heaven on earth. "Home, Sweet Home," a song written by John Howard Payne in 1823, became the most widely sung lyrics of the day, as Americans identified with the restless wanderer yearning for his childhood home.

Although most celebrations of the private dwelling were written by men, if any one person presided over the new "cult of domesticity," it was Sarah Josepha Hale, editor of *Godey's Lady's Book*, a Philadelphia-based periodical intended for middle-class readership. Her verse in praise of the home found its way into many publications and was typical of a broad effort to institutionalize the female as homemaker and queen of the house. Hale's vision, and that of almost everyone else, assumed that man's was the coarser sex; women were softer, more moral and pure. The only respectable occupation for adult females (unless they were governesses) was that of wife and mother. Dependence was not only part of woman's supposed nature, but also of English and American law. Married women had scant legal identity apart from their husbands, whose control over their wives' bodies, property, and children was all but absolute.

Like verse and prose, pictures and prints with domestic themes were published in millions of copies and in considerable variety. At midcentury, the new technology of reproducing pictures encouraged the craft businessmen Currier and Ives to establish a firm producing lithographs for magazines and books. Among the most popular of the early Currier and Ives series was one of four prints on the "seasons of life," which clearly associated happiness and success with home settings and the family.

Although most writers were too sentimental and mawkish to talk about such matters as mortgage financing and structural engineering, at the core of their thought were new notions about the actual and symbolic value of the house as a physical entity. Yale theologian Timothy Dwight was especially blunt:

> *The habitation has not a little influence on the mode of living, and the mode of living sensibly affects the taste, manners and even the morals, of the inhabitants. If a poor man builds a poor house, without any design or hope of possessing better, he will . . . conform his aims and expectations to the style of his house. His dress, his food, his manners, his taste, his sentiments, his education of his children, and their character as well as his own, will all be seriously affected by this ugly circumstance.[9]*

The single-family dwelling became the paragon of middle-class housing, the most visible symbol of having arrived at a fixed place in society, the goal to which every decent family aspired. It was an investment that many people hoped would provide a ticket to higher status and wealth. "A man is not a whole and complete man," Walt Whitman wrote, "unless he owns a house and the ground it stands on." Or, as *The American Builder* commented in 1869: "It is strange how contentedly men can go on year after year, living like Arabs a tent life, paying exhorbitant rents, with no care or concern for a permanent house." The purchase of one's home became more than a proxy for success; it also conferred moral rectitude. As Russell Conwell would later note in his famed lecture, "Acres of Diamonds," which he repeated thousands of times to audiences across the country:

> *My friend, you take and drive me— if you furnish the auto—out into the suburbs of Philadelphia, and intro-*

duce me to the people who own their homes around this great city, those beautiful homes with gardens and flowers, those magnificent homes so lovely in their art, and I will introduce you to the very best people in character as well as in enterprise in our city, and you know I will. A man is not really a true man until he owns his own home, and they that own their homes are economical and careful, by owning the home.[10]

On the simplest and most basic level, the notion of life in a private house represented stability, a kind of anchor in the heavy seas of urban life. The American population, however, was very transitory. The United States was not only a nation of immigrants, but a nation of migrants. Alexis de Tocqueville observed in 1835, "An American will build a house and sell it before the roof is on," and recently urban historians have demonstrated that in fact residence at the same address for ten years was highly unusual in the nineteenth century. The best long-term data on mobility concerns Muncie, Indiana, site of the classic *Middletown* studies. During the five years between 1893 and 1898, some 35 percent of Muncie families moved; between 1920 and 1924, the proportion rose to 57 percent; during a five-year period in the 1970s, it dropped to 27 percent. Compared to other advanced societies the figures seem to be substantial.[11]

Despite such mobility, permanent residence was considered desirable, and, then as now, homeownership was regarded as a counterweight to the rootlessness of an urbanizing population. The individual house was often no more than one in a series of houses, yet it assumed to itself the values once accorded only the ancestral house, establishing itself as the temporary representation of the ideal permanent home. Although a family might buy the structure planning to inhabit it for only a few years, the Cape Cod, Colonial Revival, and other traditional historical stylings politely ignored their transience and provided an architectural symbolism that spoke of stability and permanence.

Business and political leaders were particularly anxious for citizens to own homes, based on the hope, as Friedrich Engels had feared, that mortgages would have the effect of "chaining the workers by this property to the factory in which they work." A big employer like the Pennsylvania Railroad reportedly was unafraid of strikes because its employees "live in Philadelphia and own their homes, and therefore, cannot afford to strike." Or, as the first president of the Provident Institution for Savings in Boston remarked, "Give him hope, give him the chance of providing for his family, of laying up a store for his old age, of commanding some cheap comfort or luxury, upon which he sets his heart and he will voluntarily and cheerfully submit to privations and hardship."[12]

Marxists and feminists saw this threat because they did not share the vision of tranquil, sexually stratified domesticity in isolated households. In Europe Charles Fourier agreed with Engels that the family was based on the domestic enslavement of women, while in the United States, Charlotte Perkins Gilman, Melusina Fay Peirce, Victoria Woodhull, and a group of *"material feminists"* proposed a complete transformation of homes and cities to end sexual exploitation. Their formula for a "grand domestic revolution" included kitchenless houses and multi-family dwellings. The idea was that some women would cook all the food or do all the laundry, and that regular salaries would attend such duties. On both sides of the Atlantic Ocean, communitarian socialists conducted hundreds of experiments with alternative lifestyles, and many of the most active spokesmen specifically denounced the ideal of the female as the full-time homemaker and the man as absent breadwinner. As a Fourierist journal remarked in

1844, the semirural cottage "is wasteful ineconomy, is untrue to the human heart, and is not the design of God, and therefore it must disappear." As Fourier wished, in many areas of the world and among working class and minority populations in the United States, larger groupings would often be more important than the nuclear unit for reproduction, child-raising, and the economic functioning of the individual.[13]

The isolated household became the American middle-class ideal, however, and it even came to represent the individual himself. As Clare Cooper has noted, just as the body is the most obvious manifestation and encloser of a person, so also is the home itself a representation of the individual. Although it is only a box and often the unindividualized result of mass production and design, it is a very particular box and is almost a tangible expression of self. Men and women find in their homes the greatest opportunity to express their personal taste. Gaston Bachelard has gone further and suggested that much as the house and nonhouse are the basic divisions of geographical space, so the self and the nonself represent the basic divisions of psychic space. Not surprisingly, Anglo-Saxon law and tradition regard a man's home as his castle and permit him to slay anyone who breaks and enters his private abode. The violation of the house is almost as serious as the violation of the self.[14]

Reading 5   The Female World of Cards and Holidays: Women, Families, and the Work of Kinship[1]

MICAELA di LEONARDO*

Why is it that the married women of America are supposed to write all the letters and send all the cards to their husbands' families? My old man is a much better writer than I am, yet he expects me to correspond with his whole family. If I asked him to correspond with mine, he would blow a gasket. [LETTER TO ANN LANDERS]

Women's place in man's life cycle has been that of nurturer, caretaker, and helpmate, the weaver of those networks of relationships on which she in turn relies. [CAROL GILLIGAN, In a Different Voice][2]

Feminist scholars in the past fifteen years have made great strides in formulating new understandings of the relations among gender, kinship, and the larger economy. As a result of this pioneering research, women are newly visible and audible, no longer submerged within their families. We see households as loci of political struggle, inseparable parts of the larger society and economy, rather than as havens from the heartless world of industrial capitalism.[3] And historical and cultural variations in kinship and family forms have become clearer with the maturation of feminist historical and social-scientific scholarship.

Two theoretical trends have been key to this reinterpretation of women's work and family domain. The first is the elevation to visibility of women's nonmarket activities—housework, child care, the servicing of men, and the care of the elderly—and the definition of all these activities as *labor*, to be enumerated alongside and counted as part of overall social reproduction. The second theoretical trend is the nonpejorative focus on women's domestic or kin-centered networks. We now see them as the products of conscious strategy, as crucial to the functioning of kinship systems, as sources of women's autonomous power and possible primary sites of emotional fulfillment, and, at times, as the vehicles for actual survival and/or political resistance.[4]

Recently, however, a division has developed between feminist interpreters of the "labor" and

Many thanks to Cynthia Costello, Rayna Rapp, Roberta Spalter-Roth, John Willoughby, and Barbara Gelpi, Susan Johnson, and Sylvia Yanagisako of *Signs* for their help with this article. I wish in particular to acknowledge the influence of Rayna Rapp's work on my ideas.

*di Leonardo, Micaela. 1987. "The Female World of Cards and Holidays: Women, Families, and the Work of Kinship." *Signs: Journal of Woman in Culture and Society* (12:2):440–453. © 1987 by the University of Chicago. All rights reserved.

the "network" perspectives on women's lives. Those who focus on women's work tend to envision women as sentient, goal-oriented actors, while those who concern themselves with women's ties to others tend to perceive women primarily in terms of nurturance, other-orientation—altruism. The most celebrated recent example of this division is the opposing testimony of historians Alice Kessler-Harris and Rosalind Rosenberg in the Equal Employment Opportunity Commission's sex discrimination case against Sears Roebuck and Company. Kessler-Harris argued that American women historically have actively sought higher-paying jobs and have been prevented from gaining them because of sex discrimination by employers. Rosenberg argued that American women in the nineteenth century created among themselves, through their domestic networks, a "women's culture" that emphasized the nurturance of children and others and the maintenance of family life and that discouraged women from competition over or heavy emotional investment in demanding, high-paid employment.[5]

I shall not here address this specific debate but, instead, shall consider its theoretical background and implications. I shall argue that we need to fuse, rather than to oppose, the domestic network and labor perspectives. In what follows, I introduce a new concept, the work of kinship, both to aid empirical feminist research on women, work, and family and to help advance feminist theory in this arena. I believe that the boundary-crossing nature of the concept helps to confound the self-interest/altruism dichotomy, forcing us from an either-or stance to a position that includes both perspectives. I hope in this way to contribute to a more critical feminist vision of women's lives and the meaning of family in the industrial West.

In my recent field research among Italian-Americans in Northern California, I found myself considering the relations between women's kinship and economic lives. As an anthropologist, I was concerned with people's kin lives beyond conventional American nuclear family or household boundaries. To this end, I collected individual and family life histories, asking about all kin and close friends and their activities. I was also very interested in women's labor. As I sat with women and listened to their accounts of their past and present lives, I began to realize that they were involved in three types of work: housework and child care, work in the labor market, and the work of kinship.[6]

By kin work I refer to the conception, maintenance, and ritual celebration of cross-household kin ties, including visits, letters, telephone calls, presents, and cards to kin; the organization of holiday gatherings; the creation and maintenance of quasi-kin relations; decisions to neglect or to intensify particular ties; the mental work of reflection about all these activities; and the creation and communication of altering images of family and kin vis-à-vis the images of others, both folk and mass media. Kin work is a key element that has been missing in the synthesis of the "household labor" and "domestic network" perspectives. In our emphasis on individual women's responsibilities within households and on the job, we reflect the common picture of households as nuclear units, tied perhaps to the larger social and economic system, but not to *each other.* We miss the point of telephone and soft drink advertising, of women's magazines' holiday issues, of commentators' confused nostalgia for the mythical American extended family: it is kinship contact *across households,* as much as women's work within them, that fulfills our cultural expectation of satisfying family life.

Maintaining these contacts, this sense of family, takes time, intention, and skill. We tend to think of human social and kin networks as the epiphenomena of production and reproduction: the social traces created by our material lives. Or, in the neoclassical tradition, we see them as part of leisure activities, outside an economic purview except insofar as they involve consumption behavior. But the creation and maintenance of kin and quasi-kin networks in advanced industrial societies is *work;* and, moreover, it is largely women's work.

The kin-work lens brought into focus new perspectives on my informants' family lives. First, life histories revealed that often the very existence of kin contact and holiday celebration depended on the presence of an adult woman in the household. When couples divorced or mothers died, the work of kinship was left undone; when women entered into sanctioned sexual or marital relationships with men in these situations, they reconstituted the men's kinship networks and organized gatherings and holiday celebrations. Middle-aged businessman Al Bertini, for example, recalled the death of his mother in his early adolescence: "I think that's probably one of the biggest losses in losing a family— yeah, I remember as a child when my Mom was alive . . . the holidays were treated with enthusiasm and love . . . after she died the attempt was there but it just didn't materialize." Later in life, when Al Bertini and his wife separated, his own and his son Jim's participation in extended-family contact decreased rapidly. But when Jim began a relationship with Jane Bateman, she and he moved in with Al, and Jim and Jane began to invite his kin over for holidays. Jane single-handedly planned and cooked the holiday feasts.

Kin work, then, is like housework and childcare: men in the aggregate do not do it. It differs from these forms of labor in that it is harder for men to substitute hired labor to accomplish these tasks in the absence of kinswomen. Second, I found that women, as the workers in this arena, generally had much greater kin knowledge than did their husbands, often including more accurate and extensive knowledge of their husbands' families. This was true both of middle-aged and younger couples and surfaced as a phenomenon

in my interviews in the form of humorous arguments and in wives' detailed additions to husbands' narratives. Nick Meraviglia, a middle-aged professional, discussed his Italian antecedents in the presence of his wife, Pina:

> *Nick:* My grandfather was a very outspoken man, and it was reported he took off for the hills when he found out that Mussolini was in power.
>
> *Pina:* And he was a very tall man; he used to have to bow his head to get inside doors.
>
> *Nick:* No, that was my uncle.
>
> *Pina:* Your grandfather too, I've heard your mother say.
>
> *Nick:* My mother has a sister and a brother.
>
> *Pina:* Two *sisters!*
>
> *Nick:* You're right!
>
> *Pina:* Maria and Angelina.

Women were also much more willing to discuss family feuds and crises and their own roles in them; men tended to repeat formulaic statements asserting family unity and respectability. (This was much less true for younger men.) Joe and Cetta Longhinotti's statements illustrate these tendencies. Joe responded to my question about kin relations: "We all get along. As a rule, relatives, you got nothing but trouble." Cetta, instead, discussed her relations with each of her grown children, their wives, her in-laws, and her own blood kin in detail. She did not hide the fact that relations were strained in several cases; she was eager to discuss the evolution of problems and to seek my opinions of her actions. Similarly, Pina Meraviglia told the following story of her fight with one of her brothers with hysterical laughter: "There was some biting and hair pulling and choking . . . it was terrible! I shouldn't even tell you. . . ." Nick, meanwhile, was concerned about maintaining an image of family unity and respectability.

Also, men waxed fluent while women were quite inarticulate in discussing their past and present occupations. When asked about their work lives, Joe Longhinotti and Nick Meraviglia, union baker and professional, respectively, gave detailed narratives of their work careers. Cetta Longhinotti and Pina Meraviglia, clerical and former clerical, respectively, offered only short descriptions focusing on factors of ambience, such as the "lovely things" sold by Cetta's firm.

These patterns are not repeated in the younger generation, especially among younger women, such as Jane Bateman, who have managed to acquire training and jobs with some prospect of mobility. These younger women, though, have *added* a professional and detailed interest in their jobs to a felt responsibility for the work of kinship.[7]

Although men rarely took on any kin-work tasks, family histories and accounts of contemporary life revealed that kinswoman often negotiated among themselves, alternating hosting, food-preparation, and gift-buying responsibilities—or sometimes ceding entire task clusters to one woman. Taking on or ceding tasks was clearly related to acquiring or divesting oneself of power within kin networks, but women varied in their interpretation of the meaning of this power. Cetta Longhinotti, for example, relied on the "family Christmas dinner" as a symbol of her central kinship role and was involved in painful negotiations with her daughter-in-law over the issue: "Last year she insisted—this is touchy. She doesn't want to spend the holiday dinner together. So last year we went there. But I still had my dinner the next day . . . I made a big dinner on Christmas Day, regardless of who's coming—candles on the table, the whole routine. I decorate the house myself too . . . well, I just feel that the time will come when maybe I won't feel like cooking a big dinner—she should

take advantage of the fact that I feel like doing it now." Pina Meraviglia, in contrast, was saddened by the centripetal force of the developmental cycle but was unworried about the power dynamics involved in her negotiations with daughters- and mother-in-law over holiday celebrations.

Kin work is not just a matter of power among women but also of the mediation of power represented by household units.[8] Women often choose to minimize status claims in their kin work and to include numbers of households under the rubric of family. Cetta Longhinotti's sister Anna, for example, is married to a professional man whose parents have considerable economic resources, while Joe and Cetta have low incomes and no other well-off kin. Cetta and Anna remain close, talk on the phone several times a week, and assist their adult children, divided by distance and economic status, in remaining united as cousins.

Finally, women perceived housework, child care, market labor, the care of the elderly, and the work of kinship as competing responsibilities. Kin work was a unique category, however, because it was unlabeled and because women felt they could either cede some tasks to kinswoman and/or could cut them back severely. Women variously cited the pressures of market labor, the needs of the elderly, and their own desires for freedom and job enrichment as reasons for cutting back Christmas card lists, organized holiday gatherings, multifamily dinners, letters, visits, and phone calls. They expressed guilt and defensiveness about this cutback process and, particularly, about their failures to keep families close through constant contact and about their failures to create perfect holiday celebrations. Cetta Longhinotti, during the period when she was visiting her elderly mother every weekend in addition to working a full-time job, said of her grown children, "I'd have the whole gang here once a month, but I've been so busy that I haven't done that for about six months." And Pina Meriviglia lamented her insufficient work on family Christmases, "I wish I had really made it traditional... like my sister-in-law has special stories."

Kin work, then, takes place in an arena characterized simultaneously by cooperation and competition, by guilt and gratification. Like housework and child care, it is women's work, with the same lack of clear-cut agreement concerning its proper components: How often should sheets be changed? When should children be toilet trained? Should an aunt send a niece a birthday present? Unlike housework and child care, however, kin work, taking place across the boundaries of normative households, is as yet unlabeled and has no retinue of experts prescribing its correct forms. Neither home economists nor child psychologists have much to say about nieces' birthday presents. Kin work is thus more easily cut back without social interference. On the other hand, the results of kin work—frequent kin contact and feelings of intimacy—are the subject of considerable cultural manipulation as indicators of family happiness. Thus, women in general are subject to the guilt my informants expressed over cutting back kin-work activities.

Although many of my informants referred to the results of women's kin work—cross-household kin contacts and attendant ritual gatherings—as particularly Italian-American, I suggest that in fact this phenomenon is broadly characteristic of American kinship. We think of kin-work tasks such as the preparation of ritual feasts, responsibility for holiday card lists, and gift buying as extensions of women's domestic responsibilities for cooking, consumption, and nurturance. American men in general do not take on these tasks any more than they do housework and child care—and probably less, as these tasks have not yet been the subject of intense public debate. And my informants' gender breakdown

in relative articulateness on kinship and workplace themes reflects the still prevalent occupational segregation—most women cannot find jobs that provide enough pay, status, or promotion possibilities to make them worth focusing on—as well as women's perceived power within kinship networks. The common recognition of that power is reflected in Selma Greenberg's book on nonsexist child rearing. Greenberg calls mothers "press agents" who sponsor relations between their own children and other relatives; she advises a mother whose relatives treat her disrespectfully to deny those kin access to her children.[9]

Kin work is a salient concept in other parts of the developed world as well. Larissa Adler Lomnitz and Marisol Pérez Lizaur have found that "centralizing women" are responsible for these tasks and for communicating "family ideology" among upper-class families in Mexico City. Matthews Hamabata, in his study of upper-class families in Japan, has found that women's kin work involves key financial transactions. Sylvia Junko Yanagisako discovered that, among rural Japanese migrants to the United States, the maintenance of kin networks was assigned to women as the migrants adopted the American ideology of the independent nuclear family household. Maila Stivens notes that urban Australian housewives' kin ties and kin ideology "transcend women's isolation in domestic units."[10]

This is not to say that cultural conceptions of appropriate kin work do not vary, even within the United States. Carol B. Stack documents institutionalized fictive kinship and concomitant reciprocity networks among impoverished black American women. Women in populations characterized by intense feelings of ethnic identity may feel bound to emphasize particular occasions—Saint Patrick's or Columbus Day—with organized family feasts. These constructs may be mediated by religious affiliation, as in the differing emphases on Friday or Sunday family dinners among Jews and Christians. Thus the personnel involved and the amount and kind of labor considered necessary for the satisfactory performance of particular kin-work tasks are likely to be culturally constructed.[11] But while the kin and quasi-kin universes and the ritual calendar may vary among women according to race or ethnicity, their general responsibility for maintaining kin links and ritual observances does not.

As kin work is not an ethnic or racial phenomenon, neither is it linked only to one social class. Some commentators on American family life still reflect the influence of work done in England in the 1950s and 1960s (by Elizabeth Bott and by Peter Willmott and Michael Young) in their assumption that working-class families are close and extended, while the middle class substitutes friends (or anomie) for family. Others reflect the prevalent family pessimism in their presumption that neither working- nor middle-class families have extended kin contact.[12] Insofar as kin contact depends on residential proximity, the larger economy's shifts will influence particular groups' experiences. Factory workers, close to kin or not, are likely to disperse when plants shut down or relocate. Small businesspeople or independent professionals may, however, remain resident in particular areas—and thus maintain proximity to kin—for generations, while professional employees of large firms relocate at their firms' behest. This pattern obtained among my informants.

In any event, cross-household kin contact can be and is effected at long distance through letters, cards, phone calls, and holiday and vacation visits. The form and functions of contact, however, vary according to economic resources. Stack and Brett Williams offer rich accounts of kin networks among poor blacks and migrant Chicano farmworkers functioning to provide emotional support, labor, commodity, and cash exchange—a funeral visit, help with laundry, the gift of a dress or piece of furniture.[13] Far different in degree are exchanges such as the loan of a vacation home, multifamily boating trip, or the provision of free professional services—examples from the kin networks of my wealthier informants. The point is that households, as labor- and income-pooling units, whatever their relative wealth, are somewhat porous in relation to others with those whose members they share kin or quasi-kin ties. We do not really know how class differences operate in this realm; it is possible that they do so largely in terms of ideology. It may be, as David Schneider and Raymond T. Smith suggest, that the affluent and the very poor are more open in recognizing necessary economic ties to kin than are those who identify themselves as middle class.[14]

Recognizing that kin work is gender rather than class based allows us to see women's kin networks among all groups, not just among working-class and impoverished women in industrialized societies. This recognition in turn clarifies our understanding of the privileges and limits of women's varying access to economic resources. Affluent women can "buy out" of housework, child care—and even some kin-work responsibilities. But they, like all women, are ultimately responsible, and subject to both guilt and blame, as the administrators of home, children, and kin network. Even the wealthiest women must negotiate the timing and venue of holidays and other family rituals with their kinswoman. It may be that kin work is the core women's work category in which all women cooperate, while women's perceptions of the appropriateness of cooperation for housework, child care, and the care of the elderly varies by race, class, region, and generation.

But kin work is not necessarily an appropriate category of labor, much less gendered labor, in all societies. In many small-scale societies, kinship is the major organizing principle of all social life, and all contacts are by definition kin contacts.[15] One cannot, therefore, speak of labor that does not involve kin. In the United States, kin work as a separable category of gendered labor perhaps arose historically in concert with the ideological and material constructs of the moral mother/cult of domesticity and the privatized family during the course of industrialization in the eighteenth and nineteenth centuries. These phenomena are connected to the increase in the ubiquity of productive occupations *for men* that are not organized through kinship. This includes the demise of the family farm with the capitalization of agriculture and rural-urban migration; the decline of family recruitment in factories as firms grew, ended child labor, and began to assert bureaucratized forms of control; the decline of artisanal labor and of small entrepreneurial enterprises as large firms took greater and greater shares of the commodity market; the decline of the family firm as corporations—and their managerial work forces—grew beyond the capacities of individual families to provision them; and, finally, the rise of civil service bureaucracies and public pressure against nepotism.[16]

As men increasingly worked alongside of non-kin, and as the ideology of separate spheres was increasingly accepted, perhaps the responsibility for kin maintenance, like that for child rearing, became gender-focused. Ryan points out that "built into the updated family economy . . . was a new measure of voluntarism." This voluntarism, though, "perceived as the shift from patriarchal authority to domestic affection," also signaled the rise of women's moral responsibility for family life. Just as the "idea of fatherhood itself seemed almost to wither away" so did male involvement in the responsibility for kindred lapse.[17]

With postbellum economic growth and geographic movement women's new kin burden involved increasing amounts of time and labor.

The ubiquity of lengthy visits and of frequent letter-writing among nineteenth-century women attests to this. And for visitors and for those who were residentially proximate, the continuing commonalities of women's domestic labor allowed for kinds of work sharing—nursing, childkeeping, cooking, cleaning—that men, with their increasingly differentiated and controlled activities, probably could not maintain. This is not to say that some kin-related male productive work did not continue; my own data, for instance, show kin involvement among small businessmen in the present. It is, instead, to suggest a general trend in material life and a cultural shift that influenced even those whose productive and kin lives remained commingled. Yanagisako has distinguished between the realms of domestic and public kinship in order to draw attention to anthropology's relatively "thin descriptions" of the domestic (female) domain. Using her typology, we might say that kin work as gendered labor comes into existence within the domestic domain with the relative erasure of the domain of public, male kinship.[18]

Whether or not this proposed historical model bears up under further research, the question remains, Why do women do kin work? However material factors may shape activities, they do not determine how individuals may perceive them. And in considering issues of motivation, of intention, of the cultural construction of kin work, we return to the altruism versus self-interest dichotomy in recent feminist theory. Consider the epigraphs to this article. Are women kin workers the nurturant weavers of the Gilligan quotation, or victims, like the fed-up woman who writes to complain to Ann Landers? That is, are we to see kin work as yet another example of "women's culture" that takes the care of others as its primary desideratum? Or are we to see kin work as another way in which men, the economy, and the state extract labor from women without a fair return? And how do women themselves see their kin work and its place in their lives?

As I have indicated above, I believe that it is the creation of the self-interest/altruism dichotomy that is itself the problem here. My women informants, like most American women, accepted their primary responsibility for housework and the care of dependent children. Despite two major waves of feminist activism in this century, the gendering of certain categories of unpaid labor is still largely unaltered. These work responsibilities clearly interfere with some women's labor force commitments at certain life-cycle stages; but, more important, women are simply discriminated against in the labor market and rarely are able to achieve wage and status parity with men of the same age, race, class, and educational background.[19]

Thus for my women informants, as for most American women, the domestic domain is not only an arena in which much unpaid labor must be undertaken but also a realm in which one may attempt to gain human satisfactions—and power—not available in the labor market. Anthropologists Jane Collier and Louise Lamphere have written compellingly on the ways in which varying kinship and economic structures may shape women's competition or cooperation with one another in domestic domains.[20] Feminists considering Western women and families have looked at the issue of power primarily in terms of husband-wife relations or psychological relations between parents and children. If we adopt Collier and Lamphere's broader canvas, though, we see that kin work is not only women's labor from which men and children benefit but also labor that women undertake in order to create obligations in men and children and to gain power over one another. Thus Cetta Longhinotti's struggle with her daughter-in-law over the venue of Christmas dinner is not just about a competition over altruism, it is also about the creation of future obligations. And

thus Cetta's and Anna's sponsorship of their children's friendship with each other is both an act of nurturance and a cooperative means of gaining power over those children.

Although this was not a clear-cut distinction, those of my informants who were more explicitly antifeminist tended to be most invested in kin work. Given the overwhelming historical shift toward greater autonomy for younger generations and the withering of children's financial and labor obligations to their parents, this investment was in most cases tragically doomed. Cetta Longhinotti, for example, had repaid her own mother's devotion with extensive home nursing during the mother's last years. Given Cetta's general failure to direct her adult children in work, marital choice, religious worship, or even frequency of visits, she is unlikely to receive such care from them when she is older.

The kin-work lens thus reveals the close relations between altruism and self-interest in women's actions. As economists Nancy Folbre and Heidi Hartmann point out, we have inherited a Western intellectual tradition that both dichotomizes the domestic and public domains and associates them on exclusive axes such that we find it difficult to see self-interest in the home and altruism in the workplace.[21] But why, in fact, have women fought for better jobs if not, in part, to support their children? These dichotomies are Procrustean beds that warp our understanding of women's lives both at home and at work. "Altruism" and "self-interest" are cultural constructions that are not necessarily mutually exclusive, and we forget this to our peril.

The concept of kin work helps to bring into focus a heretofore unacknowledged array of tasks that is culturally assigned to women in industrialized societies. At the same time, this concept, embodying notions of both love and work and crossing the boundaries of households, helps us to reflect on current feminist debates on women's work, family, and community. We newly see both the interrelations of these phenomena and women's roles in creating and maintaining those interrelations. Revealing the actual labor embodied in what we culturally conceive as love and considering the political uses of this labor helps to deconstruct the self-interest/altruism dichotomy and to connect more closely women's domestic and labor-force lives.

The true value of the concept, however, remains to be tested through further historical and contemporary research on gender, kinship, and labor. We need to assess the suggestion that gendered kin work emerges in concert with the capitalist development process; to probe the historical record for women's and men's varying and changing conceptions of it; and to research the current range of its cultural constructions and material realities. We know that household boundaries are more porous than we had thought—but they are undoubtedly differentially porous, and this is what we need to specify. We need, in particular, to assess the relations of changing labor processes, residential patterns, and the use of technology to changing kin work.

Altering the values attached to this particular set of women's tasks will be as difficult as are the housework, child-care, and occupational-segregation struggles. But just as feminist research in these latter areas is complementary and cumulative, so researching kin work should help us to piece together the home, work, and public-life landscape—to see the female world of cards and holidays as it is constructed and lived within the changing political economy. How female that world is to remain, and what it would look like if it were not sex-segregated, are questions we cannot yet answer.

Reading 6   Mexican American Women Grassroots Community Activists: "Mothers of East Los Angeles"*

MARY PARDO

The relatively few studies of Chicana political activism show a bias in the way political activism is conceptualized by social scientists, who often use a narrow definition confined to electoral politics.[1] Most feminist research uses an expanded definition that moves across the boundaries between public, electoral politics and private, family politics; but feminist research generally focuses on women mobilized around gender-specific issues.[2] For some feminists, adherence to "tradition" constitutes conservatism and submission to patriarchy. Both approaches exclude the contributions of working-class women, particularly those of Afro-American women and Latinas, thus failing to capture the full dynamic of social change.[3]

The following case study of Mexican American women activists in "Mothers of East Los Angeles" (MELA) contributes another dimension to the conception of grassroots politics. It illustrates how these Mexican American women transform "traditional" networks and resources based on family and culture into political assets to defend the quality of urban life. Far from unique, these patterns of activism are repeated in Latin America and elsewhere. Here as in other times and places, the women's activism arises out of seemingly "traditional" roles, addresses wider social and political issues, and capitalizes on informal associations sanctioned by the community.[4] Religion, commonly viewed as a conservative force, is intertwined with politics.[5] Often, women speak of their communities and their activism as extensions of their family and household responsibility. The central role of women in grassroots struggles around quality of life, in the Third World and in the United States, challenges conventional assumptions about the powerlessness of women and static definitions of culture and tradition.

In general, the women in MELA are long-time residents of East Los Angeles; some are bilingual and native born, others Mexican born and Spanish dominant. All the core activists are bilingual and have lived in the community over thirty years. All have been active in parish-sponsored groups and activities; some have had experience working in community-based groups arising from schools, neighborhood watch associations, and labor support groups. To gain an appreciation of the group and the core activists, I used ethnographic field methods. I interviewed

*Pardo, Mary. 1990. "Mexican American Women Grassroots Community Activists: 'Mothers of East Los Angeles.'" *Frontiers* 11 (1):1–7. FRONTIERS Editorial Collective. Reprinted by permission.

six women, using a life history approach focused on their first community activities, current activism, household and family responsibilities, and perceptions of community issues.[6] Also, from December 1987 through October 1989, I attended hearings on the two currently pending projects of contention—a proposed state prison and a toxic waste incinerator—and participated in community and organizational meetings and demonstrations. The following discussion briefly chronicles an intense and significant five-year segment of community history from which emerged MELA and the women's transformation of "traditional" resources and experiences into political assets for community mobilization.[7]

THE COMMUNITY CONTEXT: EAST LOS ANGELES RESISTING SIEGE

Political science theory often guides the political strategies used by local government to select the sites for undesirable projects. In 1984, the state of California commissioned a public relations firm to assess the political difficulties facing the construction of energy-producing waste incinerators. The report provided a "personality profile" of those residents most likely to organize effective opposition to projects:

> *middle and upper socioeconomic strata possess better resources to effectuate their opposition. Middle and higher socioeconomic strata neighborhoods should not fall within the one-mile and five-mile radii of the proposed site. Conversely, older people, people with a high school education or less are least likely to oppose a facility.[8]*

The state accordingly placed the plant in Commerce, a predominantly Mexican American,

low-income community. This pattern holds throughout the state and the country: three out of five Afro-Americans and Latinos live near toxic waste sites, and three of the five largest hazardous waste landfills are in communities with at least 80 percent minority populations.[9]

Similarly, in March 1985, when the state sought a site for the first state prison in Los Angeles County, Governor Deukmejian resolved to place the 1,700-inmate institution in East Los Angeles, within a mile of the long-established Boyle Heights neighborhood and within two miles of thirty-four schools. Furthermore, violating convention, the state bid on the expensive parcel of industrially zoned land without compiling an environmental impact report or providing a public community hearing. According to James Vigil, Jr., a field representative for Assemblywoman Gloria Molina, shortly after the state announced the site selection, Molina's office began informing the community and gauging residents' sentiments about it through direct mailings and calls to leaders of organizations and business groups.

In spring 1986, after much pressure from the 56th assembly district office and the community, the Department of Corrections agreed to hold a public information meeting, which was attended by over 700 Boyle Heights residents. From this moment on, Vigil observed, "the tables turned, the community mobilized, and the residents began calling the political representatives and requesting their presence at hearings and meetings."[10] By summer 1986, the community was well aware of the prison site proposal. Over two thousand people, carrying placards proclaiming "No Prison in ELA," marched from Resurrection Church in Boyle Heights to the 3rd Street bridge linking East Los Angeles with the rapidly expanding downtown Los Angeles.[11] This march marked the beginning of one of the largest grassroots coalitions to emerge from the Latino community in the last decade.

Prominent among the coalition's groups is "Mothers of East Los Angeles," a loosely knit group of over 400 Mexican American women.[12] MELA initially coalesced to oppose the state prison construction but has since organized opposition to several other projects detrimental to the quality of life in the central city.[13] Its second large target is a toxic waste incinerator proposed for Vernon, a small city adjacent to East Los Angeles. This incinerator would worsen the already debilitating air quality of the entire county and set a precedent dangerous for other communities throughout California.[14] When MELA took up the fight against the toxic waste incinerator it became more than a single-issue group and began working with environmental groups around the state.[15] As a result of the community struggle, AB58 (Roybal-Allard), which provides all Californians with the minimum protection of an environmental impact report before the construction of hazardous waste incinerators, was signed into law. But the law's effectiveness relies on a watchful community network. Since its emergence, "Mothers of East Los Angeles" has become centrally important to just such a network of grassroots activists including a select number of Catholic priests and two Mexican American political representatives. Furthermore, the group's very formation, and its continued spirit and activism, fly in the face of the conventional political science beliefs regarding political participation.

Predictions by the "experts" attribute the low formal political participation (i.e., voting) of Mexican American people in the U.S. to a set of cultural "retardants" including primary kinship systems, fatalism, religious traditionalism, traditional cultural values, and mother country attachments.[16] The core activists in MELA may appear to fit this description, as well as the state-commissioned profile of residents least likely to oppose toxic waste incinerator projects. All the women live in a low-income community. Furthermore, they identify themselves as active and committed participants in the Catholic Church; they claim an ethnic identity—Mexican American; their ages range from forty to sixty; and they have attained at most high school educations. However, these women fail to conform to the predicted political apathy. Instead, they have transformed social identity—ethnic identity, class identity, and gender identity—into an impetus as well as a basis for activism. And, in transforming their existing social networks into grassroots political networks, they have also transformed themselves.

TRANSFORMATION AS A DOMINANT THEME

From the life histories of the group's core activists and from my own field notes, I have selected excerpts that tell two representative stories. One is a narrative of the events that led to community mobilization in East Los Angeles. The other is a story of transformation, the process of creating new and better relationships that empower people to unite and achieve common goals.[17]

First, women have transformed organizing experiences and social networks arising from gender-related responsibilities into political resources.[18] When I asked the women about the first community, not necessarily "political," involvement they could recall, they discussed experiences that predated the formation of MELA. Juana Gutiérrez explained:

> *Well, it didn't start with the prison, you know. It started when my kids went to school. I started by joining the Parents Club and we worked on different problems here in the area. Like the people who come to the parks to sell drugs to the kids. I got the neighbors to have meetings. I would go knock at the doors, house to house. And I told them that we*

should stick together with the Neigh-borhood Watch for the community and for the kids.[19]

Erlinda Robles similarly recalled:

I wanted my kids to go to Catholic school and from the time my oldest one went there, I was there every day. I used to take my two little ones with me and I helped one way or another. I used to question things they did. And the other mothers would just watch me. Later, they would ask me, "Why do you do that? They are going to take it out on your kids." I'd say, "They better not." And before you knew it, we had a big group of mothers that were very involved.[20]

Part of a mother's "traditional" responsibility includes overseeing her child's progress in school, interacting with school staff, and supporting school activities. In these processes, women meet other mothers and begin developing a network of acquaintanceships and friendships based on mutual concern for the welfare of their children.

Although the women in MELA carried the greatest burden of participating in school activities, Erlinda Robles also spoke of strategies they used to draw men into the enterprise and into the networks:[21]

At the beginning, the priests used to say who the president of the mothers guild would be; they used to pick 'um. But, we wanted elections, so we got elections. Then we wanted the fathers to be involved, and the nuns suggested that a father should be president and a mother would be secretary or be involved there [at the school site].[22]

Of course, this comment piqued my curiosity, so I asked how the mothers agreed on the nuns' suggestion. The answer was simple and instructive:

At the time we thought it was a "natural" way to get the fathers involved because they weren't involved; it was just the mothers. Everybody [the women] agreed on them [the fathers] being president because they worked all day and they couldn't be involved in a lot of daily activities like food sales and whatever. During the week, a steering committee of mothers planned the group's activities. But now that I think about it, a woman could have done the job just as well![23]

So women got men into the group by giving them a position they could manage. The men may have held the title of "president," but they were not making day-to-day decisions about work, nor were they dictating the direction of the group. Erlinda Robles laughed as she recalled an occasion when the president insisted, against the wishes of the women, on scheduling a parents' group fundraiser—a breakfast—on Mother's Day. On that morning, only the president and his wife were present to prepare breakfast. This should alert researchers against measuring power and influence by looking solely at who holds titles.

Each of the cofounders had a history of working with groups arising out of the responsibilities usually assumed by "mothers"—the education of children and the safety of the surrounding community. From these groups, they gained valuable experiences and networks that facilitated the formation of "Mothers of East Los Angeles." Juana Gutiérrez explained how preexisting networks progressively expanded community support:

You know nobody knew about the plan to build a prison in this community until Assemblywoman Gloria Molina told me. Martha Molina called me and said, "You know what is happening in your area? The governor wants to put a prison in Boyle Heights!" So, I called a Neighborhood Watch meeting at my house and we got fifteen people together. Then, Father John started informing his people at the Church and that is when the group of two to three hundred started showing up for every march on the bridge.[24]

MELA effectively linked up preexisting networks into a viable grassroots coalition.

Second, the process of activism also transformed previously "invisible" women, making them not only visible but the center of public attention. From a conventional perspective, political activism assumes a kind of gender neutrality. This means that anyone can participate, but men are the expected key actors. In accordance with this pattern, in winter 1986 an informal group of concerned businessmen in the community began lobbying and testifying against the prison at hearings in Sacramento. Working in conjunction with Assemblywoman Molina, they made many trips to Sacramento at their own expense. Residents who did not have the income to travel were unable to join them. Finally, Molina, commonly recognized as a forceful advocate for Latinas and the community, asked Frank Villalobos, an urban planner in the group, why there were no women coming up to speak in Sacramento against the prison. As he phrased it, "I was getting some heat from her because no women were going up there."[25]

In response to this comment, Veronica Gutiérrez, a law student who lived in the community, agreed to accompany him on the next trip to Sacramento.[26] He also mentioned the comment to Father John Moretta at Resurrection Catholic Parish. Meanwhile, representatives of the business sector of the community and of the 56th assembly district office were continuing to compile arguments and supportive data against the East Los Angeles prison site. Frank Villalobos stated one of the pressing problems:

We felt that the Senators whom we prepared all this for didn't even acknowledge that we existed. They kept calling it the "downtown" site, and they argued that there was no opposition in the community. So, I told Father Moretta, what we have to do is demonstrate that there is a link (proximity) between the Boyle Heights community and the prison.[27]

The next juncture illustrates how perceptions of gender-specific behavior set in motion a sequence of events that brought women into the political limelight. Father Moretta decided to ask all the women to meet after mass. He told them about the prison site and called for their support. When I asked him about his rationale for selecting the women, he replied:

I felt so strongly about the issue, and I knew in my heart what a terrible offense this was to the people. So, I was afraid that once we got into a demonstration situation we had to be very careful. I thought the women would be cooler and calmer than the men. The bottom line is that the men came anyway. The first times out the majority were women. Then they began to invite their husbands and their children, but originally it was just women.[28]

Father Moretta also named the group. Quite moved by a film, *The Official Story,* about the courageous Argentine women who demonstrated for the return of their children who disappeared during a repressive right-wing military dictatorship, he transformed the name "Las Madres de la Plaza de Mayo" into "Mothers of East Los Angeles."[29]

However, Aurora Castillo, one of the cofounders of the group, modified my emphasis on the predominance of women:

> *Of course the fathers work. We also have many, many grandmothers. And all this is with the support of the fathers. They make the placards and the posters; they do the security and carry the signs; and they come to the marches when they can.*[30]

Although women played a key role in the mobilization, they emphasized the group's broad base of active supporters as well as the other organizations in the "Coalition Against the Prison." Their intent was to counter any notion that MELA was composed exclusively of women or mothers and to stress the "inclusiveness" of the group. All the women who assumed lead roles in the group had long histories of volunteer work in the Boyle Heights community; but formation of the group brought them out of the "private" margins and into "public" light.

Third, the women in "Mothers of East L.A." have transformed the definition of "mother" to include militant political opposition to state-proposed projects they see as adverse to the quality of life in the community. Explaining how she discovered the issue, Aurora Castillo said,

> *You know if one of your children's safety is jeopardized, the mother turns into a lioness. That's why Father John got the mothers. We have to have a well-organized, strong group of mothers to protect the community and oppose things that are detrimental to us. You know the governor is in the wrong and the mothers are in the right. After all, the mothers have to be right. Mothers are for the children's interest, not for self-interest; the governor is for his own political interest.*[31]

The women also have expanded the boundaries of "motherhood" to include social and political community activism and redefined the word to include women who are not biological "mothers." At one meeting a young Latina expressed her solidarity with the group and, almost apologetically, qualified herself as a "resident," not a "mother," of East Los Angeles. Erlinda Robles replied:

> *When you are fighting for a better life for children and "doing" for them, isn't that what mothers do? So we're all mothers. You don't have to have children to be a "mother."*[32]

At critical points, grassroots community activism requires attending many meetings, phone calling, and door-to-door communications—all very labor-intensive work. In order to keep harmony in the "domestic" sphere, the core activists must creatively integrate family members into their community activities. I asked Erlinda Robles how her husband felt about her activism, and she replied quite openly:

> *My husband doesn't like getting involved, but he takes me because he knows I like it. Sometimes we would have two or three meetings a week. And my husband would say, "Why are you doing so much? It is*

really getting out of hand." But he is very supportive. Once he gets there, he enjoys it and he starts in arguing too! See, it's just that he is not used to it. He couldn't believe things happened the way that they do. He was in the Navy twenty years and they brainwashed him that none of the politicians could do wrong. So he has come a long way. Now he comes home and parks the car out front and asks me, "Well, where are we going tonight?"[33]

When women explain their activism, they link family and community as one entity. Juana Gutiérrez, a woman with extensive experience working on community and neighborhood issues, stated:

Yo como madre de familia, y como residente del Este de Los Angeles, seguiré luchando sin descanso por que se nos respete. Y yo lo hago con bastante cariño hacia mi comunidad. Digo "mi comunidad," porque me siento parte de ella, quiero a mi raza como parte de mi familia, y si Dios me permite seguiré luchando contra todos los gobernadores que quieran abusar de nosotros. (As a mother and a resident of East L.A., I shall continue fighting tirelessly, so we will be respected. And I will do this with much affection for my community. I say "my community" because I am part of it. I love my "raza" [race] as part of my family; and if God allows, I will keep on fighting against all the governors that want to take advantage of us.)[34]

Like the other activists, she has expanded her responsibilities and legitimated militant opposition to abuse of the community by representatives of the state.

Working-class women activists seldom opt to separate themselves from men and their families. In this particular struggle for community quality of life, they are fighting for the family unit and thus are not competitive with men.[35] Of course, this fact does not preclude different alignments in other contexts and situations.[36]

Fourth, the story of MELA also shows the transformation of class and ethnic identity. Aurora Castillo told of an incident that illustrated her growing knowledge of the relationship of East Los Angeles to other communities and the basis necessary for coalition building:

And do you know we have been approached by other groups? [She lowers her voice in emphasis.] You know that Pacific Palisades group asked for our backing. But what they did, they sent their powerful lobbyist that they pay thousands of dollars to get our support against the drilling in Pacific Palisades. So what we did was tell them to send their grassroots people, not their lobbyist. We're suspicious. We don't want to talk to a high-salaried lobbyist; we are humble people. We did our own lobbying. In one week we went to Sacramento twice.[37]

The contrast between the often tedious and labor-intensive work of mobilizing people at the "grassroots" level and the paid work of a "high salaried lobbyist" represents a point of pride and integrity, not a deficiency or a source of shame. If the two groups were to construct a coalition, they must communicate on equal terms.

The women of MELA combine a willingness to assert opposition with a critical assessment of their own weaknesses. At one community meeting, for example, representatives of several oil companies attempted to gain support for placement of an oil pipeline through the center of East Los Angeles. The exchange between the women in the audience and the oil representative was heated, as women alternated asking questions about the chosen route for the pipeline:

> "Is it going through Cielito Lindo [Reagan's ranch]?" The oil representative answered, "No." Another woman stood up and asked, "Why not place it along the coastline?" Without thinking of the implications, the representative responded, "Oh, no! If it burst, it would endanger the marine life." The woman retorted, "You value the marine life more than human beings?" His face reddened with anger and the hearing disintegrated into angry chanting.[38]

The proposal was quickly defeated. But Aurora Castillo acknowledged that it was not solely their opposition that brought about the defeat:

> We won because the westside was opposed to it, so we united with them. You know there are a lot of attorneys who live there and they also questioned the representative. Believe me, no way is justice blind. . . . We just don't want all this garbage thrown at us because we are low-income and Mexican American. We are lucky now that we have good representatives, which we didn't have before.[39]

Throughout their life histories, the women refer to the disruptive effects of land use decisions made in the 1950s. As longtime residents, all but one share the experience of losing a home and relocating to make way for a freeway. Juana Gutiérrez refers to the community response at that time:

> Una de las cosas que me caen muy mal es la injusticia y en nuestra comunidad hemos visto mucho de eso. Sobre todo antes, porque creo que nuestra gente estaba mas dormida, nos atrevíamos menos. En los cincuentas hicieron los freeways y así, sin más, nos dieron la noticia de que nos teníamos que mudar. Y eso pasó dos veces. La gente se conformaba porque lo ordeno el gobierno. Recuerdo que yo me enojaba y quería que los demás me secundaran, pero nadia quería hacer nada. (One of the things that really upsets me is the injustice that we see so much in our community. Above everything else, I believe that our people were less aware; we were less challenging. In the 1950s—they made the freeways and just like that they gave us a notice that we had to move. That happened twice. The people accepted it because the government ordered it. I remember that I was angry and wanted the others to back me but nobody else wanted to do anything.)[40]

The freeways that cut through communities and disrupted neighborhoods are now a concrete reminder of shared injustice, of the vulnerability of the community in the 1950s. The community's social and political history thus informs perceptions of its current predicament; however, today's activists emphasize not the powerlessness of the community but the change in status and progression toward political empowerment.

Fifth, the core activists typically tell stories illustrating personal change and a new sense of entitlement to speak for the community. They have transformed the unspoken sentiments of individuals into a collective community voice. Lucy Ramos related her initial apprehensions:

I was afraid to get involved. I didn't know what was going to come out of this and I hesitated at first. Right after we started, Father John came up to me and told me, "I want you to be a spokesperson." I said, "Oh no, I don't know what I am going to say." I was nervous. I am surprised I didn't have a nervous breakdown then. Every time we used to get in front of the TV cameras and even interviews like this, I used to sit there and I could feel myself shaking. But as time went on, I started getting used to it.

And this is what I have noticed with a lot of them. They were afraid to speak up and say anything. Now, with this prison issue, a lot of them have come out and come forward and given their opinions. Everybody used to be real "quietlike."[41]

She also related a situation that brought all her fears to a climax, which she confronted and resolved as follows:

When I first started working with the coalition, Channel 13 called me up and said they wanted to interview me and I said OK. Then I started get-ting nervous. So I called Father John and told him, "You better get over here right away." He said, "Don't worry, don't worry, you can handle it by yourself." Then Channel 13 called me back and said they were going to interview another person, someone I had never heard of, and asked if it was OK if he came to my house. And I said OK again. Then I began thinking, what if this guy is for the prison? What am I going to do? And I was so nervous and I thought, I know what I am going to do!

Since the meeting was taking place in her home, she reasoned that she was entitled to order any troublemakers out of her domain:

If this man tells me anything, I am just going to chase him out of my house. That is what I am going to do! All these thoughts were going through my head. Then Channel 13 walk into my house followed by six men I had never met. And I thought, Oh, my God, what did I get myself into? I kept saying to myself, if they get smart with me I am throwing them ALL out.[42]

At this point her tone expressed a sense of resolve. In fact, the situation turned out to be neither confrontational nor threatening, as the "other men" were also members of the coalition. This woman confronted an anxiety-laden situation by relying on her sense of control within her home and family—a quite "traditional" source of authority for women—and transforming that control into the courage to express a political position before a potential audience all over one of the largest metropolitan areas in the nation.

People living in Third World countries as well as in minority communities in the United States face an increasingly degraded environment.[43] Recognizing the threat to the well-being of their families, residents have mobilized at the neighborhood level to fight for "quality of life" issues. The common notion that environmental well-being is of concern solely to white middle-class and upper-class residents ignores the specific way working-class neighborhoods suffer from the fallout of the city "growth machine" geared for profit.[44]

In Los Angeles, the culmination of postwar urban renewal policies, the growing Pacific Rim trade surplus and investment, and low-wage international labor migration from Third World countries are creating potentially volatile conditions. Literally palatial financial buildings swallow up the space previously occupied by modest, low-cost housing. Increasing density and development not matched by investment in social programs, services, and infrastructure erode the quality of life, beginning in the core of the city.[45] Latinos, the majority of whom live close to the center of the city, must confront the distilled social consequences of development focused solely on profit. The Mexican American community in East Los Angeles, much like other minority working-class communities, has been a repository for prisons instead of new schools, hazardous industries instead of safe work sites, and one of the largest concentrations of freeway interchanges in the country, which transports much wealth past the community. And the concerns of residents in East Los Angeles may provide lessons for other minority as well as middle-class communities. Increasing environmental pollution resulting from inadequate waste disposal plans and an out-of-control "need" for penal institutions to contain the casualties created by the growing bipolar distribution of wages may not be limited to the Southwest.[46]

These conditions set the stage for new conflicts and new opportunities, to reform old relationships into coalitions that can challenge state agendas and create new community visions.[47]

Mexican American women living east of downtown Los Angeles exemplify the tendency of women to enter into environmental struggles in defense of their community. Women have a rich historical legacy of community activism, partly reconstructed over the last two decades in social histories of women who contested other "quality of life issues," from the price of bread to "Demon Rum" (often representing domestic violence).[48]

But something new is also happening. The issues "traditionally" addressed by women—health, housing, sanitation, and the urban environment—have moved to center stage as capitalist urbanization progresses. Environmental issues now fuel the fires of many political campaigns and drive citizens beyond the rather restricted, perfunctory political act of voting. Instances of political mobilization at the grassroots level, where women often play a central role, allow us to "see" abstract concepts like participatory democracy and social change as dynamic processes.

The existence and activities of "Mothers of East Los Angeles" attest to the dynamic nature of participatory democracy, as well as to the dynamic nature of our gender, class, and ethnic identity. The story of MELA reveals, on the one hand, how individuals and groups can transform a seemingly "traditional" role such as "mother." On the other hand, it illustrates how such a role may also be a social agent drawing members of the community into the "political" arena. Studying women's contributions as well as men's will shed greater light on the networks dynamic of grassroots movements.[49]

The work "Mothers of East Los Angeles" do to mobilize the community demonstrates that people's political involvement cannot be predicted by their cultural characteristics. These women have defied stereotypes of apathy and used ethnic, gender, and class identity as an impetus, a strength, a vehicle for political activism. They have expanded their—and our—understanding of the complexities of a political system, and they have reaffirmed the possibility of "doing something."

They also generously share the lessons they have learned. One of the women in "Mothers of East Los Angeles" told me, as I hesitated to set up an interview with another woman I hadn't yet met in person,

> *You know, nothing ventured nothing lost. You should have seen how timid we were the first time we went to a public hearing. Now, forget it, I walk right up and make myself heard and that's what you have to do.*[50]

Chapter

3 Immigrant and Ethnic Families

Reading 7   Immigrant Families in the City*

MARK HUTTER

The period of time from 1880 to 1924, when immigration laws placed severe limitation on movement into the United States, witnessed a massive exodus of people from southern and eastern Europe. This "new" immigration was from countries like Austria-Hungary, Greece, Italy, Poland, Rumania, Russia, and Serbia (now a part of Yugoslavia). Immigrants from these countries were joined by others from China and Japan, Mexico, French Canada, and the West Indies. It contrasts with the peoples of the "old" immigration, those who arrived between 1820 (when federal statistics of origin were first recorded) and 1880. That was made up almost entirely of northwest Europeans who came from countries such as England, Ireland, Scotland, France, Germany, Norway and Sweden.

Total immigration in the three decades before the Civil War totaled five million. Between 1860 and 1890 that number doubled, and between 1890 and the beginning of the first world war in 1914, it tripled. The peak years of immigration were in the early twentieth century, with over a million people entering annually in 1905, 1906, 1907, 1910, 1913, and 1914. The main explanation for this massive movement of people to the United States was that the countries of origin of the "new" immigrants were experiencing population explosions and disloca-

tions. By the later part of the nineteenth century, the pressures of overpopulation, combined with the prospects of economic opportunity in the United States and the availability of rapid transportation systems that included railroads and steamships, set the wheels of world migration moving. Maldwyn Allen Jones, whose study *American Immigration* (1960) has been a standard work on the subject, comments on the shared motives of the culturally diversified immigrants for coming to America:

The motives for immigration... have been always a mixture of yearning— for riches, for land, for change, for tranquillity, for freedom, and for something not definable in words.... The experiences of different immigrants groups... reveal a fundamental uniformity. Whenever they came, the fact that they had been uprooted from their old surroundings meant that they faced the necessity of coming to terms with an unfamiliar environment and a new status. The story of American immigration is one of millions of enterprising, courageous folk, most of them humble, nearly all of them unknown by name to

*Hutter, Mark. 1986–1987. "Immigrant Families in the City." *The Gallatin Review* 6(Winter): 60–69.

history. Coming from a great variety of backgrounds, they nonetheless resembled one another in their willingness to look beyond the horizon and in their readiness to pull up stakes in order to seek a new life. (Jones 1960, pp. 4–5)

There was a great deal of variation in immigrant family migration arrangements. Some immigrant groups coming from Scandinavian societies and from Germany came as nuclear families responding to America's needs to settle and farm the vast lands of middle western America. For these groups settlement often meant the almost complete reconstitution of Old World rural village life and family patterns in rural America (Hareven and Modell 1980). One extreme example of this practice were the Hutterites, a German religious group that lived in Russia and migrated to the United States in the late nineteenth century. They settled in isolated rural agricultural sections in order to maintain their distinctive family patterns. These include early marriage, exceptionally high fertility, and near universal remarriage after widowhood. The Hutterite community was a highly cooperative family economy ruled by a family patriarch that operated through kinship affiliations created by the high fertility and strict laws of intermarriage. This isolated group could and has maintained itself until today because of its ability to find marriage partners within the group.

As agricultural opportunities in rural America declined and as the demand for skilled and especially unskilled urban workers grew, the "new" immigrations from southern and eastern Europe concentrated in the industrial cities of the Northeast and the Midwest. It was in these urban areas where job opportunities were plentiful and where the chances of success were greatest. Young unattached males became the mainstay of the migration population. The ethnic

historian Thomas J. Archdeacon (1983) reports that, in the decades between 1840 and 1899, males constituted 58 to 61 percent of the arrivals. By contrast, the importance of single males accounts for the statistic that 70 percent of the newcomers between 1900 and 1909 and that two out of every three between 1910 and 1914 were males. The proportion of males to females did not take place evenly across the immigrant nationalities. Jews displayed the best balance with an almost fifty-fifty split. Southern Italians, on the other hand, had more than three times as many males as females. The sex ratio among Greeks, the most extreme group, indicated that for every one Greek female there were 11 Greek men. Such sex ratio imbalances obviously set limits on the possibility of family life during this time period.

The ultimate success of an immigrant group depended in large part on its ability to reestablish a normal pattern of family life in America. This initially proved quite difficult. Severe problems confronted the immigrant families in America. The huge influx of immigrants to the American cities gave new meaning and visibility to urban poverty. Ghetto housing was awful; inadequate buildings were cheaply and quickly built to meet immediate needs, which proved to be inadequate. People lived in overcrowded, dirty, unsanitary, and poorly ventilated and poorly heated apartment dwellings that were still expensive because of the demand. Boarders and lodgers were numerous and helped provide some of the needed monies to pay the rent. It was not uncommon for beds to be used around the clock, with day-shift workers using them at night and night-shift workers using them during the day.

The horrible living conditions were dramatically exposed in the muckraking works of such novelists as Upton Sinclair, whose famous novel *The Jungle* exposed the grinding poverty in the Slavic communities in Chicago located within the stench of the blood and entrails of cattle being slaughtered in the neighborhood stockyards, and also of the journalistic accounts of newsmen like Lincoln Steffens whose book, *The Shame of the Cities,* refers to the ghetto slums as literally looking like hell. The journalist Jacob Riis, himself an immigrant from Denmark, wrote and photographed the urban poverty of New York's ghetto life in his classic work, *How the Other Half Lives.* His graphic descriptions of the barren and filthy firetraps of New York's tenements startled the nation. The following passage from his book is typical of what life was like in one of these buildings:

> —*Cherry Street. Be a little careful please. The hall is dark and you might stumble over the children.... Not that it would hurt them; kicks and cuffs are their daily diet. They have little else. Here where the hall turns and dives into utter darkness is a step, and another, another. A flight of stairs. You can feel your way, if you cannot see it. Close? Yes! What would you have? All the fresh air that ever enters these stairs comes from the hall-door that is forever slamming, and from the windows of dark bedrooms that in turn receive from the stairs their sole supply of the elements God meant to be free, but man deals out with such niggardly hand.... The sinks are in the hallway, that all the tenants may have access—and all be poisoned alike by their summer stenches.... Hear the pumps squeak! It is the lullaby of tenement house babies. In summer, when a thousand thirsty throats pant for a cooling drink in this block, it is worked in vain. But the saloon, whose open door you passed in the hall, is always there. The smell of it has followed you up. Here is a door. Listen! That short hacking cough, that tiny, helpless wail—what do they mean? They mean... a sadly familiar story—before the day is at an end. The child is dying with measles. With half a chance it might have lived; but it had none. That dark bedroom killed it. (Riis, 1890/ 1957, pp. 33–34).*

A common theme in the popular literature of that time were stories of wives forgotten in the old country and of families torn asunder by the clash of the old ways of life with the new. The editorial columns of the immigrant press frequently reported on the life struggles of its readers. Many newspapers had "advice" columns with its editors serving as lay clergy, social worker, friend, and relative to those who had nowhere else to turn. The "Bintel Brief" ("Bundle of Letters") of the *Jewish Daily Forward* has become the most famous of these advice columns. Through it, readers wrote of their marital and family problems, the impact of poverty on their lives, religious conflicts in terms of attitudes and behavior, and other life concerns. The following two letters, the first from 1906 and the second from 1910, were reprinted in *A Bintel Brief* (Metzker 1971) and are illustrative of such advice columns:

1906

Worthy Mr. Editor,

I was married six years ago in Russia. My husband had not yet been called up for the military service, and I married him because he was an only son and I knew he would not be taken as a soldier. But that year all originally exempted men were taken in our village. He had no desire to serve Czar Nickolai and since I didn't want that either, I sold everything I could and sent him to London. From there he went to America:

At first he wrote to me that it was hard for him to find work, so he couldn't send me anything to live on. I suffered terribly. I couldn't go to work because I was pregnant. And the harder my struggles became, the sadder were the letters from my husband. I suffered from hunger and cold, but what could I do when he was worse off than I?

Then his letters became fewer. Weeks and months passed without a word.

In the time I went to the rabbi of our town and begged him to have pity on a deserted wife. I asked him to write to a New York rabbi to find out what had happened to my husband. All kinds of thoughts ran through my mind because in a big city like New York anything can happen. I imagined perhaps he was sick, maybe even dead.

A month later an answer came to the rabbi. They had found out where my husband was but didn't want to talk with him until I could come to America.

My relatives from several towns collected enough money for my passage and I came to New York, to the rabbi. They tricked my husband into coming there too. Till the day I die I'll never forget the expression on my husband's face when he unexpectedly saw me and the baby.

I was speechless. The rabbi questioned him for me, sternly, like a judge, and asked him where he worked and how much he earned. My husband answered that he was a carpenter and made twelve dollars a week.

"Do you have a wife, or are you single?" the rabbi asked. My husband trembled as he answered, "I have committed a crime," and he began to wipe his eyes with a handkerchief. And soon a detective appeared in the rabbi's house and

arrested my husband, and the next day the story appeared in the Jewish newspapers. Then some good women who had pity on me helped me. They found a job for me, took me to lectures and theaters. I began to read books I had never realized existed.

In time I adjusted to life here. I am not lonely, and life for me and my child is quite good. I want to add here, too, that my husband's wife came to me, fell at my feet and cried, but my own problems are enough for me.

But in time my conscience began to bother me. I began to think of my husband, suffering behind bars in his dark cell. In dreams I see his present wife, who certainly loves him, and her little boy living in dire need without their breadwinner. I now feel differently about the whole thing and I have sympathy for my husband. I am even prepared, when he gets out of jail, to wish him luck with his new life partner, but he will probably be embittered toward me. I have terrible pangs of conscience and I don't know what I can do. I hope you will print my letter, and answer me.

Cordially,
Z.B.

Answer:

In the answer to this letter, the woman is comforted and praised for her decency, her sympathy for her husband and his second wife. Also it is noted that when the husband is released he will surely have no complaints against her, since he is the guilty one in the circumstances, not she.

1910

Worthy Editor

My husband [here the name was given] deserted me and our three small children, leaving us in desperate need. I was left without a bit of bread for the children, with debts in the grocery store and the butcher's and last month's rent unpaid.

I am not complaining so much about his abandoning me as about the grief and suffering of our little children, who beg for food, which I cannot give them. I am young and healthy. I am able and willing to work in order to support my children, but unfortunately I am tied down because my baby is only six months old. I looked for an institution which would take care of my baby, but my friends advise against it.

The local Jewish Welfare Agencies are allowing me and my children to die of hunger, and this is because my "faithful" husband brought me over from Canada just four months ago and therefore I do not yet deserve to eat our bread.

It breaks my heart but I have come to the conclusion that in order to save my innocent children from hunger and cold I have to give them away.

I will sell my beautiful children to people who will give them a home. I will sell them, not for money, but for bread, for a secure home where they will have enough food and warm clothing for the winter.

I, the unhappy young mother, am willing to sign a contract, with my heart's blood, stating that the children belong to the good people who will treat them tenderly. Those who are willing and able to give my children a good home can apply to me.

Respectfully,
Mrs. P [The full name and
address are given]
Chicago

Answer:

What kind of society are we living in that forces a mother to such desperate straits

that there is no other way out than to sell her three children for a piece of bread? Isn't this enough to kindle a hellish fire of hatred in every human heart for such a system?

The first to be damned is the heartless father, but who knows what's wrong with him? Perhaps he, too, is unhappy. We hope, though, that this letter will reach him and he will return to aid them.

We also ask our friends and readers to take an interest in this unfortunate woman and to help her so that she herself can be a mother to her children. (Metzker 1971, pp. 50–52, 104–105).

In the late nineteenth and early twentieth century as a result of the public outcry generated by the exposures by social-minded individuals like Sinclair, Steffens and Riis, and such tragedies as the Triangle Shirtwaist Factory fire that claimed the lives of one hundred and forty-six people, reforms were directed to change the living and working environments of immigrants. These movements included tenement-house reforms, workmen's compensation, the abolition of child labor, and the protection of women and children in industry.

However, the pervasive poverty in rapidly growing industrial cities led many to the erroneous conclusion that it was the immigrants themselves who were to blame for their poverty. Blame was not placed on the economic circumstances that the immigrants had to confront. This belief led to the development of a wide number of social programs aimed directly at changing the immigrant families themselves. Social reformers created both private and public welfare agencies to help alleviate the problems of the sick, the poor, and the delinquent or criminal. Immigrant families and especially their children became the major targets for discipline and reformation, and programs were designed to intervene in the affairs of immigrant families. The concern was to Americanize them into what they saw as the great American melting pot where the cultural variations of the given immigrant group would be altered to the standard American way of life.

The settlement house, a private social welfare agency, is a typical example of how some of these practices became articulated. The term "settlement" meant giving the immigrant newcomers the wherewithal to survive in a modern industrial city. Located right in the heart of the immigrant communities, it sought to help the immigrant families cope with poverty and improve their living standards. Settlement house workers tried to teach English, American social customs, and, when necessary, the rudiments of household management, health care, and sanitation. They encouraged family member involvement in work and household roles that often conformed to their own middle class standards of family morality. When successful, as in the case of Jane Addams of Chicago's Hull House, they integrated their work without undermining the immigrant's native culture. Unfortunately, much too frequently, workers saw as their primary task the eradication of "non-American" cultural points of view as to family traditions regarding marital roles and parent child relationships.

Education was seen as the key institution to eradicate immigrant cultures and to achieve Americanization. For example, in the years before World War I Henry Ford required all of his foreign workers to attend English school. For a five year period, 1915–1920, the federal Bureau of Education subsidized a Division of Immigrant Education, which encouraged school districts throughout the nation to establish special Americanization programs. The response was favorable and many state governments provided funds for the education of immigrants. During this period and continuing afterwards, numerous public school systems instituted night classes in which foreign students could learn English and gain knowledge of American government to acquire citizenship (Archdeacon 1983).

For the Americanization of immigrant children, the school system became the prime vehicle to help accomplish this task. Education meant more than simply teaching proper English and the three "Rs" of reading, "riting," and "rithmetic," but also meant socializing children to "American" ways of life, habits of cleanliness, good housekeeping, nutrition, and social graces. Children were also graded on their level of acculturation to American values, as measured by behavior in school. State legislation was passed making compulsory attendance laws more stringent to help ensure that children were adequately exposed to the assimilative influences of the schools. Settlement house workers also played a role here by assisting in the supervision of school attendance and observance of child labor laws.

However, it was the immigrants themselves, especially the immigrant family system that was primarily responsible for the success of the "new" immigration in "making it" in America. Let's see how this came about. By 1920 almost sixty percent of the population of cities of more than 100,000 inhabitants were first or second generation ethnic Americans (Sellers 1977). The immigrant settled in ethnic enclaves which people referred to as "Little Italys," "Polanias," "Little Syrias," and "Jewtowns." Each enclave reflected its distinctive ethnic flavor with its own church, stores, newspapers, clothing, and gestural and language conventions. The Chicago newspaper journalist, Mike Royko, reminiscing on his own Slavic community background recalls that you could always tell where you were "by the odors of the food stores and the open kitchen windows, the sound of the foreign or familiar language, and by whether a stranger hit you in the head with a rock" (Seller 1977, p. 112).

The establishment of immigrant "ghettos" in cities reflects a stage in the development of American cities where there was a great need for occupational concentration as a result of the expansion of the industrial economy in the late 19th century (Yancey, Ericksen, and Juliani 1976). Low-paid industrial immigrant workers were forced by economic pressures to live close to their places of work. The particular choice of residence and occupation was strongly influenced by the presence of friends and relatives in a process that has been called "chain migration." Chain migration refers to the connections made between individuals in countries of origin and destination in the process of international migration and to the process in which choices of residence and occupation were influenced by friends and relatives.

Networks of friends and relatives established in America maintained their European kinship and friendship ties and transmitted assistance across the Atlantic. Relatives acted as recruitment, migration, and housing resources, helping each other to shift from the often rural European work background to urban industrial work. A number of social historians (Anderson 1971; Hareven 1975; Yans-McLaughlin 1971) have observed that nineteenth as well as twentieth century migrants chose their residential and occupational destinations in large part because of the presence of kin group members in the new area.

Chain migration can be seen as facilitating transition and settlement. It ensured a continuity in kins contacts, and made mutual assistance in cases of personal and family crises an important factor in the adjustment of immigrants to the new urban American environment. Workers often migrated into the new industrial urban centers keeping intact or reforming much of their kinship ties and family traditions. As previously mentioned, a prevalent practice was for unmarried sons and daughters of working age, or young childless married couples to migrate first. After establishing themselves by finding jobs and housing they would tend to send for other family members. Through their contacts at work or in the community they would assist their newly arrived relatives or friends with obtaining jobs and housing.

The fact that so many single individuals came to America alone accounts for the fact that turn of the century urban households of immigrants often included people other than the nuclear family. These people were not kinship related but were strangers. These strangers were boarders and lodgers who for various reasons came to America alone and for a period of time lived with fellow immigrants. This practice of taking in boarders and lodgers proved extremely valuable in allowing new migrants and immigrants to adapt to urban living (Hareven 1983).

The family can be seen as being an important intermediary in recruitment of workers to the new industrial society. Family patterns and values often carried over to the urban setting, and provided the individual with a feeling of continuity between one's rural background and new industrial city. Initially, selected individuals migrated, then families migrated in groups, and often entire rural communities reconstituted themselves in ethnic enclaves. They helped recruit other family members and countrymen into the industrial work force. Migration to industrial communities, then, did not break up traditional kinship ties; rather the family used these ties to facilitate their own transition into industrial life. Tamara Hareven (1983) after examining the historical evidence concludes that it is grossly incorrect to assume that industrialization broke up traditional kinship ties and destroyed the interdependence of the family and the community.

In summary, the 50 year dramatic growth period of 1876–1925 of the industrial urban centers of the Northeast and Midwest can be attributed to the social and family organization of the newly arriving immigration groups. Rather than view this period in terms of social disorganization we would argue that insufficient attention has been placed on the nature of social interactional patterns that were developing among the immigrant groups in American cities. We owe the spectacular rise of world cities like New York City to the vitality of the immigrants and their social support structures.

Reading 8   What Kinds of Immigrants Have Come to the Philadelphia Area, Where Did They Settle, and How Are They Doing?*

ROBERT J. YOUNG

Dramatic changes in the Immigration Law of 1965, fully implemented in gradual stages by 1968, struck at the very roots of an oppressive immigration policy mandated by national legislation between 1921 and 1924. The National Origins Immigration Act, legislated and consolidated in those years, blatantly enshrined the racial and ethnic prejudices of national policymakers. Those ethnic and racial groups designated as less desirable, mainly Southern and Eastern European, were virtually eliminated from the immigrant stream. The Italian, Polish, and other eastern European groups that had been dominant elements in the pre-WWI immigrant flow were limited after 1921 to numbers so low that these and virtually all other immigrant communities atrophied. Philadelphia, like other major metropolitan areas, experienced the end of an era of massive immigration that had created one of this city's greatest strengths and resources—its patchwork of stable ethnic neighborhoods clustered around churches, synagogues, schools, and shopping districts.

As oppressive as the National Origins Act had been it had little effect on the Asian-American communities. For all practical purposes they had been so consistently discriminated against in immigration legislation that they had long since been effectively eliminated from the immigrant flow. Discriminatory legislation on the West Coast, from the 1880s onward into the first decade of the 20th century, compounded by the Chinese Exclusion Act at the national level in 1882 and the 1907 Gentlemen's Agreement in Theodore Roosevelt's administration, not only brought Asian immigration to a halt but resulted in a reverse flow. Therefore, by 1921, Asian-American communities were already isolated, inward looking, or virtually on their way to extinction by death or intermarriage with other minority groups, for example, the Asian-Indian-Mexican pattern in California.[1] Philadelphia's only recognizable Asian-American community, the Chinese, clustered in its Chinatown, was a rather typical example of a national phenomenon of an aging, disproportionately male Asian-American population, numerically in decline.[2] Only in isolated Japanese-American enclaves on the West Coast, in San Francisco or the territory of Hawaii, was the situation different.

I note these historical details not only because, as an historian, I recognize the value of reflecting on the historical experiences of immigrant communities to understand how we and

*Young, Robert J. 1989. "What Kinds of Immigrants Have Come to the Philadelphia Area, Where Did They Settle and How are They Doing?" A version of this paper was presented at the conference, *"Who Are These Strangers Among Us?"; Recent Immigration to the Delaware Valley.* Sponsored by The Balch Institute for Ethnic Studies and The Nationalities Service Center of Philadelphia, PA.

they interpret their presence, but because I wish to emphasize the Asian-American immigrant experiences in the Delaware Valley in the post-1965 period. I leave it to others to discuss the equally important experiences of other recent arrivals, largely of European origins, who are making their contributions to our society. Certainly a significant Greek immigration which crested in the 1970s, successive and continuing waves of Russian-Jewish immigrants and the more recent phenomenon of renewed Irish migration, are all significant developments in the increasingly complex ethnic mix in the Delaware Valley. However, I have chosen to center my attention on the Asian immigrant populations not only because of my on-going relationship with several Asian communities in both official and unofficial capacities but because they represent a particularly unique experience in the recent history of immigration in the Delaware Valley. Moreover, since, unlike the aforementioned ethnic groups, they did not arrive to find established religious, education, or cultural institutions ready to welcome them, they have gone through the immigrant experience without the initial assistance, mentors, and expertise often available to these others.

A new era of massive immigration was ushered in when the National Origins immigration legislation was replaced by the Immigration Act of 1965. Not even the most farseeing national legislators anticipated the dramatic demographic changes that would result and the inherently positive impact this would have on American society. Responding largely to issues of social justice, in an era that turned its back on racism, the framers of the 1965 legislation created an immigration policy that rejected national origins as a criterion, fostered reunification of families, and allowed special consideration for the highly skilled. Only belatedly did it become apparent that this legislation, which was undoing historic bias that had largely blocked Asian immigration,

was simultaneously creating an elitist migration that would, within a decade, establish a significant Asian-American presence in or around every major city in the United States.[3] Asian communities never before represented in U.S. society, as well as those which had been previously present but not widely distributed, grew suddenly and dynamically. Obviously, a new era in the history of Asian-Americans had begun not only at the national level but in the Delaware Valley. It was the beginning of an era both unprecedented and dramatic in its implications!

In virtually all instances those Asian immigrants who arrived after 1965 found themselves on new ground without established social, religious, or cultural institutions that older established European immigrant communities had long since developed. In other instances newly arrived Asian immigrants found remnants of earlier Asian-American communities and their institutions more American than Asian. Often a gap of thirty or forty years between immigration experiences created tensions as new met old. Philadelphia, much like other American cities with small but established Asian-American communities, experienced some of this. Anyone familiar with the politics and concerns of Philadelphia's Chinatown could quickly list numerous instances in which new arrivals and older residents differ sharply over issues of land usage, commercial development, or the direction of cultural institutions. Such differences were to be expected not only because of "turf" issues but because of the size and diversity of the arriving immigrant flow.

The first great surge of Asian immigration, which followed the implementation of the Immigration Act of 1965, had special characteristics that dominated the picture of arriving Asian immigrants nationally and locally for much of the next decade. These special characteristics were a result of several factors not least of all a critical shortage of medical personnel, at the regional and national level, which generated a need for nurses and doctors. Additionally, since the Immigration Act of 1965 included a provision that gave preference to immigrants with critical skills there was little impediment and often numerous incentives for Asian professionals to migrate. These arrivals were clearly an elite in terms of education and professional backgrounds.[4] Largely college-educated, with disproportionate numbers of doctors and engineers among them, they found little difficulty in establishing themselves. Almost overnight, Asian-Indian, Chinese, Korean, and Filipino professional communities emerged where none had really existed before. Initially in Philadelphia, as at the national level, the new arrivals clustered around the academic institutions, hospitals, and research centers, which either provided employment or opportunities for "recredentialing"—a significant problem in the various medical fields. Only briefly clustered around the University of Pennsylvania, Drexel Institute, Einstein Northern Division, and Temple University, they soon departed for the suburbs to enjoy the upper-middle class lifestyle which their education and incomes made possible. By and large this "First Wave" did not cluster in the city or suburbs; they initially created few cultural institutions and quickly got on with the task of enjoying the American dream in every economic sense of the word. Dispersed to the close suburbs in Bucks, Delaware, and Montgomery counties and South Jersey, their regular contact with ethnic communities was often the Saturday trip to the ethnic grocery store and Sunday visits with friends. Widely scattered and economically integrated, they formed no recognizable or distinguishable ethnic concentrations. With both husband and wife typically employed in professional level jobs, the new arrivals had relatively easy access to society in the work-a-day world. Placing absolutely no pressure on community resources or social services, the First

Wave passed into the mainstream without serious difficulties and barely noticed. Not only were they an unmitigated blessing in terms of skills and as taxpayers but a virtual reverse foreign aid program. As noted by one distinguished Asian ambassador,[5] the thousands of fully trained doctors and engineers emigrating to the U.S. in the 1960s and 1970s represented a massive pool of skills on which the U.S. economy came to depend as did its medical and public health facilities.

As the Immigration Act of 1965 was fully implemented between 1965 and 1968, the size and composition of all Asian immigrant communities grew nationally as they did in the Delaware Valley. The entire 10,000 per nation special visa quota was utilized by China, India, Korea, and the Philippines by the mid-1970s. Fueled by the national doctors' shortage and an equally significant shortage of engineers, this elitist flow continued to the point that in the Delaware Valley as well as in numerous areas across the country every hospital emergency room and all colleges teaching engineering had become dependent on the immigrant flow. By 1975 it was also apparent that the earlier arrivals, many of whom had intentions to return after their U.S. experience, were making a decision to stay and were deeply involved in the process of raising families. It is at about this time, and at least partially in response to the Bicentennial Celebration, that numerous ethnic groups consciously began to ponder the issue of being a "hyphenated" American and the task of raising their children as Asian-Americans. An enormous number of ethnic cultural and educational efforts emerged at this point in all Asian immigrant communities in the Philadelphia area.[6]

Subtle changes in patterns of immigration were beginning to occur as this First Wave began the process of establishing educational, cultural, and religious institutions. The First Wave, as they became citizens, became significant sponsors of relatives in keeping with immigration statues that encouraged reunification of families. In essence a point had been reached that allowed for immigration patterns familiar in past U.S. history—family members bringing family members. This "Second Wave," still very much an elite in terms of past U.S. immigration patterns, was made up almost entirely of high school and college-educated individuals[7] who either settled into white collar jobs of a clerical nature or business in instances where language skills stood in the way of lateral moves. It is this Second Wave that was responsible for the sudden growth nationally of ethnically identifiable neighborhoods in major cities such as New York's Queens or Los Angeles' "Korea Town." Although nothing equivalent developed in the Philadelphia area, several Asian ethnic clusters began to emerge and widely distributed business activities became observable. In West Philadelphia the cluster of food, clothing, and service-related shops and restaurants on or adjacent to 41st and Walnut, which represent a growing Asian-Indian presence, a hub of Korean activity in Logan on and adjacent to Broad Street, which provided the usual ethnic grocery-restaurant mix but also a network of banking and business facilities and most notable, the rapid expansion of Chinatown, were signs of change. An even more significant presence was manifested in the neighborhoods of Philadelphia, Center City, and in the older suburbs as Asian merchants—especially Korean —made significant investments in "Mom and Pop" type businesses, the ubiquitous fruit stands of Center City and various services, especially dry cleaning establishments. Intent upon a future in business, many of these capital-short, college-educated merchants seized the opportunities at the bottom and moved rapidly to fill gaps in the neighborhoods left by the departure of an earlier generation of shopkeepers, largely immigrants or the children of immigrants. In many instances this resulted in linkages with traditional business

communities anxious to retire from the city. The speed with which the transition to Korean ownership occurred in some areas of the city is attributable also to a growing recognition that old and new immigrants shared certain common values, which led each to seek out the other. In Logan, the West Girard Avenue business area, the Columbia Avenue district, and many others, retiring Jewish businessmen sought out Korean merchants through informal contacts. There was also a parallel development that was having equally important implications. Although it has been little referred to by those studying Asian immigration in the 1970s, the arrival of prosperous and even wealthy immigrants who took advantage of the possibilities to do business was a significant development. Special legislation in the Immigration Act of 1965 had allowed foreign investors able to prove assets of at least $40,000 and an immigrant visa. Traditional business communities in India, Hong Kong, and the Philippines reacted immediately! Massive investments were made in real estate and banking. Even as the investment capital requirement was raised from $40,000 to $250,000, this visa category was fully utilized. Even more important, it represented an entree for future growth of dynamic business communities able to function at a regional or even national level. The much commented upon "motel Patels"[8] were only one of the most observable of many such traditional business communities to have emerged during this period as both a national and regional phenomenon.

Collectively the First Wave and Second Wave shifted traditional centers of Asian-American influence ever eastward. In the process, cities such as New York and Chicago became centers of the so-called "New Immigration" while the Delaware Valley shared in this development. As the First Wave subsided when the doctor and engineer shortages ended in the mid-1970s, a significant change occurred as the

Second Wave, with its entrepreneurial and white-collar elements, came to dominate the flow. Another observable change at this point was a shift in the age composition of all of the Asian-American communities as earlier elements aged and elderly dependents arrived to join immigrant adult children. In the process, the rate of immigration did not slacken but surged. By the end of the 1970s the four Asian countries responsible for most Asian immigrants (China, India, Korea, and the Philippines) were utilizing the entire 20,000 visas[9] allotted to each state, with some being represented by thousands more on the basis of skills that resulted in special preference visas.

It is during the 1970s that this Second Wave played a significant role in the creation of eth-nic neighborhoods in many American cities. Although, for a variety of reasons, this phenomenon is not well represented in Philadelphia, the ethnic clusters referred to earlier were lesser examples of this pattern. The huge stock of affordable housing in the Delaware Valley and accessibility to the automobile are certainly part of the reason why clustering was less practical or necessary. However, an equally important element is the rapid social mobility of virtually all the Asian immigrant communities in the Philadelphia area. The 1970s and, even more so, the 1980s saw rapid movement to better areas within the city and, for many, outside the city. By the late 1970s the Northeast section of Philadelphia was a major magnet for inner-city moves as was the Olney area. Older inner suburbs such as Cheltenham and Upper Darby, as well as areas in Lower Bucks county, received significant numbers of relocating Asian immigrants. All Asian immigrant communities shared in this restructuring.

Political events in Vietnam in 1975 radically changed the mix of Asian immigration to the United States and Philadelphia as the initial surge of hundreds of thousands of refugees from Southeast Asia joined the immigrant stream. Unlike groups that had preceded them, and traumatized by war and flight, they arrived destitute and remained subject to the whims of relocation agencies. The proximity of Philadelphia to Indiantown Gap Resettlement Camp made the Delaware Valley one of the major receiving areas for Vietnamese refugees. Despite an inhospitable climate and limited employment opportunities at the time, Philadelphia became and remained a major resettlement center.[10] Throughout the period 1975–1981 the area received tens of thousands of refugees. And even after 1981 there has been a steady, although lesser flow, which includes a significant but undocumented number of "internal migrants" drawn by the potential for entry level jobs.

The 1975 arrivals, impoverished to the extreme—but eminently middle-class in skills and education—were poured into decaying areas of West, North, and South Philadelphia by various resettlement agencies. Lacking English-language skills and with few job related skills, they competed with other minorities in deteriorating areas of the city that faced economic decline and rising rates of unemployment. Traumatized by multiple problems of adaptation and sudden downward mobility, large numbers of these refugees suffered something close to communal depression.[11] Probably the greatest burden, however, was the absence of mentors to "translate" the society to the newcomers and complete absence of familiar institutions. Throughout the remainder of the 1970s and 1980s, the continual arrival of ever more refugees, often not as well educated or resourceful,[12] compounded the problems of earlier arrivals.

The particularly heavy renewed influx of refugees from Southeast Asia, between 1979 and 1981, also tended to leave the earliest arrivals very much to their own resources. Having been involved in resettlement efforts in those days, I remember vividly the poor living conditions of recent arrivals, the constant pressures of adjustment, destabilization of family life, and the almost frenetic movement and relocation of people within the city, the state, and the country as the new arrivals sought better conditions and family reunification. I also well remember the terrible realities that many faced after the meager resettlement allowance and the first month's advance on rent ran out.[13] But what I remember most was the ill-advised policy of dispersing the refugees throughout the Delaware Valley just as an informal national policy advocated distribution of that population throughout the nation.[14] In each case these policies delayed the stabilization of the refugee population, which regrouped anyway in the next few years. For Philadelphia the regroupment lead to Vietnamese clusters in the vicinity of St. Francis de Sales parish in West Philadelphia, which increasingly functioned as a center for educational and cultural activities. For many Vietnamese, large numbers of whom were Catholic, the presence of a Vietnamese priest at a parish such as this, or the existence of a neighborhood parochial school, served as an initial linkage to the larger society and a base of support.[15]

The continuing influx of Southeast Asian refugees from Vietnam, Cambodia, and Laos into West Philadelphia and South Philadelphia eventually created the largest identifiable Asian clusters, which took place alongside the Korean enclave in Logan and Chinatown as the closest Philadelphia examples of Asian ethnic neighborhoods. However, even these enclaves showed few signs of permanence and may yet be but passing phenomena unless there are sudden infusions of new arrivals. As I will note a bit later most of these concentrations of Asian ethnic populations that developed between 1975 and 1985 are showing significant signs of mobility, which may challenge their existence, with the one notable exception of Chinatown.

As this discussion has implied, the story of recent Asian immigration to the United States and the Delaware Valley is complex and subject to numerous variables. Even in providing this brief historical background, it is obvious that it is important to note not only which state the immigrant came from but also when he came, and under what conditions. As we are now almost 25 years removed from the initial change in immigration law that resulted in the dynamic growth of Asian immigrant communities, we must begin to consider "generations" in each community based on chronological age and years of residence in the United States. To discuss where these immigrants settled and how they are doing, I must consider "generations" as one of the most important of many significant elements. In each Asian immigrant community resident in the Philadelphia area, there are obvious, if not yet documented, signs of upward mobility in terms of housing, income, and, in virtually all groups, education. If we are to go beyond generalizations to specifics, it is important to note which immigrant community we are discussing and when they arrived as well as under which conditions they arrived. The experiences of the Vietnamese refugee population are notably different from those of the Asian-Indian. The younger brothers and sisters of Asian professionals who came in the First Wave, and constitute the Second Wave, also have significant differences in their experience. Likewise even in the refugee populations there are notable differences in the experiences depending on whether one arrived in 1975, 1980, or recently.

Although it will take the national census in 1990 to document many of the observations I am about to make about the Asian immigrant communities in the Delaware Valley, I have no doubt about the outcome. I am sure that the 1990 census will show an extraordinarily local success story even more graphic than my experiential observations and very much in accord with national patterns among Asian immigrants. Even though the numbers of Asian immigrants involved in the Philadelphia area are dwarfed by those in Los Angeles, New York, and Chicago, I am sure that the overall results are at least as positive and in some instances better here.

Perhaps the easiest group to deal with is the First Wave. They arrived as an elite to fill well compensated jobs at a time when the United States and the region enjoyed full employment. Largely affluent suburbanites, clustered in the near suburbs, and favoring locations such as Cherry Hill, Cheltenham, Lower Merion, and areas in Delaware, Chester, and Bucks counties, all are almost universally homeowners with children who were born or at least raised in the United States. These groups, regardless of national origins, are characterized by their emphasis on quality education for their children and often disproportionate expenditures on the same. Now pretty much the older generation in every sense of the word, they tend to be the office-holders in the numerous cultural, religious, and educational organizations that each national group created. Secure in their professions, affluent, and long resident in the United States, their greatest collective concern seems to be the on-going adjustment to being the parents of children growing up in two cultures. In the last few years many of these have also had to accept the unexpected and often unplanned for arrival of elderly relatives who lack the language or social skills to adjust to living in the United States. Although this problem may sound like merely a variation on the growing problem of elder care in America, it has complex elements especially if the grandchildren at home no longer speak the mother tongue or traditional expectations for care of a parent are impossible. Remember that none of the Asian immigrant communities accept nursing homes as an answer. Often the result is an elderly parent spending long hours in isolation at home. As these communities age, this is an obvious emerging problem.

If there is a "sameness" to the experience of the First Wave, there is a notable diversity to the experience of the Second Wave. One of the most notable variables was the level of English language skills acquired prior to arrival. Arrivals from India and the Philippines, by and large, had these and found it relatively easy to enter white collar occupations. Large numbers of Koreans, who represented the fastest growing Asian immigrant community in the Delaware Valley,[16] did not. Problems with English largely explain why the Korean community, despite an overwhelmingly college-educated population, moved into retail sales. Once again this was both a regional and a national phenomenon. Moreover, arriving at a time when numerous small business properties were available due to retirement or abandonment, this was an opportunity available for a limited capital outlay. The Korean version of the Horatio Alger story, which saw progression from sidewalk fruitstand to inner city "Mom and Pop" grocery store to wholesaler/distributor or suburban storeowner, was played out hundreds of times in the 1970s and 1980s in the Philadelphia area. As the Korean immigrant population increased there was almost no inner city neighborhood without a Korean "Mom and Pop" grocery store. Columbia Avenue, Girard Avenue, North Broad Street, and, eventually, areas in West and South Philadelphia were blanketed by the increasingly obvious examples of Korean entrepreneurship. By the end of the 1970s this became a suburban phenomenon as well—with clusters of Korean-owned shops radiating out from the city along Lancaster Pike and in aging shopping areas in the older suburban communities of Delaware, Montgomery, and Bucks counties. Most of these businesses had in common long hours and labor intensive activities often requiring total family involvement. The typical Korean-owned business is a six-day-a-week job. Korean businessmen's associations, which only formed in the 1970s, soon boasted thousands of members.[17] Most recent estimates are that there are over 5,000 Korean-owned businesses in the Delaware Valley. Over 2,000 of these are in the suburbs, while approximately 3,000 are in Philadelphia.[18] This continued increase in Korean-owned business in the Delaware Valley since 1980 shows no sign of diminishing. The fact that virtually all these businessmen either own businesses or are acquiring them, where virtually none existed as recently as twenty years ago, says volumes about how they are doing economically.

Upward mobility in economic terms has also translated into residential mobility. Residential enclaves such as those adjacent to 4600–4800 North Broad Street are rapidly giving way to new enclaves in better neighborhoods in Olney, the far Northeast, Cheltenham, and Upper Darby. I foresee the possibility that, before long, that area will remain only as a center for business activities and social organizations even though there is a continuing stream of new arrivals. The near future will show a growing trend of Koreans commuting to their stores from city neighborhoods perceived to be safer or from nearby suburbs. Above all, the shift to the suburbs will be influenced by the quality of schools. As one educator in Delaware county told me, "Koreans choose schools, not neighborhoods."[19] The shift to the suburbs is so pronounced that several realtors in Delaware County now engage a Korean salesman for properties in the 69th Street business area and the adjacent residential area because of the recent influx of Korean businessmen either leaving homes in Philadelphia or leaving Philadelphia entirely. The same pressures also explain selective hiring of Asian-Indian salesmen.

The shift to the suburbs, which we noted as a growing movement among Korean immigrants, is also apparent in each of the other Asian immigrant communities. An older, inner suburb such as Upper Darby—an historic stepping-stone out of the city for earlier immigrant groups—appears to be functioning in much the same way for the newest arrivals. It is in areas like this that we are seeing the development of Pan-Asian enclaves adjacent to existing European immigrant communities, which have also expanded since 1965. The basic attraction is affordable housing in safe neighborhoods with viable public school systems. In neighborhoods such as Millborne and Upper Darby the Second Wave flows together with significant elements of the refugee population that arrived in the period shortly after 1975. The most graphic illustration of this trend can be gleaned from, among other things, school records in Upper Darby and adjacent areas. A particularly dramatic example of this trend is offered by enrollment figures at the Upper Darby Middle School, which has historically received the bulk of school-aged immigrant children or the children of immigrants.[20] Between 1982 and 1985 the Asian-American population increased from 5.0 percent to 8.1 percent. In 1986 it increased to 12.4 percent. In 1988 the figure reached 14.9 percent. This school, which has foreign-born students representing thirty-four countries, has thirty-two students born in Vietnam, twenty-two from Korea, eighteen from India, and twelve from Cambodia as its four largest Asian groups. What is interesting, although it is too recent a statistic to be able to evaluate, is the slight drop in Asian-American representation in 1989 to 12.1 percent. An interesting observation, which came through in interviews, may eventually explain this. It was observed that earlier arrivals—especially Koreans—are now able to afford the larger homes and more expensive real estate further out. Broomall has become the destination for many Koreans these last two years, while others, especially Vietnamese, are shifting to more affluent areas of Upper Darby such as Drexel Hill, where they are often attracted by the large homes, which provide room for extended-family living. A possible additional factor may be the rapid increase in formerly low-cost housing prices in Upper Darby since 1986, which has largely resulted in Asian-American demand. These pressures may in the short run delay the suburban move for some and encourage yet further the parallel trend, especially among more recent refugees from Southeast Asia, to acquire homes within Philadelphia adjacent to declining ethnic neighborhoods in Southwest and South Philadelphia or along Roosevelt Boulevard. The rapid development of a Vietnamese enclave in Southwest Philadelphia during the last three or four years and Vietnamese and Cambodian enclaves in South Philadelphia and the lower Northeast, is paralleled by movements of all Asian immigrant groups who have the means into the Oxford Circle area or the far Northeast. Areas in Northeast Philadelphia have become almost the equivalent of a move to older suburbs for middle-income groups in the Second Wave and refugee populations.

Despite obvious signs of rapid residential mobility each of the groups has created institutions that draw on surrounding communities. The Korean community is probably the most dynamic and visible in this regard because its businessmen's, cultural, and religious organizations are present almost everywhere in the Delaware Valley. More than a dozen Korean Protestant churches in Philadelphia and congregations in Bucks and Delaware counties are the most obvious and visible manifestations of new permanent institutional structures.[21] Korean businessmen organized along lines of specialization are equally important as a source of community mobilization.[22] Less visible are the signs of cooperation with existing institutions, which for inner-city Asian immigrants who are Catholic often take the form of ties to the local parishes. Many of these such as Holy Child in North Philadelphia, Holy Redeemer in Chinatown, St. Francis de Sales in West Philadelphia, or St. Alice's in Delaware county offer services in regional or national languages, at regular intervals, some utilizing clergy from Asian communi-

ties. Recently arrived priests from Korea and India, together with established Vietnamese clergy, represent a return to a pattern of the past when immigrant clergy followed immigrant congregations to the new country.[23]

In the midst of this glowing picture of upward mobility on the part of recent Asian immigrant and refugee populations, we must pause to acknowledge that even the most successful populations have problems and difficulties. The tensions that arise in families caught between cultures,[24] the pressure on children to excel, racial incidents, and, in many if not most cases, the six-day-a-week or two-career pattern all take a toll. It is also necessary to consider those who are not part of this pattern of upward mobility. The presence of special programs at University City High, Furness High, and at South Philadelphia High School, to encourage Asian students to stay in school and avoid drugs says something about other realities.[25] Those refugees who arrived without literacy skills in their own language and no English language skills have often languished on the bottom rungs of the ladder of success. Groups such as the Hmong, as well as large numbers of formerly rural Cambodians and Laotians, are faced by serious continuing problems of adaptation, while their younger generation is often deeply influenced by sometimes negative peer pressures from the surrounding American environment. There is also the growing concern in all the Asian communities that the public schools do not treat their cultures adequately or sympathetically, which often results in racist stereotyping bred from ignorance.[26]

In all Asian-American immigrant and refugee communities the maturation of an American-born generation is a major concern as parent-child relations and issues such as marriage often create tension-filled interludes.[27] Although it may seem to be appropriate to say that these and all the other problems noted were also faced by most earlier immigrant populations, this does not make the present experience less difficult for those experiencing the pressures now.

What is the future of Asian migration to and the growing complexity of Asian-American populations in the Delaware Valley? First, and most apparent, is the fact that a critical mass has emerged. Each of the Asian refugee and immigrant populations in the area has sunk roots, established citizenship, and now serves as a base for future immigration into the area. We can assume the Chinese, Indian, Korean, and Filipino populations will continue to grow at rates approaching the national levels, with larger proportions of those representing the attributes of the Second Wave. Each of these Asian ethnic populations will probably show fewer signs of elitism in terms of earning power and education as the principle of family reunification, as enshrined in the Immigration Act of 1965, becomes dominant. Given the labor shortage in the Delaware Valley and the continuing need for entry level employees in the service and business industries, there will be plenty of opportunities for these—especially as the second generation provides linkages and expanded opportun-ities. The fact that the Delaware Valley is already attracting significant numbers of internal migrants of Southeast Asian origins testifies to a growing recognition of these local possibilities.[28]

When speaking of Southeast Asian communities we should also note the future possibility of renewed massive immigration from Vietnam under the Orderly Departure Program (O.D.P.). Although the recent closing of refugee camps in Thailand has probably brought to an end significant emigration of Cambodians and Laotians, the O.D.P. flow from Vietnam shows not only no sign of ending but real possibilities for sudden expansion. Although so far the number of arrivals in the Delaware Valley has been largely limited to Amer-Asians and their families, recent improvements in U.S.-Vietnam relations show signs that a rapid expansion of the O.D.P. may be in the offing—and at a time when budget cutbacks have stripped refugee resettlement programs of adequate funding.[29] As American officials began to interview freed political prisoners in Ho Chi Minh City on October 5, 1989 in preparation for the departure of the first 3,000 for the United States, it was revealed that "another 100,000 former prisoners and their families have requested entry into the United States."[30] Since it is estimated that these refugees, for which the U.S. government acknowledges a responsibility, totals over 500,000, it can be assumed that the Vietnamese community in the Delaware Valley will soon experience yet another wave of new arrivals.

As we look to the future then, we can clearly see that the Asian-American presence in the Delaware Valley is well established and growing. I anticipate that the 1990 Census will show growth rates that have more than doubled the size of each of the Asian-American ethnic populations since 1980[31]—a trend that will most certainly continue through the 1990s. Along with these developments it is to be anticipated that these ethnic groups, whether individually or at times collectively, will function as ethnic groups that have preceded them. One should expect political mobilization to meet group goals as an increasingly obvious Americanization process proceeds alongside the development of a critical mass of political leadership talents. The recent rash of publicized concerns[32] of Asian ethnics and Asian-Americans with regard to schools and police, among others, are to be viewed as the beginning of a greater and more complete community involvement, which represents the maturation of an immigrant experience.

Appendix: Asian/Pacific Islanders/1980 Philadelphia Region

Population all races	1980 Asian/Pacific Islanders	Percentage	1970 Asian/Pacific Islanders
United States	226,545,805	3,726,440	1.6	1,538,721
Pennsylvania	11,863,895	70,514	0.6	20,081
New Jersey	7,364,823	109,383	1.5	23,333
Maryland	4,216,975	67,949	1.6	17,944
Delaware	594,338	4,627	0.8	1,495

Breakdown by nationality

	United States	Pennsylvania	New Jersey	Maryland	Delaware
Chinese	812,178	13,769	23,492	15,037	1,174
Filipino	781,894	9,640	24,470	15,037	1,174
Japanese	716,331	4,422	10,263	4,656	412
Asian Indian	387,223	17,230	30,684	13,788	1,227
Korean	357,393	12,597	13,173	14,783	501
Vietnamese	245,025	8,127	2,846	4,162	171
Hawaiian	172,346	909	579	630	77
Samoan	39,520	87	112	6	5
Guamaian	30,695	164	199	323	45
Other Asians					
Total	183,835	4,569	3,565	2,721	226
Asian	166,377	4,426	3,489	2,660	226
Pacific Islanders	17,005	133	76	58	—

SOURCE: U.S. Census Bureau, Philadelphia Office, August 15, 1986.

Reading 9   The Expanded Family and Family Honor*

RUTH HOROWITZ

Three months prior to Ana's cotillion, or *quince-cañera* (fifteenth birthday celebration),[1] everything appeared to be ready. Sponsors to pay for almost all aspects of the religious ceremony and the party afterward had been found. Relatives, *compadres* (godparents), and friends had been enlisted to help: an uncle was paying for the food, an aunt was paying for the liquor, a grandmother was buying her dress, baptismal godparents were buying the cake, and two of their daughters were going to "stand up" (serve as an attendant) for the church procession. Other relatives and friends were enlisted as godparents to pay for the flowers, a *cojín* (pillow) to kneel on in the church, a *diadema* (diadem or tiara), the bands, the photographs, and several other incidentals. As Ana had chosen to have the dinner and dance in the gym of the local community center, she did not have to rent a hall. An order for two hundred invitations had been placed at the engravers with the names of all the attendants printed on an inserted sheet.

In addition to finding enough relatives and friends of the family to pay for the affair, Ana had found the requisite fourteen young couples, *damas* (women) and *chambelaones* (men), to stand up in matching dresses and tuxedos. This is frequently a difficult task, as each of the young women has to buy her own dress (generally $45 to $100), which Ana, like most celebrants, picked out of a catalog of bridesmaid dresses. The cost of the rented tuxedo is often $40. A cotillion is an expense for everyone. Ana had already stood up for two of the young women, who were returning the favor, and she was scheduled to participate in four more. Finding fourteen couples who could afford and would agree to stand up for the affair was difficult. In addition, she wanted to exclude from the males any potential troublemakers. As it was, two of the young women were standing up with their brothers, who were in different gangs, and another's escort was in a rival gang, but none were known as troublemakers at parties.

Problems began several weeks before the affair. An aunt's family dropped out, claiming they could not afford to pay for the band because they had to attend the funeral of a relative in Mexico. Excuses such as this are common, but the day was rescued when Ana's mother agreed to try to pay for the band herself.

One week prior to the cotillion Ana discovered that her mother had hired only a Mexican *ranchera* (Mexican country music) band and not

*Horowitz, Ruth. 1983. "The Expanded Family and Family Honor." Pp. 52—76 in *Honor and the American Dream: Culture and Identity in a Chicano Community*. New Brunswick, NJ: Rutgers University Press. Copyright © 1983 by Rutgers, The State University. Reprinted by permission of Rutgers University Press.

a rock group. Ana did not want a cotillion without a rock group, and a local band was finally located forty-eight hours before the party. Then one of the couples decided that they could not afford to pay for the clothes and dropped out. Another couple broke up and an escort had to be found on short notice. While anxious about having only thirteen couples, Ana claimed it was better than seven or eight, as some had. Her problems were not over. An aunt informed her mother that she had seen Ana kissing her boyfriend, and her mother threatened to cancel the event because she did not want to endure the questions about Ana's virginity that public knowledge of her activities might engender. If the affair had been cancelled, the strength of the family network might have been questioned.

A cotillion is a public affirmation both of a young woman's virginity and of her kin's ability to work together to pay for such an event. Not all fifteen year olds have cotillions. Many families cannot afford them. Moreover, rumors often claim that a young woman holding a cotillion is trying to prove that she is still a virgin when she no longer is one. On the other hand, failing to have a cotillion is frequently considered a good indication that the young woman is no longer a virgin and may even be pregnant.

The evening before the affair required major organization, as beans and rice had to be prepared for two to three hundred guests and the gym had to be decorated. Retiring at two in the morning, everyone was awake by six. Clothes had to be ironed for her six brothers and sisters and both Ana and her older sister had to buy shoes the day of the affair. Her family congratulated themselves for having chosen to buy fried chicken rather than spending the considerable effort to cook the more traditional *mole* (a spicy baked chicken in sauce), though a few guests later commented on its absence.

Ana marched down the church aisle in her long white dress and veil on the arm of her uncle,

following the thirteen couples and the new godparents. As she knelt with her boyfriend before the priest, Ana and the others resembled a wedding party. She did not kiss him but quietly left her flowers at a side altar and prayed there to the Virgin Mary. Her mother was pleased that seventy-five guests attended the church ceremony and that close to two hundred attended the party, many of whom brought presents. Wandering around the room while the photographer took pictures, one could hear compliments about the open bar, the dresses Ana had chosen, and the Mexican band.

Several of the members of the Lions gang arrived after dinner, having learned of the party from their member Ten Pen, whose sister stood up for Ana. On their best behavior and wearing their good clothes, they sat quietly drinking and, when the rock band played slow tunes, got up to dance. No incidents occurred, unlike several weeks before, when a groom fought at his own wedding and was arrested when the fight continued outside the hall. Ana's cotillion was dubbed a success by all. After the party, the photographs were admired over and over.

This event symbolizes much of what is valued in the Chicano family: the close, interdependent family network and the family's success in finances, in containing the sexual activities of the daughter so that she not only remains a virgin but is perceived as such, and in following the proper forms of social interaction. Expectations based on symbols of the expanded family, male domination, virginity, motherhood, and formalism determine the meanings of social relationships within and outside the family. The family relationships should be strong, the males should be dominant, the unmarried women must remain virgins, and the married women should center their lives around motherhood. Courtesy toward and respect for others, particularly elders, is expected of everyone. Some expectations closely resemble those found in Mexican villages,[2] others are affected by United States institutions. In either case, situations of normative ambiguity create dilemmas for concrete action, and the economic status of community residents creates problems for which new cultural resolutions are constantly devised and tested.

While familial social relationships have been somewhat altered, traditional arrangements remain strong. According to Bott (1971, p. 265) "geographical mobility *alone* should be enough to disrupt the sort of close-knit networks one finds in homogeneous working-class areas, and such disruption should be accompanied by greater jointness in the husband-wife relationship."[3] On 32nd Street the move from other areas of the United States or from Mexico has not greatly altered traditional arrangements. The worlds of the men and the women remain largely segregated and traditionally oriented yet interdependent. This is attributable to a number of factors: relatives often came together or followed one another; close networks were expanded to include *compadres* (children's godparents), who were often friends and/or neighbors; and the cultural symbols that give meaning to social relationships were frequently stronger than many of the forces of change. It is situations where the circumstances (ecological, social, or economic) have changed that highlight the strengths and weakness of the collective expectations. What *should* be done may become unclear, be revised, or be reaffirmed. Let us look at these dilemmas and the evolving solutions.

A COHESIVE FAMILY

The kinship network on 32nd Street can best be termed an "expanded family" in the model described by Gans (1962). While many relatives of varying generations tend to live nearby and interact continuously, each household is comprised of a nuclear family unit. A similar structure is found throughout the Chicano population regardless of social class and is the expected standard for families.[4] In Mexico, particularly among the urban poor, the ties of kinship have been augmented to include *compadres* (fictive kin) through treating the godparents of the children as part of the expanded family network.[5] While there is some indication that the importance of fictive kin as an extension of family relationships is lessening in some areas of the United States today,[6] in other communities it remains important.[7] On 32nd Street, the relationship between the godparents of a child's baptism and the child's parents remains particularly important for many families. *Padrinos* (godfathers) and *madrinas* (godmothers) are remembered on mother's and father's day and celebrate birthdays and many holidays with their godchildren. The interaction among generations and the closeness among age groups serve in part to maintain cultural continuity in Mexico and in the United States.

The expanded family is the normative familial form for all classes, whether or not it includes fictive kin in the United States as in Mexico. An important aspect of the expanded family network is one of continuous exchanges that are not governed by laws of supply and demand. Not only is the relationship with friends who have engaged in these exchanges strengthened by being named *compadres,* but the mutual obligations further strengthen the relationship of the entire expanded family unit both as a symbol of their cohesiveness and because they need each other. The content of the exchanges varies slightly by social class among Chicanos (Sena-Rivera 1979). While the extent of economic interdependence and the exchange of personal services vary by social class, the family in all social classes remains the primary source of emotional and social support and is a major source for feelings of self-worth.[8] Sena-Rivera argues that economic interdependence is strongest for the most affluent and the least affluent families, that "interdependence in personal services is universal . . . but . . . follows socio-economic class lines (actual necessity rather than performance as an end in itself)" (p. 127). On 32nd Street the exchange of economic and personal services is frequently necessary for survival. Exchanges of money and individual skills are frequently made among kin and fictive kin. Turning for help to outside agencies such as public welfare or a public employment agency is regarded as a failure of a family's solidarity and worth. Ana's mother, for example, feared a public disgrace for the family when an aunt's family could not assist by paying for the band at the cotillion.

Having a large, close family that can be augmented by *compadres* who can and will readily help in time of need is very highly valued. Being seen as a cohesive family transcends economic success.[9] In such a family on 32nd Street and in other Chicano communities members lend each other money, locate a car mechanic, and help out in innumerable other situations.[10] "We can hardly keep track of all the money that goes around between us anymore. We just assume it's about equal," a young couple declared while discussing the state of their finances and their families' aid.

Much tension and weight are placed on the family relationship, which sometimes cannot support the demands made on it. At times these demands may lead to conflicts. With the lack of economic resources available to a nuclear family unit, its financial situation can easily become overextended, as when Ana's uncle dropped out, leaving her mother with additional expenses that were more than she could afford. This situation strained the family's relationship for several months until Ana's uncle was again able to help them. Economic pressures can disrupt the ongoing flow of resources and social relationships.

Being a cohesive family does not mean that members do not have problems. Amelia's family

is close and they help each other frequently by exchanging favors and with mutual social and emotional support. Amelia is one of nine children (aged eight to thirty). Though her mother frequently drinks heavily, which embarrasses her, the children were very close to their mother and were upset at her first absence, when, as a local representative, she went to Washington for a conference. When one of the daughters married and moved into the basement apartment, her sister felt the double bed was too large for one person and had a younger sister sleep with her. A second married sister lives upstairs, another lives ten blocks away, and the sons all live within a few blocks. All the sons and daughters congregate almost daily at their mother's home. Amelia considers her family to be a cohesive one. They constantly help each other, just as Ana's family did in providing aid to make her cotillion successful, and reaffirming their image as a strong family.

Those families who do not have relatives or *compadres* on whom to rely must turn to public welfare in time of financial problems or must ask for support, thereby publicly acknowledging their humiliation. The neighborhood is attuned to such events, and news of them is quickly shared.[11] One of the members of the Lions gang frequently attempted to invite himself to dinner at other homes. The other gang members often refused and laughed at his attempts, ridiculing him for his inability to obtain readily a meal from the usual sources—relatives. While eating at relatives' homes is common, no one *asks* to do so; relatives or *compadres* are expected to offer meals to anyone at their homes at mealtime. A person who can survive without money for a long period by going from relative to relative, is viewed as having a cohesive family. A responsible individual does make some attempt to reciprocate, though no accounting is kept and the help received may not be reciprocated for a long period of time. However, even within the family, overdependence can lead to tension, as there is little money to go around.

Compadres and relatives usually make up an emotional and social support group. Women move freely back and forth between homes—cooking together, talking, taking care of one another's children, shopping, and going out together for entertainment. They have frequent Tupperware, makeup, toy, and clothes demonstrations at relatives' or *compadres'* homes. A young woman described one such party:

> They're lots of fun. We girls get together and play lots of games, talk, laugh a lot, and buy too many things. Our husbands don't always like that when we have to pay up. Everyone dresses up to come and we laugh and gossip a lot.

Holidays, birthdays, and other special occasions are usually celebrated with *compadres,* relatives, and their children. A special dinner is prepared, and people eat in several shifts if no table is large enough to accommodate all the guests. Attending a Thanksgiving dinner, which includes not only turkey and sweet potatoes but rice, beans, and chili sauce, at the Mendoza home with two sets of *compadres* (each of the three families had seven children, then all below seventeen years old), guests ate in three of four shifts. The children played and ran in and out, while the women discussed problems of child rearing in the kitchen and then joined the men to dance to Latin music.

Not everyone is pleased with the close familial ties. For those who wish to do things differently, close ties may be viewed as prying, not helpful. Tina, a twenty-five-year-old mother of two boys explained:

> I hate living around the corner from my mother-in-law. She always wants to know what's happening over here. It's my family and I'll run it as I choose. I like some of my relatives but having them all over here asking for things constantly is too much.

Several months later I bumped into Tina after she had moved from the eastern to the western side of the community. She declared that living so near her mother-in-law had become too unpleasant and she had moved at the first opportunity. Tina gave her sister-in-law all her old dishes and furniture when she moved into the downstairs apartment. Both declared that they were happier in their new apartments in the same building. While a close family is highly valued, privately it displeases those who wish to be different.

The strong network of intergenerational relationships provides a means by which traditions can be readily passed on. Few childrearing manuals are used, and intergenerational aid encourages traditional practices. Young girls spend time helping their mothers and learning the mothering role. Girls frequently take on household responsibilities and care for their younger siblings before becoming mothers themselves.[12] At ten or twelve, girls frequently are party to discussions among their mothers' friends and between their mothers and grandmothers about family life and relationships. The intergenerational interaction and the strong emotional support these relationships provide are a solid basis for the maintenance of traditional sex role relationships within the family, upon which the code of honor is based.

MANHOOD

Manhood is expressed through independence, personal strength, control over situations, and domination. This image of manhood, particularly in relationship to femininity, has been traced by some scholars to the culture of Spain, where the desire for precedence in interpersonal relationships and authority over the family are important symbols of manliness.[13] Others trace it to the culture of the Aztecs, where women were expected to be subordinate and submissive to men, while a third group argues that male domination was a result of colonialism.[14] Though the traditional symbols of manhood have not changed substantially in the transition to 32nd Street and have significant implications for men's relationships as fathers, husbands, sons, and brothers,[15] male domination as worked out within the family does not weaken the critical position of the mother.

The role of the Mexican father/husband has been described as one of domination and control over his wife and daughters. Studies of Mexican towns demonstrate that men are seen as people who cannot be "gotten around."[16] Fathers are seen as rigid, closed, and distant.[17] Sons become independent at an early age.[18] Some of these descriptions are similar to those of relationships for fathers and husbands in the 32nd Street community while others are not. The symbols of manhood articulate many of the salient meanings of social relationships within the family. The father/husband, as the dominant member of the household, must maintain the honor of his wife and daughters. To dishonor them reflects not only on them but also on his ability to maintain his self-respect as an independent and dominant individual. He alone must be responsible for supporting his family and must not publicly appear to become dependent on a working wife. The husband/father as the family head and the son as an independent young man both expect to be served by the women in the household and to come and go as they please. Sara, an eighteen year old, explained:

My brother, he comes rushing in and sits down at the table expecting a hot dinner no matter what time it is, just like my father. . . . You know he gets it every time and we have to make it.

No one found it extraordinary that one wife, who worked an early shift (7:00 A.M. to 3:00 P.M.), was expected to prepare dinner for her husband, who finished his shift at 11 P.M. and arrived home to eat at 4:00 A.M., after several hours of drinking. If she was asleep he woke her, and she had to cook and still get their seven children ready for school and be at work by 7:00 A.M.. A spotless house was also expected and provided.

Though the men can demand and usually receive services (cooking, cleaning, and so forth) of the women when they want, the men are dependent on the women to provide these services. Men are taught that cooking, washing clothes, and cleaning are women's and *not* men's work. For example, when one male youth pulled out the ironing board to iron his pants, his sisters took it away from him and laughed and teased him for wanting to do "woman's work." They all thought him strange and talked about him behind his back. His father even gave him a lecture. A man who does "woman's work" must be unable to find a woman to do that work, and therefore must be less than a man, or must be unduly controlled by his woman. This male dependence actually gives a woman a significant source of power.

Husbands

While a husband may have extramarital affairs, he should not publicly flaunt them because it would demonstrate lack of respect for his wife.[19] In one family with seven children the mother caught her husband three times with the same fifteen-year-old woman. The oldest son beat his father. "It was OK, my mother doesn't like him either. He tricks [goes out with other women] on her all the time." This man could barely support his family, making the situation worse for him.

His wife frequently said she would leave him but she never did. Though this is not typical, similar situations exist.

Moreover, some wives argue that men are "free spirits." A scene at a large community dance illustrated some of the manipulations and interactions that occur between husbands, wives, lovers, and friends. The rock music emanating from the packed gym could be heard several blocks away and eliminated conversation. Margie sat at a table with a girlfriend and a friend of her new husband, Dino, trying not to follow Dino's movements as he wandered around the room. He stopped to slap palms every few feet and pulled a young woman out to the floor to dance a fast dance. Walking by me he complained to a female friend that Margie did not care for him or their new baby properly. He stopped by another young woman and invited her out after the dance. He then sauntered over to his wife and pulled her out to the floor for a slow number. Her expression was sulky as they walked back to the table, where he told her that if they had any money left he was going out with his male friends later. She silently found a few bills. He handed half of them back and wandered away.

Many people were aware of what was going on, but no one said anything. Finally, Dino came back and asked me to take him and his wife to get their baby at his sister's. Margie really did not want to leave yet and was silent in the car. When Dino claimed it was Margie's job to get the baby from his sister, she told him that it was his baby too. Dino got out and said that taking care of the baby was her responsibility; he worked. Looking depressed, Margie said she wished Dino would come home with her.

Dino told me to hurry to take him back to the dance after we dropped off Margie. At the discothèque downtown Dino spent the few dollars he had. Afterward he and his girlfriend went to a married couple's house. When he went home the next day he told his wife that he had passed out at a male friend's. She understood, he said. I heard later from friends that she threw several pots at him. Two years later she left him and went back to school.

While not all husbands have girlfriends, many wives believe that as long as their men come home to them, husbands should be allowed to do what they want. Christina, a friend of Margie's, claimed that Dino left Margie for six months because she tried to keep too many tabs on him.

You can't control what a man does and you got to accept him the way he is. Men are free spirits and as long as they come home to you, why should you worry? If they bring in some money and you cook, clean, sew, and are ready for them, why should they leave? Margie made a mistake that night at their party. She shouldn't have left when they had that fight, because she should have known that Dino would just stay there with one of his girlfriends. She holds him in too tight.

While wives may not like the fact that their husbands leave them home, many believe men must be free to roam.

As the person who must maintain his dominance and control the household, the husband is responsible for supporting the family without the help of his wife. Given the poorly paid jobs available, the wages of a working wife or daughter frequently become an economic necessity. Over 40 percent of the community women work, though many of them have working husbands or fathers (Schensul 1972).

Within this cultural context, men are caught in what appears to be an unresolvable dilemma. A working wife is a public indication that the husband is unable to support his family and therefore lacks control in the family and dominance over his wife, who could become economically independent. But the alternatives to an employed wife are few and not much better. A hungry and poorly clothed family does not enhance a man's reputation, nor does depending on support from the expanded family for any length of time without reciprocation. Caught in this dilemma, many husbands prefer to let their wives work and explain their actions within the traditional cultural context. By stating that they are still in control, that they let their wives work, and then only to pay for incidental expenses while the men remain the main breadwinners, their actions are legitimized. For example, while two men in their thirties were sitting in a bar discussing whether wives should work, one said to the other, "I would never let my wife work while I got this good job, but a lot of guys are getting laid off now and my wife didn't get bad money before we got married." The second responded, "I got her working now 'cause we need a new washer and dryer to help her out. Now she has to go to the laundromat." Both men criticized another man whose wife was working though he had a well-paying job and the couple had a "good home." Only if a man explains that he is still in control is a working wife considered legitimate. The fact that women work is still articulated in terms of male domination, and the women infrequently use their employment to change the husband-wife relationship.

Fathers and Sons

A son, like any man, is expected to be independent and dominant in any social relationship with women. In the family this means he should come and go as he pleases, as his father does. Staying near home is not regarded as proper. One eleven year old who always remained on his front steps was told by his father to "go hang somewhere else." What he does outside with his peers is seen largely as his own business. Some parents do not know that their sons are gang members and may know little of their sons' lives outside the home, to the point of not recognizing their "street names." One gang member told me to tell his parents that I met him in a settlement house because they did not know he was a Lion. Should a son begin to jeopardize his job potential by getting into too much trouble, his parents are faced with a dilemma. To interfere is to question his autonomy and threaten his manhood. Paradoxically, a father who refuses to control his son's behavior fails to fulfill his role as dominant family member. A situation of normative ambiguity exists: if he interferes, he violates his son's independence; if he does not, he demonstrates his lack of control. There is no higher order of rules to resolve this striking moral incongruity. Each situation must be negotiated.

The youths are aware of their parents' dilemma. One son expressed the dilemma in the following manner:

> My old lady [mother] gets really upset with me running around in the street 'til real late 'cause she's got so many things to worry about. I shouldn't do it 'cause of my old lady but can't help it; besides my old man he's out a lot anyways doin' his thing.

Felipe at fifteen was rarely punished, though he was often absent from school. He was a man, according to his father, and should be granted independence outside the home. The father felt that he had no authority over his sons and could not tell them how to organize their lives. Only inside the walls of his home did he feel he had a right to control his sons' activities. If Felipe talked back to his father or mother, or came in noisy and drunk, then his father felt he had a right to act. As a man, he had a right to maintain order in his home; otherwise, he felt he had no say. Another father felt similarly about his son. After trying for a long time to encourage his son to continue his education, the father decided that he could not use punishment to force his sixteen-year-old son to attend school.[20]

> I know my son is real smart, his teachers told me that many times, but he and his friends leave school every day before they finish. He says it's boring. He's a good artist—I told him he could go to art school but he says the teachers are all fags [homosexuals]. He has to finish school to get anywhere, but I can't force him. He's a man.

Other fathers put their sons in military schools or send them to Mexico, resolving the dilemma. The father remains in control and the son retains some independence by living away from home.

This dilemma is a triggering situation in that either solution carries implications for the parents' (largely the father's) identity in the eyes of their sons and other people in the community. If the father tries to control his son's activities, he will become known as a strict disciplinarian who is denying his son's independence. Community members will see him as someone who takes the American dream seriously but may be making his son into less of a man. If he leaves his son on his own, the son may perceive his father as distant and tough but allowing him to pursue his activities as he sees fit, as an independent man. In that case, community residents may see the father as helping to develop an independent, honorable man but failing to maintain his own manhood by losing control over his son's activities.

Neither resolution is entirely successful and both may add to the distance between the father and his children. Fathers are generally marginally involved in the care of older children except

as disciplinarians. This does not mean that there is a lack of mutual respect, only that the relationship is perceived to some degree in terms of discipline and control.[21] "During the week we have fun, but when my father's home on Sunday we can't go nowhere or do anything. He just plays his lousy music," claimed a fifteen-year-old boy. His father works the afternoon shift (he makes more money doing so) and is rarely home and awake when his children are. "When we were young my father always took us places, now he takes us nowhere," explained a twelve-year-old boy. Fathers play with babies and hug their young sons and daughters but remain at some distance from their older children. A fourteen-year-old girl complained:

> My father hardly does anything with us. He gives the little kids anything they want and he lets my oldest brother do anything he wants, but we can't go anyplace and he never takes us anywhere. He doesn't even talk to us and he only talks to my oldest brother at night sometimes.

Faced with a number of dilemmas as fathers, husbands, or sons, men must negotiate situational solutions. As a husband, a man must support his family and not allow his wife to work in order to remain dominant, but he is frequently faced with poor job prospects and an insufficient paycheck. New rationalizations and norms legitimate a wife's work and maintain the man's honor. The father-son relationship is replete with dilemmas of independence and domination, with no culturally acceptable solution to the situation of normative ambiguity. The father must decide in each situation whether to discipline his son or encourage the son's autonomy. His choice affects not only his relationship with his son but how he is viewed publicly. Moreover, most fathers realize the importance of education and the potential for getting into trouble in the streets while they also see the importance of the male peer group and male independence.

VIRGINITY

The Virgin Mother is among the most salient religious symbols in Mexico. She is more important than the adult Christ in many Mexican religious ceremonies. For example, *el día de la Virgen de Guadalupe* (December 12) is an important celebration both in Mexico and on 32nd Street, when even men who rarely attend church go to mass.[22] In Mexico City women walk on their knees the several miles from the downtown to the Virgin in Guadalupe's shrine. The sexual purity of women—the faithfulness of a wife to her husband or the virginity of an unmarried woman—is symbolized by the Virgin Mother. The honor of a man is besmirched if a daughter is not a virgin at marriage or a wife is unfaithful. His honor is inexorably tied to that of his family. In Mexican villages, the role of an honorable woman, both as a mother and as a daughter, is that of a *mujer abnegada,* a self-sacrificing, dutiful woman (Diaz 1966, p. 78). While the symbol of the Virgin Mother is used in evaluating women's relationships on 32nd Street, some expectations have changed from those of the traditional Mexican village.

According to Mexican tradition, maintaining a young woman's public image as a virgin requires that she be accompanied on social occasions by a chaperone (usually an older or younger relative). On 32nd Street, chaperonage of unmarried women has largely been eliminated though wives are often accompanied by their young children when visiting or shopping. The result is that everyone is aware that most women can escape the watchful eyes of their kin. Consequently, maintenance both of a woman's virginity or faithfulness and of community perception of that state are difficult. Most families are concerned with the movements of their daughters but cannot completely restrict their

activities, though a few families do attempt to retain tight control.

Brothers and other relatives act as unofficial chaperones for young women. They will often stop young women from drinking, watch their sisters if they are with young men, or tell all their friends to stay away. For example, at a party sixteen-year-old Sara asked me:

> *Please tell me if you see my brother because I can't drink with him around, he'll beat me. Me and my sisters are not supposed to drink, he doesn't like that. You know when we go to dances on the north side, we got to sneak 'cause if he ever found out he would follow us around and we'd never get to go anywhere.*

The importance that parents give to a daughter's identity as a virgin is revealed in the following example. Alicia, when she was fourteen, hid her pregnancy from her parents until her sixth month. Her parents sent her to an aunt and uncle in Mexico to whom she was supposed to give the child. Realizing how much she wanted to keep the baby, her aunt persuaded Alicia's parents to let her keep the child. When she returned home seven months pregnant, Alicia was not permitted to leave the house. Anytime a visitor arrived, she hid, first under the bed and then, when she became too big, under the sink in the kitchen. Labor pains started when she was hiding in the garage. Later her parents almost took over the upbringing of her son, taking him as a deduction on their income tax even after Alicia went to work and referring to him as their son, though everyone knew who the parents were.

Parents are faced with what seems to many an unresolvable dilemma. If they follow the traditional honor-based code and refuse to allow their daughter to go out unsupervised, then her virginity remains publicly unquestioned and the honor of her family is upheld. The wider society and many of the local institutions, whether organized by members of the wider society or by local residents, provide legitimation for allowing a young woman some degree of freedom. Both the schools and the churches sponsor dances that are sparsely supervised. Local community groups also sponsor dances with American rock bands. Parents are invited to attend yet discouraged from participating or actually attending by the type of music and the dim lighting. This local legitimation of more freedom for young women places parents in a problematic situation. Freedom heightens the risk of the daughter losing her virginity or being perceived as having lost it. But if they closely supervise her activities, they risk alienating her. Again a situation of normative ambiguity exists and the resolution must be situationally negotiated between parents and their daughters.

The parental dilemma is exacerbated by the expectation that men will take what they can from women. Men are defined as dominant and women defined as submissive; consequently, only male relatives can be trusted with women. One father succinctly expressed these views:

> You know what all men are after. . . .
> It's natural for them to go out and get
> it anyway they can. I don't trust any
> of the young punks around here.
> They take it and run. There are too
> many unmarried pregnant girls
> around here. The young girls don't
> know how to handle themselves.

Parents are confronted directly with the dilemma when young women ask permission to attend a party or dance with friends. Parents often employ the tactic of nondecision. They postpone any decision until the last moment. Then, when their daughter is ready to go out, they deny her permission. Other times the responsibility is shifted back and forth between mother and father and then changed again at the last moment. This lack of resolution can result in dissatisfaction on both sides. Many young women stop asking. "I just go where I please without asking permission. She [her mother] would just stare at me in silence when I asked, so what's the point in asking?" a nineteen year old explained. By going out on their own, young women risk being appraised as nonvirgins.

Some families are able to retain strict control over their daughters. Lana, for example, must ask permission to sit in front of her house and rarely is allowed to go anywhere. She was particularly upset when she was not permitted to go anywhere or do anything on her birthday.

> I don't ever get anything, like one
> time my father gave me ten dollars
> five days after my birthday and I
> threw it back at him and I told him
> that I don't want his ten dollars. I
> didn't ask you for money. He said
> this was a way to pay me back for
> what I'd done for them. I told them
> that they didn't owe me anything. All
> I wanted for my birthday was some
> fun like a picnic at the beach. I didn't
> want any money. I just wanted
> someone to remember and have
> some fun. I'm never allowed to go to
> the movies. I do all the cooking and
> cleaning. My mother comes in and
> takes a bath and watches TV.

Another mother timed her daughter's return from school every day; it took eight minutes to walk home and if her daughter was not home within twelve minutes after the last bell, the mother went out looking for her. While this case is extreme, other families only allow their daughters to attend parties or dances under the supervision of a mature older relative. Most of the young women, however, have enough freedom to do what they want during the hours they are permitted outside the house. Many skip school to attend parties or be alone with their boyfriends.

Unable to resolve the dilemma with their parents, many young women marry in order to leave home. Marriage is one of the few culturally legitimate means for young women to leave home and still maintain their honor and that of their families. For example, Mita's parents did not approve of the man she wanted to marry. She resented the fact that they physically restrained her from going out with him. At one point they threatened to send her to Texas to stay with her relatives. They followed through on the threat as far as taking her to the station but did not actually send her. Mita later moved out of her house to live with a married girlfriend and planned a wedding on her own. The week before the wedding her parents took her to Mexico on a false pretext and kept her there for a month. Finally, a few months later they gave up their efforts and let the couple marry. Mita explained:

> They want me to marry a doctor or something but I want to get married now. . . . I can't stand my parents telling me do this, do that. At night my mother makes sure we're [Mita and her younger sister] in bed and if we get up for a drink of water, she starts following us around and tells us to get back to bed. We have to sneak anything we do.

Parental permission for their daughter to go out affects the public evaluation not only of the parents but of their daughter. If she is permitted to attend parties, she is at a much greater risk of being appraised as a nonvirgin even if she actually retains her virginity. Parents frequently increase the risk of such erroneous perceptions by failing to take a strong stand if their daughter sneaks out. It is the public perception of her sexual purity that reflects upon the parents. If she is perceived as a nonvirgin, then her family's honor is questioned. Only complete parental control over her behavior minimizes the risk of her being perceived as a nonvirgin or of actually losing her virginity. As such control is difficult to maintain in modern urban society, it is more an ideal than a reality.

MOTHERHOOD

Motherhood is the most culturally acceptable identity available to women. The role of independent career woman is not culturally acceptable. Women must be either wives, sisters, or mothers to men. Motherhood is seen not as a last resort but rather as a highly honored role. The Mexican image of the Virgin Mother, loving and dependable, the person with whom the child satisfies desires for nurturing and acceptance, is the 32nd Street model of motherhood.[23] Motherhood is the basis of the strongest bonds of blood ties.[24] These bonds are much stronger than those of husbands and wives or fathers and children.

The husband-wife bond is based on procreation and expression of love but little on companionship. The expectation that men will dominate in all situations makes it difficult to develop companionable relationships between men and women even in marriage, as sociability usually develops between equals. (Moreover, any time a man and a woman who are not related through blood ties are together, it is expected that they will become sexually involved, because men dominate women and, lacking equality and the possibility of friendship, the only reason they would be together is as sexual partners.)[25] Most socializing occurs in single-sex groups, and the expanded family network fulfills companionship functions. But children's ties with their mothers are natural and lifelong:[26]

they never become distant with age, as do ties with their fathers, who discipline and control them. While the dynamics of the father-child interaction is in part determined by the child's willingness to obey him and demonstrate respect for him, mothering places no such conditions on the parent-child relationship.

Loyalty and support for his mother was demonstrated by a young man who had become addicted to heroin and entered a methadone program only after stealing from his mother:

> I used to steal all the time from my brothers and sisters and went through my old man's coat pockets many times . . . even stole his watch once and pawned it, but you know when I took some bread [money] from my old lady, then I knew I had to do something. Taking from your old lady's real bad.

The mother remains the central and most stable feature in a son's life. He depends on her for nurture and emotional support and she on him for support and the ultimate protection of her honor. As a son his honor is dependent on hers; any aspersion cast on her honor reflects on his own.

In an extreme case of maintaining a mother's honor, a son killed his father after repeatedly catching him with teenage women. Some community residents felt the murder was justifiable, that the father's behavior was dishonorable and the resolution culturally acceptable. But the community was not unanimous in defining the situation as one where the family honor was at stake. Some residents felt that murder was not a necessary or legitimate resolution and that the son was a criminal who deserved to be jailed. His mother, though, worked continuously for his release. Sentenced as a juvenile, he was out in less than three years.

Young women vicariously experience the mother role through their continual associations with relatives and *comadres* and their babies. They are frequently enthusiastic about their own mother having additional children. Fifteen-year-old Celia, one of seven children declared:

> Man, I want my mother to have a kid so I can take care of it. I love babies. I like to baby-sit for the little kid next door, she's so smart. Now my mother's comadre is having a kid so maybe I'll be able to help, but they live all the way by 40th Street, but then maybe I can stay by their house sometimes.

At sixteen, Celia became pregnant and married.

The traditional expectation that a woman's unique role is to be a mother with many children creates a conflict for those young women who have interests outside the home. Some reject motherhood. One nineteen-year-old college student, the eldest of seven, despised the traditional female role of daughter and mother:

> I had to change diapers for my three youngest brothers and sisters. They were such a mess and were so much trouble. I hate them for it. I wish my mother didn't have them. What did she need so many kids for anyway? It would have been a lot better without the last two. They were always crying and wanting attention . . . comb their hair, wash them, feed them, change their diapers, and put them to sleep. . . . They're my mother's kids. She should be responsible for them. I'm not their mother . . . if my mother gets married again and has another kid I'll die. One time I told her I wasn't going to have any kids.

She really got angry and said God will punish me. It was up to Him, not me. She didn't speak to me for a week. I'm not going to have any kids. They're just trouble.

Celia's oldest sister, a student, added another problem to the list:

It wouldn't be good for my mother to have more kids. They cost money and it would be like the dog; everyone would get excited for a while and then bored and not want to take care of it. [Celia objected here.] I don't want to take care of it. I'd move out.

The view of the two students are not generally accepted and often considered immoral. They violate all expectations of femininity and the family. Though it is becoming more common for young women to desire to limit family size, in part because of the expense of bringing up children, older people and many younger ones see this not only as tampering with "God's will" but also as comparing things that cannot be compared: economics and family. These young women are openly denying the importance of motherhood and appear to equate the family's worth with that of money. For most, social and economic success are not valued above motherhood. Problems arise only for those young women who are beginning to strive for success in the wider society. The exclusion of motherhood is still regarded as deviant.

CHIVALRY AND RESPECT

Chivalry and etiquette are not regarded as critical for most of American society today. Except for some fictional British detectives, such as Dorothy Sayres's Lord Peter Wimsey, symbols of etiquette and chivalry are rare today, but the precise form of social relationships remains important for the residents of 32nd Street. The formalities of social interaction are essential in an honor-based subculture, where even the slightest word or movement may be seen as placing a person in a demeaning situation.[27] Etiquette "sets limits and protects us from having to expose ourselves in ways which may be detrimental to our public image" (Goodenough 1963, p. 197). Formal rules provide order for everyday social interactions, creating some sense of security and stability in potentially problematic situations. Rules channel impulse, passion, and desire into ways of acting that are recognized as having a particular social meaning in a particular social setting. "Form surrounds and sets bounds to our privacy, limiting its excesses, curbing its explosions, isolating and preserving it" (Paz 1961, p. 32). Formal rules of etiquette create a distance between actors, minimizing the potential for questions about precedence and the need to prove invulnerability in a situation. For example, following rules against staring at others can prevent a person from defining a situation as a challenge to his claim to precedence.[28]

Following an elaborate set of formal rules of etiquette is expected in both Chicano and Mexican families. Foster (1967, p. 96), describing a Mexican village, states, "From early childhood one learns to be 'correct.' Children when confronted with a family friend or a stranger are told *dále la mano* [step up and shake hands]." On 32nd Street swearing is not tolerated in the home by either females or males. Swearing often results in a slap or a belt across the seat, administered by a mother, father, or older sister or brother. Nor is insolence or rudeness tolerated in the home. Doors must be closed nicely. An older person must be greeted and taken leave of with a courtesy that would please Emily Post. The following exchange took place when I brought a male friend to meet the Lions at the park. After I introduced him, each of the Lions greeted my friend with "I'm very glad to meet you" as they shook hands. Courtesies such as taking woman's arm when walking in the street and always walking on the curb side are performed by most men. The first time one of the Lions held my arm as we crossed an icy patch on the sidewalk, I turned to him astounded and asked if he always did such things. He replied that he usually did, as he had been instructed to do so since he was a child. Similar behavior was frequently demonstrated at weddings and cotillions.

Adherence to the rules of etiquette is a sign of respect when dealing with persons older than oneself. Punishment is expected if these rules are not followed. Ronny, a member of the Lions gang, was made to lean over the edge of the bathtub by his mother and was beaten with a belt when he arrived home drunk and telling wild stories. "She only does that when I come home real drunk. I usually sober up before I go home. I deserve it when I come in high." His mother felt she had no control over his drinking, but when he demonstrated a lack of respect by coming inside her home drunk and disorderly, she would and could discipline him.

Not only do formal interactions help youths to maintain order between generations, between the sexes, and between men, but youths who successfully employ the rules of etiquette at home are well received by all adults, while those who demonstrate a lack of manners within the home are denigrated by the community regardless of behavior outside the home. Those who know when to use their manners are those who gain the respect of others, even among gang members. Consequently, the use of common rules of etiquette not only demonstrates respect for others and channels behavior but is also highly valued by others in the community.

It is clear that the important symbols of family life are solidarity, male domination, virginity, motherhood, and respect. In the context of an urban community within a highly industrialized and educated society, some of the expectations derived from these symbols become distorted, are ambiguous, or are in conflict. While some of the problematic situations can be resolved within the traditional culture, for other situations all solutions seem less than perfect. Much of the ambiguity and conflict is found in the expectations concerning sex role behavior and child-parent relationships.

In the urban context youths are granted many freedoms and hold few responsibilities. These expectations are validated and supported by the media, by the schools, and even to some extent by the Catholic church. The situation places continual pressure on parents to allow their children more freedom while encouraging youths to demand those freedoms. Moreover, women are encouraged to work, particularly because of financial need.

The cohesive family with its strong network of relatives and *compadres* provides economic supports to help deal with financial realities, emotional supports to deal with normative ambiguity and conflict, and social supports and mechanisms to maintain the traditional symbols of sex role relationships and nearly traditional behavior patterns. With the support of the expanded family, actors negotiate difficult situations of normative ambiguity and conflict. Sometimes the process is painful, emotionally charged, and the consequence unsatisfactory to both parties; a son is physically punished or a daughter is locked in her room. Members of the expanded family may provide advice and emotional support or may invite the unruly son or daughter of a relative or *compadre* to live with them. Families do their best to keep members out of the social welfare and justice systems.

Youths are caught between the traditional model of social relationships and the Chicago urban reality: the streets, the school, the media, and the job scene. With the freedom they take or are given, the youths are faced with many dilemmas as they venture beyond the confines of the communal and familial order.

4 Social Policy and Families

Reading 10   Poverty and Family Structure: The Widening Gap between Evidence and Public Policy Issues*

WILLIAM JULIUS WILSON (WITH KATHRYN NECKERMAN)

In the early and mid-1960s social scientists such as Kenneth B. Clark, Lee Rainwater, and Daniel Patrick Moynihan discussed in clear and forceful terms the relationship between black poverty and family structure and sounded the alarm even then that the problems of family dissolution among poor blacks were approaching catastrophic proportions.[1] These writers emphasized that the rising rates of broken marriages, out-of-wedlock births, female-headed families, and welfare dependency among poor urban blacks were the products not only of race-specific experiences, but also of structural conditions in the larger society, including economic relations. And they underlined the need to address these problems with programs that would attack structural inequality in American society and thereby, in the words of Moynihan, "bringing the Negro American to full and equal sharing in the responsibilities and rewards of citizenship."[2]

There is a distinct difference in the way the problems of poverty and family structure were viewed in the major studies of the 1960s and the way they are viewed today, however. Unlike the earlier studies, discussions in the current research of the relationship between black family instability and male joblessness have been overshadowed by discussions that link family instability with the growth of income transfers and in-kind benefits. Because, as we demonstrate in this essay, the factors associated with the rise of single-parent families—not only among blacks, but among whites as well—are sufficiently complex to preclude overemphasis on any single variable, the recent trend among scholars and policy makers to neglect the role of male joblessness while emphasizing the role of welfare is especially questionable. But first let us examine the problem of poverty and family structure in its historical context.

POVERTY AND FAMILY STRUCTURE IN HISTORICAL PERSPECTIVE

In the early twentieth century the vast majority of both black and white low-income families were intact. Although national information on family structure was not available before the publication of the 1940 census, studies of early manuscript census forms of individual cities and counties make it clear that even among the very poor, a substantial majority of both black and white families were two-parent families. Moreover, most of the women heading families in the late nineteenth and early twentieth centuries were widows. Evidence from the 1940 census indicates that divorce and separation were relatively uncommon.[3]

It is particularly useful to consider black families in historical perspective because social scientists have commonly assumed that the recent trends in black family structure that are of concern in this essay could be traced to the lingering effects of slavery. E. Franklin Frazier's classic statement of this view in *The Negro Family in the United States* informed all subsequent studies of the black family, including the Moynihan report.[4] But recent research has challenged assumptions about the influence of slavery on the character of the black family. Reconstruction of black family patterns from manuscript census forms has shown that the two-parent, nuclear family was the predominant family form in the late nineteenth and early twentieth centuries. Historian Herbert Gutman examined data on black family structure in the northern urban areas of Buffalo and Brooklyn, New York; in the southern cities of Mobile, Alabama, of Richmond, Virginia, and of Charleston, South Carolina; and in several counties and small towns during this period. He found that between 70 percent and 90 percent of black households were "male-present" and that a majority were nuclear families.[5] Similar findings have been reported for Philadelphia, for rural Virginia, for Boston, and for cities of the Ohio Valley.[6] This research demonstrates that neither slavery, nor economic deprivation, nor the migration to urban areas affected black family structure by the first quarter of the twentieth century.

However, the poverty and degraded conditions in which most blacks lived were not with-out their consequences for the family. For the most part, the positive association between intact family structure and measures of class, such as property ownership, occupation, or literacy, generally reflected the higher rate of mortality among poor men.[7] Widowhood accounted for about three-quarters of female-headed families among blacks, Germans, Irish, and native white Americans in Philadelphia in 1880.[8] In addition, men sometimes had to live apart from their families as they moved from one place to another in search of work.[9] Given their disproportionate concentration among the poor in America, black families were more strongly affected by these conditions and therefore were more likely than white families to be female headed. For example, in Philadelphia in 1880, 25.3 percent of all black families were female headed, compared to only 13.6 percent of all native white families.

The earliest detailed national census information on family structure is available from the 1940 census. In 1940 female-headed families were more prevalent among blacks than among whites, and among urbanites than among rural residents for both groups. Yet, even in urban areas, 72 percent of black families with children under eighteen were male headed. Moreover, irrespective of race and residence, most women heading families were widows.

The two-parent nuclear family remained the predominant type for both blacks and whites up to World War II. As shown in Table 1, 10 percent of white families and 18 percent of black families were female headed in 1940. The relative stability in gross census figures on female-headed families between 1940 and 1960 obscures the beginnings of current trends in family breakup. More specifically, while widowhood fell significantly during those two decades, marital dissolution was rising.[10] Furthermore, the portion of out-of-wedlock births was growing. By the 1960s, the proportion of female-headed families had begun to increase significantly among blacks, rising from 22 percent in 1960 to

28 percent in 1970, and then to 42 percent by 1983. This proportion also rose among white families, from 8 percent in 1960 to 12 percent in 1983. The increase in female-headed families with children under eighteen is even more dramatic. By 1983, almost one out of five families with children under eighteen were headed by women, including 14 percent of white families, 24 percent of Spanish-origin families, and 48 percent of black families.[11] To understand the nature of these shifts, it is necessary to disaggregate these statistics and consider factors such as changes in fertility rates, marital status, age structure, and living arrangements.

TABLE 1   Percentage of Female-Headed Families, No Husband Present, by Race and Spanish Origin, 1940–1983

Year	White	Black	Spanish origin	Total families
1940	10.1	17.9	—	—
1950	8.5	17.6[a]	—	9.4
1960	8.1	21.7	—	10.0
1965	9.0	24.9	—	10.5
1970	9.1	28.3	—	10.8
1971	9.4	30.6	—	11.5
1972	9.4	31.8	—	11.6
1973	9.6	34.6	16.7	12.2
1974	9.9	34.0	17.4	12.4
1975	10.5	35.3	18.8	13.0
1976	10.8	35.9	20.9	13.3
1977	10.9	37.1	20.0	13.6
1978	11.5	39.2	20.3	14.4
1979	11.6	40.5	19.8	14.6
1980	11.6	40.2	19.2	14.6
1981	11.9	41.7	21.8	15.1
1982	12.4	40.6	22.7	15.4
1983	12.2	41.9	22.8	15.4

SOURCES: U.S. Bureau of the Census, *Current Population Reports,* series P-20, nos. 153, 218, 233, 246, 258, 276, 291, 311, 326, 340, 352, 366, 371, 381, and 388, "Household and Family Characteristics" (Washington, D.C.: Government Printing Office, 1965, 1970–1984); and idem, *Current Population Reports,* series P-20, nos. 267 and 290 "Persons of Spanish Origins in the United States" (Washington, D.C.: Government Printing Office, 1974 and 1975).

[a]Black and other.

CHANGING FAMILY STRUCTURE AND DEMOGRAPHIC CORRELATES

The unprecedented increases in the proportion of births out of wedlock are a major contributor to the rise of female-headed families in the black community. In 1980, 68 percent of births to black women ages fifteen to twenty-four were outside of marriage, compared to 41 percent in 1955. According to 1981 figures, almost 30 percent of all young single black women have home a child before the age of twenty.[12] The incidence of out-of-wedlock births has risen to unprecedented levels for young white women as well, although both rates and ratios remain far below those for black women (see Table 2).

These increases in births outside of marriage reflect trends in fertility and marital status, as well as changes in population composition. Age-specific fertility rates for both white and black women have fallen since the peak of the baby boom in the late 1950s. Even fertility rates for teenagers (ages fifteen to nineteen) have fallen overall. What these figures obscure, however, is that the fertility rates of young unmarried women have risen or declined only moderately, while those of married women of these ages have fallen more substantially (see Table 2). In addition, growing proportions of young women are single. For instance, the percentage of never-married women increased dramatically between 1960 and 1980, from 29 percent to 47 percent for whites, and from 30 percent to 69 percent for blacks.[13] Recent data show not only that the incidence of premarital conception has increased, but also that the proportion of those premarital pregnancies legitimated by marriage has decreased.[14] Thus, out-of-wedlock births now comprise a far greater proportion of total births than they did in the past, particularly for black women (see Table 2). The black "illegitimacy ratio" has increased so precipitously in recent years not because the rate of

Table 2   Fertility Rates and Ratios by Race and Age, 1960–1980

Age-group and year	Fertility rate		Marital fertility rate		Nonmarital fertility rate		Illegitimacy ratio	
	Black	White	Black	White	Black	White	Black	White
Ages 15–19								
1960	158.2	79.4	659.3	513.0	76.5	6.6	421.5	71.6
1965	136.1	60.7	602.4	443.2	75.8	7.9	492.0	114.3
1970	133.4	57.4	522.4	431.8	90.8	10.9	613.5	171.0
1975	106.4	46.4	348.0	311.8	86.3	12.0	747.2	229.0
1980	94.6	44.7	344.0	337.6	83.0	16.0	851.5	329.8
Ages 20–24								
1960	294.2	194.9	361.8	352.5	166.5	18.2	199.6	21.9
1965	247.3	138.8	293.3	270.9	152.6	22.1	229.9	38.4
1970	196.8	145.9	267.6	244.0	120.9	22.5	295.0	51.8
1975	141.0	108.1	192.4	179.6	102.1	15.5	399.5	60.9
1980	145.0	112.4	232.8	198.2	108.2	22.6	560.2	114.9
Ages 25–29								
1960	214.6	252.8	225.0	220.5	171.8	18.2	141.3	11.4
1965	188.1	189.8	188.6	177.3	164.7	24.3	162.8	18.8
1970	140.1	163.4	159.3	164.9	93.7	21.1	180.6	20.7
1975	108.7	108.2	130.8	132.4	73.2	14.8	226.8	26.2
1980	115.5	109.5	149.7[a]	148.4[a]	79.1	17.3	361.7	50.2

SOURCES: National Center for Health Statistics, *Vital Statistics of the United States,* annual volumes 1960–1975 and 1984 (Washington, D.C.: Government Printing Office).

[a]Marital fertility rates for 1980 are unavailable; 1979 figures are substituted.

extramarital births has substantially increased, but because the percentage of women married and the rate of marital fertility have both declined significantly.

The decline in the proportion of women who are married and living with their husbands is a function of both a sharp rise in separation and divorce rates and the substantial increase in the percentage of never-married women. The combined impact of these trends has been particularly drastic for black women as the proportion married and living with their husbands fell from 52 percent in 1947 to 34 percent in 1980.[15] As set out in Table 3, black women have much higher separation and divorce rates than white women, although the differences are exaggerated because of a higher rate of remarriage among white women.[16] Whereas white women

are far more likely to be divorced than separated, black women are more likely to be separated than divorced. Indeed, a startling 22 percent of all married black women are separated from their husbands.[17]

Just as important a factor in the declining proportion of black women who are married and living with their husbands is the increase in the percentage of never-married women. Indeed, as shown in Table 3, the proportion of never-married black women increased from 65 percent in 1960 to 82 percent in 1980 for those ages fourteen to twenty-four and from 8 percent to 21 percent for those ages twenty-five to forty-four. On the other hand, while the proportion of black women who are separated or divorced increased from 22 percent in 1960 to 31 percent in 1980 for those ages twenty-five to forty-four, and from 17 percent to 25 percent for those ages forty-five to sixty-four, the fraction divorced or separated actually fell for younger women.

For young women, both black and white, the increase in the percentage of never-married women largely accounts for the decline in the proportion married with husband present (see Table 3). For black women ages twenty-five to forty-four, increases in both the percentage of never-married women and in marital dissolution were important; for white women of the same age-group, marital dissolution is the more important factor. Marriage has not declined among white women ages forty-five to sixty-four; however, among black women in the same age-group, the proportion married with husband

present has fallen, due mainly to increases in marital dissolution.

Although trends in fertility and marital status are the most important contributors to the rise of female-headed families, the situation has been exacerbated by recent changes in the age structure, which have temporarily increased the proportion of young women in the population, particularly in the black population. Whereas in 1960, only 36 percent of black women ages fifteen to forty-four were between fifteen and twenty-four years of age, by 1975 that proportion had increased to 46 percent; the comparable increase for white women was from 34 percent in 1960 to 42 percent in 1975.[18] These changes in the age structure increase the proportion of

TABLE 3 Marital Status of Women by Race and Age, 1947–1980

Age-group and marital status	1947 White	1947 Black	1960 White	1960 Black	1970 White	1970 Black	1980 White	1980 Black
Ages 14–24								
Married[a]	33.5	30.9	33.6	25.7	29.6	21.3	26.8[b]	13.1[b]
Never married	62.9	59.5	63.3	65.0	66.4	72.3	68.6	82.4
Separated/divorced/ husband absent	3.3	8.4	3.0	9.0	3.8	6.2	4.5	4.3
Widowed	0.4	1.3	0.1	0.3	0.1	0.1	0.1	0.2
Ages 25–44								
Married	80.3	67.2	85.1	64.9	85.0	62.0	75.5	44.7
Never married	11.5	10.5	6.8	8.2	6.3	12.2	9.8	21.3
Separated/divorced/ husband absent	5.8	14.4	6.3	22.4	7.6	22.2	13.6	30.8
Widowed	2.4	8.0	1.8	4.5	1.2	3.6	1.1	3.2
Ages 45–64								
Married	70.2	57.6	74.1	52.8	73.5	54.1	74.0	46.0
Never married	8.0	5.3	6.4	5.3	5.9	4.7	4.4	6.8
Separated/divorced/ husband absent	5.0	8.3	5.7	16.6	7.3	20.4	9.8	25.4
Widowed	16.8	28.5	13.7	25.3	13.3	20.4	11.8	21.8

SOURCES: U.S. Bureau of the Census, *Current Population Reports,* series P-20, no. 10, "Characteristics of Single, Married, Widowed and Divorced Persons in 1947" (Washington, D.C.: Government Printing Office, 1948); idem, *Current Population Reports,* series P-20, nos. 153, 218, "Marital Status and Family Status" (Washington, D.C.: Government Printing Office, 1960 and 1970); idem, *Current Population Reports,* series P-20, no. 365, "Marital Status and Living Arrangements, March 1980" (Washington, D.C.: Government Printing Office, 1981).

[a]Married, husband present.

[b]Includes only ages 15–24.

births occurring to young women and, given the higher out-of-wedlock birth ratios among young women, inflate the proportion of all births that occur outside of marriage as well.

Finally, the rise in the proportion of female-headed families reflects an increasing tendency for women to form independent households rather than to live in subfamilies. Until recently, Census Bureau coding procedures caused the number of subfamilies to be significantly under-estimated;[19] therefore, an accurate time series is impossible. However, other research suggests that women are becoming more likely to form their own households. For example, Cutright's analysis of components of growth in female-headed families between 1940 and 1970 indicates that 36 percent of the increase in numbers of female family heads between the ages of fifteen and forty-four can be attributed to the higher propensity of such women to form their own households.[20] Bane and Ellwood show that these trends continued during the 1970s.[21] In the period 1969 to 1973, 56 percent of white children and 60 percent of black children born into single-parent families lived in households headed by neither mother nor father (most lived with grand-parents). During the years 1974 to 1979, those proportions declined to 24 percent for white children and 37 percent for black children.

Thus, young women comprise a greater proportion of single mothers than ever before. For example, while in 1950, only 26 percent of black female family heads and 12 percent of white female family heads were under the age of thirty-five, in 1983 those proportions had risen to 43 percent for blacks and 29 percent for whites. The number of black children growing up in fatherless families increased by 41 percent between 1970 and 1980, and most of this growth has occurred in families in which the *mother has never been married.*[22] This is not surprising, according to Bane and Ellwood's research: whereas the growth of the number of single

white mothers over the last decade is mainly due to the increase in separation and divorce, the growth of the number of single black mothers is "driven by a dramatic decrease in marriage and increase in fertility among never-married women."[23] In 1982 the percentage of black children living with both parents had dipped to 43 percent, only roughly half of the proportion of white children in two-parent homes.

As Bane and Ellwood point out, "Never married mothers are more likely than divorced, separated or widowed mothers to be younger and be living at home when they have their children."[24] Younger mothers tend to have less education, less work experience, and thus fewer financial resources. Therefore they are more likely initially to form subfamilies, drawing support from parents and relatives. However, it appears that most children of single mothers in subfamilies spend only a small part of their lives in such families. On the basis of an analysis of data from the Panel Study of Income Dynamics (PSID) for the period 1968 to 1979, Bane and Ellwood suggest that by the time children born into subfamilies reach age six, two-thirds will have moved into different living arrangements. Among blacks, two-thirds of the moves are into independent female-headed families, whereas among whites two-thirds are into two-parent families. However, whether the focus is on subfamilies or on independent female-headed families, less than 10 percent of white children and almost half of the black children born into non-two-parent families remain in such families "for their entire childhood."[25] And, as discussed in the next section, these families are increasingly plagued by poverty.

THE POVERTY STATUS OF FEMALE-HEADED FAMILIES

...The rise of female-headed families has had dire social and economic consequences because these families are far more vulnerable to poverty than are other types of families. Indeed, sex and marital status of the head are the most important determinants of poverty status for families, especially in urban areas. The poverty rate of female-headed families was 36.3 percent in 1982, while the rate for married-couple families was only 7.6 percent. For black and Spanish-origin female-headed families in 1982, poverty rates were 56.2 percent and 55.4 percent respectively.[26]

Female-headed families comprise a growing proportion of the poverty population. Individuals in female-headed families made up fully a third of the poverty population in 1982. Forty-six percent of all poor families and 71 percent of all poor black families were female headed in 1982. These proportions were higher for metropolitan areas, particularly for central cities, where 60 percent of all poor families and 78 percent of all poor black families were headed by women.[27] The proportion of poor black families headed by women increased steadily from 1959 to 1977, from less than 30 percent to 72 percent, and has remained slightly above 70 percent since then. The total number of poor black female-headed families continued to grow between 1977 and 1982, increasing by 373,000; the proportion of the total number of poor black families did not continue to increase only because of the sharp rise in the number of male-headed families in poverty during this period (from 475,000 to 622,000 in 1982). The proportion of poor white families headed by women also increased from less than 20 percent in 1959 to a high of almost 40 percent in 1977, and then dropping to 35 percent in 1983.

Female-headed families are not only more likely to be in poverty, they are also more likely than male-headed families to be persistently poor. For example, Duncan reports, on the basis of data from the Michigan PSID, that 61 percent of those who were persistently poor over a ten-year period were in female-headed families, a propor-

tion far exceeding the prevalence of female-headed families in the general population.[28]

CAUSES OF THE RISE IN FEMALE-HEADED FAMILIES

As the foregoing discussion suggests, to speak of female-headed families and out-of-wedlock births is to emphasize that they have become inextricably tied up with poverty and dependency, often long term. The sharp rise in these two forms of social dislocation is related to the demographic changes in the population that we discussed in the previous section. For example, the drop in the median age of women heading families would lead one to predict a higher rate of poverty among these families, all other things being equal. We only need to consider that young women who have a child out of wedlock, the major contributor to the drop in median age of single mothers, are further disadvantaged by the disruption of their schooling and employment.

However, while a consideration of demographic changes may be important to understand the complex nature and basis of changes in family structure, it is hardly sufficient. Indeed, changes in demographic factors are generally a function of broader economic, political, and social trends. For example, the proportion of out-of-wedlock births has risen among young black women, as a result of a decline in both marriage and marital fertility, coupled with relative stability of out-of-wedlock birth rates (i.e., the number of births per 1,000 unmarried women). This increase in the proportion of extramarital births could be mainly a function of the increasing difficulty of finding a marriage partner with stable employment, or of changes in social values regarding out-of-wedlock births, or of increased economic independence afforded women by the availability of income transfer payments. Broader social and economic forces may also be influencing married women to have

fewer children.... In this section we will delin-
eate the role of broader social and economic
forces not only on trends in family formation in
the inner city, but on national trends in family
formation as well. In the process we hope to
establish the argument that despite the complex
nature of the problem, the weight of existing evidence suggests that the problems of male joblessness could be the single most important factor underlying the rise in unwed mothers among
poor black women. Yet, this factor has received
scant attention in recent discussions of the
decline of intact families among the poor. Let us
first examine the contribution of other factors,
including social and cultural trends and the
growth of income transfers, which in recent
years has become perhaps the single most popular explanation of changes in family formation
and family structure.

The Role of Changing Social and Cultural Trends

Extramarital fertility among teenagers is of particular significance to the rise of female-headed
families. Out-of-wedlock birth rates for teens are
generally not falling as they are for older
women. Almost 40 percent of all illegitimate
births are to women under age twenty.[29] Moreover, adolescent mothers are the most disadvantaged of all female family heads because they
are likely to have their schooling interrupted,
experience difficulty finding employment, and
very rarely receive child support. They are also
the most likely to experience future marital
instability and disadvantages in the labor market.

Any attempt to explain the social and cultural factors behind the rise of out-of-wedlock
teenage fertility must begin with the fact that
most teenage pregnancies are reportedly
unwanted. Surveys by Zelnik and Kantner have
consistently shown that the majority of premarital pregnancies are neither planned nor wanted.
In 1979, for instance, 82 percent of premarital

pregnancies in fifteen- to nineteen-year-olds
(unmarried at the time the pregnancy was
resolved) were unwanted.[30]

However, unpublished tabulations from a
recent Chicago study of teenage pregnancy indicate that adolescent black mothers reported far
fewer pregnancies to be unwanted than did their
white counterparts. Moreover, as Dennis Hogan
has stated, the Chicago data suggest that "it is
not so much that single motherhood is unwanted
as it is that it is not sufficiently 'unwanted.'
Women of all ages without a strong desire to prevent a birth tend to have limited contraceptive
success.[31] This argument would seem especially
appropriate to poor inner-city black neighborhoods. In this connection, Kenneth Clark has
argued that

> In the ghetto, the meaning of the ille-
> gitimate child is not ultimate dis-
> grace. There is not the demand for
> abortion or for surrender of the child
> that one finds in more privileged
> communities. In the middle class,
> the disgrace of illegitimacy is tied to
> personal and family aspirations. In
> lower-class families, on the other
> hand, the girl loses only some of her
> already limited options by having an
> illegitimate child; she is not going to
> make a "better marriage" or improve
> her economic and social status
> either way. On the contrary, a child
> is a symbol of the fact that she is a
> woman, and she may gain from hav-
> ing something of her own. Nor is the
> boy who fathers an illegitimate child
> going to lose, for where is he going?
> The path to any higher status seems
> closed to him in any case.[32]

Systematic evidence of expected parenthood prior to first marriage is provided in two

studies by Hogan. Drawing upon data collected in a national longitudinal survey of high school students conducted for a National Center for Educational Statistics study (described from here on as the High School and Beyond data), Hogan found that whereas only 1 percent of the white females and 1.4 percent of the white males who were single and childless in 1980 expected to become parents prior to first marriage, 16.5 percent of black females and 21 percent of black males expected parenthood before first marriage. In a follow-up study that focused exclusively on black female adolescents and excluded respondents "who were pregnant or near marriage at the time of the initial interview [1980]," Hogan found that only 8.7 percent expected to become single mothers in 1980, and of these, 19.5 percent actually became unmarried mothers by 1982.[33] On the other hand, of the 91 percent who reported that they *did not* expect to become unmarried mothers, only 7.4 percent gave birth to a child by 1982. Unpublished data from this same study reveal that 20.1 percent of the black girls becoming single mothers by 1982 *expected* to do so in 1980.[34] Thus, although only a small percentage of these adolescent girls expected to become single mothers, those who expressed that view were almost three times as likely to become single mothers as the overwhelming majority who did not.

A number of social structural factors that may influence the development of certain behavior norms may also be directly related to single parenthood. Hogan's research shows that girls from married-couple families and those from households with both mother and grandparent are much less likely to become unwed mothers than those from independent mother-headed households or nonparental homes. The fact that the rate of premarital parenthood of teens who live with both their single mothers and one (usually the grandmother) or more grandparents is as low as that of teens who live

in husband-wife families suggests that "the critical effects of one-parent families are not so much attributable to the mother's example of single parenthood as an acceptable status as to the poverty and greater difficulty of parental supervision in one-adult families."[35] Furthermore, Hogan and Kitagawa's analysis of the influences of family background, personal characteristics, and social milieu on the probability of premarital pregnancy among black teenagers in Chicago indicates that those from nonintact families, lower social class, and poor and highly segregated neighborhoods have significantly higher fertility rates. Hogan and Kitagawa estimated that 57 percent of the teenage girls from high-risk social environments (lower class, poor inner-city neighborhood residence, female-headed family, five or more siblings, a sister who is a teenager mother, and loose parental supervision of dating) will become pregnant by age eighteen compared to only 9 percent of the girls from low-risk social backgrounds.[36]

Social structural factors also appear to affect the timing of marriage. Hogan reports that although black teenagers expect to become parents at roughly the same ages as whites, they expect to become married at later ages. Analysis of the High School and Beyond data reveals that when social class is controlled, black adolescents have expected age-specific rates of parenthood that are only 2 percent lower than those of whites, but expected age-specific rates of marriage that are 36 percent lower.[37] While Hogan notes that many whites are delaying marriage and parenthood because of educational or career aspirations, he attributes blacks' expectations of late marriage to the poor "marriage market" black women face. Indeed, available research has demonstrated a direct connection between the early marriage of young people and an encouraging economic situation, advantageous government transfer programs, and a balanced sex ratio.[38] These conditions are not only more likely to apply for young whites than for young blacks, but as we try to show, they have become increasingly problematic for blacks.

This evidence suggests therefore that attitudes and expectations concerning marriage and parenthood are inextricably linked with social structural factors. Since we do not have systematic longitudinal data on the extent to which such attitudes and aspirations have changed in recent years, we can only assume that some changes have indeed occurred and that they are likely to be responses to broader changes in the society. This is not to ignore the import of normative or cultural explanations, rather it is to underline the well-founded sociological generalization that group variations in behavior, norms, and values often reflect variations in group access to channels of privilege and influence. When this connection is overlooked, explanations of problems such as premarital parenthood or female-headed families may focus on the norms and aspirations of individuals, and thereby fail to address the ultimate sources of the problem, such as changes in the structure of opportunities for the disadvantaged.

It is also important to remember that there are broader social and cultural trends in society that affect in varying degrees the behavior of all racial and class groups. For instance, sexual activity is increasingly prevalent among all teenagers. Growing proportions of adolescents have had sexual experience: according to one survey, the proportion of metropolitan teenage women who reported having premarital intercourse increased from 30 percent in 1971 to 50 percent in 1979. These proportions have risen particularly for white adolescents, thereby narrowing the differentials in the incidence of sexual activity. And they have more than offset the increase in contraceptive use over the past decade, resulting in a net increase in premarital pregnancy.[39] Rising rates of sexual activity among middle-class teens may be associated with various social

and cultural trends such as the "sexual revolution," the increased availability of birth control and abortion, and perhaps the growing sophistication of American adolescents, or their adoption of adult social behavior at an increasingly early age. While these trends may also have influenced the sexual behavior of teens from disadvantaged backgrounds, it is difficult to assess their effects independent of the complex array of other factors. Our meager state of knowledge permits us only to say that they probably have some effect, but we do not have even a rough idea as to the degree.

Although our knowledge of the effect of social and cultural trends on the rise of extramarital fertility is scant, we know a little more about the effect of some of these trends on marital dissolution. Multivariate analyses of marital splits suggest that women's labor-force participation and income significantly increase marital dissolution among white women.[40] Labor-force participation rates of white women have nearly doubled from 1940 to 1980 (from 25.6 percent to 49.4 percent), in part due to a decline in marriage and in part to an increase in labor-force participation among married women, particularly those with children. The labor-force participation of black women has also increased, but not as dramatically (from 39.4 percent in 1940 to 53.3 percent in 1980);[41] black women have always worked in greater proportions than white women, a pattern that still holds today for all age-groups except women ages sixteen to twenty-four, an age category with high fertility rates.

Accompanying the increasing labor-force participation of women has been the rise of the feminist movement, which validates work as a source of both independence from men and personal fulfillment, and which has provided practical support not only through legal and political action but also through its role in promoting organizational resources for women in the labor market. Feminism as a social and cultural movement may have directly influenced the marriage decisions of women; it may also have indirectly affected these decisions through its role in womens' more active participation in the labor market. In the absence of systematic empirical data, the effect of the feminist movement on the marital dissolution of women, particularly white women, can only be assumed.

It can be confidently asserted, however, that women's increasing employment makes marital breakup financially more viable than in the past. Although marital dissolution means a substantial loss of income, and sometimes severe economic hardship—median income of white female-headed families in 1979 was $11,452, compared to $21,824 for white married-couple families[42]—most white women can maintain their families above poverty with a combination of earnings and income from other sources such as alimony, child support, public-income transfers, personal wealth, and assistance from families. In 1982, 70 percent of white female-headed families were living above the poverty line.[43] In addition, many white single mothers remarry. For most black women facing marital dissolution, the situation is significantly different, not only because they tend to have fewer resources and are far less likely to remarry, but also because the major reasons for their increasing rates of marital disintegration have little to do with changing social and cultural trends.

The Role of Welfare

A popular explanation for the rise of female-headed families and out-of-wedlock births has been the growth of liberal welfare policies, in particular, broadened eligibility for income transfer programs, increases in benefit levels, and the creation of new programs, such as Medicaid and food stamps. Charles Murray, for example, argues that relaxed restrictions and increasing benefits of AFDC enticed lower-class women to forego marriage or prolong childlessness in order to qualify for increasingly lucrative benefits.[44] Likewise, Robert Gordon depicts "welfare provisions as a major influence in the decline in two-adult households in American cities."[45]

The effect of welfare on out-of-wedlock births and marital instability became even more of an issue after the costs and caseloads of public assistance programs dramatically increased during the late 1960s and early 1970s. Since that time, a good deal of research has addressed this issue. Because all states have AFDC and food stamp programs, there can be no true test of the effects of welfare on family structure: there is no "control" population that has not been exposed to these welfare programs. However, substantial interstate variations in levels of AFDC benefits and in eligibility rules have provided opportunities for researchers to test the effects of program characteristics. Most studies have examined the level of welfare benefits as one of the determinants of a woman's choice between marriage and single parenthood. Some use aggregate data; others use individual-level data; still others examine the effect of providing cash transfers to intact families under special conditions, such as the Income Maintenance Experiments. But whether the focus is on the relationship between welfare and out-of-wedlock births or that between welfare and marital dissolution, the results have been inconclusive at best.

Many of the studies concerning welfare and out-of-wedlock births have compared illegitimacy rates or ratios across states with varying AFDC benefit levels. Cutright found no association between out-of-wedlock birth rates and benefit levels in 1960 or 1970. Using aggregate data, Winegarden's state-level analysis showed no association between measures of fertility and benefit levels, although he did report a small positive association with benefit availability. Fechter and Greenfield and Moore and Caldwell both used state-level cross-sectional data in a multivariate analysis and found no effects of welfare benefit levels on out-of-wedlock births. Finally, Vining showed that for blacks, the illegitimacy ratio in the South was only slightly lower than in non-southern states, despite levels of AFDC payments that were less than half those of the rest of the country; for whites, the difference was somewhat larger.[46]

This type of research is vulnerable to the criticism that, in Vining's words, "the overall incidence of illegitimacy could have been rising over time in concert with an overall rise in welfare payments, despite the lack of correlation between cross-state variation of illegitimacy and cross-state variation in welfare levels at any point in time."[47] However, despite frequent references in the literature to rising welfare expenditures, benefit levels have fallen in real terms over the past ten years, while illegitimacy ratios have continued to rise. Both Cutright and Ellwood and Bane examined changes over time in state benefit levels and in illegitimate birth rates and found no association.[48]

Other studies using different approaches and data sets have also yielded inconclusive, largely negative, results. Placek and Hendershot analyzed retrospective interviews of three hundred welfare mothers and found that when the women were on welfare, they were significantly *less* likely to refrain from using contraceptives, *less* likely to desire an additional pregnancy, and *less* likely to become pregnant. Similarly, Presser and Salsberg, using a random sample of New York women who had recently had their first child, reported that women on public assistance desired fewer children than women not on assistance, and were less likely to have planned their first birth. Based on a longitudinal study of low-income New York City women, Polgar and Hiday reported that women having an additional birth over a two-year period were no more likely to be receiving welfare at the start of the period

than women who did not get pregnant. Moore and Caldwell reported no relationship between characteristics of AFDC programs and out-of-wedlock pregnancy and childbearing from a microlevel analysis of survey data.[49] Ellwood and Bane examined out-of-wedlock birth rates among women likely and unlikely to qualify for AFDC if they became single mothers, and found no significant effect of welfare benefit levels; a comparison of married and unmarried birth rates in low- and high-benefit states also yielded no effects.[50]

Finally, results from the Income Maintenance Experiments have been inconclusive. Reports from the New Jersey experiments indicate no effect. In the Seattle and Denver experiments, effects of income maintenance payments on fertility varied by race/ethnicity: white recipients had significantly lower fertility, Mexican-Americans had higher fertility, and blacks showed no effect.[51] Because of the relatively short duration of the study, it is not clear if maintenance payments affected completed fertility or simply the timing of births.

The results of studies focusing on the relationship between welfare and family stability have also been inconclusive. Researchers using aggregate data ordinarily look for correlations between rates of female family headship and size of AFDC payments, while controlling for other variables. In some studies, the unit of analysis is the state; in others, most notably Honig and Ross and Sawhill, various metropolitan areas were examined.[52] Analytic models used in most of these studies are similar, but disagreement over specification of the variables and other aspects of the analysis has produced mixed results. Honig found positive effects for AFDC payments on female family headship, although by 1970 the effects had diminished; Minarik and Goldfarb reported insignificant negative effects; Ross and Sawhill found significant positive effects for nonwhites, but not for whites; and

Cutright and Madras found that AFDC benefits did not affect marital disruption, but did increase the likelihood that separated or divorced mothers would head their own households.[53]

As Ellwood and Bane observed, despite the sophistication of some of these multivariate analyses of aggregate data, the analyses have "largely ignored the problems introduced by largely unmeasurable differences between states."[54] Introducing a unique and resourceful solution to these problems, they present estimates of welfare effects based on comparisons of marital dissolution and living arrangements among mothers likely and unlikely to be AFDC recipients, and among women who are or are not mothers (and thus eligible for AFDC), in high- and low-benefit states. They also examine changes over time in benefit levels and family structure. The findings based on these three different comparisons are remarkably similar. Ellwood and Bane estimate that in 1975, a $100 increase in AFDC benefits would have resulted in a 10 percent increase in the number of divorced or separated mothers, with a more substantial effect for young women; the same increase in AFDC benefits would have contributed to an estimated 25 percent to 30 percent increase in the formation of independent households, again with much more substantial effects for young mothers.[55]

Studies using individual-level data have yielded mixed results, with some finding modest effects, and some reporting no effect at all of welfare on marital dissolution or family headship. Hoffman and Holmes analyzed Michigan PSID data and reported that low-income families living in states with high AFDC benefits were 6 percent more likely than the average to dissolve their marriages, while similar families in states with low-benefit levels were 6 percent less likely to do so. Ross and Sawhill, in a similar analysis of the same data, found no significant welfare effects, even in a regression per-

formed separately for low-income families. In a recent study, Danziger et al. modeled headship choices using data from 1968 and 1975 *Current Population Surveys* and concluded that a reduction in welfare benefits would result in only a slight decrease in the number of female household heads; the authors also reported that the increase in female-headed families between 1968 and 1975 was greater than the model would have predicted given the changes in the relative economic circumstances of female heads and married women occurring during that period.[56] It seems likely that the decreasing supply of "marriageable men" (examined below) is a constraint on women's marriage decisions that is not accounted for in the model.

Studies of intact families receiving income transfers under the Income Maintenance Experiments show that providing benefits to two-parent families did not tend to reduce marital instability: the split rates for these families were higher, not lower, than those of comparable low-income families, although the results were not consistent across maintenance levels. The Income Maintenance Experiments "increased the proportion of families headed by single females. For blacks and whites, the increase was due to the increase in dissolution; for Chicanos, the increase was due to the decrease in the marital formation rates." Groeneveld, Tuma, and Hannan speculate that nonpecuniary factors such as the stigma, transaction costs, and lack of information associated with the welfare system caused the income maintenance program to have a greater effect on women's sense of economic independence.[57]

To sum up, this research indicates that welfare receipt or benefit levels have no effect on the incidence of out-of-wedlock births. Aid to Families with Dependent Children payments seem to have a substantial effect on living arrangements of single mothers, but only a modest impact on separation and divorce. The extent to which welfare deters marriage or remarriage among single mothers is addressed only indirectly, in studies of the incidence of female-headed households, and here the evidence is inconclusive.

However, if the major impact of AFDC is on the living arrangements of single mothers, it could ultimately have a greater influence on family structure. As we emphasized in our discussion of Hogan's research on the premarital parenthood of adolescents, young women from independent mother-headed households are more likely to become unwed mothers than those from married-couple families and those from female-headed subfamilies living in the homes of their grandparents.[58]

Nonetheless, the findings from Ellwood and Bane's impressive research, and the inconsistent results of other studies on the relationship between welfare and family structure, and welfare and out-of-wedlock births, raise serious questions about the current tendency to blame changes in welfare policies for the decline in the proportion of intact families and legitimate births among the poor. As Ellwood and Bane emphatically proclaim, "Welfare simply does not appear to be the underlying cause of the dramatic changes in family structure of the past few decades."[59] The factor that we have identified as the underlying cause is discussed in the next section.

The Role of Joblessness

Although the structure of the economy and the composition of the labor force have undergone significant change over the last forty years, the labor-force participation patterns of white men have changed little. The labor-force participation rate of white men declined from 82 percent in 1940 to 76 percent in 1980, in part because of a drop in the labor-force activity of men over the age of fifty-five (from 83.9 percent to 72.2 percent for those ages fifty-five to sixty-four).[60]

Labor-force participation of white men ages twenty-four and under actually increased over the past decade.

For blacks, the patterns are different. The labor-force participation of black men declined substantially, from 84 percent in 1940 to 67 percent in 1980.[61] Labor-force trends for older black men parallel those of white men of the same ages. But a decline in labor-force participation of young black men and, to a lesser extent, prime-age black men has occurred, while the participation of comparable white men has either increased or remained stable.

Economic trends for black men, especially young black men, have been unfavorable since the end of World War II. While the status of young blacks who are employed has improved with the percentage of white-collar workers among all black male workers, rising from 5 percent in 1940 to 27 percent in 1983, the proportion of black men who are employed has dropped from 80 percent in 1930 to 56 percent in 1983. Unemployment rose sharply for black male teenagers during the 1950s and remained high during the prosperous 1960s; similarly, unemployment rates for black men twenty to twenty-four years of age rose sharply during the mid-1970s and have remained high. In 1979, when the overall unemployment rate had declined to 5.8 percent, the rate for black male teenagers was 34.1 percent.[62] In addition, while blacks have historically had higher labor-force participation levels, by the 1970s labor-force participation of black men had fallen below that of white men for all age-groups, with particularly steep declines for those ages twenty-four and younger...

The adverse effects of unemployment and other economic problems on family stability are well established in the literature. Studies of family life during the Great Depression document the deterioration of marriage and family life following unemployment. More recent research, based on longitudinal data sets such as the PSID and the National Longitudinal Study or on aggregate data, shows consistently that unemployment is related to marital instability and the incidence of female-headed families. Indicators of economic status such as wage rates, income, or occupational status may also be related to marital instability or female headedness, although the evidence is not as consistent. For instance, while Cutright's analysis of 1960 census data indicates that divorce and separation rates are higher among lower-income families, Sawhill et al. find that unemployment, fluctuations in income, and lack of assets are associated with higher separation rates, but that the level of the husband's earnings has an effect only among low-income black families. However, Cohen reports that when the husband's age is controlled, the higher the husband's earnings, the less likely both black and white couples are to divorce.[63]

Nonetheless, the weight of the evidence on the relationship between the employment status of men, and family life and married life suggests that the increasing rate of joblessness among black men merits serious consideration as a major underlying factor in the rise of black single mothers and female-headed households. Moreover, when the factor of joblessness is combined with high black-male mortality and incarceration rates,[64] the proportion of black men in stable economic situations is even lower than that conveyed in the current unemployment and labor-force figures.

The full dimensions of this problem are revealed in Figures 1 through 6, which show the effect of male joblessness trends, in combination with the effects of male mortality and incarceration rates, by presenting the rates of employed civilian men to women of the same race and age-group.[65] This ratio may be described as a "male marriageable pool index." The number of women is used as the denominator in order to convey the situation of young women in the "marriage market." Figures 1 to 3, for men sixteen to twenty-four years of age, show similar patterns: a sharp decline in the nonwhite ratios beginning in the 1960s, which is even more startling when compared with the rising ratios for white men. Figures 4 to 6, for men twenty-five to fifty-four years of age, show a more gradual decline for black men relative to white men. Clearly, what our "male marriageable pool index" reveals is a long-term decline in the proportion of black

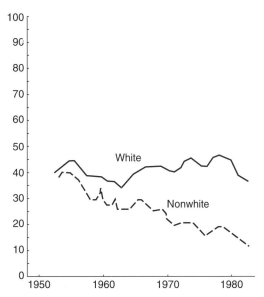

FIGURE 1   Employed men per 100 women of the same age and race—sixteen and seventeen years of age, 1954–82.

Sources: U.S. Bureau of Labor Statistics, *Handbook of Labor Statistics,* Bulletin 2070 (Washington, D.C.: Government Printing Office, 1980); idem, *Employment and Earnings.* The denominators, the number of women by age and race, are taken from U.S. Bureau of the Census, *Current Population Reports,* series P-25, no. 721, "Estimates of the United States by Age, Sex, and Race, 1970 to 1977" (Washington, D.C.: Government Printing Office, 1978); and idem, *Current Population Reports,* series P-25, "Estimates of the Population of the United States by Age, Sex, and Race, 1980 to 1982" (Washington, D.C.: Government Printing Office, 1983).

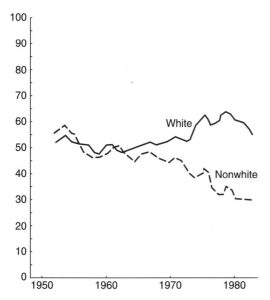

FIGURE 2   Employed men per 100 women of the same age and race—eighteen and nineteen years of age, 1954–82. Sources: see Fig. 1.

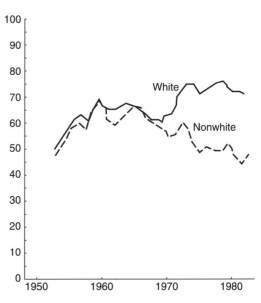

FIGURE 3   Employed men per 100 women of the same age and race—twenty and twenty-four years of age, 1954–82. Sources: see Fig. 1.

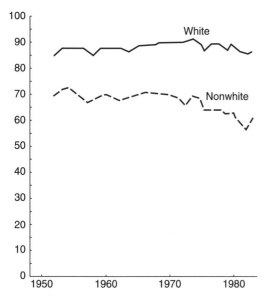

FIGURE 4   Employed men per 100 women of the same age and race—twenty-five and thirty-four years of age, 1954–82. Sources: see Fig. 1.

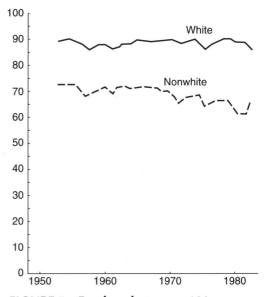

FIGURE 5   Employed men per 100 women of the same age and race—thirty-five and forty-four years of age, 1954–82. Sources: see Fig. 1.

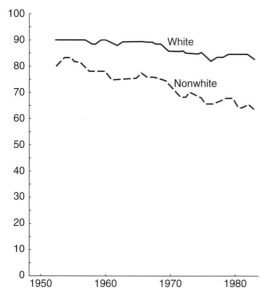

FIGURE 6   Employed men per 100 women of the same age and race—forty-five and fifty-four years of age, 1954–82. Sources: see Fig. 1.

men, and particularly young black men, who are in a position to support a family.

As we noted above, the relationship between joblessness and marital instability is well established in the literature. Moreover, available evidence supports the argument that among blacks, increasing male joblessness is related to the rising proportions of families headed by women.[66] By contrast, for whites, trends in male employment and earnings appear to have little to do with the increase in female-headed families. Although lower-income families have higher rates of marital dissolution, trends in the employment status of white men since 1960 cannot explain the overall rise in white separation and divorce rates.

It seems likely that the chief cause of the rise of separation and divorce rates among whites is the increased economic independence of white women as indicated by their increasing employment and improving occupational status. It is not that this growing independence gives

white women a financial incentive to separate from or to divorce their husbands; rather, it makes dissolution of a bad marriage a more viable alternative than in the past. That the employment status of white males is not a major factor in white single motherhood or female-headed families can perhaps also be seen in the higher rate of remarriage among white women and the significantly earlier age of first marriage. By contrast, the increasing delay of first marriage and the low rate of remarriage among black women seem to be directly tied to the increasing labor-force problems of men.

CONCLUSION

In the 1960s scholars readily attributed black family deterioration to the problems of male joblessness. However, in the last ten to fifteen years, in the face of the overwhelming focus on welfare as the major source of black family breakup, concerns about the importance of male joblessness have receded into the background. We argue in this essay that the available evidence justifies renewed scholarly and public policy attention to the connection between the disintegration of poor families and black male prospects for stable employment.

We find that when statistics on black family structure are disaggregated to reveal changes in fertility rates, marital status, age structure, and residence patterns, it becomes clear, first of all, that the black "illegitimacy ratio" has increased rapidly not so much because of an increase in the incidence of out-of-wedlock births, but mainly because both the rate of marital fertility and the percentage of women married and living with their husbands has declined significantly. And the sharp reduction of the latter is due both to the rise in black divorce and separation and to the increase in the percentage of never-married women. Inextricably connected with these trends are changes in the age structure, which have increased the fraction of births to young women and thereby inflated the proportion of all births occurring outside of marriage. The net result has been a 41 percent increase in the number of black children growing up in fatherless families during the 1970s, with most of this increase occurring in families in which the mother has never been married. Furthermore, the substantial racial differences in the timing of first marriage and the rate of remarriage underscore the persistence of black female headedness. And what makes all of these trends especially disturbing is that female-headed families are far more likely than married-couple families to be not only poor, but mired in poverty for long periods of time.

Although changing social and cultural trends have often been invoked to explain some of the dynamic changes in the structure of the family, they appear to have more relevance for shifts in family structure among whites. And contrary to popular opinion, there is little evidence to provide a strong case for welfare as the primary cause of family breakups, female-headed households, and out-of-wedlock births. Welfare does seem to have a modest effect on separation and divorce, especially for white women, but recent evidence suggests that its total effect on the size of the population of female householders is small. As shown in Ellwood and Bane's impressive study, if welfare does have a major influence on female-headed families, it is in the living arrangements of single mothers.[67] We explained why this could ultimately and indirectly lead to an increase in female family headship.

By contrast, the evidence for the influence of male joblessness is much more persuasive. Research has demonstrated, for example, a connection between the early marriage of young people and an encouraging economic situation. In this connection, we have tried to show that black women are more likely to delay marriage and less likely to remarry. We further noted that although black teenagers expect to become parents at about the same ages as whites, they expect to marry at later ages. And we argue that both the black delay in marriage and the lower rate of remarriage, each of which is associated with high percentages of out-of-wedlock births and female-headed households, can be directly tied to the labor-market status of black males. As we have documented, black women, especially young black women, are facing a shrinking pool of "marriageable" (i.e., economically stable) men.

White women are not faced with this problem. Indeed, our "male marriageable pool index" indicates that the number of employed white men per one hundred white women in different age categories has either remained roughly the same or has increased since 1954. We found little reason, therefore, to assume a connection between the rise in female-headed white families and changes in white male employment. That the pool of "marriageable" white men has not shrunk over the years is reflected, we believe, in the earlier age of first marriage and higher rate of remarriage among white women. For all these reasons, we hypothesize that increases in separation and divorce among whites are due chiefly to the increased economic independence of white women and related social and cultural factors.

Despite the existence of evidence suggesting that the increasing inability of many black men to support a family is the driving force behind the rise of female-headed families, in the last ten to fifteen years welfare has dominated explanations of the increase in female headship. The commonsense assumption that welfare regulations break up families, affirmed by liberals and conservatives alike, buttressed the welfare explanations of trends in family structure. The Subcommittee on Fiscal Policy of the Joint Economic Committee initiated a program of research on the topic in 1971; according to Cutright and Madras, recognition of the increasing monetary value of noncash benefits, in the context of economic theories of marriage,[68] persuaded the subcommittee that welfare was related to the rise of female-headed families despite inconclusive evidence. And despite frequent references to rising social welfare expenditures, the real value of welfare benefits has declined over the past ten years while the number and proportion of female-headed families continues to climb.

Only recently has it been proposed that the rise in female-headed families among blacks is related to declining employment rates among black men.[69] Evidence such as that displayed in Figures 1 to 6 and in other studies discussed in this essay makes a compelling case for once again placing the problem of black joblessness as a top-priority item in public policy agendas designed to enhance the status of poor black families.

Reading 11   Family Decline in America*

DAVID POPENOE

As a social institution, the family has been "in decline" since the beginning of world history, gradually becoming weaker through losing social functions and power to other institutions such as church, government, and school. Yet during the past 25 years, family decline in the United States, as in other industrialized societies, has been both steeper and more alarming than during any other quarter century in our history. Although they may not use the term "decline," most family scholars now agree, with a growing tinge of pessimism, that the family during this period has undergone a social transformation. Some see "dramatic and unparalleled changes" while others call it "a veritable revolution."[1]

Agreement about the dramatic nature of family change over the past few decades, together with a pessimistic assessment of it, represent a recent shift of viewpoint on the part of many scholars. In the 1970s, in sharp contrast to the prevailing mood of the general public, the outlook of many family experts was one of complacency. For example, in their 1981 book *What's Happening to the American Family?*, economists Sar Levitan and Richard Belous noted that "currently fashionable gloom and doom scenarios miss the essential process of adjustment and change" and that "a critical analysis of the evidence does not paint such a dire

picture, and thus a heartfelt 'hurrah' is in order."[2]

Yet after reviewing the events of the 1980s, their optimistic mood shifted strikingly. The second edition of this book, published in 1988, contains much apprehensive talk of "radical changes in family structure." The authors conclude, with some apologies for the "more sanguine scenario" of the earlier edition, that "American families are besieged from all sides" and "widespread family breakdown is bound to have a pervasive and debilitating impact not only on the quality of life but on the vitality of the body politic as well."[3]

The recent social transformation of the family has been so momentous that, in my opinion, we are witnessing the end of an epoch. Today's societal trends are bringing to a close the cultural dominance of what historians call the modern (I will use the term "traditional") nuclear family, a family situated apart from both the larger kin group and the workplace; focused on the procreation of children; and consisting of a legal, lifelong, sexually exclusive, heterosexual, monogamous marriage, based on affection and companionship, in which there is a sharp division of labor, with the female as full-time housewife and the male as primary provider and ultimate authority. Lasting for only a little more than a century, this family form emphasized the male as

*Popenoe, David. 1990. "Family Decline in America." Pp. 39–51, from *Rebuilding the Nest,* edited by David Blakenhorn et al., Milwaukee, WI: Family Service America. Copyright 1990. Reprinted with permission.

"good provider," the female as "good wife and mother," and the paramount importance of the family for child rearing. (Of course, not all families were able to live up to these cultural ideals.) During its cultural heyday, the terms "family," "home," and "mother" ranked extraordinarily high in the hierarchy of cultural values.[4]

In certain respects, this family form reached its apogee in the middle of the 20th century. By the 1950s—fueled in part by failing maternal and child mortality rates, greater longevity, and a high marriage rate—it is probably the case that a higher percentage of children than ever before were growing up in stable, two-parent families.[5] Similarly, this period witnessed the highest ever proportion of women who married, bore children, and lived jointly with their husbands until at least age 50.[6]

FLIGHT FROM THE NUCLEAR FAMILY

In the 1960s, however, four major social trends emerged to signal a widespread "flight" from both the ideal and the reality of the traditional nuclear family: rapid fertility decline, the sexual revolution, the movement of mothers into the labor force, and the divorce revolution. None of these changes was new to the 1960s; each represented a tendency that was already evident in earlier years. However, a striking acceleration of these trends occurred in the 1960s, which was made more dramatic by the fact that during the 1950s these trends had leveled off and in some cases even reversed their directions.[7]

The Decline in Fertility

First (taking up these four trends without reference to their relative importance or causal priority), fertility declined in the United States by almost 50% between 1960 and 1989, from an average of 3.7 children per woman to only 1.9. Although fertility has been gradually diminishing for several centuries (the main exception

being the two decades following World War II), the level of fertility during the past decade was the lowest in U.S. history and below that necessary for the replacement of the population. As a percentage of the total population, children over the past 25 years have dropped from more than a third to about one-fourth.[8]

Growing dissatisfaction with parenthood is now evident among adults in our culture, along with a dramatic decrease in the stigma associated with childlessness.[9] Some demographers now predict that between 20% and 25% of today's young women will remain completely childless, and nearly 50% will be either childless or have only one child.[10]

The Sexual Revolution

Second, what is often called the sexual revolution has shattered the association of sex and reproduction.[11] The erotic has become a necessary ingredient of personal well-being and fulfillment, both in and outside marriage, as well as a highly marketable commodity. The greatest change has been in the area of premarital sex: from 1971 to 1982, the proportion of unmarried girls in the United States aged 15–19 who engaged in premarital sexual intercourse jumped from 28% to 44%.[12] This behavior reflects a widespread change in values: in 1967, 85% of Americans "condemned premarital sex as mortally wrong," compared with only 37% in 1979.[13] The sexual revolution has been a major contributor to the striking increase in unwed parenthood. Nonmarital births jumped from 5% of all births in 1960 (22% of births among blacks) to 22% in 1985 (60% of births among blacks). This is the highest rate of nonmarital births ever recorded in the United States.

Working Married Mothers

Third, although unmarried women have long been in the labor force, the past quarter century has witnessed a striking movement into the paid work force of married women with children.[14] In

1960, only 19% of married women with children younger than 6 were in the labor force (39% with children between 6 and 17); by 1986, this figure had climbed to 54% (68% of those with older children).[15]

Increased Divorce Rate

Fourth, the divorce rate in the United States over the past 25 years (as measured by the number of divorced persons per 1,000 married persons) has nearly quadrupled, increasing from 35 to 130. This increase has led many to refer to a divorce revolution.[16] A landmark of sorts was passed in 1974, when for the first time in American history more marriages ended in divorce than in death.[17] The probability that a marriage contracted today will end in divorce ranges from 44% to 66%, depending upon the method of calculation.[18]

Reshaped Family Experience

These four trends signal a widespread retreat from the traditional nuclear family in its terms of a lifelong, sexually exclusive unit, focused on children, with a separate-sphere division of labor between husband and wife. Unlike most previous family change, which reduced family functions and diminished the importance of the kin group, the family change of the past 25 years has tended to break up the "nucleus" of the family unit—the bond between husband and wife. Nuclear units, therefore, are losing ground to single-parent families, serial and stepfamilies, and unmarried and homosexual couples.[19]

The number of single-parent families, for example, has risen sharply as a result not only of marital breakup, but also of marriage decline (fewer persons who bear children are getting married) and widespread abandonment by males. In 1960, only 9% of children in the United States younger than 18 were living with one parent; by 1986, this figure had climbed to nearly one-fourth of all children. (The comparable figures for blacks are 22% and 53%, respectively.) Of children born between 1950 and 1954, only 19% of whites (48% of blacks) had lived in a single-parent family by the time they reached age 17. But for children born in 1980, the figure is projected to be 70% (94% for blacks).[20]

During the past quarter century there has also been a retreat from family living in general. For instance, the percentage of "nonfamily" households (households other than those containing two or more persons living together and related by blood, marriage, or adoption) has nearly doubled, from 15% to 28% of all households. Approximately 85% of these new households consist of a person living alone.[21]

To summarize the state of the family today compared with that of 25 years ago:

- fewer persons are marrying and they are marrying later in life
- those marrying are having fewer children
- more marriages end in divorce

Trends such as these have dramatically reshaped people's lifetime family experiences, that is, their connectedness to the institution of the family. The proportion of an average person's adult life spent with spouse and children was 62% in 1960, the highest in our history. Today it has dropped to 43%, the lowest point in our history.[22]

In the United States, the changing family structure has helped to continue, and in some ways exacerbate, the tragedy of child poverty. Since 1974, the poverty rate among children has exceeded that among the elderly, and 40% of all poor people in this nation today are children.[23] According to a recent estimate, one out of every four American preschoolers in 1987 was living below the poverty line.[24]

In addition to family structural change, the psychological character of the marital relationship has also changed substantially over the years.[25] Traditionally, marriage has been understood as a social obligation—an institution designed mainly for economic security and procreation. Today, marriage is understood mainly as a path toward self-fulfillment: self-development is seen to require a significant other, and marital partners are picked primarily to be personal companions. Put another way, marriage is becoming deinstitutionalized. No longer comprising a set of norms and social obligations that are widely enforced, marriage today is a voluntary relationship that individuals can make and break at will. As one indicator of this shift, laws regulating marriage and divorce have become increasingly more lax.[26]

As psychological expectations for marriage grow ever higher, dashed expectations for personal fulfillment fuel our society's high divorce rate. Divorce also feeds upon itself. The higher the divorce rate, the more "normal" it becomes, with fewer negative sanctions to oppose it, and the more potential partners become available. In general, psychological need, in and of itself, has proved to be a weak basis for stable marriage.

These family trends are all interrelated. They are also evident, in varying degrees, in every industrialized Western country, which suggests that their source lies not in particular political or economic systems but in the broad cultural shift that has accompanied industrialization and urbanization. Although scholars do not agree on all aspects of this shift, clearly an ethos of radical individualism has emerged in these societies, in which personal autonomy, individual rights, and social equality have gained supremacy as cultural ideals. In keeping with these ideals, the main goals of personal behavior have shifted from commitment to social units of all kinds (families, communities, religions, nations) to personal choices, lifestyle options, self-fulfillment, and personal pleasure.[27]

FAMILY CHANGE AS FAMILY DECLINE

Despite the dramatic nature of the recent social transformation of the family, many family experts are still reluctant to refer to the transformation as "family decline." This is unfortunate, because the concept of the family as a declining or weakening institution provides a "best fit" for many of the changes that have taken place. The concept also alerts us to examine the consequences of a rapidly changing institution.

During the past 25 years, the institution of the family has weakened substantially in a number of ways. Individual family members have become more autonomous and less bound by the family group, and the group has become less cohesive. Fewer of its traditional social functions are now carried out by the family; these have shifted to other institutions. The family has lost more power and authority to other institutions, especially to the state and its agencies. The family has grown smaller, less stable, and has a shorter life span; people are therefore family members for a smaller percentage of their life. The outcome of these trends is that people have become less willing to invest time, money, and energy in family life. It is the individual him- or herself, not the family unit, in whom the main investments are increasingly made.[28]

Why, then, are so many family scholars reluctant to speak of family decline? The short answer is that to speak of family decline within the intellectual community in recent years has been to be accused of opposing equality for women.

The dominance of the traditional nuclear family in the 1950s helped to fuel the modern women's movement. Reacting strongly to the lingering patriarchy of this family form, as well as to its separate-sphere removal of women from the labor market, the women's movement came to view the traditional nuclear family in very negative terms.[29] Today those who believe in greater equality for women—and that includes most academics and other intellectuals—favor an egalitarian family form, with substantial economic independence for wives. With respect to these characteristics, the flight from the traditional nuclear family is regarded as progress, not decline.

To speak of decline under these circumstances, therefore, is perceived as being implicitly in favor of a discredited family form, one that oppressed women. Indeed, the term "decline" has been used most forcefully by those conservatives who tend to view every recent family change as negative and who have issued a clarion call for a return to the traditional nuclear family.

But properly used, the term "decline" should not carry such ideological baggage. To empirically conclude that the family is declining should not automatically link one to a particular ideology of family or gender. Moreover, not all decline is negative in its effects; decline is not necessarily the opposite of progress. All sorts of institutional forms that were once fully accepted have declined: theocracies, hereditary monarchies, imperialism. The results of their decline have been by no means merely regressive. It is important to distinguish an empirical trend, such as the weakening of an institution, from both its positive and negative consequences.

THE SOCIAL CONSEQUENCES OF FAMILY DECLINE

How are we to evaluate the social consequences of recent family decline? At the outset, it must be stressed that the issue is extremely complex. Society has been ill-served by the simplistic, either/or terms used by both the political right and left in the national debate.

Certainly, one should not jump immediately to the conclusion that family decline is necessarily bad for our society. A great many positive aspects of the recent family changes stand out as noteworthy. During this same quarter century of family decline, women (and many minorities) have clearly improved their status and probably the overall quality of their lives. Much of women's gain in status has come through their release from family duties and increased participation in the labor force. In addition, given the great emphasis on psychological criteria for choosing and keeping marriage partners, it can be argued persuasively that those marriages today that endure are more likely than ever before to be emotionally rewarding companionships.[30]

This period has also seen improved health care and longevity as well as widespread economic affluence, all of which have produced, for most people, a material standard of living that is historically unprecedented. Some of this improvement is due to the fact that people are no longer so dependent on their families for health care and economic support; they no longer are so imprisoned by social class and family obligation. When in need, they can now rely more on public care and support, as well as self-initiative and self-development.

Despite these positive aspects, the negative consequences of family decline are real and profound. The greatest negative effect, in the opinion of nearly everyone, is on children. Because children represent the future of a society, any negative consequences for them are especially significant. Substantial, if not conclusive, evidence indicates that, partly due to family changes, the quality of life for children in the past 25 years has worsened.[31] Much of the problem is of a psychological nature and thus is difficult to measure quantitatively.

Perhaps the most serious problem is a weakening in many families of the fundamental assumption that children are to be loved and valued at the highest level of priority. The general disinvestment in family life that has occurred has commonly meant a disinvestment in children's welfare. Some refer to this as a national "parent deficit." Yet the deficit goes well beyond parents to encompass an increasingly less child-friendly society. The parent deficit is all too easily blamed on newly working women. But it is men who have left the parenting scene in large numbers, a phenomenon one scholar has called "A disappearing act by fathers."[32] More than ever before, fathers are denying paternity, avoiding their parental obligations, and absent from home (at the same time there has been a slow but not offsetting growth of the "housefather" role).[33] Indeed, a persuasive case can be made that men began to abandon the "good provider" role at about the same time that many women started to relinquish the role of the full-time homemaker.[34] Thus, men and women may have been equally involved in triggering the recent flight from the traditional nuclear family.

The breakup of the nuclear unit has been the focus of much concern. Virtually every child desires two biological parents for life, and substantial evidence exists that child rearing is most successful when it involves two parents, both of whom are strongly motivated for the task.[35] This is not to say that other family forms can not be successful, only that as a group they are not as likely to be successful. This is also not to say that the two strongly motivated parents must be organized in the patriarchal and separate-sphere terms of the traditional nuclear family.

Regardless of family form, a significant change has occurred over the past quarter century in what can be called the social ecology of childhood.[36] Advanced societies are moving ever farther from what many hold to be a highly desirable child-rearing environment consisting of the following characteristics: a relatively large family that does a lot of things together, has many routines and traditions, and provides a great deal of quality contact time between adults and children; regular contact with relatives, active friendships in a supportive neighborhood, and contact with the adult world of work; little concern on the part of children that their parents will break up; and the coming together of all these ingredients in the development of a rich family subculture that has lasting meaning and strongly promulgates family values such as cooperation and sharing.

As this brief sketch of the changing ecology of childhood suggests, not only the family has been transformed, but also the community environment in which families exist. Children are especially sensitive to their local environments; yet adults, too, have a big stake in the quality of their surroundings.

The family has always been a fundamental and probably essential unit of what some call "civil society"—the local society made up of kin and friendship networks, neighborhoods, religious institutions, and voluntary associations. Civil society provides meaning and attachment for people's lives and helps to protect them from the impersonal forces of market and state.[37] As the market and state "megastructures" grow ever more powerful, the need for the mediating structures of civil society becomes that much more compelling, both for psychic survival and political freedom.[38] Although reasonable doubt can be expressed about the empirical accuracy of the common phrase "as the family goes, so goes the nation," I am not so doubtful about the phrase "as the family goes, so goes civil society."

FAMILY DECLINE AND TODAY'S POLICY DEBATE

What should be done to counteract or remedy the negative effects of family decline? This is the most controversial question of all, and the most difficult to answer.

The problems of purposive social action are enormous. In remedying the negative effects, it is never easy to avoid canceling out the positive benefits. Also, if family decline in fact stems from a broad cultural shift, it will not be easy to modify. The underlying trend may simply have to play itself out. It could be, of course, that the problems we are seeing result not from the intrinsic character of the cultural shift, but rather from its extreme rapidity. From this perspective, as the changes become complete and society settles down, we may be able to adjust without great difficulty to the new conditions.

Let us assume, however, that purposive social action is both called for and can have a useful outcome. Among the broad proposals for change that have been put forth, two extremes stand out prominently in the national debate: (1) a return to the structure of the traditional nuclear family characteristic of the 1950s and (2) the development of extensive governmental family policies.

Aside from the fact that it is probably impossible to return to a situation of an earlier time, the first alternative has major drawbacks. Such a shift would require many women to leave the work force and to some extent become "deliberated," an unlikely occurrence indeed. Economic conditions necessitate that even more women take jobs, and cultural conditions stress ever greater equality between the sexes.

In addition to such considerations, the traditional nuclear family form, in today's world, may he fundamentally flawed. As an indication of this, one should realize that the young people who led the transformation of the family during the 1960s and 1970s were brought up in 1950s families. If the 1950s families were so wonderful, why didn't their children seek to emulate them? In hindsight, the 1950s families seem to have been beset with problems that went well beyond patriarchy and separate spheres. For many families the mother–child unit had become increasingly isolated from the kin group, the neighborhood, and community, and even from the father, who worked a long distance away. This was especially true for women who were fully educated and eager to take their place in work and public life. Maternal child rearing under these historically unprecedented circumstances became highly problematic.[39]

Despite such difficulties, the traditional nuclear family is still the family of choice for millions of Americans. They are comfortable with it, and for them it seems to work. It is reasonable, therefore, at least not to place roadblocks in the way of couples with children who wish to conduct their lives according to the traditional family's dictates. Women who freely desire to spend much of their lives as mothers and housewives, outside the labor force, should not be economically penalized by public policy for making that choice. Nor should they be denigrated by our culture as second-class citizens.

The second major proposal for change that has been stressed in national debate is the development of extensive governmental programs offering monetary support and social services for families, especially for the new "nonnuclear" families. In some cases these programs assist with functions that families are unable to perform adequately; in other cases, the functions are taken over, transforming them from family to public responsibilities.

This is the path followed by the European welfare states, but it has been less accepted by the United States than by any other industrialized nation. The European welfare states have been far more successful than the United States in minimizing the negative economic impact of family decline on family members, especially children. In addition, many European nations have established policies making it much easier for women (and increasingly men) to combine work with child rearing.[40] With these successes in mind, it seems inevitable that the United

States will (and I believe should) move gradually in the direction of European countries with respect to family policies, just as we are now moving gradually in that direction with respect to medical care.

There are clear drawbacks, however, in moving too far down this road. If children are to be best served, we should seek to make the family stronger, not to replace it. At the same time that welfare states are minimizing some of the consequences of family decline, they may also be causing further decline of the family unit. This phenomenon can be witnessed today in Sweden, where the institution of the family has probably grown weaker than anywhere else in the world.[41] On a lesser scale, the phenomenon has been seen in the United States in connection with our welfare programs. Fundamental to the success of welfare-state programs, therefore, is keeping the ultimate goal of strengthening families uppermost in mind.

A NEW SOCIAL MOVEMENT

Although each of the above alternatives has some merit, I suggest a third alternative, which is premised on the fact that we cannot return to the 1950s family, nor can we depend on the welfare state for a solution. Instead, we should strike at the heart of the cultural shift that has occurred, point up its negative aspects, and seek to reinvigorate the cultural ideals of "family," "parents," and "children" within the changed circumstances of our time. We should stress that the individualistic ethos has gone too far, that children are being woefully shortchanged, and that, in the long run, strong families represent the best path toward self-fulfillment and personal happiness. We should bring again to the cultural forefront the old ideal of parents living together and sharing responsibility for their children and for each other.

What is needed is a new social movement whose purpose is the promotion of families and family values within the new constraints of modern life. It should point out the supreme importance of strong families to society, while at the same time suggesting ways that the family can better adapt to the modern conditions of individualism, equality, and the labor force participation of both women and men. Such a movement could build on the fact that the overwhelming majority of young people today still put forth as their major life goal a lasting, monogamous, heterosexual relationship that includes the procreation of children. It is reasonable to suppose that this goal is so pervasive because it is based on a deep-seated human need.

The reassertion of this personal goal as a highly ranked cultural value is not a legislative alternative; politics necessarily must respond to the obvious diversity in American life. But it is an alternative ideally suited to the leadership of broad-based citizens' groups. The history of recent social movements in America provides good reason for hope that such an initiative can make an impact. Witness the recent cultural shifts toward female and minority-group equality and the current move toward environmental protection, each of which has been led by popular movements focusing on fundamental social values. The time seems ripe to reassert that strong families concerned with the needs of children are, under modern conditions, not only possible but necessary.

Reading 12   History and Current Status of Divorce in the United States*

FRANK F. FURSTENBERG, JR.

As far back as the nineteenth century, when divorce was still uncommon in the United States, Americans worried about the consequences of marital dissolution for children.[1] Then as now, opinion divided between critics of liberalized divorce practices who worried that reform would undermine the capacity of parents to protect and nurture children and reformers who believed that divorce is a necessary mechanism to ensure matrimonial success.[2] None of the participants in these debates a century or more ago, however, contemplated an era when divorce would become an intrinsic part of our marriage system or a time when close to half of all those who entered marriage would voluntarily end their unions.

This article explores the demographic and social changes that have come about in American families as a result of the "divorce revolution," a phrase that Weitzman used to characterize the remarkable shift in marriage and divorce practices that occurred in the last third of the twentieth century.[3] This change, dramatic as it sometimes appears, was actually a gradual one that is firmly rooted in American cultural values. True, the divorce revolution has occurred among most developed nations.[4] Nonetheless, the pace

of change and the prevalence of marital disruption and family reconstitution is distinctly American. By a considerable margin, the United States has led the industrialized world in the incidence of divorce and the proportion of children affected by divorce.[5] Part of the mission of this article is to understand why this is so.

The first section of this article describes trends in divorce and remarriage and comments on the growing pattern of informal unions that complicates our interpretation of recent patterns of marriage, divorce, and remarriage. The commonalities and differences between family patterns in the United States and those in other industrialized nations are discussed. The second section of the article identifies some important sources of the transformation in marriage practices. Although other articles in this volume deal more directly with the consequences of divorce for children, this article, in the third section, provides a demographic context for this discussion by comparing the family experiences of different cohorts of children as they have encountered increasing levels of marital instability. In doing so, it highlights the very different types of family patterns that occur among whites, African Americans, and Hispanics. In the final section,

*Furstenberg, Frank, F. Jr. 1994. "History and Current Status of Divorce in the United States." *The Future of Children* Children and Divorce 4 (Spring) 1:29–43. Reprinted with permission of the Center for the Future of Children of the David and Lucile Packard Foundation.

some themes that emerge throughout the article are addressed, including what sorts of trends might occur in the near future and whether various policy initiatives can influence the future of the family, the patterns of parenting, and the welfare of children who face high degrees of uncertainty in their family arrangements.

HISTORICAL CHANGES IN DIVORCE AND REMARRIAGE

Until the latter part of the nineteenth century, divorce was largely proscribed by law and shunned in practice much as still happens today in many nations including some European countries such as Italy and Ireland.[6] Most marital disruptions occurred not as a result of divorce but from desertion or informal separation. Because population surveys were not available prior to the middle part of the twentieth century, it is difficult to know how often de facto divorce took place in the United States. But, it seems likely that all but a small minority of marriages survived until the death of one or another partner, an event that typically occurred much earlier than it does today.[7] Some have argued that the rise of divorce was partly prompted by increasing survival rates, which placed a greater strain on the ability of couples to manage marital stress or maintain marital contentment.[8] However, there is no firm evidence to support this conjecture.

Divorce rates in the United States began to rise shortly after the Civil War and continued on a steady upward course for more than a century. Over this time rates have fluctuated, often falling in poor economic times and generally surging after major wars. But these short-term variations have been far less consequential to the long-term pattern of constant growth.[9] Nearly two decades ago, Preston and McDonald calculated the likelihood of divorce for each marriage cohort beginning in 1867 and continuing until the mid-1960s.[10] Their results showed a continuous trend of dissolution among successive marriage cohorts. Roughly 5% of marriages ended in divorce just after the Civil War compared with an estimated 36% in 1964. Thus, the pattern of prevalent divorce was firmly in place in this country even before the divorce revolution of the 1960s.

Nonetheless, there was a sharp increase in the incidence of divorce from the mid-1960s to the late 1970s. During a span of a decade and a half, divorce rates for married women more than doubled (from 10.6 per 1,000 in 1965 to 22.8 in 1979), pushing the risk of divorce much higher for all marriage cohorts, especially those who wed after the mid-1960s.[11] Some researchers speculated that a majority of all marriages contracted in the 1970s and after would end, especially when both informal separations and formal divorces were counted.[12] Other researchers reached more conservative estimates but still projected that more than two in every five marriages would end in divorce when divorce rates reached their peaks in the middle 1970s.[9]

Divorce rates began to level off in the late 1970s and actually declined by about 10% during the 1980s.[13] As mentioned earlier, fluctuations of this sort are common historically and do not necessarily signal a reversal in divorce trends. Nonetheless, most demographers think that divorce is not likely to continue its upward pattern, at least in the near term. There are several demographic explanations for the failure of divorce rates to increase after the 1970s which do not necessarily imply that Americans today are becoming more committed to staying married than they were in the previous two decades.

The huge cohort of baby boomers, reacting to changing economic opportunities, postponed marriage.[9,14] A larger proportion opted to obtain more schooling and wait to form a family.[15] Marriage age for women rose from just above 20 in the mid-1950s to 24.4 in 1992, an increase of more than four years.[16] It has long been known that early marriage and lower education are associated with marital instability.[17] Thus, the pattern of delayed marriage might have had a role in curbing the rates of divorce.

Another potent source of marital disruption, associated with early marriage, is premarital pregnancy. Fewer marriages today occur as a result of a premarital pregnancy.[18] It also seems plausible that the greater availability of contraception and abortion in the 1970s may have discouraged the formation of early unions, reducing the number of ill-considered marriages, though evidence to support this hypothesis is not available.

Furthermore, the population has been getting older as the baby boomers mature. Older couples in longstanding marriages have a lower propensity to divorce.[19] Thus, as the baby boomers reach middle age, a larger proportion of those married have passed through the high-risk years, when their marriages are young and relatively more fragile.

Finally, growing rates of cohabitation before marriage may have brought down the rate of divorce. As more and more couples elect to live together prior to marrying, it seems likely that many unions that would have ended in divorce end before marriage occurs. That is, a growing number of Americans are divorcing without marrying, making the official divorce statistics a less reliable barometer of union stability.[20]

For all these reasons, it is probable that the modest drop in divorce rates does not indicate a higher propensity toward marital stability. Instead, the composition of those marrying has changed in ways that only make it appear that marriages are becoming more stable.

Remarriage

Not so many years ago, it was common for family experts to reassure those who were alarmed at the steady increase in divorce rates by pointing out that divorce typically is not a terminal event but a transition from one marriage to the next. So it was said that couples who separated lost faith in a particular marriage but not in the institution of matrimony.[21] In 1975, close to three-fourths of all women in their fifties who had experienced a divorce had remarried. For formerly married men, the occurrence of remarriage was even higher, about four in five eventually remarried, owing to the greater pool of eligible partners. (It is easier for men to attract younger partners than it is for women.) But recently, the rate of remarriage has been declining.[22]

In part, the trend toward lower remarriage rates may reflect the greater tendency to postpone second unions as both men and women may be more willing and able to live as single persons. But recent evidence from the National Survey of Families and Households (NSFH) suggests the rate of recoupling has not declined notably.[23] Many divorced persons have become more cautious about reentering matrimony, preferring instead to cohabit in informal and more fluid unions. This pattern, discussed below, poses particular problems for children who are, to an increasing extent, being raised by quasi-stepparents who are often transitional figures in their households.

The lower rates of remarriage may reflect a growing reluctance to formalize unions after a failed first marriage. Couples who remarry are known to have a higher risk of divorce than couples entering first marriages. And divorces from second marriages occur more quickly than from first unions. Cherlin has shown that the proportion of couples who will marry, divorce, remarry, and redivorce has risen eightfold during the course of this century, climbing from barely 2% of those who were born in the first decade of the twentieth century to 16% of those born after 1970.[9]

Cherlin described the changing patterns of marriage, divorce, and remarriage for four birth cohorts of women. For all but the most recent cohort, the proportion ever marrying remained relatively stable while the prevalence of divorce, remarriage, and redivorce progressively increased. In the youngest cohort, women born after 1970, Cherlin projects that marriage (and remarriage) will decline significantly and divorce will remain high among women who elect to marry or remarry.

Racial/Ethnic Differences in Patterns of Divorce and Remarriage

Rising rates of marital instability have been experienced by all Americans regardless of socioeconomic status, race, religious affiliation, or region of the country. However, the extent of marital instability differs enormously among various social groups. It is beyond the scope of this article to explore in detail the patterns described above for different social classes, religious groups, or regions of the country. It is hard to ignore, however, racial/ethnic differences in patterns of marriage, divorce, and remarriage because the experiences for whites, African Americans, and some Hispanic groups are so very disparate.

African Americans have long exhibited different patterns of family formation.[24] As far back as the nineteenth century, blacks were more likely to marry earlier, had a higher incidence of premarital pregnancy and nonmarital childbearing, formed less stable unions, and were less likely to remarry when disruption occurred. Scholars disagree on the origin of these patterns.[25] Some believe that they are rooted in different notions of kinship brought to America; others argue that distinctive patterns of family formation emerged in slavery; and still others contend that these family differences did not really take hold until after Emancipation, when black Americans were exposed to economic discrimination and racism. Still others argue that the differences are more recent in origin.[26]

Whatever the particular origin or combination of origins, there is convincing evidence that African Americans are much less likely to marry, more likely to divorce, and less likely to remarry when divorce occurs.[27] More than 90% of whites will marry compared with about 75% of African Americans; of those who do wed, African Americans have a substantially higher risk of divorce.[13] Ten years after marriage, 47% of blacks have separated or divorced compared with 28% of non-Hispanic whites. Blacks are also far less likely to remarry after separating. As a result, African Americans spend far less time in marriage than do whites.[28]

Much less information exists on the marriage patterns of other racial and ethnic groups. Census data on Hispanics suggest that their levels of marriage, divorce, and remarriage fall somewhere between those of whites and those of blacks.[13] However, official statistics actually conceal as much as they reveal about the behavior of different Latino groups. There is reason to suspect that as much difference exists between Cubans or Mexican Americans and Puerto Ricans as between whites and blacks in rates of marriage and marital stability.[29] Still, such as it is, the evidence on Hispanic subgroups reveals similar trends to those described for blacks and whites in the United States.

In sum, virtually all population subgroups have experienced a postponement of marriage, a steady increase in divorce, and a decrease in remarriage after divorce. Cohabitation as a prelude, aftermath, and perhaps alternative to marriage has become more common. These patterns are more evident among African Americans.

Childbearing

The declining institution of marriage has important ramifications for patterns of childbearing. Typically, now, marriage no longer regulates the timing of sex, and to an increasing degree, it no longer regulates the timing of first birth.[30] Nonmarital childbearing has become more prominent over the past several decades as rates of marital childbearing have declined and rates of nonmarital childbearing have held steady or increased. In 1960, only 5% of all births occurred to unmarried women; in 1990, this proportion had risen to 28%.[31] The increase for whites has been tenfold, from 2% to 20% in this 30-year period.

Figure 1 depicts the remarkable rise in the number of first births among women between the ages of 15 and 34 which have occurred before marriage for whites, blacks, and Hispanics. Among each of the racial/ethnic subgroups, the increase has been remarkable over the past 30 years. For whites this number rose from 8.5% for births occurring in the early 1960s to 21.6% for those that took place in the late 1980s. The rise for blacks was even more spectacular, going from 42.4% in the early 1960s to 70.3% in the late 1980s. The proportion for Hispanics doubled during the same period, going from 19.2% to 37.5%. Clearly, out-of-wedlock childbearing has become a far more important source of single parenthood for all Americans and especially so for African Americans, who now have a sizable majority of first births before marriage.[18] (See Figure 1.)

International Comparisons

The weakening of marriage as a social institution is not unique to the United States. Most developed countries are witnessing similar demographic trends.[32] In some instances, the retreat from marriage is even more pronounced. For example, in Scandinavia cohabitation has become a widely accepted alternative to marriage.[33] France and England have higher proportions of out-of-wedlock births than occur in the United States, though a higher proportion of these births occur to parents who are cohabiting than in this country.[34]

Divorce rates have also risen sharply in a number of European nations, though none equals this country in the prevalence of divorce.

Still, about a third of marriages in Northern Europe will end in divorce; in England and Scandinavia, as many as two in five marriages may dissolve.[35] Thus, explanations for the de-institutionalization of marriage cannot reside solely in the special features of American culture or society.

EXPLAINING CHANGING MARRIAGE PATTERNS

Much recent scholarly activity has been devoted to accounting for the declining strength of the marriage institution. The centrality of marriage and the nuclear family in the middle part of the twentieth century makes it especially puzzling to explain what appears to be the rapid erosion of a high cultural commitment to lifelong monogamy.[9,36] As we have already seen, the view that change came suddenly and only recently is certainly spurious. Many of the elements that were undermining the particular model of marriage prevalent in the 1950s have been evident for some time.

An explanation does not point to a single source of change. A configuration of many changes, some long-standing and others more recent, have shifted the balance of individual interests away from forming permanent unions to more fluid and flexible arrangements. The most important of these was undoubtedly the breakdown of the gender-based division of labor that led men to invest in work and women to specialize in domestic activity.[37]

In the United States these changes occurred in a culture that has long trumpeted the virtues of individual choice and, more recently, personal freedom and self-actualization.[38] Little wonder that Americans lead other nations in the divorce revolution.[39] Our ideology of individualism may have helped to grease the main engine of change, the movement of women into the labor force which subverted the model of marriage as an

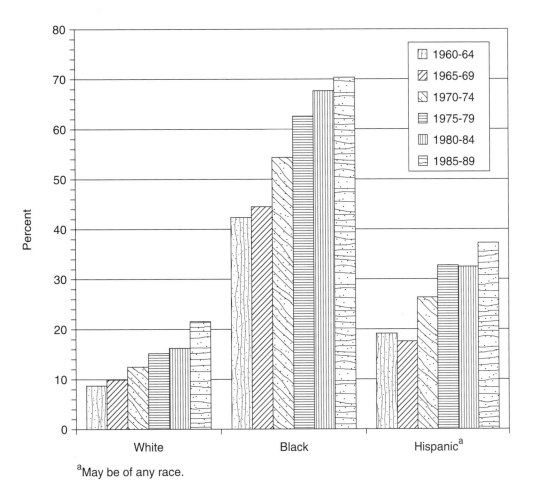

ᵃMay be of any race.

FIGURE 1   Percentage of First Births Occurring Before First Marriage Among Women 15 to 34 Years Old: 1960–64 Through 1985–89

Source: U.S. Bureau of the Census. *Households, families, and children: A 30-year perspective.* Current Population Reports, Series P-23, No. 181. Washington, DC: U.S. Government Printing Office, 1992, Figure 6.

exchange of goods and services between men and women.

Other simultaneous developments may have hastened the breakdown of the nuclear family. The sexual revolution in no small measure made marriage seem less attractive. As premarital sex with decreased risk of pregnancy became more accessible in the 1960s, the lure of early marriage lessened. The spread of birth control to unmarried youth and the availability of abortion played a part, but the growing visibility of sex that occurred in the post-Kinsey era was probably as influential as the availability of methods of fertility control in changing sexual practices.

Finally, the shift of public opinion favoring more liberal divorce laws may have fed the process of change.[9] Clearly, the laws were a response to a growing demand for divorce.[40] Increases in marital disruption preceded the legal changes or even the opinion favoring changes.[41] However, the laws, in turn, consolidated opinion institutionalizing alternative marriage forms, replacing the permanent monogamy with conjugal succession and, of late, even more conditional arrangements.

Apart from the development of new norms, marital instability promotes more instability as individuals become more wary about the prospects of permanency. They prepare for the contingency of being alone by spending time alone, and they hedge their bets by entering temporary partnerships.[42] As they do, they develop more resources for independence and a greater commitment to living alone unless they are highly contented in unions. Thus, the standards for what constitutes a gratifying relationship may have been rising to higher levels, some would say to unrealistically higher levels. Whether this is true or not, most Americans, perhaps women especially, are now less willing than they once were to settle for "good enough" marriages because they have the option of seeking more gratifying relationships or of living alone in the event that such relationships prove elusive.[43]

DIVORCE AND THE CHANGING FAMILY EXPERIENCES OF CHILDREN

The implications of these new marriage patterns for children has been the subject of enormous attention and mounting concern.[44] Close to a majority of children growing up today are likely to spend some time living in a single-parent family before reaching adulthood.[23,45] And, at least one in five will acquire a stepparent or surrogate parent. Family instability is not novel to the lat-

ter part of the twentieth century. Uhlenberg calculated that about one quarter of all children growing up in 1900 lost a parent by death.[46] If another 7% or 8% encountered a voluntary separation, then close to one in three spent time in a single-parent household during childhood. By mid-century, families had become more stable: the rapid decline of mortality was offset to some degree by rising voluntary dissolution and slightly higher rates of nonmarital childbearing. Still, the total disruptions probably did not affect more than one quarter of all children.[47]

Since the 1950s, when rates of stability were at their highest point, the risk of family disruption has more than doubled, owing to much higher rates of divorce and separation and, more recently, an explosion of nonmarital childbearing. Several estimates of children's probability of experiencing parental separation or divorce conclude that at least two in five children will see their parents separate before their late teens.[20,48] More than one quarter of children are born to unmarried couples, generally couples who are not living together when the birth occurs. Of course, there is some overlap between these two populations, but still, close to half of all children will spend time in a single-parent household before age 18.

This staggeringly high figure does not even tell the whole story. Among African Americans, the proportion of children who live continuously with two biological parents throughout childhood is certainly less than one in five and may be as low as one in ten.[49] Although data are unavailable on the experiences of different Latino groups during childhood, based on family composition, it is safe to assume that the difference among Hispanic populations is at least as great as the variation between Hispanics and either whites or African Americans. Puerto Rican patterns resemble those of African Americans while Mexican Americans appear to have even higher stability than white non-Hispanics.[50]

Marital disruption or nonmarital child-bearing for many children initiates a complex family career.[47] Most are likely to see one or both parents live with a partner for a time. Some of these partnerships eventuate in marriage; others dissolve and are succeeded by new relationships. Some remarriages persist while others end in divorce. At least one quarter of all children growing up today are likely to acquire a stepparent by marriage, and others will live with a quasi-stepparent. Beyond their household, children also may see their noncustodial parent enter new relationships. Thus, a high proportion of children growing up today will have more than two parents by the time that they reach age 18. Many more will gain additional parents in adulthood.

There has been considerable debate over the consequence of family flux on children's development and well-being. Many researchers stress the considerable costs incurred by children who are not raised in a nuclear family. Others cite the fact that most studies show relatively modest effects on children's adjustment in later life and observe that divorce represents an improvement in family circumstances for some children.[51]

Given the diversity of experience among children whose parents do not live together, it is difficult to arrive at a simple bottom line when assessing the effects of divorce. The starting point for families is so different, ranging all the way from instances where parents barely are acquainted to those who never live together to those who have lived together but are unsuccessful in collaborating to those who collaborate well before they separate but poorly afterwards to those who continue to collaborate effectively as parents even when they are no longer partners.

A growing body of research has examined how parents manage to raise children when they live apart.[52] More than half of all noncustodial parents effectively drop out, maintaining little or no contact with their children after divorce and providing little in the way of economic support. One survey in 1981 revealed that a majority of noncustodial parents saw their children infrequently or not at all.[53] Reports on child support also confirmed that a majority of noncustodial fathers contributed little or no support to their children—even those with formal support agreements.[54]

Over the past decade, there appear to have been some indications that paternal involvement after divorce may be increasing as laws both permit shared responsibility and enforce paternal obligations.[47] Unmarried fathers, too, may be experiencing the same opportunities and pressures for greater economic and emotional investment. Evidence from several longitudinal studies indicates that fathers who may be disconnected when children are young may become more involved with their offspring later in life.[55] Still, the preponderance of data indicates that a high number of nonresident fathers (and a substantial minority of nonresident mothers) disengage from their children when they do not live in the household.

At the heart of the problem is that many regard parenthood as part of a "package deal" that is inextricably linked with marriage or a marriage-like relationship. Men, in particular, often relate to their children in large part through their wives or partners. The disintegration of that relationship reduces noncustodial parents' willingness to invest resources in their children. This is especially so after remarriage, when parents often feel supplanted and disadvantaged by a new figure.

As many studies have shown, the withdrawal of economic support often has devastating effects on the living standards of mothers and children.[3,56] Though it is clear that stricter enforcement of child support will not lift all children in female-headed families out of poverty, the distributional effects would be substantial.[57] There is ample evidence that women and their children are far worse off after divorce than men and that noncustodial fathers are not paying their fair share.[58]

The effects of paternal participation on children's emotional development are less clear, though many experts believe that children are better off when their noncustodial parents remain involved.[59] In fact, the evidence for this assumption is equivocal at best. It may be that the level of paternal involvement is too low to produce a benefit or that greater involvement is accompanied by more conflict and ineffective collaboration.[60]

Despite a growing pattern of joint custody and shared responsibility, most formerly married and never-married parents do not cooperate effectively: they do not consult with one another, share information, support each other's efforts, or provide consistent monitoring and discipline.[53] Thus, the general axiom that children are better off when both parents are involved, even if they do not work well together, needs further consideration by researchers and clinicians.

A growing body of evidence also suggests that remarriage can pose complications for children even though they benefit economically when the parent with whom they live remarries.[47] The economic status of households headed by a remarried couple appears to be similar to that of couples in first marriages though few investigators have given careful consideration to the potentially greater economic demands on parents in second marriages. Still, there is no doubt that remarriage often lifts women and children out of poverty, probably because women are much less likely to reenter marriage if their potential partners have limited resources.

Remarriage not only reverses, to a large extent, the economic slide resulting from divorce but also introduces a new set of challenges for children. Remarriage can upset a stable family situation. It may, at least temporarily,

divert attention and time that children may be receiving from their parents and perhaps create frictions between stepparents and nonresident parents. Family life can become more complex, uncertain, and possibly conflict-ridden, especially when households join children from different families.[61]

Most studies show that children in stepfamilies do not do better than children in single-parent families; indeed, many indicate that on average children in remarriages do worse.[60,62] Remarriage creates a new family form that has been described by Cherlin as "incompletely institutionalized."[63] Family rights and obligations are less clearly defined and understood than in nuclear households. The absence of normative consensus extends beyond the household. A growing body of research suggests that kinship ties among steprelations are more discretionary and probably less enduring.[64] A positive aspect for children in stepfamilies is that they have access to a larger network of kin; a negative aspect is that these relations may be less reliable and committed to extending support and sponsorship.

Several recent studies of the effects of divorce and remarriage on kinship relations in later life indicate that marital disruption may be giving our kinship system a matrilineal tilt.[65] Children are less likely to give and receive time and money from their fathers and their fathers' kin than from their mothers and mothers' kin. Remarriage restores a measure of balance between maternal and (step)paternal lines, but only to a limited extent. In sum, divorce truncates the kinship network, and remarriage only partly repairs it.

Despite the evident disadvantages of marital disruption for children—loss of economic status, instability of parenting figures, and the complexity of new family arrangements—it is important to recognize that most studies show that the differences between children who grow up with both biological parents in the home and those who spend some time in non-nuclear families are relatively modest.[47,60] Unquestionably, marital disruption raises the risks of adverse consequences; but contrary to popular impression, the vast majority of children who experience life in single-parent families and step-families do well in later life. This result suggests that we have not given enough attention to understanding when and why disruption matters or, perhaps, to some of the advantages for children whose parents improve their family situation by divorce.[66]

THE IMPLICATIONS OF MARRIAGE FAMILY PATTERNS FOR CHILDREN'S WELFARE

Demographers and sociologists have had little success in forecasting family trends. However, there are many reasons for believing that the United States and other Western industrialized nations will continue to experience high levels of marital instability. Western family systems, and the United States in particular, place a high premium on individual choice and marital happiness.[39,67] The combination of imposing extremely high standards for intimate relationships while providing social and economic alternatives to those who are not achieving the desired standard of marital closeness is a virtual formula for producing high rates of marital instability. The breakdown of the gender-based division of labor accompanied and solidified the divorce revolution, a revolution that had already begun in the United States owing to Americans' well-documented taste for conjugal contentment. It created alternatives for couples (women especially) who were discontent in marriage and, in turn, probably helped to change the standards for a satisfactory marital relationship.

If this explanation for why divorce is so prevalent in the West is basically correct, there is reason to be pessimistic about containing divorce, either through moral suasion or public policy measures. Even a generation ago, when severe social and legal sanctions against divorce were still in place, rates of marital dissolution were relatively high in the United States, as high as they are in most European countries today. Restoring those sanctions, reimposing stricter divorce laws, and mobilizing social opinion against those who end their marriages probably would not persuade individuals to remain in unrewarding relationships.

Raising the barriers to divorce might convince some couples to postpone marital dissolution for the sake of their children. Whether the net effect of such efforts would benefit children is very much an open question. Existing research strongly suggests that children in poor quality marriages with high conflict do as poorly, if not worse, than children in marriages that dissolve.[60] On the other hand, children living with parents who are merely disaffected probably benefit from having them remain together. How much children would be protected by a return to the *status quo ante,* a regime with more restrictive divorce practices, is a matter for speculation.[68]

One likely consequence of restoring stricter divorce laws might be a further decline in marriage and an increase in nonmarital childbearing unless, of course, some effort was made to restigmatize unmarried parenthood. Recently, some attempts have been made to discourage the acceptance of single-parenthood. The most dramatic of these was the discussion initiated by Vice-President Dan Quayle to condemn the fictional character of Murphy Brown for having an out-of-wedlock child.[69] However, long before the public debate over Murphy Brown's decision, various public campaigns had been mounted to reduce nonmarital childbearing among teenagers. None of these, including national efforts by the Urban League and the

Children's Defense Fund, have been notably successful.[70] This is not to say that public opinion cannot shift as a result of political dialogue. However, moral exhortation, however well-intentioned, is not easily accomplished in a society that is highly diverse and socially segmented. If many devout Catholics cannot be dissuaded from having premarital sex, using contraception, or even obtaining abortions, we should not hold out much hope of raising cultural sanctions against divorce and nonmarital childbearing.

Many have argued that recent efforts to strengthen child support enforcement may increase the men's sense of family obligations.[71] Part of the rationale of the Family Support Act of 1988 was to shift some of the costs of child care to men, relieving the high burden that women bear for child support and the mounting public costs of programs like Aid to Families with Dependent Children (AFDC).[72] Some have argued that, as legal and social pressures for men to support their children mount, males may be less likely to desert their families because the economic costs of doing so will be greater. Similarly, the knowledge that they will be required to provide child support may make males more careful about impregnating partners with whom they have only casual ties.[71]

Stricter child support obligation is unlikely to have more than a modest effect on increasing marital stability or reducing nonmarital childbearing.[73] On the positive side, these laws—and the publicity surrounding them—convey an ethic of responsibility to children. However, the certainty of child support could make men more hesitant about entering marriage and women less reluctant to leave unsatisfactory unions. The net effect may be to reinforce the current retreat from marriage. Indeed, since the passage of the Family Support Act of 1988, marriage rates have continued to drop, marriage age has continued to rise, divorce rates have remained stable, and

nonmarital childbearing has risen. This is not to say that the Family Support Act has contributed to these trends, but, not surprisingly, this legislation and the publicity surrounding it seem to have had little effect on the family formation patterns of Americans.

Are there ways of stemming the erosion of marriage? At present, most public policy discussion has revolved around ways of discouraging divorce and nonmarital childbearing, largely through public rhetoric, rather than by designing measures to make marriage a more attractive and viable arrangement. Perhaps this emphasis is predictable because it is unclear how much can be done to shore up the institution of marriage. Besides, Americans are generally chary about policies designed to promote particular family arrangements.

At a minimum, most parents support some form of family life education in the schools that involves more careful consideration of the responsibilities and rewards of parenthood, that raises issues of gender roles and the difficulties of managing marriage. Efforts to prepare young people for parenthood, for entering and maintaining stable relationships are not highly controversial, but there is little evidence that family life education fosters commitment to marriage or encourages planned parenthood.

Much more controversial is the growing pressure to extend various welfare measures—common in some European nations—aimed at aiding parents with dependent children. Job security and income supplements for parents who are part-time workers, day care, parental leave, and family support allowances are economic measures designed to relieve strain on overburdened parents. Whether they also help to reduce marital breakup is not known. It might be argued that these types of family support programs make single-parent life more manageable and, thus, do little to reduce the breakup of parental unions.

Assuming that the breakdown of a gender-based division of labor is, at least, partly responsible for the destabilization of marriage from the 1960s to the present, some observers have insisted that a revision of gender roles is required to renew the institution of marriage. Family researchers have noted that considerable resistance exists to changes in the domestic division of labor.[74] Some have seen the surge of divorce as a reflection of the problems of adjusting to changing gender expectations and have argued that, with more egalitarian marriages, marital discontent may decline. How to bring about changes in marital roles through public policy is not obvious.

Clearly, there is a place for public education, but such efforts are likely to be effective only if accompanied by structural change in opportunities. Even if this occurs, it is not certain that changing gender expectations will result in more stable and secure family lives for children. Greater sensitivity to gender inequality may actually continue to raise expectations about equity in marriage. At least in the short term, expectations may continue to rise more quickly than behavior. In other words, men may assume a greater share of the domestic burdens, but their contributions may be judged by more exacting standards if they continue to fall short of true equality.

In sum, it is difficult to identify plausible policies to strengthen the institution of marriage by making divorce and nonmarital childbearing measurably less attractive or marital stability more attractive. Accordingly, it is hard to foresee a rapid reversal of current family patterns in the direction of greater family stability.

Therefore, it may be necessary to consider alternative approaches to strengthening the situation of parents and children who are economically and socially disadvantaged by living in particular family forms. At least part of the deficit associated with growing up in a single-parent household results from rapid income loss and chronic poverty created by the loss of a parent who is both a wage earner and a supplier of unpaid domestic labor.

There are some policies that might help to reduce the huge income spread between two-parent and single-parent families and thereby improve the life chances of children who grow up in a nonnuclear family. Foremost among these is the provision of an effective child support assurance plan that provides income to children whose parents cannot or do not contribute to their support. Other measures, such as low-cost child care, health care, and workplace benefits to reduce the conflict between work and family roles, could also help overburdened single parents. I noted earlier that all of these measures might also contribute to the formation and preservation of unions between parents or parent surrogates. In short, these supports to parents are proposed to benefit children regardless of whether or not parents marry and stay married.

American citizens generally agree that we share responsibility for protecting our children's future.[75] Presently, however, there is little public consensus on what that responsibility involves. More than our European counterparts, we Americans are inclined to voice strong moral concerns about the family and the well-being of children. But, our willingness to act on these concerns is undermined both by ideological disagreement and by distrust of government-sponsored interventions. At least for the time being, America's children are being held hostage to our inability to reach any kind of public consensus on a course for the future.

Part II

Gender Relations: Inequality, Sexuality, and Intimacy

Gender relations both within and outside of marriage and the family have been influenced by the ideology of patriarchal authority, which has been deeply entrenched in political, social, and economic institutions. Patriarchy has affected premarital, marital, and familial relationships and has been articulated in attitudes and behavior regarding sexuality, intimacy, power, and privilege.

However, the ideological revolutions regarding marriage and the family combined with the processes of industrialization and urbanization have produced a major reconceptualization of gender role relations within the last two hundred years. Social scientists (Ariès 1962; Shorter 1975; Stone 1977) have observed that prior to that period, the Western European and American nuclear family was not intimate and did not encourage domesticity or privacy. The inseparable and indistinguishable facets of social life were family and community. The notion of family privacy was practically unknown. Indeed, the very concept of the nuclear family did not emerge until the seventeenth century. The low valuation of the family in preindustrial Western society occurred because of the individual's almost total involvement with the community. The general situation was one in which most activities were public and one where people were rarely alone. The lack of privacy attributed to this overwhelming community sociability hindered the development of the family as we know it.

The family in this preindustrial period and extending into much later periods was patriarchal and authoritarian, and demanded deference. Husbands had virtually absolute power and control over wives and children. The relationship between husband and wife was not as intimate or private as it is today. In addition, the status and treatment of women varied with their involvement in economically productive work. When a woman contributed economically, she had more power and control over her own life. When she did not, her life was that of a domestically confined slave, servile and subservient to her master—her husband. The absolute power of the husband held true not only in economic terms but also in

163

moral matters. Both women and children were relegated to subordinate legal positions that were based on the economic and political control of the husbands and fathers.

The rise of the national state, ideological changes that included emerging ideas about liberty and the importance of the individual, combined with the Industrial Revolution all contributed to changes in the way marriage and the family were conceptualized. Traditional patriarchal relations were gradually replaced by romantic love, compassionate marriage, and an affectionate and permissive mode of child rearing. Edward Shorter (1975) labels the changes in the period after 1750 as the "Sentimental Revolution." The Sentimental Revolution ushered in a new emotional component to gender relations in three areas: courtship, the mother-child relationship, and the relationship of the family with the community.

The emergent emphasis on affection, friendship, and the romantic love ideology began to characterize courtship. As a result, marriage became more and more a matter of free choice rather than an arrangement determined by the parents on the basis of economic and social considerations. Attitudes toward children underwent a similar change, with new sentiments of affection and love emerging and neglect and indifference decreasing. An increase in the growth of maternal care and the development of a more loving attitude toward children by their mothers resulted. These shifting sentiments brought about a change in the relationship of the family to the community. Affection and caring tied the husband-wife relationship tighter and began to replace lineage, property, and economic considerations as the foundation of the marriage. Simultaneously, the couple's involvement with the community lessened.

In summary, the historical evidence illustrates two processes at work: the first is the couple's almost complete withdrawal from the community; the second is the corresponding strength of the ties of the couple with each other and with their children and close relatives. Taken together, these processes are often seen to have disturbed the grip of patriarchy on marriage and the family. The readings in this part of the book will investigate whether this has in fact occurred in the areas of dating and courtship (Chapter Five), sexuality, intimacy, and power (Chapter Six), and in the interrelationship of gender roles, work, and the family (Chapter Seven).

Most social historians believe that the modern American family emerged with the American Revolution and formed its major components by 1830. The four predominant characteristics of the American family are marriage based on affection and mutual respect, low fertility, child-centeredness, and what historian Carl Degler (1980) has called the "doctrine of the two spheres." This doctrine held that the primary role of the wife was child care and the maintenance of the household (the private sphere) while the husband's was work outside the home (the public sphere). Anchoring this doctrine was the belief that while the wife may be the moral superior in the relationship, legal and social power rests with the husband. The direct consequence is the subordination of women's roles to their husbands'. To deal with subordination, women carved out a source of power based on the emerging importance of mutual affection, love, and sexuality as integral components of modern marriage. As we shall see, a number of our readings will examine this development within an analysis of dating and courtship processes and in the expressions of sexuality.

An analysis of American courtship processes reflects historical changes that have shifted decision making from parental control to the couple themselves. This shift reflects the emerging nineteenth-century attitude that marriage should be based on personal happiness and the affection of the partners for each other. As marriage began to be equated with love and individualism, the growing acceptance of affection as the primary ground for marriage became an essential factor in the change in women's roles and a potential source of power and autonomy within the family. A woman could appeal to her husband's affection for her, and she, in turn, could manipulate that affection to increase her power or influence within marriage and the household.

Similarly, the expression of sexuality both within and outside of the courtship process took on a power component. The Victorian notion of the "passionlessness" woman can be seen as serving to improve women's status. Nancy Cott (1979) contends that the downplaying of sexuality could be used as a means of limiting male domination. The de-emphasis of feminine sexuality was replaced by an emphasis on women's moral and spiritual superiority over males and was used to enhance their status and widen their opportunities.

The doctrine of the two spheres that developed in the nineteenth century defined the essence of maleness as occupational involvement and the pursuit of worldly and material success. Women, on the other hand, were defined in terms of home—wife and mother—involvement and moral virtue. As a consequence, the idealization of masculine and feminine behavior affected courtship to the extent that romantic love took on greater importance as the criterion for marriage than ever before. Yet, ultimately, the doctrine of the two spheres continued to foster obstacles to friendship between the sexes, often resulting in a reliance on same sex friendships. Further, it severely handicapped the development of emotional bonds within courtship.

In the opening reading (13) of Chapter Five, "Dating and Courtship," Beth L. Bailey examines the economy of dating in the first three decades of the twentieth century. Her analysis reflects, in part, the work of Willard Waller, who in an influential 1937 article discussed the "rating and dating complex" that seemed to exist in colleges. Waller described a mutually exploitative dating system in which male students sought sexual gratification while women sought to enhance their prestige by going out with the more desirable men and being taken to restaurants, theaters, amusements, etc. As a result, dating became a bargaining relationship with exploitative and antagonistic overtones. Waller further speculated that the gender-role antagonisms generated by the dating system were continued in courtship, love, and marriage, and led to undesirable emotional tensions throughout the couples' lives. He conceptualized the "principle of least interest" to describe how unequal emotional involvement could lead to the person with "least interest" exploiting the other throughout their relationship.

Egon Mayer's discussion (Reading 14) of intermarriage between Jews and Christians revolves around the issues of individualism and love versus tradition and family continuity. An underlying issue is the maintenance of ethnic identity in intermarriages and the continuation of that identity in future generations.

The concluding reading (15) in this chapter is Adele Bahn and Angela Jaquez's "One Style of Dominican Bridal Shower." The authors provide an ethnographic account of what, at first glance, seems to be a festive celebration with no serious intent. However, the underlying meaning of bridal showers for these Dominican women living in New York City revolves around the anticipatory socialization of the prospective wife into four roles. The shower is seen to reflect old and new norms that prescribe and reinforce the traditional roles for the bride, including the role of a woman among women, the sexual role, the homemaker role, and the subservient role of the wife vis-a-vis the husband.

Chapter Six, "Sexuality, Intimacy, and Power," opens with a social-historical examination of etiquette books (Reading 16). The authors, Pearl W. Bartelt, Mark Hutter, and David W. Bartelt, argue that etiquette books have played an instrumental role in developing a gender-specific behavioral guideline for women. Etiquette books are examined to see how they have articulated rules regarding gender-role behavior in public places, at work, and in the home. These books are seen to have perpetuated the power and status of men and maintain women in subordinated positions.

Francesca M. Cancian explores the "feminization of love" in Reading 17. The feminized perspective defines love in terms of emotional expressiveness, verbal self-disclosure, and affection. Women are identified with this perspective. In contrast, the definition largely ignores love manifested by instrumental help or the sharing of physical activities that has been identified with masculine behavior. She argues that, by conceptualizing love in this manner, polarized gender-role relationships that contribute to social and economic inequality occur. Cancian calls for an androgynous perspective that rejects the underlying ideology of separate spheres and validates masculine as well as feminine styles of love.

Kath Weston in her book, *Families We Choose,* draws on her ethnographic field research of gays and lesbians in the San Francisco Bay Area to examine the kinship character of the ties among close friends and lovers and the political and ideological battles that were waged so that these ties would receive social and legal recognition. Weston documents how gay men and lesbians developed families and separated parenting and family formation from heterosexual relationships. In this selection from her book, Reading 18, Weston examines the ideological transformation that saw "gay" and "family" as mutually antithetical categories move to one in which these categories are used in combination to describe a particular form of kinship relation.

Arlie Russell Hochschild (Reading 19) examines the contemporary dual-career family. This paper was later elaborated in her widely praised book, *The Second Shift,* published in 1989. Hochschild is concerned with how cultural definitions of "appropriate" domestic roles and labor-force roles affect marital dynamics. She observes that contemporary economic trends have altered women's lives much more than they have altered men's lives.

Women have found themselves in new circumstances: They are working full time in the paid labor force, yet, at the same time, they are seen as primarily involved in domestic work. As a result, women are experiencing a "culture lag" in the larger world and a "gender lag" in the home. There is a lag regarding both attitudes and behavior towards women's paid work and domestic work. Women are confronted with a "second shift" of domestic labor because husbands are generally not increasing their work involvement with the home. Further, men have not emotionally supported women's role change to the same extent that women have. Hochschild analyzes this phenomenon through her concept of the "economy of gratitude." The concept is used to analyze whether husbands and wives have the same reality definitions about whether a given act requires an expression of appreciation and gratitude or not. The implications of differential reality definitions are then discussed by Hochschild.

Chapter Seven, "Gender Roles, Work, and the Family," contains three readings (20, 21, 22) focusing on gender relationships in terms of the different allocations and divisions of labor that exist between outside work and the home. In various ways the readings selected here all illustrate the continued pervasiveness of patriarchal ideology. Again, the notion of the two spheres of men's place in the workforce and of women's place in the home affects the nature and character of marital, familial, and kinship relationships and involvements.

Jesse Bernard, in her often-cited work on the "good provider" (Reading 20), traces the historical development of male familial roles in the United States. Essentially, the good-provider role defined a man as one whose wife did not have to, or should not, enter the labor force. The good-provider role is seen to have implications for both men and women. For men, the consequence of the good-provider role helped develop the predominant concept of male identity in terms of work and career activities. Consequently, the development of this specialized role removed women from labor-force participation and income-producing activities and made possible their total involvement with child-rearing and domestic household activities. The results of changes in the good-provider role in the last 25 years for both men and women are examined by Bernard.

Marjorie L. DeVault (Reading 21) focuses on the significance of the social structures of class and how it impacts on women's household roles and their ability to feed the family. The effort and skill required to perform "feed-work" is examined through a comparison of affluent homemakers and homemakers living in households sustained on poverty-level incomes. DeVault's work can be seen in terms of the underlying societal assumptions on how families are formed and sustained. Nurturance, in this regard, can be seen as a basis of group life and sociability. The effects of material conditions on women's experiences of sustaining the family in the context of social class makes DeVault's work particularly valuable in understanding internal family dynamics.

Mareena McKinley Wright (Reading 22) takes issue with the underlying assumptions of the conceptualization of the dual spheres of gender roles. This model, first articulated in the nineteenth century and still current today, saw men's work defined in terms of their involvement in economic activities and relationships based on money. Women, according to this model, were relegated to the household with emphasis on child-care and domestic activities. Her relationships were based on love and affection. Wright utilizes oral histories of older white rural women to develop a multidimensional continuum model of women's work that ranges from and has characteristics of both the public and the private. Wright believes that the inadequacies of the separate-spheres model have implications in the way that the society has failed to understand the true nature of women's and men's work and its inadequacy to develop strategies for aged individuals and children needing care.

References

Ariès, Philippe. 1962. *Centuries of Childhood: A Social History of Family Life.* Translated by Robert Baldick. New York: Knopf.

Cott, Nancy. 1979. "Passionlessness: An Interpretation of Victorian Sexual Ideology, 1790–1850." Pp. 162–181 in *A Heritage of Her Own,* edited by Nancy F. Cott and Elizabeth H. Pleck. New York: Simon and Schuster.

Degler, Carl N. 1980. *At Odds: Women and the Family in America from the Revolution to the Present.* New York: Oxford University Press.

Hochschild, Arlie (with Anne Machung). 1989. *The Second Shift: Working Parents and the Revolution at Home.* New York: Viking.

Shorter, Edward. 1975. *The Making of the Modern Family.* New York: Basic Books.

Stone, Lawrence. 1977. *The Family, Sex and Marriage in England 1500–1800.* Abridged edition. New York: Harper/Colophon Books.

Waller, Willard. 1937. "The Rating and Dating Complex." *American Sociological Review* 2:727–734.

5 | Dating and Courtship

Reading 13   The Economy of Dating*

BETH L. BAILEY

The "date" made its transition from lower-class slang to upper-crust rebellion and into middle-class convention with relative ease. To most observers, the gradual change from calling to dating looked like a natural accommodation to the new realities of twentieth-century life. Dating filled a need in an urban society in which not all respectable young women had parlors in their homes and childhood friends infrequently grew up to become husband and wife. Dating quickly became, and remains, the dominant mode of American courtship.

In the early twentieth century, the gloomiest critics feared only that this new system would make it harder for youth to negotiate the true business of courtship: marriage. Poor but ambitious and worthy young men could not attract suitable partners without spending vast sums on entertainment, and every theater ticket and late supper meant less money set aside toward that minimum figure needed to marry and start a family.

The critics were right, but in some ways their criticisms were irrelevant. Dating was not about marriage and families. It wasn't even about love—which is not to say that American youth didn't continue to fall in love, marry, and raise families. But before World War II, long-term commitments lay in the future for youth,

clearly demarcated from the dating system. In the public realm, in the shared culture that defined the conventions of dating and gave meaning and coherence to individual experience, dating was not about marriage. Dating was about competition.

Through at least the first two-thirds of the twentieth century, Americans thought of courtship as a system governed by laws of scarcity and abundance, and acted in accordance with that perception. Furthermore, America's system of courtship, as much as any other sphere of national life, mirrored the vicissitudes of economic and social opportunity and demands. In the 1920s, dating provided a new frontier for public competition through consumption, and in the 1930s it accepted competitive energies denied outlet elsewhere. In the postwar years, however, youth looked to courtship for a respite from the demands of a competitive society.

These different attitudes toward the role of competition in courtship before and after World War II are expressed in two distinct forms of dating. Before the war, American youth prized a promiscuous popularity, demonstrating competitive success through the number and variety of dates they commanded. After the war, youth turned to "going steady," saying that the system provided a measure of security and escape from

*Bailey, Beth L. 1988. "The Economy of Dating." Pp. 25–30 in *From Front Porch to Back Seat: Courtship in Twentieth-Century America*. Baltimore and London: The Johns Hopkins University Press. Reprinted by permission of The Johns Hopkins University Press.

the pressures of the postwar world. The courtship experience and ideals of those who grew up
before the war were profoundly different from
those of teenagers in the postwar years, and the
differences created much intergenerational conflict. Yet, for all their disagreement, both groups
understood dating in the same terms: competition, scarcity, abundance. This understanding of
dating, as much as the system itself, was an
accommodation to modern life.

Shortly after World War II ended, Margaret
Mead gave a series of lectures on American
courtship rituals. Although the system she
described was already disappearing, she captured the essence of what dating meant in the
interwar years. Dating, Mead stressed, was not
about sex or adulthood or marriage. Instead, it
was a "competitive game," a way for girls and
boys to "demonstrate their popularity." This was
not a startling revelation to the American public.
Americans knew that dating was centered on
competition and popularity. These were the
terms in which dating was discussed, the vocabulary in which one described a date.[1]

In 1937, in the classic study of American
dating, sociologist Willard Waller gave this competitive system a name: "the campus rating complex." His study of Penn State detailed a "dating
and rating" system based on very clear standards
of popularity. To be popular, men needed outward, material signs: an automobile, the right
clothing, fraternity membership, money. Women's popularity depended on building and
maintaining a reputation for popularity. They
had to *be seen* with popular men in the "right"
places, indignantly turn down requests for dates
made at the "last minute" (which could be weeks
in advance), and cultivate the impression that
they were greatly in demand.[2]

Waller gave academic legitimacy to a practice and a label commonly employed since the
early 1920s.[3] The competitive system of rating
and dating flourished on college campuses well

before Waller's study. It was a product of many
long-term trends that had produced an awareness of youth as a discrete and definable experience and had fostered the development of a
national youth culture. In the 1920s, youth most
extravagantly celebrated their culture (for themselves and for the nation, through the attentions
of national newspapers and magazines) on college campuses. While their numbers were relatively small, the doings of college youth carried
much symbolic weight with adults and their non-
student peers, who viewed youth culture sometimes with suspicion, sometimes with envy,
almost always with fascination.

As Paula Fass argues in her study of American college youth in the 1920s, "Competition
within conformity and conformity in the service
of competition were the structuring facts of campus life in the twenties." Competition and conformity, the individual and the group, held each
other in a delicate balance. Conformity to peer
group standards set the limits of competition—
and unleashed the forces of competition within
the limits of peer culture. Sports, school spirit,
organizational rivalry, social life, and consumption allowed full play of competitive urges. But
because youth and its institutions were a separate culture in which one could participate for
only a few years, competition was without significant long-term risk. This protected competition was seen as a training ground for the struggles young people would soon face in the world
outside college. Moreover, and paradoxically,
this competition expressed itself through conformity; conformity was the ultimate sphere of
competition. It was a self-contained, self-regu-
lating, self-limiting system.[4]

Fass explores these issues primarily in
terms of organizational and institutional competition, but youth's evolving system of courtship
also perfectly expressed them. The rating-and-
dating system *was* individual competition
expressed through conformity. The competition

was individual, but in the 1920s success in courtship came to be defined by the peer group. Success was popularity. Popularity was—and could only be—defined and allocated by others.

By the 1930s, the competitive system of courtship was well entrenched. However, though the rating-and-dating system stayed much the same, it was fed from different sources in the Depression years of the 1930s. No longer was competitive youth culture seen as the training ground for success-bound youth. Instead, success in social competition compensated for fears that other avenues of competition were closed off. But that a system based on abundance, consumption, and relative protection from the realities of adult life could persist and grow stronger in the face of a national depression shows how completely it had replaced the older systems of courtship.

No matter how people conducted their private lives, from the mid-1920s to World War II the rating-dating system dominated public discourse on courtship.[5] Waller's model is validated by countless examples from the popular media. College campuses, the peer cultures in which the rating-dating complex originated, offer textbook cases. In *Mademoiselle's* 1938 college issue, a Smith senior advised incoming freshmen that they must cultivate an "image of popularity" if they wanted dates. "During your first term," she wrote, get "home talent" to ply you with letters, telegrams, invitations. College men will think, "She *must* be attractive if she can rate all that attention."[6] And at Northwestern University in the 1920s, the competitive pressure was so intense that coeds made a pact not to date on certain nights of the week. That way they could preserve some time to study, secure in the knowledge that they were not losing ground in the race for popularity by staying home.[7]

Although Waller did not see it, the technique of image building was not always limited to women. For men, too, nothing succeeded like success. *A Guide Book for Young Men about Town* advised: "It's money in the bank to have lots of girls on the knowing list and the date calendar. . . . It means more popularity for you." As proof, the author looked back to his own college days, recalling how a classmate won the title of "Most Popular Man" at a small coed college by systematically going through the college register and dating every girl in the school who wasn't engaged.[8]

At some schools, the system was particularly blatant. In early 1936, a group of women at the University of Michigan decided to rate the BMOCs (Big Men on Campus) according to their "dating value." Men had to have dated several women even to be considered for the list. Those qualifying were rated either "A—smooth; B—OK; C—pass in a crowd; D—semigoon; or E—spook." As the Damda Phi Data sorority, these women made copies of the rating list and left them around campus. *The Michigan Daily* reported that the lists were being used "quite extensively" by women to check the ratings of potential blind dates.[9] This codification helped women to conform to peer judgments of dating value (and also to gain some kind of power over the most powerful men).

The concept of dating value had nothing to do with the interpersonal experience of a date—whether or not the boy (or girl, for that matter) was fun or charming or brilliant was irrelevant. Instead, the rating looked to others: "pass in a crowd" does not refer to any relationship between the couple, but to public perceptions of success in the popularity competition. Dating a "spook" could set you back, but the C-rater would hold your place, keep you in circulation.

Subtle manifestations of the rating-dating complex reveal the stress on competition even more clearly. In 1935, the Massachusetts *Collegian* (the Massachusetts State College newspaper) ran an editorial against using the library for "datemaking." The editors concluded: "The library is the place for the improvement of the mind and not the social standing of the student."[10] Social standing, not social life: on one word turns the meaning of the dating system. That "standing" probably wasn't even a conscious choice shows how completely people took for granted that dating was primarily concerned with status, competition, and popularity. Dates were markers in this system of exchange. Success—the only goal structurally possible—was to acquire enough popularity to continue to compete.

Popularity was clearly the key—and popularity defined in a very specific way. It was not earned directly through talent, looks, personality, or importance in organizations, but by the way these attributes translated into dates. These dates had to be highly visible, and with many different people, or they didn't count. In the mid-1930s, for instance, an etiquette book for college women compared a Northwestern University organization of campus "widows" (who showed they were faithful to faraway lovers by wearing yellow ribbons around their necks and meeting to read letters and share mementos while others dated) to women who were "pinned" to one man. The author made just one caveat: the widows "stay home all the time, and the pin wearers *at least* have steady dates" (emphasis added).[11] One man was only marginally better than none.

The rating-dating system, and the definition of popularity on which it was based, was not restricted to college campuses. Originally, popular magazines and advice books had described it as a college phenomenon, but during the 1930s, the college campus ceased to be the determining factor. In 1940, a *Woman's Home Companion* article explained the modern dating system (with no mention of college campuses) to its readers: "If you have dates aplenty you are asked everywhere. Dates are the hallmark of personality and popularity. No matter how pretty you may be, how smart your clothes—or your tongue—if you have no dates your rating is low. . . . The modern

girl cultivates not one single suitor, but dates, lots of them. . . . Her aim is not a too obvious romance but general popularity."[12]

The tone of the article is unqualified approval. As the popularity-ideal passed from college youth into the culture at large, it lost its aura of difference, its suspectness. For one thing, college youth raised on rating-dating were, by the late 1930s, the ones writing the advice columns for young people. In national magazines, they standardized and perpetuated the competitive dating system.

High school students of the late 1930s and 1940s, then, were raised on rating and dating. Not only did they imitate the conventions of older youth, they were advised by some young columnists, who spoke with distinctly nonparental voices, that these conventions were natural and right. *Senior Scholastic,* a magazine used in high schools all over the United States, began running an advice column in 1936. "Boy Dates Girl," written under the pseudonym Gay Head, quickly became the magazine's most popular feature.[13]

Gay Head's advice always took the competitive system as a given. She assumed that girls would accept any *staightforward* offer of a date if not already "dated" for the evening, and that boys, in trying for the most popular girl imaginably possible, would occasionally overreach themselves. She once warned girls never to brush off any boy, no matter how unappealing, in a rude way, since "he may come in handy for an off-night."[14] An advice column for "sub-debs" in the *Ladies' Home Journal* struck the same note. The columnist advised that shunning blind dates as "public proof" of a slow social life was bad policy. Even if "imperfect," she wrote, blind dates would "help keep you in circulation. They're good press agents. They even add to your collection."[15]

Teenagers had little argument with this advice. Early debates on "going steady" in *Senior Scholastic* (which show that some students, at least, wanted a "single suitor") over-whelmingly rejected the steady-date plan. Negative responses were blunt: "If a girl goes steady she loses her gift of gab; she doesn't need to compete with others of her species" (Chicago); "Going steady is like buying the first car you see—only a car has trade-in value later on" ("Two Boys," Milwaukee); "One is a bore—I want more!" ("A Girl," Lynwood, California). A girl from Greensboro, North Carolina summed it all up:

> *Going steady with one date*
> *Is okay; if that's all you rate.*[16]

Rating, dating, popularity, competition: catchwords hammered home, reinforced from all sides until they seemed a natural vocabulary. You had to rate in order to date, to date in order to rate. By successfully maintaining this cycle, you became popular. To stay popular, you competed. There was no end: popularity was a deceptive goal. It was only a transient state, not a trophy that could be won and possessed. You competed to become popular, and being popular allowed you to continue to compete. *Competition* was the key term in the formula—remove it and there was no rating, dating, or popularity.

Reading 14   Two Can Make a Revolution*

EGON MAYER

Paul's grandmother, Ba Thi Tu, had been cooking for the Bar Mitzvah for days alongside her daughter, Josephine Tu Steinman. The menu included veal with black mushroom sauce, Vietnamese meatballs, beef chow fun, chicken and cashew nuts, rice noodles, and other Oriental delicacies. A dish calling for pork had to be eliminated, along with shellfish dishes, because they were not kosher.

This was no ordinary Bar Mitzvah fare: no chopped herring, stuffed derma, or matzoh ball soup here. This was the home-catered Bar Mitzvah feast of Paul Steinman—the son of Ron Steinman, an executive at NBC-TV News—and Josephine Steinman, formerly Ngoc Suong Tu, a Vietnamese Buddhist who converted to Judaism after she came to the United States with her husband.

That *The New York Times* chose to report on the "Bar Mitzvah with a Vietnamese Flavor" (June 29, 1983) is ample indication, of course, that such ceremonies are far from common. Indeed, such families are far from common. Jews and Vietnamese are generally not found together in large enough numbers to produce more than one or two intermarriages. But the story highlights what have become increasingly common facts of family life for Jews, as well as other minorities, since the early part of the twentieth century. America is blending, and out of its cultural caldron are emerging life-styles and new customs that defy age-old distinctions. When it comes to mate selection and the family forms that follow from it, love triumphs over tradition; inclinations triumph over timeless customs; and even religious rituals are transfigured to meet private needs and desires.

In that simple human interest story in *The Times,* which focused on the menu rather than on the ironies of the occasion, one can see reflected centuries of tension, and the fermenting of cultural forces and contending human drives coming to fruition.

Paul's Hebrew teacher was *kvelling* (rejoicing) at what appeared to her to be the fulfillment of the American dream. "A blending of two ancient cultures have met here today," Ms. Saletsky said. One is almost moved to the clichéd exultation "Love Conquers All." But as we shall see, such simple generalizations are defied by the complex realities of intermarriages.

Here, and in most other cases, too, love is no blind conqueror. It does not vanquish all other bonds or loyalties. Ron Steinman's Jewishness was important enough for him to have Ngoc Suong convert; important enough to have his children raised as Jews and educated in a Hebrew school; and important enough to have

*Mayer, Egon. 1987. "Two Can Make a Revolution." Pp. 23–58 in *Love and Tradition: Marriage Between Jews and Christians.* New York: Human Sciences Press, Inc. Used with permission.

his firstborn son go through the traditional Jewish rite of passage. In subsequent personal conversation with Ron and Josephine, it became apparent that those same Jewish sentiments were not a salient consideration in Ron's mind when he chose to marry the then Ngoc Suong. Moreover, Josephine observed that one of her deeply felt reasons for wanting to become Jewish was her Vietnamese heritage that obliges a married woman to join her fate entirely to her husband and his family. Thus, for her, conversion to Judaism was a traditional wifely obligation. At the same time, for Ron, marriage to a Vietnamese woman was very much a break from his Brooklyn Jewish family tradition. For both, albeit for different reasons and in different ways, love and marriage entailed not following the customary path of their respective families, at least as far as mate selection was concerned.

The modern vocabulary of motives for marriage emphasizes love, compatibility, and mutual fulfillment. It leaves but little room for such considerations as duty, respect for tradition, and responsibility to one's ancestors and parents. Individualism, personalism, and privatism form the cornerstones of contemporary family relationships—at least that is the conventional wisdom. In the light of that wisdom, the very concept—intermarriage—is an anachronism. What should it matter, as the question is often asked, what a person's religious, ethnic, racial, etc., background is? Only one man and one woman are united in a marriage. Ron and Ngoc Suong no doubt underwent such questioning before their marriage; at least in their own minds, if not with one another and their respective parents.

Yet their very life as a modern Reform Jewish family is a testimonial to the persistence of tradition, albeit in modern garb. The fact that she became Jewish, an American, and changed her name to Josephine is an indication of just how important it was for both of them to bridge the

cultural and religious differences that many think should not matter any more to modern men and women living in the age of hi-tech.

The brief story of Paul's Bar Mitzvah points to a multitude of insights about what it means to be a Jew in modern America; about what it means to be a member of a religious or ethnic minority in a liberal, pluralistic society; about what it means to be a family today; and, indeed, about the very nature of identity in modern society.

The story symbolizes the simultaneous drive of individuals to pursue their own individual happiness under circumstances that are made unpredictable by the impersonal forces of history (e.g., war). At the same time, the story also symbolizes the deeply rooted tenacity of traditions and the capacity of free individuals to blend and connect the most time-honored traditions in the most unconventional ways. In a sense, the story of Paul's Bar Mitzvah epitomizes the irony of Jewish survival.

The image of love emerging out of the ashes of war has always been one of profound irony. That an American-Jewish bureau chief for NBC, covering the war in Vietnam, should return to the United States with a Buddhist wife who becomes a Jew, and that they should, in turn, raise Jewish children, is truly newsworthy. At least one of the sources of the irony is war itself. That love should emerge from it is somewhat understandable, but that it should leave intact two people's attachments to their heritage, despite their experience of the war and despite their love across vastly different heritages, is remarkable. To be sure, the Steinmans' experience is virtually unique, and hardly generalizable. Yet it recalls for me my own first encounter with Jewish intermarriage as a child, in the person of one of our closest family friends—Allen Feher, or Sándor bácsi, as I called him—in my childhood in Budapest.

Sándor had been one of my father's closest friends, ever since they were teenagers in

Komárom (a small town in southwestern Czechoslovakia). They had attended yeshiva together, both being from Orthodox Jewish families. Sándor had married a few years before World War II and lived a traditional Orthodox Jewish life as a small merchant. When the Nazis entered Hungary in 1944 he happened to be away from home on business. His wife and two children were deported and never returned from the concentration camp. Sándor had gone into hiding in Budapest in the apartment of a Christian friend. There he was befriended by Irene, the daughter of a high-ranking officer in the Hungarian military, naturally, a Christian.

At the end of the war, Sándor and Irene married and had a child. Sándor abandoned his Orthodoxy and even joined the Communist Party—at least for appearance's sake. It helped him advance in the nationalized shop in which he worked. Yet, he continued to cling to a lifelong desire to go to Israel. In Communist Hungary in the late 1940s and early 1950s, that was—for all intents and purposes—a Messianic hope. But Irene, using her family contacts in the government, was able to obtain an exit visa for the three of them. In 1953 (at the close of the Stalinist era), Sándor—an intermarried Jew with a Catholic wife and daughter—immigrated to Israel, the land of his Jewish dreams. Irene never converted. She felt that she had returned to the land of Jesus and continued to live her life as an Israeli Catholic, as did her daughter.

A different war, a different continent and, surely, different personalities, yet one cannot help but feel that the same forces were working their curious chemistry in the lives of the Steinman and the Feher families. Ron and Sándor drew from the same well of tradition. And, for some as yet mysterious reason, Ngoc Suong and Irene both found it to be their desire to link their lives and fates to the ways in which their men would come to grips with their heritages. Ngoc

Suong joined Ron Steinman's religion; Irene joined Allen Feher's nation.

Surely neither couple sought to make a social revolution of any kind and would probably be surprised to see themselves spoken of as "revolutionaries." Yet their relationships, along with the multitude of other similar relationships, continue to exert transformative pressures on the ancient culture of the Jewish people, as well as on the laws of a modern nation-state, Israel.

Allen and Irene's daughter, for example, has remained a Christian, but as a young, dynamic woman, she has also served in the Israeli army. Naturally, she met and socialized with Israeli young men, virtually all of whom were Jews. For her, it was hardly a break with any social convention to fall in love with a Jewish man. But marriage for the two of them in Israel was out of the question, since matrimonial law in Israel is determined by Jewish religious regulations that prohibit such marriages. Ironically, they had to "elope" to Cyprus to marry in a Greek civil ceremony so as to be able to live as a legitimately married couple in Israel. Their case, along with untold others, remains a source of festering tension in Israeli political life.

Bar Mitzvahs like that of the Steinmans' also stretch the meaning of the ancient Jewish ritual. According to the *halacha* (the body of Jewish law made up by the commandments in the *Five Books of Moses* and their rabbinic interpretations in the Talmud and subsequent exigetical texts), Bar Mitzvah refers to the ancient legal status of adulthood at which point an adolescent is obligated to abide by the laws. The term applied only to young men who were regarded as having reached their Bar Mitzvah at the age of thirteen. There had been no comparable status for Jewish women, nor a celebration thereof, until the Conservative movement institutionalized the Bat Mitzvah in the 1920s.

Interestingly enough, the Bar Mitzvah was one of the many observances the Reform movement abandoned in the nineteenth century. The Reform movement, born out of the spirit of the enlightenment and German nationalism at the end of the eighteenth century, sought to do away with all those Jewish religious customs that could not be rendered plausible in the light of modern reason and contemporary life-style. The notion that a pubescent young man at the tender age of thirteen should somehow be regarded as a legal adult responsible for his actions was one of those implausible customs in the eyes of the Reform movement.

Consequently, some of the oldest and most respectable Reform temples in America would not permit Bar Mitzvahs to be performed as late as the 1950s, nor were Bat Mitzvahs permitted.

But ancient traditions die hard, and sometimes not at all. The need on the part of Jewish families to signify to themselves and their communities that their children are part of the Jewish fold through some kind of joyous public ceremony could not be eradicated by rational philosophy. The Bar Mitzvah has gradually made its return into the Reform movement since the 1950s. In fact, with the increasing incidence of marriages between Jews and non-Jews, particularly in the Reform community, the Bar Mitzvah has emerged as the signal Jewish ceremony by which an intermarried family publicly proclaims that their child is being raised as a Jew.

In a twist of modern Jewish family history, the Steinmans, as Reform Jews, were celebrating the Bar Mitzvah, which had lost its apparent meaningfulness for Reform Jews earlier. It now serves a highly potent social and psychological function precisely as a result of intermarriage. To be sure, not all children of intermarriages go through a Bar or a Bat Mitzvah ceremony. Indeed, most do not. My own studies have shown that in those intermarried families in which the non-Jewish spouse does not convert to Judaism, only about 15 percent of the children will go through that symbolic Jewish life cycle

ceremony. In what we call conversionary families, in which the formerly non-Jewish spouse converts to Judaism, as in the case of the Steinmans, nearly 75 percent of the children go through the ceremony; it apparently does not take many to stimulate cultural reforms.

The Steinmans' Bar Mitzvah menu also hints at an unfolding cultural revolution. Although most of America's Jews have relinquished the ethnic distinctiveness of their daily diet over the past few generations (hardly anyone really lives on chopped herring, *gefilte* fish, or *chulent* any more), such Jewish ceremonial occasions as weddings and Bar Mitzvahs are still marked by highly traditional food. For most modern American Jews, that is probably one of the salient features of these occasions: the opportunity to recollect the flavors and images of the past through their palates. But because most typical Jewish homes no longer prepare traditional Jewish foods as part of their normal diet, professional Jewish catering has emerged as an industry in its own right. Ostensibly, the function of the industry is to provide food and style consistent with the middle-class consumer values of American Jews. However, its more subtle, latent function is to serve up a feast of traditions through culinary inventiveness: to blend the taste of the immigrant with the style of the successful American.

In "olden days," it was not the caterer, but rather the women of the family who prepared the food for days and weeks before a Bar Mitzvah or a wedding. One of the objects of the ceremony was to exhibit before the larger invited community the mastery of the family of shared food values. "Look at my *kugel*," or *strudel*, or *gefilte* fish, the proud mother of a Bar Mitzvah boy would exclaim to her friends. And recipes, memories of mothers, and culinary techniques would be exchanged. But who asks a caterer for a recipe or memories of his mother?

Not surprisingly, it was Paul Steinman's Vietnamese grandmother and mother who spent their days cooking in preparation for the Bar Mitzvah. After all, where do you get a kosher caterer who cooks Vietnamese style? And the arousal of sensory memories through food is evidently no less important to the Vietnamese than it is to Jews—even if it is at a Bar Mitzvah. But the irony is this: Given the obvious importance attached to the memories of the palate by both Jews and Vietnamese, and probably all other ethnic Americans as well, what kind of memories are being built into young Paul's palate, and what kind of a Bar Mitzvah feast will he lay out for his own son?

The old adage that an army marches on its stomach may be true, but, at least from the brief account of Paul Steinman's Bar Mitzvah feast, it may also be surmised that cultural revolutions can be instigated in the kitchen.

The ironies of Paul's Bar Mitzvah and the late Sándor bácsi's marriage to Irene and immigration to Israel all point to the historical tension between love and tradition; between the drive of the individual for self-expression and fulfillment and his affinity for the norms and values of his heritage. This tension, of course, is not unique to intermarriages. It is endemic to all modern marriages. It is therefore appropriate and necessary to turn our attention briefly to the role of love and tradition in the making of modern family life.

Modern marriages, generally, and intermarriages, most particularly, are based on the feeling that two people share by being in love. In a brilliantly argued essay, Franceso Alberoni, the Italian sociologist, has suggested that the experience of falling in love is very much akin to the birth of a social movement; it is the moment that signals the birth of a new collective "we."

In an existing social structure, the movement divides whoever was united and unites whoever was divided to form a new collective sub-ject, a "we" which, in the case of falling in love, is formed by the lover-beloved couple.[1]

"No experience of falling in love exists without the transgression of a difference," writes Alberoni, and therefore, "falling in love challenges institutions on the level of their fundamental values."[2] The potential of two individuals to make a revolution is realized through love.

But love, like any other revolutionary force, can only transform people or social institutions if it is harnessed in some kind of ongoing collective enterprise such as marriage. Perhaps for this reason, love had not been allowed to play a significant role in mate selection in most societies until the last 200 years.

In a collection of essays with the title *Romanticism: Definition, Explanation and Evaluation* (1965), the historian John B. Halsted informs us that "the term Romanticism came into currency at the very beginning of the nineteenth century" and referred primarily to the works of poets and writers, later artists and composers, who gave primacy in their works to moods, feelings, passions, and enthusiasms.[3] They saw themselves as rebelling against the structures of Classicism and Rationalism. Historians of the modern family, such as Edward Shorter and Ellen K. Rothman, have shown that at more or less the same time that Romanticism was emerging as a thematic force in the world of the arts, romance—the primacy of empathy and spontaneity as well as sexuality between men and women—was emerging as an ideology on the basis of which couples would seek to form marriages and families.[4] It is in its latter, more layman's sense that we will use the terms *romance* and *romantic*.

Whereas love unites, tradition divides. The feelings of love burst through walls and spill over boundaries of conventionality. The feelings toward a tradition are quite different. No matter how passionately one may be committed to it, the sentiments inspired by tradition can be expressed only in forms and rituals that were established by others long ago. Tradition inspires conformity, just as surely as love inspires inventiveness. Tradition makes careful distinctions in time, in space and, most importantly, between categories of people. Love is oblivious to all that.

In point of fact, modern marriages are not merely based on love. More importantly, they are based on a belief; an ideology of romance that regards the deep psychological and sexual attachments that are experienced as love as socially legitimate and desirable; an adequate basis for the making of a complex relationship called marriage. A related tenet of this ideology of romance is that the social identity or group background of the beloved has no place in the emotional calculus of the loving relationship, nor should it have a role to play in the organization and quality of the marriage that ensues from loving.

But as we shall see . . . , the heritages, traditions, cultural memories, and group identities of individuals who fall in love and marry do continue to play a significant role in the individuals' self-concepts and also in the life-styles of their families.

Thus, love is only the spark that may start a revolution. But real social transformation occurs precisely when the energy of love is harnessed and integrated in the flux of established situations: the family, religion, the state, and the community. That the love of two should have such far-reaching consequences, that is a real revolution.

For all these reasons, love and tradition have never lived comfortably with one another. Tracing the history of love in the West since the time of the ancient Greeks, Morton Hunt—a historian—shows vividly, and with some sense of both its drama and its humor, that the "joining

of romantic passion, sensuous enjoyment, friendship and marriage" took nearly 2,000 years to evolve to its modern form.[5]

The general lovelessness of ancient marriages is captured in a somewhat cruel Greek adage of the sixth century before the Christian era: "Marriage brings a man only two happy days: the day he takes his bride to his bed, and the day he lays her in her grave."[6] But as late as our own twentieth century, the fictional Goldie, wife of Sholom Aleichem's *Tevyeh, The Milkman* (popularized in America as *Fiddler on the Roof*), is perplexed when her husband asks her, "Do you love me?" She replies:

> For twenty-five years I've washed your clothes, cooked your meals, cleaned your house, given you children, and milked the cow. After twenty-five years, why talk about love right now?[7]

Goldie's words are virtually a mirror image of the ancient Greek view of matrimony attributed by Morton Hunt to the famous orator Demosthenes: "Mistresses we keep for pleasure, concubines for daily attendance upon our needs, and wives to bear us legitimate children and to be our housekeepers."[8]

Undoubtedly, many more wives and husbands probably loved one another, before, as well as during the course of their married life, than one finds recorded in the annals of history. But it is also true, and far more widely established historically, that love has been but rarely considered an acceptable reason, much less an expected forerunner, of matrimony. If love was to be found at all, it was most often to be found briefly before, and frequently outside of, marriage, generally in forbidden relationships.

Marriage, however, was a moral duty and a social responsibility particularly incumbent upon men. It was through marriage that a family name, the family heritage, and property would be passed, unto posterity. Singlehood was as much frowned upon in the ancient Jewish tradition as it was in the ancient Greek and Roman traditions. Indeed, even in colonial America, bachelors were highly suspect and, in most colonies, were burdened with special taxes and generally kept under the watchful eyes of their neighbors. In Connecticut, William Kephart reports, "every kind of obstacle was put in the way of a bachelor keeping his own house.... Unless a bachelor had authority to live alone he was fined one pound (£) a week."[9]

But although marriage was a duty almost universally honored by most adults since ancient times, who actually married whom was not left to the individual. Such decisions were too important to be left in private hands, subject to personal whim or fancy. Given its strong social, moral, and religious objectives, marriages were arranged throughout most of history, in both the East and West, by parents, older siblings, and other guardians of family tradition. They made certain that the marriage partners who were chosen for their young ones were consistent with the needs and values of the family and the larger community. Naturally, under such a controlled mate selection system, marriages between Jews and Christians were virtually out of the question on both sides; only social deviants would intermarry.

To be sure, even under such a system, a son or daughter might be granted veto power by a permissive parent over a particular choice. But it is highly unlikely that more than a rare few ever had the freedom to choose a mate based entirely on their private emotional preference and without due regard to the broad conventional preferences of their families and communities. Those who violated the imperatives of custom or clan, the Romeos and Juliets of history, most often paid the price. In short, for much of our history, the dictates of tradition clearly dominated the

inclinations of the heart when it came to marriage. It is more than likely that the ancestors of Ron Steinman—as well as those of his wife, Ngoc Suong Tu—were married off in their early teen years to mates chosen by their parents.

It took several far-reaching revolutions, and about two centuries, to dismantle traditional constraints upon mate selection and to replace them with romantic idealism. By the end of the eighteenth century, writes Edward Shorter, "young people began paying much more attention to inner feelings than to outward considerations, such as property and parental wishes, in choosing marriage partners."[10]

The onset of the Industrial Revolution in the latter half of the seventeenth century began to unsettle the closely bunched lives of people in villages and farms, forcing increasing numbers to leave their highly traditional rural enclaves for larger towns and cities.

The feudal West was beginning to stir, shaking the age-old foundations of family organization. Of course, for most Jews, those early stirrings were barely noticed. They would continue to live in restricted isolation from their Christian neighbors for yet another two centuries. But a few famous "court Jews" were beginning to enter intimate political and economic arrangements with dukes and princes in Germany, which, in due time, would lead to even greater intimacies between their children and grandchildren, as one can see among the illustrious Rothschilds. Selma Stern's colorful account of the adventurous lives of the seventeenth-century court Jews amply hints at the advance of the industrial age that was beginning to pave the way for a growing intimacy between Jews and non-Jews.[11] But whether the intimacy would lead to love and marriage would depend on the relative power of tradition and love in the prevailing social norms.

With the benefit of hindsight, we now know that romanticism followed closely on the heels of the American and French revolutions, the two epoch-making revolutions at the end of the eighteenth century that ushered in the modern era. As Edward Shorter put it, in the years after 1750, "the libido unfroze in the blast of the wish to be free." Gradually the idea gained currency that marriage should be much more than a joining of hands, of fortunes, and of families—that it should be a joining of hearts.

At least as it applies to the making of marriages, the romanticism that followed in the wake of two great political revolutions probably advanced much further in the United States than elsewhere in the West. In a delicately drawn history of courtship in America, Ellen Rothman shows that parents increasingly allowed and expected their children to freely choose their own marriage partners.[12] In turn, young men and women recognized that in order to find a mate, they must first find love. Perhaps Thomas Jefferson himself might be credited (or blamed) for the ascendancy of love. After all, it was he who changed the famous slogan of liberty attributed to John Locke ("Life, Liberty, and Property") to "Life, Liberty, and the Pursuit of Happiness."

In a profound analysis of that Jeffersonian turn of phrase, Jan Lewis, a historian, has shown that the freedom to pursue personal happiness soon became a moral as well as a psychological imperative, with wide-ranging effects on both family life and religion.[13] Put succinctly, "in the decades after the Revolution, the head fell victim to the heart." Marriage was now to grow out of passionate desire and was to lead to mutual emotional fulfillment and inner peace, and not simply to outer stability and respectability.

In their *Manifesto of the Communist Party,* Karl Marx and Friedrich Engels argued that the purely economic forces of capitalism that they saw all around them in the Europe of 1848 were sweeping away age-old customs that had governed religion, family life, and social relations in general. However, a closer look at the surge of

Romanticism in that era—be it in the form of sublime poetry read in the drawing rooms of the bourgeoisie or in the form of the unbridled sexuality of the lower classes—suggests that it was not the power of capital alone (or even primarily) that was transforming social norms. Rather, it was the revolutionary new idea that each individual had the right to pursue his or her own personal happiness: that society could be so ordered that people might find true happiness in their choice of mates, and that they might try to exploit their own talents to their best possible advantage.

Today, the unconditional value of conjugal love as both the basis for and the proper object of marriage is so thoroughly taken for granted that it is difficult to imagine that it was ever otherwise, or that any alternate view of that tender emotion might be equally valid. But if such social historians as the Frenchman, Philippe Ariès; or the Canadian, Edward Shorter; or the American, Morton M. Hunt, are correct, the popular infatuation with romantic love and its close connection in the popular mind with marriage is a relatively recent phenomenon. For most of history, men and women were joined in matrimony out of more practical considerations, such as the demands of social conventionality or the needs for security.

Looking back upon traditional patterns of courtship, Shorter writes,

> *All situations in which boys and girls met for the first time were monitored by some larger group.... Young women simply did not encounter young men without other people around.*[14]

The opportunity for the spontaneous involvement of members of the opposite sex with one another was rigorously controlled so as to prevent undesirable amorous entanglements. The "other people around" were most often parents, older siblings, or even peers who could safeguard the individual against "stepping out" of the bounds of social propriety—emotionally or otherwise. Arranged marriages, which often took place among well-to-do families in Europe, be they Jews or Christians, were the surest way to prevent romance from intruding into the all-important process of family formation. Continuing his backward glance, Shorter continues,

The most important change in the nineteenth- and twentieth-century courtship has been the surge of sentiment. . . . People started to place affection and personal compatibility at the top of the list of criteria in choosing marriage partners. These new standards became articulated as romantic love. And secondly, even those who continued to use the traditional criteria of prudence and wealth in selecting partners began to behave romantically within these limits.[15]

Like stardust in the trail of a comet, the romantic revolution followed in the wake of twin social revolutions of the eighteenth and nineteenth centuries: the industrial and the democratic.

In the United States, love and the pursuit of happiness had yet another major role in transforming the society. It was to be the flame under the melting pot.

What, then, is the American, this new man? He is neither a European, nor the descendant of a European; hence that strange mixture of blood, which you will find in no other country. I could point out to you a family whose grandfather was an Englishman, whose wife was Dutch, whose son married a French woman, and whose present four sons have now four wives of different nations.[16]

This often-quoted passage, from the pen of French-American Jean De Crevocouer in his *Letters from an American Farmer* (1782), presaged by some 120 years the theme if not the title of the Jewish-American Israel Zangwill's play, *The Melting Pot* (1908).[17] As some critics of the period observed, Zangwill captured in a phrase the spirit of the nation.

The Melting Pot was a drama about a romance, a thinly veiled imitation of Shakespeare's *Romeo and Juliet,* only with a happy ending—at least for the couple. David Quixano, a Russian-born Jewish immigrant, falls in love with Vera Revendal, a Russian-born Christian; both work on the Lower East Side of New York—that quintessential immigrant ghetto of the turn of the century. For some reason, Zangwill chose the most un-Russian last names for his principal characters. Perhaps he thought that they would blend better if they were not burdened with more distinctive names. Be that as it may, the young lovers were determined to marry, despite the turbulence of their emotions and opposition of their relatives. They put off their marriage only when it was learned that Vera's father, a colonel in the Tsar's army, was personally responsible for the killing of David's family in the Kishinev *pogrom* of 1903.

However, by the end of the play love prevails over all the sorrow, bitterness, and prejudice. To paraphrase Zangwill, the shadows of Kishinev melt away in the American crucible. The young lovers walk hand in hand into the sunset against the skyline of lower Manhattan, to the background strains of "My Country 'Tis of Thee."

The play opened at the Columbia Theater in Washington, D.C. with President Theodore

Roosevelt in attendance. In fact, the play was dedicated to Roosevelt. When the final curtain fell, Arthur Mann, the historian, writes, the President shouted from his box, "That's a great play, Mr. Zangwill! That's a great play!" *The Melting Pot* went on to become a huge popular success, continues Mann.

After showing in the nation's capital, it ran for six months in Chicago, and then for 136 performances in New York City. Thereafter, for close to a decade, it played in dozens of cities across America. In 1914 it was produced in London, again before full houses and admiring audiences.[18]

The play became a text in high schools and colleges; it was produced by amateur theatrical groups frequently, and its publisher, Macmillan, reprinted it at least once a year until 1917.

One does not need a great deal of historical insight to understand why that play should have become so popular and, particularly, so highly praised by the official champions of American culture. Between 1870 and 1924 (when the Johnson Act finally stemmed the tide of mass immigration), the population of America more than doubled from about 45 million to about 110 million.[19] The growth was fueled by the entry of about 25 million immigrants, overwhelmingly from southern, eastern, and middle Europe: Jews, Slavs, Poles, Italians, Serbs, Croats, etc. In some of the larger American cities, nearly 40 percent of the population was comprised of the foreign-born and recently arrived immigrants: "The tired, the poor, the wretched refuse of the earth," as Emma Lazarus described them on the base of the Statue of Liberty.

Lincoln Steffens voiced the central question of the period in a title of an article, "What Are We Going to Do with Our Immigrants?"[20] Perforce, the answer had to be assimilation. The

pervasive and troubling division between blacks and whites, which continues as the single most salient social division in America, inevitably drew all immigrants into the general society and made their gradual assimilation a popular social goal. Ralph Waldo Emerson gave poetic voice to this sentiment.

As in the old burning of the Temple at Corinth, by the melting and intermixture of silver and gold and other metals a new compound more precious than any, called Corinthian brass, was formed, so in this continent—asylum of all nations—the energy of the Irish, Germans, Swedes, Poles, Cossacks, and all the European tribes—of the Africans, and the Polynesians—will construct a new race, a new religion, a new state, a new literature, which will be as vigorous as the new Europe which came out of the smelting pot of the Dark Ages.[21]

Although social scientists make useful distinctions between such concepts as assimilation, amalgamation, and pluralism, it is clear from all the studies of the great immigration of that period that the process of Americanization was to involve both the relinquishing of many old-world traditions and the acquisition of many new ones.

How rapidly the process would occur in the lives of particular individuals, and in the collective history of one ethnic group or another, was to vary according to biographical and social circumstances. The peddler who found himself in the hinterlands of Pennsylvania was surely Americanized more rapidly than his cousin who manned a pushcart on New York's Lower East Side. But what would ultimately make America a true amalgam—an embodiment of the ideal printed on her coinage, *E Pluribus Unum*—was to be a universal human emotion: love.

Zangwill's play owed its popularity to the fact that it held out a promise that both the masses of immigrants yearning to become full-fledged Americans and the guardians of American culture, trying to cope with the massive influx of foreign multitudes, dearly wished to believe. The fire that was to heat the melting pot was none other than love—not the love of nation or folk, nor the love of abstract ideas, but the entirely private kind of love between a man and a woman.

It was expected that contact between different ethnic groups would lead to acculturation: borrowing a custom here and there, sharing recipes, and the like. The practical necessity of working and living in America would lead to assimilation in such matters as language, education, and political and economic aspirations. But what would forge the blended American, as Roosevelt, Emerson, or Steffens envisioned him, would be none other than marriage—the union of diverse groups through the power of romantic love.

In Jewish communities, the social revolutions of the nineteenth century socially emancipated the individual Jew, thus enabling him to become an equal citizen. As the German historian Heinrich Graetz put it,

> The hour of freedom for the European Jews dawned in the revolutions of February and March, 1848, in Paris, Vienna, Berlin, in Italy, and other countries. An intoxicating desire for liberty came over the nations of Europe, more overpowering and marvelous than the movement of 1830. With imperious demands the people confronted their princes and rulers. Among the demands was the emancipation of the Jews. In all popular assemblies and proclamations, the despised Jews of yesterday were admitted into the bond of "Liberty, Equality, and Fraternity" (the slogan of the French Revolution of 1789).[22]

As a result of those revolutions, Jews streamed from confined settlements in backward towns and villages into the capitals of Europe; from narrowly restricted occupations into the full range of modern pursuits that were being opened up by the Industrial Revolution; and into a new kind of relationship with Christians—one that, at least in principle if not in fact, was based on a doctrine of social equality.

Intermarriages between free-thinking Jews and Christians followed on the heels of emancipation in an inexorable sequence. Historians surmise that the salons in the homes of Jewish bankers in Berlin and Vienna offered the first common meeting places for liberated Jews and Christians, and it was from these sociable acquaintanceships that the first intermarriages resulted. First the privilege of only the well-to-do Jews, intermarriage between Jews and Christians gradually became an available option for the broad masses of urban middle-class Jews.

Although statistics on the rate of Jewish intermarriage at the beginning of the modern era are spotty and imprecise, there are some available that clearly buttress the general impressions. In a study of marriage records right after the American Revolution, the historian Malcolm H. Stern found that in 699 marriages of Jews, 201, or about 29 percent, were intermarriages between a Jew and a Christian.[23] Similar patterns are reported by others elsewhere in the Western World.

Citing the work of such early students of Jewish social life as Drachsler, Engelman, Fishberg, and Ruppin, Milton L. Barron reports, for instance, that the percentage of intermarriages as a proportion of all marriages in which Jews were involved increased in Switzerland from 5 percent in 1888 to about 12 percent by 1920; in Hungary, the rate increased from about 5 percent in 1895 to about 24 percent by 1935; and in Germany, the rate increased from about 15 percent in 1901 to about 44 percent by 1933, on the eve of the Nazi rise to power and the passage of the draconian Nuremberg Laws that forbade marriage between Jews and Christians.[24]

Citing the work of the French demographer E. Schnurmann, Moshe Davis similarly reports that in Strasbourg, the rate of intermarriage between Jews and Christians increased from an undetermined "very low rate" to over one-third of all marriages of Jews between 1880 and 1909. The French city of Strasbourg had a substantial Jewish population at the time, so the increase in intermarriage could not be attributed to a dearth of eligible Jewish marriage partners.[25]

Jews were apparently eager to enter the mainstream of modern society through the portals of romance and matrimony with their Christian neighbors, and they were also being more readily accepted in their host societies. The separation of church and state following the revolutions in America and France, and the availability of civil marriage—there as well as in much of the rest of the Western World—further hastened the incidence of intermarriages that would not have been legal in earlier generations.

Although the statistics are spotty, as we have seen, and not as precise as most social scientists would prefer, their message is unmistakable. Jews were choosing Christian mates (most often a Jewish man choosing a Christian woman), as well as being chosen by them, in ever-increasing number. They were breaking sharply with one of the oldest and most deeply held norms of Jewish life: the norm of endogamy—the *halachic* requirement (based on biblical inductions) that Jews only marry other Jews.

The one sleeping-giant exception to this trend at the turn of the twentieth century was the Jew of Eastern Europe, about half of the world's approximately 8 to 9 million Jews at the time.

They lived in the infamous Pale of Jewish Settlement, a territory about the size of Texas on the periphery of Russia and Poland.[26] In these small, isolated, economically backward and politically enfeebled villages, they were barely touched by the great revolutions of the previous two centuries. Whereas the lives of Western Jews had undergone significant transformations since the end of the seventeenth century, particularly rapidly from the mid-eighteenth century, the lives of Eastern European Jews in the 1880s did not differ much from what they might have been in the Middle Ages. Indeed, some might say that they were probably better off in the Middle Ages than they were in the last decades of the nineteenth century.

As described by many writers, in varying hues of pain, humor, and bitterness, as well as some nostalgia, Eastern European Jewry lived a cloistered, virtually medieval existence until the first decades of the twentieth century.

Their language, Yiddish; their religious life, a highly ritualized and fundamentalist form of Orthodox Judaism laced with the mysticism of the Hasidic Jews; their economy, pre-industrial and progressively rendered impoverished by anti-Semitic decrees; their host culture, Polish and Russian peasantry wantonly anti-Semitic and given to periodic orgies of organized violence against Jews; their self-image, a moral kingdom of priests and philosophers who were destined to attain a loftier existence someday. All these features of their life served to erect an almost impregnable barrier between Jews and Christians who lived as neighbors in the villages (or *shtetlach,* as they were called in Yiddish). Social intimacy at the level of friendship was almost non-existent between them. Therefore, the possibility of intermarriage was virtually unthinkable.

And yet, if the story of *Tevyeh, the Milkman* is any indication of social realities, despite those great barriers some Jews and Catholics or Russian Orthodox peasants did fall in love; did go against the prevailing social norms and did marry, although often they did so by eloping to the West. Clearly the inclination of the individual to pursue his or her own personal happiness, even in the face of powerful opposing social norms, could not be entirely suppressed.

Nevertheless, the central point remains— marriages between Jews and Christians were far less common in the ghettoized areas of Eastern Europe than they were for Western Jewry. Arthur Ruppin, one of the early sociologists of world Jewry, has amply documented that, for instance, the proportion of intermarriages in one hundred Jewish marriages was less than 1 percent in Galicia as late as 1929. By contrast, the rate in places like Germany was 23 percent, and it was 13 to 27 percent in Budapest and Vienna. Elsewhere in Eastern Europe—in Latvia, Lithuania, White Russia, and the Ukraine—mixed marriages rarely occurred.[27] Moreover, it stands to reason that they were not any more frequent at the end of the nineteenth century than they were in the first decades of the twentieth.

However, it must be recalled that between the 1880s and the 1920s, about half of the approximately 5 million Jews who lived in Eastern Europe immigrated to the United States. Beginning with the pogroms of 1881, masses of *shtetl* Jews were quite literally chased into the modern world by the whips and swords of Russian Cossacks. Rather than try to bear it stoically, dying martyrs' deaths as their ancestors might have done, millions of Jews from the Pale chose the path of migration to the West, specifically to the United States.

Between 1881 and 1923, approximately 2.8 million Jews entered through Ellis Island, the "golden door" to America. They quickly overwhelmed the 250,000 Jews, mostly of German descent, who had comprised American Jewry up to that time. As is well known from Irving Howe's popular *World of Our Fathers,* the first generation of Eastern European immigrants set-

tled in such densely Jewish ghettos as the Lower East Side in New York, Maxwell Street in Chicago, and similar enclaves in Philadelphia, Baltimore, and Washington, D.C.[28]

Their settlement patterns, their economic circumstances, their dependence on *mame-loschen* (mother tongue, i.e., Yiddish), and the rising tide of anti-Semitism in America soon resulted in the re-establishment of the kind of ghettoized mode of social life that they had all just recently left behind in the Old World. The convergence of all these social factors resulted in a dramatic decline in the overall rate of mixed marriages for American Jews.

In contrast to the approximately 30 percent rate of Jewish mixed marriages discovered by Malcolm Stern among American Jews in the Federal period (when there were no more than 100 thousand Jews in the country, representing about one-quarter of 1 percent of the total population), the proportion of intermarriages among Jews in the first decades of this century (when they were about 3.5 percent of the total U.S. population) was less than 2 percent.[29]

At the very historical moment when Israel Zangwill was rhapsodizing about the power of love, and intermarriage in particular, and as the great emotional fire flamed under the "melting pot," more of his own people were huddling together—as were immigrant Italians, Poles, Irish, Greeks, and Chinese—than they might have been a half century earlier. The tough realities of immigrant life, and traditions of the Old-World culture that most immigrants brought with them, placed a powerful check on the romanticism of the nineteenth century; but not for long.

In a popular compilation of letters to the editor of the *Jewish Daily Forward,* the preeminent Yiddish newspaper in America since 1890, we find that from the earliest times their readers were writing to the illustrious editor of the paper about problems having to do with marriage, particularly between Jews and non-Jews. Isaac Metzker, who published the popular compilation in 1971 under the title *A Bintle Brief (*a bundle of letters), gives us a vivid flavor of some of their concerns.

1908

Worthy Editor:

I have been in America almost three years. I came from Russia where I studied in yeshiva.... At the age of twenty I had to go to America. Before I left I gave my father my word that I would walk the righteous path and be good and pious. But America makes one forget everything.

Here I became a (machine) operator, and at night I went to school. In a few months I entered a preparatory school, where for two subjects I had a gentile girl as teacher.... Soon I realized that her lessons with me were not ordinary... she wanted to teach me without pay.... I began to feel at home in her house... also her parents welcomed me warmly.... Then she spoke frankly of her love for me and her hope that I would love her.

I was confused and I couldn't answer her immediately.... I do agree with her that we are first human beings, and she is a human being in the fullest sense of the word. She is pretty, educated, intelligent, and has a good character. But I am in despair when I think of my parents. I go around confused and yet I am drawn to her. I must see her every day, but when I am there I think of my parents and I am torn by doubt.

Respectfully,
Skeptic from Philadelphia[30]

Reading this poignant letter nearly 80 years after it was written, and with the hindsight of history, one wonders what the nameless correspondent was skeptical about. Was it about his faith, about the wisdom of his parents, or the

wisdom of his attachment to them? Was it about his love for the girl or her love for him, or was it perhaps about love itself?

Another correspondent, writing to the editor just about a year later, had other problems, but seemed to be unperturbed by any skepticism.

1909

Dear Editor:

I come from a small town in Russia. I was brought up by decent parents and got a good education. I am now twenty years old and am a custom-peddler in a Southern city. Since my customers here are Colored people, I became acquainted with a young Negro girl, twenty-two years of age, who buys merchandise from me.... She is a teacher, a graduate of a Negro college, and I think she is an honorable person.

I fell in love with the girl but I couldn't go around with her openly because I am White and she is Colored. However, whenever I deliver her order, I visit with her for awhile.

In time she went away to another city to teach, and I corresponded with her. When she came home for Christmas, I told her I loved her and intended to marry her and take her North to live. But she refused me and gave me no reason. Perhaps it was because I am a White man.

I spoke about my love for her to my friends, who are supposedly decent people, and they wanted to spit in my face. To them it appeared that I was about to commit a crime.

Therefore I would like to hear your answer as to whether I should be condemned for falling in love with a Negro woman and wanting to marry her. And if you can, explain to me also her reason for refusing me.

Respectfully,
Z.B.[31]

One wonders how many young Jewish peddlers, machine operators, and night school students who had recently come to America were having their first taste of the bittersweet pulls and pinches of romance with Italians, Irish, WASPs, and blacks. One wonders, and wishes for more data. But even in the absence of such data, it is safe to say that there were many more such matches, resulting in marriages (and even occasional conversions to Judaism), than there had been in Eastern Europe.

Writing in 1920, Julius Drachsler reported that the rate of intermarriage for Jews in New York City was 2.27 percent between 1908 and 1912. However, the trend was clearly upward as one looked past the immigrant generations and outside the ghettoized areas of Jewish Settlements.[32]

The trend became most clearly defined for American Jews only as recently as 1971. It was in that year that the Council of Jewish Federations and Welfare released its landmark study of the U.S. Jewish population known as the National Jewish Population Study, or NJPS. Table 5.1 succinctly presents the key finding of that study with regard to the intermarriage trend. Although there is some scholarly debate about the precise, most current intermarriage rate,

there is no debate about the direction of the trend.

It took about sixty years, or roughly three generations, for the descendants of the Eastern European immigrants (who constitute approximately 75 to 80 percent of the total American Jewish population) to catch up in their rate of mixed marriage with those of their brethren in America and Western Europe who had been modernized in the eighteenth and nineteenth centuries.

The magnitude of the most recent rates, and the speed with which they had increased, rang out like a thunderclap in the Jewish community. In a seminal work, *Assimilation in American Life* (1964), Milton Gordon had argued that "if marital assimilation...takes place fully, the minority group loses its ethnic identity in the larger host or core society."[33] The findings of NJPS rang a powerful alarm in the minds of those concerned with Jewish group survival.

The convergence of Gordon's sociological insights and the statistical patterns discovered by the NJPS led many learned observers to a foreboding conclusion. American Jewry might become an "extinct species" as a result of marital assimilation. At the very least, so it was feared, the size and significance of an already small minority in the American mosaic might be further reduced to ultimate insignificance as a result of intermarriage. In a carefully calculated analysis, Harvard demographer Elihu Bergman cautioned in 1977 that the net effect of the increased rate of intermarriage projected out over a century would be to reduce the size of the American-Jewish population from the approximately 5.7 million in 1976 to as few as about 10 thousand by the time of the American tricentennial, in the year 2076.[34]

Nor have the concerns been based upon Jewish facts alone. In the wake of Vatican Council II, the *Decree on Ecumenism* (1966) proposed that the Catholic Church mitigate its his-

TABLE 1   Percentage of Jewish Persons Marrying Someone Who Was Not Born Jewish, out of All Jews Who Married at Given Time Periods

Time period	Jews marrying non-Jews
1900–1920	2.0
1921–1930	3.2
1931–1940	3.0
1941–1950	6.7
1951–1955	6.4
1956–1960	5.9
1961–1965	17.4
1966–1971	31.7

torically rigorous opposition to mixed marriages. By 1970, the Church no longer required in such marriages that the non-Catholic partner promise to raise the children as Catholics—much less to convert to Catholicism. The result of the liberalizing trend in the Church was to see a steady increase in Catholic intermarriages and a corresponding decline in conversions to Catholicism. Indeed, as Andrew Greeley has shown in his *Crisis in the Church* (1979), "by far the largest numbers of those who have disidentified from the Roman Catholic Church have done so in connection with a mixed marriage."[35]

If religious tradition was steadily losing its grip on cupid's arrows, the once restraining influence of ethnic traditions was faring even worse. In an influential article in the *American Sociological Review,*[36] Richard Alba showed that marriage across ethnic lines among Catholics had increased significantly with the coming of age of successive generations of the descendents of immigrants. Ethnic in-group marriage among the immigrant generations of English, Irish, German, Polish, French, and Italian Catholics quickly yielded to ethnic mixing among the second and third generations, according to Alba's deft analysis.

Among Jews, too, the breaching of the previous generations' ethnic divisions was nearly total by the end of the 1950s. As recently as the 1910s, Konrad Bercovici reports, intermarriage between a Sephardic Jew and a Russian Jew was as rare, if not rarer (and more frowned upon), as marriage between a Jew and a non-Jew.[37] Indeed, Bavarian Jews even hesitated to marry German Jews who came from nearer the Polish border, derisively referring to them with the ethnic slur "Pollacks." In turn, the Russian Jews looked down upon the Polish Jews as well as upon the Galicians and would not permit their children to marry them, reports Milton Barron. But by mid-century the inter-ethnic aversions had largely disappeared in the Jewish community, in much the same way as they had among Catholics.

In retrospect, it would seem that the wholesale crossing of ethnic boundaries *within* religious groups paved the way for the crossing of religious boundaries. The walls of tradition were being battered down by sentiment and emotional attachments, one cultural building block at a time. If those trends would continue unabated for even a few successive generations, Israel Zangwill's play about the melting pot would prove to be prophetic. The romantic ideology of the eighteenth and the nineteenth centuries would indeed sweep away the last vestiges of traditional constraint on the individual's choice of a mate. Such a fundamental change in the making of family life would prove a more profound point as well. It would prove that happiness—and, indeed, identity itself—is quite possible in the modern world without any significant rootedness in a shared tradition.

However, alongside the increasing rates of intermarriage for Jews and others, mid-century modernity was marked by other cultural trends as well. Perhaps none is more notable than the Americans' search for their diverse heritages. The period saw a spate of publications, both in the social sciences and popular literature, extolling the virtues of ethnicity and tradition. Opposing Zangwill, Michael Novak heralded *The Rise of the Unmeltable Ethnic* (1972) and the age of "White ethnicity."[38] Earlier, Herbert Gans and Michael Parenti had also seen the signs amidst the suburban and urban transitions of the 1950s and 1960s.[39] Ethnic group ties continued to play a powerful role in shaping the residential as well as friendship preferences of people long after ethnicity had been declared irrelevant in American life by the conventional wisdom.

In popular literature, the enthusiasm for nearly lost heritages reached its crescendo with the publication and subsequent serialization on TV of Alex Haley's *Roots.* It is particularly ironic that Haley dedicated his book to America's bicentennial, since it was published in 1976. The "nation of many nations," in which the culture was to blend and render indistinguishable the diversity of cultures that it comprised, was being greeted, on its bicentennial, with a massive outpouring of interest in ethnic distinctiveness and family heritage. The interest in "roots" spawned a virtual cottage industry in genealogy as a family pastime for several years. It was being fed by such books as Bill R. Linder's *How to Trace Your Family History* (1978) and, for Jews, Arthur Kurzweil's popular *Tracing Your Jewish Roots*.[40] As recently as 1984, no less a personage than the President of the United States, Ronald Reagan, created a significant "media event" by visiting the village in Ireland from whence his ancestors emigrated to the United States in the 1840s.

The "Bar Mitzvah with the Vietnamese flavor" with which this chapter began, now points to an even deeper irony. It purports to blend two cultures, Jewish and Vietnamese, very much in keeping with the American ideal of the melting pot. But it simultaneously speaks to the persistence of an unalloyed attachment to the traditions of those cultures. It particularly speaks to the persistence of Jewish identity and ritual in the lives of people—some born Jewish, some newly so—who, at least on the basis of their choice of marriage partners, would seem to have agreed that love is more important than tradition.

The Steinman Bar Mitzvah underscores the emergence of two apparently contradictory trends among modern American Jews, in particular, and perhaps among all modern ethnic Americans, in general. One is the trend described by Shorter, by Lewis, by Rothman, and by other students of the romanticization of the modern family: the triumph of the heart over the head, of love over tradition in matters of mate selection. The other is the trend of resurgent ethnicity described by Novak, by Parenti, by Glazer

and Moynihan, and by others since the 1960s. These two contradictory trends have been made even more puzzling since the mid-1970s with the resurgence of religious emotionalism and fundamentalism among those very segments of society—the young, professional, educated, and middle class—who had been thought to be immune to spiritual matters because of their modern consciousness and life-style.

As do all profound contradictions, these contradictory trends raise several compelling questions that strike at the very core of the meaning of intermarriage. Why do people choose to celebrate particular symbols or rituals of a larger tradition whose main tenets they have rejected? For example, why did Josephine Steinman want her son's Bar Mitzvah to have a "Vietnamese flavor" when she had converted to Judaism and presumably now sees herself as part of the Jewish people? Why did Ron Steinman want his wife to become Jewish, as do tens of thousands of other young Jews who marry Christians, when his sense of equality was such that he was able to fall in love with a woman who was a Buddhist? Why do the hundreds of thousands of Jews and Christians, who marry one another in defiance of their age-old ethnic and religious traditions, persist in memorializing many of those very same traditions in their holiday celebrations, in the way they rear their children, in what they read and what they eat, and in their very concept of themselves as human beings? Particularly among American Jews who have experienced such a great and rapid increase in intermarriages, why has the trend toward intermarriage *not* been accompanied by a comparable trend of disidentification from the Jewish people?

Perhaps Josephine Steinman herself was answering some of those deep questions in her own mind when she commented on the unique Bar Mitzvah menu to *The Times'* reporter, "It was a desire to put on a party in one's own image. That became particularly important with the kind of family we have. After all, there aren't many Vietnamese-Jewish families."

Of course, Mrs. Steinman is right. There aren't many Vietnamese-Jewish families, but, until the 1950s, it is not likely that one would have found culturally blended Jewish families of even less exotic mixture, such as Italian-Jewish or Irish-Jewish, which are far more common. It is not that such marriages did not occur. Of course, they did. Jews have been marrying non-Jews since biblical times. But the social stigma attached to such marriages usually compelled intermarried couples to become more or less socially invisible—at least in the eyes of the Jewish community and often in the eyes of the Christian community as well.

What stands out as remarkable about the Steinman's Bar Mitzvah is that this family has no desire or need to "pass" as either exclusively Jewish or Vietnamese, or exclusively anything else. They can create a party in their own image, indeed an entire social identity in their own image. Moreover, they can find a Reform Jewish congregation (of which they are members) that seems not only to accept but also to actually delight in this family's ability to express their Jewishness in their own unique idiom.

Rose Epstein, an old friend of the family, is quoted as commenting on the celebration, "It's a new world, isn't it? I can't get over how nice it is when people accept." Her comment is almost liturgical. It recalls the well-known Hebrew song "Hine Ma Tov U'Manaim, Shevet Achim Gam Yachad" (Behold, how good and pleasant it is when brethren dwell in unity).[41] One almost has to pinch one's self to realize that the unity of brethren rhapsodized by the Hebrew poet certainly did not envision the celebration of Bar Mitzvahs with Vietnamese cousins or chicken with cashew nuts.

Some might say the desire, as Josephine put it, to "put on a party in one's own image" proclaims nothing more profound than the contemporary consumerist values of modern upper-middle-class Americans—young, professional urbanites—whose numbers are legion in New York City and other major metropolitan areas. Perhaps they merely reflect the narcissism of the postwar baby-boomers coming of age and expressing their passionate individualism in a traditional idiom. Perhaps tradition here is nothing more than yet another vehicle for their highly personal "ego trip." Perhaps.

But, in fact, Ron and Josephine Steinman went through a long period of searching within themselves, as well as through various Jewish institutions on two continents, before they could arrive at a form of religious identification and affiliation that was harmonious with their view of life. Josephine was searching for the compassion and respect for life she had learned as a child. Ron wanted to belong to a community that reflected tolerance and social responsibility. Their personal outlooks, although drawn from vastly different cultures, were surprisingly similar. What the two wanted was to be able to link their inner felt similarity to a single tradition; in this instance, the Jewish tradition—to link the personal feelings shared by two to a tradition shared by many. The particular resolutions they have made in dealing with their dual family heritage have come at the cost of great effort and, at times, the suffering of callousness and intolerance from those closest to them.

Their search, and particular resolution, reflects an apparent need on the part of many intermarried couples to not dismiss their heritages, but, rather, to integrate them into some kind of harmonious whole. . . . The Steinmans are not alone, even if their particular cultural blend is a bit more unusual than that of others.

Amidst the general alarm among American Jews over the increasing rate of intermarriage throughout the 1970s, relatively little attention was paid to the fact that unprecedented numbers of non-Jews were becoming Jewish by choice.

The National Jewish Population Study had found that about one-third of the contemporary intermarriages involved the conversion of the non-Jewish partner. My own study of intermarried couples, conducted on behalf of the American Jewish Committee (1976–1977), confirmed those figures and also found that in about 20 percent of the intermarriages in which no conversion to Judaism had taken place, the non-Jewish spouse had more or less "assimilated" into the Jewish community through the Jewishness of the family.

Other demographic studies of Jewish communities, such as those of Floyd Fowler in Boston (1975), of Albert Mayer in Kansas City (1977), of Bruce Phillips in Denver (1982), and of Steve Cohen and Paul Ritterband in New York (1983), all show that the rate of conversion into Judaism has increased along with the increase in intermarriage.[42] In fact, the percentage of conversions from among the intermarriers has tended to run ahead of the rate of intermarriage itself. Taken together, these studies show that the rate of conversion into Judaism during the past thirty years has increased by about 300 percent.

In 1954, Rabbi David Eichhorn published a report estimating that the Reform and Conservative movements were producing between 1,500 to 1,750 "new Jews" each year through conversions.[43] In 1984, Rabbi Sanford Seltzer of the Reform Union of American Hebrew Congregations estimated, in a personal conversation, that his movement was producing between 7,000 to 8,000 "new Jews" each year. Although increases among the Conservative and Orthodox have not been as great, knowledgeable observers in those movements also point to significant increases in their conversion activities—all this, by the way, without any direct efforts by any of the movements thus far to seek out converts actively.

As . . . in the great majority of such conversionary families, a high value is placed on the maintenance of Jewish traditions, as in the Stein-

man family. But there appears also to be an inclination to express those values in a life-style and cultural idiom that reflects the non-Jewish heritage of the family as well, at least in some respects. In those intermarried families in which no conversion has taken place, considerably less value is placed on the maintenance of Jewish traditions, as one might expect. Yet even in those families, there is a tendency in a great many cases to include certain Jewish traditions in the life-style of the home, along with such non-Jewish traditions as the celebration of Christmas with Christian relatives, and possibly other Christian holidays and life-cycle events.

One Jewish-Catholic couple—the husband had actually studied for the priesthood before he became an agnostic social worker—used the occasion of their honeymoon to travel to some of the small villages of southern Italy to try to trace the husband's ancestors. Yet this couple's son had a Bar Mitzvah thirteen years later. At the time of our meeting in 1980, their home offered a comfortable display of Italian-Catholic memorabilia; reproductions of Gothic portraits of saints alongside Diane's menorah, a reproduction of Chagall's famous fiddler on the roof picture, and Danny's Hebrew books from which he was studying for his Bar Mitzvah. And Frank—who is a master of Italian cuisine—also did much of the cooking for his son's Bar Mitzvah. Apparently the Leone family also wanted a party in their own image, a Bar Mitzvah with an Italian flavor.

Perhaps one has to be a bit narcissistic to make such casual use of divergent cultural symbols to satisfy one's own sense of the good fit between traditional and personal life-style. But such an invidious psychological label as narcissism is hardly adequate to account for the lingering attachments of contemporary intermarrieds to greater or lesser fragments of their ancestral traditions. Nor are the other explanations of intermarriage as helpful as they once might have been. The proverbial power of love, which popularly accounts for the incidence of intermarriage itself, should have rendered all previous tribal loyalties for naught. Or as Zangwill put it, the melting pot should have so alloyed the couple's traditions that the new amalgam would not betray traces of its origins.

Finally, any understanding of how intermarrieds merge their ancestral traditions with their contemporary life-style must encompass the ways in which modern families, Jewish families especially, incorporate tradition into their lives. After all, the life-styles of all ethnic groups have been greatly influenced by one another, as well as by the general patterns of American culture. Just as "you don't have to be Jewish to love Levy's real Jewish rye bread,"[44] so, too, you don't have to be intermarried to have a Jamaican calypso band at a Jewish wedding or to have kosher Chinese food at a Bar Mitzvah.

At the heart of the matter lies the cardinal principle of modern consciousness: that, in American society as in most other modern societies, the individual enjoys simultaneous membership in a great variety of groups and cliques—from work to community to leisure—and yet is freer from the constraints of any of those memberships than at any previous time in history. But that very freedom impels many to seek linkages with the timeless traditions of their ancestors.

Reading 15   One Style of Dominican Bridal Shower*

ADELE BAHN AND ANGELA JAQUEZ

Unlike American bridal showers, which are used as a means of helping the couple furnish their home, or to give personal gifts to the bride, the Hispanic shower, particularly the Dominican shower, is often the means of socialization for the bride in her future status as wife. Gifts are also presented at the Dominican shower, but gifts are not the primary purpose of the shower. While seemingly frivolous and festive, the customs and activities at showers reveal serious content when analyzed for their underlying meaning—content that reflects the norms and values of society and societal expectations about the young woman about to make the transition from fiancée and bride to wife.

One important factor in Dominican culture is the Roman Catholic church, but just as important are the historical ties with Spain (and thence

*Bahn, Adele and Angela Jaquez. 1988. "One Style of Dominican Bridal Shower." Pp. 131–146 in *The Apple Sliced: Sociological Studies of New York City,* edited by Vernon Boggs, Gerald Handel and Sylvia Fava. Prospect Heights, IL: Waveland Press. Reprinted by permission of the editors.

METHODOLOGICAL NOTE: The research reported here was done through observation of bridal showers and interviews with guests, former guests, and women who had given showers.

Seven showers were attended in New York City; the brides were in the age range 19–22. Information was obtained on thirty-two additional showers through open-ended interviews in Spanish with fifty women who described showers they had given or attended in New York City or in the Dominican Republic. The interviews took place, in groups of up to eight women at a time, over coffee or tea in the junior author's apartment. The women were primarily of Dominican background, but some were of Puerto Rican, Cuban, San Salvadoran, or Colombian origin. Invitations to the showers and introductions to the women interviewed were obtained through a "snowball sample."

Our research process illustrates some special approaches needed to study ethnic phenomena in the city to which access is limited by language, sex, and age. The senior author had studied earlier the changes and continuities in the status of American brides, through a content analysis of United States bridal magazines from 1967 to 1977, the decade of the women's movement; British, French, and Italian bridal magazines were also examined. The analysis covered family patterns, marriage customs, sex roles, sexual behavior, birth control and family planning, consumption patterns, images of the wedding, prescriptions for wifehood, concepts of beauty, and symbols and images of the wedding. This provided a framework for the study of Dominican bridal showers in New York City. The senior author participated in some of the interviews when sufficient conversation was in English.

The junior author, a graduate student in sociology, is Dominican in background, bilingual, and in her 20s, characteristics that enabled her to attend the showers and conduct the interviews. She was able to establish rapport and believes that the events and conversations were not significantly affected by her presence. Rarely was she treated as an "outsider," although on one occasion the participants deliberately did not share with the researcher their pornographic pictures and written jokes. In most instances events at the showers were tape recorded and photographed. The interviews were also recorded, transcribed, and later translated into English.

with Arab culture); these underlie Dominican culture and translate into two basic values that are paramount in the coming nuptials: virginity for the woman and *machismo* (a culturally specific type of virility or manliness) for the man. These values are interrelated and in fact are the reason for the socialization at the shower.

The young woman is expected to be a virgin when she marries. Although some norms are changing, this remains an important one. She is expected to be innocent, virginal, and inexperienced. Although more freedom is allowed her here in this country, and although it varies from one Hispanic culture to another, virginity remains the ideal. Therefore, the shower functions as an introduction and socialization for the bride to a number of her future roles, particularly the sexual role.

> One is therefore led to think that most of these rites whose sexual nature is not to be denied and which [are] said to make the individual a man or woman or fit to be one—fall into the same category as certain rites of cutting the umbilical cord, of childhood, and of adolescence. These are rites of separation from the sexual world, and they are followed by rites of incorporation into the world of sexuality, and in all societies and all social groups, into a group confined to persons of one sex or the other. This statement holds true especially for girls, since the social activity of a woman is much simpler than that of a man. [1]

SOCIAL FUNCTIONS OF THE SHOWER

The primary functions of the shower had to do with socialization, socialization to at least four roles that are components of the wifely status in traditional Dominican family life. These are (1) the role of a woman among women, (2) the sexual role, (3) the homemaker role, and (4) the subservient role of the female in the marital relationship. The socialization is both implicit and explicit.

A Woman among Women

The shower itself is attended only by women (although often men are invited to come in at the end of the shower, at which time it becomes a party with music, drinking, and dancing). However, what has happened before the men arrive is kept secret from them, and all sexual decorations and related materials will have been removed.

The women are dressed in their best. Decorations, food, entertainment, and the order of festivities have been planned by women, usually close friends or relatives of the bride. There are limitations on who is invited. No one who is either too young or too old—or too staid—is invited. Often the mother and older aunts of the bride are not invited because it is felt that such guests would put a damper on the activities; the shower would have to be "too respectable." A number of middle-aged women even denied that this type of shower takes place at all! It seems out of consonance with the continuing norms for women of respectability and sexual innocence and indifference. Only women from about sixteen to thirty-five or forty are present at the showers, with the ages of most guests, as might be expected, clustering around the age of the bride.

Some of the women who plan the shower have a consciousness of tradition and duty to the bride: to inform her of what she needs to know and what is likely to happen to her.

Not all the guests are friends of the bride. Sometimes a woman who is particularly adept at being mistress of ceremonies at the shower, or who is known to have had experience at running showers, is invited even though she may not be a particular friend of the bride or even well known to the organizer of the shower, except by reputation. These women take pride in their ability to invent and create activities and decor and to set the order and sequence of the shower.

There may be a handwritten "book," a collection of dirty jokes, sayings, and tricks that is borrowed and lent for showers. New material that is particularly successful is added to the book and it even travels from New York to the Dominican Republic in the luggage of guests invited to showers there. The essence of the book is that it is shared lore passed from women to women. Some of the respondents referred to the "dirty papers" that are part of the collection (for example, the "Memorandum" set forth a little later in this essay). However, some of the women who are particularly adept at organizing showers took pride in *not* using such materials. They felt they were experienced and creative enough not to need it.

Learning the Sexual Role

The Dominican-Spanish term for "bridal shower" is *"despedida de soltera,"* which is literally translated, "Good-bye to singlehood." It is a ceremony that rarely takes place earlier than two weeks prior to the marriage ceremony and is planned by the closest friends of the bride-to-be or her relatives but not by her parents.

Formal invitations are rarely used since the planners prefer to invite the bride-to-be's friends by word of mouth. This gives them the opportunity to make suggestions about bringing something that is sexually explicit, which will embarrass the bride.

The planners make arrangements to decorate the living room of the apartment where the shower will take place either on a Friday or Saturday evening. An umbrella is affixed to a decorated chair, which is usually placed in the corner of the room. Often pornographic pictures taken from magazines are taped on the walls around the chair. The scenes they depict are both conventional and unconventional, and a number of postures are shown. The balloons that may decorate the room turn out, on closer inspection, to be condoms, blown up and tied to hang satirically from the ceiling and walls.

For the New York shower, special items may have been bought in Times Square sex shops: a plastic banana that, when opened, reveals a pink plastic penis in a constant and impossible state of erection; or a "baby pacifier" that turns out to be a tiny penis.

The refreshments may consist—besides the cakes and sandwiches prepared by friends and relatives of the guest of honor—of sausage and hot dogs arranged to look like the male sex organs and served to the guest of honor. Sometimes a root vegetable, *yautia,* which resembles a long potato, is arranged and decorated with corn silk and two small potatoes to resemble male genitalia. The vegetables are hairy and exaggerated and may also be smeared with condensed milk and ketchup or tomato paste to symbolize the semen and blood that are expected to flow on the bride's wedding night.

The guests arrive at least thirty minutes before the bride-to-be is brought in. While waiting for her, the guests engage in a lively discussion about their first night's experience. When they suspect that she is at the door, they get together in the center of the room and turn off the lights. When she enters, she is surprised. Sometimes one of the guests throws a glass of water on her, which is supposed to give her good luck. From the doorway she is led to the decorated chair, where she remains for the rest of the ceremony. As the shower continues, the bride-to-be is prepared and informed about her future roles as a wife. This includes the giving of gifts that underline her role as a housewife. She is expected to be a virgin and sexually unknowledgeable, and these expectations color the rest of the ceremony. It is also expected that she will blush and show embarrassment, horror, and astonishment at the "dirty jokes," "red tales," and "fresh tricks" that follow.

A "corsage" made of stockings in the shape of male genitalia is pinned to the bride's bosom. A dildo, sausage, or plastic hot dog may also be used. She may be forced to eat the sausage or to keep the plastic effigy in her mouth, She may be undressed to her underwear and told to put on a "baby doll" nightgown.[2] A vibrator may be used on her breast and intimate parts but no penetration occurs. The bride is shown pictures of a variety of sexual scenes and told that this is what she may expect—that this could happen to her, that she must be ready and supply "anything he wants." Typically, one of the participants is dressed like a man and imitates the groom's actions on the wedding night. If no one dresses as a man, a dildo is tied around the waist of one of the guests and this "male impersonator" "attacks" the bride. The dildo is rubbed on her face and all over her body. Aside from these overt "sexual" acts, there are guests who give her "tips" about how to please a man sexually, such as how to perform fellatio successfully.

One respondent tells of a woman dressed as a man with a dildo attached, who jumped out of the closet and enacted a rape scene. The respondent, at whose bridal shower this had occurred, claimed that it had been a valuable experience in that it had "prepared" her for her wedding night, which had been "rough." But because of these scenes, some of the guests protest that they "don't *ever* want a shower."

At any time during the shower, any of the participants can draw the bride-to-be's attention and tell her a "red joke" or read a litany to her. Litanies are anonymously written poems that use pseudonyms for the saints and contain a great deal of vulgarity. A popular litany that is used at showers both here and in the Dominican Republic is called "A Virgin's Bedside Prayer." The main character of this litany, who is sup-

posed to be the bride-to-be, asks the saints for a man who will be sexually satisfied by her.

Double-entendres are popular at the showers. The following example was obtained from a respondent and had been translated from the Spanish.

MEMORANDUM

For the ultimate goal of maintaining the high standard of social hygiene in our city, the Honorable City Mayor along with the City Council have decreed the following:

TO ALL LOVERS AND COUPLES

As of the 16th September 1980, the Mayor and City Council in a unanimous decision have declared that all lovers and couples caught in a theater, movie, park, beach, street or avenue, empty building or even in an alleyway, committing such acts as mentioned below, will be punished to the fullest extent of the law and fined accordingly:

1. *With the hand on the thigh......$ 5.00*
2. *With the hand on the thing.....$10.00*
3. *With the thing in the hand......$15.00*
4. *With the thing in the mouth....$20.00*
5. *With the mouth on the thing...$25.00*
6. *With the thing in the thing......$30.00*
7. *With the thing inside
    the thing $35.00*
8. *With the thing on the thing.....$40.00*
9. *With the thing in the
    front of the thing $45.00*
10. *With the thing behind
    the thing $50.00*

For those who are curious about what "the thing" means:

a. *It is not a bat, but it lives most of the time hanging down.*
b. *It is not an accordion; however, it shrinks and stretches.*

c. It is not a soldier, but it attacks in the front and in the back.

d. It does not think, but it has a head.

e. It is not attractive; however, occasionally it's called "beautiful."

f. It is not analgesic, but it can be used as a tranquilizer.

g. It is not a palm tree, but it has nuts.

h. It does not belong to any club or organization; however, it's known as a member.

i. It does not produce music, but is called an organ.

j. It is not a gentleman, but it will stand up for ladies.

Any comments made by the bride-to-be during the shower are recorded or written down by one of the participants. At the end of the shower they are either read aloud or played back for the couple in a private room. The comments that she makes during the ceremony are interpreted sexually. For example, she may be forced to place her finger in a glass of ice cubes for a long time, and she may cry out, "Please take it out!" By this comment, it is understood that she will be saying the same thing to the groom on her wedding night.

Typically, home-made snacks and refreshments are served while the ceremony goes on. As the climax of the shower, the bride is told to open the gifts that she has received. The gifts consist of kitchen utensils, linen, porcelain figurines, and personal items such as nightgowns. When she opens them, she is expected to thank each donor individually and to exhibit the gifts so that the others can see what she has received. Afterward, her best friend helps her to change into her street clothes.

The role of the bride-to-be at the shower is very clear, underscoring the appropriateness of her reaction to the sexual aspects of the proceedings. She is expected to scream and show horror and surprise. The response of the girl is scripted and socially prescribed. She is expected to cry and scream to be let go, and to beg for her mother to rescue her. She is expected to be modest and maidenly. Should the bride not show the proper surprise and horror, the order of festivities changes. The tricks stop and the shower becomes more conventional.[3] Such a bride is believed by many to be perhaps "experienced" and not a virgin.

If a girl is pregnant or is known to have had sexual experience, the shower takes on a more conventional form. There are gifts and some joking, but it is mild. Interestingly, some of the respondents admit that the original purpose of the shower, to socialize and educate for sex and for the anticipated first night, may not be as necessary as before.[4] Still, they feel that it should be done "for the fun of it"—for the sociability.

Homemaker Role

The women at the older edge of the age range who are attending the shower may have a different socializing purpose. Although Dominican girls are taught from an early age to cook and perform domestic tasks at home, it was the duty of the older women at the showers, especially in the Dominican Republic, to give advice on the care of house and husband, particularly the presentation of food and the treatment of the husband in terms of comfort. They may propose the ironing of sheets, for example. Their gifts are more likely to have some relationship with cleaning and housekeeping.

At the showers observed, there was very little discussion of the housekeeper role, but participants at showers in the Dominican Republic mention that it is still a component there. In the Dominican Republic the future bride is advised to talk with her future mother-in-law in order to find out what the future husband likes or dislikes, especially with regard to food. Along similar lines, she is advised to clean the house well, particularly the bedroom and bathroom since these are the two rooms that men use the most. She is advised to serve his meals properly and make sure that he has everything he needs at the table, including toothpicks, napkin, and cold water. She is also told that she should keep herself well groomed in order to hold his interest in her as a woman. She should be tolerant, kind, understanding, show him compassion, and be sweet all the time. This type of premarital conversation with the future mother-in-law does not seem to take place in this country.

The Subservient Status of Women

The marriage is said to be in the bride's hands. She is said to be solely responsible for its success and for the happiness and comfort of her husband. Traditionally, she was dependent upon him for financial and emotional support. It will be her fault if the marriage breaks up. The woman internalizes these norms and is expected to conform. If the man leaves, it is believed that she was responsible. If he strays, that is to be expected: it is "natural" for a man to have others. And as for nagging, or even mentioning the man's misbehavior, that is worse than anything he may do. The proper role is for a wife to act even more loving and understanding.

The internalization of these values is associated with the concept of machismo,[5] the superiority of the male over the female in every area. A frequent theme is the wife's inadequacy as a sexual partner. If the husband is unfaithful and needs an excuse, or is impotent, or feels some dissatisfaction, it is her fault. Her vagina is too big rather than that he is an inept lover. The size of the women's vagina is believed to be critical to the sexual satisfaction of both. She may be told to use ointments that will shrink her vagina temporarily before having sex. The size of the vagina is a subject of conversation among the girls and women and a good deal of anxiety is reflected in the conversation and jokes. There is little acknowledgment that the clitoris is the primary area of female pleasure and that more expert manipulation or adjustment might make sexual satisfaction a reality for both. Blaming the size of the vagina allows the man to say that it is the woman's fault for being "so big"—and she, internalizing his perspective, agrees.

Some respondents speak of the old days in the Dominican Republic when, in the event proof of virginity was lacking, the wife could be sent back to her parents. One respondent, whose husband trained as a physician in the Dominican Republic, notes that even recently operations have been performed, primarily on upper-middle-class women who might have had sexual experience, to restore their hymen or to at least make penetration seem difficult. Another respondent, who was a virgin at the time of her marriage ten years ago but did not bleed, notes that her husband (who is not a Dominican) still mentions it and that it is the last word in any argument they have.

The concept of *machismo* is broader than explicit sexual relations. It also covers the wife's contact with men and women in general. Under the rules of *machismo*:

1. No males are allowed to visit a woman when her husband is not at home.
2. She is not allowed to "hang out" with a group of friends.
3. She is to restrict her friendship to females.
4. She should not be too friendly with others of either sex.

Many jokes told at the shower are forms of reactions to *machismo*. Most jokes are antimale and tend to fall into two categories. The first has to do with sexual inadequacy on the part of the husband. The second has to do with his cuckoldry. In both cases, the women may be expressing the laughter of the oppressed. The jokes are a way to say that which is unsayable, that there is an unequal distribution of power.

The jokes constitute an ideological attack on a system, and make manifest another ideology: that the weaker one may also have a weapon; that "he" is not so powerful after all and "she" may have a weapon at her disposal. The antimale joke that follows has been translated from the Spanish:

APARTMENT FOR RENT

A prosperous businessman propositioned a prostitute, and she agreed to spend the night with him for the sum of five hundred dollars. When he departed the following morning, he told her that he didn't carry money with him, but he would tell his secretary to send a check with the indication that the check was for renting an "apartment." On the way to his office, he felt that the "program" did not warrant the fee and was not worth the amount agreed upon, and for that reason he ordered his secretary to send a check for two hundred dollars with the following note:

Dear Mrs.:
I am sending you a check for the renting of your apartment. I am not sending the amount agreed upon because when I rented your apartment, I was under the impression

1. That it had never been used;
2. That it had heat; and
3. That it was small.

But last night, I noticed that it had been used, that it did not have heat, and that it was excessively big.

The prostitute had hardly received the note before she sent back the check with the following note:

Dear Sir:
I am sending back your check of two hundred dollars, since I do not under-

stand how you can have imagined that such a pretty apartment would not have been previously occupied. In reference to the heat, I want to tell you that you didn't know how to turn it on, and as for the size, I am not at fault that you did not have sufficient household goods to fill it.

ETHNIC ADAPTATION IN THE BRIDAL SHOWER

In New York City, the Dominican bridal shower appears in two forms, the "pure" Dominican shower and the American-Dominican shower. A "pure," shower is characterized by Dominican hospitality and warmth shown to people in general. The Dominican tendency to share, to talk, to open themselves up makes everyone feel at home. Fewer commercially purchased items are used. For decorations, pictures taken from pornographic magazines are usually used. The dildoes are all homemade rather than bought in sex-item stores. The snacks and refreshments are personally served and the souvenirs are individually pinned on the guests. This is not always true at American-Dominican showers.

The language spoken at the "pure" Dominican showers is Spanish, whereas at the American-Dominican one, bilingualism is quite prevalent. Here the guests are found forming little social groups who chatter among themselves. They also help themselves to the snacks and refreshments. The difference, it appears, is that the "pure" shower is more strongly characterized by collectivism, while the American adaptation reflects more individualism.

The Americanized bride-to-be seems to show less shock and astonishment at the goings-on than does the "pure" Dominican bride, whose reaction is very strong, spontaneous, and full of tears. The sexually explicit material that is shown her often brings about refusals to look at or to participate in the acts. However, the American-Dominican bride-to-be responds less dramatically and seems to enjoy it all. This "take-it-on-the-chin" attitude of the Americanized bride seems to be the result of having been exposed to much more sexual information, either in school, at work, on television, or at the movies.

Another important distinction between American-Dominican showers and their "pure" counterparts is the integration of different ethnic features in the ceremony. There is a considerable influence of Puerto-Rican and Cuban culture in some showers held in New York City, whether they are "pure" or American-Dominican. This is illustrated by the types of litanies and dirty poems read at the showers. Most of the vulgar words used to describe sexual organs and acts are slang from Puerto Rico or Cuba. For example, the word "*pinga*" is Cuban slang for "penis" and "*chocha*" is a Puerto Rican slang word for "vagina." The Dominican immigrants have learned the words through social interaction with other Hispanic groups domiciled in the city. In fact, many Dominican males were nicknamed "*Chicho*" at home, but are not called that here, since for Puerto Ricans it is the slang word for "sexual intercourse." As has already been noted, vulgarity is not commonly used by Dominican women, but is quite acceptable and indeed pertinent at the showers in both countries.

The showers are rapidly being affected by the technology of modern society. The tape recorder is taking the place of written notes; the film projector is beginning to replace the sex education "classes" held at most ceremonies; and cameras are being used to record these events. This is happening not only here, but also in the Dominican Republic, probably introduced there by Dominican immigrants who travel constantly between the two places.[6]

CONCLUSION

Exploration of the showers suggests that they might be a good indicator of the degree of assimilation to American values of marital egalitarianism, even allowing for class differences within the Dominican family structure, particularly in New York but also perhaps in the Dominican Republic.[7] It used to be that "*New Yorkinas*"— girls who grew up in or came to New York— were seen to be on the track of a loose life: corrupted somehow, nonvirginal, or at least on the way to being that way. But the true "corruption" may be nonacceptance of the traditional subservient role, a major change that immigration has brought. There is a continuous exchange between the Dominican Republic and Dominicans in New York. People go back and forth. When they first came here, the old norms remained strong at first. But changes in the family structure having to do with economic and social life here in New York have changed some of the norms and have at least made others the focus of conflict.

Both men and women work here in New York. In fact, the employment opportunities for women in factories and the garment district may be better than for men. More women go to school than men. Many young women serve as the brokers for their families, dealing with city officials and social agencies and thus gaining experience and autonomy. The broker role, traditional for men in the Dominican Republic, serves here to give women power in their families; but it may also cause conflicts. For example, a woman's fiancée may retain the traditional values of Dominican family life, even though he may be earning no more than she and may be less educated. The shower, whether reflecting old or new norms, prescribes and reinforces some of the traditional roles for the bride. But she, while enjoying the attention her friends are paying her, may be making an adjustment that will not necessarily be helpful to her in her new status as a married woman in a family structure that is in flux. Changes in the social context in which the marriage will be embedded, as well as the urban environment in which she lives, require education, independence, and aggressiveness on the part of both men and women.

A CASE STUDY: MARIA'S SHOWER

José and Maria, who met at a party in Upper Manhattan, have now been going out for eight months. Their relationship had to be approved by Maria's parents, who ultimately agreed that José could visit her regularly at her home. Since they decided to have a steady relationship, it was expected that a formal engagement would follow. José bought Maria an engagement ring and presented it to her in front of her parents. Their next step was to set up a wedding date. Maria decided to get married in spring. Maria's friends and relatives were anxious to learn the exact date of the wedding. Her best friend and her future sister-in-law wanted to give her a shower. They felt that it would be good for her to participate in one, since it would be a time for her to have fun with all her friends before she got married. Two weeks prior to the wedding, the word was spread, at her job, at the church, at the local bodega, and throughout the neighborhood that she was going to have a shower. Nobody was supposed to reveal to Maria that such an event was being planned for her. It could not take place at her home because the preparations might make her suspicious. It would no longer be a surprise, as it is supposed to be. Her best friend offered her apartment in Washington Heights (Manhattan), which she and two other friends cleaned and decorated, particularly the living room. On a Saturday evening in March, one week before the wedding, the shower was held. When the planners invited other friends, they suggested that they bring dirty jokes, "fresh" gifts, and anything else that would amuse and embarrass the bride-to-be. They divided up the work, and two women made kipper and pastelitos; these were the snacks that would be served at the shower along with Pepsi-Cola and orange soda.[8]

One hour before the shower everything was ready. During this time, the guests, all females, arrived and awaited the bride-to-be's entrance at seven o'clock. Thirty-four well-dressed women of all ages, most of them in their twenties, were present at the ceremony. However, one young girl fifteen years of age was in attendance. The living room contained a decorated chair with an umbrella placed above it, a wishing well, and a table with an elaborately decorated pink cake on it. Under the chair was a tape recorder. On the wall were pornographic pictures of nude white men and women with abnormally large genitalia and of couples engaged in various stages of sexual intercourse. In the center of these pictures, a large home-made penis had been placed. It was made by one of the participants out of a nylon stocking and paper. (The woman who made it is Cuban; she stated that she loved to go to bridal showers.) Next to the cake was a doll dressed in pink with a hot dog on its head.

All of the participants were from Latin America. They began discussing their own experiences on their wedding nights. A Dominican said that she almost died of a heart attack when she saw her husband naked for the first time: "He had a big member." Another participant replied, "It's quality not quantity that counts." Some of the women admitted that they were afraid on their wedding night, and others said that they were anxious to find out what it really was like to have sex for the first time. All of the participants engaged in this type of conversation.

At the moment of the bride-to-be's arrival, one of the women said, "She's coming. Silent! Quiet!" There was a lot of tension in the air, as people tried to decide where to place themselves so as to completely surprise the bride. The light was turned off. One of the women was standing in the middle of the room with a glass of water in her hands. When the bride appeared in the doorway, the water was thrown in her face and everyone shouted, "Surprise!" The bride covered her face and began to cry. She said, "José and I have an appointment with the priest right now, but I guess that we will have to go another day."

Everyone was speaking Spanish, telling jokes, and generally having fun. The only words spoken in English were "Okay" and "Nice." A young woman took the penis from the wall and pinned it on the bride as a corsage. The bride-to-be begged, "No, please. It's ugly!" The woman replied, "You have to wear it because from now on, you're always going to have one chasing you and following you around." Another woman asked the bride to put it into her mouth. She refused to do so. Another woman took it and forced it into Maria's mouth. "There's nothing to be afraid of! Just be a good girl. This is harmless in comparison to what you're marrying." Another person asked, "Do you like it the way it is—hard like a rock?" Whenever the bride touched it, other women would say, "Oh, look how she caresses it. I knew you were going to like it."

One woman took a glass filled with ice and forced the bride's finger into it. She had to keep her finger in it until it hurt so that she could beg and scream for them to stop, saying things like, "Please stop doing this to me. I hate you. Are you crazy or something? I didn't know you were going to do this to me." Meanwhile, everything she was saying was being recorded. This was later played back for the groom at the shower's end. The women then said to him, "Listen to all the things she's going to say to you on your wedding night."

A woman picked up a penis that she had made from the protective rubber of her sewing machine and dropped it in Maria's lap, saying, "This thing loves to be between legs. You have to get accustomed to it." Another woman said, "Do you know which number is going to be your favorite? You mark my words, it will be sixty-nine." Another participant showed Maria a red baby-doll nightgown and told her, "Come on and put it on! Take off your panty-hose." Maria seemed surprised and said, "I am okay in my

dress." A woman told her, "No, you have to wear the gown, now." Two women helped her to undress and to put on the nightgown while others applauded and commented, "She is going to look good. Not bad! You're going to drive him crazy. Sexy. That's the way he wants you." A woman picked up the home-made dildo and quickly rubbed it on the bride-to-be's vulva. Another young woman who was standing up said to her, "I am going to show you the woodpecker style, but you have to be drunk to do it." She stuck her tongue in and out and said, "Pick, pick, with the tip of your tongue. Touch his ass simultaneously right in the hole." Everyone laughed, and the bride-to-be, although laughing with them, was amazed. A woman in her late thirties approached Maria, who said to the women, "Look, auntie, what these women are doing to me." Her aunt smiled at her and another woman stood up and said, "Listen to Maria's prayer. She used to say this prayer every night before she met José." A litany was read aloud and everyone laughed at each sentence. The name of the litany was "A Virgin's Bedside Prayer." After the litany had been read, the reader asked the bride-to-be, "Is this true? No, don't answer because we know it's true." Maria told them that they were "a bunch of fresh women." She was beginning to feel more comfortable. Meanwhile a copy of *Playgirl* magazine was being passed around and the women made jokes about the naked men, the size of their penises, etc. Suddenly, someone cried out, "José is coming!" Immediately, a young woman impersonating a man walked in. Everyone began to laugh. She had a home-made penis hanging from the zipper of her pants. She came up to the bride and wiped the penis across her face. Then she took Maria's hand and made her squeeze the penis. "This is yours, my love." Laughing, the bride pushed her away. Then the young girl with the "penis" began chasing all the women in the room. Everyone was having fun.

A native of Colombia had brought a film projector along to show some X-rated films. Everyone sat on the floor and the first film was shown. It was about two women engaged in a homosexual relationship. Most of the women protested and one of them said, "We don't want to see homosexuals. We want to see the real thing." Finally, the woman changed the film. Another woman said to Maria, "Pay attention, Maria!" The film showed two women engaged in various sexual acts with a man who was in a bathtub. Someone said to Maria, "You have to be ready to do it anywhere at anytime, Maria." The film showed the man ejaculating, and someone said to the bride, "Look at all that milk. You have to get accustomed to it. And look at how vulnerable a man can be when he comes!" The film ended and the kipper and pastelitos were served to the guests by two of the women in attendance.

At the time that this was happening, a thirty-five-year-old Dominican woman was giving Maria advice and telling her to wear something blue, something old, and something new on her wedding day for good luck. (It is part of the Dominican folklore to do this.) Two young women suggested that she should start opening her gifts. The first gift that she opened was a table set. Then she opened a box containing kitchen utensils and other boxes containing bathroom towels, an automatic broom, a nightgown, etc. On the whole, the gifts were household gifts, mainly items for use in the kitchen or bathroom. (There seemed to be a great deal of curiosity about who brought which gift.) The bride thanked everyone for their gifts and at 10 P.M. she was helped into her street clothes and prepared for the arrival of José. Then someone said to her, "Maria, guess who's here?" José shook hands with all the women and some of the male relatives, who came in when it was clear that the shower had ended. No one discussed what had gone on during the shower and at 11 P.M. everyone went home, including the bridal couple.

ACKNOWLEDGMENTS

The authors would like to thank Carmen Salcedo and Altagracia Mejia for the initial invitations and Vernon Boggs for his encouragement of the study.

6   Sexuality, Intimacy, and Power

Reading 16   Politics and Politesse: Gender Deference and Formal Etiquette*

PEARL W. BARTELT, MARK HUTTER, AND DAVID W. BARTELT

In the persistently hierarchical relationship between men and women, the mechanisms of control range from the wage-scale to the legal system, and from expressly sexist regulations to verbal forms of disapproval and censure. In this catalog of controls, the etiquette handbook plays a significant role. At once both an arbiter to social propriety and a guide to attaining a mystical ideal of perfect domestic order, these handbooks have played, and continue to play, a significant part in developing a gender-specific behavioral ideal for women. In this paper, we report the results of an analysis of these handbooks, and argue that these works both describe "proper" behavior for women and delimit those situations within which women should appear, and in what roles. They describe, in short, the deferential behavior necessary for women to move in an acceptable fashion in a male-dominated social structure.

The prescription of deferential behavior for women by women could be analyzed as another example of simple adaptation to structural inequality, with etiquette books providing the guidelines for "getting by," as it were. While a part of this may well be accurate, we have chosen to focus on a different aspect of the hand-book. We feel that these handbooks provide an excellent example of what Mills (1940) termed "situated actions and vocabularies of motive." That is, these handbooks provide a case in which normative structures become part of a vocabulary of motives which rationalize and defend deferential behavior as it occurs. Thus, etiquette handbooks, while playing an important structural role in the persistence of male-female hierarchies, also have an interactional meaning within the day-to-day behavior of women who defer to a male-ordered world.

As can be expected, we have addressed this analysis from the specific theoretical perspective of symbolic interactionism. We have also borrowed from the fields of literary criticism and hermeneutics in our attempt to analyze a deeper structure of etiquette texts. We feel that the symbolic interactional perspective, while traditionally astructural and ahistorical in nature (Meltzer, Petras, and Reynolds 1975), has shown a marked facility for interpreting the internal dynamics of a social relationship. There have been, in fact, attempts to broaden the perspective with analyses of face-to-face inequality (Goffman 1956), social definitions reflective of superordinate positions (Blumer 1958), and external status identifiers (Braroe 1970; Stone 1970, pp. 256–59). Work focusing on gender inequality is also present in Goffman's (1977) analysis of sexual "arrangements."

We assume in this paper that there is a persistent structural inequality involved in the social relationships between males and females. We examine here a major component of that inequality—the development of formal rules of conduct (etiquette) which provide a ready-made, and standardized, vocabulary of motives for major social situations which persistently involve women as major actors. These rules of etiquette, we assert, have inherent in them a subordinating status. These rules, further, are persistent through time—they make the subordination of women a historical feature of multiple situations, transcending any specific situation and any specific rule. Perhaps most significantly, they make the subordinate status of women an integral part of the social definition of propriety.

THE HISTORICAL CONTEXT

The Industrial Revolution shattered the domestic economy where work and family activities were integrated in the household. The rise of industrial and monopolistic capitalism separated men and women into two isolated worlds: the world of work and the world of the household. This had the effect of separating the life of the husbands from the intimacies of everyday domestic activities and estranging them from their wives and children. Economic factors coincided with a misguided Victorian partriarchialism that saw economic employment as a threat to womanly virtue and to her physical and emotional well-being (Hutter 1981).

Nineteenth-century Victorian society was organized in such a way that it heightened the dichotomy between private and public, domestic and social, female and male. Through the restrictions of the conjugal family, women tended to be

relegated to the domestic sphere. Yet, when the society placed values on men's and women's work, the tendency was to place greater value and higher priority on the public work associated with men rather than the domestic work associated with women.

Engels in his *The Origin of the Family, Public Property and the State* ([1884] 1972) was quick to point out the alienating character of women's domestic work. The gradual loss of women's economic independence led to an increased division of labor between men and women and to the subservience of women to men. Engels spells out the implications of the development of the "privatization of the family" for women:

> *her being confined to domestic work now assured supremacy in the house for man; the woman's housework lost its significance compared with the man's work in obtaining a livelihood; the latter was everything, the former an insignificant contribution . . . (Engels, [1884] 1972 p. 152)*

The privatization of the family with its withdrawal from economic and community activities led to the development of inequality within the family. This inequality was based on the sexual differentiation of labor. In the private sphere, this differentiation was encouraged by the admonitions placed on women to cease work and take almost exclusive care of small children and to sacrifice their career aspirations to those of their husbands. In the public sphere, in addition to women's forced withdrawal from the marketplace and the work force, urban public places and facilities were designed, for the most part, to inhibit or discourage women's participation in them. Normative strictures supported the social and legal constraints to perpetuate the assignment of women to the domestic, private sphere. They justified the almost exclusive involvement of men in the higher valued and higher status activities of the public sphere. The role of etiquette books in the articulation of these normative strictures is the focus of this paper.

THEORETICAL ELEMENTS: SYMBOLIC INTERACTIONISM MEETS SEXUAL POLITICS

Most interactionist treatments of non-native aspects of behavior refer back to Goffman's basic essays "On Face Work: An Analysis of Ritual Elements in Social Interaction" (1955) and "The Nature of Deference and Demeanor" (1956), in which he is concerned with rules of conduct. Rules of conduct are seen as guiding behavior in two ways: as obligations they provide moral constraints on an individual's behavior; and as expectations they provide information on the behavior of others also guided by those constraints. Thus, rules of conduct are mutual and reciprocal and provide operational guidelines for participants' behaviors in social interaction.

Goffman delineates two types of rules of conduct—that between "substance" and "ceremony." Substantive rules which guide conduct are expressed in law, morality, and ethics while ceremonial rules which guide conduct are expressed in etiquette. Goffman focuses his attention on the rules of etiquette, applying what Lindesmith, Strauss, and Denzin (1977, pp. 398–403) refer to as an "interactional loss" analysis of human interaction. That is, the participants of the interaction are concerned with assuring the regularity and order of the interaction and the maintenance of "face" or self-esteem of the participants.

Norms, or the concept of normative structures, have always been troublesome elements in theories accounting for structured social relationships—particularly ones based on conflict or inequality. Put briefly, norms are not always consistent, not always followed, and not always applied, and are seldom clear-cut and unambiguous. The concept implies, then, a structure of power and enforcement for the development, application, interpretation, and change of norms. Further theoretical problems arise when one adopts an interactionist approach, which makes the individual's adherence to social norms problematic rather than automatic. Mills, in an early article, presents one resolution of this issue, adopted as well by Lindesmith et al. (Mills 1940; Lindesmith et al. 1977, p. 275). Mills begins with the proposition that behavior does not occur in a vacuum, but in a social situation whose parameters are mutually defined by the actors in a situation. Once a situation is understood, the behavior that takes place is symbolically interpreted by the participants according to a vocabulary of motives—a set of explanations of behavior which a person attaches to himself or herself and to others in the situation. Norms are, in the context of this vocabulary, explanations of behavior conforming to some actor or actors' expectations.

Placed within a hierarchical relationship, published codes of conduct, such as etiquette, are best understood as formalized, public statements which explain the deferential behavior of subordinates, both to themselves and others. Etiquette texts provide these vocabularies for social situations which persistently involve women as major actors, and act as a set of authoritative behavioral guideposts on the social landscape. As such, they constitute an accessible indicator of persistence and change in the nature of the relationships of inequality between men and women, as well as viable illustrations of the propriety of subordination.

Goffman (1977) offers an analysis of sexual arrangements which supplements the argument we have developed thus far. He notes, "The sociologically interesting thing about a disadvantaged category is not the painfulness of the disadvantage but the bearing of the social structure on its generation and stability. The issue then, is not that women get less but under what arrangements this occurs and what symbolic reading is given to the arrangement" (1977, p. 307). Goffman considers women as a disadvantaged group with particular distinctions. First, unlike other disadvantaged adult groups women are not sequestered off into entire families or neighborhoods; they are an integral part of the family. But, through their extensive involvements with the family of orientation and the family of procreation they develop ideological commitments with their menfolk which are supportive of the advantaged position of men in society. "Women are ... separated from one another by the stake they acquire in the very organization which divides them" (Goffman 1977, p. 308). Secondly, they are held in high regard. Through ritualized conduct they are defined as being fragile and valuable and consequently they have to be sheltered through the harsher things in life. Here Goffman (1977, p. 311) articulates the importance of the "courtesy" system in expressing this condition:

In terms of what interpersonal rituals convey, the belief (in Western society) is that women are precious, ornamental, and fragile, uninstructed in, and ill-suited for, anything requiring muscular exertion or mechanical or electrical training or physical risk; further, that they are easily subject to contamination and defilement and to blanching when faced with harsh words and cruel facts, being labile as well as delicate. It follows, then, that males will have the obligation of stepping and helping (or protecting) whenever it appears that a female is threatened or taxed in any way,

shielding her from gory, grisly sights, from squeamish-making things like spiders and worms, from noise, and from rain, wind, cold, and other inclemencies. Intercession can be extended even to the point of mediating her contacts with officials, strangers, and service personnel.

Goffman's explicit enumeration of the several ways in which men intervene on women's behalf contains an implicit message as well. The multiple specific instances of male "protection" of women generate, in their very multiplicity, a sense of permanent dependence and subordination.

In a later work, *Gender Advertisements* (1979), Goffman notes the same principle of deference expressed in multiple forms. While predominately a visual text, this work examines the implicit gender deference found in the realm of advertising. The case Goffman makes is fairly straightforward, namely that the advertisement of products reproduces gender inequality in its imagery as a significant aspect of the sales process. Thus, mirroring his earlier analysis, while multiple products are advertised, and multiple forms of body language are catalogued, one must assume that the persistence of male gender dominance in virtually all gender-based advertising represents an idealization of male dominance. (The interested reader is referred to Winter, 1981, for a more systematic treatment of the reading of visual "texts" and the determination of structural relations from them.)

In this paper we wish to examine the rules of etiquette which govern the face-to-face interaction of males and females in everyday life. Etiquette books will be used as our indicator since they provide one systematic source of these rules. Our logic is consistent with that of Sherri Cavan, who states "while all appropriate rules of etiquette are not actualized in all situations at all times, these books can serve at least as a partial codification of the precepts of befitting modes of general conduct" (1970, p. 556). We will be looking at etiquette books written since early in the century to see how the rules of conduct have provided guidelines to regulate that relationship.

In particular, we will focus our attention on the hierarchical characteristics of that relationship and how it is handled in etiquette books. A major component ordering the male-female relationship is the superordinate and subordinate positions; we are interested in how this is articulated in etiquette books.

In etiquette books, the concepts of superordinate and subordinate positions are very interesting because at first glance it often appears that the subordinate is really the superordinate. The potential for confusion occurs if one equates placement on a pedestal as superordinate.

Thus, while etiquette books indicate that men should show deference and respect to women in actuality this is a subterfuge for an underlying reduction in status for women. While they advocate the "benefits" they downplay the inherent inferiority and fail to recognize that they actually limit female options. Games of deference, however, often act to keep someone in their place, namely, in a subordinate position.

Another interesting point is that the books are written for the subordinate. Paradoxically, it becomes the task of the person in this subordinate position to impose the strictures of etiquette upon others. It may be that language implying the superordinate position (respect, deference, etc.) is used to gain cooperation of women. The books themselves may be a contributing factor in the acceptance of this subordinate position.

An additional explanation illustrates why females need the etiquette books and males do not. Daniels (1975, p. 343) states that "Those in the superordinate status will find this structure undergirding their privileged condition natural or even virtually invisible. Those who are below

them are more cognizant of the costs of the system and so are less likely to feel that the system is natural." Since it is not natural for them the women need to be taught etiquette.

Henley and Freeman (1975) have observed that everyday interaction patterns reflect the subordination of women to men and are a fundamental source of social control employed by men against women. Further, by constant repetition these patterns become habitual and are taken for granted; the hierarchical power significance which underlies these patterns becomes obscure:

> *By being continually reminded of their inferior status in the interaction with others, and continually compelled to acknowledge that status in their own patterns of behavior, women learn to internalize society's definition of them as inferior so thoroughly that they are often unaware of what their status is. Inferiority becomes habitual, and the inferior place assumes the familiarity—and even desirability—of home (1975 p. 391).*

Henley and Freeman argue that if women are to fully understand the nature of sexual politics in everyday interactional patterns they must systematically analyze how they are affected by them and how they perpetuate the power and status of men. This same position of the women's involvement in the process is a part of our paper in the examination of etiquette.

Henley, in her later work (1977), discussed nonverbal behavior between males and females that involves power. She examines address, demeanor, posture, personal space, time, touching, eye contact, facial expression, and self-disclosure. Differential gesture behavior between females and males follows the same relationship as gestures between status nonequals, with males following the behavior of the superior and females following the behavior of the subordinate (Henley 1977, p. 181). Indeed, even when women follow patterns to assert dominance (as in the case of eye make-up to increase staring) the assumption of the gesture becomes interpreted sexually rather than as a gesture of dominance.

One of the more interesting techniques employed to show the importance of gesture in subordinate, superordinate positioning of females and males is a set of exercises designed for males by Williamette Bridge (Henley 1977, pp. 143–44). Here men are directed to sit, bend, run, and walk in the fashion appropriate for a female. These kinesics that are appropriate for females are just those postures which connote submission rather than power.

A similar orientation to our study is that of Gordon and Shankweiler (1971) who view marriage manuals in terms of sexual ideology. They note that the traditional definition of ideology refers to a body of beliefs and values which have a legitimating function for the status quo. Ideology tends to support and give substance to the position of dominance of one group over another. Translated into the study of sexual ideology, males are seen as the dominating group with females subservient and subordinate to them.

METHODOLOGY

After presenting the method used in this study we will turn our attention to these etiquette books and see in more illustrative detail how etiquette manuals articulated this sexist ideology. As noted earlier, our areas of concern will be behavior in public places and everyday life, domestic relations, and women and work. The preselection of these categories derived from the perspective that assumes there is a division of major worlds within which women participate—the public arena, the home, and the workplace. (See, for example, Siltanen and Stanworth 1984.)

(It should be noted that while recent etiquette books have dealt with more "modern" conditions, such as single parenting and divorce situations, these areas did not allow for the kind of historical analysis we were concerned with. Clearly, these and many other topics in these texts may prove amenable to a similar analysis. Given our concern with continuity, such a consideration lies outside the purview of this analysis.)

Obviously the etiquette books in the sample covered a large range of materials. We found that the three main areas we had selected were covered in all of the books and consistently addressed male–female relations.

The etiquette books that are in this study form a purposive sample. The books that are presented were collected from a variety of public and academic libraries throughout the Philadelphia–southern New Jersey area. The variety included a large urban university, a private liberal arts college, a four-year state college, a large urban public library, and small county affiliated borough libraries. We felt that this diversity would provide the depth of materials needed for a qualitative analysis of the materials.

These works are an indication of these libraries' current holdings and reflect a variety of historical periods. We selected library holdings since the library historically serves as a reference place for etiquette materials. We systematically extracted anecdotal records from all of the works and selected all etiquette admonition procedures that involved males and/or females specifically. We then selected those items that best illustrated the composite and diversity of all the data for a particular topic.

It was decided that only those books published from the turn of the century to the present would be used. They therefore range from a publication date of 1899 to the present and include one author's continuing updating (Vanderbilt 1957, 1972, 1974).

A HISTORY OF AMERICAN ETIQUETTE BOOKS

A brief overview of the history of American etiquette books beginning within the context of nineteenth-century industrial urban society may be of value here. As we noted at the beginning of this paper, the Industrial Revolution had a profound effect on women. For the mid-nineteenth-century family it meant the separation of men and women into two isolated worlds: the world of work and the world of the household.

In terms of involvement in city life, Victorian partriarchal ideology developed the belief that it would be best for the protection of women that they minimize their contact with it. Women were directed to develop a life comprised solely of concerns centered around the family, the home, and the school. Their contacts with the outside world, particularly economic employment, diminished and they were removed from other community involvements as well. The family's withdrawal from the community was tinged by its hostile attitude toward the surrounding city (Hutter 1983). The city was depicted as a sprawling and planless development bereft of meaningful community and neighborhood relationships. The tremendous movement of a large population into the urban industrial centers was seen to provide little opportunity for the family to form or develop deep or lasting ties with neighbors. Instead the family viewed their neighbors with suspicion and wariness. Exaggerated beliefs developed on the prevalence of urban poverty, crime, and dis-

organization. The perceived chaotic world of the city was countered by the family turning in onto itself—what Karl Marx has described as the privatization of the family.

The effects of urban industrial growth combined with what Barbara J. Berg (1978) has labeled the "women-belle ideal." The tenets of this creed held that women were inferior, that they should be denied access to the institutions of knowledge and given little responsibility. The result was the production of "an anomalous sector of society: the useless lady" (Berg 1978, p. 96). Sheila M. Rothman (1978) makes a similar observation. Rothman (1978, p. 21) argues that the consequence of the technological innovation and urban living for women was to provide them with leisure and to become consumers, not producers, of the new technology. The downtown department store was literally designed for the woman consumer. It was the notable exception that allowed for women's involvement in public urban places (Rothman 1978; Hutter 1983).

Virtuous womanhood was defined in similar ways by ministers, moralists, writers of advice books, and public lecturers as one in which there were distinct and separate tasks and reponsibilities for the sexes. The appropriate sphere for women was nurturance and caretaking. It is interesting to note that both Berg and Rothman see that the role of caretaker and nurturer was eventually extended outside the home to involvement in social welfare groups and agencies. Rothman cites Catherine Beecher, a very influential writer of advice books in the 1860s and 1870s who urged women to obtain "appropriate scientific and practical training for her distinctive profession as housekeeper, nurse of infants and the sick, educator of childhood, trainer of servants and minister of charities" and by so doing they would "develop the intellectual, social and moral powers in the most perfect manner" (1978, p. 22).

Etiquette books played an important role in the socialization process of the Victorian lady. They emphasized the importance of proper modes of acting to socially conscious Americans whether they were part of the upper class or not in the areas of deference, demeanor, and manners.

Arthur M. Schlesinger (1946), in an insightful monograph entitled *Learning How to Behave,* observed that etiquette manuals were published at the rate of five or six a year between 1870 and 1917. Their aim was to instill a more aristocratic style of behavior in the emerging middle classes. They also served to reinforce the "relative duties of superior and subordinate" (Schlesinger 1946, p. 34). A third factor, according to Schlesinger (p. 35), was desire to cultivate and sensitize American people to the social graces which were seen to lag behind their European counterparts.

The emphasis on sophisticated manners led to exhaustive specifications of what to do in every conceivable situation: how high to lift one's skirt when crossing a street ("A lady should gracefully raise her dress a little above her ankle"); when and how to bow ("The head should be bent; a mere lowering of eye-lids, affected by some people, is rude"); how to shake hands (avoid either the "pump handle shake" or the "cold clammy hand" resembling a fish); how and when to write acceptances and re-grets; how to make calls ("The formal call should not exceed fifteen minutes"); what to wear at morning functions, in the afternoon and at the ball or opera; and so on ad infinitum. Little wonder that one mentor proudly remarked that "not even a saint could, from his 'inner consciousness' alone, evolve a conception of the

thousand and one social obser-vances of modern fashionable life."

Esther B. Arestz (1970), in a popular account of etiquette notes that American etiquette books flourished during the first decade of the twentieth century; 71 etiquette books and twice that number of magazine articles were published. However, a significant change characterized these books. No longer did etiquette books claim to be written for "Society." Arestz attributed this to the low regard Americans had for the upper classes. "Society's reputation for vulgar spending and tasteless antics had gone from bad to shocking with millionaires staging dinner parties where guests in formal attire dined on horseback or drank toasts to a monkey as guest of honor" (Arestz 1970, p. 275). The focus of the new etiquette books was generally to improve the manners of middle class America.

After World War I, a major transition occurred in American social values. New wealth generated from the war was accompanied by the rejection of the rigidities of America's Victorian conventions. In addition, Prohibition, the automobile, and movies and radio, all encouraged the development of a more informal relationship between the sexes. These changes became incorporated into etiquette books without changing their basic orientations.

Etiquette books continued to be popular. Schlesinger (1946) reports that from 1918 to 1929 no less than 68 etiquette books were published and an additional 78 were published in the period from 1930 to 1945. The two most influential, Lillian Eichler's (1922) *Book of Etiquette* and Emily Post's *Etiquette: The Blue Book of Social Usage* written in 1922, sold over a million copies in the ensuing years. Schlesinger (1946) believes that their popularity stems from the continued social mobility of the social classes and "the need many earnest souls felt for a steadying hand in a period of bewildering flux in social conventions" (p. 51). The publication of numerous etiquette books has continued since the end of World War II. Amy Vanderbilt's (1957, 1974), *McCall's Magazine's* (1960), and *Vogue's* (1948) and others have been quite popular, as have the continued revised editions of Emily Post's books. Baldrige (1978) has continued Vanderbilt's tradition and Ford (1980) and Martin (1982) have entered the field. Martin, as Miss Manners, has experienced considerable popularity.

While these manuals and others of the same ilk bowed to emerging new attitudes, i.e., women smoking in public, no chaperones, the proper usage of "Ms.," there can still be seen the perpetuation and continuation of traditional social values and particularly of patriarchal ideology. They still maintain the underlying sexist ideology of female subservience. Further, for American women, the rules of etiquette are particularly demeaning. Stemming from the sexist pedestal model of their English counterparts, American etiquette books continue a patriarchal viewpoint from the Victorian era to the present. An unbroken tradition of female subservience most symbolically represented in the restriction of the women to the home in relative isolation and of courtesy based on femininity continues.

The placement of American women on the pedestal has been particularly perfidious. Unlike England where social power frequently accompanied rules of etiquette, no vestige of social power can be claimed or articulated by American etiquette rules.

We have isolated three areas where these rules are most consistent over time; behavior in public places, at work, and in the home. The ubiquity of day-to-day situations contained in these three categories, combined with the significance of everyday interactions in maintaining deference in sexual politics, leads us to argue that etiquette guides contribute significantly to the subordination of women in American society.

BEHAVIOR IN PUBLIC PLACES AND IN EVERYDAY LIFE

David Reisman (see Reisman, Glazer, and Denney 1961) has observed that in societies which are relatively stable, peoples' conformity reflects their membership in particular age groupings, clan and caste groups. Behavior patterns are well established and have endured through a considerable period of time. However, in societies undergoing rapid social change such normative guidelines are inoperative. Etiquette rules are then established to control and regulate the important relationships of life.

In everyday life situations—walking, taking a streetcar, dining in public restaurants, the theater and cultural events, traveling—there arises the necessity to develop rules governing one's behavior and to provide predictability in such relatively anonymous situations. This was particularly true in the United States during the turn-of-the-century period. America was undergoing major social and industrial changes. Cities were expanding at a phenomenal rate. People were moving to urban areas from the rural areas of the South and Midwest. There was an unprecedented wave of immigration from eastern and southern Europe. To control this disparate population in these emerging communities, etiquette manuals were developed as one attempt to teach these norms of conduct and to do so explicitly. This was an attempt to maintain the status quo.

Lyn Lofland (1973) found in a review of etiquette books from 1881 to 1962 that there was a concentration on explicit instructions for public behavior during the earlier period and a gradual decreasing concern with these matters during the later one. This reflects the instability and unpredictability which people felt in the emerging industrial cities in the United States and the growing felt regularities in the cities of the mid-twentieth century. These concerns of the early etiquette books are demonstrated in such topics as:

Street Etiquette: Recognizing friends on the street—Omitting to recognize acquaintances—Shaking hands with a lady—Young ladies conduct on the street—Accompanying visitors...—Conduct while shopping...—Carriage of a lady in public...—Meeting a lady acquaintance...—Riding and Driving... —Travelers and Traveling

These early guidebooks provide the reader with explicit instructions on how to behave in these public places. The general pattern of admonitions revolves around the areas of controlling the relationship of males and females who are strangers to each other. The following ex-cerpts from Lillian Eichler's etiquette book in 1922 is illustrative:

If a women drops her bag or gloves and they are retrieved by a passing man, it is necessary only to smile and say "Thank you." No further conversation is permissible (p. 194).

When a gentleman sees that a woman passenger is having difficulty in raising a window he need feel no hesitancy in offering to assist her. However, the courtesy ends when the window has been raised (p. 224).

Green (1922) reaches a similar position:

A man bowing and joining a woman on the street must ask permission to do so. She is at perfect liberty to gracefully decline (p. 47).

A man may offer his services to a woman in crossing a crowded thoroughfare and should raise his hat

and bow when she is safely over, but should make no comment unless she does so first. He may also offer his assistance in getting on or off a car, raising his hat and bowing without remark (p. 241).

These restrictions on peoples' behavior in public places continues to the present in more recent etiquette books. Boykin (1940, p. 229) states:

A girl traveling alone should be especially reserved with members of the opposite sex. If not her attitude may be misunderstood and she may find herself in a situation she will not enjoy.

And, again, Amy Vanderbilt (1967, p. 167) continues to argue for the control of interaction among strangers in public places:

A man touches his hat but does not look more than briefly at a woman to whom he gives up his seat (in a streetcar). He then stands as far away from her as possible and does not look in her direction.

When we shift our attention to other areas of public life—pedestrian behavior, shaking hands, opening doors, smoking in public, restaurant behavior, women's dress—we see a pattern which continues to be enunciated in contemporary etiquette books. The underlying rationale for this pattern is giving deference to women—opening doors, walking on the outside of sidewalks (to possibly prevent women being littered by splashes from the street or by garbage), asking women for permission to smoke. Underlying these deferential patterns is imputation of women's helplessness and frailty. This is, of course, accompanied by the more subtle but direct premise of women's subservience. This is the price exacted. The following guidelines illustrate this:

SEXUAL TRAFFIC

A man should always give a woman the right of way whenever it is possible, and cross behind her instead of in front of her (Hathaway 1928, p. 35).

Naturally a man always opens a door for a woman. She should draw aside when she is preceding him and permit him to do so. No gentleman is happy walking through a door a woman has opened (Wilson 1940, 18).

A man accompanying a woman "opens the door for her and holds it for her to go through. At a revolving door, he starts it off with a push and waits for her to go through." Also he "allows a woman to precede him, if single file formation is necessary, unless there is some service he can do for her by going first" (Fenwick 1948, p. 29).

Traditionally, a man preceded a woman through a revolving door in order to push the door for her. He was also the first one on the escalator, to be in a position to help the woman on and off. This ritual may still be practiced for form's sake, but if a woman reaches the conveyance first she needn't stand and wait unless she is elderly or is carrying packages and does in fact need help (Ford 1980, p. 60).

Gentlemen, to this very day, walk on the street side of the side-walk, unless they are European gentlemen, in which case they walk to the lady's left. Miss Manners, who can bear the idea that styles of clothing change, but not that the small courtesies of life do, firmly believes that the only reason men do not tip their hats is the same as the reason they no longer smack one another across the face with their gloves when they are angry: They don't have the sartorial equipment (Martin 1982, p. 84).

GREETING RITUALS

Men always shake hands... A woman does not shake hands with a man unless he happens to be an intimate friend. In this case she may offer her hand if she wishes. However, under no circumstances may she ignore the overture should the hand be extended (Gardner and Farren 1937, p. 65).

A man always removes his hat when he meets a woman and keeps it off as long as they stand talking, unless the weather is very bad (Stephenson and Millett 1936, p. 72).

A man kissing a lady on the street—in greeting or farewell (only)—should always remove his hat, no matter what the weather. He should be careful concerning this courtesy even—or perhaps I should say especially with his wife or daughter (Vanderbilt 1974, p. 20).

Men should always stand, and most women prefer to, when being introduced to older people or to high officials. A man always stands when being introduced to another man or a woman, and today at small gatherings more and more women feel comfortable standing when the men stand to be introduced to a newcomer. I think it shows both consideration and a special interest to stand and devote your full attention to someone new. It is not out of place for a woman in a group of women to stand when introduced to someone new (Ford 1980, p. 30).

A gentleman must, in these circumstances, take what he is offered. If it is a hand, shake it. If it is a cheek, kiss it. If it is a pair of lips, kiss it. If it keeps reappearing, it must be re-kissed. Remember that we are talking about a formal, public gesture, and the fact that parts of the body and ways they are used may duplicate private expressions of emotions is irrelevant. Just because gentlemen no longer have the exclusive right to initiate private kissing does not mean that they may now share in the ladies' privilege of initiating—or withholding—public kissing (Martin 1982, p. 79).

COSTUME

Women dress in keeping with their companion, not vice-versa (Hathaway 1928, p. 43).

When a man can't or won't dress for an occasion it is bad taste for the woman who he escorts to be dressed to the hilt, and while I feel a certain informality in entertaining tends to relax us all, it shouldn't relax us so much that we become completely graceless (Vanderbilt 1974, p. 268).

SMOKING

Well-bred women do not smoke when it will make them conspicuous, or when it will embarrass or offend anyone who is with them (Hathaway 1928, p. 43).

A man lights a woman's cigarette first unless there is a high wind, in which case he lights his own first, and his female companion's from his cigarette (Vanderbilt 1974, p. 19).

Underlying all these admonitions is the philosophy of female helplessness, weaknesses, and frailties. Bevans in the 1960 edition of *McCall's Etiquette Book* states that "Man's treatment of women is based on a time when women were considered muscularly (hence mentally) the inferior sex. In return for knuckling under to this attitude of male superiority, women demanded and got many special considerations based on their weaknesses and helplessness. Manners of men toward women are still to a great extent based on this ancient blackmail, although the reason for it has long since been disproven" (Bevans 1960, p. 11). A similar conclusion was reached by Elizabeth Post (1975): "Femininity is still more attractive in a woman than masculine capability and in no way denies the fact that her helplessness is a thing of the past" (Post 1975, p. 156).

We believe that this type of thinking still pervades contemporary etiquette books. The authors of these books fail to see that these deferential patterns are in reality forms of social control which perpetuate and continue the power and superior status enjoyed by men. While it is true that "wiser" people know that women are not weak and helpless and continuation of these patterns for whatever motive—femininity, courtesy, or whatever—when it is solely based on sexual differentiation criteria continues to serve as a common means of social control employed against women. The fixing of these patterns into codified vocabularies defining propriety in inherently inequitous terms, in day-to-day situations, links these definitional processes to the overarching structure of sexual politics—the persistent power differential between the sexes.

DOMESTIC RELATIONS

In the Victorian era there developed a systematic rationale for keeping women in the home. For the upper classes, domestic confinement was seen as essential for women in their societies' role of controlling and regulating social gatherings. As newly rich families began to gain eminence, these families through individual achievement in industry and commerce were supplanting the traditional rich whose positions were based on hereditary and family connections. To govern the social mobility of these new personnel an elaborated formalized society developed.

Influenced by the male dominating patriarchal ideology, women were exhorted to act as guardians of the home; men were exhorted to leave the home for the struggles of the business world, the army, the church, or politics. Women's duties were to regulate and control social gatherings and thus keep order in the ever-changing social scene. However, their sequestration in the home and the confinement of their activities to domesticate and "society" matters occurred at the same time men were expanding their influence and involvement in the new industrial world. This, ultimately, proved disastrous for women's independence and autonomy.

Having woman relegated to the home regardless of training had another disastrous effect. Her individuality and uniqueness are discounted and she is molded into a conforming domestic identity. She is never judged by or allowed to expand on her talents but is judged

instead by her "housewifery." Bem and Bem share this view in their statement that "a women's unique identity determine(s) only the periphery of her life rather than its central core" (1979, p. 34).

The rules governing sexual behavior for women were also paradoxical. The emphasis was on respectability through control of sexual behavior and desire. Victorian women gained status by denying their own sexuality and in treating the Victorian masculine sex drive as sinful. Beliefs in purity and the elaborated etiquette norms which stressed modesty, prudishness, and cleanliness and the rules governing demeanor and appearance served to provide a sense of order, stability, and status in the everyday world. However, it also served to be psychologically stultifying. Further, the placing of woman on the "virginal pedestal" and limiting her involvements to the home and excluding her from the economic sphere served to reinforce the patriarchal ideology. Through idolatry subservience emerged.

This normative pattern carried over to the less affluent classes without the same rationale. Patriarchal ideology—the placing of women on a pedestal—supported this pattern. Men's affairs were primarily in the outside world, where they had to provide the income to support the family. This financial dependency tied with the ideological dependency was effective in keeping women in their place. Etiquette books were the major supports to this philosophy. An examination of their stances over the years reflects this. What changes have occurred in more recent books is a toning down of the more explicit sexist statements to the more subtle form. The most typical assertion is that man is the provider, woman, the domesticator. The following are illustrative:

> *Man is the worker and provider, protector and the law giver; woman is*

the preserver, the teacher or inspirer, and the exemplar (Hale 1899, p. 31).

Man's work is to subdue the earth; women's to take charge of the home, to nourish and bring up children. Woman has her work and her duties but these are neither man's work nor man's duties; and just in proportion as he seeks to impose his own burdens upon her, will he find his own character degraded and debased by so doing (Hale 1899, p. 297).

After listening and looking the most important of a woman's accomplishments is the ability to maintain an intelligent, vivacious conversation with family friends and guests (Hardy 1910, p. 232).

This attitude continues from the 1920s through the 1940s:

There are a few things for girls to remember, too. Avoid the things that show a possessive instinct, such as helping a man with his coat, straightening his necktie, brushing a bit of lint from his coat, or hanging on to his arm in public. Don't call him on the telephone unless it is necessary to change some arrangements you had made with him previously (Stephenson and Millett 1936, p. 119).

The ideal attitude which should underlie all women's manners, express kindness, gentleness, good will, sensitive understanding, self respect and when it is appropriate, deference (Fenwick 1948, p. 33).

Deference is perhaps too strong a word to describe the perfect attitude, but certainly there should be a noticeable deferring on the part of the wife, toward the husband as head of the home (Fenwick 1948, p. 34).

Finally, when we would expect major reformations in the 1960s and 1970s we found none:

Although husbands should try to help with the household chores his wife should, I think, try her best to spare him the too feminine chores—washing the dishes, setting the table, or sweeping the floors (Vanderbilt 1972, p. 648).

Society holds a wife accountable to a large extent for the presence or lack of agreeable attributes in a husband. If his manners are boorish, she is expected to correct them, one way or the other, to help him get ahead. If his clothes are ill-kept and shabby, the fact is usually attributed to his wife's negligence or lack of thrift. If he's blatantly attentive to other women, society asks where his wife has failed—and it may be right (Vanderbilt 1957, p. 47; 1967, p. 511; 1972, p. 647).

There is no place where manners are more important than in marriage. We should all encourage husbands to maintain the traditional gallantry toward us, not so much for our own sakes, but for theirs. It helps a man, I think, to maintain his status at a time when so much—I'm thinking of the independence of women

—threatens him (Vanderbilt 1974, p. 27).

In sum, these manuals and others of the same ilk can be seen as perpetuating and continuing traditional social values and particularly patriarchal ideology. They still maintain the underlying sexist ideology of female subservience and continue a patriarchal viewpoint from the Victorian era to the present. As explicit behavioral guideposts, these normative vocabularies directly place a woman into a subservient role within the home. As ideal models to which many women refer, they provide an almost perfectly self-contained system of domestic labor-management relations.

WOMEN AND WORK

Let us now turn our attention to the role of women in the business world. Women particularly have found a place in the tertiary sector (office work and service jobs) and in occupations that are clearly related to traditional female sex-role activities and personality traits. There is an overwhelming concentration of women in canning and clothing factories, teaching, nursing, social work, dietetics, and at occupational levels which require little or no organizational or leadership characteristics (Yorburg 1974, p. 68). Women's employment can thus be categorized in terms of occupations which are extensions of domestic involvements (i.e., teaching, nursing, waitress, etc.) or in occupations which have a dead-end aspect to them (e.g., clerical, retail sales).

In addition to the above described characteristics the business world is structured by men. This is reflected in selective hiring practices which ensure that males are likely to find themselves working with relatively young and attractive females. Goffman (1977, p. 318) points out that "the world that men are in is a social construct, drawing them daily from their conjugal milieu to what appear to be all male settings: but these environments turn out to be strategically stocked with relatively attractive females, there to serve in a specialized way as passing targets for sexually allusive banter and for diffuse considerateness extended in both directions."

The rules of etiquette depict women in terms of the ideals of femininity which preclude them becoming involved in or competing with men on an equal footing in the business world. So these ideals have, then, a political consequence, that of relieving persons who are males from half the competition they would otherwise face (Goffman 1977, pp. 325–26).

Etiquette books are instructive on how they have perpetuated the exclusion of women from equality in the world of work. One area that might be indicative of the changing view of women and work is the advice involving the woman as wife/mother. It is interesting that in the earlier references (Hathaway 1928, pp. 31–32) one sees the wife's role as external to the business world:

During business hours a considerate wife does not interrupt her husband's work by unnecessary telephone calls and messages, nor does she treat her husband as a superior sort of errand boy who is expected to be on call at all hours of the day and night. And neither does she expect a man to jump up and do a bit of carpentry or furniture moving after he comes home tired from a day's work. If a woman could only realize the severe tension under which the average man has to work, she would be more careful to fit her demands for his help into his more leisurely moments.

In the 1950s, however, the woman is being cautioned not to let her career take precedence over her husband and family.

It's hard to face this, but no woman can find happiness putting career above her husband and family. Once she has taken on women's natural responsibilities, whatever work she undertakes must be done in a way that deprives the family the least— for some deprivation they must endure if she works at all . . . the hard truth is that more women with young children fail at making happy homes while working full-time than succeed (Vanderbilt 1957, p. 206; 1967, p. 159; 1972, p. 247).

It is important to note that this same citation is maintained in the more recent issues of her work (Vanderbilt, 1967, 1972).

The woman in business is presented as "giving up" certain aspects of femininity. This pattern is maintained throughout the literature.

Women in business should expect from men only the same courtesy that businessmen of a fine type pay to each other . . . Just because she is a woman she should not expect special privileges, nor should she let the feminine—that is, the coquettishly feminine—side of her nature be evident. This actually repels rather than attracts the man of sense and breeding, who realizes how out of place such an attitude is in a business environment (Hathaway 1928, p. 329).

Women in business should expect from men only the same courtesy that businessmen of a fine type pay to each other . . . If we stop to consider it, this is usually rather a high grade of courtesy with which any woman should be satisfied. . . . Moreover, it might be added that in business a woman should in general behave herself with about the same manner that a high grade gentleman does. Applying make-up conspicuously at one's post . . . preening oneself generally and indulging in coquettish or kittenish ways are not according to the rules of etiquette, say the experts (Stevens 1934, p. 118).

While she should be charming and womanly at all times, the feminine office worker should not expect full drawing-room courtesy from her employer and coworkers. Wise is she who realizes that in the office she is on the same footing as a man. . . . If she has tact, courtesy and poise, and conducts herself as a "lady," she will at all times receive the respect to which she is entitled (Gardner and Farren 1937, p. 108).

A woman in business is supposed to be a woman, not one of the boys. On the other hand, you must avoid being so female that you embarrass your co-workers (Bevans 1960, p. 69).

Notice that this is important because if she does not preserve her femininity she might "repel rather than attract males" (Hathaway 1928), or "embarrass coworkers" (Bevans 1960). The woman is still functioning in her day-to-day interactions for others rather than herself.

The Bevans (1960) etiquette book effectively illustrates that the status of secretary involves a change of deference patterns:

> If the employer is a man and his secretary a woman, the secretary doesn't expect him to rise, when she enters, and she properly treats him with the kind of respect she might expect from a man in a drawing room (p. 69).
>
> A man's relationship to his secretary is very different from that of a man and woman socially. He doesn't rise when she enters the room. He may precede her through doors (though most men don't). He doesn't introduce her to visitors unless there is a specific reason they should become acquainted. He calls her "Martha" before she calls him "Henry" and he invites her to use his first name if he wants her to, rather than the other way around. He is the one who starts a conversation, too. If it is a business one, she may properly open it, but chatting about outside things should wait until the boss indicates that he has time for a talk (p. 74).
>
> If a man and his secretary must work together during their stay (on a business trip), the proper thing is for the secretary to go to her employer's room, not the other way around (p. 356).

Even in the more modern works where it is stated that a secretary is not always a female, the choice of using gender-specific language is maintained. Baldrige's (1978) chapter on General Office Manners concentrates on the secretary rather than the executive:

> A good secretary is usually a firm's most important and perhaps least appreciated segment of the business. A good secretary bears a tremendous responsibility in the success of any operation with which he or she is associated. (A secretary may, of course, be male or female; the employer also. For the sake of brevity, we will refer to the secretary as "she" and the employer as "he.") (p. 474).
>
> She helps her employer do the gracious thing in his office relationships—including writing thank-you notes, sending gifts, and calling someone when the occasion warrants it—both inside the office and out of it (p. 474).
>
> Most good secretaries I know have never minded doing work that involves the personal side of their bosses' lives. In fact, most of them enjoy doing it. A woman easily becomes a member of his family in many ways, and takes vicarious enjoyment in the family's activities. However, in some firms a secretary is not supposed to perform any functions of a personal nature. If she feels her employer is loading her with too many personal things, she should speak to him about it in a very nice but frank way, so that he will not feel offended or guilty (p. 475).

This status designation really formalizes the subordinate position.

Look at how the woman in other than the secretarial role is not free from the subservient position. She is told she must guard against letting this superordinate role take over her life:

A woman who achieves executive status of some kind must guard against being dictatorial at home as well as in the office....[W]hen a woman does arrive she tends to become irritatingly important.... [S]he forgets the feminine graces and cajoleries and tries to meet him man-to-man (Vanderbilt 1957, pp. 207–208; 1967, p. 181; 1972, p. 276).

Names and titles are also a part of the business world. The suggestion is made in some of the materials that a woman retain her business name:

It is better taste for a business woman to be known professionally as "Miss Maiden Name" in public life, and "Mrs. James L. Jones" in private life (Wilson 1940, p. 136).

It has always seemed wise to me for a woman who establishes herself in business or a profession to use her maiden name. I believe this gives protection, too, to her husband, should she engage in any activities that might run counter to his own professional or business interest (Vanderbilt 1974, p. 79).

It is interesting that in the Vanderbilt (1974) reference the justification is for the protection of the male.

Even when the justification is not subservience she is cautioned to be sensitive to her "husband's ego":

A woman who keeps her maiden name professionally (or even if she retains it for everything) should be very sensitive to her husband's ego when they are in social situations where she is known and he is not. People who do not know them well will tend to assume the woman and her husband bear the same name. It is important for the wife to introduce her husband proudly and distinctly. If Mary Branton, for example, is accompanied by her husband to her firm's annual convention, she should always introduce him as John Kushell, saying his name slowly and carefully so the difference is clear. Then people will not introduce John Kushell around as John Branton (Baldrige 1978, p. 79).

The other area that one must pursue is how to address a husband and wife if she has a title such as a physician. Notice how her professional role is subservient to her social role:

A woman physician uses her Christian name with her title on her cards... Her title as physician cannot be indicated on a joint card with her husband's name (Wilson 1940, p. 136).

On a married woman doctor: If she uses husband's name professionally and he is not a doctor himself, it would seem a little belittling for her to use a joint card, which read "Mr. James Pike and Dr. Mary Pike." A joint card in his case would read "Mr. and Mrs. James Pike." If both are doctors their joint card should read Dr. and Mrs. James Pike" (Vanderbilt 1957, p. 567; 1967, p. 598; 1972, p. 765).

If he (her husband) is not a doctor (and she is) she must decide whether or not she wishes to retain the title socially, which means that letters must be addressed to "Dr. Mary and Mr. Simon Fling"—an awkward and lengthy address ... so for the sake of convenience many women doctors do prefer to be addressed as "Mrs." on social correspondence (Post 1975, p. 73).

A different solution is presented by Martin (1982). One can see, however, that the solution did not come about because of the recognition of the women's professional role:

Illicit love has given us, if nothing else, the two-line method of address, which may also be applied to married couples with different titles or names. The doctor and Mr. may be addressed as:

    Dr. Dahlia Healer

    Mr. Byron Healer

and the doctor and academician, if he uses his title socially, which not all holders of doctorates do, as:

    Dr. Dahlia Healer

    Dr. Bryon Healer

or as:

    The Doctors Healer

or as:

    The Doctors Bryon and Dahlia Healer (p. 515).

A woman must, therefore, not let her career be more important than her family, not give up her femininity, and not let her title supersede that of wife. All of this relates back to the earlier discussion of the woman maintaining her femininity and how this acts as a form of social control that maintains her subservient position. It also further demonstrates the ways in which gender-based definitions of propriety supersede, or at least supplement, work rules in the subordination of women in the workplace.

INTERACTION: SYMBOLS AND STRUCTURE

In the idealized world of the etiquette text, we have come to recognize a world of women's automatic deference to male prerogatives. Thus far, we have treated these works as normative points of reference on certain interactional states—public, domestic, and workplace. In this regard, they occupy the same societal position as a host of other such guidebooks, covering self-improvement, success, sexuality, and the stock market, to name the most obvious parallels. We prefer, however, to extend our analysis beyond this point, starting with the observation that the role of women remained consistent in the etiquette texts during almost the entire twentieth century. While the manners and mores of the society were changing, and while the specifics of many earlier social situations no longer obtain, the deference of female to male embodied in these texts has remained constant.

On the one hand, this could be simply handled as a case of cultural persistence, and further evidence for the school of thought which maintains the virtual inevitability of female subjugation (e.g., Stephens 1963; Ortner 1974). This persistence is so striking, however, that we feel that a closer look at the structure of these texts is warranted. Borrowing from the fields of literary criticism and hermeneutics, we shall attempt to analyze a deeper structure to the etiquette text (Said 1983; Ricouer 1981). For the time being we adopt the common assumption of these fields, that the organization and form of presentation of a text is at least as important as its explicit content.

Earlier in the paper, for instance, we noted that in the areas of sexual traffic, greeting rituals, costume, smoking, domestic relations, and the workplace that women were explicitly expected to defer to males. We have also noted earlier that at least one form of textual structure is remarkable, namely that public and business arenas are male-determined. Women are external to them, and surrender a part of their sexuality if they participate fully in them, especially in the world of work. In a complementary fashion, the domestic world is presented as an adjunct to the world of work, and appropriate behaviors justified in terms of that work.

At one level, this analysis simply reestablishes the points brought out a century ago by Engels, cited earlier. But the family as adjunct to the production system, and the male dominance of these worlds is still too easily viewed as the explicit aspect of the etiquette messages. We would argue that there are three additional points deserving of attention. First, aside from a persistence of deference, there is a persistence of style of the text. That is, the entire discussion of the proper form of behavior is cast in a similar nominative structure, or naming convention. The subject of etiquette is not the behavior of individuals, but the behavior of the generalized others, if you will, of "men" and "women." This stylistic device serves to objectify the nature of gender as a base for normative prescription. It places the roots for appropriate behavior not in the social order, but implicitly in a more fundamental, biological order.

This brings us to a second observation. The effect of objectifying the subjects of etiquette, i.e., men and women in concrete social situations become males and females, is to accept a system of natural law as a basis for deference and demeanor. It makes the relations between

men and women a function of chromosonal makeup—a transhistorical inequality rooted in the nature of things, as it were. The force of etiquette becomes reinforced by the "laws of nature" without specific reference to these laws, simply by the process of objectifying the gender classification scheme. In short, the internal force of an etiquette text rests on its ability to present the species *Homo sapiens* as if it were in fact two species. [We should also note that is not restricted only to the etiquette text. Hubbard (1979) has argued that the structure of evolutionary theory in biology makes a similar assumption.]

Finally, the form of the etiquette prescription is also of interest. Consistent with the above arguments, we find that specific behavioral situations are analyzed and prescribed for in terms of some general set of principles, which we may call "propriety." In this sense, the etiquette text resembles nothing so much as dialectic of circumstance and code, specific behavior and normative generalization. In itself, this is not revealing. Combined with the natural law tendencies of that general code, especially regarding gender-based propriety, it becomes more significant. We would argue, however, that the greatest significance in this relationship of behavior to code is its implicit similarity to two widely different normative structures: tort law and religious canon.

More specifically, tort law is essentially a system of jurisprudence which rests on a case system. General principles of law are applied to specific circumstances as they arise. Litigious situations are always interpreted with respect to their similarity with previous situations, and if they are truly unique, with respect to the general principles of law. Similarly, religious laws in Western society have been caught in the dilemma of orthodoxy vs. social change on the one hand, and differential orthodoxies, based on textual interpretation, on the other. Both dilemmas have resulted in the establishment of a sort of religious propriety—a general set of principles or beliefs which become translated into specific doctrines attached to specific situations. In religious law, doctrine is an equivalent to etiquette; in tort law, private property to propriety. The underlying textual organization is shared, as specific behaviors or situations are contextualized, as representations of a universal set of principles.

These equivalences are not argued to be identities. Nonetheless, they are powerful symbolic links which seem woven into the very fabric of the etiquette text. It is as if the etiquette text is written in a style which encourages it being seen as another form of natural law. While we may view the application of etiquette guidelines as being somewhat trivial, it is still significant that the style of presentation brings with it the heavy rhetorical baggage of both the legal and judicial system.

There are several links between this essentially hermeneutic analysis and other approaches to gender dominance and conflict which deserve mention. Of special note are the potential ties of this analysis to recent conceptualizations present in feminist theory. A strong parallel exists between our concept of property and propriety and MacKinnon's (1982, 1983) analysis of the objectification of sexual categories, especially as they are reflected in the legal system. Building and expanding upon works of recent French feminists (Marks and de Courtivron 1980) and the works of de Beauvoir (1953; see also Schwartzer 1984), MacKinnon argues persuasively that the process of gender objectification implicitly serves to ground male dominance in the natural order, as it were: "Sexual objectification . . . is at once epistemological and political" (1983, p. 635–36). Just as MacKinnon is able to relate the legal text to behavioral consequence and to structural antecedents, it should be possible to take the analysis of etiquette texts

as a further modality of control based on a similar textual/categorical assumption.

A work which is somewhat less directly theoretical, but which provides a slightly different perspective, is that of Hochschild (1983). In her analysis of the commercialization of human feeling, she points out that roughly half of women's jobs in the work force consist of public contact work—work which essentially deals with emotional impression management. Just as on-the-job training emphasizes a fictional emotional deference (particularly in the airline industry), etiquette texts assume the necessity of managing human relationships virtually as if they were public contact occupations. This similarity might prove useful in explaining selective recruitment into "women's work," based on the presocialization already present for situations requiring gender-based deferential behavior.

Alternatively, Collins has advanced a non-Marxian conflict theory of sexual stratification (1975, pp. 225–58), based on these systems of inequality having some roots in biological gender differences. His argument, while not a form of genetic determinism, assumes that differences in average size become socially magnified into gender stratification. While we do not necessarily agree with either the form or the substance of his theoretical argument, he has provided an alternative approach which needs to be assessed independently of this specific analysis. Indeed, some of the comments he has made regarding the status context of deference and demeanor are largely supportive of the arguments we have raised regarding the reinforcement of privilege through behavioral guidelines (1975, pp. 161–68, 187–209).

We leave the theoretical discussion, then, at a point of divergence. We feel that our analysis of etiquette texts can be fit into either conflict perspective as they represent theories of the larger social structure. Beyond the specifics of etiquette texts lie other specific areas of analysis to which symbolic interactionist techniques, or their derivatives, might be applied. It is hoped that this attempt to isolate structural and historical factors has demonstrated the utility of symbolic interaction for such analyses.

CONCLUSION

"Modern . . . lives are a series of traps," Mills once argued (1959, p. 3), and proceeded to describe a sociology whose purpose was to illuminate and resolve these traps as a way of humanizing society. His was a reminiscent echo of Marx's argument that people "made history, but seldom of their own choosing" ([1869] 1959, p. 320) as he too called for an end to coercive ideologies which masked social relationships for subordinate classes. We have argued that formal etiquette constitutes one of those traps—a vocabulary of motives which conceals politics behind politesse, and sexism behind propriety. Just as Blood noted that Victorian chivalry made "the ladies feel like queens . . . (while) the king still wielded the royal sceptre" (1972, p. 427), we have argued that the woman's pedestal found in etiquette as elsewhere conceals the real power reflected in the norms of "proper" behavior. While the evidence we have provided is anecdotal in nature, the persistence of gender-specific controls over time in our sample (dating from 1899 to the present) reveals a consistency and a pervasiveness of these norms in a variety of social situations.

In behavior in public places and in everyday life women must control their interactions with strangers and be treated in a subservient manner (door openings, cigarette lightings, etc.). In business a woman must guard against losing her femininity or letting her career supersede her family. She also must relinquish her professional title in social settings. Etiquette books are in many ways telling her to remain a female and to

remain in the subordinate position in the business world. In the area of interpersonal relations the major emphasis is on the man being the provider and the woman being involved in the domestic aspects of life. Once again women are cut off from the world at large. Goffman (1977, p. 326) summarizes our position:

Apologists can, then, interpret the high value placed on femininity as a balance and compensation for the substantive work that women find they must do in the domestic sphere and for their subordination in, if not exclusion from, public spheres. And the courtesies performed for and to women during social occasions can be seen as redress for the retiring roles they are obliged to play at these times. What could be thought good about their situation, then seems always to enter as a means of cloaking what could be thought bad about it. And every indulgence society shows to women can be seen as a mixed blessing.

The authors must conclude that etiquette books have acted to perpetuate the power and status of men and maintain women in the subordinate, subservient role. The totality of the subordination of women in this set of rules, the persistence of these rules over time, and their linkage to situations which involve extensive male-female interactions make these etiquette rules virtually an ideology of sexual subservience. It is obviously only one of many ideological elements operating in the sphere of male-female "arrangement" and, as such, is basically reflective of a more universal justification of sexual inequality. The analysis we have offered demonstrates how this particular normative vocabulary of motives operates to justify and perpetuate this type of inequality. While these etiquette books may have a limited readership, this in no way vitiates their importance in the larger context of sexual politics. Indeed, they may be taken as symbolic of prevalent attitudes regarding sexual relationships in twentieth-century American society.

ACKNOWLEDGMENTS

The authors would like to thank Lynn Kahn formerly of the Glassboro State College Women's Studies Office for the collection and review of materials and Michael Gordon for his comments on an earlier draft of the paper.

Reading 17   The Feminization of Love*

FRANCESCA M. CANCIAN

A feminized and incomplete perspective on love predominates in the United States. We identify love with emotional expression and talking about feelings, aspects of love that women prefer and in which women tend to be more skilled than men. At the same time we often ignore the instrumental and physical aspects of love that men prefer, such as providing help, sharing activities, and sex. This feminized perspective leads us to believe that women are much more capable of love than men and that the way to make relationships more loving is for men to become more like women.[1] This paper proposes an alternative, androgynous perspective on love, one based on the premise that love is both instrumental and expressive.[2] From this perspective, the way to make relationships more loving is for women and men to reject polarized gender roles and integrate "masculine" and "feminine" styles of love.

THE TWO PERSPECTIVES

"Love is active, doing something for your good even if it bothers me" says a fundamentalist Christian. "Love is sharing, the real sharing of feelings" says a divorced secretary who is in love again. In ancient Greece, the ideal love was the adoration of a man for a beautiful young boy who was his lover. In the thirteenth century, the exemplar of love was the chaste devotion of a knight for another man's wife. In Puritan New England, love between husband and wife was the ideal, and in Victorian times, the asexual devotion of a mother for her child seemed the essence of love.[3] My purpose is to focus on one kind of love: long-term heterosexual love in the contemporary United States.

What is a useful definition of enduring love between a woman and a man? One guideline for a definition comes from the prototypes of enduring love—the relations between committed lovers, husband and wife, parent and child. These relationships combine care and assistance with physical and emotional closeness. Studies of attachment between infants and their mothers emphasize the importance of being protected and fed as well as touched and held. In marriage, according to most family sociologists, both practical help and affection are part of enduring love, or "the affection we feel for those with whom our lives are deeply intertwined."[4] Our own informal observations often point in the same direction: if we consider the relationships that are the prototypes of enduring love, it seems that what we really mean by love is some combination of instrumental and expressive qualities.

Historical studies provide a second guideline for defining enduring love, specifically between a woman and a man.[5] In precapitalist

*Cancian, Francesca M. 1986. "The Feminization of Love." *Signs: Journal of Women in Culture and Society* 11(4): 692–709.

America, such love was a complex whole that included work and feelings. Then it was split into feminine and masculine fragments by the separation of home and workplace. This historical analysis implies that affection, material help, and routine cooperation all are parts of enduring love.

Consistent with these guidelines, my working definition of enduring love between adults is a relationship wherein a small number of people are affectionate and emotionally committed to each other, define their collective well-being as a major goal, and feel obliged to provide care and practical assistance for each other. People who love each other also usually share physical contact; they communicate with each other frequently and cooperate in some routine tasks of daily life. My discussion is of enduring heterosexual love only; I will for the sake of simplicity refer to it as "love."

In contrast to this broad definition of love, the narrower, feminized definition dominates both contemporary scholarship and public opinion. Most scholars who study love, intimacy, or close friendship focus on qualities that are stereotypically feminine, such as talking about feelings.[6] For example, Abraham Maslow defines love as "a feeling of tenderness and affection with great enjoyment, happiness, satisfaction, elation and even ecstasy." Among healthy individuals, he says, "there is a growing intimacy and honesty and self-expression."[7] Zick Rubin's "Love Scale," designed to measure the degree of passionate love as opposed to liking, includes questions about confiding in each other, longing to be together, and sexual attraction as well as caring for each other. Studies of friendship usually distinguish close friends from acquaintances on the basis of how much personal information is disclosed, and many recent studies of married couples and lovers emphasize communication and self-disclosure. A recent book on marital love by Lillian Rubin focuses on intimacy, which she defines as "reciprocal expression of feeling and thought, not out of fear or dependent need, but out of a wish to know another's inner life and to be able to share one's own."[8] She argues that intimacy is distinct from nurturance or caretaking and that men are usually unable to be intimate.

Among the general public, love is also defined primarily as expressing feelings and verbal disclosure, not as instrumental help. This is especially true among the more affluent; poorer people are more likely than they to see practical help and financial assistance as a sign of love.[9] In a study conducted in 1980, 130 adults from a wide range of social classes and ethnic backgrounds were interviewed about the qualities that make a good love relationship. The most frequent response referred to honest and open communication. Being caring and supportive and being tolerant and understanding were the other qualities most often mentioned.[10] Similar results were reported from Ann Swidler's study of an affluent suburb: the dominant conception of love stressed communicating feelings, working on the relationship, and self-development.[11] Finally, a contemporary dictionary defines love as "strong affection for another arising out of kinship or personal ties" and as attraction based on sexual desire, affection, and tenderness.[12]

These contemporary definitions of love clearly focus on qualities that are seen as feminine in our culture. A study of gender roles in 1968 found that warmth, expressiveness, and talkativeness were seen as appropriate for women and not for men. In 1978 the core features of gender stereotypes were unchanged although fewer qualities were seen as appropriate for only one sex. Expressing tender feelings, being gentle, and being aware of the feelings of others were still ideal qualities for women and not for men. The desirable qualities for men and not for women included being independent, unemotional, and interested in sex.[13] The only component perceived as masculine in popular definitions of love is interest in sex. .

The two approaches to defining love—one broad, encompassing instrumental and affective qualities, one narrow, including only the affective qualities—inform the two different perspectives on love. According to the androgynous perspective, both gender roles contain elements of love. The feminine role does not include all of the major ways of loving; some aspects of love come from the masculine role, such as sex and providing material help, and some, such as cooperating in daily tasks, are associated with neither gender role. In contrast, the feminized perspective on love implies that all of the elements of love are included in the feminine role. The capacity to love is divided by gender. Women can love and men cannot.

SOME FEMINIST INTERPRETATIONS

Feminist scholars are divided on the question of love and gender. Supporters of the feminized perspective seem most influential at present. Nancy Chodorow's psychoanalytic theory has been especially influential in promoting a feminized perspective on love among social scientists studying close relationships. Chodorow's argument—in greatly simplified form—is that as infants, both boys and girls have strong identification and intimate attachments with their mothers. Since boys grow up to be men, they must repress this early identification, and in the process they repress their capacity for intimacy. Girls retain their early identification since they will grow up to be women, and throughout their lives females see themselves as connected to others. As a result of this process, Chodorow argues, "girls come to define and experience themselves as continuous with others; . . . boys come to define themselves as more separate and distinct."[14] This theory implies that love is feminine—women are more open to love than men—and that this gender difference will remain as long as women are the primary caretakers of infants.

Scholars have used Chodorow's theory to develop the idea that love and attachment are fundamental parts of women's personalities but not of men's. Carol Gilligan's influential book on female personality development asserts that women define their identity "by a standard of responsibility and care." The predominant female image is "a network of connection, a web of relationships that is sustained by a process of communication." In contrast, males favor a "hierarchical ordering, with its imagery of winning and losing and the potential for violence which it contains." "Although the world of the self that men describe at times includes 'people' and 'deep attachments,' no particular person or relationship is mentioned. . . . Thus the male 'I' is defined in separation."[15]

A feminized conception of love can be supported by other theories as well. In past decades, for example, such a conception developed from Talcott Parsons's theory of the benefits to the nuclear family of women's specializing in expressive action and men's specializing in instrumental action. Among contemporary social scientists, the strongest support for the feminized perspective comes from such psychological theories as Chodorow's.[16]

On the other hand, feminist historians have developed an incisive critique of the feminized perspective on love. Mary Ryan and other social historians have analyzed how the separation of home and workplace in the nineteenth century polarized gender roles and feminized love.[17] Their argument, in simplified form, begins with the observation that in the colonial era the family household was the arena for economic production, affection, and social welfare. The integration of activities in the family produced a certain integration of expressive and instrumental traits in the personalities of men and women. Both women and men were expected to be hard working, modest, and loving toward their spouses and children, and the concept of love included instrumental cooperation as well as expression of feelings. In Ryan's words, "When early Americans spoke of love they were not withdrawing into a female byway of human experience. Domestic affection, like sex and economics, was not segregated into male and female spheres." There was a "reciprocal ideal of conjugal love" that "grew out of the day-to-day cooperation, sharing, and closeness of the diversified home economy."[18]

Economic production gradually moved out of the home and became separated from personal relationships as capitalism expanded. Husbands increasingly worked for wages in factories and shops while wives stayed at home to care for the family. This division of labor gave women more experience with close relationships and intensified women's economic dependence on men. As the daily activities of men and women grew further apart, a new worldview emerged that exaggerated the differences between the personal, loving, feminine sphere of the home and the impersonal, powerful, masculine sphere of the workplace. Work became identified with what men do for money while love became identified with women's activities at home. As a result, the conception of love shifted toward emphasizing tenderness, powerlessness, and the expression of emotion.[19]

This partial and feminized conception of love persisted into the twentieth century as the division of labor remained stable: the workplace remained impersonal and separated from the home, and married women continued to be excluded from paid employment. According to this historical explanation, one might expect a change in the conception of love since the 1940s, as growing numbers of wives took jobs. However, women's persistent responsibility for child care and housework, and their lower wages, might explain a continued feminized conception of love.[20]

Like the historical critiques, some psychological studies of gender also imply that our current conception of love is distorted and needs to

be integrated with qualities associated with the masculine role. For example, Jean Baker Miller argues that women's ways of loving—their need to be attached to a man and to serve others—result from women's powerlessness, and that a better way of loving would integrate power with women's style of love.[21] The importance of combining activities and personality traits that have been split apart by gender is also a frequent theme in the human potential movement.[22] These historical and psychological works emphasize the flexibility of gender roles and the inadequacy of a concept of love that includes only the feminine half of human qualities. In contrast, theories like Chodorow's emphasize the rigidity of gender differences after childhood and define love in terms of feminine qualities. The two theoretical approaches are not as inconsistent as my simplified sketches may suggest, and many scholars combine them;[23] however, the two approaches have different implications for empirical research.

EVIDENCE ON WOMEN'S "SUPERIORITY" IN LOVE

A large number of studies show that women are more interested and more skilled in love than men. However, most of these studies use biased measures based on feminine styles of loving, such as verbal self-disclosure, emotional expression, and willingness to report that one has close relationships. When less biased measures are used, the differences between women and men are often small.

Women have a greater number of close relationships than men. At all stages of the life cycle, women see their relatives more often. Men and women report closer relations with their mothers than with their fathers and are generally closer to female kin. Thus an average Yale man in the 1970s talked about himself more with his mother than with his father and was more satisfied with his relationship with his mother. His most frequent grievance against his father was that his father gave too little of himself and was cold and uninvolved; his grievance against his mother was that she gave too much of herself and was alternately overprotective and punitive.[24]

Throughout their lives, women are more likely to have a confidant—a person to whom one discloses personal experiences and feelings. Girls prefer to be with one friend or a small group, while boys usually play competitive games in large groups. Men usually get together with friends to play sports or do some other activity, while women get together explicitly to talk and to be together.[25]

Men seemed isolated given their weak ties with their families and friends. Among blue-collar couples interviewed in 1950, 64 percent of the husbands had no confidants other than their spouses, compared to 24 percent of the wives.[26] The predominantly upper-middle-class men interviewed by Daniel Levinson in the 1970s were no less isolated. Levinson concludes that "close friendship with a man or a woman is rarely experienced by American men."[27] Apparently, most men have no loving relationships besides those with wife or lover; and given the estrangement that often occurs in marriages, many men may have no loving relationship at all.

Several psychologists have suggested that there is a natural reversal of these roles in middle age, as men become more concerned with relationships and women turn toward independence and achievement; but there seems to be no evidence showing that men's relationships become more numerous or more intimate after middle age, and some evidence to the contrary.[28]

Women are also more skilled than men in talking about relationships. Whether working class or middle class, women value talking about feelings and relationships and disclose more than men about personal experiences. Men who deviate and talk a lot about their per-sonal experiences are commonly defined as feminine and maladjusted.[29] Working-class wives prefer to talk about themselves, their close relationships with family and friends, and their homes, while their husbands prefer to talk about cars, sports, work, and politics. The same gender-specific preferences are expressed by college students.[30]

Men do talk more about one area of personal experience: their victories and achievements; but talking about success is associated with power, not intimacy. Women say more about their fears and disappointments, and it is disclosure of such weaknesses that usually is interpreted as a sign of intimacy.[31] Women are also more accepting of the expression of intense feelings, including love, sadness, and fear, and they are more skilled in interpreting other people's emotions.[32]

Finally, in their leisure time women are drawn to topics of love and human entanglements while men are drawn to competition among men. Women's preferences in television viewing run to daytime soap operas, or if they are more educated, the high-brow soap operas on educational channels, while most men like to watch competitive and often aggressive sports. Reading tastes show the same pattern. Women read novels and magazine articles about love, while men's magazines feature stories about men's adventures and encounters with death.[33]

However, this evidence on women's greater involvement and skill in love is not as strong as it appears. Part of the reason that men seem so much less loving than women is that their behavior is measured with a feminine ruler. Much of this research considers only the kinds of loving behavior that are associated with the feminine role and rarely compares women and men in terms of qualities associated with the masculine role. When less biased measures are used, the behavior of men and women is often quite similar. For example, in a careful study of kinship relations among young adults in a southern city, Bert Adams found that women were much more likely than men to say that their parents and relatives were very important to their lives (58 percent of women and 37 percent of men). In measures of actual contact with relatives, though, there were much smaller differences: 88 percent of women and 81 percent of men whose parents lived in the same city saw their parents weekly. Adams concluded that "differences between males and females in relations with parents are discernible primarily in the subjective sphere; contact frequencies are quite similar."[34]

The differences between the sexes can be small even when biased measures are used. For example, Marjorie Lowenthal and Clayton Haven reported the finding, later widely quoted, that elderly women were more likely than elderly men to have a friend with whom they could talk about their personal troubles—clearly a measure of a traditionally feminine behavior. The figures revealed that 81 percent of the married women and 74 percent of the married men had confidants—not a sizable difference.[35] On the other hand, whatever the measure, virtually all such studies find that women are more involved in close relationships than men, even if the difference is small.

In sum, women are only moderately superior to men in love: they have more close relationships and care more about them, and they seem to be more skilled at love, especially those aspects of love that involve expressing feelings and being vulnerable. This does not mean that men are separate and unconcerned with close relationships, however. When national surveys ask people what is most important in their lives, women tend to put family bonds first while men put family bonds first or second, along with work.[36] For both sexes, love is clearly very important.

EVIDENCE ON THE MASCULINE STYLE OF LOVE

Men tend to have a distinctive style of love that focuses on practical help, shared physical activities, spending time together, and sex.[37] The major elements of the masculine style of love emerged in Margaret Reedy's study of 102 married couples in the late 1970s. She showed individuals' statements describing aspects of love and asked them to rate how well the statements described their marriages. On the whole, husband and wife had similar views of their marriage, but several sex differences emerged. Practical help and spending time together were more important to men. The men were more likely to give high ratings to such statements as: "When she needs help I help her," and "She would rather spend her time with me than with anyone else." Men also described themselves more often as sexually attracted and endorsed such statements as: "I get physically excited and aroused just thinking about her." In addition, emotional security was less important to men than to women, and men were less likely to describe the relationship as secure, safe, and comforting.[38] Another study in the late 1970s showed a similar pattern among young, highly educated couples. The husbands gave greater emphasis to feeling responsible for the partner's well-being and putting the spouse's needs first, as well as to spending time together. The wives gave greater importance to emotional involvement and verbal self-disclosure but also were more concerned than the men about maintaining their separate activities and their independence.[39]

The difference between men and women in their views of the significance of practical help was demonstrated in a study in which seven couples recorded their interactions for several days. They noted how pleasant their relations were and counted how often the spouse did a helpful chore, such as cooking a good meal or repairing a faucet, and how often the spouse expressed acceptance or affection. The social scientists doing the study used a feminized definition of love. They labeled practical help as "instrumental behavior" and expressions of acceptance or affection as "affectionate behavior," thereby denying the affectionate aspect of practical help. The wives seemed to be using the same scheme; they thought their marital relations were pleasant that day if their husbands had directed a lot of affectionate behavior to them, regardless of their husbands' positive instrumental behavior. The husbands' enjoyment of their marital relations, on the other hand, depended on their wives' instrumental actions, not on their expressions of affection. The men actually saw instrumental actions as affection.[40] One husband who was told by the researchers to increase his affectionate behavior toward his wife decided to wash her car and was surprised when neither his wife nor the researchers accepted that as an "affectionate" act.

The masculine view of instrumental help as loving behavior is clearly expressed by a husband discussing his wife's complaints about his lack of communication: "What does she want? Proof? She's got it, hasn't she? Would I be knocking myself out to get things for her—like to keep up this house—if I didn't love her? Why does a man do things like that if not because he loves his wife and kids? I swear, I can't figure what she wants." His wife, who has a feminine orientation to love, says something very different: "It is not enough that he supports us and takes care of us. I appreciate that, but I want him to share things with me. I need for him to tell me his feelings."[41] Many working-class women agree with men that a man's job is something he does out of love for his family,[42] but middle-class women and social scientists rarely recognize men's practical help as a form of love. (Indeed, among upper-middle-class men whose jobs offer a great deal of intrinsic gratification,

their belief that they are "doing it for the family" may seem somewhat self-serving.)

Other differences between men's and women's styles of love involve sex. Men seem to separate sex and love while women connect them,[43] but, paradoxically, sexual intercourse seems to be the most meaningful way of giving and receiving love for many men. A twenty-nine-year-old carpenter who had been married for three years said that, after sex, "I feel so close to her and the kids. We feel like a real family then. I don't talk to her very often, I guess, but somehow I feel we have really communicated after we have made love."[44]

Because sexual intimacy is the only recognized "masculine" way of expressing love, the recent trend toward viewing sex as a way for men and women to express mutual intimacy is an important challenge to the feminization of love. However, the connection between sexuality and love is undermined both by the "sexual revolution" definition of sex as a form of casual recreation and by the view of male sexuality as a weapon—as in rape—with which men dominate and punish women.[45]

Another paradoxical feature of men's style of love is that men have a more romantic attitude toward their partners than do women. In Reedy's study, men were more likely to select statements like "we are perfect for each other."[46] In a survey of college students, 65 percent of the men but only 24 percent of the women said that, even if a relationship had all of the other qualities they desired, they would not marry unless they were in love.[47] The common view of this phenomenon focuses on women. The view is that women marry for money and status and so see marriage as instrumentally, rather than emotionally, desirable. This of course is at odds with women's greater concern with self-disclosure and emotional intimacy and lesser concern with instrumental help. A better way to explain men's greater romanticism might be to focus on men.

One such possible explanation is that men do not feel responsible for "working on" the emotional aspects of a relationship, and therefore see love as magically and perfectly present or absent. This is consistent with men's relative lack of concern with affective interaction and greater concern with instrumental help.

In sum, there is a masculine style of love. Except for romanticism, men's style fits the popularly conceived masculine role of being the powerful provider.[48] From the androgynous perspective, the practical help and physical activities included in this role are as much a part of love as the expression of feelings. The feminized perspective cannot account for this masculine style of love; nor can it explain why women and men are so close in the degrees to which they are loving.

NEGATIVE CONSEQUENCES OF THE FEMINIZATION OF LOVE

The division of gender roles in our society that contributes to the two separate styles of love is reinforced by the feminized perspective and leads to political and moral problems that would be mitigated with a more androgynous approach to love. The feminized perspective works against some of the key values and goals of feminists and humanists by contributing to the devaluation and exploitation of women.

It is especially striking how the differences between men's and women's styles of love reinforce men's power over women. Men's style involves giving women important resources, such as money and protection that men control and women believe they need, and ignoring the resources that women control and men need. Thus men's dependency on women remains covert and repressed, while women's dependency on men is overt and exaggerated; and it is overt dependency that creates power, according to social exchange theory.[49] The feminized perspective on love reinforces this power differential by leading to the belief that women need love more than do men, which is implied in the association of love with the feminine role. The effect of this belief is to intensify the asymmetrical dependency of women on men.[50] In fact, however, evidence on the high death rates of unmarried men suggests that men need love at least as much as do women.[51]

Sexual relations also can reinforce male dominance insofar as the man takes the initiative and intercourse is defined either as his "taking" pleasure or as his being skilled at "giving" pleasure, either way giving him control. The man's power advantage is further strengthened if the couple assumes that the man's sexual needs can be filled by any attractive woman while the woman's sexual needs can be filled only by the man she loves.[52]

On the other hand, women's preferred ways of loving seem incompatible with control. They involve admitting dependency and sharing or losing control, and being emotionally intense. Further, the intimate talk about personal troubles that appeals to women requires of a couple a mutual vulnerability, a willingness to see oneself as weak and in need of support. It is true that a woman, like a man, can gain some power by providing her partner with services, such as understanding, sex, or cooking; but this power is largely unrecognized because the man's dependency on such services is not overt. The couple may even see these services as her duty or as her response to his requests (or demands).

The identification of love with expressing feelings also contributes to the lack of recognition of women's power by obscuring the instrumental active component of women's love just as it obscures the loving aspect of men's work. In a culture that glorifies instrumental achievement, this identification devalues both women and love.[53] In reality, a major way by which women are loving is in the clearly instrumental activities associated with caring for others, such as preparing meals, washing clothes, and providing care during illness; but because of our focus on the expressive side of love, this caring work of women is either ignored or redefined as expressing feelings. Thus, from the feminized perspective on love, child care is a subtle communication of attitudes, not work. A wife washing her husband's shirt is seen as expressing love, even though a husband washing his wife's car is seen as doing a job.

Gilligan, in her critique of theories of human development, shows the way in which devaluing love is linked to devaluing women. Basic to most psychological theories of development is the idea that a healthy person develops from a dependent child to an autonomous, independent adult. As Gilligan comments, "Development itself comes to be identified with separation, and attachments appear to be developmental impediments."[54] Thus women, who emphasize attachment, are judged to be developmentally retarded or insufficiently individuated.

The pervasiveness of this image was documented in a well-known study of mental health professionals who were asked to describe mental health, femininity, and masculinity. They associated both mental health and masculinity with independence, rationality, and dominance. Qualities concerning attachment, such as being tactful, gentle, or aware of the feelings of others, they associated with femininity but not with mental health.[55]

Another negative consequence of a feminized perspective on love is that it legitimates impersonal, exploitive relations in the workplace and the community. The ideology of separate spheres that developed in the nineteenth century contrasted the harsh, immoral marketplace with the warm and loving home and implied that this contrast is acceptable.[56] Defining love as expressive, feminine, and divorced from productive activity maintains this ideology. If personal relationships and love are reserved for women and the home, then it is acceptable for a manager to underpay workers or for a community to ignore a needy family. Such behavior is not unloving; it is businesslike or shows a respect for privacy. The ideology of separate spheres also implies that men are properly judged by their instrumental and economic achievements and that poor or unsuccessful men are failures who may deserve a hard life. Levinson presents a conception of masculine development itself as centering on achieving an occupational dream.[57]

Finally, the feminization of love intensifies the conflicts over intimacy between women and men in close relationships. One of the most common conflicts is that the woman wants more closeness and verbal contact while the man withdraws and wants less pressure.[58] Her need for more closeness is partly the result of the feminization of love, which encourages her to be more emotionally dependent on him. Because love is feminine, he in turn may feel controlled during intimate contact. Intimacy is her "turf," an area where she sets the rules and expectations. Talking about the relationship as she wants, may well feel to him like taking a test that she made up and that he will fail. He is likely to react by withdrawing, causing her to intensify her efforts to get closer. The feminization of love thus can lead to a vicious cycle of conflict where neither partner feels in control or gets what she or he wants.

CONCLUSION

The values of improving the status of women and humanizing the public sphere are shared by many of the scholars who support a feminized conception of love; and they, too, explain the conflicts in close relationships in terms of polarized gender roles. Nancy Chodorow, Lillian Rubin, and Carol Gilligan have addressed these issues in detail and with great insight. However, by arguing that women's identity is based on attachment while men's identity is based on separation, they reinforce the distinction between feminine expressiveness and masculine instrumentality, revive the ideology of separate spheres, and legitimate the popular idea that only women know the right way to love. They also suggest that there is no way to overcome the rigidity of gender roles other than by pursuing the goal of men and women becoming equally involved in infant care. In contrast, an androgynous perspective on love challenges the identification of women and love with being expressive, powerless, and nonproductive and the identification of men with being instrumental, powerful, and productive. It rejects the ideology of separate spheres and validates masculine as well as feminine styles of love. This viewpoint suggests that progress could be made by means of a variety of social changes, including men doing child care, relations at work becoming more personal and nurturant, and cultural conceptions of love and gender becoming more androgynous. Changes that equalize power within close relationships by equalizing the economic and emotional dependency between men and women may be especially important in moving toward androgynous love.

The validity of an androgynous definition of love cannot be "proven"; the view that informs the androgynous perspective is that both the feminine style of love (characterized by emotional closeness and verbal self-disclosure) and the masculine style of love (characterized by instrumental help and sex) represent necessary parts of a good love relationship. Who is more loving: a couple who confide most of their experiences to each other but rarely cooperate or give each other practical help, or a couple who help each other through many crises and cooperate in running a household but rarely discuss their personal experiences? Both relationships are limited. Most people would probably choose a combination: a relationship that integrates feminine and masculine styles of loving, an androgynous love.

Reading 18 Is "Straight" to "Gay" as "Family" Is to "No Family"?*

KATH WESTON

For years, and in an amazing variety of contexts, claiming a lesbian or gay identity has been portrayed as a rejection of "the family" and a departure from kinship. In media portrayals of AIDS, Simon Watney (1987:103) observes that "we are invited to imagine some absolute divide between the two domains of 'gay life' and 'the family,' as if gay men grew up, were educated, worked and lived our lives in total isolation from the rest of society." Two presuppositions lend a dubious credence to such imagery: the belief that gay men and lesbians do not have children or establish lasting relationships, and the belief that they invariably alienate adoptive and blood kin once their sexual identities become known. By presenting "the family" as a unitary object, these depictions also imply that everyone participates in identical sorts of kinship relations and subscribes to one universally agreed-upon definition of family.

Representations that exclude lesbians and gay men from "the family" invoke what Blanche Wiesen Cook (1977:48) has called "the assumption that gay people do not love and do not work," the reduction of lesbians and gay men to sexual identity, and sexual identity to sex alone. In the United States, sex apart from heterosexual marriage tends to introduce a wild card into social relations, signifying unbridled lust and the limits of individualism. If heterosexual intercourse can bring people into enduring association via the creation of kinship ties, lesbian and gay sexuality in these depictions isolates individuals from one another rather than weaving them into a social fabric. To assert that straight people "naturally" have access to family, while gay people are destined to move toward a future of solitude and loneliness, is not only to tie kinship closely to procreation, but also to treat gay men and lesbians as members of a nonprocreative species set apart from the rest of humanity (cf. Foucault 1978).

It is but a short step from positioning lesbians and gay men somewhere beyond "the family"—unencumbered by relations of kinship, responsibility, or affection—to portraying them as a menace to family and society. A person or group must first be outside and other in order to invade, endanger, and threaten. My own impression from fieldwork corroborates Frances FitzGerald's (1986) observation that many heterosexuals believe not only that gay people have gained considerable political power, but also that the absolute number of lesbians and gay men (rather than their visibility) has increased in recent years. Inflammatory rhetoric that plays on fears about the "spread" of gay identity and of AIDS finds a disturbing parallel in the imagery used by fascists to describe syphilis at mid-century, when "the healthy" confronted "the degenerate" while the fate of civilization hung in the balance (Hocquenghem 1978).

A long sociological tradition in the United States of studying "the family" under siege or in various states of dissolution lent credibility to charges that this institution required protection from "the homosexual threat." Proposition 6 (the Briggs initiative), which appeared on the ballot in California in 1978, was defeated only after a massive organizing campaign that mobilized lesbians and gay men in record numbers. The text of the initiative, which would have barred gay and lesbian teachers (along with heterosexual teachers who advocated homosexuality) from the public schools, was phrased as a defense of "the family" (in Hollibaugh 1979:55):

One of the most fundamental interests of the State is the establishment and preservation of the family unit. Consistent with this interest is the State's duty to protect its impressionable youth from influences which are antithetical to this vital interest.

Other anti-gay legislative initiative campaigns adopted the slogans "save the family" and "save the children" as their rallying cries. In 1983 the *Moral Majority Report* referred obliquely to AIDS with the headline, "Homosexual Diseases Threaten American Families" (Godwin 1983). When the *Boston Herald* opposed a gay rights bill introduced into the Massachusetts legislature, it was with an eye to "the preservation of family values" (Allen 1987).

Discourse that opposes gay identity to family membership is not confined to the political arena. A gay doctor was advised during his residency to discourage other gay people from becoming his patients, lest his waiting room become filled with homosexuals. "It'll scare away the families," warned his supervisor (Lazere 1986). Discussions of dual-career families and the implications of a family wage system usually render invisible the financial obligations of gay people who support dependents or who pool material resources with lovers and others they define as kin. Just as women have been accused of taking jobs away from "men with families to support," some lesbians and gay men in the Bay Area recalled coworkers who had condemned them for competing against "people with families" for scarce employment. Or consider the choice of words by a guard at that "all-American" institution, Disneyland, commenting on a legal suit brought by two gay men who had been prohibited from dancing with one another at a dance floor on the grounds: "This is a family park. There is no room for alternative lifestyles here" (Mendenhall 1985).

Scholarly treatments are hardly exempt from this tendency to locate gay men and lesbians beyond the bounds of kinship. Even when researchers are sympathetic to gay concerns, they may equate kinship with genealogically calculated relations. Manuel Castells' and Karen Murphy's (1982) study of the "spatial organization of San Francisco's gay community," for instance, frames its analysis using "gay territory" and "family land" as mutually exclusive categories.

From New Right polemics to the rhetoric of high school hallways, "recruitment" joins "reproduction" in allusions to homosexuality. Alleging that gay men and lesbians must seduce young people in order to perpetuate (or expand) the gay population because they cannot have children of their own, heterosexist critics have conjured up visions of an end to society, the inevitable fate of a society that fails to "reproduce."[1] Of course, the contradictory inferences that sexual identity is "caught" rather than claimed, and that parents pass their sexual identities on to their children, are unsubstantiated. The power of this chain of associations lies in a play on words that blurs the multiple senses of the term "reproduction."

Reproduction's status as a mixed metaphor may detract from its analytic utility, but its very ambiguities make it ideally suited to argument and innuendo.[2] By shifting without signal between reproduction's meaning of physical procreation and its sense as the perpetuation of society as a whole, the characterization of lesbians and gay men as nonreproductive beings links their supposed attacks on "the family" to attacks on society in the broadest sense. Speaking of parents who had refused to accept her lesbian identity, a Jewish woman explained, "They feel like I'm finishing off Hitler's job." The plausibility of the contention that gay people pose a threat to "the family" (and, through the family, to ethnicity) depends upon a view of family grounded in heterosexual relations, combined with the conviction that gay men and lesbians are incapable of procreation, parenting, and establishing kinship ties.

Some lesbians and gay men in the Bay Area had embraced the popular equation of their sexual identities with the renunciation of access to kinship, particularly when first coming out. "My image of gay life was very lonely, very weird, no family," Rafael Ortiz recollected. "I assumed that my family was gone now—that's it." After Bob Korkowski began to call himself gay, he wrote a series of poems in which an orphan was the central character. Bob said the poetry expressed his fear of "having to give up my family because I was queer." When I spoke with Rona Bren after she had been home with the flu, she told me that whenever she was sick, she relived old fears. That day she had remembered her mother's grim prediction: "You'll be a lesbian and you'll be alone the rest of your life. Even a dog shouldn't be alone."

Looking backward and forward across the life cycle, people who equated their adoption of a lesbian or gay identity with a renunciation of family did so in the double-sided sense of fearing rejection by the families in which they had grown up, and not expecting to marry or have children as adults. Although few in numbers, there were still those who had considered "going straight" or getting married specifically in order to "have a family." Vic Kochifos thought he understood why:

> It's a whole lot easier being straight in the world than it is being gay.... You have built-in loved ones: wife, husband, kids, extended family. It just works easier. And when you want to do something that requires children, and you want to have a feeling of knowing that there's gonna be someone around who cares about you when you're 85 years old, there are thoughts that go through your head, sure. There must be. There's a way of doing it gay, but it's a whole lot harder, and it's less secure.

Bernie Margolis had been sexually involved with men since he was in his teens, but for years had been married to a woman with whom he had several children. At age 67 he regretted having grown to adulthood before the current discussion of gay families, with its focus on redefining kinship and constructing new sorts of parenting arrangements.

> I didn't want to give up the possibility of becoming a family person. Of having kids of my own to carry on whatever I built up.... My mother was always talking about she's looking forward to the day when she would bring her children under the

canopy to get married. It never occurred to her that I wouldn't be married. It probably never occurred to me either.

The very categories "good family person" and "good family man" had seemed to Bernie intrinsically opposed to a gay identity. In his fifties at the time I interviewed him, Stephen Richter attributed never having become a father to "not having the relationship with the woman." Because he had envisioned parenting and procreation only in the context of a heterosexual relationship, regarding the two as completely bound up with one another, Stephen had never considered children an option.

Older gay men and lesbians were not the only ones whose adult lives had been shaped by ideologies that banish gay people from the domain of kinship. Explaining why he felt uncomfortable participating in "family occasions," a young man who had no particular interest in raising a child commented, "When families get together, what do they talk about? Who's getting married, who's having children. And who's not, okay? Well, look who's not." Very few of the lesbians and gay men I met believed that claiming a gay identity automatically requires leaving kinship behind. In some cases people described this equation as an outmoded view that contrasted sharply with revised notions of what constitutes a family.

Well-meaning defenders of lesbian and gay identity sometimes assert that gays are not inherently "anti-family," in ways that perpetuate the association of heterosexual identity with exclusive access to kinship. Charles Silverstein (1977), for instance, contends that lesbians and gay men may place more importance on maintaining family ties than heterosexuals do because gay people do not marry and raise children. Here the affirmation that gays and lesbians are capable of fostering enduring kinship ties ends up reinforcing the implication that they cannot establish "families of their own," presumably because the author regards kinship as unshakably rooted in heterosexual alliance and procreation. In contrast, discourse on gay families cuts across the politically loaded couplet of "pro-family" and "anti-family" that places gay men and lesbians in an inherently antagonistic relation to kinship solely on the basis of their nonprocreative sexualities. "Homosexuality is not what is breaking up the Black family," declared Barbara Smith (1987), a black lesbian writer, activist, and speaker at the 1987 Gay and Lesbian March on Washington. "Homophobia is. My Black gay brothers and my Black lesbian sisters are members of Black families, both the ones we were born into and the ones we create."

At the height of gay liberation, activists had attempted to develop alternatives to "the family," whereas by the 1980s many lesbians and gay men were struggling to legitimate gay families as a form of kinship. When Armistead Maupin spoke at a gathering on Castro Street to welcome home two gay men who had been held hostage in the Middle East, partners who had stood with arms around one another upon their release, he congratulated them not only for their safe return, but also as representatives of a new kind of family. Gay or chosen families might incorporate friends, lovers, or children, in any combination. Organized through ideologies of love, choice, and creation, gay families have been defined through a contrast with what many gay men and lesbians in the Bay Area called "straight," "biological," or "blood" family. If families we choose were the families lesbians and gay men created for themselves, straight family represented the families in which most had grown to adulthood.

What does it mean to say that these two categories of family have been defined through contrast? One thing it emphatically does not mean is that heterosexuals share a single coherent form of family (although some of the lesbians and gay men doing the defining believed this to be the case). I am not arguing here for the existence of some central, unified kinship system vis-à-vis which gay people have distinguished their own practice and understanding of family. In the United States, race, class, gender, ethnicity, regional origin, and context all inform differences in household organization, as well as differences in notions of family and what it means to call someone kin.[3]

In any relational definition, the juxtaposition of two terms gives meaning to both.[4] Just as light would not be meaningful without some notion of darkness, so gay or chosen families cannot be understood apart from the families lesbians and gay men call "biological," "blood," or "straight." Like others in their society, most gay people in the Bay Area considered biology a matter of "natural fact." When they applied the terms "blood" and "biology" to kinship, however, they tended to depict families more

consistently organized by procreation, more rigidly grounded in genealogy, and more uniform in their conceptualization than anthropologists know most families to be. For many lesbians and gay men, blood family represented not some naturally, given unit that provided a base for all forms of kinship, but rather a procreative principle that organized only one possible *type* of kinship. In their descriptions they situated gay families at the opposite end of a spectrum of determination, subject to no constraints beyond a logic of "free" choice that ordered membership. To the extent that gay men and lesbians mapped "biology" and "choice" onto identities already opposed to one another (straight and gay, respectively), they polarized these two types of family along an axis of sexual identity.[5]

The chart below recapitulates the ideological transformation generated as lesbians and gay men began to inscribe themselves within the domain of kinship.

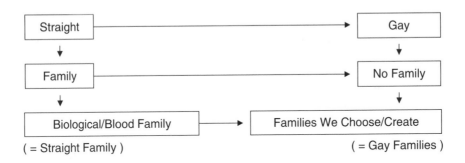

What this chart presents is not some static substitution set, but a historically motivated succession.[6] To move across or down the chart is to move through time. Following along from left to right, time appears as process, periodized with reference to the experience of coming out. In the first opposition, coming out defines the transition from a straight to a gay identity. For the person who maintains an exclusively biogenetic notion of kinship, coming out can mark the renunciation of kinship, the shift from "family" to "no family" portrayed in the second opposition. In the third line, individuals who accepted the possibility of gay families after coming out could experience themselves making a transition from the biological or blood families in which they had grown up to the establishment of their own chosen families.

Moving from top to bottom, the chart depicts the historical time, that inaugurated contemporary discourse on gay kinship. "Straight" changes from a category with an exclusive claim on kinship to an identity allied with a specific kind of family symbolized by biology or blood. Lesbians and gay men, originally relegated to the status of people without family, later lay claim to a distinctive type of family characterized as families we choose or create. While dominant cultural representations have asserted that straight is to gay as family is to no family (lines 1 and 2), at a certain point in history gay people began to contend that straight is to gay as blood family is to chosen families (lines 1 and 3).

What provided the impetus for this ideological shift? Transformations in the relation of lesbians and gay men to kinship are inseparable from sociohistorical developments: changes in the context for disclosing a lesbian or gay identity to others, attempts to build urban gay "community," cultural inferences about relationships between "same-gender" partners, and the lesbian baby boom associated with alternative (artificial) insemination.... If Pierre Bourdieu (1977) is correct, and kinship is something people use to act as well as to think, then its transformations should have unfolded not only on the "big screen" of history, but also on the more modest stage of day-to-day life, where individuals have actively engaged novel ideological distinctions and contested representations that would exclude them from kinship.

Reading 19   The Economy of Gratitude*

ARLIE RUSSELL HOCHSCHILD

A person is usually grateful to receive a gift. But what is a gift? For a gift to *be* a gift, it must *feel* like one. For it to feel like a gift, it must seem extra—something beyond what we expect normally.[1] The broader culture helps fix in the individual a mental baseline against which any action or object seems extra, and so, like a gift. Changes in the broader culture also shift the many tiny mental baselines which undergird a person's sense of a gift. The sense of genuine giving and receiving is a part of love, and so it is through the conception of a gift that the broader culture makes its way into love.

Take modern marriage. In light of changing cultural ideas about manhood and womanhood, what does a wife expect from her husband? What does she take as a gift, and so feel moved to thank him for? What does he want to be thanked for? What really feels to the husband like a gift from her? Is the gift she wants to give the one he wants to receive? Much depends on how cultural currents influence their "marital baseline"—what each partner consensually, if not consciously, expects of the other. Sometimes couples agree on the definition of a gift. But when strong cultural currents affect men and women differently, a marriage may contain two separate and conflicting baselines.

Take the example of housework in a two-job marriage. A husband does the laundry, makes the beds, washes the dishes. Relative to his father, his brother and several men on the block this husband helps more at home. He also does more than he did ten years ago. All in all he feels he has done more than his wife could reasonably expect, and with good spirit. He has given her, he feels, a gift. She should, he feels, be grateful. However, to his wife the matter seems different. In addition to her eight hours at the office, she does 80% of the housework. Relative to all she does, relative to what she wants to expect of him, what she feels she deserves, her husband's contribution seems welcome, but not extra, not a gift. So his gift is "mis-received." For each partner has perceived this gift through a different cultural prism. By creating different cultural prisms for men and women, larger social forces can impoverish a couple's private *economy of gratitude*.

An *economy of gratitude* is a vital, nearly sacred, nearly bottom-most, largely implicit layer of the marital bond. It is the summary of all *felt gifts*. Some marital economies thrive, others flounder. Crucial to a healthy economy of gratitude is a common interpretation of reality, such that what feels like a gift to one, feels like a gift

*Hochschild, Arlie Russell. 1989. "The Economy of Gratitude." Pp. 95–113 in *The Sociology of Emotions: Original Essays and Research Papers,* edited by David D. Franks and E. Doyle McCarthy. Greenwich, CT: JAI Press, Copyright © 1989 by JAI Press, Inc., Greenwich, Connecticut. Reprinted by permission.

to the other. A common interpretation of reality, in turn, relies on a shared template of prior expectation, which is laid down by cultural habits of thought. In comparison to this preexisting template of expectation, any newly grasped event or thing spontaneously stands out as more, or less, or different than what, until just now, one had expected.[2] This prior expectation and the newly grasped reality together create feeling. Sometimes we infer the prior expectation (and newly grasped reality) from the feeling, and sometimes we infer the other way around. But when we speak of a shared cultural baseline, it is this we share.

Gratitude is a form of appreciation. We appreciate many acts and objects which we take for granted. But we feel grateful for what seems to us extra. In the *Random House Dictionary of the English Language,* gratitude is synonymous with the term "indebted" or "obliged." But gratitude as used in this paper is different and more: for a person may be burdened with a surfeit of gifts which formally obliges him to return the favor—without wanting to, without gratitude. Gratitude involves a warmth, a thankfulness, a desire to return the favor. According to Joel Davitz, gratitude adds to "Thanks" the feeling of an "intense positive relationship with another person . . . a communion, a unity, a closeness, friendliness and freedom, mutual respect and interdependence."[3]

The economy of gratitude is Janus-faced. It faces outward to rapid, bewildering changes in the larger society, which filter downward from society, to community, to the two selves that compose a couple. It also faces inward to the individual's experience of gratitude and love. One way to understand the relation of social issues to private troubles, as C. Wright Mills put it, is to explore the place at which they meet—the economy of gratitude.

Let us start at the beginning of a chain of social events—with a mass exodus of women into the cash economy. In 1950, 29% of working-age women worked in the labor force while in 1980, it was 52%. In the 1950s relatively few mothers worked; now more mothers than non-mothers work. Since 1980 women have taken 80% of the new jobs in the economy. Women's movement into the cash economy has drastically changed their lives. Yet, at the same time, the traditional view that childrearing and housework are "women's work" strongly persists. The culture lags behind the economy creating what William Ogburn called a "culture lag."

Because economic trends bear most directly upon women, they change women more.[5] As a result, culturally speaking, men lag behind women in their adaptation to the new economic reality. For women the *economy* is the changing environment, while for men, *women* are the changing environment. Women are adapting more quickly to changes in economic opportunity and need, than men are adapting to changes in women. A culture lag in the wider society, then, echoes as a "gender lag" at home. There is a lag both in behavior and in attitude: while women have gone out to paid work, most men have not increased their care of the home. But, perhaps even more important, men emotionally support this change in women far less than do women.

In uniting men and women, marriage intimately unites a social stratum which has changed less with a social stratum that has changed more. Marriage thus becomes an intimate arena in which to negotiate a broader culture lag. Marriage is not a "haven in a heartless world," as Christopher Lasch suggests (1977). Rather, marriage is the major shock absorber of tensions created by wider trends bearing unevenly upon men and women.[6] These shocks are finally absorbed—and felt—as the "mis-receiving" of a gift.

In what follows, I ask how various conditions influence how people attune themselves to gratitude in similar or divergent ways. How do divergences imbalance an economy of gratitude, and so affect love? Examples in this essay are drawn from in-depth interviews with fifty-five two-job families in the San Francisco Bay Area conducted between 1978 and 1983. Both husbands and wives work 35 hours or more and care for at least one child six years or under. Twenty percent of husbands fully shared housework and parenting, while most of the rest "helped out some." I interviewed individuals separately and together.[7]

TRADITIONAL AND EGALITARIAN ECONOMIES OF GRATITUDE

A gender culture is a matter of beliefs about manhood and womanhood, and of emotive anchors attached to these beliefs. Many discrete beliefs, such as, "a woman's place is in the home," can be understood as positions on central cultural rules about gender honor. The traditional person affirms rules that accord honor to men and women in different ways (asymmetric rules of honor): the egalitarian affirms rules that accord honor in a similar way (symmetric rules of honor). More specifically, the traditional endorses an asymmetrical "conversion rule" according to which a man's status in the public realm can be converted into honor in the private realm, while women's essentially cannot. The traditional believes a woman's honor derives properly from the home, a man's from the public world. A man's public work thus "translates"; a woman's does not. To gauge a woman's honor, then, one asks: Is she married? To a good fellow? How many children? Are her children doing well? Is her home tidy? She may work outside the home, often because she has to, but this adds nothing to her honor as a woman, only something to the family coffers. To gauge a man's honor, on the other hand, one asks how much he earns? What job does he do? At what rank? In

which institution? He may do half the parenting of his children, but in the eyes of the traditional, this does not add to his honor as a man; if anything, it subtracts.

To the traditional, a man may also transfer his publicly based honor to his wife. Mr. Jones's promotion at the bank reflects well on Mrs. Jones. Especially if the wife forms part of what Hanna Papanek calls, the "two-person career," a husband's glory reflects on his wife. It is not simply that she is proud of him; in the eyes of others, her own status has risen. But according to the traditional rule, Mrs. Jones cannot, in a parallel way, transfer her own promotion to her husband—because her husband's honor as a man a) cannot depend in any way on his wife's public work, and b) because he must do better than she in *his* realm, her success may therefore *detract* from his honor. Arrangements of gender honor are such that only a man can "do social class" for the family.

In contrast, for the egalitarian, male and female honor is based equally on their participation in the public and private spheres. Women can transfer their honor to men, just as men transfer theirs to women. By these new rules, women like men can "do social class" for their family.

The communities in which most Bay Area two-job couples lived were themselves culturally plural. Most couples had friends who shared their gender rules, but acquaintances who went by different rules. One man captured this sense of cultural pluralism when he commented:

> In some social circles, it's high status to have a professional wife. I would say it is more high status to have a wife who is a highly regarded professional than one who is home cooking dinner. Yet we have a dentist friend who refuses to let his wife work. After a while, they crossed us off their list, because my wife gave his wife "too many ideas."

Only a minority of Bay Area couples in the late 1970s and early 1980s were what we could call pure traditionals in the sense that their "marital baseline"—their set of cultural assumptions—was squarely set upon traditional gender rules. Living by traditional rules, they established a traditional economy of gratitude. One such couple were Frank and Carmen Delacorte.[8] Frank is a serious, quiet 30-year-old, high school educated, cabinet maker whose national origin is El Savador and who is a Catholic. He feels that it is his job (his only job, and no one else's job) to provide for his family. Frank dislikes the unskilled work he has recently been forced to do in a box factory, but still bases his male pride on the fact that he works, and provides for his family.

Carmen, his wife, is a large voluble, dark haired woman who runs a daycare center in her home for the children of neighboring mothers who work. She does it she explains firmly, "to help Frank":

The only reason I'm working is that every time I go to the grocery store, the bill is twenty dollars more. I'm not working to develop myself or to discover my identity. No way.

Frank feels grateful that Carmen helps him do his job—without complaining. Consider the "not complaining." One evening Frank and Carmen have dinner with another couple, the wife of whom resents *having to* work as a waitress, because "the man should earn the money." To the discomfort of the Delacortes, the wife openly exposes her husband's vulnerability—given their traditional cultural baseline—he could not support his family as a man should.

Frank rides in a carpool with his foreman, an ardently outspoken traditional. As Frank hesitantly explained:

We are talking about needing extra money and I told him about the business that Carmen has (taking children into her home) and I said: "You know, you've got a house. Your wife could have a business like Carmen's. It's not too bad." His attitude was "no! no! no!...I don't want anybody saying my wife is taking care of other people's children." He feels like he lives the way most people should live—the husband working, the wife at home.

In Frank's social world, the old gender rules hold: the wife of an adequate man should not *need* to work, but to support a family in the urban working class in the early 1980s, men like Frank, in fact do need a wife's salary. Frank's economic circumstances erode the rules on which he bases his identity as a man, and make him, as a man, vulnerable to insult. Frank feels grateful, then, that his wife gives him the real gift of working without complaining about it.

For her part, Carmen feels *her* job is to care for the home and children; she expects Frank to do the outside chores and to help some, when she asks, with the inside ones. Like most working mothers, Carmen averaged fifteen hours longer each week than Frank did—it added up to an extra month a year. But as a traditional, Carmen could not formally define her "double day" as a problem. Like a number of traditional women in my study, Carmen found a way around her dilemma. She claimed incompetence. She did not drive, so Frank had to shop with her. She did not have a mechanical sense, so Frank had to get money from the automatic teller. In this way, Carmen got relief from her burdens but clung to her traditional notion of womanhood. But she did so, as Erving Goffman would note, at the expense of her "moral character." Instead of moving to new gender rules which would honor Carmen for her paid work, and Frank for his contributions at home, Carmen felt Frank's help at home as a continual series of "gifts." And given her incapacities, she felt grateful.

The Delacortes agreed on certain ritually symbolic extras, for which they felt a certain ritual gratitude. Frank occasionally brought flowers to Carmen. From time to time Carmen troubled to bake an apple pie, because it was Frank's favorite dessert. The roses and the pie were their private extras, symbols of other private gifts.

Flowers from a man to a woman, and food from a woman to a man are widely shared symbols of giving: they are *gendered gifts.* Commercial advertising exploits these gender conventions even as it extends and perpetuates them. The floral industry advertises roses as a man's gift of love to a woman. Similarly, Pillsbury advertises its flour with "Nothin' says lovin' like something from the oven—and Pillsbury says it best." Frank felt Carmen baked the pie because she knew that he personally—not 8 million viewers—loved pie. Carmen felt Frank gave her roses because he knew she—not all the women in America—loved roses. Each incorporated public gender conventions into their private economy of gratitude.

In sum, the Delacorte's economy of gratitude was archetypically traditional. Economic times strained their cultural ideas, but Carmen's way of getting Frank to help at home without changing the gender rules—also archetypical—did not break their accord on the rules. Thus what felt like a gift to the giver also felt like one to the receiver. Seldom was a gift "misreceived." Theirs was thus a rich economy of gratitude.

AN EGALITARIAN ECONOMY OF GRATITUDE

Michael Sherman is a thoughtful, upper-middle-class engineer and in the eight years of his marriage he had gradually at his wife's urging, "converted" from traditional to egalitarian gender rules. His wife, Adrienne, is a college professor. By the time their twins were born, their understanding was that both would give priority to the family and would take whatever cuts in income and career they had to.

Adrienne was not helping Michael "do social class" for their family, she was sharing that function. When Michael bathed the twins, he was helping Adrienne: he was doing what a good father and a good man does. Adrienne was not grateful for Michael's help because she expected it. But Adrienne was grateful to Michael because, in their social circle, egalitarian marriages were themselves rare. In that sense, she felt Michael had given her an "extra." Because she had struggled to establish the new rules in her marriage, and because the rules were new in her social circle and in the wider culture itself, Adrienne sensed their social fragility. She felt Michael had given her an appreciable gift in accepting her terms, when he had been brought up in family to whom caring for children was a mere diversion from a man's task of securing the family's social class.

Michael did feel he was getting behind other traditional men whose wives did more than his at home, but he did not complain; he was doing this for himself as well and for her, and for this, Adrienne was grateful.

For his part, Michael was grateful because, despite their egalitarianism, Adrienne had for six years in good spirit moved from city to city, disrupting her professional training in order to follow him.

Just as the need for a woman's wage challenged the old gender rules, so the wage gap between working men and women challenges the new rules. Although Adrienne wanted her husband to treat her work as just as important as his, her salary was half of his. This piece of economic reality undermined her cultural claim to an equal part in the "class-making" of the family. Adrienne was grateful, then, when Michael honored her work despite the wage gap.

Adrienne was, therefore, especially grateful to Michael for the little signs of deference he showed to her contributions to her field. On one occasion, Michael brought the children to a conference at which she was giving a talk. As she rose to give her talk, she saw in the audience, her beaming husband and two squirming children. But in that one moment, she felt Michael had given her a great gift.

The egalitarian woman is oddly similar to the traditional man: for a new economic reality undercuts the cultural identity of each, making each grateful to their partners for passing lightly over the "soft patches" in their gender positions.

The Delacortes and the Shermans each illustrate the tie between a cultural baseline, the definition of a gift and gratitude. For the Delacortes, gratitude emerges along old cultural tracks; for the Shermans, on the new.[9] For each, cultural thinking implies a language by which we "speak gratitude." In this sense, the Delacortes and Shermans speak in different tongues. Just as a meaning in one language is not understood in the other, so gifts in the language of gratitude are not interchangeable. Carmen Delacorte's gift of "non-complaint" is meaningless if set on the cultural baseline of a Michael Sherman. Adrienne would never complain she had to work, having fought so hard for the equal right to want to. Had she complained, Michael would have turned to talk of Adrienne's "hang up" about ambition, Adrienne's "will to fail." Nor could gifts cross the language barrier in the other cultural direction. For a gift *feels like* a gift only if the giving and receiving are defined by the same cultural baseline.

CULTURAL MISALIGNMENTS AND NON-RECEIVED GIFTS

The Delacortes and Shermans describe two cultural poles between which most couples fall into a large, confusing cultural middle ground. Unlike Carmen Delacorte, most Bay Area working women *want* to work, but unlike Adrienne Sherman, most do not fully share the family's "class-making." Unlike Frank Delacorte, most men whole-heartedly support their wives' work, but unlike Michael Sherman, did not fully share the housework and childcare.

More important, most couples differ to some degree in their idea about manhood and womanhood, and so differ in their understandings about the gendering of gifts. The "language barrier" lies *between* husband and wife. The most common form of "mis-giving" occurs when the man offers a traditional gift—hard work at the office—but the woman wants to receive a "modern" one—sharing child-rearing and housework. Similarly, the woman offers a "modern" gift—more money, while the man hopes for a traditional gift—like home cooking. As external conditions create a "gender gap" in the economy of gratitude, they disrupt the ordinary ways in which a man and woman express love.

Many marriages resemble the couple in O'Henry's story, *The Gift of the Magi*. In that story, Della and Jim are very poor but very much in love and at Christmas, each wants to buy the other a fine gift. Della has beautiful long brown hair that hangs below her waist. Jim sells his favorite gold watch in order to buy combs for her beautiful hair. At the same time, Della cuts off her hair and sells it in order to buy a chain for Jim's gold watch. Each makes a sacrifice for the other which makes them unable to receive a gift from the other. The poignance of the story lies not in the mix-up of the gifts which is, after all, farcical. The poignance rises from the reader's fear that each character will fail to *appreciate* the sacrifice of the other. The story ends happily, however, for each finds out and gives thanks. Presently, new economic pressures and old gender rules are creating in marriage a social version of *The Gift of the Magi*, but the endings are not always so happy.

In *The Gift of the Magi*, the couples exchanged gifts on Christmas, a ritual occasion set aside for gift exchange. In the story, each gift was intended and planned. Each gift was also an object, not an activity, and so seemed well removed from the realm of social roles. (Actually, though, Della's hair seems an emblem of beauty, and the feminine role, while Jim's watch seems an emblem of industry, and the male role.) Each wanted to please, and gave to the other what they knew the other would treasure. The "mis-giving" lay only in *external* circumstance —the timing and secrecy of each sacrifice.

In the ordinary domestic life of working couples, on the other hand, little time is set aside for ritual gift giving. The daily round of chores more often feels like flat, neutral, necessary doings than like meaningful gem-like offerings. Yet curiously, in the course of these "flat" doings, flashes of feeling may spontaneously emerge: on one side, "He should love this . . ." or on the other, "God, what a sweetheart." These spontaneous flashes suggest the comparison between the Christmas Eve watch chain on one hand, and a Saturday washing of the dog on the other. The pattern of those flashes along certain social tracks, the feeling of intense personal closeness, and warmth that rises from the realization—"a gift for me"—make up a real working economy of gratitude.

LIGHT AND HEAVY MEANINGS; GRATITUDE TO NURTURANCE

Sometimes a "mis-giving" stays "light" in the sense that a missed exchange does not make one or the other *feel unloved.* At other times, it cuts dangerously deep into signs by which partners know they are loved.

Consider a light "mis-giving" between Peter and Nina Loyola. Married 12 years, the parents of two, Peter is a sensitive, articulate man who ran a book store. His wife, Nina, a tall, lively woman, is a rising star in the personnel division of a large and expanding company. Like the Delacortes, they began their courtship on traditional terms. But as Nina's company grew, and as managerial opportunities for women opened up, Nina was promoted, until she began to earn three times Peter's salary.

Proud of her career and her salary, Nina was glad to contribute that much money to the family coffers. She was glad to enable Peter to do work he loved, such as running a book store rather than work he hated, but would have done for the money, like real estate. As Nina commented: "My salary and benefits make it possible for Peter to take some risks, starting a new store. I'm really glad he can do it." Nina offered Peter her high salary as a gift.

But Peter did not *receive* her high salary as a gift. Peter knew Nina meant it as a gift. He was glad he could do work he loved, and appreciated what her salary allowed them—a new home, car and private education for their eldest daughter. But he could muster only an ambivalent "thanks." For after a certain point, the old gender rule stopped him.

Peter felt *ashamed* that Nina earned much more than he. What was the source of this shame? Peter did not feel competitive with Nina, nor did he sense her competing with him. Peter appreciated her talents and accomplishments. As he put it, "Not all women could do as well as my wife has." He also appreciated her physical appearance. "She's a good looking woman," he volunteered, "I love seeing her in the morning, her hair washed, and shiny, when she's all fresh for the day." He wanted his daughter to be "just like her."

Peter felt proud *for* Nina, and proud *of* Nina, but he could not feel proud *because* of her: he could not *share* her new status. He could not feel "given to" by her. So Nina could not give her new status *to* him. Indeed, her rise in status actively reduced his—not in Nina's eyes, but in the eyes of his relatives and neighbors and old friends—and among them, especially the men.

Through Peter, with Peter's consent, these imagined others discredited Nina's gift. For they judged his honor by the old rule of asymmetrical status transfer.

Far from receiving Nina's salary as a gift, then, Peter treated her salary as a miserable secret to manage. They did not tell Peter's parents—his father, Peter explained, "would die." They did not tell Nina's parents because "she even out-earns her father." They did not tell Peter's high school buddies back in his rural home town in Southern California because "I'd never hear the end of it." Her salary was treated as a deviant act, even a bit like a crime. As Nina explained, in a near whisper:

I was interviewed for an article in Business Week, and I had to call the fellow back and ask him please not to publish my salary. When he interviewed me, I was a little proud of saying what my salary was. Then I thought, "I don't want that in there—because of Peter."

The taboo on talk of Nina's salary finally extended to themselves as well. As Nina explained, "after awhile we stopped talking about my salary. We still don't."

Another matter diminished Nina's gift. Her salary might make her expect more help from Peter at home. As Nina reported:

Occasionally I've wondered if (my salary) bothered him. Because if we're having a disagreement over something, he sometimes indicates he thinks I'm acting high and mighty, like "who do you think you are?" I say, "You never used to say that." He said, "I do think you've gotten much more assertive [nervous giggle] than you used to be." I do think Peter might equate my assertiveness with my income. I don't know in my own mind if that has anything to do with it. Or if I was just tired of doing all the housework.

If her greater salary meant he would have to do more at home, he would accept it only grudgingly.

In the climate of opinion he sensed himself to be living in, Peter felt like a "one in a hundred" kind of man. For, as he said with great feeling, "most men couldn't take it if their wives outearned them this much!" They both felt Nina was *lucky* to be married to such an unusually understanding man. So the gift, as Peter felt it was not from Nina to Peter, but from Peter to Nina. Nina, too, felt lucky because only with such an unusually understanding man could she be both successful at work and married.

Nina gave Peter the kind of gift it was a "man's place" to give a woman. Peter wanted to give Nina the high salary, and even more, to give her "the *choice* of whether or not to work." But Nina did not need the choice. Given her skills and opportunities, she would always choose to work. Instead, Nina really wanted Peter to share the housework and childcare. As it was, Nina had to ask Peter to help. Having always to ask, Nina felt Peter was doing her a favor: his participation was not a settled matter. Because she had to ask, his help did not *feel* to Nina like a gift.

Given Peter's shame about her salary, however, Nina did not want to push Peter about the housework. So she rarely asked. She herself did the lion's share of it. Nina *made up* for outearning her husband (and breaking the cultural rule) by working a double day.[10] In this way, the old rules reduced the value of new economic opportunities for women, and introduced an imbalance that might surprise Marx but not Simone de Beauvoir—in the marital economy of gratitude.

In the end, Peter benefited from his wife's salary. But he also benefited from a second order of gifts his wife owed him *because* she had given him the first gift—an "apology" said through housework.

Given how traditional most men are, a liberated man could make a fine marital bargaining chip out of his sympathy with the new rules, or even attempt at sympathy. Peter gave Nina an unusual amount of personal support for her career. What he did not give her was an acceptance of its public reflection on him. Curiously Nina was "doing it all"—being the prime provider and housekeeper too—and felt *grateful* that she could. We have here the emotional underbelly of gender ideology—not, as we might imagine, in its more popular form of anger and resentment, but in its more common form—of apology and gratitude.

Nina and Peter devised a marital dialogue that "lightened" their "mis-giving." They sidestepped the issue and exchanged other gifts. Nina also came to sympathize with Peter's view of the matter, so that they formed a united cultural baseline, according to which Peter's "mis-giving" was not a marital problem, but only Nina's personal problem of "role conflict," her personal weariness from too much to do.

In other marriages, mis-givings run deeper. Seth Stein, for example, was a hard-driving internist who worked eleven hours a day, and on three days, twelve. "I finally arranged to come home at 6:30," he explained, "when I realized I had missed the first two years of my son's growing up." Officially Seth supported his wife's career. As he commented, "I've always known my wife was a career lady." He believed that in general, too, women had as much place in the public world as men. But it was also clear that his outward rhetoric cloaked deeper and different feelings on the matter. There was a lag between his outward attitude toward his wife's career and the emotional anchor to which it was firmly tied.

For Seth acted and felt as though his work mattered far more than his wife's. This was because the reputational talk of fellow doctors, mattered dearly to Seth, and to such doctors—themselves "career-believers"—it did not matter how many times he had to read to his son the "Three Little Pigs." For Jessica, he felt, it must be different.

But Jessica had earned her own way through medical school, and now practiced as an internist. To a certain degree, Seth felt proud of his wife; he did not want her to be a housewife, or even a secretary. But the egalitarian rule stopped there at midpoint. Emotionally he resisted the rest of its social-psychological logic. His wife would be a professional, like himself. But her work would not be as important to the family or to himself, as he wanted his work to be to her and the family. (There would be no symmetrical "Status transfer.") Because his work took priority over hers, its rewards in relaxation and nurturance would take priority over hers, too. In sum, Seth was an egalitarian on the surface and a traditional underneath.[11]

As Seth drove home from a tough, long day at the office, he had the fantasy of a fresh cooked meal, wine, the children in bed, and appreciation, gratitude and nurturance from Jessica—who would be grateful for all his hard work brought her. Much to his wife's dismay, he sought no exit from his extraordinary hours, and insisted on conceiving of them as his gift to her.

Jessica wanted Seth to share the work of the home with her. Failing that, she wanted Seth to feel badly about not sharing. Even if his career could not permit, she wanted Seth *to want* to share. Failing that, she wanted Seth to set aside his concern for his own work, so he could appreciate *her* parenting. In contrast to the traditional Carmen, Jessica most of all wanted Seth to appreciate the fact that she was relinquishing time from her career, so that he could go full steam ahead in his work. As Seth explained:

Jessica has been very disappointed about my inability to do more in terms of the child rearing and my not doing 50-50. She says I don't do 50-50, that I have left the child rearing to her. Her career has suffered. She cut twice as much time, instead of me cutting time back from my career. She complains that I'm not more like some imaginary other men or men she knows. Such a man does take time with his children because he wants to and knows how important it is. I don't do enough parenting. So she's disappointed in me for not doing my share. On the other hand, she understands the spot I'm in. So she holds it in, until she gets good and pissed and then she lets me have it.

Their gratitude clash extended to nurturance. I asked Seth what he was not getting from Jessica that he had expected and wanted. He answered ruefully:

Nurturing. She don't take care of me enough. But the deal was so straight forward from day one that I'm not bitter. But when I do reflect on it, that's the thing I reflect on. I ain't got a wife taking care of me. Every once in a while I will be upset about it and long for someone who might be sitting around waiting to make me comfortable when I get home. Instead, Jessica needs her back massaged just as much as I do.

If Seth played by the cultural rules that made social room for his "career lady" wife, he could not enjoy first claim to nurturance. But Seth badly wanted that first claim, though he

was not convinced he had the *right* to want it. This was the first point in the interview that he broke into pigeon English, as if to distance himself from what he was saying, as if to say "someone less educated, someone younger, someone not me is talking."

Jessica proposed a different cultural baseline: "If you help me at home, I will feel grateful for *that* and love you." Through their different stances on the gender rules, they created a deep fracture in their understanding about what was not a gift. Both felt they were thanklessly giving gifts that were continually lost on the other. As Seth finally put it, "I work, and I work and I work, and I come home to what? Nothing." As Jessica put it, "I'm making sacrifices he doesn't even see." Their economy of gratitude had gone broke: each felt short-changed. Disappointed and deprived of "gifts," each finally resented the other. In another, yet more adversarial marriage, a similar husband explained miserably:

I could dig a twenty foot ditch and she would not notice. Barbara complains I am not doing my share. We get into arguments. We are both equally convinced that we are doing our share of chores around the house and Jude (the two year old)—in a sense—is considered a chore. One or the other of us is always thinking we're getting ripped off.

Each spouse failed to give what the other wanted, or to appreciate what the other was trying to give. Perhaps part of the answer lies in some early injury to human character. But mis-givings also seemed to occur to couples who were, in other arenas of their lives, thoughtful and giving. The larger problem lies in gender mixups in our modern *The Gift of the Magi*.

PRAGMATIC AND HISTORICAL FRAMES ON GRATITUDE

We may trace gratitude to three sources; first, to ideas about gender honor which derive from a *moral* frame of reference. Second, it may be traced to notions about what is, practically speaking, available. When a man compares his wife to other wives "out there" and finds her better or worse, he invokes a *pragmatic* frame of reference. Third, we may compare our fortunes with those of parents and grandparents, and others of the past, and so invoke a *historical* frame of reference.

In describing how gender rules have a ripple effect on marriage, we have already talked of a moral frame of reference. So let us turn now to the pragmatic and historical. When we apply a pragmatic frame of reference, we invoke ideas about how common or rare a desirable attitude or action is within a marketplace of ideas and actions. For example, women married to egalitarian husbands nearly always mentioned how "lucky" they felt they were to have a husband who was "unusually supportive" of their work, or who was "unusually willing" to share household chores, or "unusually involved with the children." Female "luck" was rooted in a comparison to other less lucky women. Compared to other women, they had it good. When men spoke of luck, which they less often did, it was relative to that of other men.

These luck-comparisons fit a certain pattern. When women tried to persuade their husbands to do more in the home, they compared their husbands to other men who did more. Husbands compared themselves to other men who did less. Underlying both comparisons, however, was a question of the gender marketplace: what was the *going rate* for male housework? For pitching in with the child rearing? For support for a wife's work?

Some working mothers also felt grateful for being actively shielded against the disapproval of kin or neighbors. Many working mothers told "shielding stories"—stories of being protected from the dishonor of breaking the traditional gender rules. One working mother was protected by a maid from the disapproval of a neighbor. Another was protected by a co-worker from the disapproval of a boss. Another had earned an advanced degree in nursing much against the advice of her mother, mother-in-law, and sister-in-law, all of whom were ardently traditional "hold-outs" against the mass movement of women into the cash economy. From time to time, her husband shielded her against this hostile microclimate of opinion. As she recounted appreciatively:

> Once when I was at the library working on a lecture, my husband's mother dropped by and asked where I was. Evan told her I was out shopping for Joey's clothes. He covered for me. Otherwise she would have been very critical of me for leaving Evan and Joey on a weekend like that.

To creep off to the library on a Saturday afternoon, leaving one's husband in charge of a three year old, under the cold judging eyes of traditional kin, was a daring act. Given her time and place, she was socially vulnerable. She therefore felt grateful that her husband protected her. For, when the relevant climate of opinion is unfavorable to women's ambitions, some unusual husbandly support becomes an extra chip in the marital bargain. This husband offered more than the "going rate" among males. He was unusual. Pragmatically speaking, his wife was "lucky."

We may also invoke a historical frame of reference. Over all, more women than men among these Bay Area couples mentioned feeling "lucky" or grateful at some aspect of their work and family arrangement. They felt lucky to have a good babysitter, lucky to have an understanding boss, or husband. They felt lucky their child so seldom got sick, lucky they needed so little sleep.

In many ways, men were objectively luckier than women. For roughly the same hours of work, women earned a third of the male wage. In addition to their full time jobs, these working mothers did nearly all the housework and childcare. Were they to divorce, these women were poised—as their husbands were not—for a great class fall. Ironically, though, women talked about luck and men did not. Why?[12]

Perhaps women unconsciously compare themselves favorably to yet more oppressed women of previous eras—their mothers or grandmothers who had fewer opportunities and rights than they. While many men have moved up the class ladder, men, as a gender, have relinquished certain privileges their fathers and grandfathers enjoyed. Relative to men in the past, they may feel "unlucky." To put it another way: (a) if life is divided into a female domestic realm and a male public realm, (b) if the female realm is devalued relative to the male, and (c) if females are now entering the male realm and males are encouraged to enter the female realm, these changes are likely to feel to women like moving "up" and to men like moving "down." History, too, provides a template of prior expectation against which we appraise our luck.

We may receive a gift from a person and feel grateful, or receive a gift from "life in general," and feel lucky. In either case the gift is a profoundly social affair. For to perceive a gift *as* a gift is to apply a background context to the present moment. This background context is partly moral: "how lucky I am compared to what the cultural rules lead me to expect." It is partly pragmatic: "how lucky I am compared to what I might have otherwise." It is partly historical: "how lucky I am compared to people of my kind in the past." We bring to bear these three frames of reference upon the ongoing stream of experi-

ence, and from time to time they produce moments of gratitude and luck.

This analysis of the social production of gratitude is not an alternative to an analysis based on power. It is an analysis of just how profound inequalities work emotionally. Power does not work *around* the feeling of gratitude: it works *through* it by establishing a moral, pragmatic and historical frame of reference which lowers a woman's template of prior expectations even as it artificially elevates that of man.

CONCLUSION AND IMPLICATIONS

Changes in the modern family alter how moral, pragmatic, and historical frames of reference are brought to bear on the ongoing flow of domestic life. Contemporary economic trends have drastically altered the reality of women's lives, much less so those of men. These trends have created a "culture lag"—a strain between the economic reality and the cultural code people apply to it. This culture lag bears powerfully on marriage. It makes of marriage a shock absorber of social tensions produced by larger social trends. Drawing on interviews from a larger study of two-job couples, I have contrasted (a) a consensual traditional economy of gratitude, (b) a consensual egalitarian economy of gratitude, (c) a larger number of marriages in which conflicting notions of gender transformed gratitude into an object of struggle.

When couples struggle over the cultural baseline of their economy of gratitude, they partly control the value of the gifts they want to exchange, and partly they do not. If a woman offers a man a homemade apple pie, they do not have to consider how the outside culture sees the apple pie. The valuing of the pie is "social" only in the sense that they have adopted an outer symbol of giving as a private one. Once done, the perception of the gift does not hinge upon the opinion of the outer world.

But couples do not have such control over the value of other gifts they may wish to exchange. Nina, in the example above, offered her higher salary to her husband. But his gender ideology prevented him from receiving it—not simply because he had a traditional notion of male honor in his head, but because his social circle was composed of people who have that notion in their heads. If he ignored what his social circle thinks of him, that act of courage enters his marital economy of gratitude. His wife will be grateful—and, in some way, will repay him. The best way to get sexism out of the economy of gratitude, then, might be to get it out of the social circles on which people—mainly men—rely for a good opinion of themselves.

Second, if marriage is the shock absorber of a dissonance between cultural and economic realities, and if this dissonance creates different viewpoints between men and women within marriage, then we need to understand "marital" problems in more broadly social ways. Certainly marriage is a union of two personalities: there's good chemistry and bad. But something fundamentally social also bedevils many modern marriages as well. For marriage is also a joining of two—often different, usually shifting—stances toward gender rules. A stance toward a gender rule affects what feels like a gift, a token of love. Much of marital dialogue is tacitly aligning his idea to her idea of how much a stint of housework, how much disapproval-shielding, or how much "taking it from the boys about your wife's higher salary"—counts in the currency of gratitude.

In modern times, the daily realities strain the traditional economy of gratitude—because most women have to work and want to be valued for it. At the same time modern realities also strain the egalitarian economy of gratitude, for many want to be equally valued for work that still earns substantially less. For traditional and egalitarian couples alike, then, the notion of a gift is culturally in flux.

The strain in modern marriage, then, may have less to do with "personal hang-ups" than with the ripple effect of larger social trends upon the understanding of a gift. The happiest of these two-job marriages, shared a common understanding of what a gift would be and their understanding also fit the current realities of their lives: even highly traditional men in happy marriages did not come home, sit at the dining room table and feel he "would be grateful" and "would feel loved" if dinner were waiting on it—for under modern circumstances, often it is not. Each found feasible equivalents for roses and apple pie.

Happy egalitarian couples sought out the social support to fully internalize the new gender rules. Most important, they did not make do with less gratitude: they found a way to exchange more gifts on new terms and in this way solved the problem of *The Gift of the Magi.*

ACKNOWLEDGMENTS

Special thanks to Adam Hochschild, Ann Swidler, Peggy Thoits, Steve Gordon, and David Franks for insightful criticism.

7 Gender Roles, Work, and the Family

Reading 20   The Good-Provider Role: Its Rise and Fall*

JESSIE BERNARD

The Lord is my shepherd, I shall not want. He sets a table for me in the very sight of my enemies; my cup runs over (23rd Psalm). And when the Israelites were complaining about hunger, they were on their way from Egypt to Canaan. God told Moses to rest assured: There would be meat for dinner and bread for breakfast the next morning. And, indeed, there were quails that very night, enough to cover the camp, and in the morning the ground was covered with dew that proved to be bread (Exodus 16:12–13). In fact, in this role of good provider, God is sometimes almost synonymous with Providence. Many people like Micawber, still wait for him, or Providence, to provide.

Granted, then, that the first great provider for the human species was God the Father, surely the second great provider for the human species was Mother, the gatherer, planter, and general factotum. Boulding (1976), citing Lee and de Vore, tells us that in hunting and gathering societies, males contribute about one fifth of the food of the clan, females the other four fifths (p. 96). She also concludes that by 12,000 B.C. in the early agricultural villages, females provided four fifths of human subsistence (p. 97). Not until large trading towns arose did the female contribution to human subsistence decline to equality with that of the male. And with the beginning of true cities, the provisioning work of women tended to become invisible. Still, in today's world it remains substantial.

Whatever the date of the virtuous woman described in the Old Testament (Proverbs 31:10–27), she was the very model of a good provider. She was, in fact, a highly productive conglomerate. She woke up in the middle of the night to tend to her business; she oversaw a multiple-industry household; *her* candles did not go out at night; there was a ready market for the high-quality linen girdles she made and sold to the merchants in town; and she kept track of the real estate market and bought good land when it became available, cultivating vineyards quite profitably. All this time her husband sat at the gate talking with his cronies.

A recent counterpart to the virtuous woman was the busy and industrious shtetl woman:

> The earnings of a livelihood is sexless, and the large majority of women ... participate in some gainful occupation if they do not carry the chief burden of support. The wife

of a "perennial student" is very apt to be the sole support of the family. The problem of managing both a business and a home is so common that no one recognizes it as special. . . . To bustle about in search of a livelihood is merely another form of bustling about managing a home; both are aspects of . . . health and livelihood. (Zborowski and Herzog 1952, p. 131)

In a subsistence economy in which husbands and wives ran farms, shops, or businesses together, a man might be a good, steady worker, but the idea that he was *the* provider would hardly ring true. Even the youth in the folk song who listed all the gifts he would bestow on his love if she would marry him—a golden comb, a paper of pins, and all the rest—was not necessarily promising to be a good provider.

I have not searched the literature to determine when the concept of the good provider entered our thinking. The term *provider* entered the English language in 1532, but was not yet male sex typed, as the older term *purveyor* already was in 1442. Webster's second edition defines the good provider as "one who provides, especially, colloq., one who provides food, clothing, etc. for his family; as, he is a good or an adequate provider." More simply, he could be defined as a man whose wife did not have to enter the labor force. The counterpart to the good provider was the housewife. However the term is defined, the role itself delineated relationships within a marriage and family in a way that added to the legal, religious, and other advantages men had over women.

Thus, under the common law, although the husband was legally head of the household and as such had the responsibility of providing for his wife and children, this provision was often made with help from the wife's personal property and earnings, to which he was entitled:

He owned his wife's and children's services, and had the sole right to collect wages for their work outside the home. He owned his wife's personal property outright, and had the right to manage and control all of his wife's real property during marriage, which included the right to use or lease property, and to keep any rents and profits from it. (Babcock, Freedman, Norton, and Ross 1975, p. 561)

So even when she was the actual provider, the legal recognition was granted the husband. Therefore, whatever the husband's legal responsibilities for support may have been, he was not necessarily a good provider in the way the term came to be understood. The wife may have been performing that role.

In our country in Colonial times women were still viewed as performing a providing role, and they pursued a variety of occupations. Abigail Adams managed the family estate, which provided the wherewithal for John to spend so much time in Philadelphia. In the 18th century "many women were active in business and professional pursuits. They ran inns and taverns; they managed a wide variety of stores and shops; and, at least occasionally, they worked in careers like publishing, journalism and medicine" (Demos 1974, p. 430). Women sometimes even "joined the menfolk for work in the fields" (p. 430). Like the household of the proverbial virtuous woman, the Colonial household was a little factory that produced clothing, furniture, bedding, candles, and other accessories, and again, as in the case of the virtuous woman, the female role was central. It was taken for granted that women provided for the family along with men.

The good provider as a specialized male role seems to have arisen in the transition from subsistence to market—especially money—

economies that accelerated with the industrial revolution. The good-provider role for males emerged in this country roughly, say, from the 1830s, when de Tocqueville was observing it, to the late 1970s, when the 1980 census declared that a male was not automatically to be assumed to be head of household. This gives the role a life span of about a century and a half. Although relatively short-lived, while it lasted the role was a seemingly rock-like feature of the national landscape.

As a psychological and sociological phenomenon, the good-provider role had wide ramifications for all of our thinking about families. It marked a new kind of marriage. It did not have good effects on women: The role deprived them of many chips by placing them in a peculiarly vulnerable position. Because she was not reimbursed for her contribution to the family in either products or services, a wife was stripped to a considerable extent of her access to cash-mediated markets. By discouraging labor force participation, it deprived many women, especially affluent ones, of opportunities to achieve strength and competence. It deterred young women from acquiring productive skills. They dedicated themselves instead to winning a good provider who would "take care of" them. The wife of a more successful provider became for all intents and purposes a parasite, with little to do except indulge or pamper herself. The psychology of such dependence could become all but crippling. There were other concomitants of the good-provider role.

EXPRESSIVITY AND THE GOOD-PROVIDER ROLE

The new industrial order that produced the good provider changed not so much the division of labor between the sexes as it did the site of the work they engaged in. Only two of the concomitants of this change in work site are selected for comment here, namely, (a) the identification of gender with work site as well as with work itself and (b) the reduction of time for personal interaction and intimacy within the family.

It is not so much the specific kinds of work men and women do—they have always varied from time to time and place to place—but the simple fact that the sexes do different kinds of work, whatever it is, which is in and of itself important. The division of labor by sex means that the work group becomes also a sex group. The very nature of maleness and femaleness becomes embedded in the sexual division of labor. One's sex and one's work are part of one another. One's work defines one's gender.

Any division of labor implies that people doing different kinds of work will occupy different work sites. When the division is based on sex, men and women will necessarily have different work sites. Even within the home itself, men and women had different work spaces. The woman's spinning wheel occupied a different area from the man's anvil. When the factory took over much of the work formerly done in the house, the separation of work space became especially marked. Not only did the separation of the sexes become spatially extended, but it came to relate work and gender in a special way. The work site as well as the work itself became associated with gender; each sex had its own turf. This sexual "territoriality" has had complicating effects on efforts to change any sexual division of labor. The good provider worked primarily in the outside male world of business and industry. The homemaker worked primarily in the home.

Spatial separation of the sexes not only identifies gender with work site and work but also reduces the amount of time available for spontaneous emotional give-and-take between husbands and wives. When men and women work in an economy based in the home, there are frequent occasions for interaction. (Consider, for example, the suggestive allusions made today to the rise in the birth rate nine months after a blackout.) When men and women are in close proximity, there is always the possibility of reassuring glances, the comfort of simple physical presence. But when the division of labor removes the man from the family dwelling for most of the day, intimate relationships become less feasible. De Tocqueville was one of the first to call our attention to this. In 1840 he noted that

> almost all men in democracies are engaged in public or professional life; and...the limited extent of common income obliges a wife to confine herself to the house, in order to watch in person and very closely over the details of domestic economy. All these distinct and compulsory occupations are so many natural barriers, which, by keeping the two sexes asunder, render the solicitations of the one less frequent and less ardent—the resistance of the other more easy. (de Tocqueville 1840, p. 212)

Not directly related to the spatial constraints on emotional expression by men, but nevertheless a concomitant of the new industrial order with the same effect, was the enormous drive for achievement, for success, for "making it" that escalated the provider role into the good-provider role. De Tocqueville (1840) is again our source:

> The tumultuous and constantly harassed life which equality makes men lead [becoming good providers] not only distracts from the passions of love, by denying them time to indulge in it, but it diverts them from it by another more secret but more certain road. All men who live in democratic ages more or less

contract ways of thinking of the manufacturing and trading classes. (p. 221)

As a result of this male concentration on jobs and careers, much abnegation and "a constant sacrifice of her pleasures to her duties" (de Tocqueville 1840, p. 212) were demanded by the American woman. The good-provider role, as it came to be shaped by this ambience, was thus restricted in what it was called upon to provide. Emotional expressivity was not included in the role. One of the things a parent might say about a man to persuade a daughter to marry him, or a daughter might say to explain to her parents why she wanted to, was not that he was a gentle, loving, or tender man but that he was a good provider. He might have many other qualities, good or bad, but if a man was a good provider, everything else was either gravy or the price one had to pay for a good provider.

Lack of expressivity did not imply neglect of the family. The good provider was a "family man." He set a good table, provided a decent home, paid the mortgage, bought the shoes, and kept his children warmly clothed. He might, with the help of the children's part-time jobs, have been able to finance their educations through high school and, sometimes, even college. There might even have been a little left over for an occasional celebration in most families. The good provider made a decent contribution to the church. His work might have been demanding, but he expected it to be. If in addition to being a good provider, a man was kind, gentle, generous, and not a heavy drinker or gambler, that was all frosting on the cake. Loving attention and emotional involvement in the family were not part of a woman's implicit bargain with the good provider.

By the time de Tocqueville published his observations in 1940, the general outlines of the good-provider role had taken shape. It called for a hard-working man who spent most of his time at his work. In the traditional conception of the role, a man's chief responsibility is his job, so that "by definition any family behaviors must be subordinate to it terms of significance and [the job] has priority in the event of a clash" (Scanzoni 1975, p. 38). This was the classic form of the good-provider role, which remained a powerful component of our societal structure until well into the present century.

COSTS AND REWARDS OF THE GOOD-PROVIDER ROLE FOR MEN

There were both costs and rewards for those men attached to the good-provider role. The most serious cost was perhaps the identification of maleness not only with the work site but especially with success in the role. "The American male looks to his breadwinning role to confirm his manliness" (Brenton 1966, p. 194).[1] To be a man one had to be not only a provider but a *good* provider. Success in the good-provider role came in time to define masculinity itself. The good provider had to achieve, to win, to succeed, to dominate. He was a bread*winner.* He had to show "strength, cunning, inventiveness, endurance—a whole range of traits henceforth defined as exclusively 'masculine'" (Demos 1974, p. 436). Men were judged as men by the level of living they provided. They were judged by the myth "that endows a money-making man with sexiness and virility, and is based on man's dominance, strength, and ability to provide for and care for 'his' woman" (Gould 1974, p. 97). The good provider became a player in the male competitive macho game. What one man provided for his family in the way of luxury and display had to be equaled or topped by what another could provide. Families became display cases for the success of the good provider.

The psychic costs could be high:

By depending so heavily on his breadwinning role to validate his sense of himself as a man, instead of also letting his roles as husband, father, and citizen of the community count as validating sources, the American male treads on psychically dangerous ground. It's always dangerous to put all of one's psychic eggs into one basket. (Brenton 1966, p. 194)

The good-provider role not only put all of a man's gender-identifying eggs into one psychic basket, but it also put all the family-providing eggs into one basket. One individual became responsible for the support of the whole family. Countless stories portrayed the humiliation families underwent to keep wives and especially mothers out of the labor force, a circumstance that would admit to the world the male head's failure in the good-provider role. If a married woman had to enter the labor force at all, that was bad enough. If she made a good salary, however, she was "co-opting the man's passport to masculinity" (Gould 1974, p. 98) and he was effectively castrated. A wife's earning capacity diminished a man's position as head of the household (Gould 1974, p. 99).

Failure in the role of good provider, which employment of wives evidenced, could produce deep frustration. As Komarovsky (1940, p. 20) explains, this is "because in his own estimation he is failing to fulfill what is the central duty of his life, the very touchstone of his manhood—the role of family provider."

But just as there was punishment for failure in the good-provider role, so also were there rewards for successful performance. A man "derived strength from his role as provider" (Komarovsky 1940, p. 205). He achieved a good deal of satisfaction from his ability to support his family. It won kudos. Being a good provider led to status in both the family and the community.

Within the family it gave him the power of the purse and the right to decide about expenditures, standards of living, and what constituted good providing. "Every purchase of the family—the radio, his wife's new hat, the children's skates, the meals set before him—all were symbols of their dependence upon him" (Komarovsky 1940, pp. 74–75). Such dependence gave him a "profound sense of stability" (p. 74). It was a strong counterpoise vis-á-vis a wife with a stronger personality. "Whether he had considerable authority within the family and was recognized as its head, or whether the wife's stronger personality...dominated the family, he nevertheless derived strength from his role as a provider" (Komarovsky 1940, p. 75). As recently as 1975, in a sample of 3,100 husbands and wives in 10 cities, Scanzoni found that despite increasing egalitarian norms, the good provider still had "considerable power in ultimate decision-making" and as "unique provider" had the right "to organize his life and the lives of other family members around his occupation" (p. 38).

A man who was successful in the good-provider role might be freed from other obligations to the family. But the flip side of this dispensation was that he could not make up for poor performances by excellence in other family roles. Since everything depended on his success as provider, everything was at stake. The good provider played an all-or-nothing game.

DIFFERENT WAYS OF PERFORMING THE GOOD-PROVIDER ROLE

Although the legal specifications for the role were laid out in the common law, in legislation, in legal precedents, in court decisions, and, most importantly, in custom and convention, in real-life situations the social and social-psychological specifications were set by the husband or, perhaps more accurately, by the community, alias the Joneses, and there were many ways to perform it.

Some men resented the burdens the role forced them to bear. A man could easily vent such resentment toward his family by keeping complete control over all expenditures, dispensing the money for household maintenance, and complaining about bills as though it were his wife's fault that shoes cost so much. He could, in effect, punish his family for his having to perform the role. Since the money he earned belonged to him—was "his"—he could do with it what he pleased. Through extreme parsimony he could dole out his money in a mean, humiliating way, forcing his wife to come begging for pennies. By his reluctance and resentment he could make his family pay emotionally for the provisioning he supplied.

At the other extreme were the highly competitive men who were so involved in outdoing the Joneses that the fur coat became more important than the affectionate hug. They "bought off" their families. They sometimes succeeded so well in their extravagance that they sacrificed the family they were presumably providing for to the achievements that made it possible (Keniston 1965).[2]

The Depression of the 1930s revealed in harsh detail what the loss of the role could mean both to the good provider and to his family, not only in the loss of income itself—which could be supplied by welfare agencies or even by other family members, including wives—but also and especially in the loss of face.

The Great Depression did not mark the demise of the good-provider role. But it did teach us what a slender thread the family hung on. It stimulated a whole array of programs designed to strengthen that thread, to ensure that it would never again be similarly threatened. Unemployment insurance was incorporated into the Social Security Act of 1935, for example, and a Full Employment Act was passed in 1946. But there proved to be many other ways in which the good-provider role could be subverted.

ROLE REJECTORS AND ROLE OVERPERFORMERS

Recent research in psychology, anthropology, and sociology has familiarized us with the tremendous power of roles. But we also know that one of the fundamental principles of role behavior is that conformity to role norms is not universal. Not everyone lives up to the specifications of roles, either in the psychological or in the sociological definition of the concept. Two extremes have attracted research attention: (a) the men who could not live up to the norms of the good-provider role or did not want to, at one extreme, and (b) the men who overperformed the role, at the other. For the wide range in between, from blue-collar workers to professionals, there was fairly consistent acceptance of the role, however well or poorly, however grumblingly or willingly, performed.

First the nonconformists. Even in Colonial times, desertion and divorce occurred:

Woman may have deserted because, say, their husbands beat them; husbands, on the other hand, may have deserted because they were unable or unwilling to provide for their usually large families in the face of the wives' demands to do so. These demands were, of course, backed by community norms making the husband's financial support a sacred duty. (Scanzoni 1979, pp. 24–25)

Fiedler (1962) has traced the theme of male escape from domestic responsibilities in the American novel from the time of Rip Van Winkle to the present:

The figure of Rip Van Winkle presides over the birth of the American imagination; and it is fitting that our first successful home-grown legend should memorialize, however playfully, the flight of the dreamer from the shrew—into the mountains and out of time, away from the drab duties of home... anywhere to avoid...marriage and responsibility. One of the factors that determine theme and form in our great books is this strategy of evasion, this retreat to nature and childhood which makes our literature (and life) so charmingly and infuriatingly "boyish." (pp. xx–xxi)

Among the men who pulled up stakes and departed for the West or went down to the sea in ships, there must have been a certain proportion who, like their mythic prototype, were simply fleeing the good-provider role.

The work of Demos (1974), a historian, offers considerable support for Fiedler's thesis. He tells us that the burdens thrust on men in the 19th century by the new patterns of work began to show their effects in the family. When "the [spatial] separation of the work lives of husbands and wives made communication so problematic," he asks, "what was the likelihood of meaningful communication?" (Demos 1974, p. 438). The answer is, relatively little. Divorce and separation increased, either formally or by tacit consent—or simply by default, as in the case of a variety of defaulters—tramps, bums, hoboes—among them.

In this connection, "the development of the notorious 'tramp' phenomenon is worth noticing," Demos (1974, p. 438) tells us. The tramp was a man who just gave up, who dropped out of the role entirely. He preferred not to work, but he would do small chores or other small-scale work for a handout if he had to. He was not above begging the housewife for a meal, hoping she would not find work for him to do in repayment. Demos (1974) describes the type:

> *Demoralized and destitute wanderers, their numbers mounting into the hundreds of thousands, tramps can be fairly characterized as men who had run away from their wives... Their presence was mute testimony to the strains that tugged at the very core of American family life... Many observers noted that the tramps had created a virtual society of their own [a kind of counterculture] based on a principle of single-sex companionship. (p. 438)*

A considerable number of them came to be described as "homeless men" and, as the country became more urbanized, landed ultimately on skid row. A large part of the task of social workers for almost a century was the care of the "evaded" women they left behind.[3] When the tramp became wholly demoralized, a chronic alcoholic, almost unreachable, he fell into a category of his own—he was a bum.

Quite a different kettle of fish was the hobo, the migratory worker who spent several months harvesting wheat and other large crops and the rest of the year in cities. Many were the so-called Wobblies, or Industrial Workers of the World, who repudiated the good-provider role on principle. They had contempt for the men who accepted it and could be called conscientious objectors to the role. "In some IWW circles, wives were regarded as the 'ball and chain.' In the West, IWW literature proclaimed that the migratory worker, usually a young, unmarried male, was 'the first specimen of American manhood...the leaven of the revolutionary labor movement'" (Foner 1979, p. 400). Exem-

plars of the Wobblies were the nomadic workers of the West. They were free men. The migratory worker, "unlike the factory slave of the Atlantic seaboard and the central states,...was most emphatically 'not afraid of losing his job.' No wife and family cumbered him. The worker of the East, oppressed by the fear of want for wife and babies, dared not venture much" (Foner 1979, p. 400). The reference to fear of loss of job was well taken; employers preferred married men, disciplined into the good-provider role, who had given hostages to fortune and were therefore more tractable.

Just on the verge between the area of conformity to the good-provider role—at whatever level—and the area of complete nonconformity to it was the non-good provider, the marginal group of workers usually made up of "the under-educated, the under-trained, the under-employed, or part-time employed, as well as the under paid, and of course the unemployed" (Snyder 1979, p. 597). These included men who wanted—sometimes desperately—to perform the good-provider role but who for one reason or another were unable to do so. Liebow (1966) has discussed the ramifications of failure among the black men of Tally's corner: The black man is

> *under legal and social constraints to provide for them [their families], to be a husband to his wife and a father to his children. The chances are, however, that he is failing to provide for them, and failure in this primary function contaminates his performance as father in other aspects as well. (p. 86)*

In some cases, leaving the family entirely was the best substitute a man could supply. The community was left to take over.[4]

At the other extreme was the overperformer. De Tocqueville, quoted earlier, was already describing him as he manifested in the 1830s. And as late as 1955 Warner and Ablegglen were adding to the considerable literature on industrial leaders and tycoons, referring to their "driving concentration" on their careers and their "intense focusing" of interests, energies, and skills on these careers, "even limiting their sexual activity" (pp. 48–49). They came to be known as workaholics or work-intoxicated men. Their preoccupation with their work even at the expense of their families was, as I have already noted, quite acceptable in our society.

Poorly or well performed, the good-provider role lingered on. World War II initiated a challenge, this time in the form of attracting more and more married women into the labor force, but the challenge was papered over in the 1950s with an "age of togetherness" that all but apotheosized the good provider, his house in the suburbs, his homebody wife, and his third, fourth, even fifth, child. As late as the 1960s most housewives (87%) still saw breadwinning as their husband's primary role (Lopata 1971, p. 91).[5]

INTRINSIC CONFLICT IN THE GOOD-PROVIDER ROLE

Since the good-provider role involved both family and work roles, most people believed that there was no incompatibility between them or at least that there should not be. But in the 1960s and 1970s evidence began to mount that maybe something was amiss.

De Tocqueville had documented the implicit conflict in the American businessman's devotion to his work at the expense of his family in the early years of the 19th century; the Industrial Workers of the World had proclaimed that the good-provider role which tied a man to his family was an impediment to the great revolution at the beginning of the 20th century; Fiedler (1962) had noted that throughout our history, in

the male fantasy world, there was freedom from the responsibilities of this role; about 50 years ago Freud ([1930]1958) had analyzed the intrinsic conflict between the demands of women and the family on one side and the demands of men's work on the other:

> Women represented the interests of the family and sexual life, the work of civilization has become more and more men's business; it confronts them with ever harder tasks, compels them to subliminations of instinct which women are not easily able to achieve. Since man has not an unlimited amount of mental energy at his disposal, he must accomplish his tasks by distributing his libido to the best advantage. What he employs for cultural [occupational] purposes he withdraws to a great extent from women, and his sexual life; his constant association with men and his dependence on his relations with them even estrange him from his duties as husband and father. Woman finds herself thus forced into the background by the claims of culture [work] and she adapts an inimical attitude towards it. (pp. 50–51)

In the last two decades, researchers have been raising questions relevant to Freud's statement of the problem. They have been asking people about the relative satisfactions they derive from these conflicting values—family and work. Among the earliest studies comparing family–work values was a Gallup poll in 1940 in which both men and women chose a happy home over an interesting job or wealth as a major life value. Since then there have been a number of such polls, and a considerable body of results has now accumulated. Pleck and Lang (1979) and Hesselbart (1978) have summarized the findings of these surveys. All agree that there is a clear bias in the direction of the family. Pleck and Lang conclude that "men's family role is far more psychologically significant to them than is their work role" (p. 29), and Hesselbart—however critical she is of the studies she summarizes—believes they should not be dismissed lightly and concludes that they certainly "challenge the idea that family is a 'secondary' valued role" (p. 14).[6] Douvan (1978) also found in a 1976 replication of a 1957 survey that family values retained priority over work: "Family roles almost uniformly rate higher in value production then the job role does" (p. 16).[7]

The very fact that researchers have asked such questions is itself interesting. Somehow or other both the researchers and the informants seem to be saying that all this complaining about the male neglect of the family, about the lack of family involvement by men, just is not warranted. Neither de Tocqueville nor Freud was right. Men do value family life more than they value their work. They do derive their major life satisfactions from their families rather than from their work.

It may well be true that men derive the greatest satisfaction from their family roles, but this does not necessarily mean they are willing to pay for the benefit. In any event, great attitudinal changes took place in the 1960s and 1970s.

Douvan, on the basis of surveys in 1957 and 1976, found, for example, a considerable increase in the proportion of both men and women who found marriage and parenthood burdensome and restrictive. Almost three fifths (57%) of both married men and married women in 1976 saw marriage as "all burdens and restrictions," as compared with only 42% and 47%, respectively, in 1957. And almost half (45%) also viewed children as "all burdens and restrictions" in 1976, as compared with only 28% and

33% for married men and married women, respectively, in 1957. The proportion of working men with a positive attitude toward marriage dropped drastically over this period, from 68% to 39%. Working women, who made up a fairly small number of all married women in 1957, hardly changed attitudes at all, dropping only from 43% to 42%. The proportion of working men who found marriage and children burdensome and restrictive more than doubled, from 25% to 56% and from 25% to 58%, respectively. Although some of these changes reflected greater willingness in 1976 than in 1957 to admit negative attitudes toward marriage and parenthood—itself significant—profound changes were clearly in process. More and more men and women were experiencing disaffection with family life.[8]

"ALL BURDENS AND RESTRICTIONS"

Apparently, the benefits of the good-provider role were greater than the costs for most men. Despite the legend of the flight of the American male (Fiedler 1962), despite the defectors and dropouts, despite the tavern habitué's "ball and chain" cliché, men seemed to know that the good-provider role, if they could succeed in it, was good for them. But Douvan's findings suggest that recently their complaints have become serious, bone-deep. The family they have been providing for is not the same family it was in the past.

Smith (1979) calls the great trek of married women into the labor force a subtle revolution—revolutionary not in the sense of one class overthrowing a status quo and substituting its own regime, but revolutionary in its impact on both the family and the work roles of men and women. It diluted the prerogatives of the good-provider role. It increased the demands made on the good provider, especially in the form of more, emotional investment in the family, more sharing of household responsibilities. The role became even more burdensome.

However men may now feel about the burdens and restrictions imposed on them by the good-provider role, most have, at least ostensibly, accepted them. The tramp and the bum had "voted with their feet" against the role; the hobo or Wobbly had rejected it on the basis of a revolutionary ideology that saw it as enslaving men to the corporation; tavern humor had glossed the resentment habitués felt against its demands. Now the "burdens-and-restrictions" motif has surfaced both in research reports and, more blatantly, in the male liberation movement. From time to time it has also appeared in the clinicians' notes.

Sometimes the resentment of the good provider takes the form of simply wanting more appreciation for the life-style he provides. All he does for his family seems to be taken for granted. Thus, for example, Goldberg (1976), a psychiatrist, recounts the case of a successful businessman:

> He's feeling a deepening sense of bitterness and frustration about his wife and family. He doesn't feel appreciated. It angers him the way they seem to take the things his earnings purchase for granted. They've come to expect it as their due. It particularly enrages him when his children put him down for his "materialistic middle-class trip." He'd like to tell them to get someone else to support them but he holds himself back. (p. 124)

Brenton (1966) quotes a social worker who describes an upper-middle-class woman: She has "gotten hold of a man who'll drive himself like mad to get money, and [is] denigrating him

for being too interested in money, and not interested in music, or the arts, or in spending time with the children. But at the same time she's subtly driving him—and doesn't know it" (p. 226). What seems significant about such cases is not that men feel resentful about the lack of appreciation but that they are willing to justify their resentment. They are no longer willing to grin and bear it.

Sometimes there is even more than expressed resentment; there is an actual repudiation of the role. In the past, only a few men like the hobo or Wobbly were likely to give up. Today, Goldberg (1976) believes, more are ready to renounce the role, not on theoretical revolutionary grounds, however, but on purely selfish ones:

> Male growth will stem from openly avowed, unashamed, self-oriented motivations.... Guilt-oriented "should" behavior will be rejected because it is always at the price of a hidden build-up of resentment and frustration and alienation from others and is, therefore, counterproductive. (p. 184)

The disaffection of the good provider is directed to both sides of his role. With respect to work, Lefkowitz (1979) has described men among whom the good-provider role is neither being completely rejected nor repudiated, but diluted. These men began their working lives in the conventional style, hopeful and ambitious. They found a job, married, raised a family, and "achieved a measure of economic security and earned the respect of . . . colleagues and neighbors" (Lefkowitz 1979, p. 31). In brief, they successfully performed the good-provider role. But unlike their historical predecessors, they in time became disillusioned with their jobs— not jobs on assembly lines, not jobs usually characterized as alienating, but fairly presti-gious jobs such as aeronautics engineer and gov-ernment economist. They daydreamed about other interests. "The common theme which sur-faced again and again in their histories, was the need to find a new social connection—to reas-sert control over their lives, to gain some sense of freedom" (Lefkowitz 1979, p. 31). These men felt "entitled to freedom and independence." Middle-class, educated, self-assured, articulate, and for the most part white, they knew they could talk themselves into a job if they had to. Most of them did not want to desert their fami-lies. Indeed, most of them "wanted to rejoin the intimate circle they felt they had neglected in their years of work" (p. 31).

Though some of the men Lefkowitz studied sought closer ties with their families, in the case of those studied by Sarason (1977), a psycholo-gist, career changes involved lower income and had a negative impact on families. Sarason's subjects were also men in high-level profes-sions, the very men least likely to find marriage and parenthood burdensome and restrictive. Still, since career change often involved a reduction in pay, some wives were unwilling to accept it, with the result that the marriage dete-riorated (p. 178). Sometimes it looked like a no-win game. The husband's earlier career brought him feelings of emptiness and alienation, but it also brought financial rewards for the family. Greater work satisfaction for him in lower pay-ing work meant reduced satisfaction with life-style. These findings lead Sarason to raise a number of points with respect to the good-pro-vider role. "How much," he asks, "does an indi-vidual or a family need in order to maintain a satisfactory existence? Is an individual being responsible to himself or his family if he pro-vides them with little more than the bare essen-tials of living?" (p. 178). These are questions about the good provider role that few men raised in the past.

Lefkowitz (1979) wonders how his down-wardly mobile men lived when they left their jobs. "They put together a basic economic pack-age which consisted of government assistance, contributions from family members who had not worked before and some bartering of goods and services" (p. 31). Especially interesting in this list of income sources are the "contributions from family members who had not worked be-fore" (p. 31). Surely not mothers and sisters. Who, of course, but wives?

WOMEN AND THE PROVIDER ROLE

The present discussion began with the woman's part in the provider role. We saw how as more and more of the provisioning of the family came to be by way of monetary exchange, the woman's part shrank. A woman could still pro-vide services, but could furnish little in the way of food, clothing, and shelter. But now that she is entering the labor force in large numbers, she can once more resume her ancient role, this time, like her male counterpart the provider, by way of a monetary contribution. More and more women are doing just this.

The assault of the good-provider role in the Depression was traumatic. But a modified ver-sion began to appear in the 1970s as a single income became inadequate for more and more families. Husbands have remained the major providers, but in an increasing number of cases the wife has begun to share this role. Thus, the proportion of married women aged 15 to 54 (liv-ing with their husbands) in the labor force more than doubled between 1950 and 1978, from 25.2% to 55.4%. The proportion for 1990 is esti-mated to reach 66.7% (Smith 1979, p. 14). Fewer women are now full-time housewives.

For some men the relief from the strain of sole responsibility for the provider role has been welcome. But for others the feeling of degradation resembles the feeling reported 40 years earlier in the Great Depression. It is not that they are no longer providing for the family but that the role-sharing wife now feels justified in making demands on them. The good-provider role with all its prerogatives and perquisites has undergone profound changes. It will never be the same again.[9] Its death knell was sounded when, as noted above, the 1980 census no longer automatically assumed that the male member of the household was its head.

THE CURRENT SCENE

Among the new demands being made on the good-provider role, two deserve special consideration, namely, (1) more intimacy, expressivity, and nurturance—specifications never included in it as it originally took shape—and (b) more sharing of household responsibility and child care.

As the pampered wife in an affluent household came often to be an economic parasite, so also the good provider was often, in a way, a kind of emotional parasite. Implicit in the definition of the role was that he provided goods and material things. Tender loving care was not one of the requirements. Emotional ministrations from the family were his right; providing them was not a corresponding obligation. Therefore, as de Tocqueville had already noted by 1840, women suffered a kind of emotional deprivation labeled by Robert Weiss "relational deficit" (cited in Bernard 1976). Only recently has this male rejection of emotional expression come to be challenged. Today, even blue-collar women are imposing "a host of new role expectations upon their husbands or lovers. . . . A new role set asks the blue-collar male to strive for . . . deep-coursing intimacy" (Shostak 1973, p. 75). It was not only vis-á-vis his family that the good provider was lacking in expressivity. This lack was built into the whole male role script. Today not

only women but also men are beginning to protest the repudiation of expressivity prescribed in male roles (David and Brannon 1976; Farrell 1974; Fasteau 1974; Pleck and Sawyer 1974).

Is there any relationship between the "imposing" on men of "deep-coursing intimacy" by women on one side and the increasing proportion of men who find marriage burdensome and restrictive on the other? Are men seeing the new emotional involvements being asked of them as "all burdens and restrictions"? Are they responding to the new involvements under duress? Are they feeling oppressed by them? Fearful of them?

From the standpoint of high-level pure-science research there may be something bizarre, if not even slightly absurd, in the growing corpus of serious research on how much or how little husbands of employed wives contribute to household chores and child care. Yet it is serious enough that all over the industrialized world such research is going on. Time studies in a dozen countries—communist as well as capitalist—trace the slow and bungling process by which marriage accommodates to changing conditions and by which women struggle to mold the changing conditions in their behalf. For everywhere the same picture shows up in research: an image of women sharing the provider role and at the same time retaining responsibility for the household. Until recently such a topic would have been judged unworthy of serious attention. It was a subject that might be worth a good laugh, for instance, as when an all-thumbs man in a cartoon burns the potatoes or finds himself bumbling awkwardly over a diaper, demonstrating his—proud—male ineptness at such female work. But it is no longer funny.

The "politics of housework" (Mainardi 1970) proves to be more profound than originally believed. It has to do not only with tasks but also with gender and perhaps more with the site of the tasks than with their intrinsic nature. A man can cook magnificently if he does it on a hunting or fishing trip; he can wield a skillful needle if he does it mending a tent or a fishing net; he can even feed and clean a toddler on a camping trip. Few of the skills of the homemaker are beyond his reach so long as they are practiced in a suitably male environment. It is not only women's work in and of itself that is degrading but any work on female turf. It may be true, as Brenton (1966) says, that "the secure man can wash a dish, diaper a baby, and throw the dirty clothes into the washing machine—or do anything else women used to do exclusively—without thinking twice about it" (p. 211), but not all men are that secure. To a great many men such chores are demasculinizing. The apron is shameful on a man in the kitchen; it is all right at the carpenter's bench.

The male world may look upon the man who shares household responsibilities as, in effect, a scab. One informant tells the interviewer about a conversation on the job: "What, are you crazy?" his hard-hat fellow workers ask him when he speaks of helping his wife. "The guys want to kill me. 'You son of a bitch! You are getting us in trouble.'... The men get really mad" (Lein 1979, p. 492). Something more than persiflage is involved here. We are fairly familiar with the trauma associated with the invasion by women of the male work turf, the hazing women can be subjected to, and the male resentment of admitting them except into their own segregated areas. The corresponding entrance of men into the traditional turf of women—the kitchen or the nursery—has analogous but not identical concomitants.

Pleck and Lang (1979) tell us that men are now beginning to change in the direction of greater involvement in family life. "Men's family behavior is beginning to change, becoming increasingly congruent with the long-standing psychological significance of the family in their lives" (p. 1). They measure this greater involve-

ment by way of the help they offer with homemaking chores. Scanzoni (1975), on the basis of a survey of over 3,000 husbands and wives, concludes that at least in households in which wives are in the labor force, there is the "possibility of a different pattern in which responsibility for households would unequivocally fall equally on husbands as well as wives" (p. 38). A brave new world indeed. Still, when we look at the reality around us, the pace seems intolerably slow. The responsibilities of the old good-provider role have attenuated far faster than have its prerogatives and privileges.

A considerable amount of thought has been devoted to studying the effects of the large influx of women into the work force. An equally interesting question is what the effect will be if a large number of men actually do increase their participation in the family and the household. Will men find the apron shameful? What if we were to ask fathers to alternate with mothers in being in the home when youngsters come home from school? Would fighting adolescent drug abuse be more successful if fathers and mothers were equally engaged in it? If the school could confer with fathers as often as with mothers? If the father accompanied children when they went shopping for clothes? If fathers spent as much time with children as do mothers?

Even as husbands, let alone as fathers, the new pattern is not without trauma. Hall and Hall (1979), in their study of two-career couples, report that the most serious fights among such couples occur not in the bedroom, but in the kitchen, between couples who profess a commitment to equality but who find actually implementing it difficult. A young professional reports that he is philosophically committed to egalitarianism in marriage and tries hard to practice it, but it does not work. He even feels guilty about this. The stresses involved in reworking roles may have an impact on health. A study of engineers and accountants finds poorer health among those with employed wives than among those with nonemployed wives (Burke and Wier 1976). The processes involved in role change have been compared with those involved in deprogramming a cult member. Are they part of the increasing sense of marriage and parenthood as "all burdens and restrictions"?

The demise of the good-provider role also calls for consideration of other questions: What does the demotion of the good provider to the status of senior provider or even mere coprovider do to him? To marriage? To gender identity? What does expanding the role of housewife to that of junior provider or even coprovider do to her? To marriage? To gender identity? Much will of course depend on the social and psychological ambience in which changes take place.

A PARABLE

I began this essay with a proverbial woman. I close it with a modern parable by William H. Chafe (1978), a historian who also keeps his eye on the current scene. Jack and Jill, both planning professional careers, he as doctor, she as lawyer, marry at age 24. She works to put him through medical school in the expectation that he will then finance her through law school. A child is born during the husband's internship, as planned. But in order for him to support her through professional training as planned, he will have to take time out from his career. After two years, they decide that both will continue their training on a part-time basis, sharing household responsibilities and using day-care services. Both find part-time positions and work out flexible work schedules that leave both of them time for child care and companionship with one another. They live happily ever after.

That's the end? you ask incredulously. Well, not exactly. For, as Chafe (1978) points out, as usual the personal is also political:

> *Obviously such a scenario presumes a radical transformation of the personal values that today's young people bring to their relationships as well as a readiness on the part of social and economic institutions to encourage, or at least make possible, the development of equality between men and women. (p. 28)*

The good-provider role may be on its way out, but its legitimate successor has not yet appeared on the scene.

Reading 21   Affluence and Poverty*

MARJORIE L. DeVAULT

Here, I will focus explicitly on the significance of class relations for the conduct of feeding work. Feeding, like most household work, is performed as direct service for family members, outside of cash-mediated relations, and is often experienced as freely given, out of "love." But the means for providing a household life are commodities that, for the most part, must be wrested from a cash-mediated market. In the United States, where there is some measure of income protection for most workers and a greatly expanded sphere of "consumption," basic necessities can be obtained more easily than in many societies. However, this observation obscures more disturbing facts: that income differences mean considerable variation in the amounts and kinds of food consumed; that many in the United States must spend a far higher percentage of their income merely to eat; and that a significant group of people continue to experience hunger and malnutrition.[1]

The establishment of an official "poverty threshold" recognizes the impossibility of providing for a family without at least a minimal cash income, and social welfare assistance provides minimal cash payments to at least some of those who cannot earn a living wage. The poverty threshold is based on a "household budget" that estimates necessary expenditures.[2] Such a budget, however, says nothing about the kind of work required to translate these minimal sums into household life for a group of people (in much the same way that time-budget studies of household work are mute on the invisible tasks of monitoring, planning, and coordinating family life). The differing material bases of household/family groups—connections to wealth and occupation, the resulting amount and stability of cash resources, and redistributions of resources by the state—all combine to construct quite different conditions for the conduct of household work. These different conditions mean that the work itself is experienced and understood differently, and that the "families" produced through housework are different as well.

In this chapter, I consider how class relations shape and are shaped by distinctive patterns of feeding work and household life. My discussion is based on a conception of social class as dynamic social process, organizing the activities of individuals and families both in very direct ways—such as through the wages flowing into households, or the demands of particular occupations—and also in less direct ways, through locations in particular neighborhoods, schools, and other social groups. My aim is to show how the social structures of class construct contexts for household life and work, and also to show how different ways of conducting household life and work are implicated in the reproduction of class relations.[3] I discuss profound differences in the work of "feeding a family," but I also take notice of the ways that these differences are obscured. I will suggest later that cultural discourses about class-less "wives" and "mothers" are powerful ideological tools that hide the realities of many women and their families.

I assume that class position, though produced primarily through occupation, is more accurately assigned to households than to individuals. The conditions and requirements for household work are contingent upon the total resources available to the household group. Most family/households gain income from wage work by one or more members. Some inherit family wealth, and virtually all benefit, though in very different ways, from government redistributions, such as provisions for tax relief and social welfare benefits. Occupational position and income are related, but they rarely coincide neatly. Thus, neither occupational categories nor income levels alone are completely satisfactory ways of "sorting" households, especially for a discussion of issues related to consumption, which are more directly tied to income than to workplace experiences. In general, those in professional/managerial occupational positions have higher incomes than those in working-class/white-collar positions. But, there is a large area of overlap between these two groups, produced partly but not entirely by the income contributions of wives who work for pay in the working-class/white-collar group. In fact, some of the class-related effects on the conduct of household work are closely related to income, while others arise from the patterns of sociability of groups linked to different types of paid work.

In the first part of this chapter, I discuss in a general way the significance of money in people's accounts of household work, and some variations in their spending and saving practices. Then, I take a closer look behind the predominant image, of the affluent homemaker, at households sustained on the meagerest incomes.

MONEY AND THE MARKET

In the most general sense, all of these people face a similar problem: the allocation of their total money resources to food and other expenses. For most people, a general level of spending on food is a settled question, a background assumption that underlies their more specific everyday strategizing about planning and purchasing. But attention to food expense is necessary for some and voluntary for others. Slightly less than half of all these interviewees (43 percent) talked of having a "budget" for food expenditures and those who did so were more heavily represented in the lower-income groups.[4] Whether they budget or not, those with very low incomes are most directly aware of economic constraints, and their awareness appears in their talk. In the poorest women's accounts, there are many spontaneous comments about money. When they reported on shopping routines, they often began by mentioning the amounts of money that structure their decisions: how much money they have each month, and how much they spend on food. These references appeared both earlier in the interviews and more often than in the accounts of more affluent informants. Margaret, a white single mother who works part-time at a low-wage job, offered as an introductory comment in the first few minutes of our interview:

> With cooking and stuff like that, we stick to chicken, hamburger meat, and hot dogs. Because we spend over $100 a week, on food alone.

Like others with limited incomes, she had developed an idiosyncratic but effective system for sticking to an informal "budget":

> Usually if I fill the basket up, it's about 130... When the basket is full, that's a little over $100. Because

I buy the same amount of stuff. But if it's getting a little over the basket, that's when I have to buy like, deodorant and toilet paper, which I don't buy every week. Or shampoo and toothpaste, And then that makes it 140, 130.

Another woman makes one large shopping trip each month, and insures that she will stay within her budget by taking with her only the amount she intends to spend:

OK, when I go I have $200 even, and that's including the tax and everything. And with that $200, that's including soap, toilet paper and all the household things. That's $200 for everything.

The $200 limit she has established reflects her earlier practice, when she relied on food stamps and had less cash income available. At the time of our interview, she was working for pay and no longer received food stamps; however, her low-wage job had not significantly increased her overall resources. She explained her reasoning about a food budget, once again structuring the account around specific money amounts:

When I got food stamps, I would spend—I'd come out spending $200. My 168 in food stamps, plus another $50 in money. That's the way it worked out. So that's the way I did it when I got a job. I just, you know, went on spending $200.

Those in households with more resources often reported a similar result—a generally stable level of expense. They talked of routinizing their purchasing decisions, and of avoiding particularly expensive foods in order to hold their expenditures at a constant level ("He doesn't get filet mignon at home," or somewhat more ambiguously, "I don't buy junk.") In addition, the shopping strategies of some of those in moderate-income households were also tied to specific amounts of money, which came into the household at particular times. But those who had more money to work with talked about these matters more abstractly, and infrequently mentioned how much they spent. For example, when Janice described her weekly shopping, she referred to the checks she and her husband received, but not to the amounts of their incomes:

I get paid every other Friday, and my husband gets paid every Friday. And the payday that I have I use my money, and on the payday that he has, that I don't, I use his. Which is a lot less than what I have, so I try to do my bigger shopping on my payday, and get as many things as I can. On his, I'll fill in with a lot of vegetables and fruits.

In part, the differences in these accounts seem to arise from differences in attitude, the reticence of more affluent interviewees reflecting a characteristically middle-class "etiquette" of keeping such information within the family. In this study, for instance, the poorest interviewees talked most directly about money, while others were more likely to talk in general terms about whether things were "tight" or "comfortable" (though all except one informant—the wealthiest—were willing to tell me the amount of their household income when asked). This pattern is consistent with other studies of very poor and very wealthy households. Carol Stack's (1974) study of poor families shows how income pooling is an adaptive survival strategy in poor communities, and suggests that as a result, knowledge about the resources available is relatively widely distributed. Rosanna Hertz (1986), by contrast, shows how affluent dual-career couples can afford to use their discretionary money to express individuality and autonomy, and how in some cases, spouses withhold information about their salaries even from each other. But these studies also suggest that such differences arise not only from attitudes toward money, but from material conditions that construct quite different relations to money in poor and affluent households. Those in very poor households must use very small amounts of cash income to maintain their households, and these minimal amounts set narrow limits for expenditure on survival needs. As a result, poor women discussing their food expenses often talked rather specifically about their rent or other household expenses as well, something that others rarely did. When I asked about her income, a black woman caring for six children produced a succinct summary of her monthly budget:

> I do get food stamps—food stamps, I get, uh, $291. And the check [from AFDC] is about 500. OK. Now my rent's about $300. Then I have the light bill, and the gas bill, and the phone bill. And then I have to figure out ways to get washing done. And somebody's always going to be needing something.

Her account displays the calculus that is ever present in these women's strategizing, the balancing of meager income against fixed expenses, unpredictable needs, and the areas—like food expense—where expenditures can sometimes be reduced through careful purchasing or extra effort. In situations like these, when there is virtually no margin beyond subsistence, even small amounts of money loom large, and particular prices are significant.

Charles and Kerr (1988) also found that poor women are more likely than others to report that cost is an important criterion for shopping decisions, and they suggest that poor women are less able to concern themselves with the "goodness" of food purchases. However, Charles and Kerr relied on a structured interview technique that required ranking such factors, and therefore made cost and "goodness" competing concerns. The accounts of informants in this study did not suggest that poor women were less concerned with the quality of food they purchased; rather, their task was to strategize about obtaining "good" food with very little expenditure.

In addition to a heightened concern about expenditure in low-income households, efforts to save money on food purchases involve different practices and have different meanings. For all of these people, food is an essential, but variable rather than fixed expense. Thus, almost everyone, from the wealthiest to the poorest households, talked about food expenditure as a possible area for saving money in order to make more available for other purchases. This mode of thought produces a surface similarity in people's accounts. Most, though not all, talked of trying to limit their food expenses, comparing prices in the store while shopping, watching for bargains and stocking up on items on sale, and purchasing cheaper generic products rather than brand-name items.[5] The interviews revealed a general trend toward greater emphasis on economizing among poor and working-class families, but also considerable individual variation.

In all groups, those who engage in these economizing practices typically describe them as necessary ("Of course now everyone is very cost conscious"), or as self-evidently intelligent or admirable behavior ("It's like a game, that I say, oh, wow, I only spent you know, a certain amount—it's oh, you did good!"). Those who do little economizing treat such practices as matters of personal inclination, and tend to minimize their value. Virtually all of the accounts, however, display considerable ambivalence about the efficacy of economizing, reflecting the difficulty of calculating actual savings when there are so many decisions to be made simultaneously. Those who are most committed to economizing do not express their ambivalence directly, but rather in extensive discussion of alternative purchasing strategies, a kind of talk that suggests continuing anxiety about saving as much as possible. For others, ambivalence is expressed more directly ("You have to watch . . . and make sure you're not spending more with your coupons"), or in negotiation with other household members. In several of the professional households, for example, husbands were especially concerned about potential savings on food, and either shopped themselves in order to save as much as possible or pressured their wives to economize more. Typically, their wives acknowledged the rationality of attending to cost, but they often expressed doubts about the value of specific practices these husbands suggested. One white woman described her partner's attention to relatively small savings with an amused tolerance:

> My husband likes to clip coupons. And I tease him about this. I say, "A lawyer? Clipping and cataloging coupons?" I said, "I don't bother with that, I don't think it's worth the money. But you're welcome to do it." So then I have to go and look for his coupons, to make him happy, see if he's got anything new.

Her report displays the uncertainty about savings that was characteristic of so many accounts, but it also shows the power of a husband's statement of economic logic. Even though she herself considers this kind of activity inessential—not "worth the money"—she finds it difficult to argue that clipping coupons is not virtuous activ-

ity, and she feels obliged to "make him happy" by using the coupons he has collected.

In spite of considerable individual variation in the extent to which shoppers attempt to save money, and their particular means for doing so, there are also fundamental differences produced by having more or less money to work with, and these begin to come into view when we look at the meanings of economizing in different sorts of households. Income levels themselves do not always convey the objective situation of particular household groups, or their subjective assessments of their situations. Families with relatively high incomes sometimes reported severe financial pressures, usually because of heavy obligations and debt. In the following discussion, therefore, I have not sorted households by income levels or class groups alone; instead I characterize several relatively distinct approaches to reasoning about economizing, which were loosely associated with both class group and income level.

Most of the wealthiest interviewees, all from professional/managerial households, made some reference to economizing, though virtually all acknowledged that they did not need to "worry about money." They took for granted a certain kind of attention to money; the underlying assumption, that one should not spend more than necessary on food, seemed not to require elaboration. But these families' incomes—and the security of stable incomes—allow rather generous definitions of what is "necessary." Like others, they sometimes talked about the boundaries to their purchasing decisions—which items they would not buy because of price. But they were less likely than others to rule out particular kinds of food and more likely to report that they decided when to buy things because of price: "If grapes cost more than $1.19, I just don't get them."

Most informants in higher-income households reported that they compare prices, watch for sales, and use some coupons or generic items. But the calculus of cost, need, and preference is quite flexible for these families, and they discuss the cost of food as one factor to be considered among others. They are concerned with the variety and quality of their food, and there is little indication in these accounts that cost places significant limits on what they buy. The practice of "stocking up" on sale items—used by others to save money on standard purchases—is often used by wealthier shoppers as an opportunity to purchase especially favored foods, expanding the household repertoire of menus, rather than simply reducing cost. A white professional man, for example, who does the shopping for his household precisely because he believes he can save more money than his wife, reported proudly: "This winter I've invested heavily in shrimp and scallop futures."

These families with more resources can accommodate their preferences more easily; saving money is desirable, but optional. While these people usually refer to the importance of economizing, they also speak without worry about decisions to forego savings for other benefits in particular situations. The voluntary character of economizing is clearest in the account of a relatively affluent white single mother, who reported that she does not worry about saving money on food because time is an even scarcer resource in her life. She explained:

> I used to go to the big supermarkets, and try to save a penny here, a penny there, you know. And occasionally I'll look at the, you know, the sale items. But I gave that up. That is the most ridiculous waste of time.

Since her divorce, as she begins a new career and cares for her two children, she chooses to go to a smaller store where she can do her shopping more quickly:

> They get you in and out! Oh—it's wonderful. And all of a sudden that

> became more important to me than any money I was saving or anything.

A final feature that appeared in the talk of a few wealthy women was a concern with the negative implications of economizing, a sense that too much attention to price might be unseemly. For example, one affluent white woman, reporting that she had purchased orange juice on sale rather than squeezing it herself, worried that I would think her "a tightwad." And a white professional woman explained that she clips coupons occasionally because her husband will use them, but that she is uncomfortable with the image of "couponing": "there are always these horrible ladies on television who, you know, 'I only spent 39¢ on my—feeding my family of four because I saved all these coupons!'... there's a lot of affect associated with my not saving coupons."

In middle-income, mostly working-class, households, relatively secure but with considerably less income than the most affluent families, typical practices of economy are more limiting. As they describe their routine shopping, these people talk of firmer boundaries to their purchasing, mentioning more items they simply never buy in order to keep their expenditures within relatively predictable limits. Laurel explained:

> We don't buy the best cuts of meat, except to entertain, we don't, you know, we buy 39¢ chickens when they're on sale, by the tens, that sort of thing.

Even when the logic of shopping is similar here and for more affluent shoppers, with special items purchased on sale, the resulting stock of foods is rather different. While those with more money reported watching for bargains on shrimp and scallops, Jean told of making standard purchases of ground beef and chicken, and buying pork chops "if they're not too expensive."

Whatever their actual purchases, those in middle-income households seem more conscious of cost as a real limit to their enjoyment of eating, and for several, "steak" served as a convenient vehicle for discussing difficulties at the boundaries. Bertie, for example, talked of the conflict between her concern with cost and her husband's preferences:

> There are a lot of things that I don't buy because they're too expensive. We do without—since beef has gotten so high. My husband is not as conscious of food prices as I am, since he doesn't buy food as much as I do. He will go out and buy steaks. I won't.

The issue is one that arises in some form in most of these households. Donna, for example, makes the same decision as Bertie, and displays more of the reasoning behind her choice:

> Like my one brother-in-law, they have steaks every week. And they never have any money. And you know, I say, at least we have food— I'd rather spend $5 on two different kinds of meat than on one steak.

Others choose in favor of taste when they can— especially if their husbands are more insistent. (Indeed, these two accounts suggest again the force of husbands' wishes, and the dilemma produced for wives who have too little money to satisfy them. Donna, whose husband was quite demanding, concluded this discussion by acknowledging that she doubted he "really likes steak that much.") But even the accounts of those who choose to spend money on more expensive items are full of an awareness that such choices are not always possible. Susan, for example, explains that "it all revolves around

how much money's coming in." She reported that when her husband was unemployed they ate "a lot of macaroni and cheese," but that now her husband gets steak. Even as she explains, the choice is tied to the possibility of facing hard times again:

> I can't see depriving my husband, or myself, of the better quality if I can afford it. Because the day might come that we'll be back at square one again.

Susan's talk of "deprivation" recalls—in a somewhat different register—the tone of the more affluent wives who were concerned not to be "tight" with their families. But while there were occasional echoes of this attitude, most of the working-class wives I spoke with talked positively about their efforts to use their resources carefully. They constructed economizing even more clearly in terms of responsibility and virtue, and seemed more anxious than wealthier informants about choices in favor of preference or convenience.

Income is less stable in these households than in professional/managerial families, and several interviewees told about times when they suffered losses. Reporting on these episodes, they described minimal meals that became standard fare and allowed them to survive. Jean, for example, described some typical meals when she and her husband were separated for a time, a few years before our interview:

> Well, pancakes and eggs. A lot of times we'd have grilled cheese sandwiches. A lot of times we'd have spaghetti, like I just—the kids love this—when I just cook plain spaghetti and mix it with butter and parmesan cheese, not tomato sauce, just that, with a salad I liked it too.

Had that a lot...Sometimes for a treat, like a big treat would be a bacon, lettuce, and tomato sandwich. I'd buy half a pound of bacon and make it last all month, you know [laughing]. I'd fry, like for four, for three sandwiches we'd have three pieces—no, we'd have like two pieces of bacon, and they'd be cut, you know, in all these little— everybody'd have like crumbled bacon. And that's how we used to do it. But it was fine, you know, we all survived.

Such difficulties inevitably reveal food as one of only a few variable categories of expense. For example, both Robin and Rick were working at the time of the interview, but their expenses for a mortgage, utilities, day care, and transportation to work were so high that food was "very low on a priority list...[though] it shouldn't be." Rick explained, "we're hurting right now. So now it's just like, three days—I'll go out and get enough food for three days." Both of them stressed the various ways they save money on purchases: driving to discount stores, comparing prices and saving coupons for items they need. But when they reach the limit of this kind of economizing, sometimes they simply cannot buy adequate food. Robin explained how they make decisions at these times:

If we repeat a meal for three days, it's no big deal to us. To see a nice piece of meat, like a steak or something, is really rare. It's usually the hamburgers and hot dogs and cheese sandwiches and stuff. We just can't afford anything else... If it gets down to it, we buy to feed the kids... And then we'll eat whatever we can scrounge together.

In several ways—including their limited diet and their dissatisfaction with it—this account was similar to those of much poorer families. Ironically, in such cases financial achievements —home ownership and the expenses associated with full-time jobs—have the effect of requiring radically reduced expenditures on food.

In households with incomes near poverty levels, or where food expenditures are especially reduced, another irony appears. Though these families are most in need of any savings produced by economizing, some of the prescribed techniques of "smart" shopping are not always appropriate or even possible. The poorest women I talked with were well aware that the stores in their neighborhoods charged more for many food items than stores in other areas. But few of them had transportation to other shopping areas. One black woman, for example, knew of several stores where she could find bargains, but had to rely on friends or her sister for transportation, or consider whether to spend extra money on a delivery service. In addition, these women often choose to buy more expensive brand-name products simply because they do not have enough cash to experiment with cheaper items and risk wasting money on unsatisfactory purchases. While more affluent shoppers could recite long lists of bargain items they had tried—some acceptable and some not—poor shoppers tended to report more conservative strategies for selecting foods, emphasizing the cost of a single mistake:

I go for quality... I'd rather go and get Del Monte corn... I have bought some of these—like they had four cans for a dollar. And when you got it, all the husks and stuff was inside it and it was just money wasted, when I could have just took that dollar and bought that one can of Del Monte... To me, it really is a waste of money.

For these women, any waste seems very consequential. Wealthier shoppers seem comfortable thinking of themselves as consumers who freely choose from items on the market, simply rejecting items not up to standard; poor shoppers are more likely to think of the market antagonistically. Affluent shoppers were aware of price differences in different stores and neighborhoods; for them, these patterns were background information they referred to as they reported where they go to shop. Shoppers with little money were mostly unable to respond to these differences by shopping elsewhere, and were more likely to talk about higher prices in the areas they could reach as unavoidable features of the market environment. One woman complained that "in some areas, you can go and buy one item this week and it's at a reasonable rate, and you come back the next week, and it's 50¢ higher," and Margaret observed that, "Especially food and stuff, things that you really need, they take advantage of it."

These poor shoppers work at "making do," in as many ways as they can. They compare prices carefully, watch for special bargains, and to the extent possible, shop where prices are most reasonable. But they are severely constrained by circumstance, usually limited to shopping in depressed neighborhoods and with no discretionary cash to subsidize economies that could be produced by traveling to cheaper outlets or experimenting with cheaper products. Their frequent references to the dangers of wasting food reveal the differences produced by their quite limited budgets in comparison to others' more ample resources. While most shoppers would like to spend less on food, these women know that they can only spend so much, and their most urgent concern is to make sure that they can make their meager allowances last. The ways in which this concern permeates the everyday experience of poor women will be explored in the next section.

POVERTY AND THE WORK OF SURVIVAL

In this section, I consider the work of five women caring for children in households sustained on minimal cash income. This group should not be taken as representative of all poor households, since that group includes more than just single-mother families. However, single-mother families make up a large and significant segment of the poor: in 1986, 60 percent of poor households were headed by single women (U.S. Bureau of the Census 1989). In the group of five I studied, three mothers lived in households of their own, and two thought of themselves and their children as independent "families," but at the time of my interviews resided with parents in what might be described as "subfamily" arrangements.[6] One woman was widowed, two separated or divorced, and two were never-married, though both of these had had relationships of some duration with their children's fathers. One reported that her children's father was often in the household, and usually shared their meals.

All these women were "on their own" in some sense. Though one described herself as engaged and planned to marry soon, the others, like many single mothers, were conscious of their difference from a more accepted form for family life. While the two women in their thirties seemed to take for granted that they would raise their children mostly on their own, the younger women—both in residence with their own parents—seemed to think of their single status as temporary, and expressed some worry about living in households that were not "proper" families. Margaret, for example, emphasized that her present living arrangement was a transitional one, and took care to explain how her routine would be different if she were living on her own: the children would set the table, for example, and she would "experiment" more and take more time with the cooking.

All but one of these women were unable, for one reason or another at the time of the interviews, to command a living wage. Two were in their early twenties, and had few marketable skills. One of these two, and one other of the five, reported she was temporarily unable to hold a paying job owing to a recent disturbance in her life (one was recently widowed and severely depressed; the other was recovering from a bout with drugs). One cared for six children, all younger than ten years old. And the only one who worked at a full-time job received such a low wage that she was able to manage only because she lived in a rent-subsidized apartment. Accounts of financial arrangements in these households reveal complex relations of adaptation, a process of piecing together enough resources to survive. All received some kind of government assistance, whether in the form of a direct payment, food stamps, or subsidized rent; several received material help from family members; and two held jobs, both of which paid minimum wage or below. These sources of income were interrelated, in ways mediated by the bureaucracy of state assistance. For example, the two women who lived with parents thereby forfeited their right to food stamps; a woman working full-time at minimum wage was ineligible for AFDC (Aid to Families with Dependent Children), while another woman worked only part-time in order to retain her benefit. These "patchwork" combinations of material resources are summarized in the table below. The information revealed is consistent with what we know of the welfare system: because increments resulting from wage work or family assistance usually mean a reduction in government aid, the total resources of each woman hover at roughly similar levels that barely provide for their subsistence.

Because they depend at least in part on direct government assistance, these women's lives must be understood in the context of the

Sources and Amounts of Income or Subsidy in Five Poor Families

Household composition	AFDC	Wages	Housing assistance	Food assistance	Estimated annual income (including FS)
Margaret + 2 children 3 in "sub-family," 9 in extended family/household (White)	$302/mo	$260/mo	Lives w/parents	Father buys food	$6,744
Ivy + 2 children 3 in "sub-family," 4 in extended family/household (Black)	$302/mo	—	Lives w/mother	Mother buys food	$3,624
DW + 2 children fiance sometimes in household (Black)	—	$500/mo	Rent subsidy	—	$6,000
Annie + 3 children 1 other child lives elsewhere with grandparent (White/ Hispanic)	$NA[a]	—	—	Food stamps $NA[a]	Unknown
LM + 6 children (Black)	$500/mo	—	—	Food stamps $291	$9,492

[a]Amounts of subsidies unrecorded.

welfare state in the United States. (Government subsidies support wealthier families as well, but less directly, and thus less intrusively.) Mimi Abramovitz (1988) shows that, historically, social welfare policy has included some provision for the support of mothers and children, but has also regulated their lives through restrictive and often moralistic policy. She argues, with others (e.g. Gough 1980; Dickinson 1986; Corrigan 1977), that the state recognizes the need to reproduce and maintain a healthy labor force, and subsidizes women's household labor in order to do so. At the same time, however, welfare provisions are designed to insure that government assistance will not become a preferred alternative to paid employment or traditional family life. They do this chiefly by limiting eligibility for subsidies to those seen as "deserving," as well as keeping payments at levels below prevailing low-wage employment options. In spite of these regulatory effects, most social welfare programs have empowering effects as well, if only limited ones. They do contribute to the subsistence of those outside the labor market, and by doing so they provide a modicum of choice and make possible some resistance to the most severe forms of exploitation.

The program of Aid to Families with Dependent Children, on which several of the women I studied depend, was established in 1935, but developed in part from earlier Mothers' Pension programs established during the Progressive Era. Abramovitz argues that these programs, which provide direct subsidies for poor women raising children alone, have been built around a "family ethic" that assumes the naturalness of gender distinctions, and assigns child care and household responsibility exclusively to women. Concern for children has been expressed in terms of the importance of "proper mothering," which has been defined and enforced through education, supervision, and threats of ineligibility for assistance or the

removal of children from poor women's homes. The biases in early Mothers' Pension programs had systematic effects: white widows received most aid, and never-married and black women were seldom on the rolls for assistance. The exclusion of large numbers of women from the programs meant that in spite of a rhetoric that supported women's household work, large groups of "undeserving" (especially black) women were channeled into low-paid wage work. Thus, the contradictions in the programs helped to mediate conflicting demands for women's household and market labor.

The operation of AFDC has reflected similar dynamics since its inception. Widespread ambivalence toward husbandless women has kept eligibility rules tight and benefit levels low. In the early years of the program, vaguely defined rules about "suitable homes" were used to justify continual scrutiny and harassment of recipients, and kept many women out of the program. During the 1960s, at least partly in response to the growth of a strong grassroots welfare rights movement (Piven and Cloward 1979; West 1981), the mechanisms of regulation shifted somewhat, opening up the program in response to pressure, and moving from a coercive to a more paternalistic kind of regulation. A rhetoric of social services to support "proper mothering" began to substitute for some of the harshest program rules, though in practice only limited service was actually provided. As AFDC expanded during the 1960s and 1970s, public and political antagonism toward its recipients grew. In spite of its regulatory agenda, the program did support and in some sense legitimate single mothers living alone with their children. Abramovitz (1988:352) summarizes:

> [I]nstead of supplying the market with low paid women workers and delegitimizing female-headed households [as program framers intended], AFDC

enabled welfare mothers to avoid dangerous marriages and jobs, to prefer public assistance to either wedlock or work, and to accept public aid as a right.

Since it was increasingly seen during the 1970s and 1980s as a challenge to the "family ethic," AFDC has been subject to a series of new modifications and restrictions. Welfare "reforms" introduced in 1981 included stricter eligibility requirements, new requirements for work outside the home, and lower real benefit levels. Thus, my interviews with AFDC recipients took place during a period of limitation and cutback in the program; inflation during the period worsened their situations as well.

The food stamp program, which supplements AFDC for two of the women I interviewed, has a similar history (DeVault and Pitts 1984). This program—which provides vouchers to be used in purchasing food items—functions chiefly as income supplementation, since it means that recipients can spend their cash income on other needs. However, like AFDC, it incorporates regulatory provisions that control recipients' use of the program: benefits are provided "in kind" (to be used for food only) rather than directly, as additional cash. While this program feature was intended primarily as a subsidy for American agriculture, it also reflects an underlying distrust of recipients and a desire to control the purchases of those in the program.[7] As supplementation to AFDC, it suggests that spending money on food ("wisely," of course) can legitimately be enforced as part of "proper mothering." The more recent Special Supplemental Food Program for Women, Infants and Children (WIC)—which provides in-kind food aid and nutrition education—emphasizes the relation of food and mothering more explicitly, and is more restrictive than the food-stamp program. (One of the women I interviewed had participated briefly in a WIC program; her experience will be discussed below.)

These social welfare provisions can be seen as part of a transition from private to "public patriarchy" (Brown 1981), with reproduction increasingly subsidized and controlled by the state instead of by individual men as family heads. Johnnie Tillmon, a welfare rights activist (cited in Abramovitz 1988:313–14), compares welfare to a "supersexist marriage":

You trade in "a" man for "the" man. But you can't divorce him if he treats you bad. He can divorce you of course, cut you off anytime he wants. But in that case "he" keeps the kids, not you. "The" Man runs everything. In ordinary marriage, sex is supposed to be for your husband. On AFDC you're not supposed to have any sex at all. You give up control over your body. It's a condition of aid…"The" man, the welfare system, controls your money. He tells you what to buy and what not to buy, where to buy it, and how much things cost. If things— rent, for instance—really cost more than he says they do, it's too bad for you.

Many welfare recipients are sharply aware of the punitive restrictions that condition the assistance available to them, especially since the emergence of a welfare rights consciousness during the 1960s. But recipients' perspectives on the system are also conditioned by prevailing cultural ideologies about work and individual achievement, as well as by the ideology built into welfare policy. Most seem to experience a complex mixture of feelings, and are subject to dissatisfaction and resentment about their situation, which can be directed both outward and inward. In the following discussion, as I examine the feeding work of the poorest women I interviewed, I will attend to the ways in which the contradictory purposes and consequences of welfare policy intersect with everyday struggles to feed and care for children.

These interviews, as a group, were the most difficult for me to conduct and analyze. I spoke, as a middle-class researcher, with women whose lives were very different from my own. Our conversations were mostly comfortable—the women generously accommodated my curiosity, and in at least some cases, seemed to welcome my listening perhaps as company. But with some distance from the interview situation, I began to realize how unprepared I was to know their lives, and how frightened I could be by their situations. These realizations developed at different times, and in different ways: sometimes unsurprisingly, as when I drove nervously into unfamiliar parts of the city; sometimes much later, as I have studied the transcripts of our conversations, noticing gaps in my understanding and questions I might have asked. Such gaps in understanding present problems for any middle-class researcher talking with those whose lives are quite different from hers (see, for example, Riessman 1987). One approach to a solution involves prolonged immersion in the lives of those studied (e.g. Stack 1974); another involves a more collaborative research strategy (e.g. Mies 1983). In this study, however, I adopted neither of these strategies, but interviewed poor women in the same relatively conventional way as others. An awareness of this problem recommends reading my account here somewhat cautiously, as an attempt to begin to see what is missing from a more middle-class view of feeding work. What we find, I will suggest, is a hint at the dark underside of women's caring work, the most brutal expression of the pitfalls built into women's inexorable responsibility for the well-being of others.

One of the features of these interviews that made them different from others is that they were less neatly compartmentalized; my conversations with these poor women often ranged far beyond their feeding routines, including larger life stories, reflections on their hopes and ambitions, and, in some cases, discussions of relations among several generations of women and children. I did not seek such comments, though I did not discourage them either. They emerged in response to the same questions I asked others, perhaps because of different understandings of the conduct of a research interview, but perhaps also in recognition of my ignorance about the conditions of these lives, from a desire to show me the context for household routine. I sometimes became caught up in the dramas of these lives, and lost my focus on feeding as we talked—other kinds of stories seemed more important. But I wonder now if this phenomenon I experienced as a "loss of focus" should be taken as an indication of a significant feature of these women's lives: the fact that feeding is only one difficult task among many, part of a total life experience that needs broader explication precisely because it does not fit a middle-class norm.

To my knowledge, these households were not visited by hunger and malnutrition, in the clinical senses. However, several comments leave this statement open to some doubt: one woman reported giving her children two meals instead of three during the winter when they slept later and were less active; another's two-year-old daughter had grown so slowly that she had been hospitalized for a time; and a third described one child who "just gobbles...down (her food)" and is always "wanting more, wanting seconds." Still, the overall sense of these accounts is one of a skillful management of quite limited resources that makes possible the survival of these household groups. In many ways, these women engage in precisely the same kinds of work activities as mothers with more resources. They pay attention to the needs and preferences of their children, they shop for provisions with which to prepare "proper" meals, and spend time planning such meals, and they work at teaching their children about proper eating, through experience and example as well as direct instruction. But the insufficiency of their cash income adds an additional layer to the web of conditions within which they do this work, and gives the provision of food a different meaning for the household group.

These women talked straightforwardly about the difficulties of their situations. As one black woman explained:

> *Being on public aid is a very—well, to me, it's, you know, a hassle. I don't like it. You know, first of all, because the amount of money you receive from public aid is not really enough to, you know, for a person to take care of their family. It's really not enough.*

They see quite clearly that their decisions are structured by the restrictive, even punitive regulations that define public aid. The only woman working full-time, for example, explained that since she has started work, she is no longer eligible for enough food assistance to make it worthwhile to apply: "I know the changes I would have to go through downtown with them—it's not worth it, when they're not going to give me, maybe $30." But as they considered their lives within this context, all of these women expressed some pride in their abilities to manage, and especially to care for their children. Some saw themselves as protecting their children in a hostile environment. For example:

> *They [the children] know that there's a single parent here, so they do try to*

> *be helpful . . . But I don't push it on them a whole lot . . . I want them to enjoy their childhood while they can, because once they start getting big then they're going to be, "Oh, it's bill time," "Oh, it's food," "Oh, it's this and that." You know, so I feel that they should stay young.*

And for Margaret, pride is tied to a sense that she manages in spite of the difficulties produced by the market:

> *I enjoy doing it. Because I know, I can feed—I can get around all these people who think they're going to, you know, BS everybody else. You know, I'm smarter than they are.*

With one exception (Ivy, who will be discussed below), these women were active and determined, working to fill in with extra effort for the money resources they lacked. One works at a low-wage telephone job she describes as "a bitch," but "better than sitting home all day"; another cares for six children and also works in a community group; and a third, Annie, reported how she keeps track of all the kids on the street in her area, serves as secretary for a neighborhood organization, and helps Spanish-speaking mothers deal with their children's problems at school.

The lives these women lead can be better understood by examining Annie's in some detail. Annie was a white woman in her late twenties, and lived in a predominantly Hispanic neighborhood with three of her four children when I interviewed her. She had been married briefly, to a Puerto Rican man, but her husband had left the family almost a decade earlier when he discovered he was too ill to provide for them. Annie had worked at a variety of low-wage jobs until she became ill herself, and then, as she recovered from surgery, began to use drugs. By the time I interviewed her, she had succeeded in quitting drugs and seemed to have reestablished a relatively stable household life. However, she reported that her health was poor and that she had had "a couple of nervous breakdowns." When I interviewed her, she was not working for pay; she explained, somewhat ruefully, that she was "supposed to be taking it easy." Much of Annie's life was structured by conditions in her neighborhood, an area with a lively and sometimes dangerous street life. Her oldest daughter, who "couldn't handle it," had been sent to live with a relative in a rural area, and Annie spent much of her time keeping an informal watch over the neighborhood's children as well as her own.

Annie acknowledges the help she receives from family and friends, but she also emphasizes her own work and her self-sufficiency: when she told about some workshops offered through her children's Head Start program, she explained, "I figured, 'Well, I'm going to play mother and father, and work, and I've got to learn something.'" She also reported that her sisters are sometimes jealous, and tell her she is "lucky," but she stresses her own effort as the source of whatever comfort she enjoys:

> They don't see how I can make it so good, and not have no money and live on welfare. But I told them, "If you budget yourself, and penny-pinch, you can do it." Because I do. I go to No-Frills, I go to Diamond's, I go to the fruit market. I mean, I don't care, if I have to walk all over the city to get it.

Accounts of "penny-pinching" were prominent in the reports of other poor women as well. Just as they were more likely than others to talk spontaneously about their overall budgets, poor women were more likely than others to include

the prices of foods they selected as they talked about their shopping. Another woman, for example, told me in detail about several "good buys" she had located in various markets:

> They have these beef sausages—I think it's a good buy, you know, you get a whole—I guess it stands as long as me—for $10. Where going to the store and getting a little piece, you got to pay almost 2 or 3 dollars... And maybe I'll go down to Quik-Stop—they have these, 30 pounds of chicken for 14, 15 dollars. Which is not a bad buy.

And Margaret described her reasoning about which brands and sizes of products would be cheapest to buy, referring from memory to the prices for different brands of toilet paper and sizes of rice packages. What is striking in these accounts, and different from others, is the frequent reference to actual sums, the attention to exact prices, which marks these women's necessarily constant concern with the distribution of whatever cash is available.

By "penny-pinching," then, Annie manages to purchase supplies, and works to produce "family meals," as others do. She explained that they all sit down together for dinner:

> The meal is on the table, and I tell them if the steam leaves the bowl before they get to the table, the bowl goes right back in the stove and they don't get any supper. So they make sure they get to the table. And then that's our group discussion, this girlfriend played with that boyfriend at school, and—I hear everything.

As she describes their routines, it is clear that she is conscious, like more affluent mothers, of using food to construct social relations and mark special events in the week. When she describes a typical meal, we can see the sense of group sociability that arises from having a "house specialty," and also the attention to individual preference that marks the family as "personal":

> Oh, that's our house specialty, macaroni and cheese. And my daughter usually makes that. I guess she's got her way of making it, because when I make it she says I don't make it right...And then plus, the 11-year-old, she doesn't like ground beef in her macaroni and cheese. So hers is made separately. They make the macaroni and cheese, the ground beef, and then before they add the ground beef, my 12-year-old will take out a big bowl and put a separate [gesturing to indicate a separate portion]—for the 11-year-old—and then she'll keep on making the rest of it.

Because she works with such limited resources, Annie must be especially clever about making use of what is available. This requirement became especially evident when I considered her organization of household space. I interviewed Annie in her apartment's "living room" (perhaps twelve by twenty-four feet), which contained not only a couch and television but also a cooking area with refrigerator, stove and small work counter, a small kitchen table for eating, and a work table where we sat for our talk and where the children do their homework. As she described her routine, Annie referred to the sense of space she has created for the family by using different areas in the room for different purposes, and enforcing different rules in each one. She explained, for instance, that on weekends breakfast is different, because she allows the children to watch cartoons while they eat:

> I don't want them to eat cereal in here [the "living" rather than "kitchen" end of the room]. They could eat here [the table where we are sitting during the interview], but I won't put the TV here because they have to study here. So on Saturdays and Sundays they have to bring a tray [to the couch]...And usually I make a banana shake...They have to bring a tray, they have to have a napkin, their roll's in a bowl... They're real good about it.

In many ways, the logic of "constructing family" is the same here as in more affluent households, though the "products" may differ—these families enjoy macaroni and cheese rather than a steak dinner or stir-fry, and treat themselves with breakfast on the couch rather than the terrace. However, in spite of the similarities, a more thorough examination of the meaning of regular family meals will show that poverty constructs a distinctive relation to food and the work of care, both for those who do the work and those who are fed. Parents in households with more resources talk about using food, thoughtfully and creatively, to signify love, comfort, and pleasure. They seem rarely to be conscious of the possibility of scarcity, but this spectre is rarely absent from the consciousness of those who live in poverty. Thus, while poor mothers also use food to mean love, comfort, and pleasure, they teach a harsher lesson as well—that survival is never to be taken for granted.

A consciousness of scarcity appeared in the talk of some working-class informants who were not technically "poor," as well as in the accounts of the poor women who are the subjects of this section, and all of these people talked about the particular significance of scarcity for children's health and well-being. When I asked how she "felt" about cooking—whether she enjoyed the work or not—a black single mother living on her clerical-worker salary replied: "I'm just glad that I can provide for my family, because you know, there are so many people who don't, children who don't have no one there to cook for them, or nothing to eat." And Robin and Rick, the two-paycheck couple beset by expenses and debts who were quoted above, reported: "If it gets down to it, we buy to feed the kids." In these households, as in others, providing food sends messages of interdependence and caring. But in these households, "caring" is also understood in terms of urgent necessity, and it loses some of the romantic gloss it often has in more affluent families. Cooking and eating, like other household activities, are organized around the exigencies of survival.

In poor households, children learn early, through direct observation, that their parents are caught up in economic circumstances over which they have little control. In spite of parents' attempts to protect children from the worst consequences of their poverty, children see their parents' frustrating labors, and they typically understand that they must often do without (Stack 1974). Parents face a dilemma: while they would like to let children "enjoy their childhood," they are also concerned to prepare them for independence. Thus, Annie's caring for her children is expressed in part through tough, energetic discipline, and determination and self-sufficiency are part of an attitude toward life that she teaches them quite directly:

> I told them, "You stand up and say 'I am somebody,' because if not, you're just going to be with the rest of them"...So my kids, they know, they stand up for themselves. If not, they get stepped on. I tell them, "That's the way it goes."

Her message to the children should be understood in the context of the family's difficulties. Like the black mothers described by their daughters in a study by Gloria Joseph, she is both "tough and tender" (1981:101). Joseph found that, while daughters recognized their mothers' shortcomings, they had tremendous respect for mothers' work, both outside and inside the home:

> [A]ggressive and harsh behaviors were acknowledged and appreciated in light of their being carried out in the context of caring for the daughters (and other family members) and trying to instill the need to be prepared and to be able to cope within a society where choices for Black women are frequently between the dregs of the keg or the chaff from the wheat. (1981:102)

Poor families like Annie's, and many black families whether poor or not, are in situations requiring that they adapt to hostile environments, and a protective "toughness" emerges as part of the caring work that maintains family members in the present and prepares them for challenges ahead.

Annie relies on her children to help with household work and to begin caring for themselves at an early age. When she worked in the afternoon, they took care of themselves after school and she would leave them a list of chores: "Sometimes I'd forget...So they'd call and say, 'What's there to do today, and what time can we go out?' Very well organized." When she is not working, Annie does most of the housework herself, but she still strategizes about how much help the children should provide, balancing their need to spend time on schoolwork against the importance of learning responsibility and household skills. This general feature of their relationship appears in a specific form in her talk about feeding them:

> *Everybody has to do something in order to eat . . . I don't never let them go without a meal, but I just tell them, "You're not going to eat if the sink is dirty. If I have to start supper with dirty dishes I won't do supper that day."*

Children in more affluent households help with chores too, usually also because their parents want them to learn responsibility and household skills.[8] But in poor families like Annie's, the necessity behind children's independence gives them a distinctive sense of the struggles their parents face. As a result, these children learn that to struggle for physical maintenance is "natural" (as Annie explained, "That's the way it goes."), while more affluent children take survival for granted, and learn to feel a sense of entitlement to the pleasures that food can provide.

The gender organization of feeding work is also expressed in a distinctive form in these poor households. Since all of these poor families were headed by single mothers, questions about a division of labor between spouses do not arise. But these mothers' sole responsibility for children can be seen as part of a larger community-level division of labor. The predominance of single-mother families among the poor in the 1980s can be attributed to a variety of factors, including high rates of male unemployment and incarceration among the poor, the relative unavailability of income assistance for two-parent families, and increasing rates of divorce and single childbearing among the population as a whole (Wilson 1987). These trends, together, tend to produce a particular pattern of gender segregation, with poor women more likely than men to be attached to household and children. Thus, poor women cook at least in part simply because they are more likely than men to live in relatively stable households with children who must be fed. Often, they cook for men who do not live with them, but join their households for meals through kin or "fictive kin" relationships (Stack 1974). Annie, for example, often cooks for a boyfriend, and sometimes for his brother as well. The men usually bring something in exchange—some soda, perhaps—but these exchange relations are delicate ones, and Annie reports that her boyfriend is sometimes embarrassed at how much his brother eats. His worry hints at expectations that surround such relations of service and exchange: they all accept that Annie should provide food for the one man she is attached to, however informally, but her responsibilities toward others are more ambiguous. Thus, even in the absence of a legal marriage relationship or even cohabitation, the relations of service and entitlement that organize feeding and eating are organized around the heterosexual couple.[9]

As we talked, Annie revealed an awareness of a gendered division of labor, and also some ambivalence about it. Her construction of her situation as a single mother—"I'm going to play mother and father"—relies both on a dichotomy between men's and women's activity and on a confidence that she can transcend the dichotomy. She reported that many of her men friends cook, and that her son has learned cooking skills in his Head Start program. But she emphasizes cooking skills for her daughters rather than her son, and she worries about his development as an acceptable man, encouraging him to spend time alone with her boyfriend. She is uncertain about changing expectations for men's and women's activity: "I was brought up with the same beliefs that my mother taught me—boys are boys and girls are girls. And boys don't do girls' things.

But nowadays it's different." Her daughters, drawing on more traditional cultural expectations, insist that their brother should not work in the kitchen:

> I've got a lot of friends that are bachelors, and I've took my daughters over and seen them, and said, "See, he cooks." So they're kinda letting him participate. But they also used to say that if he does it, he gonna be funny, you know, gay.

Annie tries to negotiate a reasonable compromise that takes account of several conflicting demands and beliefs here: her son's desire to be with the girls in the kitchen, her daughters' more traditional demands for gender segregation, her own appraisal of concrete evidence of changing patterns, and the ideology of gender equality that is taught at preschool, but not in the girls' elementary school. She encourages her daughters to be more open to male participation in housework, but she also advises her son that he is old enough to begin to "separate himself" from the girls. In their struggles over this issue, they encounter and respond to a cultural ideology that emphasizes the distinction between male and female, and in the girls' worry about homosexuality we see how the enforcement of traditionally gendered activity supports heterosexuality as well. Annie, a single woman who "plays mother and father," takes responsibility for feeding and even as she questions a gendered division of labor, reinforces it with her children.

Most of the poor women I talked with, like Annie, thought of themselves as managing relatively well, even with their limited resources; indeed, they are probably a more successful group than would be found through random sampling since those who are managing well are most likely to agree to be interviewed. The kind of maintenance work they do has often been understood as an essential contribution to communities under siege by the wider society; Patricia Hill Collins suggests that black women, for example, "see their unpaid domestic work more as a form of resistance to oppression than as a form of exploitation by men" (1990:44). The household and feeding work performed by slave women for their families (Davis 1981), by working-class mothers (Caulfield 1974), by Southern black "Mamas" for civil rights workers (Evans 1979; Jones 1985), and by poor women for networks of kin (Stack 1974) has been essential labor that contributes directly to group survival. In groups such as these, women's responsibility for feeding is significantly different from that in more privileged families: rather than a work burden that excludes middle-class white women from the more remunerative activity and status enjoyed by their male counterparts, feeding others is a work task that also provides an opportunity to promote the survival and well-being of the less privileged community, including men, children, and women themselves. But we will see below that this opportunity, which can bring honor to those women able to fulfill such roles, can also be cruelly demanding for those who are not so gifted or fortunate. One of my informants, Ivy, was in a period of considerable stress and depression, and her story highlights some of the special difficulties of being a poor mother who cannot cope so well with the difficulties of her situation.

Ivy, a black woman in her early twenties, had come to the United States from the Caribbean about ten years before I interviewed her. When we talked, she was recovering from the death of her children's father and a subsequent period of grief and disruption. In spite of public assistance and financial help from her mother, she acknowledged that feeding her children was "very hard"; it was a matter of great concern because her young daughter had been hospitalized briefly the year before for failure-to-thrive. Her daughter's hospitalization marked her as a mother in need of help, and since then she had been especially vulnerable to the scrutiny of medical and social welfare professionals. Ivy's situation illustrates the complex reality of troubles with caring work. She had real difficulties managing the care of her children, and she needed and, for the most part, welcomed expert advice. However, her reports about the help she has received reveal significant gaps between what is offered and what she can use. And to some extent, the counseling intended to help Ivy seems to have contributed to her depression and sense of inadequacy.

Though she lives with her mother, who pays for much of their food and often does the shopping, Ivy is responsible for the work at home; her mother, she explains, is tired when she returns home from her very demanding service job. Ivy takes her children to nursery school in the morning, and spends most of each day at home alone. Her account hints at the curious contradictions of a state of anxious depression. Though she does not enjoy cooking, she reports that she cleans energetically: "I'm a workaholic. As a matter of fact, I love cleaning up ... I'm not used to the type of life of sitting and relaxing, it's not me." Yet a few minutes later, when I ask if she usually cleans the dishes after supper:

No, sometimes I skip that, you know, I watch TV, or try to play with them. I don't do that very often. Or I just sit and watch TV. And you know, you get depressed now and then. You know, I try to play with them. And then after, do the dishes. Sometimes I leave them overnight, because you know, I have to conserve my energy, I'm using up so much trying to get everything done.

This excerpt illustrates a tone that characterized all of Ivy's talk in the interview: an emphasis on things she "tries" or "needs" to do, alongside apologetic accounts of how her actual practice usually falls short.

This characteristic mix of anxiety and discouragement was even more prominent in Ivy's accounts of food routines. For example, when I asked what they would eat for dinner the night of the interview:

Have to look in the freezer and decide. Because I gave them spaghetti yesterday night. Have to find something. [After a pause] I can cook, but—you know, I need to learn how to fix different varieties of stuff. It's not easy.

The same tone appears in her account of the afternoon routine:

Around 3:00 I start, just to get it out of the way. I hate to cook late, especially when I have to go pick the kids up ... I try to cook as early as I can.

And although they usually eat in front of the television, she reports that they sit at the table "now and then," and adds, "We should get into the habit."

Ivy, like anyone in a contemporary industrial society, lives surrounded by a discourse that emphasizes the importance of food in family life and women's responsibility for preparing food. She wants desperately to do better, and attends to media discussions of nutrition and food preparation, but her depression limits her ability to use what she learns. Still, this discourse appears frequently in her talk, and seems to contribute to her perception of herself as an inadequate mother. Explaining the breakfast routine, for example, she referred to something she had heard on the radio:

> There too I still have to try to get some variety. Instead of fixing them eggs, eggs, every other day. Like I heard on the radio they had this nutrition program and they said that you could—instead of fixing the same thing you could even fix spaghetti for breakfast. You know, it's nourishing. Things like that.

It is clear from other comments that these media features are not limited to nutrition information, but also reinforce the idea that food is central to the quality of family life: Ivy hopes to learn more so that the food she prepares will be like the food in books that looks so "eatable" and "delightful." And it is also clear that the media create standards for food work with which women like Ivy are obliged to compare themselves. When I asked about shopping, for example:

> Like I say, I need to get organized. Like when I shop I'll just pick up anything, that's not very good shopping. I don't really look, and read the label and you know, find out what different kinds of food, you know— You know, some people when they do their shopping they're always organized, they know exactly what they're going for.

These public sources of information create standards for all women, but those who are better able to follow these discursive prescriptions refer to them less directly, incorporating them more smoothly as "background information" into their accounts of their own routines. Ivy's difficulties living up to an image of the ideal homemaker bring the coercive character of this discursive construction more clearly into view.

Because she had been identified as a mother with problems, Ivy had received several kinds of expert advice. She was seeing a psychologist, with whom she talked about her problems with the children; she had talked with doctors (not much help, she reported) and other hospital personnel about nutrition (they had mainly provided "booklets"); and she had discussed her children's eating habits with teachers at their nursery school. She had also participated briefly in a WIC program, and mentioned that the extra food provided was "very helpful," even though she was sometimes unable to make the trip downtown to pick up her coupons at the required time. But when she talked about these relationships, she seemed curiously detached, stuck in everyday realities that seldom fit with the information provided. When I asked if the WIC program helped her learn about nutrition, for example, she acknowledged that such teaching was built into the program, but could only talk about it in a vague and general way. Her comment suggests that somehow the instruction offered through the program was only something to "listen to," and that she was never able to tell them "her part" or get answers to her own questions:

> Yeah, that was part of it, they had someone to tell you, you know, what you should feed. But I never really did get to tell them. you know, my part. You know, I was just listening to what they had to say. I didn't, like, ask them questions. I didn't take much interest in that.

I do not mean to diminish the importance of information about food and nutrition. But Ivy's problem is not primarily a lack of knowledge. She is severely depressed, with no marketable skills, isolated at home, and responsible for two small children. Given her material and psychological difficulties, the social services emphasis on instruction for homemaking seems primarily to have heightened her anxiety about the work of care.

The depression and discouragement that was so marked in Ivy's case showed up in subtler ways in all of the poor women's accounts, suggesting that however well they manage from day to day, they experience common psychological costs. All of them seemed relatively isolated: they lived in small, crowded apartments, and referred to their difficulties traveling outside their neighborhoods for appointments or to shop. All of them referred to their need sometimes to "just sit," conveying a sense of alternating periods of effort and listlessness. Perhaps most significantly, several of these women referred to their own lack of appetite and indicated that they often simply did not eat. Ivy, for example, complained, "Sometimes the food gets very boring. [Laughing a bit] You know, boring, boring, boring food." When I asked what she liked to eat, she could hardly think of anything:

> I don't know, I'm a picky person, I hardly know what I like. But I don't know—sometimes I get hungry and I look—there's food, but sometimes it's just not what I like. So you know. I look in the freezer, I look in there and there's nothing that you like to eat.

Another woman explained that she usually does not eat until mid-afternoon when the children are off to school or taking naps. Then she has "a sandwich, or maybe some junk food" [pointing to a soda and some doughnuts on the coffee table nearby]. "I like salads," she went on. "But I don't do that very often . . . I'm on a budget, so I can't just go out and get whatever I've got a taste for, you know, like just go out and get a steak or something." And Margaret reported: "I usually don't eat, because I can't—if I'm on the go all day, I can't eat. Because I just—my stomach gets goofed up. I have to be relaxed to eat."

These disruptions of appetite probably have multiple sources. It is not uncommon for women of any class to feel ambivalent about eating, for a variety of reasons (Kaplan 1980; Charles and Kerr 1988: chap. 7). In addition, these women seem to be expressing a heightened sense of the more widespread notion that women's own food is less important than that prepared for others. But the fact that these poor women were the only ones among these interviewees who spontaneously talked about simply not eating suggests that their loss of appetite is directly related to their poverty. Their comments suggest an alienation from their family work, a distaste for food that arises from the fact that it is always a problem, and unavailable as simple pleasure. Further, social welfare policy seems to invade even this intimate physiological aspect of these women's lives. The one woman who was working full-time was the only one of the poor women I interviewed who did not appear to have difficulty with her own eating, or feel guilty about it. This single exception suggests that those receiving assistance are undermined by the public dictum that they are to be valued and assisted only in their roles as "proper mothers." They actually play out this ideology in their everyday lives, working to feed their children as well as possible, but not themselves.

THE ILLUSION OF SIMILARITY

In this chapter, I have looked beyond surface similarity to examine the ways that feeding work is organized through access to cash income from different sources. The ideology of a capitalist economy emphasizes similarity in the situations of household/family groups, constructing households as "consumption units" and individuals as consumers who choose freely from what is offered on the market. In this model, each household must garner cash resources, usually by sending some members out to work for a wage. Then, household members decide how to use their resources, allocating them to the necessary expenses of sustenance and other purchases, as desired. Every consumer seems to be doing the same thing: deciding to exchange cash for some desired product. Careful budgeting—shrewd decision making about how much to exchange for what products—seems to determine how well families live.

This simple, ideological model of consumer behavior omits the structural economic factors that determine what kinds of access families have to cash resources, what kinds of products are available on the market, how their cost is determined, and how they are distributed and marketed.[10] But this simple model is the one that underlies discussions of housekeeping in advertising, expert advice for women, and much public policy discussion. The "smart shopper" is the central image in this discourse: she is the woman who carefully tends the family resources, purchasing wisely in order to "make ends meet." This "smart shopper" is class-less: whether she has plenty of money or only a little, she virtuously balances cost and need, spending only what is necessary to provide for her family.

There is, of course, a material base for this image: women (and some men) do budget and calculate as they purchase goods for their families, and many husbands and children would live considerably less comfortable lives but for women's efforts at making ends meet (Luxton 1980). However, the class-neutral character of the image obscures crucial differences in the work of provisioning and in the different kinds of "family" people are able to produce.

Economizing is activity that some people engage in voluntarily; they can make choices about when and how to economize. Others "make do" from necessity, and are rarely able to purchase what they want. Thus, concepts like consumer "choice" and "power" apply to only some consumers. The work of feeding is very different for women of different classes: the

woman with plenty of money is able to operate more like a manager, considering the market and making "executive" decisions about purchasing for the family (perhaps this is why more middle-class than working-class men seem interested in shopping for food; see Charles and Keff 1988:176), while the woman who does not have enough is more like an unprotected daily laborer, dependent on the local availability of products and unpredictable fluctuations in prices.

Also missing from this picture are those workers in the burgeoning service industries whose labor provides time-saving "conveniences" for those houseworkers who can afford them. For example, Margaret's paid work in a laundry provides essential maintenance work for others, but also limits the time she can spend with her children and renders her too exhausted to eat herself when she returns home late in the evening. Many such workers are members of disadvantaged racial and ethnic groups, and Evelyn Nakano Glenn (1990) suggests that the increasing marketization of household maintenance work reshapes a longstanding racial/ethnic division of labor. Rather than purchasing the labor of women of color directly, as domestic servants, affluent white women increasingly benefit from the labors of others less directly, and perhaps more comfortably because relations of oppression and privilege are less visible.

These differences mean that feeding and eating are experienced quite differently as well. In families with more resources, food becomes an arena for self-expression, providing a chance to experience family as a reward for achievement; in poor families, feeding and eating are themselves the achievement. Since the ability to maintain family members cannot be taken for granted, all family members are recruited into interdependence through necessity. In working-class and poor households, the person who does the work experiences its two sides quite sharply: though she often understands her activity in terms of enabling the pleasures of eating, she also works with more urgency to provide sustenance, and often has the unpleasant task of deciding which desired items must be eliminated from the family's diet.

Finally, it must be clear that, given the market distribution of food, some families enjoy plenty of healthful food, while others do not. The poor have access to such minimal cash resources that they can only obtain an adequate diet through extraordinary effort. They are often blamed for their own deprivation. Social programs are based on calculations that assume that households are managed by "smart shoppers" who will be able to stretch meager resources. Social policy simply assumes that women will do this work, and Ivy's story illustrates how thoroughly mothers are held responsible, whatever their circumstances or individual difficulties. Discourses about such programs emphasize knowledge and skill as a condition for survival, and largely ignore the energy, will, and luck that are also necessary. Thus, they help to maintain an illusion—that families share a similar experience of purchasing and preparing foods, and that differences in their diets must indicate that some are at fault, that some "deserve" healthful and satisfying meals, while others do not.

Reading 22 "I Never Did Any Fieldwork, but I Milked an Awful Lot of Cows!": Using Rural Women's Experience to Reconceptualize Models of Work*

MAREENA McKINLEY WRIGHT

Researchers studying women and work in the past 10 years have called for a redefinition of "work" (Beneria 1991; Hossfeld forthcoming; Mies 1986; Ward 1990; Ward and Pyle 1995). One way to further this redefinition of work is to develop the theoretical contours of a multidimensional continuum model of women's work, moving away from older dual spheres models and using empirical evidence obtained from oral histories of older rural women from Iowa and Missouri. As in the dual spheres model, the dimensions of a continuum model of work include where women's work takes place, what economic benefits the work provides, and what characteristics the work has.

Capitalist cultural ideologies developed in the late 19th century assumed that the social world was divided into two spheres: the public world of the capitalist economy where relationships were based on money and the private world of the family where relationships were based on love and affection. Definitions of work based on this ideology focused on waged work and ignored other forms of work such as unpaid household work (Bose 1987; Mies 1986). Social scientists in the 20th century, studying the family and women's roles, still base much of their work on this underlying ideology of dichotomous spheres without questioning its appropriateness or empirical validity (Belsky and Rovine 1988; Beneria 1991; Davis 1984; Elder and Rockwell 1976; Gerson 1985; Kreps 1976; Moen 1992); however, feminist researchers have noted the ideological basis of the separate spheres division of the world with its limited definition of work as waged work and have demonstrated that neither historical nor cross-cultural empirical evidence supports a dichotomous model (Bose 1987; Collins and Gimenez 1990; Rothstein 1994; Ward 1990). Furthermore, they have

AUTHOR'S NOTE: I thank Kathy Ward, Rachel Rosenfeld, Glen Elder, and Cindy Gimbel, in addition to the *Gender & Society* reviewers, for their insightful comments on earlier drafts.

*Wright, Mareena McKinley. 1995. "'I Never Did Any Fieldwork, but I Milked an Awful Lot of Cows!': Using Rural Women's Experience to Reconceptualize Models of Work." GENDER & SOCIETY (9)2:216–235. ©1995 Sociologists for Women in Society. Reprinted by permission of Sage Publications, Inc.

shown that a dichotomous model makes much of women's work invisible or valueless (Beneria 1991; Collins and Gimenez 1990; Glazer 1990; Ward and Pyle 1995).

Ward and Pyle (1995) suggest that women's work might be better conceptualized as a continuum ranging from formal labor market work to informal work to unpaid household work. They argue that women work in formal and informal sectors and in the household. The formal sector provides legally regulated wages and working conditions for labor and contractual relationships between labor and capital. The informal sector "is structurally heterogeneous and comprises such activities as direct subsistence, small-scale production and trade, and subcontracting to semi-clandestine enterprises and homeworkers" (Portes and Sassen-Koob 1987, 31). Informal sector work includes home-based work but not unpaid work—such as household domestic labor. Household work obviously takes place in the household.

A focus on sector alone, however, conceals other significant aspects of women's work. I look for other dimensions of work that better characterize the various labor options[1] women use and women's use of multiple labor strategies. Using a collection of oral histories of older rural women from Iowa and Missouri, I examine the labor options women use and begin to excavate the dimensional contours of a continuum model of work.

This article addresses two major questions. What labor options did this group of women use and what dimensions can we identify in these labor options that characterize a continuum model of work? Previous research provides several ideas for places to begin: the sector where the work takes place (Ward and Pyle 1995), the economic benefit of working (Collins and Gimenez 1990; Ward and Pyle 1995), and differences in work "boundaries" for men and women (Ward 1990). Based on my analyses of the women's

experiences, I identify three important dimensions present in the labor options: economic benefits, physical location, and time control characteristics.

In this analysis, I focus on women's work that has a *direct* impact on the family economy, either by providing income to the family economy or by reducing necessary expenditures. Family economy refers to the systematic mobilization and allocation of family resources such as money, time, and skills to meet family needs. While others have argued eloquently for a definition of work that includes many nonwaged activities (such as volunteer work or shopping) that do not have a direct impact on the family economy (Collins and Gimenez 1990; Hertzog et al. 1989; Mies 1986), I view my focus on work with a direct impact on the family as a first-step strategy to simplify a complex research problem.

The work described here is not an exhaustive list of all labor options available to women at all times. Women in other regions of the country no doubt had other options available to them that were not available to these women. Some options that were less important to rural white women, such as domestic work, have been more important for women of color and urban immigrant women (Buss 1985; Romero 1992). Furthermore, many of the labor options used by my informants waned in importance over time while others became more important (Adams 1991; Fink 1986; Osterud 1991); nevertheless, these labor options provide sufficient evidence to elaborate the dimensions of a work continuum and to show how these dimensional characteristics both allow and require women to combine labor options into multiple work strategies.

The focus on rural women is a distinctive feature of this research, adding to the growing body of literature that has examined farm women's work on and off the farm (Adams 1991; Fink 1986, 1992; Haney and Knowles 1988; Osterud 1994; Rosenfeld 1985). This study also expands research to include nonfarm rural women. Several key features of the rural environment provide advantages for studying labor as a continuum. First, fewer opportunities for formal labor market work exist in rural areas compared to urban areas. Second, lower population density means available jobs are likely to be farther away. Third, as farming economic cycles force farm families to rely on nonfarm income to make up income shortages during farming hard times, the farm wife often is the family member who generates nonfarm income (Conger and Elder 1994; Rosenfeld 1985). Fourth, additional constraints abound for rural women wanting to work, such as the lack of transportation and child care. As a consequence of this economically marginal environment, women needing income must be creative in developing strategies other than formal labor market work to meet family economic needs. These constraints on rural women's formal labor market work lead to a wide variety of alternative work situations, an ideal data situation for reconceptualizing women's labor as a multidimensional continuum.

DATA AND METHODS

I interviewed 35 older rural women, members of the grandparent generation of the pilot families in the Iowa Youth and Families Project, an ongoing study of family resilience to economic distress (Conger and Elder 1994). The 76 pilot families reside in agriculturally dependent, predominately white counties in central Iowa and participated in the pilot study in 1987. Of the possible 152 grandmothers, I interviewed 35 white women living in Iowa (33 women) and Missouri (2 women). My impression of the women I contacted who declined to participate was that either they were reluctant to discuss their life stories or they did not want to take the time to participate.

The study participants were born between 1905 and 1932, meaning they ranged in age from 55 to 82 years when they were interviewed. About half the women came from farm backgrounds. A little more than half lived on family farms at some time during adulthood. These women's families farmed relatively small acreages (80–160 acres), although after about 1960 families farmed relatively larger acreages (200–400 acres). Most families raised corn and soybeans at the time of the interviews, although they had previously raised a wider variety of crops, including oats and wheat.

At the time of the interviews, the majority were still married to their first (and only) husbands; the rest were widowed. Only one woman had ever been divorced. The women had completed on average 12 years of education; about 20 percent did not complete high school. Half of the women had married by age 20. On average, the women had four children.

This informant pool limits the generalizability of my findings. First, I know only about women with children *and* grandchildren. Never-married women and childless women may use different labor options or may experience constraints in a different way than do women with husbands and children. Second, the informants all lived independently and enjoyed relatively good health at the time of the interview. Since working experiences have an impact on health (Pavalko, Elder, and Clipp 1993), this group may not include women whose labor options negatively affected their health. One final limitation of the informant pool is that all the women I interviewed were white. Given minority women's historically different work lives the model of work described here cannot be generalized to all women without considering the different experiences of women of color.

The life history interviews for this project were semistructured reminiscences covering the entire life course of the informants. Women answered questions about their residence, household composition, marital events, births and deaths of significant others, and important activities, including paid and unpaid work over their lifetimes. I interviewed most women in one visit, with the majority of the interviews lasting around two hours, but several interviews required more than one visit. Total interview times ranged from one to six hours. Interviews were taped and partially transcribed.[2]

From these life histories and using a grounded theory approach (Strauss and Corbin 1990), I first developed descriptions of the important ways the informants engaged in labor including formal and informal market work, home-based work, and housework. Next, using the women's descriptions of their work, I looked for characteristics of each option that affected women when they used that option. I looked both for characteristics of work that I identified as important and for characteristics the women identified as salient. I could group these characteristics into several dimensions that varied, depending on the type of option. Finally, I looked for the dimensions' consequences for women and for strategies women used to balance these consequences with their family responsibilities.

A qualitative approach allowed me to learn about each woman as part of an ongoing life with a history of experiences. The open-ended format permitted each woman to establish categories of salience for her life and experiences rather than relying on those imposed by a structured interview format.

RURAL WOMEN'S LABOR OPTIONS

The women I studied used a wide variety of labor options to meet their families' economic needs. These options varied over time and circumstances. Most women engaged in multiple labor options at least some of the time and often most of the time. The labor options I identified included formal labor market work, family business work, domestic work, farm fieldwork, chicken/egg production, milking, gardening, piecework, craft work, caregiving, and housework.

Formal labor market work. These women engaged in several formal labor market activities during their lives, including clerical work, nursing, teaching, factory work, restaurant work, and retail sales. Only three women had never worked in the formal labor market; most women worked in the formal labor market before marriage, and all but one woman left the formal labor market at the time they married. Although about a quarter worked in the formal labor market while they had children under the age of six years, most women returned to formal labor market work at some time after their children were old enough for school, either intermittently or continuously.

Kathy's experience presents a good example of formal labor market work in women's lives. Kathy quit nursing after she married in 1945, partly because many nursing jobs at that time required nurses to be single. After her children entered school, Kathy took a job as a county nurse. After several years, she became a school nurse and continued that position until she retired. After retirement, Kathy took a part-time job at a nursing home in a nearby community, where she was still working at the time of our interview.

Family businesses. Several women worked outside the home in family businesses. Sharon and Bobbie ran the offices of their husbands' businesses. Laura worked more than full-time, side by side with her husband, in their newspaper business. Rita operated a beauty shop. Work in a family business had characteristics similar to formal labor market work. For example, some women received wages and other benefits from the businesses; however, most women working in family businesses did not receive benefits directly, but benefited indirectly through the business profits.

Domestic work. Eighteen women performed domestic work in other people's homes, typically as teenagers or young adults. Besides doing housekeeping chores such as cooking, dishwashing, or ironing, they also helped with seasonal chores such as gardening or canning.

Fieldwork. Women often worked in childhood as laborers on their family farms. They plowed, cultivated, harvested, and took care of livestock. Caroline, born in 1924, started working in the fields when she was about five or six years old. Her father farmed a lot of acreage, and so he needed every child's labor:

> *We were all taught very young that the farming was first, and we had to do it, because that was the only way that Dad could hold on to the farm at that time, with the Depression and everything, with all the children and everything. So, we was out there working, as soon as we could get big enough to hold on to a pair of lines, well, we was out there farming.*

As wives, many women performed fieldwork. For example, Roberta worked full-time in the fields with Fred. When her children were three and two years old, she left them in a grove of trees next to the field while she worked:

> *I felt kinda strange, leaving that young of children, you know, by themselves, but, it was cheaper for me to be in the field than to try to hire somebody when you didn't have the money to hire with.*

Chickens. Two-thirds of the farm wives and several nonfarm wives raised chickens and eggs to sell; most other farm wives raised chickens and eggs for family consumption. Women hatched the eggs, brooded the baby chicks, fed and watered the chickens, collected the eggs, then peddled them and sometimes the meat to grocery stores. Chickens were a lot of trouble, and many of the women who raised chickens did not like them:

> M: *Did you do chickens?*
> F: *Oh, we had a hundred or two. I hated 'em. Oh, I never got so I liked chickens. If I have nightmares to this day, I've got chickens that are dyin' somewhere, chickens that are smotherin', chickens that are crowding. Oh, I hated chickens.*

Milking. Women were more likely to be involved in dairy work when they were children than when they were wives, since in the past parents typically gave daughters responsibility for milking and feeding. Edith told me: "I never did any fieldwork, but I milked an awful lot of cows!" Later, as adults, husbands usually did most of the milking and feeding if the families operated dairies. Wives primarily took responsibility for cream separating and butter making, but only occasionally for milking or feeding. Additionally, both farm and nonfarm women reported keeping a milk cow to provide milk and butter for their families.

Gardening. Most women raised gardens, primarily for family use but also sometimes for sale. As a child, Winnie assisted her parents in raising tomatoes and cucumbers to sell to restaurants and hotels. Carrie had an acreage planted with raspberries, which she and her children sold to friends and neighbors and from a roadside stand. Fanny and her children also sold surplus produce from a roadside stand.

Piecework. Several women took in piecework, most commonly typing, which they did at home in between their other duties. Patty typed for the company for which she had worked before marriage; Winnie typed for a company for which she later worked full-time. Through piecework, women could maintain ties with businesses for which they might return to formal labor market work at a later time. Other kinds of piecework included tinting photographs, taking in laundry and mending, and making shoe repairs.

Crafts. Several women made crafts at home, which they sold to friends and neighbors and in places such as beauty shops or flea markets. Most women who made crafts began selling them in middle age, as a hobby expanded into a business. For example, Teresa made tissue box covers, and Rita made pillowcases into dolls. Grace, after losing her portrait-tinting trade, began painting china. Roberta worked with her husband manufacturing and hand painting toys.

Caregiving. Women performed many tasks related to taking care of their children and sometimes other people. Most women took care of their own children, even when they did other labor. Nearly two-thirds of the women took care of people other than their children, usually in middle age after the children were grown. The cared-for people included parents, aunts, uncles, in-laws, siblings, grandchildren, and husbands. Some women cared for more than one person at the same time. Robin was taking care of her husband at home and her mother who lived down the street. At the time of her interview, Rita was caring for three people: her father-in-law, her husband's uncle, and an aunt-in-law.

Many women provided in-home child care either occasionally or on a full-time basis. This activity fit very well with having young children

of one's own. It provided both a little extra money and playmates for the women's children. Most women provided child care part-time or intermittently and usually only when they had small children of their own; however, after her husband died and her own children left home, Julia provided day care in her home for up to nine children. She told me she needed something to keep her busy.

Housework. Housework is a constant in most women's lives (Cowan 1983; Oakley 1974; Strasser 1982), and the women in this study provide no exception. Beginning in childhood, daughters had responsibility for assisting their mothers with cooking, cleaning, laundry, and gardening. Daughters' earliest responsibilities involved water: pumping or drawing it from a well or cistern, carrying it into the house, heating it, and carrying used water out of the house. Young children also took responsibility for carrying in firewood or coal and corncobs for tender and for carrying out ashes. Daughters helped with washing dishes, cleaning house, making beds, sweeping, dusting, and the myriad other chores required to keep a house.

In adolescence, some daughters took greater responsibility for the housework, while their mothers worked outside the home or suffered illnesses. Bernice spent a lot of time on housework:

> *Mother was always just getting over an operation, and Dad and I took over the household work. I did a lot of cooking. We'd get up of a morning and wash, and I'd hang the washing out before we went to school, and I did a lot of the homework and everything.*

Julia stayed out of school for a year to help her sickly mother; thus, some daughters began full-time housekeeping in adolescence. After they married, all the women in this study took primary responsibility for their families' house-keeping, even when working outside the home.

Women reported great variation in when and how they performed their housework. Some maintained high standards of cleanliness, while others told me that they did not keep their houses as clean as they thought they should:

> I never did dust to suit [my mother].
> I don't dust to suit myself, as far as
> that goes!

As a form of housework, women also engaged in labor-intensive productive activities rather than purchasing products ready made. Most of the study women lived their childhoods during the years of the Great Depression and, thus, are part of a generation dedicated to frugality and making do (Elder 1974). As adults, they continued to practice these spartan skills:

> We went without, you know, a lot. I
> made all their clothes and didn't buy
> prepared foods.

DEVELOPING THE CONTOURS OF A MULTIDIMENSIONAL CONTINUUM MODEL OF WORK

Given these labor options, we can begin to sketch out some important dimensions of work that make up a continuum model. First we can see that the *economic benefits* of work vary, from generating a wage to providing goods or services directly to the family to saving money. Second, we observe that work takes place in a variety of *locations,* including businesses, other people's homes, roadside vegetable stands, farm fields, chicken sheds, and houses. Third, women have varying degrees of *control* over different aspects of their labor options, such as when and how the work is done. These three dimensions interact to create patterns of possibility and necessity that contribute to women's use of multiple labor

strategies, either by allowing women to combine labor options or by requiring women to combine options. They also contribute to a greater likelihood that women will have *too much* work to do.

Economic Benefits

While many labor options generated income through wages or profits, women and their families also benefited directly from labor options that reduced necessary expenses for the family economy, leaving family resources available for other needs. Labor options, thus, could range from *income generating* to *expenditure reducing.*

Sometimes a woman's work both generated income and reduced expenditures. Roberta worked full-time in the fields with her husband, reducing farm expenditures because her labor substituted for hired labor; however, her labor contributed as much as her husband's to the value of the crops produced. Kate helped out at her husband's restaurant on special occasions and when employees were sick, reducing the cost of labor to the business; however, reduced labor costs translated into greater bottom-line profits for Kate's family.

The women I studied generated income for their family economies in a number of ways. Most worked in the formal labor market for wages at some time during their lives. Some women also worked away from home in family businesses, doing domestic work in someone else's home or doing farm labor on someone else's farm. Farm daughters and farm wives worked in the fields and performed other farm chores on family farms. Women raised chickens and sold the meat or eggs, milked cows and sold butter and cream, and raised produce to sell. Within their own homes, they worked for others, caring for children, doing piecework such as typing, or making crafts.

Women's expenditure-reducing options often entailed the same tasks as did income-generating work. Women produced and preserved food for their families, such as garden produce, eggs, meat, and milk. They also produced other goods, such as clothing or household furnishings. Keeping house and caring for their own children and other family members, especially the sick and aged, consumed the most amount of time.

According to my participants, everyone in their families engaged in income generation and expenditure reduction at various times, regardless of their age or gender; however, men usually produced goods and services in exchange for cash, while women and children usually produced goods and services for family use. Throughout their adult lives, these women engaged in income-generating and expenditure-reducing activities, often simultaneously, in a dynamic process in which women shifted between income generation, expenditure reduction, and combinations of both over time.

Women's work usually generated less income than did men's work. As a consequence, women often needed to combine two or three labor options to get the optimal mix of income generation and expenditure reduction. Expenditure-reducing work usually provided a lower net benefit to family economies than did income-generating work, and only women from the most affluent families could rely on expenditure-reducing work alone. For example, Maude cared for her grandchildren and her invalid husband, took in laundry and mending, and drove a school bus part-time to maintain an adequate family income. In this way, the limited economic benefit women received from their labor options often required that they use multiple work strategies.

Physical Location

While physical location might seem related to sector, they are not *isomorphic*—that is, having all the same relevant qualities. Sector is not just a literal "where." As a concept, sector has less to do with *where* the work takes place as with *what* kind of relationship worker and capital have with

each other and *how* that relationship is regulated by the government (see Portes and Sassen-Koob 1987). The physical location of formal sector work is partly a consequence of governmental regulation. For example, in the United States, federal regulations make giving out piecework difficult for formal labor market employers. Sector and physical location are correlated, but they are not two names for the same concept.

This distinction between sector and physical location clarifies our understanding of women's labor decisions, especially those involving multiple labor strategies. I found that women's work took place in a variety of locations. Most of the women I interviewed worked in places such as businesses, factories, or retail stores at some time during their lives. This roughly corresponds to the formal sector. Women also worked in family businesses away from their residences. Women worked on farms, both their own families' farms and the farms of extended kin and neighbors. Many women worked in the gardens or farmyards, raising chickens, milking cows, and gardening. Some women worked in the homes of extended family members and/or nonfamily members. These kinds of work roughly correspond to informal sector work discussed in the women in development literature (e.g., Rothstein 1994; Truelove 1990; Ward 1990), although the family farmwork might also be considered household sector work. Women also worked at various labor options inside their own houses, such as providing child care or doing piecework as well as the never-ending household tasks of cooking, cleaning, and caring for children. These kinds of work span both informal sector work (piecework) and household sector work.

Looking at physical location separately from sector reveals two previously unremarkable features of women's work that affect women's use of multiple labor strategies. First, physical location and economic benefit covary, but the correlation is not perfect. That is, women generate income away from home and at home, and women reduce expenditures away from home and at home; however, most labor options performed away from home generated income, while more of the labor options done at home reduced expenditures (see Table 1). Furthermore, location could directly affect economic benefits. When Lucy drove 60 miles to her job at a processing plant, she netted less income because of her traveling expenses.

Second, location had important consequences for women's ability to combine two or more labor options. Women could combine different options that took place in the same location more easily than they could combine options that occurred in different locations. When some other responsibility constrained them in their choice of location, the women often chose to add on another option that could be performed in the same location. Bobbie talked about deciding to do in-home day care:

> I didn't like the responsibility. But, it gave my last one somebody to play with while the others [were in school] 'cause he's three years behind the others. So I guess if I's gonna be at home with my own, then I might as well take on another one.

Since the decision to care for her children herself kept her from using a labor option in another location (working in the formal labor market, in this case), Bobbie chose another labor option that she could do at home.

Time Control Characteristics

I found three time characteristics of labor options that varied across options and affected the amount of control a woman had over when she performed that option. These included who initiated the option, who had primary responsibility for the work, and who controlled the timing of the work. These characteristics consequently limited women's range of labor option choices and tended to make women's time more available to other people such as husbands or children. In this discussion, we need to distinguish between the time (covering weeks, months, or years) when women are using a par-

TABLE 1   Labor Options in the Intersection of Physical Location and Economic Benefit

Location	Income generation	Mixed	Expenditure reduction
Away from home	Formal labor market work Domestic work Fieldwork for nonfamily	Family business	Caring for aged parent
Farm and yard	Gardening Milking Chickens	Fieldwork for family farm Gardening Milking Chickens	Gardening Milking Chickens
In the house	Piecework Crafts Child care for others		Housework Child care Sewing Food preservation

ticular labor option, the time (during the day) when women do a particular task of a labor option, and women's total time. I refer to the first as labor option timing, to the second as task timing, and to the third as women's time.

Labor option timing initiated by others versus that initiated by self. The person who initiated the labor option made it available, thus controlling the labor option timing. Brigit was able to go to work in a factory only because the factory had job openings and subsequently hired her; thus, someone other than the woman herself initiated formal labor market work and controlled when she could engage in that labor option. Contractors also usually initiated the piecework rather than the woman herself. Alternatively, the woman herself initiated labor options such as raising chickens, making crafts, or selling garden surplus, given that a market existed for the products. These kinds of labor options allowed women to control the labor option timing. Some labor options could be initiated by either the woman worker or the person using her labor, depending on the circumstances. For example, Velda decided that she would provide the personal care her mother-in-law needed, while Sarah's mother-in-law asked Sarah to take care of her.

Who initiated the work directly affected women's use of multiple work strategies by affecting their labor option timing. Other-initiated work required women to wait until the opportunity to work became available. Self-initiated labor options allowed women to add more easily on another labor option to supplement or replace income, because they could decide on their own to start doing these labor options without waiting for another option to become available. For example, when Bobbie left work to stay home with her children, she began providing day care for other children in her home. Self-initiated work helped women maintain multiple work strategies.

Primary responsibility for labor option versus helper. In options such as housecleaning or child care, women usually took primary responsibility for the option, although they might receive assistance from husbands, children, or others:

M: Who took care of the kids while you were gone [to work on the night shift]?

L: My husband. I had them in bed there, and then he was with them at night.

M: And so when did you sleep?

L: I slept when the kids took their morning naps, and then their afternoon naps.... And then, if I would have a day where I didn't get much sleep, then I'd take a nap after supper, until I went to work.

In other options, women served as helpers, but they did not make decisions about when or how the work should be accomplished. For example, many farm wives helped their husbands in the fields, but their husbands made most of the decisions about issues such as when to plow, plant, cultivate, or harvest. Still other work situations, such as doing domestic work for relatives, involved an intermediate level of responsibility for the work. For example, when Carrie did domestic work for her grandmother, she had responsibility for certain jobs such as washing dishes or ironing, but her grandmother had some input into how and when Carrie would accomplish the tasks.

Primary responsibility for a task constrained women's time more than did helping, affecting their ability to use multiple work strategies. Roberta, who helped her husband with fieldwork, could more easily combine that labor option with her child care and housekeeping responsibilities than could Winnie, who supervised a lab full-time for a chemical company. "Helping" labor options usually took less of women's time, leaving women freer to do other labor options as well; however, these options also left women more vulnerable to interruptions, and women did not always receive as much help as they gave, as Roberta explained:

M: How much time do you think [your husband] spent helping you with your chores?
R: Not as much time as I helped outside [laughs]!

Task timing controlled by others versus that controlled by women. Women doing waged work often had a supervisor who regulated task timing issues, from when the women did particular tasks to when they could go to the toilet. Formal labor market work structured women's time, while other options such as piecework or housework left their time relatively unstructured and flexible. Bobbie noted the differences between formal labor market work and household work:

M: How do you like [being a housewife]?
B: I love it.
M: Better than working?
B: Well...one thing about a household, if you don't wanna wash today, big deal. You'd get fired if you said I don't wanna type a letter.... You have a lot more freedom being a housewife, I think.

Controlling the task timing affected women's ability to combine labor options in multiple work strategies. When Brigit worked at a factory, she focused her attention on that task and nothing else while at the job. She could not care for her baby at the same time. Choosing factory work as a labor option closed the door to any other use of her time while at work. In other kinds of work in which women controlled task timing, their attention could be divided between several tasks, a vital ingredient for maintaining multiple work strategies. For example, when Winnie typed at home for a company, she decided when during the day she did the work. She could stop as necessary to attend to some other tasks such as feeding a baby or running an errand for her husband, or she could type in the evenings when her other responsibilities had gone to bed. When Winnie typed at an office, she had much less control over task timing. She had to be in the office when the business was open, and she could not easily leave her work to take care of other responsibilities (see Table 2).

Controlling task timing had positive consequences for women in terms of being able to maximize economic benefits through combining two or more labor options; however, this control had negative consequences as well, especially by overloading women with demands on their time. First, greater task timing control increased the likelihood that women *would* combine several labor options, using up more of their time and contributing to their work overload. Second, women with greater task timing control *could* stop doing one task easily to attend to another demand. Controlling task timing made women appear to have more time, which might then be co-opted by someone else, such as a spouse. Fanny went out to the field one day (for some minor reason that she could not recall). She was wearing a dress, but the next thing she knew she had spent the whole day tractoring. She got a terrible sunburn: "You don't drive a tractor in a dress!" Fanny had prepared to do a task appropriate for a dress but was commandeered into tractoring because the other things she had to do could be put off until later.

Consequently, women often ended up doing their primary responsibilities *and* helper tasks for other people. This contributed to women

TABLE 2   Labor Options in the Intersection of Physical Location and Task Timing Control

Location	Controlled by others	Partially controlled by self	Controlled by self
Away from home	Formal labor market work Domestic work Fieldwork for nonfamily	Family business Caring for aged parent	
Farm and yard		Fieldwork for family farm Milking Chickens	Gardening
In the house		Piecework Child care for others	Housework Child care Sewing Food preservation Crafts

doing more work overall. For example, Caroline told me how her mother helped her father with harvesting corn:

Mother always worked out in the field with Dad.... Mainly, she would pick corn with him, and they picked corn by hand then.... She took her kids—her babies—with her, and he fixed a box on the back of the wagon, and she'd put pillows and blankets in there and wrap the baby good, and when the baby would get hungry or anything or want to nurse, well, Mother, she, they'd stop, and Mother would nurse the baby.... Then they'd take [the load of corn] in, maybe at dinner time, and then Mother, she'd take the baby and go on into the house, and she'd prepare dinner.... When Dad come in from unloading the load of corn, then she would have the dinner prepared, and then as soon as they got through eating dinner, they'd just take the baby and go right back out to the field again.... After they got through with supper that night, she'd do the dishes. So she had quite a life.

In other words, she worked side by side with her husband in the fields all day, and because the housework could be put off until after they had finished harvesting for the day, she did all the housework too. Controlling the task timing of their work made women more likely to be overloaded with work.

These characteristics of task timing demonstrate more clearly why women's work has more "permeable" boundaries than does men's work (Ward 1990). Men engage in work that cannot easily be set aside to help a child with homework, to go to town for a machine part, or to go over to Grandpa's place to fix his supper. Women often engage in work that is easily set aside. Gardening can be put off, chickens can be fed early or late; housework can wait. Work that can be set aside probably will be.

DISCUSSION

Economic benefits, location, and time control dimensions have serious consequences for women's work experiences. First, limited economic benefits from the labor options women use tend to funnel them into multiple work strategies where they combine several labor options to maximize economic benefit. Second, location also encourages multiple labor strategies because women often have responsibilities that restrict them to a particular location where labor options have lower benefits, such as household work, for which they compensate by adding on other labor options. Third, women's other responsibilities, especially those of child care, encourage them to seek out labor options having flexible option timing and task timing so that they *can* combine options; however, labor options with flexible time constraints tend to provide relatively lower economic benefits, and they also contribute to women's work overload.

On the one hand, informal labor market forms of work, especially work performed at home, have positive consequences for women, such as greater control over the timing and performance of work and enhancing women's ability to combine various kinds of work with other family and household responsibilities in multiple labor strategies. Also, informal labor market work allows women to maintain ties with potential formal labor market employers. On the other hand, this ability to use multiple labor strategies also subjects women to a "triple shift" burden (Hossfeld forthcoming) where they must combine market, household, and informal work in multiple work strategies. Research in currently developing countries and urban areas in the United States demonstrates other negative consequences of informal labor market work, such as low wages, exploitative working conditions, long hours, and health risks (Boris and Daniels 1989; Chaney and Castro 1989; Enloe 1989).

Replacing old models of work with a multidimensional continuum model changes the way we perceive a number of issues. It allows us to observe some of the mechanisms operating in women's labor decision-making process. It suggests new ways of thinking about women's life course patterns. And by providing us with a definition of work that more accurately reflects observed experience, it casts doubt on some of

our current social policies, especially those regarding the care of children and the elderly.

A continuum model reveals new details of women's labor decision making by highlighting two important parameters of this process. First, women's work decisions are not either/or. Much of the literature of women's work looks at what women do as *either* paid market work *or* unpaid household work. But I found that many times women do multiple kinds of work *at the same time*—not just household *or* market work, but household *and* market work, and chickens besides. Discourse on women's "second shift" has made the important point that many women have responsibility for both market work and household work (Hochschild 1989). Hossfeld (forthcoming) further discusses the possibility of a "triple shift" for urban women. My research shows that this triple shift is a feature of rural women's lives as well, especially women living in economically marginal environments and times. A multidimensional model demonstrates that women can and do engage in multiple forms of work simultaneously.

Second, a continuum model reveals that labor decisions have overlapping effects; deciding to do her own child care takes up time that reduces the amount of income a woman can generate and that leads to deciding to add another home-based labor option, such as piecework or providing child care for other people. That decision leaves her available for going to town to get a tractor part, so that she must set aside the piecework, which means she has to stay up late to get the piecework done. A continuum model allows us to look at this as a process rather than as a status and allows us to better understand how *and why* women juggle multiple demands for work at home and elsewhere. Much previous research on women's work has focused strictly on work status—in or out of the formal labor market. Many also consider the presence or absence of children; however, the stories reported here clearly show that income generation and child care responsibilities interact in a much more complex fashion than can be documented by simple employed/housewife coding schemes. To observe the underlying process, we need detailed data to document the process.

A better understanding of this processual nature of women's work offers potential benefits to researchers studying the life course in general. Life course research focuses on patterns of events and transitions between events or statuses in people's lives (Elder 1985; Hagestad 1990). Studies of women's lifetime labor patterns assume that women's household or formal labor market work represents a status entered or exited via a discrete event. The data presented here suggest that work transitions may be less abrupt than previously conceptualized. Women may move gradually from one labor option to another, and a change in labor option may reflect not a change in work status but a change in work strategy.

The multidimensional continuum model further affects the way we do life course research and the conclusions we draw from our research findings. The M-shaped curve of women's labor force participation patterns provides a good example. Researchers have observed that the labor force participation of women born before World War II shows high rates of employment among women in their early 20s, a sharp decline in rates among women in their late 20s and early 30s, then a gradual increase across the middle ages, and a gradual decline among women in their 50s and 60s. Women born after the war, while showing a plateau in labor force participation during their 20s, tend to have patterns resembling men's labor force participation (McLaughlin et al. 1988).

Using an underlying dual spheres model, researchers attribute the sharp decline to women leaving the labor force, the public sphere, to bear and care for children, a private sphere occupa-

tion (Elder and Rockwell 1976). Women's return to the public sphere as their children grow up causes the increase in labor force participation in middle age. In a dichotomous model, explanations for time spent in one sphere depend on time spent in the other sphere, an either/or algorithm.[3]

A continuum model directs us to look for both/and explanations (Collins 1990) that address women's movement in the continuum, from working at the telephone company as a typist, to caring for the children at home, to typing at home for the telephone company, to working part-time at a book store, to working full-time at the bookstore, to doing housework, to caring for aging parents. Having children at home affects these shifts, but other factors affect them as well: family economic need, the availability of work, and the ability to combine different labor options into multiple work strategies. A continuum allows us to view work as both/and rather than as either/or: women can do *both* this labor option *and* that labor option at one time rather than *either* formal market work *or* household work. These insights offer great potential for better understanding life course processes.

Finally, reconceptualizing work as a multidimensional continuum transforms our definition of work from an activity that generates a wage (and benefits a capitalist) to an activity that generates a variety of benefits for women and their families, both income generating and expenditure reducing. It contradicts old notions that household work is somehow different or less significant to society than is waged work.

A continuum model offers a different way of looking at the world. Instead of looking at the world as either/or public/private, we see the world as a continuous piece of experience in which people move from the extreme public end to the extreme private end, but most of the time people (women *and* men) are operating in parts of the world that have characteristics of both the public and the private.

Which definition we choose to apply to work influences not only our research but also social and business policy. Social scientists did not "invent" the separate spheres model; rather, it arose out of capitalist ideological beliefs in the 19th century (Bose 1987; Mies 1986). Capitalism needed most forms of work to be viewed as nonpublic so that capitalists did not need to take financial responsibility for things such as child care and elder care. With these old unquestioned ideological blinders, society frequently fails to recognize and value the economic contributions of women's (and men's) unpaid caregiving activities both to their families and to society at large, because these activities have been relegated to the private/affective sphere. Now we find ourselves facing a situation in which we have increasing numbers of aged individuals and children needing care, increasing numbers of women engaged in waged work outside the home, and no strategies to deal with societywide financial demands for these unmet caregiving needs (Abel 1991). Because we have not considered women's caregiving as work, we now cannot deal with it as work. As social scientists, we cannot transform cultural ideologies by a simple change of conceptual models; however, we can begin the process by incorporating into our research models whose underlying assumptions reflect observed experience.

Part III

Generational Relationships

Part II of this reader was largely devoted to examining the marriage and family dynamics of gender relationships. We now shift our attention to readings that study relationships between family members of different ages.

All human societies are differentiated on the basis of age and sex. Throughout history, the social roles of men and women have been separate, as have the roles of children, adults, and the aged. The family is composed of members of various ages who are differentially related. Most sociological accounts of the family have emphasized how age differentiation of family members enhances their solidarity. The interdependence of family members has been seen to foster emotional attachments, structural solidarity, and family cohesion. Yet, inherent in this differential age structure is the potential for conflict and tension.

Differential age structures have always been linked to status discrepancies in power, privilege, and prestige. Just as a power dimension is often articulated in gender relationships, families can be viewed in terms of hierarchical social structures in which older generations or older siblings hold positions of power, authority, and prestige over their younger counterparts. There are various degrees of family stratification by age. But the universal tendency is for the elders to exercise control over younger family members.

The articles contained in the two chapters that make up this part of the book will examine how families define sets of people according to age. These age categories influence family members' relations to one another. Distinguishing family members by age also has implications for the conceptualization of persons placed in particular age groups. The conceptualizations of childhood and adolescence, adulthood, and the aged reflect conceptualizations of the family, and they should be seen in terms of cultural diversity and social-historical context.

Philippe Ariès in his classic study, *Centuries of Childhood: A Social History of Family Life* (1962), put forth the striking theme that Western ideas about childhood and family life have changed and developed from the Middle Ages to modern times. Ariès sought to document how in medieval life the child was integrated into the community. It was not until

311

the development of bourgeois capitalist society that the segregation of children occurred. He argued that, in the earlier period, children were treated as small adults. As soon as they were capable of being without their mothers, children interacted in the adult world, sharing the same world of work and play. By the age of seven or eight, they were treated as if they had the same mental capacities for understanding and feeling as their adult counterparts.

The lack of awareness of the particular nature of childhood and the full participation of children in adult life is associated with the nature of the family and the community. Ariès depicted the medieval community as intense; no one was left alone because the high density of social life made isolation virtually impossible. This sociability practically nullified the reality and the conceptualization of the private home and the private family. The distinct sense of privacy so characteristic of modern-day families was absent.

Ariès saw the transition to the modern conceptualization of the child beginning to emerge during the seventeenth century. Economic changes led to a revival of interest in education. This, in turn, introduced the idea that a period of special preparation was necessary before individuals could assume their place as adults. Children began to be treated differently, they were expected to behave differently, and their nature was viewed as being different. Children were now coddled, and a greater interest and concern for their moral welfare and development became common.

Ariès emphasized that this emerging concept of childhood developed and was given expression in the emergence of the bourgeois family. He argued that, from a relatively insignificant institution during the Middle Ages, there developed a growing belief in the virtue of the intimate and private nuclear family. The rise of the private family and the growth of the sentimental bonds among its members consequently came about at the expense of the public community.

The continued inward development of the family and its creation of a private sphere of life removed from the outside world was intertwined with the increased importance given to children. The outside community came to be viewed with suspicion and indifference. Proceeding into the industrial era, the family began to withdraw its nonproductive members, women and children, from involvement with the surrounding community. The increased division of labor of family members and the consequent isolation of women and children within the home resulted.

Here again, the broad historical survey of Western patterns of parenthood and child-rearing needs to be modified through an examination of the experiences of racial ethnic families in the United States. In Chapter Eight, "Patterns of Parenthood, Childhood, and Adolescence," Bonnie Thornton Dill (Reading 23) first examines the experience of parent-hood among racial ethnic women within an historical perspective. She builds on the earlier examination of the separate-spheres doctrine that relegated women to household work characterized by childbearing, childrearing, and domestic labor—"reproductive labor." She observes that this model was based on patriarchal authority in which men's economic activities allowed them to control the family. Women, while having few legal rights, were protected under the umbrella of patriarchy—the "politics and politesse" of patriarchy as Bartelt, Hutter, and Bartelt (Reading 16) describe it—in their designated roles of wives, mothers, and daughters. This model was essentially the pattern prevalent among eighteenth- and nineteenth-century white women. The circumstances of racial ethnic women were quite different.

Dill examines reproductive labor among African American, Chinese American, and Mexican American women in the United States during the nineteenth century. She observes that the concept of reproductive labor must be modified when applied to women of color. Productive labor, i.e., paid work, was required for these women to sustain their families. They never experienced the "cult of domesticity"; instead their lives were characterized by the "double day" of work and family involvements. Special attention is given in the article to how racial ethnic women's work in maintaining the family was a source of resistance to the cultural assaults of the larger society.

Viviana Zelizer (1985) in her book *Pricing the Priceless Child* traces the emergence of the modern conceptualization of the child by documenting a shift in the value of American children since the 1870s from economically useful assets to economically "useless" but emotionally "priceless" love objects. In Reading 24, she observes that the changing economic character of baby adoption and the more recent use of surrogacy has historically moved from a buyer's market to a bullish baby's market. This change is seen to reflect the "profound cultural transformation in children's economic and sentimental values" during this time period. Zelizer further argues that surrogacy is a further extension of the sentimental search for a child to love. By specifying the racial and cultural characteristics of the sought-for surrogate mother, parents aim for the "deliberate manufacture of a particular, suitable child."

In addition to historical transformation in the attitudes toward and the conceptualization of children, attitudes and values regarding the saliency of the parental role have also changed. This has been most dramatically evident in the current heated debate regarding abortion. The United States has witnessed a revolution in the abortion situation for the last twenty-five years. Many states have liberalized their abortion laws. As a severe reaction, a "right to life" movement has emerged as the most powerful single-issue force in American politics. In recent years, there has been a noticeable reversal of court decisions, reflecting an increasing number of state legislatures undoing the past liberalizing laws.

Kristin Luker (1984) in a very important work, *Abortion and the Politics of Motherhood,* argued that female pro-choice and pro-life advocates hold different world views regarding gender, sex, and the meaning of parenthood. Moral positions on abortion are seen to be tied intimately to views of sexual behavior, the care of children, family life, technology, and the importance of the individual. Luker identifies pro-choice women as educated, affluent, and liberal. In contrast, pro-life women support traditional concepts of women as wives and mothers. Luker believes that the abortion debate is so passionately fought "because it is a referendum on the place and meaning of motherhood."

Another major contemporary concern regarding the nature of parenthood, childhood, and adolescence is reflected by the rise in teenage pregnancy and parenthood. In the United States, these teenage mothers are many times more likely than other women with young children to live below the poverty level. Kristin Luker (Reading 25) observes that the complicated link between poverty and teen pregnancy raises questions about our political culture as well as our public choices. She examines the commonly held belief that teen pregnancy is a major cause of poverty and that reducing one would reduce the other. She calls for a broadening of understanding of societal dynamics rather than simply focusing on the perceived failures of teenagers to control their sexual impulses. She views teen pregnancy in terms of how race and class are factors that limit opportunities, restricting horizons and the boundaries of hope.

Chapter Nine, "The Family and the Elderly," is concerned with the nature of generational relationships between the elderly and the family. Earlier, we commented that the universal tendency has been for elders to exercise control over younger family members. Indeed in more traditional societies that are less susceptible to social change, the elderly have been seen as the repositories of strategic knowledge and religious custom, controlling the ownership of property, and having major influence over kinship and extended family rights and obligations. But, with the movement toward modernization, individualism, and the private family there has been a significant decline in the influence, power, and prestige that the elderly have in the family. The elderly have relatively little importance in an industrial society that emphasizes individual welfare, social and economic progress and change, and that is opposed to the ideology of family continuity and tradition.

However, recent research has demonstrated that the significant decline in the mortality rate, especially in the later decades of the twentieth century, has fundamentally changed the character of the relationship among elders, their children, and grandchildren. This decline has given contemporary grandparenthood new meaning and has accounted for the rise of the four-generation family. This demographic change has greatly increased the potential for family interaction across more than two generations.

Ethel Shanas (Reading 26) focuses on the "new pioneers" among the elderly and their families—the members of four-generation families. Shanas observes that the implications for the emergence of a four-generation-family system are not fully appreciated. Opportunities exist for the development of innovative and satisfying kinship ties across the generations, but the disruptive potential of the older generations straining the emotional and economic resources of the younger generations is quite real.

Andrew Cherlin and Frank Furstenberg, Jr. (1986) studied a representative nationwide sample of American grandparents. They note that quality-of-life improvements for many older people have brought about changes in the grandparent-grandchild relationship. The authors discuss how grandparents are at a stage where they desire to maintain autonomy while at the same time participate in the family life of their children and grandchildren. They further observe that social class is relatively unimportant in grandparenthood. In Reading 27, we reprint a selection from their book *The New American Grandparent,* which has the informative subtitle "A Place in the Family, a Life Apart." In this selection, Cherlin and Furstenberg also discuss the future of grandparenthood.

The last two articles in this chapter focus on elderly with different ethnic backgrounds. Florentius Chan (Reading 28) reports on the experiences of elderly Asian and Pacific Islanders, many of whom are foreign-born and are newly arrived immigrants or refugees. The popular image is of the veneration of elders by Asians and Pacific Islanders. However, as Chan observes, problems of cultural adjustment and the shattering of support networks in America result in very disruptive family and social patterns for these people.

Joan Weibel-Orlando (Reading 29) also examines how the cultural context affects generational relations. Through a study of Native Americans in California and a reservation in South Dakota, the author shows that there is a variety of grandparenting models. However, compared to Americans of European descent, Native Americans have less-restricted boundaries between genealogical generations. Weibel-Orlando also documents how generational relationships are affected not only by the traditional patterns but also by needs generated out of stresses imposed by their present poverty.

REFERENCES

Ariès, Philippe. 1962. *Centuries of Childhood: A Social History of the Family.* New York: Knopf.
Cherlin, Andrew, and Frank Furstenberg, Jr. 1986. *The New American Grandparent: A Place in the Family, a Life Apart.* New York: Basic Books.
Luker, Kristin. 1984. *Abortion and the Politics of Motherhood.* Berkeley, CA: University of California Press.
Zelizer, Viviana A. 1985. *Pricing the Priceless Child.* New York: Basic Books.

Chapter 8

Patterns of Parenthood, Childhood, and Adolescence

Reading 23   Our Mothers' Grief: Racial Ethnic Women and the Maintenance of Families*

BONNIE THORNTON DILL

REPRODUCTIVE LABOR[1] FOR WHITE WOMEN IN EARLY AMERICA

In eighteenth- and nineteenth-century America, the lives of white[2] women in the United States were circumscribed within a legal and social system based on patriarchal authority. This authority took two forms: public and private. The social, legal, and economic position of women in this society was controlled through the private aspects of patriarchy and defined in terms of their relationship to families headed by men. The society was structured to confine white wives to reproductive labor within the domestic sphere. At the same time the formation, preservation and protection of families among white settlers was seen as crucial to the growth and development of American society. Building, maintaining, and supporting families was a concern of the State and of those organizations that prefigured the State. Thus, while white women had few legal rights as women, they were protected through public forms of patriar-

chy that acknowledged and supported their family roles of wives, mothers, and daughters because they were vital instruments for building American society.

The groundwork for public support of women's family roles was laid during the colonial period. As early as 1619, the London Company began planning for the importation of single women into the colonies to marry colonists, form families, and provide for a permanent settlement. The objective was to make the men "more settled and less moveable...instability would breed a dissolution, and so an overthrow of the Plantation" (cited in Spruill 1972, p. 8).

In accordance with this recognition of the importance of families, the London Company provided the economic basis necessary for the development of the family as a viable and essential institution within the nascent social structure of the colonies. Shares of land were allotted for both husbands and wives in recognition of the fact that "in a new plantation it is not known whether men or women be the most necessary" (cited in Spruill 1972, p. 9).

*Dill, Bonnie Thornton. 1988. "Our Mothers' Grief: Racial Ethnic Women and the Maintenance of Families." Journal of Family History, Volume 13, Number 4, pages 415–431. Copyright © 1988 by JAI Press Inc. All rights of reproduction in any form reserved. Reprinted by permission.

This pattern of providing an economic base designed to attract, promote and maintain families was followed in the other colonial settlements. Lord Baltimore of Maryland "...offered to each adventurer a hundred acres for himself, a hundred for his wife, fifty for each child, a hundred for each man servant, and sixty for a woman servant. Women heads of families were treated just as men" (Spruill 1972, p. 11).

In Georgia, which appealed to poorer classes for settlers more than did Virginia or Maryland, "...among the advantages they offered men to emigrate was the gainful employment of their wives and children" (Spruill 1972, p. 16).

In colonial America, white women were seen as vital contributors to the stabilization and growth of society. They were therefore accorded some legal and economic recognition through a patriarchal family structure.

> *While colonial life remained hard, ... American women married earlier [than European women], were less restricted by dowries, and often had legal protection for themselves and their children in antenuptial contracts (Kennedy 1979, p. 7).*

Throughout the colonial period, women's reproductive labor in the family was an integral part of the daily operation of small-scale family farms or artisan's shops. According to Kessler-Harris (1981), a gender-based division of labor was common, but not rigid. The participation of women in work that was essential to family survival reinforced the importance of their contributions to both the protection of the family and the growth of society.

Between the end of the eighteenth and mid-nineteenth century, what is labeled the "modern American family" developed. The growth of industrialization and an urban middle class, along with the accumulation of agrarian wealth

among Southern planters, had two results that are particularly pertinent to this discussion. First, class differentiation increased and sharpened, and with it, distinctions in the content and nature of women's family lives. Second, the organization of industrial labor resulted in the separation of home and family and the assignment to women of a separate sphere of activity focused on childcare and home maintenance. Whereas men's activities became increasingly focused upon the industrial competitive sphere of work, "women's activities were increasingly confined to the care of children, the nurturing of the husband, and the physical maintenance of the home" (Degler 1980, p. 26).

This separate sphere of domesticity and piety became both an ideal for all white women as well as a source of important distinctions between them. As Matthei (1982) points out, tied to the notion of wife as homemaker is a definition of masculinity in which the husband's successful role performance was measured by his ability to keep his wife in the homemaker role. The entry of white women into the labor force came to be linked with the husband's assumed inability to fulfill his provider role.

For wealthy and middle-class women, the growth of the domestic sphere offered a potential for creative development as homemakers and mothers. Given ample financial support from their husband's earnings, some of these women were able to concentrate their energies on the development and elaboration of the more intangible elements of this separate sphere. They were also able to hire other women to perform the daily tasks such as cleaning, laundry, cooking, and ironing. Kessler-Harris cautions, however, that the separation of productive labor from the home did not seriously diminish the amount of physical drudgery associated with housework, even for middle-class women.

> *It did relegate the continuing hard work to second place, transforming*

the public image of the household by the 1820s and 1830s from a place where productive labor was performed to one whose main goals were the preservation of virtue and morality...Many of the "well-run" homes of the pre-Civil War period seem to have been the dwelling of overworked women. Short of household help, without modern conveniences, and frequently pregnant, these women complained bitterly of their harsh existence (Kessler-Harris 1981, p. 39).

In effect, household labor was transformed from economic productivity done by members of the family group to home maintenance; childcare and moral uplift done by an isolated woman who perhaps supervised some servants.

Working-class white women experienced this same transformation but their families' acceptance of the domestic code meant that their labor in the home intensified. Given the meager earnings of working-class men, working-class families had to develop alternative strategies to both survive and keep the wives at home. The result was that working-class women's reproductive labor increased to fill the gap between family need and family income. Women increased their own production of household goods through things such as canning and sewing; and by developing other sources of income, including boarders and homework. A final and very important source of other income was wages earned by the participation of sons and daughters in the labor force. In fact, Matthei argues that "the domestic homemaking of married women was supported by the labors of their daughters" (1982, p. 130).

The question arises: Why did white working-class families sacrifice other aspects of this nineteenth-century notion of family, such as privacy and the protection of children, to keep wives as homemakers within the home? Zaretsky (1978) provides a possible answer:

The Victorian emphasis on the sanctity of the family and on the autonomy of women within the family marked an advance for women of all classes over the interdependent but male dominated subsistence farm of the 18th century...most of women's adult life was taken up with childrearing. As a result, a special respect for her place within the home, and particularly for her childrearing activities was appreciated by working class women (p. 211).

Another way in which white women's family roles were socially acknowledged and protected was through the existence of a separate sphere for women. The code of domesticity, attainable for affluent women, became an ideal toward which nonaffluent women aspired. Notwithstanding the personal constraints placed on women's development, the notion of separate spheres promoted the growth and stability of family life among the white middle class and became the basis for working-class men's efforts to achieve a family wage, so that they could keep their wives at home. Also, women gained a distinct sphere of authority and expertise that yielded them special recognition.

During the eighteenth and nineteenth centuries, American society accorded considerable importance to the development and sustenance of European immigrant families. As primary laborers in the reproduction and maintenance of family life, women were acknowledged and accorded the privileges and protections deemed socially appropriate to their family roles. This argument acknowledges the fact that the family structure denied these women many rights and privileges and seriously constrained their individual growth and development. Because women gained social recognition primarily through their membership in families, their personal rights were few and privileges were subject to the will of the male head of the household. Nevertheless, the recognition of women's reproductive labor as an essential building block of the family, combined with a view of the family as the cornerstone of the nation, distinguished the experiences of the white, dominant culture from those of racial ethnics.

Thus, in its founding, American society initiated legal, economic, and social practices designed to promote the growth of family life among European colonists. The reception colonial families found in the United States contrasts sharply with the lack of attention given to the families of racial-ethnics. Although the presence of racial-ethnics was equally as important for the growth of the nation, their political, economic, legal, and social status was quite different.

REPRODUCTIVE LABOR AMONG RACIAL-ETHNICS IN EARLY AMERICA

Unlike white women, racial-ethnic women experienced the oppressions of a patriarchal society but were denied the protections and buffering of a patriarchal family. Their families suffered as a direct result of the organization of the labor systems in which they participated.

Racial-ethnics were brought to this country to meet the need for a cheap and exploitable labor force. Little attention was given to their family and community life except as it related to their economic productivity. Labor, and not the existence or maintenance of families, was the critical aspect of their role in building the nation. Thus they were denied the social structural supports necessary to make *their* families a vital element in the social order. Family membership was not a key means of access to participation in the wider society. The lack of social, legal, and

economic support for racial-ethnic families intensified and extended women's reproductive labor, created tensions and strains in family relationships, and set the stage for a variety of creative and adaptive forms of resistance.

AFRICAN-AMERICAN SLAVES

Among students of slavery, there has been considerable debate over the relative "harshness" of American slavery, and the degree to which slaves were permitted or encouraged to form families. It is generally acknowledged that many slaveowners found it economically advantageous to encourage family formation as a way of reproducing and perpetuating the slave labor force. This became increasingly true after 1807 when the importation of African slaves was explicitly prohibited. The existence of these families and many aspects of their functioning, however, were directly controlled by the master. In other words, slaves married and formed families but these groupings were completely subject to the master's decision to let them remain intact. One study has estimated that about 32% of all recorded slave marriages were disrupted by sale, about 45% by death of a spouse, about 10% by choice, with the remaining 13% not disrupted at all (Blassingame 1972, pp. 90–92). African slaves thus quickly learned that they had a limited degree of control over the formation and maintenance of their marriages and could not be assured of keeping their children with them. The threat of disruption was perhaps the most direct and pervasive cultural assault[3] on families that slaves encountered. Yet there were a number of other aspects of the slave system which reinforced the precariousness of slave family life.

In contrast to some African traditions and the Euro-American patterns of the period, slave men were not the main provider or authority figure in the family. The mother-child tie was basic and of greatest interest to the slaveowner because it was critical in the reproduction of the labor force.

In addition to the lack of authority and economic autonomy experienced by the husband-father in the slave family, use of the rape of women slaves as a weapon of terror and control further undermined the integrity of the slave family.

It would be a mistake to regard the institutionalized pattern of rape during slavery as an expression of white men's sexual urges, otherwise stifled by the specter of the white womanhood's chastity... Rape was a weapon of domination, a weapon of repression, whose covert goal was to extinguish slave women's will to resist, and in the process, to demoralize their men (Davis 1981, pp. 23–24).

The slave family, therefore, was at the heart of a peculiar tension in the master-slave relationship. On the one hand, slaveowners sought to encourage familial ties among slaves because, as Matthei (1982) states: "...these provided the basis of the development of the slave into a self-conscious socialized human being" (p. 81). They also hoped and believed that this socialization process would help children learn to accept their place in society as slaves. Yet the master's need to control and intervene in the familial life of the slaves is indicative of the other side of this tension. Family ties had the potential for becoming a competing and more potent source of allegiance than the slavemaster himself. Also, kin were as likely to socialize children in forms of resistance as in acts of compliance.

It was within this context of surveillance, assault, and ambivalence that slave women's reproductive labor took place. She and her menfolk had the task of preserving the human and family ties that could ultimately give them a reason for living. They had to socialize their children to believe in the possibility of a life in which they were not enslaved. The slave woman's labor on behalf of the family was, as Davis (1971) has pointed out, the only labor the slave engaged in that could not be directly appropriated by the slaveowner for his own profit. Yet, its indirect appropriation, as labor crucial to the reproduction of the slaveowner's labor force, was the source of strong ambivalence for many slave women. Whereas some mothers murdered their babies to keep them from being slaves, many sought within the family sphere a degree of autonomy and creativity denied them in other realms of the society. The maintenance of a distinct African-American culture is testimony to the ways in which slaves maintained a degree of cultural autonomy and resisted the creation of a slave family that only served the needs of the master.

Gutman (1976) provides evidence of the ways in which slaves expressed a unique Afro-American culture through their family practices. He provides data on naming patterns and kinship ties among slaves that flies in the face of the dominant ideology of the period. That ideology argued that slaves were immoral and had little concern for or appreciation of family life.

Yet Gutman demonstrated that within a system which denied the father authority over his family, slave boys were frequently named after their fathers, and many children were named after blood relatives as a way of maintaining family ties. Gutman also suggested that after emancipation a number of slaves took the names of former owners in order to reestablish family ties that had been disrupted earlier. On plantation after plantation, Gutman found considerable evidence of the building and maintenance of extensive kinship ties among slaves. In instances where slave families had been disrupted, slaves in new communities reconstituted the kinds of family and kin ties that came to characterize black family life throughout the South. These patterns excluded, but were not limited to, a belief in the importance of marriage as a long-term commitment, rules of exogamy that included marriage between first cousins, and acceptance of women who had children outside of marriage. Kinship networks were an important source of resistance to the organization of labor that treated the individual slave, and not the family, as the unit of labor (Caulfield 1974).

Another interesting indicator of the slaves' maintenance of some degree of cultural autonomy has been pointed out by Wright (1981) in her discussion of slave housing. Until the early 1800s, slaves were often permitted to build their housing according to their own design and taste. During that period, housing built in an African style was quite common in the slave quarters. By 1830, however, slaveowners had begun to control the design and arrangement of slave housing and had introduced a degree of conformity and regularity to it that left little room for the slave's personalization of the home. Nevertheless, slaves did use some of their own techniques in construction and often hid it from their masters.

> Even the floors, which usually consisted of only tamped earth, were evidence of a hidden African tradition: slaves cooked clay over a fire, mixing in ox blood or cow dung, and then poured it in place to make hard dirt floors almost like asphalt...In slave houses, in contrast to other crafts, these signs of skill and tradition would then be covered over (Wright 1981, p. 48).

Housing is important in discussions of family because its design reflects sociocultural attitudes about family life. The housing that slaveowners provided for their slaves reflected a view of Black family life consistent with the stereotypes of the period. While the existence of slave families was acknowledged, it certainly was not nurtured. Thus, cabins were crowded, often containing more than one family, and there were no provisions for privacy. Slaves had to create their own.

> Slave couples hung up old clothes or quilts to establish boundaries; others built more substantial partitions from scrap wood. Parents sought to establish sexual privacy from children. A few ex-slaves described modified trundle beds designed to hide parental lovemaking...Even in one room cabins, sexual segregation was carefully organized (Wright 1981, p. 50).

Perhaps most critical in developing an understanding of slave women's reproductive labor is the gender-based division of labor in the domestic sphere. The organization of slave labor enforced considerable equality among men and women. The ways in which equality in the labor force was translated into the family sphere is somewhat speculative. Davis (1981), for example, suggests that egalitarianism between males and females was a direct result of slavery when she says:

> Within the confines of their family and community life, therefore, Black people managed to accomplish a magnificent feat. They transformed that negative equality which emanated from the equal oppression they suffered as slaves into a positive quality: the egalitarianism characterizing their social relations (p. 18).

It is likely, however, that this transformation was far less direct than Davis implies. We know, for example, that slave women experienced what has recently been called the "double day" before most other women in this society. Slave narratives (Jones 1985; White 1985; Blassingame 1977) reveal that women had primary responsibility for their family's domestic chores. They cooked (although on some plantations meals were prepared for all of the slaves), sewed, cared for their children, and cleaned house, all after completing a full day of labor for the master. Blassingame (1972) and others have pointed out that slave men engaged in hunting, trapping, perhaps some gardening, and furniture making as ways of contributing to the maintenance of their families. Clearly, a gender-based division of labor did exist within the family and it appears that women bore the larger share of the burden for housekeeping and child care.

By contrast to white families of the period, however, the division of labor in the domestic sphere was neither reinforced in the relationship of slave women to work nor in the social institutions of the slave community. The gender-based division of labor among the slaves existed within a social system that treated men and women as almost equal, independent units of labor.[4] Thus Matthei (1982) is probably correct in concluding that:

> Whereas . . . the white homemaker interacted with the public sphere through her husband, and had her work life determined by him, the enslaved Afro-American homemaker was directly subordinated to and determined by her owner . . . The equal enslavement of husband and wife gave the slave marriage a curious kind of equality, an equality of oppression (p. 94).

Black men were denied the male sources of a patriarchal society and therefore were unable to turn gender distinctions into female subordination, even if that had been their desire. Black women, on the other hand, were denied support and protection for their roles as mothers and wives and thus had to modify and structure those roles around the demands of their labor. Thus, reproductive labor for slave women was intensified in several ways: by the demands of slave labor that forced them into the double-day of work; by the desire and need to maintain family ties in the face of a system that gave them only limited recognition; by the stresses of building a family with men who were denied the standard social privileges of manhood; and by the struggle to raise children who could survive in a hostile environment.

This intensification of reproductive labor made networks of kin and quasi-kin important instruments in carrying out the reproductive tasks of the slave community. Given an African culture heritage where kinship ties formed the basis of social relations, it is not at all surprising that African American slaves developed an extensive system of kinship ties and obligations (Gutman 1976; Sudarkasa 1981). Research on Black families in slavery provides considerable documentation of participation of extended kin in childrearing, childbirth, and other domestic, social, and economic activities (Gutman 1976; Blassingame 1972; Genovese 1974).

After slavery, these ties continued to be an important factor linking individual household units in a variety of domestic activities. While kinship ties were also important among native-born whites and European immigrants, Gutman (1976) has suggested that these ties:

> were comparatively more important to Afro-Americans than to lower-class native white and immigrant

Americans, the result of their distinctive low economic status, a condition that denied them the advantages of an extensive associational life beyond the kin group and the advantages and disadvantages resulting from mobility opportunities (p. 213).

His argument is reaffirmed by research on Afro-American families after slavery (Shimkin et al. 1978; Aschenbrenner 1975; Davis 1981; Stack 1974). Sudarkasa (1981) takes this argument one step further and links this pattern to the African cultural heritage.

Historical realities require that the derivation of this aspect of Black family organization be traced to its African antecedents. Such a view does not deny the adaptive significance of consanguineal (kin) networks. In fact, it helps to clarify why these networks had the flexibility they had and why, they, rather than conjugal relationships came to be the stabilizing factor in Black families (p. 49).

With individual households, the gender-based division of labor experienced some important shifts during emancipation. In their first real opportunity to establish family life beyond the controls and constraints imposed by a slavemaster, family life among Black sharecroppers changed radically. Most women, at least those who were wives and daughters of able-bodied men, withdrew from field labor and concentrated on their domestic duties in the home. Husbands took primary responsibility for the fieldwork and for relations with the owners, such as signing contracts on behalf of the family. Black women were severely criticized by whites for removing themselves from field labor because

they were seen to be aspiring to a model of womanhood that was considered inappropriate for them. This reorganization of female labor, however, represented an attempt on the part of Blacks to protect women from some of the abuses of the slave system and to thus secure their family life. It was more likely a response to the particular set of circumstances that the newly freed slaves faced than a reaction to the lives of their former masters. Jones (1985) argues that these patterns were "particularly significant" because at a time when industrial development was introducing a labor system that divided male and female labor, the freed black family was establishing a pattern of joint work and complementary of tasks between males and females that was reminiscent of the preindustrial American families. Unfortunately, these former slaves had to do this without the institutional supports that white farm families had in the midst of a sharecropping system that deprived them of economic independence.

CHINESE SOJOURNERS

An increase in the African slave population was a desired goal. Therefore, Africans were permitted and even encouraged at times to form families subject to the authority and whim of the master. By sharp contrast, Chinese people were explicitly denied the right to form families in the United States through both law and social practice. Although male laborers began coming to the United States in sizable numbers in the middle of the nineteenth century, it was more than a century before an appreciable number of children of Chinese parents were born in America. Tom, a respondent in Nee and Nee's (1973) book, *Longtime Californ'* says: "One thing about Chinese men in America was you had to be either a merchant or a big gambler, have lot of side money to have a family here. A working man, an ordinary man, just can't!" (p. 80).

Working in the United States was a means of gaining support for one's family with an end of obtaining sufficient capital to return to China and purchase land. The practice of sojourning was reinforced by laws preventing Chinese laborers from becoming citizens, and by restrictions on their entry into this country. Chinese laborers who arrived before 1882 could not bring their wives and were prevented by law from marrying whites. Thus, it is likely that the number of Chinese-American families might have been negligible had it not been for two things: the San Francisco earthquake and fire in 1906, which destroyed all municipal records; and the ingenuity and persistence of the Chinese people who used the opportunity created by the earthquake to increase their numbers in the United States. Since relatives of citizens were permitted entry, American born Chinese (real and claimed) would visit China, report the birth of a son, and thus create an entry slot. Years later the slot could be used by a relative or purchased. The purchasers were called "paper sons." Paper sons became a major mechanism for increasing the Chinese population, but it was a slow process and the sojourner community remained predominantly male for decades.

The high concentration of males in the Chinese community before 1920 resulted in a split household form of family. As Glenn observes:

> In the split household family, production is separated from other functions and is carried out by a member living far from the rest of the household. The rest—consumption, reproduction and socialization—are carried out by the wife and other relatives from the home village ... The split household form makes possible maximum exploitation of the workers ... The labor of prime-age male workers can be bought relatively cheaply, since the cost of reproduction and family maintenance is borne partially by unpaid subsistence work of women and old people in the home village (Glenn 1981, pp. 14–15).

The women who were in the United States during this period consisted of a small number who were wives and daughters of merchants and a larger percentage who were prostitutes. Hirata (1979) has suggested that Chinese prostitution was an important element in helping to maintain the split-household family. In conjunction with laws prohibiting intermarriage, Chinese prostitution helped men avoid long-term relationships with women in the United States and ensured that the bulk of their meager earnings would continue to support the family at home.

The reproductive labor of Chinese women, therefore, took on two dimensions primarily because of the split-household family form. Wives who remained in China were forced to raise children and care for in-laws on the meager remittances of their sojourning husband. Although we know few details about their lives, it is clear that the everyday work of bearing and maintaining children and a household fell entirely on their shoulders. Those women who immigrated and worked as prostitutes performed the more nurturant aspects of reproductive labor, that is, providing emotional and sexual companionship for men who were far from home. Yet their role as prostitute was more likely a means of supporting their families at home in China than a chosen vocation.

The Chinese family system during the nineteenth century was a patriarchal one wherein girls had little value. In fact, they were considered only temporary members of their father's family because when they married, they became members of their husband's families. They also had little social value: girls were sold by some poor parents to work as prostitutes, concubines, or servants. This saved the family the expense of raising them, and their earnings also became a source of family income. For most girls, however, marriages were arranged and families sought useful connections through this process.

With the development of a sojourning pattern in the United States, some Chinese women in those regions of China where this pattern was more prevalent would be sold to become prostitutes in the United States. Most, however, were married off to men whom they saw only once or twice in the 20- or 30-year period during which he was sojourning in the United States. Her status as wife ensured that a portion of the meager wages he earned would be returned to his family in China. This arrangement required considerable sacrifice and adjustment on the part of wives who remained in China and those who joined their husbands after a long separation.

Kingston (1977) tells the story of the unhappy meeting of her aunt, Moon Orchid, with her husband from whom she had been separated for 30 years.

For thirty years she had been receiving money from him from America. But she had never told him that she wanted to come to the United States. She waited for him to suggest it, but he never did (p. 144).

His response to her when she arrived unexpectedly was to say:

"Look at her. She'd never fit into an American household. I have important American guests who come inside my house to eat." He turned to Moon Orchid, "You can't talk to them. You can barely talk to me." Moon Orchid was so ashamed, she held her hands over her face. She

wished she could also hide in her dappled hands (p. 178).

Despite these handicaps, Chinese people collaborated to establish the opportunity to form families and settle in the United States. In some cases it took as long as three generations for a child to be born on United States soil.

In one typical history, related by a 21 year old college student, great-grandfather arrived in the States in the 1890s as a "paper son" and worked for about 20 years as a laborer. He then sent for the grandfather, who worked alongside great-grandfather in a small business for several years. Great-grandfather subsequently returned to China, leaving grandfather to run the business and send remittance. In the 1940s, grandfather sent for father; up to this point, none of the wives had left China. Finally, in the late 1950s father returned to China and brought his wife back with him. Thus, after nearly 70 years, the first child was born in the United States (Glenn 1981, p. 14).

CHICANOS

Africans were uprooted from their native lands and encouraged to have families in order to increase the slave labor force. Chinese people were immigrant laborers whose "permanent" presence in the country was denied. By contrast, Mexican-Americans were colonized and their traditional family life was disrupted by war and the imposition of a new set of laws and conditions of labor. The hardships faced by Chicano families, therefore, were the result of the United States colonization of the indigenous

Mexican population, accompanied by the beginnings of industrial development in the region. The treaty of Guadalupe Hidalgo, signed in 1848, granted American citizenship to Mexicans living in what is now called the Southwest. The American takeover, however, resulted in the gradual displacement of Mexicans from the land and their incorporation into a colonial labor force (Baffera 1979). In addition, Mexicans who immigrated into the United States after 1848 were also absorbed into the labor force.

Whether natives of Northern Mexico (which became the United States after 1848) or immigrants from Southern Mexico, Chicanos were a largely peasant population whose lives were defined by a feudal economy and a daily struggle on the land for economic survival. Patriarchal families were important instruments of community life and nuclear family units were linked together through an elaborate system of kinship and godparenting. Traditional life was characterized by hard work and a fairly distinct pattern of sex-role segregation.

> *Most Mexican women were valued for their household qualities, men by their ability to work and to provide for a family. Children were taught to get up early, to contribute to the family's labor to prepare themselves for adult life ... Such a life demanded discipline, authority, deference— values that cemented the working of a family surrounded and shaped by the requirements of Mexico's distinctive historical pattern of agricultural development, especially its pervasive debt peonage (Saragoza 1983, p. 8).*

As the primary caretakers of hearth and home in a rural environment, *Las Chicanas* labor made a vital and important contribution to family survival. A description of women's reproductive labor in the early twentieth century can be used to gain insight into the work of the nineteenth-century rural woman.

> *For country women, work was seldom a salaried job. More often it was the work of growing and preparing food, of making adobes and plastering houses with mud, or making their children's clothes for school and teaching them the hymns and prayers of the church, or delivering babies and treating sicknesses with herbs and patience. In almost every town there were one or two women who, in addition to working in their own homes, served other families in the community as curanderas (healers), parteras (midwives), and schoolteachers (Elasser 1980, p. 10).*

Although some scholars have argued that family rituals and community life showed little change before World War I (Saragoza 1983), the American conquest of Mexican lands, the introduction of a new system of labor, the loss of Mexican-owned land through the inability to document ownership, plus the transient nature of most of the jobs in which Chicanos were employed, resulted in the gradual erosion of this pastoral way of life. Families were uprooted as the economic basis for family life changed. Some immigrated from Mexico in search of a better standard of living and worked in the mines and railroads. Others who were native to the Southwest faced a job market that no longer required their skills and moved into mining, railroad, and agricultural labor in search of a means of earning a living. According to Camarillo (1979), the influx of Anglo[5] capital into the pastoral economy of Santa Barbara rendered obsolete the skills of many Chicano males who had worked as ranchhands and farmers prior to the urbanization of that economy. While some women and children accompanied their husbands to the railroad and mine camps, they often did so despite prohibitions against it. Initially many of these camps discouraged or prohibited family settlement.

The American period (post-1848) was characterized by considerable transiency for the Chicano population. Its impact on families is seen in the growth of female-headed households, which was reflected in the data as early as 1860. Griswold del Castillo (1979) found a sharp increase in female-headed households in Los Angeles, from a low of 13% in 1844 to 31% in 1880. Camarillo (1979, p. 120) documents a similar increase in Santa Barbara from 15% in 1844 to 30% by 1880. These increases appear to be due not so much to divorce, which was infrequent in this Catholic population, but to widowhood and temporary abandonment in search of work. Given the hazardous nature of work in the mines and railroad camps, the death of a husband, father or son who was laboring in these sites was not uncommon. Griswold del Castillo (1979) reports a higher death rate among men than women in Los Angeles. The rise in female-headed households, therefore, reflects the instabilities and insecurities introduced into women's lives as a result of the changing social organization of work.

One outcome, the increasing participation of women and children in the labor force was primarily a response to economic factors that required the modification of traditional values. According to Louisa Vigil, who was born in 1890:

The women didn't work at that time. The man was supposed to marry that girl and take of her... Your grandpa never did let me work for nobody. He always had to work, and we never

did have really bad times (Elasser 1980, p. 14).

Señora Vigil's comments are reinforced in Garcia's (1980) study of El Paso. In the 393 households he examined in the 1900 census, he found 17.1% of the women to be employed. The majority of this group were daughters, mothers with no husbands, and single women. In the cases of Los Angeles and Santa Barbara, where there were even greater work opportunities for women than in El Paso, wives who were heads of households worked in seasonal and part-time jobs and lived from the earnings of children and relatives in an effort to maintain traditional female roles.

Slowly, entire families were encouraged to go to railroad workcamps and were eventually incorporated into the agricultural labor market. This was a response both to the extremely low wages paid to Chicano laborers and to the preferences of employers who saw family labor as a way of stabilizing the workforce. For Chicanos, engaging all family members in agricultural work was a means of increasing their earnings to a level close to subsistence for the entire group and of keeping the family unit together. Camarillo (1979, p. 93) provides a picture of the interplay of work, family, and migration in the Santa Barbara area in the following observation:

The time of year when women and children were employed in the fruit cannery and participated in the almond and olive harvests coincided with the seasons when the men were most likely to be engaged in seasonal migratory work. There were seasons, however, especially in the early summer when the entire family migrated from the city to pick fruit. This type of family seasonal harvest was evident in Santa Barbara by the 1890s. As walnuts replaced al-monds and as the fruit industry expanded, Chicano family labor be-came essential.

This arrangement, while bringing families together, did not decrease the hardships that Chicanas had to confront in raising their families. We may infer something about the rigors of that life from Jesse Lopez de la Cruz's description of the workday of migrant farm laborers in the 1940s. Work conditions in the 1890s were as difficult, if not worse.

We always went where the women and men were going to work, because if it were just the men work-ing it wasn't worth going out there because we wouldn't earn enough to support a family... We would start around 6:30 a.m. and work for four or five hours, then walk home and eat and rest until about three-thirty in the afternoon when it cooled off. We would go back and work until we couldn't see. Then I'd clean up the kitchen. I was doing the housework and working out in the fields and taking care of two chilren (quoted in Goldman 1981, pp. 119–120).

In the towns, women's reproductive labor was intensified by the congested and unsanitary conditions of the *barrios* in which they lived. Garcia (1980) described the following conditions in El Paso:

Mexican women had to haul water for washing and cooking from the river or public water pipes. To feed their families, they had to spend time marketing, often in Cuidad Juarez across the border, as well as long,

hot hours cooking meals and coping with the burden of desert sand both inside and outside their homes. Besides the problem of raising chil-dren, unsanitary living conditions forced Mexican mothers to deal with disease and illness in their families. Diptheria, tuberculosis, typhus and influenza were never too far away. Some diseases could be directly traced to inferior city services... As a result, Mexican mothers had to devote much energy to caring for sick children, many of whom died (pp. 320–321).

While the extended family has remained an important element of Chicano life, it was eroded in the American period in several ways. Griswold del Castillo (1979), for example, points out that in 1845 about 71% of Angelenos lived in extended families and that by 1880, fewer than half did. This decrease in extended families appears to be a response to the changed economic conditions and to the instabilities generated by the new sociopolitical structure. Additionally, the imposition of American law and custom ignored and ultimately undermined some aspects of the extended family. The extended family in traditional Mexican life consisted of an important set of familial, religious, and community obligations. Women, while valued primarily for their domesticity, had certain legal and property rights that acknowledged the importance of their work, their families of origin and their children. In California, for example:

Equal ownership of property be-tween husband and wife had been one of the mainstays of the Span-ish and Mexican family systems. Community-property laws were writ-ten into the civil codes with the intention of strengthening the economic controls of the wife and her relatives. The American government incorporated these Mexican laws into the state constitution, but later court decisions interpreted these statutes so as to undermine the wife's economic rights. In 1861, the legislature passed a law that allowed the deceased wife's property to revert to her husband. Previously it had been inherited by her children and relatives if she died without a will (Griswold del Castillo 1979, p. 69).

The impact of this and other similar court rulings was to "strengthen the property rights of the husband at the expense of his wife and children" (Griswold del Castillo 1979, p. 69).

In the face of the legal, social, and economic changes that occurred during the American period, Chicanas were forced to cope with a series of dislocations in traditional life. They were caught between conflicting pressures to maintain traditional women's roles and family customs and the need to participate in the economic support of their families by working outside the home. During this period the preservation of some traditional customs became an important force for resisting complete disarray.

According to Saragoza (1983), transiency, the effects of racism, and segregation, and proximity to Mexico aided in the maintenance of traditional family practices. Garcia has suggested that women were the guardians of Mexican cultural traditions within the family. He cites the work of anthropologist, Manuel Gamio who identified the retention of many Mexican customs among Chicanos in settlements around the United States in the early 1900s.

These included folklore, songs and ballads, birthday celebrations, saints'

day, baptism, weddings, and funerals in the traditional style. Because of poverty, a lack of physicians in the barrios, and adherence to traditional customs, Mexicans continued to use medicinal herbs. Gamio also identified the maintenance of a number of oral traditions, and Mexican style cooking (Garcia 1980, p. 322).

Of vital importance to the integrity of traditional culture was the perpetuation of the Spanish language. Factors that aided in the maintenance of other aspects of Mexican culture also helped in sustaining the language. However, entry into English-language public schools introduced the children and their families to systematic efforts to erase their native tongue. Griswold del Castillo reports that in the early 1880s there was considerable pressure against the speaker of Spanish in the public school. He also found that some Chicano parents responded to this kind of discrimination by helping support independent bilingual schools. These efforts, however, were short-lived.

Another key factor in conserving Chicano culture was the extended family network, particularly the system of *compadrazgo* or godparenting. Although the full extent of the impact of the American period on the Chicano extended family is not known, it is generally acknowledged that this family system, though lacking many legal and social sanctions, played an important role in the preservation of the Mexican community (Camarillo 1979, p. 13). In Mexican society, godparents were an important way of linking family and community through respected friends or authorities. Named at the important rites of passage in a child's life, such as birth, confirmation, first communion, and marriage, *compadrazgo* created a moral obligation for godparents to act as guardians, to provide financial assistance in times of need, and to substitute in case of the death of a parent. Camarillo (1979) points out that in traditional society these bonds cut across class and racial lines.

> The rites of baptism established kinship networks between rich and poor—between Spanish, mestizo and Indian—and often carried with them political loyalty and economic-occupational ties. The leading California patriarchs in the pueblo played important roles in the compadrazgo network. They sponsored dozens of children for their workers or poorer relatives. The kindness of the padrino and madrina was repaid with respect and support from the pobladores (pp. 12–13).

The extended family network—which included godparents—expanded the support groups for women who were widowed or temporarily abandoned and for those who were in seasonal, part- or full-time work. It suggests, therefore, the potential for an exchange of services among poor people whose income did not provide the basis for family subsistence. Griswold del Castillo (1980) argues that family organization influenced literacy rates and socioeconomic mobility among Chicanos in Los Angeles between 1850 and 1880. His data suggest that children in extended families (defined as those with at least one relative living in a nuclear family household) had higher literacy rates than those in nuclear families. He also argues that those in larger families fared better economically, and experienced less downward mobility. The data here are too limited to generalize to the Chicano experience as a whole but they do reinforce the actual and potential importance of this family form to the continued cultural autonomy of the Chicano community.

CONCLUSION: OUR MOTHERS' GRIEF

Reproductive labor for Afro-American, Chinese-American, and Mexican-American women in the nineteenth century centered on the struggle to maintain family units in the face of a variety of cultural assaults. Treated primarily as individual units of labor rather than as members of family groups, these women labored to maintain, sustain, stabilize, and reproduce their families while working in both the public (productive) and private (reproductive) spheres. Thus, the concept of reproductive labor, when applied to women of color, must be modified to account for the fact that labor in the productive sphere was required to achieve even minimal levels of family subsistence. Long after industrialization had begun to reshape family roles among middle-class white families, driving white women into a cult of domesticity, women of color were coping with an extended day. This day included subsistence labor outside the family and domestic labor within the family. For slaves, domestics, migrant farm laborers, seasonal factory-workers, and prostitutes, the distinctions between labor that reproduced family life and which economically sustained it were minimized. The expanded workday was one of the primary ways in which reproductive labor increased.

Racial-ethnic families were sustained and maintained in the face of various forms of disruption. Yet they and their families paid a high price in the process. High rates of infant mortality, a shortened life span, the early onset of crippling and debilitating disease provided some insight into the costs of survival.

The poor quality of housing and the neglect of communities further increased reproductive labor. Not only did racial-ethnic women work hard outside the home for a mere subsistence, they worked very hard inside the home to achieve even minimal standards of privacy and cleanliness. They were continually faced with disease and illness that directly resulted from the absence of basic sanitation. The fact that some African women murdered their children to prevent them from becoming slaves is an indication of the emotional strain associated with bearing and raising children while participating in the colonial labor system.

We have uncovered little information about the use of birth control, the prevalence of infanticide, or the motivations that may have generated these or other behaviors. We can surmise, however, that no matter how much children were accepted, loved, or valued among any of these groups of people, their futures in a colonial labor system were a source of grief for their mothers. For those children who were born, the task of keeping them alive, of helping them to understand and participate in a system that exploited them, and the challenge of maintaining a measure—no matter how small—of cultural integrity, intensified reproductive labor.

Being a racial-ethnic woman in nineteenth century American society meant having extra work both inside and outside the home. It meant having a contradictory relationship to the norms and values about women that were being generated in the dominant white culture. As pointed out earlier, the notion of separate spheres of male and female labor had contradictory outcomes for the nineteenth-century whites. It was the basis for the confinement of women to the household and for much of the protective legislation that subsequently developed. At the same time, it sustained white families by providing social acknowledgment and support to women in the performance of their family roles. For racial-ethnic women, however, the notion of separate spheres served to reinforce their subordinate status and became, in effect, another assault. As they increased their work outside the home, they were forced into a productive labor sphere that was organized for men and "desperate" women who were so unfortunate or immoral that they could not confine their work to the domestic sphere. In the productive sphere, racial-ethnic women faced exploitative jobs and depressed wages. In the reproductive sphere, however, they were denied the opportunity to embrace the dominant ideological definition of "good" wife or mother. In essence, they were faced with a double-bind situation, one that required their participation in the labor force to sustain family life but damned them as women, wives, and mothers because they did not confine their labor to the home. Thus, the conflict between ideology and reality in the lives of racial-ethnic women during the nineteenth century sets the stage for stereotypes, issues of self-esteem, and conflicts around gender-role prescriptions that surface more fully in the twentieth century. Further, the tensions and conflicts that characterized their lives during this period provided the impulse for community activism to jointly address the inequities, which they and their children and families faced.

ACKNOWLEDGMENTS

The research in this study is the result of the author's participation in a larger collaborative project examining family, community, and work lives of racial-ethnic women in the United States. The author is deeply indebted to the scholarship and creativity of members of the group in the development of this study. Appreciation is extended to Elizabeth Higginbotham, Cheryl Townsend Gilkes, Evelyn Nakano Glenn, and Ruth Zambrana (members of the original working group), and to the Ford Foundation for a grant that supported in part the work of this study.

Reading 24   From Baby Farms to Baby M*

VIVIANA A. ZELIZER

The Baby M deal would astonish any nineteenth-century baby trader. Not because of inflation in baby prices and not even because of Baby M's unusual mode of conception. The amazing fact, from a nineteenth-century perspective, is that Baby M has such eager and paying customers. For in the 1870s, there was no such market for babies. The only profitable undertaking was, as the *New York Times* described it in 1873, the "business of getting rid of other people's [unwelcome] babies." For about ten dollars, baby farmers took in these generally illegitimate children. With babies' high rates of mortality, the turnover was quick, and business brisk. Indeed, one report estimated that a "tradeswoman in tiny lives" could make as much as $10,000 a year.

Selling babies, on the other hand, was a rare and largely unprofitable transaction: often no more than a twenty-five-cents deal. In an 1890 case, an agent of the New York Society for the Prevention of Cruelty to Children pretended interest in obtaining a two-week-old baby. The baby farmer demanded two dollars but quickly settled for half. "She ... urged [the agent] to take the infant at once and at his own price." It was, unquestionably, a buyer's market.

Yet, by the 1920s and 1930s, "baby-hungry" couples were eagerly paying $1,000 or more to purchase an infant. As a 1939 article in *Collier's* put it: "It's [a] bonanza ... there's gold in selling babies." The trade slogan of one baby seller in

Chicago was "It's cheaper and easier to buy a baby ... than to have one of your own." Today, the going rate for a healthy white infant in the black market is up to $50,000. "Special-order" Baby M cost the Sterns $25,000 plus the now surely steep legal fees. And this is just a down payment. It will take at least an additional $150,000 to provide Baby M with the first eighteen years of a proper upper-middle-class upbringing.

Lost in the emotional immediacy of the Baby M dispute are two more general and fundamental issues that underlie the surrogacy controversy. First, what explains our bullish baby market? Why were late-nineteenth-century mothers forced to pay baby farmers to get rid of a baby they did not want or could not afford, while today a Mrs. Whitehead is paid to produce a baby for others? Is it just a matter of the scarcity of babies? Second, what, precisely, defines the legitimacy or illegitimacy of baby markets? Are surrogacy fees necessarily a degrading payment or "dirty money"? Then, are adoption fees, foster care payments, and "gray" baby markets, also "dirty money"?

I argue that the socially and morally problematic nature of the surrogacy baby market is not primarily, as Neuhaus suggests, that sacred items are "placed in a contract and sealed by money," nor even that surrogacy is rigged against poor women. More significantly, surrogacy

*Zelizer, Viviana. 1985. "From Baby Farms to Baby M." *Society* 25(3): 23–28. Reprinted by permission of Transaction Publishers.

unequivocally reveals our discriminatory valuation of children. Babies are made on "special-order" because children already available on the adoption market are not "good" enough—too old, too sick, or of the wrong skin color. In this respect, surrogacy is only a technical innovation. In fact, it is just the latest stage of a very special adoption market which began in the 1920s.

CREATION OF A BABY MARKET

The creation of a market for babies in the 1920s was not the result of clever promotion and only partly a consequence of an increasing shortage of infants. The startling appreciation in babies' monetary worth was intimately tied to the profound cultural transformation in children's economic and sentimental value between the 1870s and 1930s; specifically, the emergence of the economically worthless but emotionally priceless child.

In eighteenth-century rural America the birth of a child was welcomed as the arrival of a future laborer and as security for parents later in life. By the mid-nineteenth century, the construction of the economically worthless child was completed among the urban middle class. It took longer among working-class families which, even in the late nineteenth century, depended on the wages of older children and the household assistance of younger ones. Child labor laws and compulsory education gradually destroyed the class lag. By the 1930s, lower-class children joined their middle-class counterparts in a new nonproductive world of childhood, a world in which the sanctity and emotional value of a child made child labor taboo.

The "exchange" value of children changed accordingly. Nineteenth-century foster families took in useful children expecting them to help out with farm chores and household tasks. It was considered a fair bargain. After all, if children worked for their own parents, why not work for surrogate caretakers? Not surprisingly, the premium was for children older than ten, old enough to be useful. In this context, babies were "unmarketable," and hard to place except in foundling asylums or on commercial baby farms.

The redefinition of children's value at the turn of the century challenged established instrumental assumptions. If child labor was no longer legitimate, a working home was an anachronism. If children were priceless, it was obnoxious to profit from their misfortune. Thus, baby farming was singled out as a uniquely mercenary "traffic in children." Child-welfare workers actively sought to replace instrumental parenting of any kind with a new approach to adoption more suitable for the economically "useless" sacred child. Parents were urged by *Children's Home Finder* in 1897 not to take a child "for what you can get out of him, but, rather, for what you can put into him." By the 1920s and 1930s, a new consensus was reached. The only legitimate rewards of adoption were emotional, as the *New York Times* put it in 1926: "an enlargement of happiness to be got in no other way." As one grateful adoptive father told a *Good Housekeeping* reporter in 1927, "Talk about children owing their parents anything! We'll never be able to pay what we owe that baby."

Sentimental adoption created an unprecedented demand for children under three, especially for infants. In 1910, the press already discussed the new appeal of babies, with *Cosmopolitan* warning, "there are not enough babies to go around." The Home-Finding Committee of the Spence Nursery, an agency organized for the placement of infants, was surprised to discover that, "instead of our having to seek these homes, they have sought us, and so great is the demand for babies that we cannot begin to meet it." By 1937, infant adoption was being touted as the latest American fad. *Pictorial Review* noted: "The baby market is booming.... The clamor is for babies, more babies. . . . We behold an amazing phenomenon: a country-wide scramble on the part of childless couples to adopt a child." Ironically, while the economically useless nineteenth-century baby had to be protected because it was unwanted, the priceless twentieth-century baby, "needs protection as never before . . . [because] too many hands are snatching it."

The priceless child was judged by new criteria; its physical appeal and personality charms replaced earlier economic yardsticks. After talking to several directors of orphan asylums, the *New York Times* concluded in 1909 that "every baby who expects to be adopted . . . ought to make it a point to be born with blue eyes. . . . The brown-eyed, black-eyed, or grey-eyed girl or boy may be just as pretty . . . but it is hard to make benevolent auxiliaries of the stork believe so." The greatest demand was for little girls. Soon after launching its popular Child-Rescue Campaign in 1907, promoting foster home care, the *Delineator* commented that requests for boys were half that for girls: "a two-year old, blue-eyed, golden haired little girl with curls, that is the order that everybody leaves. It cannot be filled fast enough."

The gender and age preferences of twentieth-century adoptive parents were clearly linked to the cultural revolution in fostering. While the earlier need for a useful child put a premium on strong, older children, preferably male; the later search for a child to love led to babies and, particularly, pretty little girls. It was not the innate smiling expertise of females, but established cultural assumptions of women's superior emotional talents which made girls so uniquely attractive for sentimental adoption.

PRICING THE PRICELESS CHILD

The sentimentalization of adoption had an unanticipated and paradoxical effect. By creating a demand for babies, it also stimulated a new kind of baby market. While nineteenth-century mothers had paid baby farmers to accept their unwanted baby, twentieth-century adoptive parents were willing to pay to obtain an infant. "Baby traffickers" thus found an additional line of business; making money not only from the surrender of babies, but doubling their profits by then selling them to their new customers. As a result, the value of a priceless child became increasingly monetized and commercialized. Ironically, the new market price for babies was set exclusively by their noneconomic, sentimental appeal.

By 1922, the dramatic findings of "A Baby a Day Given Away," a study conducted by the New York State Charities Aid Association, put commercialized adoption directly in the national public spotlight. The six-months investigation of newspaper advertisements offering and requesting children for adoption, revealed an "indiscriminate exchange of children." An average of a baby a day was being disposed of in New York, "as casually as one would give away a kitten"; many sold at "bargain-counter" prices. It was not a peculiar New York arrangement. In the classified advertisement column of almost any Boston newspaper, noted Ida Parker in *Fit and Proper?* in 1927, "together with items relating to automobiles, animals, amusements . . . may often be found the child offered for adoption."

Three years later, the notorious prosecution of a New York baby farmer shocked the nation, further raising the visibility of commercial child placement. Helen Augusta Geisen-Volk was charged and indicted for child substitution and for starving infants to death. The young wife of a well-to-do manufacturer added fuel to the scandal by publicly confessing that, unknown to her husband, Mrs. Geisen-Volk had sold her an infant for seventy-five dollars. None of the crimes committed by Geisen-Volk were new to the baby-farming business; similar accusations were made as early as the 1870s. More unusual were the severity of the reaction and the degree of public interest in the case.

Commercial child placement emerged as a significant social problem in the 1920s in large part because it violated new professional standards in adoption. Without proper supervision by a licensed child-placing agency, adoption could be dangerous both for children and their adoptive parents. Selling children undermined not only professional adoption; it also betrayed the new standards of sentimental adoption. It was a sacrilege to price a priceless child. Worse than a criminal, Mrs. Geisen-Volk was indicted by the judge as a "fiend incarnate." As a probation officer told *New York Times* reporters, "the woman...has no maternal affections...[babies] to her...are articles of merchandise to be bartered or exchanged. The defendant represents a revolting anomaly in humankind."

Harshly denounced as an "iniquitous traffic in human life," and a "countrywide shame," the black market in babies flourished in the 1930s and 1940s. As demand for adoptable children grew, the booming traffic in infants reached a new stage. It was now a seller's market. Therefore, the mother of an unwanted child no longer needed to pay to dispose of her baby. Instead, entrepreneurial brokers approached her, offering to pay medical and hospital expenses and often a bonus in exchange for her baby. Even in independent placements arranged without profit, it became common practice to pay the hospital and medical expenses of the natural mother.

In 1955 a congressional investigation conducted by Senator Estes Kefauver officially pronounced baby-selling a national social problem. The price tag of a black-market baby climbed, from an estimated $1,000 in the 1930s to $5,000 in the late 1940s. By 1951 some babies sold for as much as $10,000. The rising money value of infants was partly determined by a reduced supply. As the dramatic decline in the national birthrate, which began early in the nineteenth cen-

tury, continued into the 1930s, fewer babies were available for adoption. Contemporary observers also suggested that the increased demand for babies was partly the result of higher rates of infertility among American couples. Growing concern with the preservation of the family unit further contributed to the baby shortage. After 1911, the mothers' pension movement allowed widows, and in some cases deserted wives or mothers, or keep their children. Reformers also encouraged unmarried mothers to keep their babies. As a result, the supply of adoptable infants shrunk, and the waiting lists of adoption agencies grew longer. Unwilling to wait two or more years for a child, parents turned to the black market.

Scarcity alone does not determine value. A reduced supply raised the price of babies only because there was a growing number of enthusiastic buyers for white, healthy babies. The market capitalized on, but did not create, the infatuation with priceless babies. In sharp contrast, older children found few customers. Deprived of their former labor value, they were excluded from the new emotional market. Therefore, while the agencies' waiting list for babies had the names of hundreds of impatient parents, it was virtually impossible to find homes for children older than six, who had become both economically and sentimentally useless. Handicapped and minority children were also excluded from the adoption market.

PAYING FOR BABIES: A SPECIAL CURRENCY

The sentimentalization of adoption in the twentieth century, thus, led paradoxically to a greater commercialization and monetization of child life. As the market for child labor disappeared, a market price developed for children's new sentimental value. Childless couples were now willing to pay thousands of dollars to obtain a child's love, smiles, and emotional satisfactions. In 1975, a second congressional hearing on black-market practices estimated that more than 5,000 babies were sold each year in the United States, some for as much as $25,000. Sellers retained bargaining leverage. As one black-market lawyer told a prospective customer, "Take it or leave it. I have five other couples." The capitalization of children's value extended into legitimate child placement. Reversing a long-standing policy, many agencies in the 1940s introduced adoption fees.

Today, surrogacy arrangements introduce a new "custom-made" market for children. Fees are paid not just to obtain someone else's baby but to produce a brand new one. For some economists, this further monetization of child life makes sense. Indeed, Landes and Posner advocate the outright legalization of baby-selling as the best solution to the baby shortage. An undiluted price system, they argue, would match adoptive parents with adoptable children more efficiently than agencies. Landes and Posner, in the 1978 *Journal of Legal Studies,* dismiss "moral outrage" or "symbolic" objections against baby sales, as antiquated and impractical.

Yet moral objections to baby payments cannot be easily appeased. For many, the exchange of children should be regulated only by altruism, never for profit. Indeed, money is what makes surrogacy particularly unsavory. Without payment, surrogacy can be an innovative act of altruism; making babies as a gift for childless couples. But $10,000 turns the giver into a salaried agent, and the baby into commercial chattel. From this perspective, surrogate parenthood can be legitimized simply by making it unprofitable. For instance, last May in Michigan, a sixteen-member national panel of doctors, lawyers, and clergymen, convened by State Senator Connie Binsfield to discuss legislation covering reproductive technologies, recommended that surrogate parenthood not be outlawed, but that the

"production of babies for money, or a fee beyond reasonable expenses" be banned. Similarly, in Nebraska, a bill proposed by State Senator Ernest Chambers of Omaha, would accept the legality of surrogate relationships, but would declare that any commercial surrogate contract could not be enforced through the state's judicial system. Surrogate babies, declared Chambers in the *New York Times,* "become commodities like corn or wheat, things which can be purchased in the futures market."

Are surrogacy fees necessarily degrading? Does it only take a payment to transform a baby into a commodity? Ironically, both supporters and opponents of baby-selling answer affirmatively; thus equally accepting the inevitable power of money. They only differ in their evaluation of the process: economists welcome the rationalization of baby exchanges while anti-market ideologists bemoan the monetization of child life. All agree that once money is exchanged, the sale of children is qualitatively indistinct from the sale of cars. After all, in both cases, the payoff is identical: cold cash.

This is a narrow view of money. Money does serve as the key instrument of the modern market, transforming objects or even emotions and the value of life into quantifiable, objective sums. But money also exists outside of the sphere of the market, profoundly shaped by culture and social structure. Despite the physical anonymity of dollar bills, not all dollars are equal. We routinely assign different meanings and uses to particular monies. A paycheck, for instance, is "marked" as a different kind of money than a lottery winning. The money we obtain as compensation for an accident is not quite the same as the royalties from a book. A gift of money from a friend is distinct from our employer's Christmas bonus or a grandparents' Christmas check. Different monies are used differently: for instance, a wife's pin money was traditionally reserved for special purchases such as clothing or vacations and kept apart from the "real" money earned by her husband. Different uses can transform the meaning of money. What if Mrs. Whitehead, for instance, had intended to use her $10,000 as a donation to an infertility clinic? That would certainly mark the money differently than if she planned to use it for a Florida weekend, or simply for groceries. Such distinctions are not imposed by rational economic guidelines, but emerge from our cultural and social context.

Baby payments are a special category of money, shaped by the cultural definition of children as priceless. We also distinguish between legitimate and illegitimate baby purchases. Black-market sales, for example, are unacceptable because they treat children in the same impersonal, economizing manner used for less sacred commercial products. Yet a different kind of market exists which is, in most cases, legal and compatible with sentimental adoption. In this gray market, placements are arranged without profit by parents, friends, relatives, doctors, and lawyers. Within this context, professional fees for legal or medical services are acceptable. Justifying such payments during the 1975 congressional hearings on black-market practices, the executive director of the Child Welfare League of America explained, "Money exchanges hands, but it is only to pay for actual costs. There is no thought of profit." Thus, while the black market is defined as a degrading economic arrangement; a modified, legitimate market exists for the exchange of children.

Adoption fees are another category of "special money." Until the 1940s, agencies only accepted "gratitude donations" from adoptive parents. The Children's Home Society of Virginia, for instance, according to the 1941 *Child Welfare League of America Bulletin,* told parents, "that a gift from them in such an amount as they choose will be gratefully received, but that it must be made as a gift and not as payment for services." The society's directors refused to even discuss any definite sum with foster families. The boundary between adoption and purchase was preserved by defining the money as an elective gift and a symbol of gratitude, not a price.

The shift from donations to fees was, therefore, a sensitive matter. Yet the system was accepted. How was the adoption fee distinguished from a purchase price? In large measure, the differentiation hinged on defining the payment as compensation for professional services, not in exchange for a child. A fee was also legitimized as a symbolic payment, a material expression of gratitude. Adoption fees were usually portrayed as a psychological crutch for parents, rather than a commercial device for agencies; for example, from the *Child Welfare League of America Bulletin*: "For any human being to be in the position of asking another . . . for a child . . . is to admit inadequacy. . . . Payment of the fee may ease some of the discomfort arising from this deeply humiliating experience." Parents' voluntary contributions of additional monies to the agency, beyond the stipulated fee, further reinforced the boundary between the adoption fees and a purchasing price. Their elective gift of money served as a symbolic reminder that adopting a child is not an ordinary business deal.

The uniqueness of payments involving children is also apparent in their "rental." For example, at the beginning of the century, wet nurses employed by the foundling asylums were often accused of regarding their infant boarders simply as a source of income. Yet, while these "pay babies" were indeed a source of much needed income, it was defined as a very special payment. A Russell Sage report in 1914 remarked that "renting" out a baby to these poor New York women was often more a sentimental event than a business deal.

Similarly, when boarding homes for older children were first introduced at the turn of the century, boarding fees were defined as "dirty money," tempting foster parents into taking children for profit. This ambivalence over paid parenting was persistent. For instance, periodic efforts to raise board payments by defining the foster mother as an employee of the agency met with resistance and ultimately failure. In the 1940s, a special committee from the Washington Council of Social Agencies, urged payment of a service fee to foster parents in return for their contributions over and above the physical care and maintenance of the child. But the service fee was opposed because it transformed mothering into a marketable job.

"SPECIAL-ORDER" BABIES

Adequate monetary incentive seems to have an effect on the number of foster homes available and even on the success of fostering. Yet foster parents—most of whom are recruited from lower-middle-class or working-class families—remain uneasy about asking for payment. They often find ways to transcend the instrumental parenting contract. In many cases, for instance, foster parents use their own funds for a foster child's incidental expenses; extra clothing, transportation, allowance, toys, or parties.

The gray market, adoption fees, and board payments illustrate some of the cultural contours of baby payments. Pricing the priceless child is a unique commercial venture; child "rental" and child sales are profoundly constrained by twentieth-century conceptions of children. The money involved is partly payment, but it can also also be a symbolic expression of sentimental concern.

Surrogacy fees are the latest addition to this inventory of special monies. They remain in a definitional limbo. For opponents of surrogacy, surrogacy fees are no different than black-market price tags, unsuitable to measure the value of a child's life. Some see it as a perverse

form of pin money for housewives, paying extra expenses by making a baby. But there is a moral arrogance as well as sociological blindness in the absolutist indictment of surrogacy payments. This money can indeed be "dirty" cash, used to entice poor women into renting their wombs for the rich. It can even be used by the surrogate to blackmail childless couples.

Is that how surrogate mothers define their payment? Most do acknowledge that they would not have entered the arrangement without compensation. Some seem to perceive it as an ordinary wage: "We wanted money to pay some bills and take a vacation," explained one housewife. But surrogates clearly mark the special quality of this money, sometimes refusing even to define it as a payment in exchange for a baby. A mother who was paid $10,000 and delivered twins was quoted by the *New York Times* as saying, "Believe me,... there are easier ways to make ten thousand dollars that involve a lot less time and a lot less pain."

The fee is defined by many surrogates as the childless couple's expression of gratitude for their special gift of a baby. Indeed, a study of 125 surrogate mothers found that while 89 percent of the women said they would require a fee for their service, in no case was money the only reason for "baby-making." One woman who had had an abortion now wanted, according to *Psychology Today,* "to give the gift of a live baby to a loving couple." Others simply liked being pregnant. Surrogates are well aware of the vulnerable boundary between a noble payment and a mercenary fee. Some mark the special quality of the surrogacy fee by allocating the money to particularly unselfish expenses. Mrs. Whitehead, for instance, intended to use the $10,000 toward a college education for her two other children. As another surrogate mother explained in the *New York Times*: "If the money was just for me I'd feel as if I'd sold her [the baby], and it would be dirty money."

Distinguishing between monies by differential uses occurs with other kinds of special payments. For instance, in cases of compensation for the accidental death of a young child, plaintiffs often ritualize the monetary award by donating it to charity, safety organizations, or scholarships for needy children. Baby payments, much as "death" money, are different than ordinary cash. We need to understand better the meaning of surrogacy fees. How does the father define this money? What about the baby brokers? How do their fees differ from the payment to the mother? How is a "just" surrogacy fee determined? Dr. Richard Levin, the head of Kentucky's Surrogate Parenting Associates (quoted in *The Surrogate Mother* by Noel P. Keane with Dennis L. Breo), explains that he has a "moral problem with paying a surrogate mother too much—as with one woman who...wanted $100,000—or not enough." But what makes $10,000 acceptable? Would a small token fee be defined as more appropriate? Or would an extraordinarily large sum—comparable to some wrongful-death settlements in child death cases—be a more dignified quantity?

The moralistic indictment of surrogacy fees obscures the complex reality of such payments. The involvement of money does not necessarily convert all exchanges into ordinary sales. The surrogate payment may be a venal and dehumanizing payoff but it can also symbolize an acceptable retribution. Thus, with proper regulation, money does not necessarily pollute the surrogacy baby market. The class bias in surrogacy arrangements, which is the focus of Neuhaus's argument, is a potentially more damaging feature of the surrogacy market. Poor women, traditionally the wet nurses and baby minders of the rich, would now also become their baby makers. Subsidized surrogacies, much like subsidized adoptions, however, could make the benefits of surrogacy available to poor infertile women. That would only equalize the buyers. It is improbable, although not impossible, that affluent women would serve as surrogates.

In the cases of surrogacy, the inequities between parents are less fundamental than the explicit discrimination between children. Surrogacy is not just a sentimental search for any child to love, but the deliberate manufacture of a particular, suitable child. As one observer has pointed out, the advertisements to hire a surrogate do not follow any affirmative action plan. This "help-wanted" ad specifies: "English background," "Northern European," "white," "Caucasian." The desired product is a white infant, with no physical or mental handicaps. In the 1920s rush to adopt babies, some wealthy Americans had their English-rose, golden-haired baby girls imported from London. Today, they can be made in America. They even carry the genetic insurance provided by the adoptive father's sperm.

Surrogacy further marks the distinction between priceless, desirable children and "unsuitable" children that was established earlier in the century. While babies are made to order, the National Committee for Adoption estimates that a minimum of 36,000 hard-to-place children, some because they are sick, some disturbed, others because they are black, and still others because they are too old, cannot find an adoptive home. Surrogacy contracts often make the concern with quality-control quite explicit. Some contracts include provisions for amniocentesis and obligatory abortion if the results are not agreeable to the genetic father. But what if, despite all precautions, a child is born defective? Would Baby M be disputed with equal passion if she were not a cute, healthy baby—the ultimate priceless child?

Private adoption of unwanted children cannot be mandated by the state. Neither should the search for a child—even through surrogate arrangements—be outlawed by the state, although it must be closely regulated and officially supervised. But we need to collectively recognize the curious and even cruel limits to our sentimentalization of childhood. We must invest emotionally and financially in finding ways to nurture—either in family groups or collective arrangements—those children who need care but are not infants, not white, or not healthy enough. The shortage of such care is as severe as the shortage of cute and healthy white babies.

Reading 25   Dubious Conceptions: The Controversy over Teen Pregnancy*

KRISTIN LUKER

The conventional wisdom has it that an epidemic of teen pregnancy is today ruining the lives of young women and their children and perpetuating poverty in America. In polite circles, people speak regretfully of "babies having babies." Other Americans are more blunt. "I don't mind paying to help people in need," one angry radio talk show host told Michael Katz, a historian of poverty, "but I don't want my tax dollars to pay for the sexual pleasure of adolescents who won't use birth control."

By framing the issue in these terms, Americans have imagined that the persistence of poverty and other social problems can be traced to youngsters who are too impulsive or too ignorant to postpone sexual activity, to use contraception, to seek an abortion, or failing all that, especially if they are white, to give their babies up for adoption to "better" parents. Defining the problem this way, many Americans, including those in a position to influence public policy, have come to believe that one attractive avenue to reducing poverty and other social ills is to reduce teen birth rates. Their remedy is to persuade teenagers to postpone childbearing, either by convincing them of the virtues of chastity (a strategy conservatives prefer) or by making abortion, sex education, and contraception more freely available (the strategy liberals prefer).

Reducing teen pregnancy would almost certainly be a good thing. After all, the rate of teen childbearing in the United States is more similar to the rates prevailing in the poor countries of the world than in the modern, industrial nations we think of as our peers. However, neither the problem of teen pregnancy nor the remedies for it are as simple as people think.

In particular, the link between poverty and teen pregnancy is a complicated one. We do know that teen mothers are poorer than women who wait past their twentieth birthday to have a child. But stereotypes to the contrary, it is not clear whether early motherhood causes poverty or the reverse. Worse yet, even if teen pregnancy does have some independent force in making teen parents poorer than they would otherwise be, it remains to be seen whether any policies in effect or under discussion can do much to reduce teen birth rates.

These uncertainties raise questions about our political culture as well as our public choices. How did Americans become convinced that teen pregnancy is a major cause of poverty and that reducing one would reduce the other? The answer is a tale of good intentions, rising cultural anxieties about teen sex and family breakdown, and the uses—and misuses—of social science.

*Luker, Kristin. 1991. "Dubious Conceptions: The Controversy Over Teen Pregnancy." *The American Prospect* 5:73–83. Reprinted with permission from *The American Prospect,* Spring 1991. © New Prospect Inc.

HOW TEEN PREGNANCY
BECAME AN ISSUE

Prior to the mid-1970s, few people talked about "teen pregnancy." Pregnancy was defined as a social problem primarily when a woman was unmarried; no one thought anything amiss when an eighteen- or nineteen-year-old got married and had children. And concern about pregnancies among unmarried women certainly did not stop when the woman turned twenty.

But in 1975, when Congress held the first of many hearings on the issue of adolescent fertility, expert witnesses began to speak of an "epidemic" of a "million pregnant teenagers" a year. Most of these witnesses were drawing on statistics supplied by the Alan Guttmacher Institute, which a year later published the data in an influential booklet, *Eleven Million Teenagers.* Data from that document were later cited—often down to the decimal point—in most discussions of the teenage pregnancy "epidemic."

Many people hearing these statistics must have assumed that the "million pregnant teenagers" a year were all unmarried. The Guttmacher Institute's figures, however, included married nineteen-year-olds along with younger, unmarried teenage girls. In fact, almost two-thirds of the "million pregnant teenagers" were eighteen and nineteen-year olds; about 40 percent of them were married, and about two-thirds of the married women were married prior to the pregnancy.

Moreover, despite the language of epidemic, pregnancy rates among teenagers were not dramatically increasing. From the turn of the century until the end of World War II, birth rates among teenagers were reasonably stable at approximately 50 to 60 births per thousand women. Teen birth rates, like all American birth rates, increased dramatically in the period after World War II, doubling in the baby boom years to a peak of about 97 births per thousand teenaged women in 1957. Subsequently, teen birth rates declined, and by 1975 they had gone back

down to their traditional levels, where, for the most part, they have stayed (see figure).

Were teen births declining in recent decades only because of higher rates of abortion? Here, too, trends are different from what many people suppose. The legalization of abortion in January of 1973 made it possible for the first time to get reliable statistics on abortions for women, teenagers and older. The rate among teenagers rose from about 27.0 to 42.9 abortions per 1,000 women between 1974 and 1980. Since 1980 teen abortion rates have stabilized, and may even have declined somewhat. Moreover, teenagers account for a declining proportion of all abortions: in the years just after *Roe v. Wade,* teenagers obtained almost a third of all abortions in the country; now they obtain about a quarter. A stable teen birth rate and a stabilizing teen abortion rate means that pregnancy rates, which rose modestly in the 1970s, have in recent years levelled off.

What has been increasing—and increasing dramatically—is the percentage of teen births that are out-of-wedlock (see figure). In 1970 babies born out of wedlock represented about a third of all babies born to teen mothers. By 1980 out-of-wedlock births were about half; and by 1986 almost two-thirds. Beneath these overall figures lie important racial variations. Between 1955 and 1988 the out-of-wedlock rate rose from 6 to 24.8 per thousand unmarried, teenage, white women, while for unmarried, nonwhite teenagers the rate rose from 77.6 to 98.3 per thousand. In other words, while the out-of-wedlock birth rate was rising 25 percent among nonwhite teens, it was actually quadrupling among white teens.

The immediate source for this rise in out-of-wedlock teen pregnancy might seem to be obvious. Since 1970 young women have increasingly postponed marriage without rediscovering the virtues of chastity. Only about 6 percent of teenagers were married in 1984, compared to 12 percent in 1970. And although estimates vary,

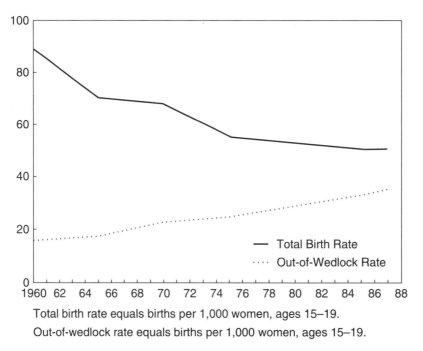

Total birth rate equals births per 1,000 women, ages 15–19.

Out-of-wedlock rate equals births per 1,000 women, ages 15–19.

Trends in Teen Birth Rates

SOURCES: National Center for Health Statistics, *Annual Vital Statistics,* and *Monthly Vital Statistics Reports;* U.S. DHEW, Vital and Health Statistics, "Trends in Illegitimacy, U.S. 1940–1965."

sexual activity among single teenagers has increased sharply, probably doubling. By 1984 almost half of all American teenage women were both unmarried and sexually active, up from only one in four in 1970.

Yet the growth of out-of-wedlock births has not occurred only among teens; in fact, the increase has been more rapid among older women. In 1970 teens made up almost half of all out-of-wedlock births in America; at present they account for a little less than a third. On the other hand, out-of-wedlock births represent a much larger percentage of births to teens than of births to older women. Perhaps for that reason, teenagers have become the symbol of a problem that, to many Americans, is "out of control."

Whatever misunderstandings may have been encouraged by reports of a "million preg-

nant teenagers" a year, the new concept of "teen pregnancy" had a remarkable impact. By the mid-1980s, Congress had created a new federal office on adolescent pregnancy and parenting; 23 states had set up task forces; the media had published over 200 articles, including cover stories in both *Time* and *Newsweek*; American philanthropy had moved teen pregnancy into a high priority funding item; and a 1985 Harris poll showed that 80 percent of Americans thought teen pregnancy was a "serious problem" facing the nation, a concern shared across racial, geographic, and economic boundaries.

But while this public consensus has been taking shape, a debate has emerged about many of its premises. A growing number of social scientists have come to question whether teen pregnancy causes the social problems linked to it. Yet these criticisms have at times been interpreted as either an ivory-tower indifference to the fate of teen parents and their babies or a Panglossian optimism that teen childbearing is just one more alternate lifestyle. As a result, clarity on these issues has gotten lost in clouds of ideological mistrust. To straighten out these matters, we need to understand what is known, and not known, about the relation of teen pregnancy to poverty and other social problems.[1]

DISTINGUISHING CAUSES FROM CORRELATIONS

As the Guttmacher Institute's report made clear, numerous studies have documented an association between births to teenagers and a host of bad medical and social outcomes. Compared to women who have babies later in life, teen mothers are in poorer health, have more medically treacherous pregnancies, more stillbirths and newborn deaths, and more low-birthweight and medically compromised babies.

Later in life, women who have babies as teenagers are also worse off than other women. By their late twenties, women who gave birth as teenagers are less likely to have finished high school and thus not to have received any subsequent higher education. They are more likely to have routine, unsatisfactory, and dead-end jobs, to be on welfare, and to be single parents either because they were never married or their marriage ended in divorce. In short, they often lead what the writer Mike Rose has called "lives on the boundary."

Yet an interesting thing has happened over the last twenty years. A description of the lives of teenage mothers and their children was transmuted into a causal sequence, and the often-blighted lives of young mothers were assumed to flow from their early childbearing. Indeed, this is what the data would show, if the women who gave birth as teenagers were the same in every way as women who give birth later. But they are not.

Although there is little published data on the social origins of teen parents, studies have documented the effects of social disadvantage at every step along the path to teenage motherhood. First, since poor and minority youth tend to become sexually active at an earlier age than more advantaged youngsters, they are "at risk" for a longer period of time, including years when they are less cognitively mature. Young teens are also less likely to use contraceptives than older teenagers. Second, the use of contraception is more common among teens who are white, come from more affluent homes, have higher educational aspirations, and who are doing well in school. And, finally, among youngsters who become pregnant, abortions are more common if they are affluent, white, urban, of higher socio-economic status, get good grades, come from two-parent families, and aspire to higher education. Thus, more advantaged youth get filtered out of the pool of young women at risk of teen parenthood.

Two kinds of background factors influence which teens are likely to become pregnant and give birth outside of marriage. First is inherited disadvantage. Young women from families that are poor, or rural, or from a disadvantaged minority, or headed by a single parent are more likely to be teen mothers than are their counterparts from more privileged backgrounds. Yet young mothers are not just disadvantaged; they are also discouraged. Studies suggest that a young woman who has other troubles—who is not doing well in school, has lower "measured ability," and lacks high aspirations for herself—is also at risk of becoming a teenaged mother.

Race plays an independent part in the route to teen motherhood. Within each racial group, according to Linda Waite and her colleagues at the Rand Corporation, teen birth rates are highest for those who have the greatest economic disadvantage and lowest academic ability. The effects of disadvantage, however, vary depending on the group. The Rand study found that among young high-ability, affluent black women from homes with two parents, only about one in a hundred become single, teenage mothers. For comparable whites, the risk was one in a thousand. By contrast, a poor, black teenager from a female-headed household who scores low on standardized tests has an astonishing one in four chance of becoming an unwed mother in her teens. Her white counterpart has one chance in twelve. Unwed motherhood thus reflects the intersecting influences of race, class, and gender; race and class each has a distinct impact on the life histories of young women.

Since many, if not most, teenage unwed mothers are already both disadvantaged and discouraged before they get pregnant, the poor outcomes of their pregnancies as well as their later difficulties in life are not surprising. Consider the health issues. As the demogapher Jane Menken pointed out some time ago (and as many other studies have corroborated), the medical complications associated with teen pregnancy are largely due not to age but to the poverty of young mothers. As poor people, they suffer not from some biological risk due to youth, but from restricted access to medical care, particularly to prenatal care. (To be fair, some research suggests that there may be special biological risks for the very youngest mothers, those under age fifteen when they give birth, who constitute about 2 percent of all teen mothers.)

Or, to take a more complicated example, consider whether bearing a child blocks teenagers from getting an education. In the aggregate, teen mothers do get less education than women who do not have babies at an early age. But teen mothers are different from their childless peers along exactly those dimensions we would expect independently to contribute to reduced schooling. More of them are poor, come from single-parent households, and have lower aspirations

for themselves, lower measured ability, and more problems with school absenteeism and discipline. Given the nature of the available data, it is difficult to sort out the effects of a teen birth apart from the personal and social factors that predispose young women to both teen motherhood and less education. Few would argue that having a baby as a teenager enhances educational opportunities, but the exact effect of teen birth is a matter of debate.

Educational differences between teen mothers and other women may also be declining, at least in terms of graduating from high school. Legislation that took effect in 1975 forbade schools to expel pregnant teens. Contrary to current skepticism about federal intervention, this regulation seems to have worked. According to a study by Dawn Upchurch and James McCarthy, only 18.6 percent of teenagers who had a baby in 1958 subsequently graduated from high school. Graduation rates among teen mothers reached 29.2 percent in 1975; by 1986 they climbed to 55 percent. Teen mothers were still not graduating at a rate equal to other women (as of 1985, about 87 percent of women ages 25 to 29 had a high school diploma or its equivalent). But over the decade prior to 1986, graduation rates had increased more quickly for teen mothers than for other women, suggesting that federal policies tailored to their special circumstances may have made a difference.

Since education is so closely tied to later status, teasing out the relationship between teen pregnancy and schooling is critical. The matter is complicated, however, because young people do many things simultaneously, and sorting out the order is no easy task. In 1984 Peter Morrison of the Rand team reported that between a half and a third of teen mothers in high school and beyond dropped out before they got pregnant. Upchurch and McCarthy, using a different and more recent sample, found that the majority of female dropouts in their study left school before they got pregnant and that teens who got pregnant while still in school were not particularly likely to drop out. On the other hand, those teens who first drop out and then get pregnant are significantly less likely to return to school than other dropouts who do not get pregnant. Thus the conventional causal view that teens get pregnant, drop out of school, and as a result end up educationally and occupationally disadvantaged simply does not match the order of events in many people's lives.

THE SEXUAL ROOTS OF PUBLIC ANXIETY

Teen pregnancy probably would not have "taken off" as a public issue quite so dramatically, were it not for the fact it intersects with other recent social changes in America, particularly the emergence of widespread, anxiety-producing shifts in teen sex. Academics debate whether there has been a genuine "sexual revolution" among adults, but there is no doubt in regard to teenagers. Today, by the time American teenagers reach age twenty, an estimated 70 percent of the girls and 80 percent of the boys have had sexual experiences outside of marriage. Virtually all studies confirm that this is a dramatic historical change, particularly for young women. (As usual, much less is known about the historical experiences of young men.) For example, Sandra Hofferth and her colleagues, using nationally representative data from the 1982 National Survey of Family Growth, found that women navigating adolescence in the late 1950s had a 38.9 percent chance of being sexually active before marriage during their teenage years. Women who reached their twentieth birthday between 1979 and 1981, in contrast, had a 68.3 percent likelihood.

Yet even the statistics do not capture how profoundly different this teen sexuality is from that of earlier eras. As sources such as the Kinsey Report (1953) suggest, premarital sex for many American women before the 1960s was

"engagement" sex. The woman's involvement, at least, was exclusive, and she generally went on to marry her partner in a relatively short period of time. Almost half of the women in the Kinsey data who had premarital sex had it only with their fiances.

But as the age at first marriage has risen and the age at first intercourse has dropped, teen sexuality has changed. Not surprisingly, what scattered data we have about numbers of partners suggest that as the period of sexual activity before marriage has increased, so has the number of partners. In 1971, for example, almost two-thirds of sexually active teenaged women in metropolitan areas had had only one sexual partner; by 1979 fewer than half did. Data from the 1988 National Survey of Family Growth confirm this pattern for the nation as a whole, where about 60 percent of teens have had two or more partners. Similarly, for metropolitan teens, only a small fraction (about 10 percent) were engaged at the time of their first sexual experience, although about half described themselves as "going steady."

Profound changes in other aspects of American life have complicated the problem. Recent figures suggest that the average age at first marriage has increased to almost 24 years for women and over 25 years for men, the oldest since reliable data have been collected. Moreover, the age of sexual maturity over the last century has decreased by little under six months each decade owing to nutritional and other changes. Today the average American girl has her first menstrual period at age twelve and a half, although there are wide individual variations. (There is less research on the sexual maturity of young men.) On average, consequently, American girls and their boyfriends face over a decade of their lives when they are sexually mature and single.

As teenagers pass through this reproductive minefield, the instructions they receive on how to conduct themselves sexually are at best mixed. At least according to public opinion polls, most Americans have come, however reluctantly, to accept premarital sex. Yet one suspects that what they approve is something closer to Kinsey-era sex: sexual relations en route to a marriage. Present-day teenage sex, however, starts for many young people not when they move out of the family and into the orbit of what will be a new family or couple, but while they are still defined primarily as children.

When young people, particularly young women, are still living at home (or even at school) under the control, however nominal, of parents, sexual activity raises profound questions for adults. Many Americans feel troubled about "casual" sex, that is, sex which is not intimately tied to the process by which people form couples and settle down. Yet many teenagers are almost by definition disqualified as too young to "get serious." Thus the kinds of sexuality for which they are socially eligible—sex based in pleasure, not procreation, and in short-term relationships rather than as a prelude to marriage— challenge fundamental values about sexuality held by many adults. These ambiguities and uncertainties have given rise to broad anxieties about teen sexuality that have found expression in the recent alarm about teen pregnancy.

RAISING CHILDREN WITHOUT FATHERS

While Americans have had to confront the meaning and purpose of sexuality in the lives of teenagers, a second revolution is forcing them to think about the role—and boundaries—of marriage and family. Increasingly for Americans, childbearing and, more dramatically, childrearing have been severed from marriage. The demographer Larry Bumpass and his colleagues have estimated that under present trends, half or more of all American children will spend at least part of their childhood in a single-parent (mainly

mother-only) family, due to the fact that an estimated 60 percent of recent marriages will end in divorce.

At the same time, as I indicated earlier, out-of-wedlock births are on the rise. At present, 26 percent of all births are to single women. If present trends continue, Bumpass and others estimate, almost one out of every six white women and seven out of ten black women will give birth to a child without being married. In short, single childbearing is becoming a common pattern of family formation for all American women, teenagers and older.

This reality intersects with still another fact of American life. The real value of inflation-adjusted wages, which grew 2.5 to 3.0 percent a year from the end of World War II to at least 1973, has now begun to stagnate and for certain groups decline; some recent studies point to greater polarization of economic well-being. Americans increasingly worry about their own standard of living and their taxes, and much of that worry has focussed on the "underclass." Along with the elderly and the disabled, single women and their children have been the traditional recipients of public aid in America. In recent years, however, they have become especially visible among the dependent poor for at least two reasons. First, the incomes of the elderly have improved, leaving behind single mothers as a higher percentage of the poor; and second, the number of female-headed households has increased sharply. Between 1960 and 1984, households headed by women went from 9.0 percent to 12.0 percent of all white households, and from 22.0 percent to 43 percent of all black households. The incomes of about half of all families headed by women, as of 1984, fell below federal poverty levels.

Raising children as a single mother presents economic problems for women of all ages, but the problem is especially severe for teenagers with limited education and job experience.

Partly for that reason, teenagers became a focus of public concern about the impact of illegitimacy and single parenthood on welfare costs. Data published in the 1970s and replicated in the 1980s suggested that about half of all families supported by Aid to Families with Dependent Children (AFDC) were started while the mother was still a teenager. One estimate calculated that in 1975 the costs for these families of public assistance alone (not including Medicaid or food stamps) amounted to $5 billion; by 1985, that figure increased to $8.3 billion.

Yet other findings—and caveats—have been ignored. For example, while about half of all AFDC cases may be families begun while the woman was still a teenager, teens represent only about 7 percent of the caseload at any one time. Moreover, the studies assessing the welfare costs of families started by teens counted any welfare family as being the result of a teen birth if the woman first had a child when under age twenty. But, of course, that same woman—given her prior circumstances—might have been no less likely to draw welfare assistance if, let us say, she had a baby at age twenty instead of nineteen. Richard Wertheimer and Kristin Moore, the source of much of what we know about this area, have been careful to note that the relevant costs are the marginal costs—namely, how much less in welfare costs society would pay if teen mothers postponed their first births, rather than foregoing them entirely.

It turns out, not surprisingly, that calculated this way, the savings are modest. Wertheimer and Moore have estimated that if by some miracle we could cut the teen birth rate in half, welfare costs would be reduced by 20 percent, rather than 50 percent, because many of these young women would still need welfare for children born to them when they were no longer teens.

Still other research suggests that most young women spend a transitional period on welfare, while finishing school and entering the job market. Other data also suggest that teen mothers may both enter and leave the welfare ranks earlier than poor women who postpone childbearing. Thus teen births by themselves may have more of an effect on the timing of welfare in the chain of life events than on the extent of welfare dependency. In a study of 300 teen mothers and their children originally interviewed in the mid-1960s, Frank Furstenberg and his colleagues found seventeen years later that two-thirds of those followed up had received no welfare in the previous five years, although some 70 percent of them had received public assistance at some point after the birth of their child. A quarter had achieved middle-class incomes, despite their poverty at the time of the child's birth.

None of this is to deny that teen mothers have a higher probability of being on welfare in the first place than women who begin their families at a later age, or that teen mothers may be disproportionately represented among those who find themselves chronically dependent on welfare. Given the disproportionate number of teen mothers who come from socially disadvantaged origins (and who are less motivated and perhaps less able students), it would be surprising if they were not overrepresented among those needing public assistance, whenever they had children. Only if we are to argue that these kinds of women should never have children—which is the implicit alternative at the heart of much public debate—could we be confident that they would never enter the AFDC rolls.

RETHINKING TEEN PREGNANCY

The original formulation of the teen pregnancy crisis seductively glossed over some of these hard realities. Teen motherhood is largely the province of those youngsters who are already disadvantaged by their position in our society. The major institutions of American life—families, schools, job markets, the medical system—are not working for them. But by framing the issue as teenage pregnancy, Americans could turn this reality around and ascribe the persistence of poverty and other social ills to the failure of individual teenagers to control their sexual impulses.

Framing the problem as teen pregnancy, curiously enough, also made it appear universal. Everyone is a teenager once. In fact, the rhetoric has sometimes claimed that the risk of teen pregnancy is universal, respecting no boundaries of class or race. But clearly, while teenage pregnancies do occur in virtually all walks of life, they do not occur with equal frequency. The concept of "teen pregnancy" has the advantage, therefore, of appearing neutral and universal while, in fact, being directed at people disadvantaged by class, race, and gender.

If focussing on teen pregnancy cast the problem as deceptively universal, it also cast the solution as deceptively simple. Teens just have to wait. In fact, the tacit subtext of at least some of the debate on teen pregnancy is not that young women should wait until they are past their teens, but until they are "ready." Yet in the terms that many Americans have in mind, large numbers of these youngsters will never be "ready." They have already dropped out of school and will face a marginal future in the labor market whether or not they have a baby. And as William J. Wilson has noted, many young black women in inner-city communities will not have the option of marrying because of the dearth of eligible men their age as a result of high rates of unemployment, underemployment, imprisonment, and early death.

Not long ago, Arline Geronimous, an assistant professor of public health at the University of Michigan, caused a stir when she argued that teens, especially black teens, had little to gain (and perhaps something to lose) in postponing pregnancy. The longer teenagers wait, she noted, the more they risk ill health and infertility, and the less likely their mothers are to be alive and able to help rear a child of theirs. Some observers quickly took Geronimous to mean that teen mothers are "rational," affirmatively choosing their pregnancies.

Yet, as Geronimous herself has emphasized, what sort of choices do these young women have? While teen mothers typically report knowing about contraception (which they often say they have used) and knowing about abortion, they tell researchers that their pregnancies were unplanned. In the 1988 National Survey of Family Growth, for example, a little over 70 percent of the pregnancies to teens were reported as unplanned; the teenagers described the bulk of these pregnancies as wanted, just arriving sooner than they had planned.

Researchers typically layer their own views on these data. Those who see teens as victims point to the data indicating most teen pregnancies are unplanned. Those who see teens as acting rationally look at their decisions not to use contraceptives or seek an abortion. According to Frank Furstenberg, however, the very indecisiveness of these young people is the critical finding. Youngsters often drift into pregnancy and then into parenthood, not because they affirmatively choose pregnancy as a first choice among many options, but rather because they see so few satisfying alternatives. As Laurie Zabin, a Johns Hopkins researcher on teen pregnancy, puts it, "As long as people don't have a vision of the future which having a baby at a very early age will jeopardize, they won't go to all the lengths necessary to prevent pregnancy."

Many people talk about teen pregnancy as if there were an implicit social contract in America. They seem to suggest that if poor women would just postpone having babies until they were past their teens, they could have better lives for themselves and their children. But for teenagers already at the margins of American life, this is a contract that American society may be hard put to honor. What if, in fact, they are acting reasonably? What can public policy do about teen pregnancy if many teenagers drift into childbearing as the only vaguely promising option in a life whose options are already constrained by gender, poverty, race, and failure?

The trouble is that there is little reason to think any of the "quick fixes" currently being proposed will resolve the fundamental issues involved. Liberals, for example, argue that the answer is more access to contraception, more readily available abortion, and more sex education. Some combination of these strategies probably has had some effect on teen births, particularly in keeping the teen pregnancy rate from soaring as the number of sexually active teens increased. But the inner logic of this approach is that teens and adults have the same goal: keeping teens from pregnancies they do not want. Some teens, however, do want their pregnancies, while others drift into pregnancy and parenthood without ever actively deciding what they want. Consequently, increased access to contraceptives, sex education, and abortion services are unlikely to have a big impact in reducing their pregnancies.

Conservatives, on the other hand, often long for what they imagine was the traditional nuclear family, where people had children only in marriage, married only when they could prudently afford children, and then continued to provide support for their children if the marriage ended. Although no one fully understands the complex of social, economic, and cultural factors that brought us to the present situation, it is probably safe to predict that we shall not turn the clock back to that vision, which in any event is highly colored by nostalgia.

This is not to say that there is nothing public policy can do. Increased job opportunities for both young men and young women; meaningful job training programs (which do not slot young women into traditional low-paying women's jobs); and child support programs (See Theda Skocpol, "Sustainable Social Policy, Fighting Poverty Without Poverty Programs," *TAP,* Summer 1990) would all serve either to make marriage more feasible for those who wish to marry or to support children whose parents are not married. But older ages at first marriage, high rates of sex outside of marriage, a significant portion of all births out of wedlock, and problems with absent fathers tend to be common patterns in Western, industrialized nations.

In their attempts to undo these patterns, many conservatives propose punitive policies to sanction unmarried parents, especially unmarried mothers, by changing the "incentive structure" young people face. The new welfare reform bill of 1988, for example, made it more difficult for teens to set up their own households, at least in part because legislators were worried about the effects of welfare on the willingness to have a child out of wedlock. Other, more draconian writers have called for the children of unwed teen parents to be forcibly removed and placed into foster care, or for the reduction of welfare benefits for women who have more than one child out of wedlock.

Leave aside, for the moment, that these policies would single out only the most vulnerable in this population. The more troublesome issue is such policies often fall most heavily on the children. Americans, as the legal historian Michael Grossberg has shown, have traditionally and justifiably been leery of policies that regulate adult behavior at children's expense.

The things that public policy could do for these young people are unfortunately neither easy to implement nor inexpensive. However, if teens become parents because they lack options, public policy towards teen pregnancy and teenage childbearing will have to focus on enlarging the array of perceived options these young people face. And these must be changes in their real alternatives. Programs that seek to teach teens "future planning," while doing nothing about the futures they can expect, are probably doomed to failure.

We live in a society that continues to idealize marriage and family as expected lifetime roles for women, even as it adds on the expectation that women will also work and be self-supporting. Planning for the trade-offs entailed in a lifetime of paid employment in the labor market and raising a family taxes the skills of our most advantaged young women. We should not be surprised that women who face discrimination by race and class in addition to that of gender are often even less adept at coping with these large and contradictory demands.

Those who worry about teenagers should probably worry about three different dangers as Americans debate policies on teen pregnancy. First, we should worry that things will continue as they have and that public policy will continue to see teens as unwitting victims, albeit victims who themselves cause a whole host of social ills. The working assumption here will be that teens genuinely do not want the children that they are having, and that the task of public policy is to meet the needs of both society and the women involved by helping them not to have babies. What is good for society, therefore, is good for the individual woman.

This vision, for all the reasons already considered, distorts current reality, and as such, is unlikely to lower the teen birth rate significantly, though it may be effective in keeping the teen birth rate from further increasing. To the extent that it is ineffective, it sets the stage for another risk.

This second risk is that the ineffectiveness of programs to lower teen pregnancy dramatically may inadvertently give legitimacy to those who want more punitive control over teenagers, particularly minority and poor teens. If incentives and persuasion do not lead teenagers to conduct their sexual and reproductive lives in ways that adults would prefer, more coercive remedies may be advocated. The youth of teen mothers may make intrusive social control seem more acceptable than it would for older women.

Finally, the most subtle danger is that the new work on teen pregnancy will be used to argue that because teen pregnancy is not the linchpin that holds together myriad other social ills, it is not a problem at all. Concern about teen pregnancy has at least directed attention and resources to young, poor, and minority women; it has awakened many Americans to their diminished life chances. If measures aimed at reducing teen pregnancy are not the quick fix for much of what ails American society, there is the powerful temptation to forget these young women altogether and allow them to slip back to their traditional invisible place in American public debate.

Teen pregnancy is less about young women and their sex lives than it is about restricted horizons and the boundaries of hope. It is about race and class and how those realities limit opportunities for young people. Most centrally, however, it is typically about being young, female, poor, and non-white and about how having a child seems to be one of the few avenues of satisfaction, fulfillment, and self-esteem. It would be a tragedy to stop worrying about these young women—and their partners—because their behavior is the measure rather than the cause of their blighted hopes.

Chapter 9 — The Family and the Elderly

Reading 26   Older People and Their Families: The New Pioneers*

ETHEL SHANAS

The theme of this paper is the relationship of older people and their families in the contemporary United States. The title, which really encapsulates the theme, was suggested to me by a thoughtful article by David W. Plath, an anthropologist on the faculty of the University of Illinois at Urbana-Champaign. In discussing the elderly in Japan, Professor Plath (1972) points out that the aged, in Japan, as in many other countries, are treated ambivalently. On the one hand, there are the Confucian precepts that demand honor for the elderly, and for parents in particular. On the other hand, there are the social strains that arise from an increase in both the numbers and the proportion of the elderly in the Japanese population. In his final paragraph, Professor Plath (1972, p. 150) writes:

Modern society, in Japan as in many nations, has bestowed longevity. It has turned old people loose into new life-span territory. But it has equipped them only with medieval maps, full of freaks and monsters and imaginary harbors. The aged are the true pioneers of our time, and pioneer life is notoriously brutal.

I have often considered this statement and its implications for the American aged. Ours is a society which, as Irving Rosow states (1976, pp. 457–482), "systematically undermines the position of the elderly and deprives them of major institutional functions." Our society is oriented toward youth. We deprive older people of work, their major source of income, and thus make it impossible for them to compete for goods and services in the marketplace. For older persons who prefer not to work forever, and they are the majority, we downgrade their leisure-time activities and view these as trivial. We accept in the young modes of behavior we condemn or at least frown upon among those in the middle or later years. Barefoot college students on the street do not draw a second glance; barefoot older persons are considered, at best, eccentric and, at worst,

*Shanas, Ethel. 1980. "Older People and Their Families: The New Pioneers." *Journal of Marriage and the Family* 42(1): 9–15. Copyrighted 1980 by National Council on Family Relations, 3989 Central Ave. NE, Suite 550, Minneapolis MN 55421. Reprinted by permission.

Burgess Award Address presented at the annual meeting of the National Council on Family Relations in Boston, Massachusetts on August 6, 1979. The 1975 Survey of the Elderly was supported by the U.S. AoA, grant number 90-A-369, and the U.S. Social Security Administration, grant number 10-P-57823. Gloria Heinemann had major responsibility for the preparation of the tabular data.

mentally incompetent. Discussions about university tenure are confused by the implicit assumption that somehow tenured faculty are all unproductive "old fogies," whereas the ranks of assistant professors abound with unrecognized geniuses. Politicians, as well as performers, undergo hair transplants and hope this will help them look younger. Despite the fact that the men sent to the moon were middle-aged (because, in that strange environment, experience and judgment were deemed to be of utmost importance), we continue to downgrade attributes such as theirs in those we describe as "old."

I agree that the aged in the United States are deprived of major institutional functions. At the same time, I question whether the aged in this country are living in a world with only imaginary harbors as Professor Plath suggests. Are these new pioneers perhaps finding their way to safe havens after all? And, if they are, where are these safe havens for the elderly?

In this paper, I shall try to answer these questions by a consideration of the relations of older persons in the United States and their age distribution. Following this, I shall consider, first, the physical proximity of older persons to their children, siblings, and other relatives; second, family help patterns; third, the four-generation family and some of the role ambiguities it raises for its members; and, finally, what progress the aged as new pioneers are making in their voyage to a safe harbor. Some of the data to be given here comes from the United States Bureau of the Census; the findings on the proximity of older persons and their families, on family help patterns, and on the four-generation family come from three successive nationwide probability surveys of the noninstitutionalized population aged 65 and over, the first of which dates back to 1957, and the most recent of which was completed in 1975. In surveys such as these there are no volunteer subjects. The probability design is such that the chances are 19 out of 20

that the true proportion of any variable will be within the range of estimate reported here, plus and minus one standard deviation. These data then are based on what older people report about themselves, not on what other people say about them.

I should like in this paper to pay tribute to Ernest Watson Burgess, the 1942 president of the National Council on Family Relations, for whom this lecture is named. It was my privilege, first as a student and then as a colleague, to know and work with this extraordinary man. Ernest Burgess died in December, 1966, at the age of 80. From 1916 until his formal retirement in 1951 he taught in the Department of Sociology at the University of Chicago. After his retirement, until the age of 78, he continued as a consultant at the Industrial Relations Center at that university. Many of the retirement preparation programs now so widely used in government and industry grew out of Dr. Burgess' post-retirement occupation. Ernest Burgess was an innovator in the study of urban sociology, delinquency, gerontology and the family. He himself never married, but many of us were his "intellectual" children and he remained concerned about our work, our welfare, and our families, as long as he lived. At the end, his colleagues and his former students were his family, and they (particularly Donald J. Bogue of the Department of Sociology at the University of Chicago) took the responsibility of providing care and attention to a beloved teacher and sociological pioneer.

THE NUMBERS AND PROPORTIONS OF OLDER PERSONS

Let us turn to some consideration of the numbers and proportions of older persons in the United States. When is a person old? There is no simple answer to this question. Some 20 years ago the identical question was asked of a cross-section of the American public, aged 21 and over. The findings of that survey are still relevant today. Regardless of his calendar age, the public viewed a man as "young" or "middle-aged" as long as he was vigorous and active. A woman's age, however, was considered to be more closely related to her calendar age. A man, then, is as old as his activities; a woman as old as her birthdays (Shanas 1962). In this country, a calendar age, 65, is used to define the beginning of old age. Other countries use different ages, some less than 65, some more. The use of age 65 rather than another age, for instance, 70, as the mark of old age, then, is a man-made artifact. When the United States enacted its Social Security Legislation in 1935, 65 was selected as the age at which full retirement benefits were available to workers. Sixty-five thus became institutionalized as the threshold of old age.

All the research available, however, shows that people grow old at different rates. One person may be physically old at 60 while another is "young" at 75. The older the age cohort, the less alike are its individual members. There are more differences in functional capacity among persons aged 80 to 90, for example, than among a group of 20-year-olds. Scholars in the field have posited the need for a definition of old age based on function rather than one based on the calendar. However, what the components of such a definition should be are as yet undetermined (Birren and Renner 1977).

Using the calendar definition of old age common in this country, persons aged 65 and over, and, more particularly, persons aged 75 and over, are increasing both in their number and as a proportion of the total population of the United States. We need only look about us in our daily life to see that old people are increasingly visible. For many of us, this visibility of the old is a personal experience, because we have parents and grandparents who may be well over 65. When I began teaching some 30 years ago very

few of my senior year students had living grandparents. Now, most of my students have at least one living grandparent, and some even have living great-grandparents.

Census reports document this change in family composition. In 1950, there were about 12.3 million people aged 65 and over. These persons constituted about 8.1 percent of the population, or about one in every 12 or 13 persons. By 1980, there will be about twice as many persons aged 65 and over as there were in 1950, 24.5 million, and they will constitute about 11 percent of the population, or one in every nine Americans. Among every hundred Americans of all ages, then, "11 will be 65 years of age or more."

People aged 80 and over were rare in the United States at the turn of the century. In 1900, most old people were the "young" old, those under 70 or 75. At that time, there were about 21 to 24 persons aged 80 and over for every 100 persons aged 60 to 64. Three-quarters of a century later, the "old-old" had become common. In 1975, there were 49 persons aged 80 and over for every 100 persons aged 60 to 64 (Siegel 1976). The ratio of persons 80 and over to persons 60 to 64 has more than doubled since 1900. Those 80 and over are the great-grandparent generation. There are now more than 2 million Americans 85 years of age and over (Siegel 1976). It is difficult to visualize 2 million people. For comparison purposes it may help to recall that only three of our large cities, New York, Chicago and Los Angeles, have more than 2 million residents.

For those who fear that the United States will become a country of old people in the foreseeable future, that these longevous new pioneers will be the "take-over" generation, demographers forecast that the rapid rise in the proportion of the population aged 65 and over is past. To quote Jacob Siegel of the Bureau of the Census (1976, pp. 1–68), "Statements made in the press and elsewhere that over one-third of the population of the United States will be over

65 years of age in another quarter to half century are unfounded." However unfounded these prophecies about the future, the fact remains that there has been a tremendous growth in the numbers of older people during the past three-quarters of a century, and that these increased numbers have had their effect on contemporary family relationships.

OLDER PARENTS AND THEIR CHILDREN

Among those aged 65 and over today, only about four of every five have living children. Of those who have children, half have only one or two, and half have three or more (Shanas 1978). The old person with children has had different life experiences than the person with no children. These differences continue into old age. The person with children is not *only* a parent; as a parent, he is part of a lineage. Often he or she is the beginning of a lineage of three, four, or even five generations. Ninety-four percent of old people with children are grandparents; 46 percent, great-grandparents. Almost half of all persons aged 65 and over in this country who have living children are thus members of four-generation families. The likelihood of being a great-grandparent increases with age, and among those 80 and over, almost three-fourths are great-grandparents. On the other hand, there are great-grandparents among the "young-old" too. One-fourth of those aged 65 and 66 in 1975 are already great-grandparents (Shanas 1978).

THE LIVING ARRANGEMENTS OF PERSONS OVER 65

Before beginning this discussion of the living arrangements of older people, it is necessary to distinguish between family and household as these terms are used in this essay. For most older people, the family is that group of individuals to whom they are related by blood and marriage. This definition of the family implies that the family includes more than the individual's immediate family, that is, spouse, children, and perhaps siblings. For an older person, his family may include those persons somewhat distantly related by blood or marriage, such as cousins of various degrees, or in-laws, all of whom may be perceived as family members. Nothing in this definition of the family as a network of kin implies that a family must live under the same roof. Those living under the same roof comprise a household. While households of unrelated old people who exchange services and who give one another emotional support as though they were family members are becoming more common, only a small fraction of the elderly live in such arrangements.

Most older people in the United States live in the community, only about 5 to 6 percent live in institutions. About two of every three older men are married and living with their wives. Primarily because women outlive men, only about one of every three older women is married and living with her husband.

In the United States, both older people and their adult children place a value on independent living. Older people stress their desire for such living arrangements. They want to live close enough to children so that they can see them and, especially, see their grandchildren, but they also want to maintain their own households as long as possible. Adult children, for their part, stress their own need for privacy. These desires for independence and privacy are reflected in the living arrangements of older people. Among all older married persons, whether they have children or not, only 12 percent live in a household that includes one or more of their children, while 17 percent of unmarried persons, the single, widowed and divorced, live in such households. Two-thirds of all unmarried persons, whether men or women live alone (Shanas 1978). This two-thirds of all unmarried persons encompasses one of every seven older men, and one of every three older women (Siegel 1976; Glick 1979).

It is not possible to live with children if one has no children. The discussion which follows then focuses on those older people who have children, about four of every five of the noninstitutionalized elderly. While the proportion of old people who live with their children has decreased over the last 20 years, the proportion living close to children has increased substantially. In 1975, the proportion of old people living in the same household with one of their children was 18 percent. Thirty-four percent of all persons over 65 with children, however, live apart from children, but within 10 minutes distance from at least one of them. As a result, in 1975, half of all people with children (52 percent) lived either in the same household with a child, or next door, down the street or a few blocks away. Old people who live alone are commonly considered a particularly vulnerable group among the elderly. Yet, among those old people who have children and who live alone, half are within 10 minutes distance of a child (Shanas 1979b).

Living near adult children is no guarantee that the older parent will see his or her children. In a national interview study in 1975, however, half of all old people with children, including those with children in the same household, saw one of their children the day they were interviewed or the day before that. Three-fourths of older people with children had seen at least one of their children during the week before they were interviewed. Old people (with children) who live alone are equally as likely as those who live in larger households to have seen a child the previous day or within the past week.

Relatives other than children also play an important role in the family life of old people. In 1975, about eight of every 10 old people had living siblings. Those now 75 years of age were themselves part of an average family of five children. With the increase in longevity, many of these brothers and sisters have also survived to old age. Old persons who have never married are especially likely to be close to their siblings. Many live in the same household. Furthermore, while about only one-third of all persons with siblings had seen a brother or sister the week before they were interviewed, among those who had never married, three-fourths saw a brother or sister (Shanas 1979b).

In addition to visiting with children and siblings, old people visit with other relatives who are not among their direct descendants. In 1975, about three of every 10 older persons said that they had seen some relative who was neither a child, a grandchild nor a brother or sister during the previous week.

We know very little about the quality of the interchange either in the households shared by older people and their adult children or in the visits between older people and their children and other relatives. Old people living in the same household with children or relatives may find such an arrangement satisfactory or they may find it unpleasant. In a national survey made some 20 years ago, those older parents who lived in households separate from their children were the most likely to oppose living with a child; those already living in the same household with a child were the least likely to oppose this mode of life. Those older persons who lived with adult children were the most likely of all old persons to say that this is the preferred living arrangement for older people (Shanas 1962). I would guess that we would find much the same attitudes about living arrangements among older people were we to repeat these questions today. People tend to approve of the living arrangement in which they find themselves.

In much the same way, we do not know whether the visits between older people and their children and relatives are brief or lengthy, friendly and warm, or acrimonious and hostile (Shanas 1979b). What we do know is that older parents and their adult children and other relatives do see one another, and that some exchange takes place between them. The nature of such an exchange may just be, as people say, "a visit," or it may involve actual help and services between the generations.

HELP PATTERNS AMONG THE ELDERLY AND THEIR KIN

Help and services across the generations is a continuing feature of family life in the United States (Shanas 1973; Sussman and Burchinal 1962). In 1975, seven of every 10 persons aged 65 and over with children report they gave help to their children, the same proportion reported help to their grandchildren, and five of every 10 reported help to their great-grandchildren. At the same time that old people report giving help to their descendants, a substantial proportion of old persons, again seven of every 10, report receiving help from children. The kinds of help received from children and the help given to children are very similar. These include help with home repairs and housework, care in illness, and various kinds of gifts. In addition, help to children by older people included taking care of grandchildren. Only about two-thirds of those who said they helped their grandchildren or great-grandchildren reported that they actually gave such help during the month before they were interviewed. The nature of such help was personal care described as "baby-sitting," or "having the children stay with me," making things for the grandchildren or great-grandchildren, and giving them money or other gifts.

It should be borne in mind that often the sharing of a home by older parents and an adult child is a form of help although it is usually not reported as such by older people. Such home sharing may mean that the older parent is providing shelter and care for divorced or widowed adult children and their children, in turn, or that adult children are providing shelter and care for indigent or sick parents. As adult children have children of their own they reach a better understanding with their parents. Turning to parents for help seems to become easier. The family, in turn, persists as a major source of help to the elderly in case of illness and in necessary negotiations with bureaucracy despite the fact that, in the United States and in other industrial countries, arrangements are available for outside agencies to fulfill these functions (Shanas 1979a). Parents, as they become unable to satisfy their needs, continue to turn first to their children for care and services.

THE EMERGENCE OF THE FOUR-GENERATION FAMILY

I want now to discuss the true new pioneers among the elderly and their families. These are the members of the four-generation family. Half of all persons over 65 in the United States with living children are members of such four generation families. Such families are now commonplace, but, as the data on the numbers and proportions of old people have shown, earlier in this century such families were rare. Many persons now in their seventies, eighties and nineties, the great-grandparent generation, will say "I never expected to live so long." In their youth, and even in their young adulthood, very old people were few. Those now among the "old-old" (Neugarten 1974), have no role models that they can use to fashion their own present day roles. In our society, as Irving Rosow (1976 p. 466) has put it, persons "are not socialized to the fate of aging." The lives of the older members of the four-generation families, the presence of great-grandchildren can provide joy and a sense of fulfillment. It can also serve as a source of bewilderment as the life-styles of the young become more and more different from those of the older generation.

The adult children of the oldest generation, those in the grandparent generation, find themselves in the middle. They, too, are new pioneers. Those middle-aged persons who have perhaps looked forward to the time when their children would be grown as a time for freedom from major family responsibilities, now find themselves with new responsibilities, the care and often the financial support of elderly parents. Many persons in the grandparent generation are experiencing some of the stresses associated with their own aging, retirement from work, lessened income, and perhaps health problems. Yet they are expected to be, and often are, the major social support of their own parents. The needs of their own children and grandchildren indeed may conflict with the needs of their elderly parents.

The generation in the middle are parents to their own children; they sometimes must assume the parental roles for their grandchildren and, yet, at the same time, they must be dutiful and loving children to their own parents. The strain attendant to such a role may be considerable. The members of the four-generation family, as it has emerged in contemporary life, are plagued by role ambiguities and by unanticipated demands from its members. Who is the matriarch in such four-generation families? Is it the great-grandmother or is it the grandmother who holds the family together? Which of these two is called "Granny" by great-grandchildren, and which is given another descriptive title? Just as the old tell us that they never expected to live so long, so the generation in the middle tell us that "I've raised my family. I want to spend time with my husband or wife. I want to enjoy my grandchildren. I never expected that when I was a grandparent, I'd have to look after my parents."

SUMMARY AND DISCUSSION

Old people and their families are the new pioneers of our era. They have ventured into uncharted areas of human relationships, and developed systems of exchange and interaction without help or guidance from the so-called helping agencies in our industrial society. Astronauts and space vehicles have guidance systems. Old people and their families have only those traits which distinguish human beings from other animals: love, sympathy, the ability to empathize one with the other.

Between the turn of the century and the present, the number of persons aged 65 and over has increased eightfold; their proportion in the population has increased threefold. The status of old people has increased not at all. It may even have become lessened, as what was once scarce, a very old person, has become commonplace. In most areas, in the marketplace, in the area of work, in social intercourse, the only status of those aged 65 or more is that they are old. Sometimes they are seen as "funny" old people who behave inappropriately in the eyes of younger persons. At other times, they are "cute" old, bright productive and active persons, and, thus, assumed to be like clever children. Society has deprived old people both of responsibility and of function and thus provided the basis for the roleless role of the elderly (Rosow 1976).

There is one area, however, in which old people do have a role and a safe haven. That safe harbor is within the family. The family—spouse, siblings and other kin—serves to integrate old people into society. If people have children, they live close to at least one of their children and see at least one child often. If people have no children, other relatives, siblings, nieces, nephews, or cousins often assume some of the helping functions of children. Friends and neighbors provide social support for people without kin who live alone. Pseudofamilies function to invite people without kin to join them at traditional family gatherings, at Thanksgiving and Christmas parties. The four-generation family, plagued with role ambiguities, supports its members, both young and old, with informal as well as formal help.

The safe harbor for the elderly is constantly under siege.

Analysis of contemporary and future models of the family structure of the elderly in the United States indicate that, despite the fact that the family is now serving as a major source of help to its elderly members, certainly as the major source of care to those who need nursing and home care, *the trend toward further bureaucratization of services to the elderly seems inevitable (Shanas 1977, p. 18).*

As more women work, there will be fewer available family caretakers. Yet, as families become less able to fulfill the role of helpers to their aged members, they will seek to modify the bureaucratic structure so that it functions in a way that is more satisfactory to both old people and their kin. The future is uncharted for the old as it is for all of us. Family and kinship ties, however, have been amazingly resilient through the millennia. They may be different for old people in the future from what they are now, but they will continue to provide safe harbor for their members however long they may live.

Reading 27   The Future of Grandparenthood*

ANDREW CHERLIN AND FRANK FURSTENBERG, JR.

Almost three years to the day after our initial visit, we returned to the senior citizen center where we had begun our study of American grandparents. During the interim, we had designed a questionnaire, conducted a nationwide survey by telephone, visited personally with grandparents around the country, analyzed our data, and written most of this book. Still, we wanted to listen to grandparents one last time, to test whether their words would now have a familiar ring, and to clear up a few lingering issues.

So, feeling now like veterans rather than the novices of 1982, we once again parked our car in front of the converted store and went inside to meet a new group of Jewish grandparents. There had been some changes in the neighborhood. In the past few years, several Jewish families had emigrated to this city from the Soviet Union. Our informants were in awe of the relationships between the Russian-Jewish grandparents and their families. One woman, Mrs. Berg, told us:

We have quite a few Russian friends. Now these friends, invariably the mothers are living with the sons, the daughters, with grandchildren— they're all together. I have noticed such a difference among our Russian

friends, who have only been in this country four or five years—these are new immigrants. The grandchildren have great reverence for the grandparents; they live together. When they go on vacation they take the grandparents with them! I'm just shocked! When they go out eating, they take the grandparents with them! When you go to a restaurant, you will see the grandparents with them. And this is such a new experience because we don't go eating with our children. They go their way, we go our way. It's a special occasion when you go out with your children—an anniversary, a birthday.

Her husband added:

The [Russian] grandparents are very much involved with the families of their children. They assume such a responsibility. We know a woman who was a famous surgeon in Russia, she's here in America, and she has that same feeling that she has to take of her grandchild if the mother goes away. She's always obligated to

*Cherlin, Andrew and Frank Furstenberg, Jr. 1986. "The Future of Grandparenthood." Pp. 185–207 in *The New American Grandparent: A Place in the Family, a Life Apart.* New York: Basic Books. Reprinted by permission of the authors.

that little girl. Now, you wouldn't find the same thing in America.

The grandparents in the room contrasted this great degree of togetherness, respect, and mutual obligation with the weaker ties they experienced with their own children and grandchildren. Mr. Berg asked:

Does it appear to you that we're disenchanted?

Interviewer: Do you think you're disenchanted?

Yes. Disenchanted with the way we expected the family continuity to be—you know, when we were younger, when we had children, and the way it turned out. The lessening of the relationship, the distance between us, the wide abyss between the way my grandchildren think and the way we feel. And the kind of reverence we had toward an old, intelligent, crude grandfather. I had reverence for him because he was my grandfather.

After a number of these contrasts between the fullness of the grandparent-grandchild relationship among the Russian immigrants and the thinness among the Americans, plus some complaining about the material advantages immigrant families had secured through special assistance programs, one of us asked whether anyone in the group would trade places with the immigrants in order to have their type of relationship. The question was met with immediate cries of "No Way!", "No," "I'm satisfied." The questioner pursued the point further: "Why wouldn't you trade places? There are all these strong family ties." A woman replied, "I don't think I could live with my children," and a chorus of "No" and "No way" followed.

Another woman said simply, "It's too late." And in an important sense, she was right. The immigrants' family relationships reminded the Jewish-American grandparents of the idealized picture that they conjure up when asked what family life was like when they were children. Whether or not this picture is accurate as a description of the past, it is clear to most grandparents that it cannot serve as a model for their families today—that, indeed, they would reject this model if it were offered. For the discussion at the senior center illustrated a central contradiction in the lives of American grandparents: like most other Americans, they want intimate, satisfying, stable family ties, but at the same time they want to retain their independence from kin. They want affection and respect from their children and grandchildren, but they do not want to be obligated to them. The price paid for strong family ties by the Russian immigrants—and by family members in developing countries around the world—is a substantial loss of autonomy. It is a price most American grandparents are not willing to pay.

In this regard, they are becoming more and more like their children and grandchildren. Joseph Veroff, Elizabeth Douvan, and Richard A. Kulka analyzed two national surveys about American's feelings of well-being and life satisfaction, conducted in 1957 and 1976. Overall, they found that feelings of well-being among Americans in 1976 were tied to personal growth more than in 1957. Life satisfaction was linked more closely to interpersonal intimacy and less closely to participation in organizations such as the church or social roles such as worker or husband. Moreover, self-reliance and self-expression became more important sources of fulfillment. And as for the greater importance of self-reliance:

This is no more clearly highlighted than in the case of older people in

*the society of 1976 who have joined
the rest of their population in seeking
self-sufficiency as a crucial life value
for well-being more than older people in 1957.*[1]

We would argue that this change in the basis of
older people's sense of well-being is rooted in
material changes . . . : the great rise in their standard of living, the increase in longevity,
improvements in transportation and communication, and the like. As a result of these trends,
many more older Americans have the opportunity to live independent lives. Given this opportunity, they—like their children and grandchildren—are seizing it. Another grandparent at
the senior center told us:

*When we were raising children, we
figured when the children got married and moved to their own locales,
we'd be free to do as we please. All
our lives, we've worked for the kids,
to make sure they had an education
and everything else. Then we find
out when we're grandparents they
say, "Uh, Mom, Pop, how about
babysitting? We're going away for a
couple of days." Once in a while this
is fine, but we wouldn't want to be
tied down to that like three or four
times a year. And when my wife was
baby-sitting for my granddaughter, I
was against it because she was coming here to the center on Wednes-
days. She was giving up her day; it
killed the day even though she was
only baby-sitting for five hours or
so. . . . And she's depriving herself of
her pleasures.*

The sense that they deserve to have their
pleasures now because they worked hard to raise

their children was widespread among the grandparents in our study. Having paid their dues,
many—like the grandfather just quoted—felt
that they need not be "tied down" too often, need
not oblige all their children's demands. Perhaps
grandparents in other cultures, if faced with the
same opportunities for independence, would
make different choices. For example, older people in Taiwan still live with their adult children
in substantial, though slowly declining, numbers
despite rapid economic development.[2] But personal autonomy has long been a central value in
American life, as observers from the time of
Tocqueville have noted. And this emphasis on
autonomy extends to family relations as well. In
a recent study of American individualism, Robert N. Bellah and his colleagues wrote that "free
choice in the family, which was already greater
in Tocqueville's day than it had been before, is
now characteristic of the decisions of all members of the family except the youngest children."[3] Given the central place of personal
autonomy in American culture and the improved
material circumstances of older people, the shift
among grandparents toward greater independence seem inexorable.

We would also argue . . . that the increasing
independence of the generations promotes the
growth of the compassionate style of interaction
between grandparents and grandchildren. Informal, affectionate, warm relations are more likely
when grandparents and grandchildren are relatively equal in social status, as anthropological
studies suggest. Thus, the greater independence
of grandparents—their reluctance to assume
responsibility except in times of crisis, their
exclusion by parents from decision-making,
their overall lack of authority—leads to a greater
emphasis on personal intimacy and emotional
satisfaction with grandchildren. Here again, as
the Veroff, Douvan, and Kulka study makes
clear, their behavior mirrors that of Americans in
general. Grandparents, newly freed from the

constraints of economic dependence, blessed with longer lives, and imbued with American values, have joined their juniors in the pursuit of sentiment. The new American grandparent wants to be involved in her grandchildren's lives, but not at the cost of her autonomy.

Some would fault grandparents of this behavior. Arguing on behalf of stronger family ties, conservative critics of the contemporary family have called for a return to "traditional" family values, including the restoration of the authority of old over young and of husbands over wives. Although we respect the moral concern that underlies this position, our research has convinced us that the chances for a large-scale restoration of these traditional values are near zero—particularly insofar as grandparents are concerned. The most outspoken advocate for closer ties between grandparents and grandchildren has been child psychiatrist Arthur Kornhaber. . . . He has warned of a "new social contract" that has, in his opinion, weakened the family:

> A great many grandparents have given up emotional attachments to their grandchildren. They have ceded the power to determine their grandparenting relationship to the grandchildren's parents and, in effect, have turned their backs on an entire generation.[4]

In the book he wrote with journalist Kenneth L. Woodward, he calls for a return to "an ethos which values emotions and emotional attachments," particularly between grandparents and grandchildren.[5]

Kornhaber's critique, though well intentioned and not without basis, is strong on rhetoric but weak on the facts. First, he downplays the positive features of social change. For example, his charge that grandparents have abandoned emotional attachments to their grandchildren is false, as the evidence in this book has amply demonstrated. Again and again, our interviews showed that grandparents have strong attachments to their grandchildren. In a majority of cases, this bond takes the form of a compassionate relationship based on regular (though not daily) contact and an informal style of interaction. The grandparents in our survey reported overwhelmingly . . . that their relationships with the study children were "closer" and "more friendly" than their own relationships with their grandparents had been when they were children. We learned that grandparents with compassionate relationships expressed great contentment with the emotional rewards of grandparenthood, even if they were not completely satisfied with the amount of time they were able to spend with their grandchildren. [We] discovered that the major enemy of grandparents is geographical distance. When grandchildren live nearby, grandparents see them often, even if they do not get along with the children's parents.

Kornhaber . . . does not think today's compassionate relationships qualify as "real" relationships—thus his charge that grandparents have abandoned their family commitments. But they certainly felt like real relationships to the grandparents we spoke with. One should at least consider the possibility that the greater emphasis on companionship has had the salutary effect of diminishing the stiff, formal style that often dominated intergenerational relations in the past and increasing the salience of love and affection in intergenerational relations today.

Similarly, there is little recognition that the greater independence of the older population usually is experienced by them and most of their children as a positive development. What seems to Kornhaber as detachment is perceived by many grandparents as self-reliance, a quality much valued in American culture. Just a generation or two ago, far fewer grandparents had the economic resources and the good health necessary to live long, independent lives. Now that more do, is it fair to criticize them for enjoying the autonomy that is so highly prized in American society? The older among today's grandparents came of age during the Great Depression and lived through the hardships of World War II. They raised large families during the baby boom and worked to put their children through college. Consequently, it is not surprising that most older Americans are generally content with the trouble-free, independent lives that they now lead. Is there not a great social achievement here, namely, an advance in the quality of life for a previously disadvantaged group of Americans?

Conservative arguments about the family are often stated as if, without any major changes in social structure, moral exhortation alone could alter people's behavior patterns. Kornhaber and Woodward . . . are aware that the strong intergenerational ties of the past that they so admire were rooted in economic cooperation among families working hard to subsist. They further acknowledge that as material conditions have improved, intergenerational ties have become less intense. Yet they reject the linkage between material conditions and family relationships, calling merely for the spread of an ethos than would restore the intensive emotional ties of the idealized three-generational unit, as if the power of moral suasion were sufficient to bring about the changes they favor. It is not. To attain the goal they seek, one must consider, in addition, what changes in the social structure would be necessary—and what the social and economic costs would be.

Let us consider, then, what it might take to establish widely the kind of deeper, stronger ties between grandparents and grandchildren that Kornhaber—and, other things being equal, almost everyone else—would like to see. To begin with, our society would have to discourage if not restrict people's geographical movements. Our analyses [have] shown that involved relationships between grandparents and grandchildren depend most heavily on very frequent contact,

which in turn depends very heavily on living nearby. A massive relocation would be required to put enough grandparents and grandchildren near enough to allow for a great increase in contact. Presumably, young adults move to pursue better opportunities, thus improving the general welfare (by more efficiently matching their skills to jobs); and older people relocate for health and recreational reasons. Are we prepared to reduce employment opportunities for improved grandparent-grandchild relations? Would we really consider urging workers to remain in depressed labor markets so that their children would have regular contact with grandparents? How many older people who have worked hard all their lives could be dissuaded from retiring to a condominium in the Sunbelt? We doubt that many Americans would respond to these appeals.

Moreover, even if such appeals were successful, they would not suffice. The involvement of grandparents in families of the past was enhanced when they retained a substantial amount of authority over the lives of their children, often based upon the ownership or control of economic resources. Even today in many developing countries, elders have a great deal of influence over the timing of the major events in their children's lives due to their control over resources.[6] In order to foster intense intergenerational ties, then, our society would have to give the older generation substantial control over resources and allow for older people to have more influence over their children's choice of spouse, timing of marriage, type of work, and place of residence. We suspect that few Americans would accept this degree of influence in their own family decisions.

THE GAINS FROM INTERGENERATIONAL TIES

These, then, are the steps it would take to restore the authority of grandparents as it is sometimes believed to have existed in the past. We stress the "believed" because family historians have cast doubt on the notion that American families ever functioned like families in Japan, India, or China, where reverence and respect for ancestors remains high even today. Still, it is likely that family elders more often wielded influence in day-to-day family dealings a century ago than they do today. Teenaged children were expected to contribute to their parents' support, and elderly parents often continued to receive material support from their adult children and their children's children. Money and services flowed in two directions within the family—to children when they were young and then back to parents as they aged.

Family scholars are not quite certain just when and why this reciprocal flow of resources changed. Some believe that the change occurred gradually as parents lost the ability to employ their children in the family farm or business. Others think that the sustained period of economic growth following World War II reduced the need for intergenerational transfers. Probably, too, the Social Security system, which was devised to insure the economic well-being of the elderly, helped to undermine the traditional pattern of intergenerational exchange. By the middle of this century, relatively few adult children continued to turn over portions of their earnings to their parents. Increasingly, older parents were able to support themselves, and growing numbers of them were able to assist their adult children in establishing careers and launching families.

What do grandparents gain from intergenerational relations today? First, . . . an indirect exchange still is taking place through the Social Security system. The middle generation is paying generously to support the elderly, while preserving the cultural fiction that the elderly are taking care of themselves. This belief reinforces the high value Americans place on the autonomy of family members. Grandparents do not want to

rely on their children and grandchildren for economic security.

Second, grandparents are repaid by their children and grandchildren in sentimental currency—love and affection. While we cannot fully document it, we believe that this form of exchange probably has increased over the past several decades. We have argued that emotional ties between the elderly and their grandchildren are more valued than ever before. This does not necessarily mean that they are more gratifying—though we suspect that they often are—but that the standards of what constitutes a "close" relationship have been elevated. As in contemporary marriage, more emotional satisfaction is now expected in intergenerational relations. Yet, as in marriage, the pursuit of sentiment, though personally rewarding, can be elusive and frustrating. As inflation in standards can lead to doubts and disappointments. When our respondents told us about their strong feelings for their grandchildren, we sometimes sensed reservations about whether the feelings were reciprocated. Some grandparents felt less than secure about their place in the family.

Third, grandparents are able to bask in what they perceive as the special achievements of their grandchildren. Though they may see them infrequently, grandparents boast of their grandchildren's success in school, on the athletic field, or in church activities. In the homes we visited, we were shown trophies, merit badges, certificates, and newspaper clippings. We were regaled with stories of school plays, honor rolls, and lucrative summer employment. It was clear that grandchildren's accomplishments had helped to make life worthwhile. To be sure, grandparents understand, as do parents, that children are achieving for themselves. But grandparents are a central part of the audience. Indeed, parents encourage them to share the children's accomplishments. And one of the benefits of this form of exchange is that grandparents who live in

Florida or Arizona can receive it nearly as well as those who live next door.

Our conclusion, then, is that there will be no "return" to "traditional" grandparent-grandchild relations on a large scale—and that this is not altogether bad. Substantial benefits have accrued to grandparents and their adult children as a result of the movement toward greater autonomy and companionship. Moreover, the symbolic rewards of grandparenthood are important, even though they are less substantive than the exchange of goods and services. In addition, the costs of widely establishing a strong, influential relationship between grandparents and their progeny are so high that few would support the necessary actions. This is not to deny that real costs are attached to the current state of family relations or that some grandparents have misgivings or discontents about their roles. All family arrangements entail certain costs; we are probably more aware of the costs of ours than ever before. Rather, we wish to emphasize here that even if there are structural weaknesses in the American family (as few would deny), grandparents are not likely to be the agents of change or useful instruments of public policy. Their influence in most families is modest, and the prospects for greatly increasing that influence are slim. Those searching for a means of strengthening the American family will probably have to look elsewhere.

COUNTERCURRENTS

Still, there are some countervailing tendencies that may act to increase modestly the importance of the grandparental role. Those who are inclined to exhortations on behalf of strong bonds between grandparents and grandchildren might take heart from our finding that grandparents with a greater family consciousness saw their grandchildren more often and exchanged more services. These findings showed that there

is significant variation in family values among American grandparents, holding economic factors constant. But just how one might foster the spread of a more familistic orientation—assuming that was a shared policy objective—is unclear.

More important, for better or worse, is the trend toward frequent divorce. [D]ivorce in the middle generation creates a need for assistance from the older generation and how grandparents, particularly on the custodial side, respond to that need. The crisis of divorce calls into action the latent support network of the family, in which grandparents play a central part. In essence, divorce recreates a functional role for grandparents similar to the roles they had when higher parental mortality and lower standards of living necessitated more intergenerational assistance. One result . . . is that children in divorced families today tend to develop stronger ties to their custodial grandparents than children in intact families develop with either set of grandparents.

The effect of divorce demonstrates once again that strong, functional intergenerational ties are linked to family crises, low incomes, and instability rather than to health, prosperity, and stability. There is a trade-off here, and we suspect that almost everyone would prefer to see fewer family crises—and less divorce—even at the cost of a weakening of intergenerational ties. Consequently, the latent nature of intergenerational support in most intact families today—the "family watchdog" role of grandparents, in Lillian Troll's phrase—should be seen as an advance in social welfare. It reflects the greater prosperity and (at least until the recent rise in divorce) stability of the nuclear unit and the greater material well-being of the older generation. It would be nice to have one's cake and eat it, too—that is, to have prosperity and family stability and also to retain strong intergenerational ties. But the strong bonds of the past, when they did exist, derived from day-today participation in a common family enterprise. Without the need for such participation, intergenerational ties emphasize loving, affectionate, compassionate relations with a fund of additional resources held in reserve.

Nevertheless, divorce is creating a more functional role for grandparents in millions of American families. At current rates, about two-fifths of all American children will witness their parents' divorce.... Since most older people have more than one child, the odds are increasingly high that a grandparent will watch at least one child divorce after the birth of grandchildren. The small silver lining in this otherwise dark cloud is that many grandchildren will experience closer ties to some of their grandparents. But... this benefit is distributed quite unequally, from the grandparents' point of view. Maternal grandparents, whose daughters usually retain custody following a divorce, stand to benefit most; but paternal grandparents stand to lose. Although some paternal, noncustodial grandparents do establish closer ties, they more commonly become symbolic figures who see their grandchildren infrequently and on ritual occasions. Nor... is this situation amenable to legal remedies. High rates of divorce, coupled with current custody patterns, could increase the relative importance of the maternal line in American kinship, an unanticipated, unwanted, though not necessarily harmful effect. All in all, divorce is far from an ideal way to strengthen intergenerational ties.

Another potential crosscurrent is the increasing relative wealth of older Americans. Because of... economic trends..., the elderly are now a relatively advantaged, though not affluent, group. Should these trends continue, more grandparents will be able to play the role of economic protectors of their grandchildren. They also may be more motivated to do so, as we will discuss, if birth rates remain low and grandchildren are in short supply. The family watchdogs

will have more resources with which to act when trouble arises. Even so, we would not expect grandparents in intact families to have more authority over the major decisions in their children's lives. That kind of authority cannot be bought; it requires day-to-day involvement in the grandchildren's lives. Many of today's independent grandparents do not want this type of involvement, nor do their children want them to have it. And some of the grandparents who would like day-to-day involvement live too far away to get it. The typical types of financial aid are likely to be lump-sum transfers for special needs—such as orthodontics, college tuition, or a downpayment on a home—rather than smaller, regular payments. Indeed, only one-fourth of the most affluent grandparents in our survey (those with total family incomes of twenty thousand dollars or more in 1982) reported that they had provided any financial support to the study child's parents in the previous twelve months; and more than half of them did so "occasionally" or "seldom" (as opposed to "regularly").

Thus, grandparents are likely to be increasingly important as a source of financial reserves —an insurance policy against family crises or a source of assistance for major purchases—but not as a source of regular income support. This role is consistent with the independence both grandparents and their adult children value so highly. Occasional large transfers of assets allow grandparents to make an important contribution while retaining most of their regular flow of income for their own use. Occasional transfers also allow adult children to receive valuable assistance without feeling that they are dependent on their parents for support. And by compartmentalizing financial transfers, this system does not interfere with the preferred day-to-day emphasis on companionship.

On a national scale, one might ask whether these intrafamily transfers are likely to redress the growing imbalance between the well-being of children and the well-being of the elderly. Samuel H. Preston has demonstrated that during the 1960s and 1970s, the relative economic position of the elderly improved. In 1970, according to Preston, 16 percent of children under fourteen were living in poverty, compared to 24 percent of persons over sixty-five. But by 1982 the situation had reversed: 23 percent of children were poor, compared to just 15 percent of the elderly. When in-kind payments such as Medicare and food stamps are taken into account, according to Preston, the gap widens further: 17 percent of children were poor in 1982, compared to just 4 percent of the elderly.[7] The gap is a result, in part, of the great increases in Social Security and pension payments.... It also results from the growth of single-parent families and from the greater postponement of childbearing among more well-to-do families. Can we rely on private transfers from grandparents to grandchildren to help close the gap?

In our opinion, private, intrafamily transfers can be of only limited help. To be sure, moderately affluent grandparents whose children divorce often will be called upon to help out financially. [G]randparents on the custodial side after a divorce were more likely to be providing support than other grandparents, even several years after the divorce. But the problem is that many disadvantaged children have disadvantaged grandparents. Out-of-wedlock births to teenagers, for example, occur disproportionately in the lower-income segment of the population; in some cases, the paternal grandparents may not even acknowledge (or know about) their son's paternity. In order to reduce substantially the disparity between children and the elderly, grandparents would have to take responsibility for assisting other people's grandchildren whom they do not know and who do not live in their neighborhoods. There is no reason to believe that this will occur on an individual level, not because grandparents are selfish but because,

like most other Americans, they confine their personal generosity to their own families and their own communities. Even a sudden plunge in the divorce rate would not eliminate the gap. A fifteen-year study of family economics by the University of Michigan showed that only part of the reduction of children's economic well-being relative to the elderly is a result of changes in family structure.[8] Consequently, the only way to reduce the gap directly is by some type of aggregate transfer from the elderly—or from the even better-off adult population of working age—to children. Policy makers cannot look to private intergenerational transfers to mitigate the poverty that disadvantaged children face.

Grandparents: Supply and Demand

An additional trend that may have a substantial impact on the future of grandparenthood is the sharp decline in the birth rate since the 1950s. At current rates, the average American woman will give birth to fewer than two children, and continued low birth rates will create a growing imbalance between the numbers of grandparents and grandchildren. To illustrate, suppose we had done our survey, in 1900, when the birth rate was higher and life expectancy was lower. [W]e would have found that grandparents were in short supply: there were only twenty-seven persons age fifty-five and over for every one hundred children fourteen and under. Moreover, those grandparents who were fortunate enough to have survived were less affluent and had fewer resources to give to their grandchildren. Now let us suppose that we were to redo our survey in the year 2000, and let us assume further that the birth rate has remained low, that gains in adult life expectancy have continued, and the economic situation of the elderly has not deteriorated. We would find that the demand for grandchildren would have increased as more persons lived relatively affluent, long lives but that the supply of grandchildren would have decreased sharply. [T]he Bureau of the Census predicts that by the year 2000 persons fifty-five and over will actually outnumber children fourteen and under.

Thus, the demographic and economic bases of the grandparent-grandchild relationship at the end of this century are likely to be reversed from what existed at the beginning of the century. In the earlier period, grandparents had more claimants on their emotional and material resources and fewer resources to give; in the near future they will have more resources but far fewer claimants. A few generations ago some grandparents must have been overwhelmed by the number of grandchildren they had, but in the 1990s many more will be underwhelmed. On average, given continued low fertility, an older person will have nearly two living adult children, each of whom will have nearly two children. But these averages will conceal important variations. For example, demographer Charles F. Westoff estimates that if current rates continue, about one-fourth of all young women will not bear children.[9] If so, then a substantial minority of older persons will find that only one of their children will give birth to grandchildren—often just one or two.

This short supply of grandchildren may alter the strategies that grandparents pursue. Fewer grandparents will have the option of letting circumstances—such as geographical proximity or how well they get along with their daughters-in-law—determine the nature of their relationships with their grandchildren. The strategy we label selective investment . . . will not be possible as often. Instead, there will be more incentive for grandparents to invest heavily in their first or second grandchild, on the theory that there may not be any others, even if the grandchild does not live nearby. Yet it is very difficult for grandparents to overcome the barriers of distance or a poor relationship with daughters-in-law. There could be an increasing proportion of grandparents who have remote

relationships with all their grandchildren. But if older people remain relatively well-off economically and fertility remains low, we would expect to see more grandparents engage in large expenditures such as airplane trips and joint vacations that might maintain ties despite great distances. Grandparents may also become even more accommodating in their relations with their children—even more circumspect, for example, about the norm of noninterference—in order to maintain family ties. Another alternative would be for grandparents to compensate by embracing stepgrandchildren as the best available substitute. [T]he bonds between stepgrandparents and stepgrandchildren appear to vary sharply according to custody arrangements and to the age of the children when their parents remarry. Continued low fertility may promote the assimilation into the family of stepgrandchildren who today might be considered marginal.

All this suggests that the fit between the number of older family members, the resources available to them, and the numbers of children in their families—between the demand for grandchildren and the supply of same—may have improved and then worsened during this century. At the turn of the century, when grandparents were less numerous and less well-off, the demand for grandparents who could devote time, energy, and resources to their grandchildren may have exceeded the supply. By the end of the century the supply of able, healthy, well-off potential grandparents is likely to exceed the demand. We would speculate that sometime in the very recent past, probably in the 1970s, the balance between the resources and desires of grandparents and the needs of grandchildren may have been at a peak. The grandparents of the 1970s were the first to benefit from the extraordinary increases in Social Security payments that began in the mid-1960s. They also had large numbers of grandchildren because they had given birth to the large baby-boom cohorts in the 1950s. This conjuncture of longevity, relative affluence, and large families may prove to be unique. To a degree, it allowed grandparents to increase their personal autonomy without sacrificing intimacy—to lead in-dependent lives without foregoing intergenerational ties. From the grandchildren's perspective, to be sure, the trends look different: they may benefit in the near future from the increased attention their scarcity seems likely to bring. Thus, a low birth rate, like a high divorce rate, may act to increase somewhat the salience of grandparents to grandchildren's lives. But grandparents as a group, it seems to us, never had it as good as they did in the recent past, and they may never have it as good again.

FORMULATING A NEW DEFINITION OF THE ROLE

Finally, then, what are we to make of the ambiguous situation of the new American grandparent? First, we must reject the notion that grandparenthood is a meaningless, unimportant role. On the contrary, being a grandparent is deeply meaningful. But it must be understood that what makes life experiences "meaningful" in our society has changed in recent decades. Like most other Americans, grandparents increasingly find meaning in their lives through personal fulfillment: they seek self-reliance, and they seek emotionally satisfying interpersonal relationships. Their relationships with grandchildren fit these criteria. Eschewing the role of the authority figure, grandparents concentrate instead on developing relationships based largely on love and affection. Most succeed in establishing rewarding, companionate relationships without compromising the autonomy they also value. Some social commentators argue that we ought to emphasize additional criteria when evaluating our personal well-being—for example, the extent to which we are engaged in efforts to assist others, or the degree to which we have last-

ing, stable bonds to family and community. But these arguments, valid though they may be, cannot change the fact that grandparents, in their own terms, find compassionate relationships meaningful and satisfying. Whether or not it ought to be so, the pursuit of sentiment is central to the meaning of grandparenthood today.

Nevertheless, some grandparents play an active role in helping to rear their grandchildren and in exchanging services with them. Sixteen percent of the grandparents in our survey had this type of "involved" relationship with the study children. Since the grandchildren in the study essentially were selected randomly, an additional fraction of the grandparents must have had involved relationships with other grandchildren not in the study. In order for grandparents to have this functional role, however, a special set of circumstances must exist. Most important, the grandchildren must live quite close by; our findings suggest that, with few exceptions, grandparents cannot take on parentlike authority unless they see their children and grandchildren very frequently. It also helps if the grandparents are younger—hence better able to cope physically with the duties of caring for children—and if they get along well with the grandchild's mother. And it helps if there is a specific need for the grandparents' assistance, as is the case when a divorce occurs in the middle generation. There is not much chance of an involved relationship developing between a sixty-eight-year-old grandmother and a granddaughter who lives with her mother and father an hour's drive away; too many structural constraints prevent it, even if the grandmother wanted it. Thus, it is unrealistic to expect that large numbers of grandparents could play a strong, authoritative, ever-present role in their grandchildren's upbringing.

Is this to be lamented? Readers must answer that question according to their own moral views. But let us make a few observations that, we believe, should temper any feelings of disappointment about the infrequency of strong, functional intergenerational ties. First, . . . the idealized picture of the strong, supportive grandparent of the past is overdrawn. As recently as the turn of the century, far fewer grandchildren had the opportunity to know their grandparents, and most did not live with them. It is misleading to compare the reality of the present to a nostalgic image of the past. Second, it is common for grandparents today to serve as the protectors of their grandchildren—as sources of support in reserve. This latent support may never be activated; but, like a good insurance policy, it is important nevertheless. In fact, given the growing affluence of the elderly, the rise in divorce, and the declining numbers of grandchildren, the protector role is likely to become more salient in the future. Third, the evidence . . . suggests that even if more grandparents played a key functional role, they would have a relatively modest influence over the values of their grandchildren. When even parents have a difficult time combating the influence of the media or the peer group, we cannot expect grandparents to be very effective.

What has happened over the past decades is that grandparents have been swept up in the same social changes that have altered the other major family relationships—wife and husband, parent and child. The increasing economic independence, the greater emphasis on self-reliance, and the search for sentiment that have changed marital relations—making them both more oriented toward intimacy and more brittle—have also changed grandparental relations. In addition, we have seen how the limitations of grandparent-grandchild relations mirror in many ways the difficulties of parent-child relations. Indeed, the final lesson we wish to draw from our study is that the situation of grandparents today demonstrates the pervasiveness of family change. Rooted in our changing social structure and our changing values, the tension between personal autonomy and family bonds now affects all important family relationships. For grandparents, this tension means that they must try to balance their desire for emotionally satisfying relationships with their grandchildren, on the one hand, against their wish to lead, at long last, independent lives. The resolution of this tension is the fundamental problem facing American families today. As our study suggests, there can be no return to the "traditional" family values of the past without alterations in our social structure that few would tolerate. And yet the maintenance of family ties remains important to most of us. This is a problem that requires the attention of all family members and of our society as a whole; we cannot expect grandparents, acting alone, to solve it for us.

Reading 28 To Be Old and Asian: An Unsettling Life in America*

FLORENTIUS CHAN

The 1980 census reported that there were 211,736 older Asian and Pacific Islanders aged 65 and over living in the United States. This figure is expected to increase significantly by 1990. The majority of these elderly are foreign-born and many of them are newly arrived immigrants or refugees. Like most of the Asians in this country, they usually live in or near big cities such as San Francisco, Los Angeles and New York.

The Asian elderly who were born in this country have experiences similar to those of other elderly Americans. Typically, they live by themselves and have fairly regular contact with their grown-up children.

The situation of elderly immigrants and refugees, however, is quite different, as is now well known to the mental health professionals who assist them with their problems of adjustment to life in America. Most of the refugees and immigrants who came to this country when already elderly did not intend to come here in the first place. They accompanied children who migrated to this country or followed later when their children sponsored their entry to the United States. They did not know very much about this country and were not well prepared for the changes about to confront them.

As they left their home countries these elderly persons experienced a series of significant losses. Their support networks of relatives and friends were shattered by war or were left behind when they departed. Their status in society and family changed dramatically, along with cultural and financial changes that deeply affected every aspect of their lives.

Elderly refugees from Vietnam, Cambodia and Laos faced additional problems. Unlike most other immigrants, they could not reasonably expect to be able to return to their countries of origin if adjustment to life in the United States proved too difficult.

Severe adjustment problems often induce in the elderly Asians a sense of having lost control over their lives and daily events, increasing their dependency and depression.

Most elderly Asian persons have great difficulty learning English. Except for those who live in Chinatowns or other ethnic communities, English is a necessity if they are to engage in even simple conversations with neighbors, take buses, read newspapers, understand TV programs and carry on the ordinary activities of everyday life. The language problem may keep them at home with little to do, making them

*Chan, Florentius. 1988. "To Be Old and Asian: An Unsettling Life in America." *Aging* 358:14–15. Reprinted with permission.

In the balance of this article, the term Asian refers to immigrants and refugees from Asia and the Pacific Islands.

dependent on their children or others as interpreters and intermediaries.

Lack of transportation is another major problem. Very few Asian elderly own cars or have drivers' licenses, and if they can't read street signs or subway maps, they probably can't use public transportation. Even keeping appointments with doctors or welfare agencies may be very difficult. The expression "no legs" is commonly used by the Asian elderly who complain of severe handicaps due to lack of transportation.

Problems of cultural adjustment tend to underlie all the other difficulties that Asian elderly immigrants and refugees face. In their home countries they were generally respected and consulted for their wisdom and experience. They usually lived with their adult children and grandchildren and received any care they needed from them. They participated actively in making household decisions and disciplining grandchildren, while enjoying a position of authority in the home.

Their position in this country, however, may be quite different. Although they often live with their children or relatives, the older generation's knowledge may be considered obsolete and their wisdom may be ignored by the younger family members. The elders' religious practices, such as burning paper money and sacrificing live chickens, may seem totally out of place here. They may be allowed to play little role in household decisions. When they get sick they may be regarded as a burden, especially if they do not have health insurance or Medicaid coverage.

Elderly Asian men often come to feel bored and useless because they have few friends and activities and cannot get involved in household events. Elderly Asian women may be challenged on their childrearing practices when they babysit their grandchildren. Their methods and thinking may seem old-fashioned or unsuitable.

Arguments and disagreements tend to erupt more when they are living with their daughters-in-law than when with their sons-in-law. They complain that their daughters-in-law do not live up to traditional virtues and expectations. And the daughters-in-law tend to find the elderly women too bossy and stubborn.

Following are some notes from case histories illustrating some of the difficulties Asian elderly persons face:

• A homeless, divorced 80-year-old Filipino man came to the community mental health clinic complaining of sleep disturbance, poor memory and anxiety. He has four children but refuses to live with them, saying they do not respect him and mistreat him. Social Security disability income is his main financial resource. He carries his bags of belongings from place to place and has been mugged several times.

• A 63-year-old married Vietnamese woman sought help at the mental health clinic for depression. She and her husband came to the United States in 1985, sponsored by one of their sons. They have five children, two in Vietnam, one in a Thai camp, and two in the United States. They stayed with the son who lived in California until he rejected them because his wife didn't want them in her home any longer. The other married son who lives in Texas also refused to accept them. The couple is now dependent on general relief funds and has very serious financial problems.

• A healthy 84-year-old Vietnamese widow has lived in this country since 1978. She was a wealthy business woman in Vietnam. She does not want to live with her children because she does not get along well with them. Currently she lives alone and is able to take care of herself. A devout Buddhist, she maintains an altar with a statue of the Buddha and burns incense there every day. She is extremely concerned that if she should die in this country her soul would never rest. Her children would not visit her burial place often, she believes, and would not burn money there, as is the tradition—they would probably only bring flowers. She speaks of returning to Vietnam in four more years. In Vietnam her soul could rest in peace, she feels. Her greatest fear is that she may die suddenly before returning to Vietnam. Sometimes she goes to the community social services agency to ask for help with a translation or local transportation. At those times she usually tells the community worker she has no friends and feels very lonely.

Such problems and conflicts are not unique, of course, to Asian immigrants and refugees. But they do call for culturally-sensitive assistance of a special kind, tailored to the needs of the older Asians and the process of adjustment they are undergoing.

Reading 29   Grandparenting Styles: Native American Perspectives*

JOAN WEIBEL-ORLANDO

Much of the grandparenting literature and especially the small collection of works specifically about Native American grandparenting examine shifts in statuses and roles which aging women experience in relation to their parents, children, grandchildren, and society in general (Amoss 1981; Nahemow 1987; Shanas and Sussman 1981; Schweitzer 1987; Tefft 1968; Teski 1987). Primarily focused on social culture and psychological outcomes for aging women of the status, grandmother, these studies, with a few noteworthy exceptions, assume grandparenthood to be shaped largely by social and biological factors over which the aging woman has little personal control. Grandparenthood, however, is neither defined by the narrow constraints of biological and reproductive attainments nor executed solely within the parameters of cultural consensus. Rather, grandparental roles among contemporary North American Indians are expressed across a range of activities, purposes, and levels of intensity. The ways these components fit together are so varied as to be identified as distinct grandparenting styles. These five grandparenting styles are identified below as: cultural conservator, custodian, ceremonial, distanced, and fictive.

Freedom of choice in the creation of one's particular brand of grandparenthood is considerable. Some American Indian grandparents petition their children for the privilege of primary care responsibilities for one or more grandchildren with considerable success. When parents are reluctant to relinquish care of a child to its grandparents, individuals who relish continuing child care responsibilities past their childbearing years activate alternative strategies of both traditional and contemporaneous origin. Establishment of fictive kinship, provision of foster parent care, and involvement in cultural restoration programs in the public schools are among the alternative roles available to older American Indians whose grandchildren, either because of distance or parental reluctance, are not immediately accessible to them.

The findings presented here are based on the reflections of the North American Indian grandparents with whom I have worked since 1984 and my observations of their interactions with their grandchildren. The grandparenting styles listed above are defined by seven factors: (1) the quality and intensity of the relationship across the grandparent/grandchild generations; (2) the grandparents' perceptions of what grand-

*Weibel-Orlando, Joan. 1990. "Grandparenting Styles: Native American Perspectives." Pp. 109–125 in Jay Sokolovsky (ed.), *The Cultural Context of Aging.* Westport, CT.: Greenwood Press. Reprinted with permission of Greenwood Publishing Group, Inc., Westport, CT.

parenting goals should be *vis-à-vis* their grandchildren; (3) accessibility of the grandchildren by the grandparents; (4) social and familial integration of the grandparents; (5) personal life course goals of the grandparents; (6) social, economic, and psychological stability of the children's parents; and (7) the age at which grandparenthood is attained.

While custodial, fictive, ceremonial, and distanced grandparenting styles are evidenced cross-culturally, I suggest that the cultural conservator grandparenting style, if not particularly North American Indian, is essentially a phenomenon of general ethnic minority-group membership. Fearing loss of identity as a people because of the relentless assimilationist influences of contemporary life, many ethnic minority members view their elders as cultural resources for their children. Grandparents as cultural conservators constitute both a cultural continuity in that responsibility for the enculturation of the youngest generation was traditionally the role of the grandparents across American Indian tribal groups (Amoss 1981; Schweitzer 1987). Cognizant of the heady influences which attract their urbanized, educated, and upwardly mobile children away from tribal pursuits, many contemporary American Indian grandparents understand their roles as conservators and exemplus of a world view and ethos that may well disappear if they do not consistently and emphatically impart it to and enact it for their grandchildren. The ideological, enculturational, and behavioral components of this grandparenting style are particular foci of this chapter.

DESCRIPTION OF THE SAMPLE

Contemporary North American Indian life has been an abiding interest of mine ever since I first "discovered" American Indians living in Los Angeles (Weibel 1978). In the ensuing years I chronicled the effects of the Federal Indian Relocation Program and urban life on the thousands of American Indian families who migrated to Los Angeles since the 1950s particularly as it impinged on family life, health, and ethnic identity.

To my surprise and delight I found that at least half of the people I had met during early fieldwork periods were no longer living in Los Angeles. Upon retirement strong family, economic, friendship, and aesthetic ties pulled increasing numbers of older, "urban" American Indians back to tribal homelands. Retiree's reduced incomes go further in American Indian communities where the cost of housing, utilities, medical services, and some foodstuffs are federally subsidized. Rural family lands and ancestral homes provide the older American Indians much relished sanctuary from the hustle-bustle of urban city life. And lifelong friends and family provide easily accessed affectional supports, in contrast to the increasingly attenuated ones in urban centers. Recognizing this unexpected phenomenon, I happily shifted my research efforts to where the exurbanite, American Indian elders had "gone home."

Since the summer of 1984, when this study began, I have mentioned twenty-six North American Indians who had lived for at least twenty years in either the West Coast urban centers of Los Angeles or San Francisco or in rural areas at least 500 miles away from their original homelands.[1] All of the interviewees had returned to their childhood homelands less than five years before they were interviewed.

The shift of research sites to South Dakota and Oklahoma was predictable. Aside from being two of the three most heavily represented territorial groups in Los Angeles, the Sioux and the Muskogeans were also among the very first relocatees to come to Los Angeles (Weibel 1978). It was reasonable to assume, then, that they would be most heavily represented in the retirement age American Indians I could identify. Aside from widely separated traditional territories the Sioux and Muskogeans represent two distinct cultural traditions (Kroeber 1939).

The Sioux, who at the time of European contact were nomadic, big game hunters of the northern plains, contemporarily maintain seven tribal reservations in North and South Dakota. No one has written more persuasively about Sioux personality development than has the psychoanalyst Erik Erikson (1963). Yet, in over fifty pages of text dealing with Sioux childrearing patterns, Erikson provides no clue as to the role of the grandparents in the enculturation of the Sioux child. There are, however, lengthy discussions of the mother's role in shaping the world view of the developing child. William Powers (1977) suggests that the bilateral nature of contemporary Sioux kinship reckoning masks an earlier matrilineal pattern. From my observations of contemporary Sioux childrearing practices and the predominance of both mother and grandmother and the shadowlike nature of fathers' and grandfathers' involvement in the enculturation process, I suggest that now, as then, the Sioux family presents a strongly matrifocal profile.

Traditionally, the clear division of labor by sex (men did the hunting, women maintained the hearth and home) resulted in the absence of the Sioux men from the hearth for long stretches of time. When the men were on the hunt or off on raiding forays, the women were left to their own devices in the rearing of the young. With work of her own to do on behalf of her husband and family (preparing hides, gathering seeds and tubers, and curing meats), young Sioux mothers often left weaned toddlers in the care of their older siblings or other female members of the three- or, occasionally, four-generation band or residential unit. Often from the same generation as the children's biological grandmothers, these women as well as the biological grandmothers who shared their daughter's *tipis,* would be addressed by their charges as *unci,* the Lakota term for grandmother. It is assumed, then, that Sioux grandmothers had as much input into the enculturation of the young child historically as they do today.

The Muskogean-speaking people (Creeks, Chickasaws, and Choctaws) of this sample were originally village farmers from the southeastern states of Georgia, Alabama, and Louisiana (Driver 1969). In the 1830s, however, their ancestors were summarily removed from their thriving communities and resettled in the territory which now comprises most of Oklahoma's southeastern quadrant (Foreman 1934).

Again, what data we have about childrearing practices and grandparenthood among these tribal groups are extremely sketchy and provide only hints as to possible enculturation practices during historical times. We do know that all three tribal groups were clearly matrilineal. Families were matrifocal as well as matrilocal. The typical family constellation consisted of three generations living in the ancestral village home or in its near vicinity and carrying out a yearly round of agricultural chores on behalf of the most senior female head of household. Use of large agricultural plots were passed through the matrilineage, though husbands and brothers worked the gardens outside the protection of the village palisades. When the men were not gardening or holding elaborate fertility rites around the agricultural calendar, they engaged in the many and continuing intertribal skirmishes and, by the eighteenth century, numerous wars with offending European interlopers (Driver 1969; Foreman 1934).

As with the Sioux, then, the Muskogean men were usually otherwise occupied and, therefore, took minimal interest in the care of the young children. We can assume that, as among the Sioux, much of the parenting responsibility of young children fell under the purview of "women's work." The younger Muskogean women, too, had their quota of work. Smaller family gardens within the village compounds were the responsibility of the women (Driver 1969). It seems likely that grandmothers would be expected to tend children while their parents gardened and prepared food.

Though the two culture areas represented by the people in this sample are widely disparate traditional ecological adaptations, they share several important cultural traits: division of labor by sex, predominance of the three-generation extended family residence pattern, and relative absence of male involvement in the care of off-spring during early childhood. I, therefore, sug-gest that childrearing patterns and, particularly, the role of the grandparents in that process in these two culture areas were probably as similar historically as they are contemporaneously.

The twelve Indian men and sixteen Ameri-can Indian women in the sample ranged in age from fifty-six to eighty-three in 1984. Twelve people (seven women and five men) are Sioux and were living on the Pine Ridge Reservation in South Dakota when I first interviewed them. Fourteen participants live in the area tradition-ally known as Indian Territory in southeastern Oklahoma. Five of these (two men and three women) are members of the Creek and Seminole tribes. Six (three women and three men) are Choctaw, and one man and two women are Chickasaw.

The twenty-eight participants represent sev-enteen households. Five women and one man were single heads of households. Out of fourteen families who had biological grandchildren, only five did not have grandchildren living with grandparents. Of these five families, all had grandchildren who still lived on the West Coast or at least five-hundred miles away, with their parents.

Seven families live in the type of three-generational family setting Harold Driver (1969:236) described as the modal North Amer-ican Indian household configuration. One family had at least one member from each of its four generations living under one roof. Eight grand-parents were the primary caretakers for at least one grandchild. In seven cases, the parents of the grandchildren were not living in the primary

caretaking households at the time of the inter-views. In an eighth case, the mother lived at home but worked full-time. Here, the resident grandmother was the primary caretaker of the three grandchildren in the household during the workweek.

The number of grandchildren in the house-hold ranged fairly evenly between one and five. One family cared for a great grandchild at least half of the day while his mother attended high school classes. All fourteen biological grandpar-ents had other grandchildren who were not liv-ing in their homes at the time of the interview.

These demographics illustrate that a sub-stantial percentage of American Indian grand-parents still assume primary caretaker responsi-bility for their grandchildren. Additionally, the multigenerational household still appears to be the modal family composition in the two focal tribal groups.

GRANDPARENTING STYLES

What little literature there is on the role of the North American Indian grandparents in the enculturation of their grandchildren during his-toric times (sixteenth to nineteenth centuries) tends to be sketchy, ambiguous, and highly romanticized. Grandparents are depicted as storytellers (Barnett 1955:144), mentors to girls about to become socially acknowledged as women (Elmendorf and Kroeber 1960:439) and to boys old enough to embark upon the first of many vision quests (Amoss 1981), and caretak-ers of children left orphaned by disease, war, or famine (Schweitzer 1987). In all cases the liter-ature depicts Indian grandparents as protective, permissive, affectionate, and tutorial in their interactions with their grandchildren. Only most recently has Pamela Amoss (1986) offered an intriguing analysis of the ambiguous nature of Northwest Coast Native American myths about grandmothers. In these legends the old women have the power both to protect and to destroy their progeny.

The generally acknowledged model of Indian grandparenting presented above fits most closely the cultural conservator and custodial models to be discussed. In both cases, I suggest that such grandparenting styles in contemporary American Indian family life spring from the same conditions and concerns that shaped historical grandparenting modes: practical issues of division of labor and the efficacy of freeing younger women so that they can participate more fully in the economic sector of the tribal community; nurturance of unprotected minors so as to the continuance of the tribe as a social entity, and the belief that old age represents the culmination of cultural experience. Elders are thought to be those best equipped to transmit cultural lore across generations, thus ensuring the cultural integrity of the group.

In the sections to follow, five observed grandparenting styles are defined and illustrated by excerpts from life-history interviews with individuals who exemplify a particular grandparenting style. These grandparenting styles are not mutually exclusive categories. Rather, the grandparents who shared their life histories with me, over time, have manifested attributes of several caretaking styles both with the same children and across their assortment of other grandchildren, both biological and fictive. The case studies presented represent the individual's modal executions of grandparenting which constitute their most consistent grandparenting style.

Although this chapter deals mainly with women as grandparents, there are ten men in the study who interact on a continuing basis with their grandchildren, so it seems more precise to label these relational styles grandparenting, rather than grandmothering, styles. The grandfathers, although present in the homes, are much less absorbed in the ordering of their grandchil-dren's lives than are their wives. As described in nineteenth-century ethnographic accounts of American Indian family life, the grandfather, like the father, is more likely to be the soft, affectionate, shadow figure in the family constellation who leaves the discipline and socialization of the grandchildren to his wife or her brothers (Pettitt 1946). Rarely, and in this study only in the case of two men who were religious leaders, did grandfathers take on assertive roles *vis-à-vis* their grandchildren's socialization. Today, as in the nineteenth-century accounts of North American Indian family life, raising children is women's work.

The Distanced Grandparent

Of the seventeen families in this study, only three are best described by the term distanced grandparent. In all three cases the grandchildren are living either on the West Coast with their parents or far enough away to make regular visits difficult. Nor do summer school vacations herald extended visits from the grandchildren in these families. Occasionally, the grandparents will make the trip west to visit their grandchildren. These visits, however, are infrequent and do not have the ritual qualities of the scheduled visits of the ceremonial grandparents. The distance between grandparent and grandchild is geographical, psychological, and cultural. For the most part, the distanced grandparents understand the lack of communication with their grandchildren as the effect of changed lifestyles on their children and grandchildren. As one Choctaw grandmother told me: "Oh, they've got their own thing in the city. You know, they have their friends, and their music lessons and school activities. They'd get bored out here if they couldn't get to a mall or the movies."

In one case, the grandfather had had a child from a failed first marriage whom he has not seen since her birth. He has been told that she has had children of her own whom he also has not seen. This instance of both geographical and psychological distance, while more common among American Indian men, is highly unusual and almost nonexistent among American Indian grandmothers. For example, one Sioux grandmother not only knew all of her grandchildren from her children's formal marriages or publicly acknowledged, long-term liaisons but also all of her biological grandchildren from her sons' informal sexual encounters. In fact, the issue of grandparental responsibility to a new grandchild was such a strong cultural tenet that she sought out the assistance of a medicine man in determining the truth when a young woman presented herself as the mother of one of her son's children and the young man refused to acknowledge the paternity of the child. Of importance to the Sioux grandmother was that the child would know who his family was and that she would not shirk her grandparental responsibilities to the child because of her son's indifference.

The distanced grandparent, then, is a relatively rare phenomenon among North American Indian families. I find no reference to this kind of grandparenting style in the literature on traditional American Indian family life. If it occurred, it was usually viewed as a cultural aberration due to separation of family members through capture by enemies, death, or marriage out of the group. Rather, the distanced grandparent appears to be an effect of an earlier (1950s to the 1970s) migration of American Indians into urban centers. The distancing is gradual, accumulative, and only exacerbated by the second and third generations remaining in the cities to work, go to school and become acclimated to urban life when grandparents decide to return to their homelands upon retirement.

Most American Indian families would still view this relative lack of contact between extended family members as an aberration. American Indians speak proudly of their familistic propensities, often comparing themselves favorably to what they see as the more nucleated, individualistic, and isolated Anglo-American family configuration. Indeed, the popular literature on American family life tends to perpetuate this comparison (Holmes 1986). That three of seventeen families exhibit this grandparenting pattern suggests countervailing tendencies; the continuing vitality of cultural tenets which promote strong intergenerational ties in both culture areas versus the growing negative influence of postmortem migration patterns on intergenerational cohesion.

The Ceremonial Grandparent

Only two cases of this grandparenting style were identified. In both cases the grandchildren live some distance from the grandparents who, as with the distanced grandparents, have returned to their ancestral homes after living for many years in urban centers. The quality, frequency, and purpose of their family visits, however, distinguish their grandparenting style from the distanced grandparent. These families tend to visit with regularity. Every year, summer vacations are planned to include a sojourn with the grandparents. Flowers, gifts of money, clothing, or plane and bus tickets are forwarded to the grandparents at most holidays and birthdays.

When grandchildren visit grandparents, or vice versa, the host communities are alerted. The entire family attends a steady round of ethnic ceremonial gatherings and social activities at which announcements of their visits are made and applauded. Frequently, the public announcements make references to the distances traveled and the venerable ages of the visiting or visited grandparents. That these features of intergenerational visits are equally and enthusiastically applauded by the spectators underscores the importance of cultural values, such as family cohesion and reverence for one's elders, which are ritually enacted and legitimized by these public displays of the ceremonial grandparents.

Ceremonial grandparenting is expressed in other public forms as well. Grandparents are often asked to say prayers, lead honoring dances, or stand and allow the community to honor them in ceremonies which dramatize the traditional attitudes of respect and reverence for those who have had the spiritual power to live to old age. Families gain honor and visibility in their communities for fostering the health and well-being of their ancient members. Therefore, the ceremonial prerogatives of old age are sought out and perpetuated both by the elderly person as one way of maintaining a public presence and by the elderly person's family as one way of enhancing group membership and family status within their ethnic group.

Ceremonial grandparents provide ideal models of "traditional" (correct) intergenerational behavior for their children, grandchildren, and the community. In time-limited interactions with their grandchildren, the venerated grandparents embody and enact those behaviors appropriate to their age and prestige ranking in the community. By watching the ceremonial displays of age and family cohesiveness the children learn the appropriateness of veneration of the elderly and how adherence to community mores qualifies older individuals for displays of respect and love in old age. The children are taught to display appropriate ceremonial behavior toward their elders: assisting the unsteady of gait to the dance floor, fetching food and cold drinks for them, and formally presenting them with gifts and performance in special ceremonies such as the Siouan powwows and giveaways and the Muskogean church "sings."

The ceremonial aspect of contemporary American Indian grandparenting is certainly consistent with historical accounts of public behavior toward tribal elders (Schweitzer 1987). In fact, insistence on public veneration of the elderly may now be exaggerated so as to underscore, once again, what is assumed to be the more positive approach to aging in American Indian culture *vis-à-vis* Anglo society. Both American Indians and non-Indians are aware of mass-media ruminations about the American preoccupation with youth and the warehousing of its elderly. As a counter to this, there is an insistence on elder spiritual leaders at Sun Dance processions and communal prayers at powwows and sings. In general both aged men and women are expected to be in attendance at public events so as to be recognized and honored simply for being there at their advanced age. Such events tend to convince community members and non-Indians alike that American Indians know how to treat their elders.

The Fictive Grandparent

Fictive grandparenting is an alternative to the lack or absence of biological grandchildren. All three examples of fictive grandparenting in this sample are women. Two of the women had biological grandchildren living on the West Coast whose parents would not relinquish their care to the grandmothers. Solutions to their grandchildless homes included a variety of ingenious strategies. One Sioux woman applied for and received foster home accreditation. During the first two years of her return to reservation life she harbored seven different, nonrelated children in her home for periods of four to eighteen months. At one time she had four foster children living with her at the same time.

> Well, I got to missing my grandchildren so much. And none of my kids would let me have one of their kids to take care of so I decided I had to do something. And there's so much need out here...you know...with all the drinking, and wife abuse, and neglect of the children and all that...so I felt I could provide a good home for these pitiful Sioux

kids whose families couldn't take care of them. So I applied for the foster parent license. I was scared that maybe they would say I was too old at sixty-five. But, you know, within a week after I got my license I got a call from them. And they had not one, but two kids for me to take. (Sioux woman, sixty-seven, Pine Ridge, South Dakota)

One Choctaw woman, a teacher's assistant in the public school system, became involved in the development of teaching materials designed to introduce American Indian and non-Indian students to traditional Choctaw life. Simple readers and instructional sheets in English that provide study outlines for the acquisition of traditional Choctaw dances, games, and foods have now evolved into a full-fledged Choctaw language-learning course. The grandmother's skill as a Choctaw-speaking storyteller has allowed her access to dozens of kindergarten to third-grade children who fill the widening gap she recognizes between herself and her West Coast-based grandchildren.

I think it is very important for the young children, both Choctaw and non-Indian, to learn about traditional Choctaw culture. In this way they have something to be proud of. They won't think of themselves the way the non-Indians think of them— dirty, dumb savages—but as people who had a rich and beautiful culture which they can be proud of and that was taken away from them for no good reason. I feel as if I am passing on my heritage to not only my grandchildren as it would have been done traditionally but to all of the grandchildren who will ever have me as a

teacher. (Choctaw woman, sixty-five, Broken Bow, Oklahoma)

One grandchildless woman had an informally adopted son living with her who was young enough to be her grandchild. (She was eighty-three and he was twenty-five when interviewed in 1984 and still living in Los Angeles.) He subsequently accompanied her to Oklahoma when she decided to return to her hometown in 1985. "He needed a home. And he didn't want to live with his mother no more. And we didn't know where his dad was. And all I had was my daughter, who works all day and is practically blind, so she isn't much help around the place when she gets home at night. I needed someone around here who can look after me, drive me places, help me with the shopping, and all that. So I adopted him when he was around seventeen and he's been with me every since" (Creek woman, eighty-three, Los Angeles, California).

Fictive grandparenting was not initiated by any of the men in this study. That is not to say, however, that men do not facilitate these types of relationships upon occasion. In fact, some older men, particularly if they are in command of medicinal or spiritual lore, will apprentice young men who they later adopt as kin if there is no blood tie between. Older women tend to initiate fictive kin ties for the broader personal, emotional social, cultural, and purely pragmatic reasons stated above.

The Custodial Grandparent

As Linda Burton and Vern Bengtson (1985) rightly and importantly point out, grandparenthood is not a status to which the universe devoutly aspires. The ease and enthusiasm with which the status is acquired depends, to a great extent, on timing, personal career paths, aspirations of both parents and new grandparents, and the relative stability of the extended family structure. Though Burton and Bengtson's findings are based on black family studies, much the same can be said of the range of responses to grandparenthood among the American Indian grandparents I have interviewed. Marjorie Schweitzer points out that, "It is customary for [American Indian] grandparents to raise grandchildren who have been left without a father or mother or both. It is also customary for grandparents to raise grandchildren when parents work, a parent is sick, away on a job relocation or when it eases the burden of too many children" (1957:173). I suspect custodial grandparenting can be identified across cultures where unanticipated family trauma (divorce, death, unemployment, abandonment, illness, neglect, or abuse) separates child and parents.

Three families in this study are best described by the term custodial grandparenthood. In all three cases, the grandchildren were children of daughters who had either died, had their children taken from them by the court system, or had been abandoned by the children's fathers and could not keep the families intact with their meager earnings or child welfare stipends. In all cases, the grandparents' roles as primary caretakers were solicited either by the children's parents or the courts, not by lonely grandparents rattling about in their empty nests.

In one family the grandmother was not only caring for a daughter's three children but also one son's child, as well as a great-grandchild, when I interviewed her. The custodial role essentially has been forced upon her by the misconduct or lack of interest of two of her children. She begrudgingly accepts the role as the duty of a moral Christian woman and in the best interest of her several troubled and abandoned grandchildren.

When is it ever going to end, that's what I would like to know? All my life I've had these kids off and on. Especially with my daughter's kids

...Atoka has been with me since she was a year and a half. Her mother would go out and would be partying and someone was left with the child. But that person took off and left Atoka by herself. And the neighbors called me to tell me the child was all by herself, crying. The judge wouldn't let her [the daughter] have her back so he gave her to me. Lahoma, she's been with me since she was born, I guess. Pamela went with somebody. I think she was placed in a home, then she would come to stay with me for a while, then her mother would take her back, and then get into trouble again and the whole thing would start all over again. (Choctaw woman, fifty-seven, Broken Bow, Oklahoma)[2]

Recognizing that her children, and especially her drug-dependent daughter, take advantage of her nurturant nature, this woman explains the moral responsibility she feels for the welfare of her grandchildren: "In L.A. sometimes I would go out to one of the Indian bars just to do something else besides working and taking care of kids. So I'd pay someone to watch the kids and I'd go out for a few hours. But every time I was at a party or a bar in the back of my mind I'd think, 'What if something happened to me? What if I get in an accident? What's going to happen to those kids?' You know, most people don't think like that."

For the cultural conservator, having a houseful of grandchildren is an expected privilege of old age. In contrast, the custodial grandmother is often relatively young and unprepared to take on the caretaking responsibilities culturally appropriate to the status of grandmother. In this case the woman's perceptions of her custodial grandmothering range from an appreciation of the comfort and companionship she received from her favorite grandson to annoyance and frustration with having to assume the extra burden of her sixteen-year old granddaughter's unwanted pregnancy. These child-care responsibilities are particularly irksome as they are thought to be inappropriate to the current stage of her life career trajectory: "I shouldn't be doing this [taking care of children]. Not at my age. I should be just taking it easy and going here and there. Now Donny, he's no problem. He's real sweet and bright—he's got a brain. He's a lot of company for me. But, then, there's my sixteen-year-old granddaughter. She's going to have a baby. And guess who's going to take care of that baby when it comes?"

The bitter inflection of the grandmother's last words underscores her resentment and sense of futility in this matter. Pressured by cultural norms and familial needs, this fifty-seven year-old soon-to-be great-grandmother feels powerless to act on her own personal behalf. Suffused since childhood with fundamental Christian values (charity, self-denial, motherhood, the sanctity of the family) and spurred on by the promise of heavenly rewards to those who endure an earthly martyrdom, she resentfully accepts her custodial great-grandmotherhood as her "cross to bear."

The Cultural Conservator Grandparent

Being raised by one's grandparents is not an enculturative phenomenon unique to either twentieth-century rural or urban American Indian experience.

In fact, grandmothers as primary caretakers of first and second grandchildren is a long-established native American child-care strategy. Leo Simmons tells us that "old Crow grandmothers were considered essential elements in the household, engaged in domestic chores" (1945:84) while helping young mothers who were burdened with work. And Marjorie

Schweitzer explains that "within the framework of the extended family a special relationship existed between grandparents and grandchildren which began at birth and lasted a lifetime. Children were cared for by grandparents and, in turn, the family cared for the old when they were feeble" (1987:169).

The cultural conservator role is a contemporary extension of this traditional relationship. Rather than accept an imposed role, the conservator grandparents actively solicit their children to allow the grandchildren to live with them for extended periods of time for the expressed purpose of exposing them to the American Indian way of life. Importantly, the cultural conservator is the modal grandparenting style among the families in this study.

Six families are best described by this term. One Sioux woman, who had two of her grandchildren living with her at the time of the interview, exemplifies the cultural conservator grandparenting style. The enthusiasm about having one or more grandchildren in her home for extended periods of time is tempered by the realization that, for her own children who grew up in an urban environment, the spiritual magnetism of reservation life is essentially lost. She regards their disdain for tribal life with consternation and ironic humor and consciously opts for taking a major role in the early socialization of her grandchildren. She views her children as being just "too far gone (assimilated) for any attempt at repatriation on her part. Her role as the culture conservator grandmother, then, is doubly important. The grandchildren are her only hope for effecting both personal and cultural continuity: "The second- or third-generation Indian children out [in Los Angeles], most of them never get to see anything like... a sun dance or a memorial feast or giveaway or just stuff that Indians do back home. I wanted my children to be involved in them and know what it's all about. So that's the reason that I always try to keep my grandchildren whenever I can" (Sioux woman, sixty-seven, Pine Ridge, South Dakota).

She recognizes the primary caretaking aspects of her grandmotherhood as not only a traditionally American Indian, but also as a particularly Lakota thing to do: "The grandparents always took...at least the first grandchild to raise because that's just the way the Lakota did it. They [the grandparents] think that they're more mature and have had more experience and they could teach the children a lot more than the young parents, especially if the parents were young.... I'm still trying to carry on that tradition because my grandmother raised me most of the time up until I was nine years old."

She remembers her grandparents enculturative styles as essentially conservative in the sense that those things they passed on to their grandchildren were taken from traditional Sioux lore. The grandparents rarely commanded or required the grandchild's allegiance to their particular world view. Rather, instruction took the form of suggestions about or presentation of models of exemplary behavior. "Well, my grandfather always told me what a Lakota woman wouldn't do and what they were supposed to do. But he never said I had to do anything." She purposely continues to shape her grandmotherhood on the cultural conservator model of her own grandparents. "I ask [my children] if [their children] could spend the summer with me if there isn't school and go with me to the Indian doings so that they'll know that they're Indian and know the culture and traditions. [I'm] just kind of building memories for them."

Those cultural and traditional aspects of Sioux life to which this grandmother exposes her city-born grandchildren include a wide range of ceremonial and informal activities. The children go everywhere with her. An active participant in village life, she and her grandchildren make continual rounds of American Indian church meet-

ings, senior citizens lunches, tribal chapter hearings, powwows, memorial feasts, sun dances, funerals, giveaways, and rodeos. The children attend a tribe-run elementary school in which classes are taught in both English and Lakota. The children actively participate in the ceremonial life of the reservation, dancing in full regalia at powwows and helping their grandmother distribute gifts at giveaways and food at feasts. Most importantly, those grandchildren who live with her for long periods of time are immersed in the daily ordering of reservation life. Through the grandmothers firm, authoritative tutelage, complemented by their gentle and affectionate grandfather, and through the rough-and-tumble play with rural age-group members who, for the most part, can claim some kinship with the urban-born visitors, they learn, as did nineteenth-century Sioux children (through observation, example, and experimentation), their society's core values and interactional style.

As stated earlier, the grandparenting styles are not mutually exclusive categories. Rather, this woman's primary caretaking responsibility, at times, has taken on elements of the custodial model. She describes her reservation home in relation to her children's Los Angeles homes in much the same way she remembers her own grandparental home. Her modest prairie ranch home takes on qualities of sanctuary—a place of calm regularity, and wholesomeness. She sharply contrasts the stability of her home with the characteristic turbulence of her children's urban social and psychological context: "I think I have a stable home and I can take care of them. Especially if the mother and father are having problems. This next June, Sonny [her daughter's son] will be with me two years, and last November Winoma was with me one year, so she's been with me a year and a half. That's how long I've had them. But this is an unusual situation. The parents...are going to get a divorce. That's why

I didn't want them around there [Los Angeles] while this was going on. I think they're better off with me."

Marjorie Schweitzer (1987) suggests that adults, especially women, welcome becoming a grandparent and are proud to claim that status. For the cultural conservator, primary caretaking is a role eagerly negotiated with children. For the Sioux woman in question, having her youngest grandchildren in her home and under her absolute custody for extended periods of time is just one more example of her acceptance and enactment of behaviors expected of properly traditional older Sioux women. Her active grandmotherhood fulfills what she sees as an important cultural function not only for herself but also for her future generations. She exercises that function in ways that would have been familiar to her arch-conservative grandparents —a cultural continuity she finds particularly satisfying. "I think it's a privilege to keep my grandchildren. When they're grown up, they'll remember and talk about when I lived with my grandmother.... Like I talk about living with my grandmother."

CONCLUSIONS

The five divergent perceptions and expressions of grandparenthood presented here are clearly consequences of the individuals sense of personal control and initiative in shaping the style in which they would carry out their grandparenthood. Clear parallels to the distanced and custodial grandparenting styles can be found in the descriptions of contemporary American grandparenthood (Cowgill and Holmes 1972; Myerhoff 1978; Stack 1974; Burton and Bengtson 1985; Simic 1987). I suggest that those factors which prompt these interactional styles among American Indian families—migration, psychological estrangement between the parental gen-

erations, and relative psychological and economic stability of the parental household—also produce instances of these grandparenting styles among non-Indian families. Interestingly, neither style is the cultural ideal for either American Indians or non-Indians. The popular literature deplores the psychological distance between generations, yet also finds the child reared by grandparents as culturally and psychologically disadvantaged. While American Indians equally deplore the distanced grandparenting style, the child in the custody of a grandparent is seen as potentially advantaged by that experience.

Incidence of the ceremonial grandparenting style among non-Indians is not clearly indicated in the literature, although, I suggest, it does exist in some form (the inclusion of grandparents in national and religious holiday celebrations, for instance). Where ceremonialism between grandparents and grandchildren occurs in Anglo-American families, however, it is prompted by different motivations. As the literature suggests, the noninterfering, affectionate grandparents who live independently in their own homes at some distance from the nuclear parental family is the Anglo-American cultural ideal (Holmes 1986; Simic 1987). In contrast, the ceremonial grandparenting style among North American Indians is a compromise—at once pleasing and incomplete. It is symbolic behavior, enactment of one aspect of American Indian family life, in the wake of others.

Both the fictive and cultural conservator grandparenting styles are particularly American Indian adaptations. Neither of these grandparenting styles is apparent in the literature on Anglo-American grandparenting. Current motivations for both styles are consistent with historical ones. Pragmatic concerns for providing emotional and economic supports in the absence of biologically mandated ones prompt fictive kinship designations today as in the nineteenth century. And the need to care for children while parents work and to fulfill a sense of continuing participation in family and community life prompted the cultural conservator grandparenting style then as now.

Today, however, presenting one's grandchildren with traditional cultural lore has become a critical issue of cultural survival *vis-à-vis* a new and insidious enemy. Faced by consuming cultural alternatives and unmotivated or inexperienced children, American Indian grandparents can no longer assume the role of cultural conservator for their grandchildren as practiced historically. Rather, grandparents, concerned with continuity of tribal consciousness, must seize the role and force inculcation of traditional lore upon their grandchildren through a grandparenting style best described as cultural conservation.

The status, grandparent, is imbued with considerable sociostructural weight in that it, across cultures, automatically confers both responsibility and rewards to the individual upon the birth of the grandchild. The roles associated with grandparenthood, however, can be and are negotiated. Satisfaction with both status and role is an artifact of the individual's sense of creating a grandparenthood consistent with both personal and cultural expectations.

Part IV

Families in Crisis and Change

In this part of the reader, we examine two problematic aspects of marriage and family life. The ensuing selections will illustrate how patriarchy has been a major contributor to marital and familial tensions and problems. Patriarchal ideology supported by economic, social, political, and religious institutions often enables men to exert the upper hand in many aspects of marital and family relationships. Similarly, the domination of older family members over younger ones has often been the consequence of age stratification processes operating in family systems. In Chapter Ten, "Family Stress, Crisis, and Violence," the first two deal with the ultimate abuse of marital and familial patterns of stratification and power—family violence.

Intimate violence, whether it takes the form of wife battering or child abuse, can be seen as an irrational outgrowth of the excesses of patriarchal authority. The legitimation of male prerogatives, privilege, authority, and power can be abused, and in the case of wife battering, it is. This results in the severe mistreatment of women. Contemporary American society has just recently discovered the prevalence of marital abuse, which has been hidden from history because the belief that "normal" marriages are happy and well adjusted and that violence is an aberration has led to the underestimation of such abuse. This misunderstanding has further led to the treatment of marital abuse erroneously as a psychologically determined pathology and not as a social phenomenon.

Similarly, child abuse can be seen as a negative consequence of the conceptualization of children and adolescents as essentially inferior and subordinate human beings. Structural characteristics of the private nuclear family also play important contributory roles. Governmental policies and the underlying assumptions of the helping professions, too, often work against the best interests of children.

Murray A. Straus has been one of the most active sociologists in the study of family violence. In an important essay, "Societal Morphogenesis and Intrafamily Violence in Cross-Cultural Perspective," Straus (1977) outlined the major factors that account for family violence. The first three factors relate to internal family dynamics and include the extent of time involvements of family members with each other, the number of activities and interests that the family members share, and the intensity of their involvements and attachments. The fourth factor is sexual inequality, which links male dominance with wife beating. The privacy of the family is listed as the fifth factor. Straus argues that the private family insulates its members from the social control of neighbors and extended kin. He then builds on the relationship between family violence and aggression and various societal patterns. Using cross-cultural data as his source, Straus develops the view that the more pervasive the existence of societal violence, the higher is the level of family violence. Further, there seems to exist a reciprocal relationship between the aggression and violence in the society and the level of violence within the family.

Another point of interest is Straus's assertion that there is a strong link between violence in one family role with violence in other family roles. Thus, in families where violence between husband and wife is prevalent, parents will more likely be violent toward their children. Further, battered or abused children often become parents who batter and abuse their children. Finally, we should note that the growing concern of abuse of elderly parents by their grown children can be seen as a manifestation of the inadequacies of the private family and the declining significance of the elderly in contemporary society.

John M. Johnson and Kathleen J. Ferraro, two sociologists who work out of the symbolic interaction perspective of social psychology, are concerned with how individuals continually adapt to situations and how these adaptations affect self concepts. In Reading 30, Johnson and Ferraro study the experiences of battered women, who find themselves living through episodic outbursts of violence from their mates. The consequences of that victimization on their sense of identity is the focus of their concern.

In the next reading (31), Johnson extends the analysis of the conceptualization of childhood to an understanding of the changing concept of child abuse. He further elaborates by discussing the child maltreatment movement and its impact on family life. What complicates the treatment of child abuse is the prevailing tension between the rights of parents and the intervention of social agencies. Since the privatization of the family, parental rights regarding the rearing of children have been of paramount importance. However, in cases of child maltreatment, society finds itself in a dilemma. Although it may be in the victimized child's best interest, society is reluctant to interfere with parental prerogatives and often leaves the child in the family and subject to further neglect and abuse. Taking the child from the home, on the other hand, often means subjecting the child to inadequate foster-care programs and institutional facilities. Johnson's paper is concerned with this dilemma.

The concluding reading (32) in this chapter examines the effects of homelessness on family relationships. The homeless family became a visible phenomena on the American scene in the 1980s. Government figures on the number of homeless range from 350,000 to 2,000,000. Advocates of the homeless put the figure much higher, into the double digits—10 to 20 million. The variation in these estimates is attributable to the difficulty in getting accurate assessments of people who are highly transient and often unwilling to be counted. Who are these homeless people? The evidence that has been collected indicates that they vary greatly from the "old" homeless who populated the nation's Skid Rows of the 1950s and 1960s who were almost all white males with an average age of around fifty years. The new homeless are characterized by extreme poverty and little family support. They are much younger—around thirty years of age—25 percent are women, and proportionately, African Americans and Hispanics constitute an increasing number of them (Rossi, 1994).

The primary reason for the upsurge in homelessness is related to the structural changes occurring in the economy as it moves from a manufacturing base with large numbers of low-skill manual jobs to a service base requiring higher educational attainment and greater occupational skills (Rossi, 1994). The deteriorating value of AFDC payments and the crisis in affordable housing are contributing factors. The most significant change in the demographic composition of the new homeless was the appearance of homeless families. These families are identified as being single-parent, mostly young mothers in their twenties, with very young children. How these economic changes have impacted on families is given a human dimension in the excerpt (Reading 32) from Steven Vanderstaay's (1992) *Street Lives: An Oral History of Homeless Americans.* "Karla" is the oral history of a woman with two children; Mark and Linda Armstrong are the parents of teenage children.

The final chapter of the book, Chapter Eleven, "Divorce, Single Parenthood, and Remarriage," contains three readings. Divorce is a major form of marital dissolution. It represents an ultimate manifestation of marital and familial instability. Divorce has been viewed by some as an indicator of the breakdown of the American family and as a reflection of societal decline. Conversely, others see it as the outcome of a positive individual act, ultimately beneficial to all members and, as such, a sign of societal strength.

Diane Vaughan in her work on "uncoupling" (Reading 33) analyzes the social-psychological consequences of divorce. Her research findings have subsequently been incorporated in her best-selling book, *Uncoupling: How Relationships Come Apart.* Vaughan's analysis of "uncoupling" is influenced by Peter L. Berger and Hansfried Kellner's (1964) "Marriage and the Construction of Reality."

Berger and Kellner believe that the contemporary character of marriage originated in the development of a private sphere of existence that is separated from the controls of such public institutions as politics and economics. Marriage is designed to be a haven of security and order. It is a world in which the husband and wife can create their own social reality and social order. This is seen to be of crucial importance to wage earners—it provides them with an environment in which they can gain a sense of control in contrast to their jobs, which are often viewed in terms of powerlessness and unfulfillment, or to politics, which is viewed cynically.

Berger and Kellner argue that the reality of the world is sustained through interaction with significant others. An individual who is deprived of relationships with significant others will feel a sense of anomie and alienation. The marriage relationship is designed to provide a "nomic" versus an "anomic" situation. Here intimacy can occur and a meaningful world can be constructed. In marriage the two participants come together and redefine themselves through the unfolding of the marital relationship and the involvement they have with others.

Vaughan recognizes the extreme importance that marriage has for an individual's emotional and intimate well-being and one's sense of identity. Indeed, marriage American-style demands that psychological intimacy and love become the cornerstones of marriage. As a consequence, the "uncoupling" process that leads to divorce marks a major turning point in the lives of those affected. Vaughan examines this process and sees it in terms of a series of transitions that range from the dissolution of the marital identity to the formation of a somewhat problematic new identity.

The effects of divorce on children and adolescents has long been a concern of sociologists. These effects have become an even more urgent matter in light of the continued high divorce rate in the United States and the fact that an increasing number of children are affected. In 1960 the number of children involved in divorce was 500,000; thirty years later it doubled to more than 1 million. It is estimated that nearly half of all children under the age of eighteen will experience divorce in the 1990s. Paul R. Amato (Reading 34) provides us with a comprehensive examination of the life-span adjustment of children to their parents' divorce. He states that these children exhibit more conduct problems, more symptoms of psychological maladjustments, lower academic achievement, more social difficulties, and poorer self-concepts compared to children who live in continuously intact two-parent families. Some of the key factors that relate to children's adjustment include the amount and quality of contact with noncustodial kin, the custodial parents' psychological adjustment and parenting skills, the level of inter-parental conflict before and after divorce, the degree of economic hardship that children are exposed to, and the number of stressful events that accompany and follow divorce. He believes that these factors can be used as guides to assess the probable impact of various legal and therapeutic interventions to improve the well-being of children of divorce.

The study of remarriage has increasingly become an interest of sociologists. There is a myth surrounding remarriage that says the second marriage is more successful than the first—that "love is better the second time around." According to popular opinion, this is so because remarried individuals are now older, wiser, and more mature. Also, it is assumed that divorced persons who remarry will work harder to ensure a more successful second marriage. Yet, as Andrew Cherlin reports (Reading 35), the divorce rate for persons who remarry after divorce is higher than for persons who marry for the first time. According to this researcher, insufficient institutional supports and guidelines to ensure optimal success of these marriages account for the high rate of divorce among remarrieds with children. Cherlin observes that family members of such remarriages face unique problems that do not exist in first-marriage families. He believes that the origins of these problems lie in the complex structure of remarried families and the normative inadequacies to define these familial roles and relationships. Cherlin's seminal article points out the necessity for a more systematic investigation of remarriage.

References

Berger, Peter L. and Hansfried Kellner. 1964. "Marriage and the Construction of Reality." *Diogenes* 46(1–25).

Rossi, Peter H. 1994. "Troubling Families: Family Homelessness in America." *American Behavioral Scientist* 37 (January) 3:342–395.

Straus, Murray A. 1977. "Social Morphogenesis and Intrafamily Violence in Cross-Cultural Perspective." *Annals of the New York Academy of Sciences* 285:719–730.

Vanderstaay, Steven. 1992. *Street Lives: An Oral History of Homeless Americans.* Philadelphia, PA: New Society Publishers.

Vaughan, Diane. 1986. *Uncoupling: How Relationships Come Apart.* New York: Oxford University Press.

10 Family Stress, Crisis, and Violence

Reading 30 The Victimized Self: The Case of Battered Women*

JOHN M. JOHNSON AND KATHLEEN J. FERRARO

In existential sociology the self is not fixed but continually changes and adapts to new situations. The self is essentially open to the world of experience, both positive and negative. When the existential self is confronted with challenging or taxing circumstances, it does not usually recoil or shatter. Instead, it struggles to incorporate new experiences into its evolving reality. Battered women provide an excellent example of this. The victimization experienced by battered women illustrates how the existential self moves from one identity to another under varying conditions.[1] Contrary to much of the research and mass-media reporting about battered women, they do not become victims simply by being the recipients of physical violence. In fact, many women live their entire lives experiencing episodic outbursts of violence from their mates without developing the feelings and identity of a victimized self.[2]

The victimized self is a complex mixture of feelings and thoughts based on the individual's overriding feeling of having been violated, exploited, or wronged by another person or persons. It develops when an individual feels a fundamental threat to his or her very being or existence. The actions or situations people interpret as fundamental threats are varied. Some women feel deeply threatened by verbal assaults, while others may come close to death regularly without feeling themselves to be victims (Ferraro 1979).

THE VICTIMIZATION PROCESS

Women who experience repeated violence or abuse without feeling victimized make use of rationalizations and belief systems that allow them to maintain a feeling of being in a good, normal, or at least acceptable marriage. For example, some women play the role of a "caring wife" and view situations of violence as occasions for taking responsibility to "save" their husbands. Others deny the injuries done to them, even relatively serious ones, and act as if the violence had not occurred. Some will acknowledge the existence of the abuse but reject the husband's responsibility, blaming instead external factors, such as unemployment, alcoholism, or mental illness. Others may feel they "had it coming," an attitude commonly based on feelings of submission to the husband's traditionally defined absolute dominance in the home. And some appeal to higher or institutional loyalties, such as religion, the church, or the sanctity of family life. All of these rationalizations are used by individuals to make sense of their feelings, to make rational what might otherwise be seen as irrational. For some women, these rationalizations can sustain a marriage through a lifetime of violence or abuse. Some may go to their graves believing in them, as did over 3,600 victims of family homicides in 1980 (Ferraro 1982).

Some battered women experience a turning point when the violence or abuse done to them comes to be felt as a basic threat, whether to their physical or social self or to both. Such turning points may stem from dramatic events or crises. They may additionally originate from progressive, gradual realizations by women. In all cases, however, the experience of the turning point produces retrospective interpretations of past events, where individuals creatively seek out new understandings of "what went wrong." What had been rationalized as acceptable is recast as dangerous, malicious, perhaps life-threatening. Before this point, many women may have felt guilt concerning their own complicity in their family situations and perhaps hopefulness that things would improve over time. But these feelings commonly change to feelings of fear and despair. The experience of the turning point produces changes in feelings and interpretations. A new sense of self emerges to meet these emergent conditions. While the development of a victimized self is commonly temporary for individuals, at this juncture the self becomes organized around the perceived facts of victimization. Once women develop a victimized self—a new feeling of being exploited and a new interpretation of the causes and consequences of this exploitation—they may become sufficiently motivated to leave violent situations.

An individual's adoption of a victimized self is all-consuming. For the immediate present it tends to override (but not necessarily destroy) other aspects of the self. It becomes an organizing perspective by which all other aspects of life are interpreted or reinterpreted. It has some similarities to what Everett C. Hughes termed "master status," and indeed, for some rare individuals, the victimized self may assume such importance for long periods of time, perhaps even for the remainder of the person's life. But for most, the victimized self is temporary. After leaving a violent relationship a woman soon begins to take practical steps toward recovery and the rebuilding of her life. She must either set up a new, independent household, arrange for marriage counseling, or return to the marriage with renewed optimism that things will be different. These actions militate against continuance of the individual's sense of victimization. Thus, the victimized self tends to be temporary, certainly for those who mobilize their personal and social resources for change.

The victimized self emerges during moments of existential threat, and it dissolves when one takes actions to construct new, safer living conditions. The victimized self emerges when the rationalizations of violence and abuse begin to lose their power; it becomes the all-consuming basis for however long it takes to transcend this period of crisis and threat. It tends to dissolve, over time, for those who change their lives in new, creative ways, although the sense of victimization never disappears altogether. For all who experience it, it becomes incorporated into an individual's biography as lived experience.

CATALYSTS IN THE VICTIMIZATION PROCESS

When the process of victimization begins, events that previously had been defined as acceptable, although unpleasant, aspects of the relationship begin to take on new meanings. Violence, which had been rationalized as either insignificant in its consequences, beyond the abuser's control, or necessary to the relationship or some other value, is now redefined as abuse or battering.

Changing the definition of events is not an isolated process. It is linked to other aspects of the relationship, and, when these aspects change, specific events within the relationship undergo retrospective reinterpretation. As in cases of non-violent divorce, what was previously accepted as part of the marriage becomes a focus for discontent (see Rasmussen and Ferraro 1979).

There are a number of catalysts that can trigger this redefinition process. Some authors have noted that degree of severity is related to a woman's decision to leave a violent situation (Gelles 1976). However, it is known that women can suffer extremely severe violence for many years without leaving (Pagelow 1981). What does seem significant is a sudden change in the *level of severity.* Women who suddenly realize that their lives are literally in danger may begin the victimization process. At the point where death is imminent, rationalizations to protect the relationship often lose their validity. Life itself is more important to maintain than the relationship. A woman beaten by an alcoholic husband severely over many years explained her decision to leave on the basis of a direct threat to her life:

> It was like a pendulum. He'd swing to the extremes both ways. He'd get drunk and beat me up, then he'd get sober and treat me like a queen. One day he put a gun to my head and pulled the trigger. It wasn't loaded. But that's when I decided I'd had it. I sued for separation of property. I knew what was coming again, so I got out. I didn't want to. I still loved the guy, but I knew I had to for my own sanity.

Of course, many homicides do occur, and in such cases the wife has obviously not correctly interpreted increases in severity as a threat to her life. Increases in severity do not guarantee a reinterpretation of the situation, but they may play a part in the process.

Another catalyst for changing one's definition of violence may be a *change in its visibility.* Creating a web of rationalizations in order to overlook violence is accomplished more easily if no outsiders are present to question their validity. Since most violence between couples occurs in privacy, victims do not have to cope with conflicting interpretations from outsiders. In fact, they may have difficulty in convincing others that they have a problem (Martin 1976; Davidson 1979). However, if the violence does break through the bounds of privacy and occur in the presence of others, it may trigger a reinterpretation process. Having others witness the degradation of violence is humiliating, for it is a public statement of subordination and powerlessness. It may also happen that an objective observer will apply a different definition to the event than what is consistent with the victim's prior rationalizations, and the mere existence of this new definition will call into question the victim's ideas.

The effect of external definitions on a battered woman's beliefs about her situation varies with the source and form of external definitions. The opinions of those who are highly regarded by the victim, either by virtue of a personal relationship or an occupational role, will be the most influential. Disbelief or an unsympathetic response from others tends to suppress a woman's belief that she has been victimized and to encourage her to accept what has happened as normal. However, when outsiders respond with unqualified support and condemnation of the abuser, their definitions can be a potent catalyst toward victimization. Friends and relatives who show genuine concern for the woman's well-being may initiate an awareness of danger that contradicts previous rationalizations. As one woman reported:

> *My mother-in-law knew what was going on, but she wouldn't admit it.... I said, "Mom, what do you think these bruises are?" and she said, "Well, some people just bruise easy. I do it all the time, bumping into things.".... and he just denied it, pretended like nothing happened ... but this time, my neighbor knew what happened, she saw it, and when he denied it, she said, "I can't believe it! You know that's not true!" ...and I was so happy that finally somebody else saw what was goin' on, and I just told him that this time I wasn't gonna come home!*

Shelters for battered women are one source of external definitions that contribute to the victimization process. They offer refuge from a violent situation, a place where a woman may contemplate her circumstances and what she wants to do about them. Within a shelter she will come into contact with counselors and other battered women, who are familiar with the rationalization process and with the reluctance to give up the image of a good marriage. In counseling sessions, rap groups, and informal conversations with other residents, women will hear horror stories from others who have already defined themselves as victims. They will be encouraged to express anger over their abuse and to reject responsibility for the violence. A major goal of many shelters is to help women overcome feelings of guilt and inadequacy so that they will make choices in their own best interests. In this atmosphere, violent incidents are reexamined and defined as assaults in which the woman was *victimized* (Ferraro 1981).

The emergence of shelters as a place to escape from violent marriages has also established a catalyst for the victimization process simply by providing a *change in resources.* When there is no practical alternative to remaining married, there is no advantage in defining oneself as a victim. When resources become available, however, it may be beneficial to reassess the value of remaining in the marriage. Roy (1979) found that the most commonly stated reason for remaining in a violent marriage was having no place else to go. Certainly, a change in resources, then, would alter one's response to violence. Not only shelters, but a change in personal circumstances, such as having the last child leave home, getting a grant for school, or finding a job, can be the catalyst for beginning to think differently about violence.

Apart from external influences, there may be *changes in the relationship itself* that initiate the victimization process. Walker (1979), in her discussion of the stages of a battering relationship, has noted that violent incidents are usually followed by periods of remorse and solicitude. Such phases can be very romantic and thus bind the woman to her husband. But as the battering progresses, this phase may shorten or disappear altogether, eliminating the basis for maintaining a positive outlook on the marriage. When the man realizes that he can get away with violence, he may view it as his prerogative and no longer feel and express remorse. Extended periods devoid of any show of kindness or love may alter the woman's feelings toward her attacker so that she eventually begins to define herself as a victim. One shelter resident described her disenchantment with her marriage this way:

> *At first, you know, we used to have so much fun together. He has kind've, you know, a magnetic personality, he can be really charming. But it isn't fun anymore. Since the baby*

came, it's changed completely. He just wants me to stay at home, while he goes out with his friends. He doesn't even talk to me, most of the time.... No, I don't think I really love him anymore, not like I did.

Changes in the nature of the relationship may result in a loss of hope that things will get better and lead to feelings of despair. As long as a woman can cling to a hope that the violence will stop, she can delude herself about it. But when these hopes are finally destroyed and she feels only despair, she may begin to interpret violence as victimization. The Al-Anon philosophy, which is designed for spouses of alcoholics, who are often also victims of abuse, emphasizes the importance of "hitting bottom" before a person can make real changes in his or her life. The director of an Al-Anon-organized shelter explained hitting bottom to me:

Before the Al-Anon program can really be of benefit, a woman has to hit bottom. When you hit bottom, you realize that all of your own efforts to control the situation have failed; you feel helpless and lost and worthless and completely disenchanted with the world. Women can't really be helped unless they're ready for it and want it. Some women come here when things get bad, but they aren't really ready to be committed to Al-Anon yet. Things haven't gotten bad enough for them, and they go right back. We see this all the time.

She stressed that it is not the objective level of violence that determined hitting bottom but, rather, the woman's feelings of despair. Before one can develop a real, effective sense of victim-

ization, it is necessary to feel that the very foundations of the self have been threatened or attacked, that one's very life or social being is endangered. It isn't until that primordial threat has been experienced that it is likely that the individual will be mobilized for effective action, the kind sufficient to break love-bounds or to change external circumstances. Many do not reach this point. In 1980 over 3,600 persons were killed in family homicides. This figure alone indicates that the interpretive processes discussed here are problematic ones for individuals. Violence may never be interpreted as life-threatening even if it eventually has mortal consequences.

THE TURNING POINT

The victimization process involves redefining past events, their meanings, and one's role in them. Violent incidents must be interpreted as violations of one's rights, as unjustified attacks on one's self, and as the responsibility of the attacker in order for a victimized self to emerge. Whatever the original context of the violence, it is now viewed as the most explicit expression of a generalized pattern of abuse. The positive aspects of the relationship fade into the past, the interactional subtleties and nuances become blurred, and the self becomes organized around victimization.

For some, the awareness of the victimized self may begin with a relatively dramatic event, a "turning point," perhaps similar to what anthropologists have termed "culture shock," that heightened existential awareness associated with meeting persons from foreign cultures, when attempts at communication lay bare the artificiality of social conventions. For others, the process may be more gradual. In either case, the result is similar: for the individual, an awareness of the social reality previously taken for granted. For all individuals, almost all of the time, daily life has a certain obdurate, taken-for-granted quality to it. The substance of what is taken for granted varies from culture to culture, even between individuals within a given culture, whether one is an artist or a hod carrier. But for all persons, most of their lives have this taken-for-granted quality, which is occasionally interrupted or broken by crises of one sort or another. The effect of such crises is to reacquaint the individual with the precariousness of this taken-for-granted reality. This is a time of heightened self-consciousness, when things and events, previously assumed to have an "objective" character, seem to be merely human in their nature. Individuals who experience this crisis in their daily life commonly begin elaborate reconstructions and reinterpretations of past events and individuals in their lives. Different features of events are highlighted. Individuals previously idealized are now "demonized," as Jack Douglas has termed it, as facts of their (putative) character are fashioned in such a manner as to make sense of their evil victimizing. For some persons, perhaps only a few major portions of their lives are reinterpreted (such as the meanings of one's courtship and marriage, following a subsequent reinterpretation of battering), while for others the reinterpretation may be "global," encompassing all aspects of one's life and identity, which are now cast in a new light and subject to new understandings. Such a global reconstruction rarely occurs quickly. It commonly takes months, even years. But initiation of the process involves temporarily adopting a victimized self as a "master status" (Hughes 1958), an interpretive frame that overrides all others in importance for the person and provides the foundation for all lesser interpretations. "Being a victim" is a way of relating to the world, a way of organizing one's thoughts and feelings about daily events and persons. Old things are seen in a new way. Old feelings are felt differently now. Old meanings are experienced in a different light. A woman who discussed her marriage while staying at a shelter illustrates this process of reinterpreting the past:

> When I look back on it now, of course, I can see how all along he'd do anything to control me. First it was little things, like wanting me not to wear makeup, then it got so he criticized everything I did. He wouldn't let me drive or handle our money. He wouldn't even let me buy the kids' Christmas presents. I think he wanted me to be his slave, and so he started beating on me to make sure I was scared of him.

Achieving a new sense of a victimized self commonly prepares the way for practical action. While it is true that some individuals seem to find solace and comfort in their interpretations of victimization as such, this is not true for most of those who feel victimized. Feeling victimized threatens one's self, one's sense of competence, and this is usually related to practical actions to see that the victimization stops or does not reoccur. The practical actions taken by individuals vary greatly. One battered woman might leave her husband, establish an independent existence, and perhaps undergo counseling to change relationship patterns that had become habitual over the years. Another might return to the marriage, accepting the husband's claims that he has changed and that he will never hurt her again. Some of those who are victimized join together with others for many purposes, such as setting up self-help groups (e.g., Al-Anon), or for social-movement organization and action. The feeling of victimization underlies social-movement participation in many cases and some political actions as well. Wars, revolutions, and many social movements have started with the feelings of the victimized self.

THE EMOTIONAL CAREER OF THE VICTIMIZED SELF

The cognitive aspects of accepting a victimized self, such as rejecting rationalizations and reinterpreting the past, are tied to the feelings that are created by being battered: The emotional career of the victimized self begins with guilt, shame, and hopefulness, moves to despair and fear, shock and confusion, and finally to relief and sometimes even elation. These feelings are experienced by women who first rationalize violence, then reach a turning point, and finally take action to escape. At any point in her emotional career a woman may decide to cling to rationalizations and a violent marriage. Only about half of the women who enter shelters actually progress along this emotional career to the point of feeling relief that they are no longer in danger. The career path, then, should be viewed as a continuum rather than a fixed sequence through which all battered women pass.

When men beat their wives, they usually have some explanation for their violence even if that explanation seems nonsensical to outsiders. Women are told that their abuse is a natural response to their inadequacies. They are made to feel that they are deficient as women, since they are unable to make their husbands happy. Battered women often feel quite guilty about their marital problems. They feel largely responsible for their husbands' violence and make efforts to control anything that might trigger their displeasure. They feel that the violence is a reflection of their own incompetence or badness. Feelings of guilt and shame are part of the early emotional career of battered victims. At the same time, however, they feel a kind of hopefulness that things will get better. Even the most violent man

is nonviolent much of the time, so there is always a basis for believing that violence is exceptional and that the "real" man is not a threat.

First of all, the first beatings, you can't believe it yourself. I'd go to bed, and I'd cry, and I just couldn't believe this was happening, and I'd wake up the next morning thinking, that couldn't have happened, or maybe it was my fault, it's so unbelievable, that this person that you're married to and you love would do that to you, but yet you can't leave either because ya know, for the other 29 days of the month that person loves you and is with you.

These feelings of guilt and shame mixed with hopefulness give way to despair when the violence continues and the relationship loses all semblance of a loving partnership. At the point of despair, the catalysts described above are most likely to influence a battered woman to make a change.

The turning point in the victimization process, when the self becomes organized around a fundamental threat, is characterized by a penetrating fear. Women who do see their husbands' actions as life-threatening experience a fear that consumes all thoughts and energies. It is felt physiologically in general body achiness, a pain in the pit of the stomach, and tension headaches. There is physical shaking, chills, and inability to eat or sleep. Sometimes the fear is expressed as a numbed shock, in which little is felt or communicated. The belief that her husband is intent on inflicting serious bodily harm explodes the prior self, which is built on rationalizations and the myth of a "good marriage." The self is left without a reality base, in a crisis of ambiguity. The woman is no longer the wife she defined herself to be, but she has not had time to create new meanings for her life. She feels afraid, alone, and confused.

At that point, I was just panicked, and all I kept thinking was, "Oh God, he's gonna kill me." I could not think straight, I was so tired and achey, I couldn't deal with anything, find a place to move and all that. Thank God my friends took me in and hid me. They took me by the hand and led me through the motions for a few days, just took care of me, because I really felt just sick.

The victimized self is highly vulnerable. Battered women escaping violent situations depend on the nurturance and support of outsiders, sometimes strangers in shelters, to endure the period of fear and shock that follows leaving the marriage. In cases where women do not feel the support of others, an abuser's pleas to come home and try again are especially appealing and often effective. People in great pain and confusion will turn to those who offer warmth. If a violent husband is the only person who appears to offer that warmth, a battered woman will probably return to the relationship. However, if she is able to find and accept a temporary refuge with friends, relatives, or a shelter, she will be in a situation much more conducive to the relief that follows in the wake of a crisis endured. Once situated in a safe location, with supportive people, fear for her life subsides. Then, perhaps, she will feel relieved to lay down a burden she has carried for months or years. She will be free of the continuous concern to prevent violence by controlling all potentially disturbing events. This sudden relief sometimes turns to feelings of elation and exhilaration when women who have repressed their own desires find themselves free to do as they please. Women in shelters often

rejoice at such commonplace events as going shopping, getting their hair done, or taking their children to the park without worrying about their husbands' reactions.

Boy, tomorrow I'm goin' downtown, and I've got my whole day planned out, and I'm gonna do what I wanna do, and if somebody doesn't like it, to Hell with them! You know, I'm having such a good time, I shoulda done this years ago!

The elation that accompanies freedom serves as a wellspring of positive action to begin a new life. The difficult tasks of finding a new home, getting divorced, and, often, finding a job are tackled with energies that had previously been directed toward "keeping the peace." As these activities begin, however, the self moves away from victimization. Active involvement with others to obtain one's own desires is inconsistent with the victimized self. The feelings and perceptions of self required to leave a violent marriage wither away as battered women begin to build a new self in a new situation.

CONCLUSION

Feeling victimized is for most individuals a temporary, transitory stage. There are good reasons for this. While it is of great importance for victimized individuals to achieve and create new understandings of their present and past, and while this itself alleviates some of the sufferings of victimization, there are certain incompatibilities between feeling victimized and being oriented toward practical actions to change one's situation in the world. Feeling victimized implies, for most persons, significant passivity in accepting external definitions and statuses. To change such a situation involves the individual in active, purposive, creative behavior. Since victimization represents a primordial threat to the self, individuals are highly motivated to change these circumstances, and these actions by themselves diminish the sense of victimization. The specific time frame for this transitory period varies. For most wars, revolutions, and social movements, it may be a matter of months or years. For individuals caught in the throes of a violent marriage for decades, the process may take longer, even the remainder of their lives. It makes little difference, however, whether or not the practical actions achieve "success," whether success is defined in terms of revolutionary victory, the success of a social-movement organization, or moving into a new relationship in which violent or abusive acts are absent. The very process of taking practical action inevitably diminishes the individual's sense of victimization and in many cases even brings the emotional career of the victimized self to an end.

There are both similarities and differences between the form of victimization described here and other forms. Battered children, for example, often reinterpret childhood abuse when they reach adulthood; these reinterpretations thus do not occur as the by-product of a turning point in the course of the abuse, as is the case in violent marriages. Those who are assaulted by strangers, such as victims of muggings or rapes, may experience the existential threat to the self in much the same way as battered women do, but there is no prior relationship to reinterpret as a consequence of assuming a victimized self. The feelings and perceptions of these other victimized selves remain largely unexplored. Future studies, detailing the cognitive and emotional experiences of various types of victims, would make possible a more complete, generalized analysis of the victimized self than can be gained by focusing only on battered women.

Reading 31   The Changing Concept of Child Abuse and Its Impact on the Integrity of Family Life*

JOHN M. JOHNSON

During the brief span of twenty-five years in the United States, the concept of child abuse has changed dramatically. It has gone from an obscure and hotly contested topic found in arcane medical journals to a position of routine mass-media publicity. Twenty-five years ago most medical doctors, including pediatricians, resisted the legitimacy of the child abuse concept. Today it is widely accepted and discussed by all professionals. It is widely discussed among the citizens as well, and even small schoolchildren talk about child abuse or neglect. Occasionally these children initiate reports to school or police officials, alleging injuries to themselves or others. Clearly these are indices of a massive social change that has occurred over a relatively short period of time.

The social changes concerning child abuse and neglect are intertwined with a "statistical explosion" of officially recognized and officially documented cases. This dramatic increase has led popular and scientific writers to assert a social problem of "epidemic" proportions. The first national study of the incidence of child abuse in the United States was done in 1962 by the American Humane Association. This study documented, for the first eleven months of 1962, a total of 662 cases that were serious enough to warrant some kind of court proceedings. We can thus, by extrapolation, place the 1962 incidence of child abuse at about 720 cases.[1]

The year 1963 marks the beginning of legislative initiative in the field of child abuse. The next decade saw much legislative, governmental, and programmatic action, with the establishment, at the end of the year, of the National Center on Child Abuse and Neglect. Their official statistics for 1973 show an incidence of about 60,000 officially recorded cases of child abuse, a national increase of over 8,300 percent in about ten years. Two years later they produced a national incidence of about 80,000 cases. And the 1976 study by the Department of Health, Education and Welfare put the annual rate at about a million new cases of child abuse and neglect. At the beginning of the 1980s in the United States, estimates of our incidence rate (number of new cases per year) for child abuse and neglect vary between 1 million to 4.5 million cases, and estimates of the prevalence (number of cases at any one time) are commonly two or three times that number. This is the "new math" of family violence in the United States.

Child maltreatment, now the more general term, includes child battering, abuse, neglect, failure to thrive, malnutrition, emotional abuse or neglect, sexual abuses, and a range of other acts or conditions. Child maltreatment is also today a large social movement that includes the activities of many groups: officials, professionals, media personalities, and private citizens. Partisans who promote the causes of the child maltreatment movement want us to think that the officially produced statistics on incidence and prevalence are objective, empirical facts. They wish us to think that a determination of child maltreatment is a scientific assessment made by a trained professional. They wish us to think that assessments of child maltreatment are done without regard to the assessor's values, and that the official statistics are collected without regard for political definitions or realities. But these are the rhetorical promotions of those with partisan interests in this area, those who wish to enlist our support for the political reality they have constructed since the early 1960s. None of these rhetorical claims can be supported by the facts.

Child maltreatment is not an unproblematic, empirical fact. It is a political definition of state legislatures. State officials are the ones mandated by law to respond to and bureaucratically process the child maltreatment claims brought to their attention. They are the ones who take the immediate, practical action in specific cases. They do so on the basis of their professional, bureaucratic, and personal values, as mitigated by situational constraints and resource practicalities. The national incidence and prevalence statistics on child maltreatment do not make any intelligible sense, because they combine incomparable state political definitions and practical decisions by bureaucratic officials at the local level. To understand the proper context of the present situation, it is important to gain a historical perspective on how children have been treated over the centuries. Such a historical perspective not only produces a sense of the relativity of judgments concerning child maltreatment but—and this is more important—provides a grasp of the essentially political and normative nature of a phenomenon so commonly presented as something else. The beating of children is an old phenomenon, but child maltreatment as a social movement that has mapped out new mandates for state authority and intervention is a relatively new phenomenon.

THE ORIGINS OF CHILDHOOD

Today it is taken for granted that "childhood" is a distinct, and even special, state of life. While the centuries have witnessed relatively little change in the manner by which infants and small children have biologically and physically grown, the social and cultural meanings associated with and imputed to "childhood" have changed greatly over time. For about 90 percent of all human history for which there are some records, societies have condoned and practiced infanticide, the intentional killing of infants. Infanticide was practiced for reasons of birth control, religious ceremony, or social policy. The earliest historical records of infanticide date to 7,000 B.C. in Jericho.[2] Infanticide was practiced for well over 8,000 years, and began to disappear only during the Middle Ages. In ancient Sparta, a public official examined newborns to attest to their health and worthiness to draw upon limited societal resources. The unworthy were thrown into the "Valley of Infants." Roman law forbade the raising of deformed infants. Even in later centuries, when the Christian churches redefined and prohibited infanticide, it was practiced clandestinely, and deaths were attributed to "over-laying," or accidental suffocation by the mother.[3]

Recent laws prohibiting infanticide can be found as late as 1843 in Germany, 1870 in Russia, and 1875 in India. Today the practice is largely clandestine and unofficial.

After the Middle Ages, abandonment of infants emerged as a common practice in western cultures. Harris estimates that by 1820 in France about 40,000 infants per year were being legally abandoned by their parents.[4] In the United States the New York Foundling Asylum was established in 1869 to save abandoned infants, who numbered about 1,400 in 1873.[5]

The growth of Christianity is associated with the emergence and development of many forms of child "discipline." The Puritan concept held that newborns, like adults, were born into a state of sin and depravity; hence strict measures were needed to acquaint the young with the ways of God.[6] Physical punishment, restraint, bodily mutilations, whippings, beatings, and the use of many instruments to bring these about were considered "normal" for members of Western cultures between the 1700s and 1900s. Many of these practices and ideologies thrive today. Radbill observes, "It was always taken for granted that parents and guardians had every right to treat their children as they saw fit."[7] This was additionally emphasized by the following thumb rule from American common law:

> If one beats a child until it bleeds,
> then it will remember the words of
> its master. But if one beats it to death,
> then the law applies.[8]

The fundamental ambiguities of legal applications are illustrated by one of the most famous child maltreatment cases in history. In 1875 the American Society for the Prevention of Cruelty to *Animals* (ASPCA) in New York City was asked to intervene for the purpose of protecting Mary Ellen, a nine-year-old girl who had been neglected, beaten, and even slashed with scissors by her foster parents. Earlier efforts to intervene had failed, because the parental rights to child discipline had been heretofore considered absolute by the law. So the ASPCA was asked to intervene to protect Mary Ellen on the argument that she was a member of the animal kingdom, and thus the legitimate recipient of laws already on the books to protect animals. The case received wide media publicity, and paved the way for the founding of the Society for the Prevention of Cruelty to Children (SPCC) in 1876. In the following years, the SPCC emerged as one important element of the growing social movement to prohibit child labor; their efforts were thus directed more to the abuses by employers of children, and only rarely did they concern themselves with the abuses of natural parents. There would have been relatively little public sentiment for the latter at the time. There were 161 local chapters of the SPCC by the turn of the century. These were later consolidated into the Children's Division of the American Humane Association.

THE MODERN DISCOVERY OF CHILD ABUSE

Historical evidence presents a long record of child victimization. The first medical or scientific studies of parental "abuse," however, can be dated from the 1888 article on acute periosteal swelling by Dr. S. West.[9] Later there was the 1946 study by Dr. John Caffey, analyzing the relationship between long bone fractures and subdural hematoma, the hemorrhaging that follows a head injury.[10] These early studies appeared to produce little publicity or concern.

Two medical studies done during the 1950s gained greater recognition.[11] Both asserted, in effect, that certain patterns of traumatic childhood injuries were caused by parental irresponsibility, neglect, indifference, or immaturity. This was an important departure for the medical profession, which, at an earlier time, had interpreted similar injuries as the result of "unspecified" causes.

A watershed point occurred with the 1962 publication of an article, "The Battered Child Syndrome," by C. Henry Kempe and his colleagues at the University of Colorado Medical School.[12] This research, published in a most prestigious and respected medical journal, was accompanied by an official editorial asserting the seriousness of this new medical problem. The characteristic features of the syndrome included traumatic injuries to the head and long bones, commonly done to children under three years of age by parents who had themselves been beaten or abused as children. These parents commonly denied the mistreatment of their own children. The publication of this research article was an important step in legitimizing this problem as an appropriate area of medical intervention.[13] An interesting question is why the medical profession's policy and involvement occurred at this time rather than an earlier one. Pfohl[14] argues that the entrepreneurial efforts of the occupational group of pediatric radiologists were important elements of the social movement at this early stage.

EARLY LEGISLATION

One critical social movement organization is the American Humane Association. The AHA has been active in all phases of the child maltreatment movement from the very beginning. They have conducted research, drawn up early "model legislation" for all governmental levels, published and publicized research and program information, provided "expert witnesses" to state legislatures contemplating legislative initiatives, and served important gatekeeping and liaison functions among and between all the professions through their conferences, workshops, and other communications. Most of these activities occurred under the 24-year leadership of Vincent de Francis, a key figure in the child maltreatment movement. He was one of the participants in an important meeting that occurred in January 1962 in Washington, D.C., at the Department of Health, Education and Welfare (HEW). The purpose of this meeting was to begin exploring the possibility of federal and/or state legislation on child abuse. Included in this meeting were Children's Bureau and HEW officials, members of the pediatric section of the American Medical Association, de Francis of the American Humane Association, and some private parties.[15] The main thrust of this meeting was to encourage legislative initiative to protect medical doctors from potential legal action in cases where they made reports of child maltreatment.

An eventual outcome of the 1962 meeting was a draft of "model legislation," which could be taken back to state legislatures, concerning child abuse reporting, liabilities, mandates, and responsibilities. The year 1963 is an important one for child abuse legislation, as eighteen states proposed and eleven states passed enabling bills on child abuse. During the next two years, thirty-six more states followed, and within the first five years fifty of the U.S. states and territories passed some form of child abuse legislation. This is an impressive social change to occur in such a relatively short period of time. It is interesting to contrast the child abuse legislation with the efforts to pass the Equal Rights Amendment (ERA), which failed to gain the needed two-thirds majority required for a constitutional amendment within a period of *ten years.* The contrast shows that, unlike the hotly contested and disputed ERA, child abuse and neglect are "least common denominator social problems" for large numbers of the American public, involving few conflicts and heated confrontations.[16] They are the kinds of problems everyone can be against. The prevailing definitions and realities of child maltreatment and the appropriate policy response are not contested by the major political parties, ideological positions, major churches, or professional and educational institutions.

As legal phenomena, child abuse and neglect are defined at the *state* level of government and, as with most other state definitions, the statutory concepts and mandates differ greatly from one jurisdiction to another. The early legislation generally mandated the *reporting* by physicians of child abuse or neglect. Many states established penalties for failures to report suspected cases. The new laws at first included few changes to existing statutes concerning delinquency, dependency, neglect, and criminal penalties. Since the early legislative period (1963–65), however, all of the state laws have been changed, modified, or revised on these and many other crucial issues.

THE AMBIGUOUS POLITICAL DEFINITIONS OF ABUSE

By 1965, reporting of child abuse and neglect had been mandated by forty-three of the fifty states.[17] By 1967, forty-nine states had the new laws.[18] As a reasonable assumption, one might think that if something is against the law, and hence the subject of potential legal sanction, the phenomenon in question would be clearly defined. How could officials (or professionals) define, identify, or classify something if the law requiring their identifications did not define it? But this is precisely the case for child abuse and neglect. By 1974, only eighteen of the fifty-three states and U.S. territories specifically defined child abuse and neglect in their statutes.[19] The state laws reflect very little consensus on even the most fundamental terms. The 1975 analysis by Sanford Katz observed the following:

A large majority of the jurisdictions (45) do not have a statutory definition for the term "neglect" and/or "neglected child." Only eight states define "neglect".... and less than half of the jurisdiction (22) have a "neglected child" definition.... Twenty-three states use some other definition to refer to a "neglected child," such as "deprived child," "dependent or neglected," or "dependent child."[20]

On common sense grounds, it is easy to understand how a perception of child neglect" might be intertwined with an observer's personal values, since a judgment of "neglect" implies a concept of a "normal home," which is subject to great ambiguity. A physical child battery, however, is hardly less ambiguous or problematic. Western legal traditions have long assessed legal culpability on the basis of determining the *intention* to commit an act. If it can be determined that an individual was fully and legally capable of intending his or her actions, and did in fact do so on a given occasion, then we properly hold that individual accountable for his or her action. If, by contrast, the individual was not capable of intending the action, whether because of reduced capacity, insanity, or mental illness, he or she is held blameless, even for the same action. If the individual is judged capable of forming intentions, but found by a judicial process not to have done so on a specific occasion, then the individual is held blameless. Examples of the latter may be "accidents," that is, events that may indeed produce harmful consequences, even death, but where the judgment is that the act was not a willful or intentional one. The determination of the caretakers' intention is not just one of many factors to be considered in making an assessment about child battering; it is *definitive*. It is only possible to distinguish a "child battery" from an "accident" by making an assessment of the caretakers' intention to do the act. As an internal mental state of the individual at the time of engaging in an act, intent is not directly observable by an outsider, and is thus inherently problematic (or uncertain). An added complication is that those who are called in to investigate claims about child abuse are invariably called in after the fact, when direct evidence of the actor's internal mental state is impossible, and indirect evidence often ambiguous, contradictory, or uncertain. For these and many other reasons, then, even the assessments of a physical beating are commonly very problematic ones.

It is easier to formulate and operationalize an abstract definition when one is dealing with a more restricted phenomenon, such as a physical battery. New levels of complexity and ambiguity are introduced when the focus is more broad, as in "child neglect." For neglect, again, the issues surrounding definition are of primary importance and logically take precedence over epidemiological or etiological questions. Nevertheless, there is no agreement about the parameters of child neglect. In some respects the definition of neglect is of greater significance than that of battering or abuse, since informed "guesstimates" place the ratio of neglect to abuse cases from three-to-one[21] to ten-to-one.[22] Guesstimates such as these commonly sidestep the logically and empirically prior question of definition by taking as an instance of neglect anything so defined by officials at the local levels, by whatever criteria they may have used.

Those who focus on neglect emphasize either the condition(s) of the parent(s), such as alcoholism, drug abuse, or psychological problems, or some specific harm to the children, such as an identifiable physical or psychological harm. To be neglectful means that the parent has failed in some manner to exercise responsibility over those means within their control. This latter idea about control introduces another level of discretionary judgment into an already complex

equation. What about the family that is trying conscientiously and sincerely to provide the basic necessities, but is still unable to do so because of their present condition of poverty, illness, or unemployment? To what extent is their poverty or employment status "within their control"? How does one judge "conscientious" or "sincere" in such a situation? Officials and professionals who routinely make such assessments play an important "gatekeeping" role in the screening of potential child neglect cases.[23] Many studies now show that various kinds of racial, ethnic, social class, and occupational biases creep into such assessments, with the general finding being that official gatekeepers are more likely to "normalize" those persons, behaviors, and situations seen as close to their own lives or circumstances, but are more likely to officially label and bureaucratically process those experienced as more remote from them.[24] This is one of the important factors accounting for the usual overrepresentation of poor and minority persons in official caseloads.[25]

Few states have clear definitions, as we have seen. And there is certainly no agreement between states on definitions. Despite this, however, there have been several important changes to the child abuse and neglect laws since the 1963–65 period of legislative initiative. These changes have occurred in all states. By the 1980s, states have changed, modified, or revised their child abuse and neglect laws two or three times in most cases. One important change concerns the progressive expansion of the mandate to report suspected cases of abuse or neglect. Whereas the early laws commonly required only physicians to report, most laws today require many other professionals as well—any physician (including interns and residents), surgeon, dentist, osteopath, chiropractor, podiatrist, nurse, druggist, pharmacist, laboratory technician, acupuncturist, schoolteacher or school administrator, social worker, and/or "any other person."

Another important change involves the increase in the penalties for not reporting. Granting immunity from criminal or civil liability for those who report suspected cases of abuse or neglect is another critical change, now found in all of the state laws. Also, granting doctors and other professionals waivers from the legal or ethical restrictions against revealing confidential communications represents another way by which the law has been changed to encourage reporting to and processing by official, bureaucratic agencies. There have been some other legal changes, too, including revisions of the evidentiary criteria to be used in court cases involving abuse or neglect. These changes have for the most part enhanced and facilitated organizational goals rather than individual or family rights.

Providing incentives as well as sanctions to report abuse and neglect cases, while at the same time ignoring critical matters of defining what it is that is to be reported, has produced many ironic results at local and state levels. After the passage of new laws at the state level, it is common for local and state agencies to experience an initial short-term rate increase of several hundred, even several thousand, percent.[26] This has been observed for crime rates as well, and on many occasions, those cities or states with the highest crime rates are those in the process of rationalizing their reporting procedures, or in the process of documenting some "need" for federal or state financial assistance. For child maltreatment, such short-term increases often overwhelm the local bureaucratic resources for responding to or investigating new reports. Such a situation greatly increases the chances of making a "Type II error," that is, failing to diagnose child abuse or neglect when it is in fact present.[27] In given local situations, this may mean that the efforts to stop child maltreatment through enhanced reporting efforts may cause deleterious consequences that may have been otherwise

avoided. The bureaucratic welfare state produces many such ironies.

Child maltreatment is not some symptomatic feature of American society, or even of the 1960s and 1970s, but *allegations* of mass maltreatment arose during those two decades. Child maltreatment is thus more usefully seen as a social movement, one that has achieved success at several levels. As such, the current movement is a recent manifestation of the earlier "child saving" movement,[28] a turn-of-the-century moral crusade that asserted the symbolic dominance of middle-class, Christian values. Moral crusades are an indisputable tradition in American history.

The child maltreatment social movement achieved many successes at various state and local levels, as we have seen. The greatest success, however, and the greatest impetus for the movement, came with the 1974 passage of federal legislation: the Child Abuse Prevention and Treatment Act, also informally known as the "Mondale Bill" after its primary sponsor. This federal law (PL. 93-247) established a National Center on Child Abuse and Neglect, located within the Department of Health, Education and Welfare. The official mandates of the National Center included changes to conduct research on the causes, incidence, and prevalence of child abuse and neglect, and also to compile and publish a summary of pertinent knowledge in this field.[29] It is additionally important to understand that this bill provided $85 million of resources for the child maltreatment movement over a four-year period. This money was spent for research, publication, and program initiative. The latter typically occurred under the auspices of a "demonstration project," whereby the federal government would provide the "seed money" to get a program started and operational for a specified period, usually two to three years, on the theory that once program effectiveness had been established, local funding sources would then step in to continue the program. The $85 million provided a major resource leading to the institutionalization of the child maltreatment social movement. New programs dealing with child maltreatment were started in hospitals,[30] clinics,[31] volunteer programs,[32] day care centers,[33] and entire communities.[34] Programs such as these greatly enhanced local officials' abilities to gain contact with heretofore undefined abuse or neglect cases, through the mechanisms the practitioners term "case finding." And they also greatly enhanced the gatekeeping role of decision makers in local agencies.

AGENCY SCREENING AND CASE FINDING

A somewhat naive view about child abuse and its relationship to community agencies assumes that what is called child abuse or neglect is relatively straightforward and unproblematic. Abuse and neglect are seen to define specific acts, with "abusive" and "neglectful" being considered characteristics of specific individuals who engage in them. Community agencies are assumed to adopt a passive or reactive response to abusive or neglectful acts that precede their interventions in space and time. Community agencies are thought to represent a functional response to the problem, tending to control it.

The available evidence fails to support any of the above assumptions. The formal definitions of abuse and neglect are very ambiguous and problematic. There is very little agreement on the meanings of maltreatment even among the professionals who intervene in such cases. An early study of Viano[35] found dissimilar attitudes and perceptions among the professionals involved. More recently, a very thorough research project found significant differences in the perceptions of child abuse and neglect between the four major occupational groups involved in the investigation, identification, and

treatment of maltreatment cases: police, social workers, lawyers, and pediatricians.[36] Some of these differences appeared to be related to the different occupational tasks the professionals commonly performed. This understanding is what led Gelles to propose that "the occupational and organizational mandate of a community agency determines how active it will be in identifying cases of child abuse, how likely the employees of the agency are to label particular cases abuse, and the types of cases which are labeled abuse."[37]

The various occupational groups that find themselves in a situation of receiving, investigating, or otherwise processing child maltreatment cases develop an "occupational ideology" about those cases. This ideology includes a set of perceptions, thoughts, feelings, values, and work experiences that become taken for granted by those in a given work setting. The traditional ideology of social workers tends to be supportive and humanitarian, for example, whereas police and prosecutors tend to be more punitive and legalistic in their orientation.[38] Whatever the abstract or ideological values, however, virtually all child abuse screening occurs in some kind of *organizational context*. This commonly involves sets of formal and informal rules that are routinely used to organize work tasks, recipe knowledge of "the way we do things around here," and limited resources to pursue one course of action over another. Such considerations form a practical work context for all decisions, often determining what gets done in specific instances, even independently of other professional or occupational values. Child protective service professionals may investigate a claim of child neglect and determine that the removal of the child is warranted, for example. But perhaps, at that moment, there are no resources available to effect such a decision (such as emergency or regular foster homes). In such a situation, the placement of the child is highly unlikely, unless the case involves an immediate threat to life, which is rare, or the potential for media publicity.

Child maltreatment investigations in public agencies are always made within a context of limited time and resources. Rare exceptions to this involve those "child abuse horror stories" that receive disproportionate mass media publicity.[39] These involve dramatic injuries or circumstances. One example originated from Cleveland, Tennessee, where a father forced his three-year-old daughter to remain awake and walking for three days. When she asked for water, he forced Tabasco sauce down her throat and stomped on her feet. She died of exhaustion. Another case, out of Long Beach, California, involved the discovery of a seven-year-old girl who had been tied to a chair in her room for her entire life. She had been forced to sleep in her own feces; when found, she weighted only 35 pounds and was unable to talk. A third case, from Los Angeles, involved an infant found to have more than 600 cigarette burns over her body. These are the dramatic, horrible child abuse cases. When they occur, there is usually an instantaneous consensus about what should be done to save the child from immediate danger. But these dramatic cases are statistically very rare, and their unrepresentative publication via the mass media presents a distorted picture of the more routinely encountered cases.

The usual child maltreatment cases routinely encountered in the everyday operations of official agencies tend to involve ambiguities, uncertainties, conflicting accounts about what occurred (or why), nonserious injuries, and living conditions that render judgments cloudy. For these kinds of cases, which clearly constitute the overwhelming statistical majority as well as the dominant work tasks of those confronted with them, there is much room for discretion. Police, emergency room physicians, child protective services' social workers, public health nurses,

and others who receive allegations of abuse or neglect essentially serve as "gatekeepers," determining which cases will be screened in or out of the system. At all levels the discretion is great, and decisions are essentially free of review. Officials who make these determinations do so on the bases of their occupational ideology, personal values, and immediate practical situation within the bureaucratic organization. In a situation such as this, an uncanny correspondence exists between the official assessments and the resources available at the moment to "do something."

The gatekeeping functions of local agency decisions are illustrated by the concept of "case finding." This refers to the entrepreneurial initiative exercised by officials to recruit new cases, which would not otherwise be there, into the child protective services' caseloads. Case finding is a concept well known to social work professionals. References to the practice can be found throughout the academic and professional literature. Large numbers of social workers and other health services workers openly advocate the discovery and recruitment of new cases through case finding, on the theory that this is a way to bring needed services to those who either would not know to ask about them or who might be mistaken about whether such interventions would serve their best interests. The very concept and practice of case finding, however, disproves the naive view that officials only passively respond to reports that predate their interventions.

One needs hardly to emphasize that large numbers of citizens do not share the naive view about official interventions in child maltreatment cases. Many individuals and families feel a great sense of injustice concerning the official investigations or interventions in their lives. Such feelings have been common in many minority communities for decades now. In such communities a feeling of discrimination and injustice has persisted for years. The available research tends to support this feeling, showing that official decision-making processes recruit disproportionate numbers of poor and minority families into their caseloads. With respect to decisions on specific cases, perhaps there have always been a few instances of officials who make "Type I errors," that is, who incorrectly label someone a child abuser. But in recent years these numbers have grown to the point where aggrieved parties have organized for counteraction. In Phoenix, Arizona, for example, there is a group known as PAPS, or Parents Against Protective Services. The founders of this group claim a membership of about 2,200 parents who have been angered by the treatment they have received at the hands of child protective services. The very existence of such organizations carries important implications. It shows that the steadily increasing power of the state to intervene in family life has reached such a point that organized opposition to it has developed. It also indicates that the state interventions now extend considerably beyond the traditional target groups for official social control: the poor and certain ethnic communities.

THE IMPACT OF THE CHILD MALTREATMENT MOVEMENT ON THE INTEGRITY OF FAMILY LIFE

All persons familiar with the current facts on child abuse and neglect express agreement on this important point: Existing definitions are imprecise and ambiguous, and there is no consensus about their meanings. What remains hotly disputed, however, is whether this state of affairs represents a desirable or undesirable situation. Those who see advantages to the open-ended nature of the definitions, for example, argue that this permits the flexibility needed to "individualize" decision making in specific

cases. A respected scholar in the field of family law, Harry Krause, argues as follows:

> *Due to the varied nature of the situations to be covered, the neglect and dependency laws are rarely specific. A legal finding of neglect typically is a composite of many factors and requires a highly individualized judgment on all of the circumstances of each specific case. Statutes* need *to be flexible to provide the necessary broad discretion to the courts.*[40]

Advocates of the "open definition" consider it advantageous because decision makers can be sensitive to contextual, local, and emergent features of the situation. There is an implicit assumption here, however, that officials not only act in good faith, but with the "best interests" of the community foremost in mind at all times. At this stage in our history, such claims are more usefully seen as just ignorant—or as self-interested claims by those who wish to extend the powers and authorities of the welfare state, in what they must presume to be their own best interests.

Opponents of "open definitions" are less sanguine about official good faith and judicial wisdom. They tend to emphasize the potential for injustice that resides in statutory ambiguity and official discretion. Michael Wald, who drafted the child protective model legislation promoted by the American Bar Association, is one who advocates such a stance:

> *Most state statutes define neglect in broad, vague language, which would seem to allow virtually unlimited intervention.... The definitions of neglect offered by legal scholars are equally broad.... The absence of precise standards for state intervention is said to be a necessity, even a*

virtue. . . . It is both possible and desirable to define neglect in more specific terms and with reference to the types of damage that justify intervention. . . . Vague laws increase the likelihood that decisions to intervene will be made in situations where the child will be harmed by intervention. Because the statutes do not reflect a considered analysis of what types of harm justify the risk of intervention, decision making is left to the ad hoc analysis of social workers and judges. . . . Their decisions often reflect personal values about children which are not supported by scientific evidence and which result in removing children from environments in which they are doing adequately. Only through carefully drawn statutes, drafted in terms of specific harms to the child, can we limit the possibility of intervention in situations where it would do more harm than good .[41]

These continuing disputes about definitions and the proper authority for state intervention have important consequences. They also provide evidence of the critical impact of the child maltreatment movement on American family life. Never before in history has the power of the state expanded so rapidly into the domain of the family. Never before have so many of the traditional rights and obligations of family life eroded so rapidly. Never before have so many families been caught up in the net of official investigation and case processing, our best estimates today tell us that about 1 million U.S. families receive an official investigation that results in a *substantiated* claim of abuse or neglect *each year.*[42] Several million others are investigated by official agents, which is in and of itself a great source of

anxiety, stress, conflict, and stigma. The legal custody and control of children has been taken away from more and more parents through court proceedings, although there is some evidence that these trends are reversing in more recent years. More and more children are now removed from their homes and "placed" in a foster home or other institution; one needs only the most superficial familiarity with this situation to see that such placement decisions tend to follow resource availability; that is, as new facilities or resources are added to the institutional network, more and more of these placement decisions are seen by officials as "needed," or even "necessary."

We are forever interested in the questions about how our society compares to others, or whether the times we live in are better or worse than before. Is there more or less justice for families today? Is the family stronger or weaker? Are our policies more or less humane? These are often the important questions that animate our academic and research interests. Unfortunately perhaps, the evidence about all of these issues is mixed. A historical perspective tends to produce a complex, mixed judgment. Certainly we no longer practice the forms of infanticide, abandonment, enslavement, bodily mutilation, or severe corporal discipline so common throughout history. Most people would see this as representing an improved, more humane condition. On the question of state authority and intervention in family life, the evidence is again mixed. The United States no longer invests forms of virtually unreviewed discretion as we find in the office of the tithingman in Massachusetts in the 1670s, who was given the mandate to personally inspect local families for their moral rectitude and religious obedience.[43] We no longer condone the removal of children from their families, by private parties, without any due process or legal hearing, to be given or sold to other families. Yet this was a sanctioned policy of U.S.

Societies for the Prevention of Pauperism at the turn of the century.[44] When seen in this context, perhaps some of the recent legal cases concerning child maltreatment may be judged more humane.

Historical relativism provides a necessary view, but it should not produce in us a paralysis of perspective or action. There is little doubt that basic family relations are once again caught in the throes of social change, and that the integrity of family life is threatened in new and fundamentally different ways. The recent experience with the Child Maltreatment Movement in the United States forces on us one inescapable conclusion: We must stop thinking that governmental actions merely represent functional responses to family problems, tending to control them. Recent empirical evidence leads us to see that governmental efforts may serve to create and sustain some kinds of problems, and specifically in the case of official interventions into family life, they may make problems worse for the individuals involved. This realization produces a new circumspection and caution about the role of governmental action in resolving family problems, and paves the way for more informed political action.

Reading 32   Karla and the Armstrongs: Two Oral Histories of Homeless American Families*

STEVEN VANDERSTAAY

KARLA—ST. LOUIS, MISSOURI

*"We'll start with what happened,"
Karla begins. Young, bright, a mother
of two children, she is part of a
growing phenomenon: single-parent
mothers on assistance who cannot
afford a place to live.*

*Cities handle such families dif-
ferently. New York City houses many
women like Karla in so-called welfare hotels, while other cities place
them in barracks-style emergency
shelters or housing projects. Karla
could find nowhere to go.*

*Karla is an African American in
her twenties. We met at a Salvation
Army shelter for homeless families.*

I was working up until the time I had my
second baby. I lived with my mom but we
weren't getting along. She took care of the first
child but the second, that was too much. Then
she felt that once I had the children . . . well, her
words were, "Two grown ladies can never manage in the same house." So I got on AFDC and
went to stay with my littlest girl's aunt.

Well, three weeks ago now, her landlord
called and said the building didn't pass inspection. See, the building was infested with bugs
and mice.

I didn't have any money saved 'cause I was
spending all the AFDC and food stamps on us. I
do have qualifications for a lot of jobs, but
they're all $3.35. And it's not worth getting a job
where you have no medical or dental insurance,
not if you have kids. It's not worth giving up
welfare. I would work at $3.35 if they let me
keep Medicaid and the food stamps, but they
don't. They'll cut you off.

But AFDC's not enough to live on either. I
started looking for another place but all the
apartments I could afford were just like the one
we were living in. It wasn't worth leaving one
condemnation to go to another.

Then my daughter's aunt, she moved in with
her sister. There was no way I could afford an
apartment on my own, not and eat too—and like I
said, they were all as bad as the first place. So me
and the kids—I have a 3-year-old and a 9-month-
old—we just stayed in the building. They boarded
it up but we got in through the back window.

There was this older lady that lived next
door. We were friends and if she could have

*Vanderstaay, Steven. 1992. "'Karla' & 'The Armstrongs, Mark and Linda.'" Pp. 170–176 in *Street Lives: An Oral His-
tory of Homeless Americans.* Philadelphia, PA: New Society Publishers, 4527 Springfield Ave., Phila., PA. Reprinted
with permission.

416

helped me she would have. But she already had her four grown kids, plus their kids, livin' with her in a two-bedroom apartment. There's a lot of that these days.

She gave us blankets, though, and I wrapped us up in them. We'd stay outside all day, do something—go to the library or I'd take 'em to the museum. Something. Nights we'd go back into the apartment, light candles, and sleep.

Then it rained real bad. And it was cold. The electrical was off, the gas was off, we were going by candlelight. Mice and rats came out really bad. I woke up one morning and there was a mouse on my 9-month-old's head . . . we couldn't stay in there.

So we went outside, walked around all day. Night came and we slept in a car I found. We were wet and both my kids caught a cold real bad. I took 'em to the emergency room and we slept at the hospital.

The next night we were in this laundromat . . . it was so awful. I was crying, the kids were still sick. And my oldest, Robert, he asked a lot of questions. "Momma, why did we sleep in the car? Why are we outside? It's raining, Momma, I'm cold. I don't feel good."

I couldn't explain. And we had been out for the last three days, never being able to rest. He hadn't eaten anything that night 'cause I didn't have any more money.

Then the man at the laundromat, he gave me $4 to get Robert something to eat. And I stole my baby a can of milk.

THE ARMSTRONGS, MARK AND LINDA— SEATTLE, WASHINGTON

The Armstrongs lived in Bellevue, a young, largely affluent city east of Seattle, until a medical emergency and the sudden loss of Mark's job forced the family to seek emergency housing.

Since Bellevue has little emergency housing, the Armstrongs were advised to seek shelter in nearby Seattle. Eventually, the family was moved to a large public housing project in the city's Central District. Each morning they awake at 5:00 for the long bus ride back to Bellevue for work and school.

Mark and Linda both work, as do their teenage children. Speaking to them, I am struck that they are the quintessential American family: hardworking, supportive, patriotic, loving. And now homeless. The Armstrongs' difficulties—underemployment, housing, grocery bills, health costs, insurance problems—mirror those of other homeless families driven from affluent communities.

They are African Americans in their early thirties.

Mark:

I designed and built conveyor belts, and was good at it. I was making over $15 an hour. And I can go back there right now and get you a letter of recommendation from the company and let you read what they wrote about me. That in itself tells you what kind of worker I am.

The company went out of business. Bang! Didn't even know it was coming. I was between jobs three or four months. I could have found work right away if I wanted to make minimum wage, but I got pretty high standards for myself. I don't even want to make what I'm making now. We could barely afford rent then, how can we now? But when you got kids to feed and bills to pay, you have to do the best you can.

But minimum wage—that's insulting. I don't knock it for high school students. They're getting training, learning about working, making their pocket money. That's fine. But you take a person . . . I got six kids. $3.35, $4 an hour, I spend more than that wage in a day's time on a grocery bill. I mean you can accept some setbacks, but you can't tell a person, "I don't care if you've been making $15 something an hour, the minimum is what you've got to make now." If I hand you this letter, give you my resumé, my military record, show you the kind of worker I am, talk about my family, how can you degrade me by offering me the minimum wage?

Then we had trouble with the house we were renting. And, well, the biggest part of it was hospital bills. My son had to have emergency surgery. Since the company was going out of business it let the insurance lapse, so I got stuck with the bill. Spent every penny we had saved and there's still fourteen hundred dollars on it. You would think by being medical that it wouldn't affect the credit, but it does.

Now I'm working with Safeway's warehouse. I work in the milk plant. Swing shift. Sometimes I'm off at 12:30, 1:00 at night, and then turn right around and go back at 8:30 the next morning. Yeah, it's hard sometimes. I'm not making half of what I used to. I'm a helper—I used to have people working for me. I'd worked my way up through the ranks. But like I was saying, you adjust, you do what you have to do. I'm the kind of person, I get with a company I want to stay, be a part of it. I like to get along with people and work, get my hands dirty. See something accomplished. I'm low man on the totem pole but I'll stay and work my way up.

The warehouse, it's refrigerated on one end and kind of hot on the other. They make their own milk cartons out of plastic so you have to deal with heat and cold. You have to know how to dress 'cause you're dealing with both extremes.

Linda:

I've been a custodian, nurse's aid; now I work at K-Mart. I still have to bus back to the East side [Bellevue] every day. It's okay but I'm looking for something else. You know, it's $4 an hour, and there's no benefits, no discounts at the store, nothing like that.

And I'm in school now, too. I'm going for business training, probably computers or administration. When school starts I'll either bring the little ones there with me or have one of the older ones bring them home.

Working full-time and going to school. Six kids, seventeen on down to twelve. Three in high school, three in grade school. Two of them work at Jack in the Box. They've been working the same shift but my oldest, he's on the football team, so he might be working at a different time than my daughter. And then there's the church, and those football games. Yes we're busy! Just an all-American family. One that's hit a string of bad luck, that's all.

The hardest thing is getting up early enough to bus back over there. As soon as school gets started that's really going to be a problem. It might be a couple of hours, both ways. And if they find out our kids are living here they'll want them in school in Seattle. But they like the schools there and I like them. They're better. And that's where we've lived, that's where we work.

But we get by. The kids, they cook, they clean, they wash and iron their own clothes. And the older ones, they all work. We're so proud of them. Oh, we have the same problems everybody else has, with teenagers and so forth. But we get through 'em. Just thank God they're not on drugs. That's the biggest problem here.

Mark:

When we had to move and lost the house, when I lost my job, we told the kids the truth, the flat out truth. With no misconception; none whatsoever. Kids are not dumb. If you lie to kids, why should they be honest with you? They know exactly what we're going through and they know why.

Same thing when we moved here—six kids, three rooms, writing all over the walls, the drugs and crime. We tried to avoid the move but we didn't have any choice. They knew exactly where we were moving to, as best as I could explain it. We told them we didn't want to come, but if it came down to it we were coming. And we did.

Now my worst fear...there's so much drugs in this area. And people think every apartment in the projects is a drug house. They knock on the doors, knock on the windows—they stop me out there and ask where it is. It's here, so close to us all the times. And all the shooting and fighting...you can look out the window any given night and see the police stopping people and searching everyone.

If I can't look out my door and see my kids, I send for 'em. And I'm afraid when I can't see 'em. 'Cause when they get to shootin' and fightin' and carryin'-on a bullet don't got no names on it. Sometimes when I come in from work, three, four o'clock in the morning, I wonder just when they're going to get me. But my worst fear, my worst fear is the kids.

Linda:

Over in Bellevue they think if you can't afford it then you shouldn't be there. You know, who cares if you work there.

The first house that we had, we were the first blacks in the neighborhood. When I moved over there I said, "Where the black people?" [laughs, then moves her head from side to side as if searching]...no black people? Then the neighbors, they got to looking, came out, they were surprised, too. "Oooh, we got black people over here now" [laughs]. The kids were the only black kids around.

Mark:

People don't want to rent to a family. And you know the kind of rent they're asking over there

in Bellevue, that's not easy to come up with. And you need first, last month's rent, security.... And then people automatically assess, they stereotype you. Maybe sometimes it's 'cause we're black—I'm not saying this is true, I'm saying that sometimes I *felt* that the reason we didn't get a place was because we were black. But most of the time it's the family. People would rather you have pets than kids these days.

One guy, he had six bedrooms in this house. But he didn't want a family. Why would you have six bedrooms if you didn't want to rent to a family? May not be legal, but they do that all the time.

Now there is some validity in what they say about children tearing up things. But the child is only as bad as you let him be. You're the parent, he's going to do exactly what you let him do and get away with. If my kids tear something up I'll pay for it. But me, I tell my kids that if I have to replace something they've destroyed, then one of their sisters or brothers isn't going to get something they need. And when they do something they answer to me.

I'm not bitter...I mean I'm somewhat so. I'm not angry bitter. It's just that I don't like dragging my kids from one place to the next, and I don't think we've been treated right. We had to take places sight-unseen, just to get 'em. We paid $950 a month, and during the wintertime $300, $400 a month for electric and gas bills. Then bought food, kept my kids in clothes. How you supposed to save to get ahead with all that?

And the house, when we moved in the landlords said they'd do this and that, fix this and that. Said we would have an option to buy it. We said, "Okay, and we'll do these things." We had an agreement.

We never got that chance to buy, and they never fixed those things. But we kept paying that $950 a month. They had a barrel over us: we needed some place to go. And they made a small fortune those years. A month after we moved out we went by: all those things they wouldn't do were done.

Before that the guy decided to sell his house, just like that, and we had to move. It was December, wintertime. For a while we were staying with her mother in a two-bedroom. Nine people. We had to be somewhere so we took that second place before we had even seen it.

Everybody has to have a place to live. And people will do what they have to do to survive. A lot of things that you see going on around here are for survival [he sweeps his hand, indicating the housing projects]. I'm not taking up for them, there's a lot of things happening here that I oppose. But where there's a will there's a way, you know.

Divorce, Single Parenthood, and Remarriage

Reading 33   Uncoupling: The Social Construction of Divorce*

DIANE VAUGHAN

Berger and Kellner (1964) describe marriage as a definitional process: two autonomous individuals come together with separate and distinct biographies and begin to construct for themselves a subworld in which they will live as a couple. A redefinition of self occurs as the autonomous identity of the two individuals involved is reconstructed as a mutual identity. This redefinition is externally anticipated and socially legitimated before it actually occurs in the individual's biography.

Previously, significant conversation for each partner came from nonoverlapping circles, and self-realization came from other sources. Together, they begin to construct a private sphere where all significant conversation centers in their relationship with the other. The coupled identity becomes the main source of their self-realization. Their definitions of reality become correlated, for each partner's actions must be projected in conjunction with the other. As their worlds come to be defined around a relationship with a significant other who becomes *the* significant other, all other significant relationships have to be reperceived, regrouped. The result is the construction of a joint biography and a mutually coordinated common memory.

Were this construction of a coupled identity left only to the two participants, the coupling would be precarious indeed. However, the new reality is reinforced through objectivation, that is, "a process by which subjectively experienced meanings become objective to the individual, and, in interaction with others, become common property, and thereby massively objective" (Berger and Kellner 1964, p. 6). Hence, through the use of language in conversation with significant others, the reality of the coupling is constantly validated.

Of perhaps greater significance is that this definition of coupledness becomes taken for granted and is validated again and again, not by explicit articulation, but by conversing around the agreed [upon] definition of reality that has been created. In this way a consistent reality is maintained, ordering the individual's world in such a way that it validates his identity. Marriage, according to Berger and Kellner, is a constructed reality which is "nomosbuilding" (1964, p. 1). That is, it is a social arrangement that contributes order to individual lives, and therefore should be considered as a significant validating relationship for adults in our society.

Social relationships, however, are seldom static. Not only do we move in and out of relationships, but the nature of a particular relationship, though enduring, varies over time. Given that the definitions we create become socially validated and hence constraining, *how do individuals move from a mutual identity, as in marriage, to assume separate, autonomous identities again?* What is the process by which new definitions are created and become validated?

The Berger and Kellner analysis describes a number of interrelated yet distinguishable stages that are involved in the social construction of a mutual identity; for example, the regrouping of all other significant relationships. In much the same way, the *demise* of a relationship should involve distinguishable social processes. Since redefinition of self is basic to both movement into and out of relationships, the social construction of a singular identity also should follow the patterns suggested by Berger and Kellner. This paper is a qualitative examination of this process. Hence, the description that follows bears an implicit test of Berger and Kellner's ideas.

The dimensions of sorrow, anger, personal disorganization, fear, loneliness, and ambiguity that intermingle every separation are well known.[1] Their familiarity does not diminish their importance. Though in real life these cannot be ignored, the researcher has the luxury of selectivity. Here, it is not the pain and disorganization that are to be explored, but the existence of an underlying orderliness.

Though the focus is on divorce, the process examined appears to apply to *any* heterosexual relationship in which the participants have come to define themselves and be defined by others as a couple. The work is exploratory and, as such, not concerned with generalizability. However, the process may apply to homosexual couples as well. Therefore, the term "uncoupling" will be used because it is a more general concept than divorce. Uncoupling applies to the redefinition of self that occurs as mutual identity unravels

into singularity, regardless of marital status or sex of the participants.

The formal basis from which this paper developed was in-depth, exploratory interviews. The interviews, ranging from two to six hours, were taped and later analyzed. All of the interviewees were at different stages in the uncoupling process. Most were divorced, though some were still in stages of consideration of divorce. Two of the interviews were based on long-term relationships that never resulted in marriage. All of the relationships were heterosexual. The quality of these interviews has added much depth to the understanding of the separation process. The interviewees were of high intellectual and social level, and their sensitivity and insight have led to much valuable material, otherwise unavailable.

A more informal contribution to the paper comes from personal experiences and the experiences of close friends. Further corroboration has come from autobiographical accounts, newspapers, periodicals, and conversations, which have resulted in a large number of cases illustrating certain points. Additional support has come from individuals who have read or heard the paper with the intent of proving or disproving its contentions by reference to their own cases.

Since the declared purpose here is to abstract the essential features of the process of uncoupling, some simplification is necessary. The separation of a relationship can take several forms. To trace all of them is beyond the scope of this study. Therefore, to narrow the focus, we must first consider the possible variations.

Perhaps the coupled identity was not a major mechanism for self-validation from the outset of the union. Or the relationship may have at one time filled that function, but, as time passed, this coupled identity was insufficient to meet individual needs. Occasionally this fact has implications for both partners simultaneously, and the uncoupling process is initiated by both. More frequently, however, one partner still finds the marriage a major source of stability and identity, while the other finds it inadequate. In this form, one participant takes the role of initiator of the uncoupling process. However, this role may not consistently be held by one partner, but instead may alternate between them, due to the difficulty of uncoupling in the face of external constraints, social pressure not to be the one responsible for the demise of the marriage, and the variability in the self-validating function of the union over time. For the purpose of this study, the form of uncoupling under consideration is that which results when one partner, no longer finding the coupled identity self-validating, takes the role of initiator in the uncoupling process. The other partner, the significant other, still finds the marriage a major source of stability and identity.

UNCOUPLING: THE INITIATION OF THE PROCESS

I was never psychologically married. I always felt strained by attempts that coupled me into a marital unit. I was just never comfortable as "Mrs." I never got used to my last name. I never wanted it. The day after my marriage was probably the most depressed day of my life, because I had lost my singularity. The difference between marriage and a deep relationship, living together, is that you have this ritual, and you achieve a very definite status, and it was that that produced my reactions—because I became in the eyes of the world a man's wife. And I was never comfortable and happy with it. It didn't make any difference who the man was.

An early phase in the uncoupling process occurs as one or the other of the partners begins to question the coupled identity. At first internal, the challenging of the created world remains for a time as a doubt within one of the partners in the coupling. Though there is a definition of coupledness, subjectively the coupledness may be experienced differently by each partner. Frequently, these subjective meanings remain internal and unarticulated. Thus, similarly, the initial recognition of the coupling as problematic may be internal and unarticulated, held as a secret. The subworld that has been constructed, for some reason, doesn't "fit."

A process of definition negotiation is begun, initiated by the one who finds the mutual identity an inadequate definition of self. Attempts to negotiate the definition of the coupledness are likely to result in the subjective meaning becoming articulated for the first time, thus moving the redefinition process toward objectivation. The secret, held by the initiator, is shared with the significant other. When this occurs, it allows both participants to engage in the definitional process.

Though the issue is made "public" in that private sphere shared by the two, the initiator frequently finds that a lack of shared definitions of the coupled identity stalemates the negotiations. While the initiator defines the marriage as a problem, the other does not. The renegotiation of the coupled identity cannot proceed unless both agree that the subworld they have constructed needs to be redefined. Perhaps for the significant other, the marriage as it is still provides important self-validation. If so, the initiator must bring the other to the point of sharing a common definition of the marriage as "troubled."

ACCOMPANYING RECONSTRUCTIONS

Though this shared definition is being sought, the fact remains that, for the initiator, the coupled identity fails to provide self-validation.

In order to meet this need, the initiator engages in other attempts at redefining the nature of the relationship. Called "accompanying reconstructions," these *may* or *may not* be shared with the significant other. They may begin long before the "secret" of the troubled marriage is shared with the other, in an effort to make an uncomfortable situation more comfortable without disrupting the relationship. Or they may occur subsequent to sharing the secret with the significant other, as a reaction to the failure to redefine the coupledness satisfactorily. Time order for their occurrence is not easily imposed—thus, "accompanying reconstructions."

The initiator's accompanying reconstructions may be directed toward the redefinition of (1) the coupledness itself, (2) the identity of the significant other, or (3) the identity of the initiator. A change in definition of either of the three implies a change in at least one of the others. Though they are presented here separately, they are interactive rather than mutually exclusive and are not easily separable in real life.

The first form of accompanying reconstruction to be considered is the initiator's redefinition of the coupledness itself. One way of redefining the coupledness is by an unarticulated conversion of the agreed-upon norms of the relationship.

> *I had reconceptualized what marriage was. I decided sexual fidelity was not essential for marriage. I never told her that. And I didn't even have anyone I was interested in having that intimate a relationship with—I just did a philosophical thing. I just decided it was O.K. for me to have whatever of what quality of other relationship I needed to have. Something like that—of that caliber—was something I could never talk to her about. So I did it all by myself. I read things and decided*

> *it. I was at peace with me. I knew that we could stay married, whatever that meant. O.K., I can stay legally tied to you, and I can probably live in this house with you, and I can keep working the way I have been. I decided I can have my life and still be in this situation with you, but you need some resources, because I realize now I'm not going to be all for you. I don't want to be all for you, and I did tell her that. But I couldn't tell her this total head trip I'd been through because she wouldn't understand.*

Or, the coupledness may be redefined by acceptance of the relationship with certain limitations. Boundaries can be imposed on the impact that the relationship will have on the total life space of the initiator.

> *I finally came to the point where I realized I was never going to have the kind of marriage I had hoped for, the kind of relationship I had hoped for. I didn't want to end it, because of the children, but I wasn't going to let it hurt me any more. I wasn't going to depend on him any more. The children and I were going to be the main unit, and, if he occasionally wanted to participate, fine—and if not, we would go ahead without him. I was no longer willing to let being with him be the determining factor as to whether I was happy or not. I ceased planning our lives around his presence or absence and began looking out for myself.*

A second form of accompanying reconstruction occurs when the initiator attempts to redefine the significant other in a way that is more compatible with his own self-validation needs. The initiator may direct efforts toward specific behaviors, such as drinking habits, temper, sexual incompatibilities, or finance management. Or, the redefinition attempt may be of a broader scope.

> *I was aware of his dependence on the marriage to provide all his happiness, and it wasn't providing it. I wanted him to go to graduate school, but he postponed it, against my wishes. I wanted him to pursue his own life. I didn't want him to sacrifice for me. I wanted him to become more exciting to me in the process. I was aware that I was trying to persuade him to be a different person.*

Redefinition of the significant other may either be directed toward maintaining the coupledness, as above, or moving away from it, as is the case following.

> *The way I defined being a good wife and the way John defined being a good wife were two different quantities. He wanted the house to look like a hotel and I didn't see it that way. He couldn't see why I couldn't meet his needs... When he first asked for a divorce and I refused, he suggested I go back to school. I remembered a man who worked with John who had sent his wife back to school so she could support herself, so he could divorce her. I asked John if he was trying to get rid of me. He didn't answer that. He insisted I go, and I finally went.*

A third form of accompanying reconstruction may be directed toward the redefinition of the initiator. Intermingled with attempts at redefinition of the significant other and redefinition of the coupledness itself is the seeking of self-validation outside the marriage by the initiator. A whole set of other behaviors may evolve that have the ultimate effect of moving the relationship away from the coupledness toward a separation of the joint biography.

SELF-VALIDATION OUTSIDE THE MARRIAGE

What was at first internally experienced and recognized as self-minimizing takes a more concrete form and becomes externally expressed in a search for self-maximization. Through investment of self in career, in a cause requiring commitment, in a relationship with a new significant other, in family, in education, or in activities and hobbies, the initiator develops new sources of self-realization. These alternative sources of self-realization confirm not the coupled identity but the singularity of the initiator.

Furthermore, in the move toward a distinct biography, the initiator finds ideological support that reinforces the uncoupling process. Berger and Kellner (1964, p. 3) note the existence of a supporting ideology which lends credence to marriage as a significant validating relationship in our society. That is, the nuclear family is seen as the site of love, sexual fulfillment, and self-realization. In the move toward uncoupling, the initiator finds confirmation for a belief in *self* as a first priority.

> *I now see my break with religion as a part of my developing individuality. At the time I was close friends with priests and nuns, most of whom have since left the church. I felt a bitterness toward the church for its definition of marriage. I felt constrained toward a type of marriage that was not best for me.*

Whether this ideology first begins within the individual, who then actively *seeks* sources of self-realization that are ideologically congruent, or whether the initiator's own needs come to be met by a serendipitous "elective affinity" of ideas (Weber, 1930), is difficult to say. The interconnections are subtle. The supporting ideology may come from the family of orientation, the women's movement, the peer group, or a new significant other. It may grow directly, as through interaction, or indirectly, as through literature. No matter what the source, the point is that, in turning away from the marriage for self-validation, a separate distinct biography is constructed in interaction with others, and this beginning autonomy is strengthened by a supporting belief system.

The initiator moves toward construction of a separate subworld wherein significant conversation comes from circles which no longer overlap with those of the significant other. And, the significant other is excluded from that separate subworld.

> I shared important things with the children that I didn't share with him. It's almost as if I purposefully punished him by not telling him. Some good thing would happen and I'd come home and tell them and wouldn't tell him.

The initiator's autonomy is further reinforced as the secret of the troubled marriage is shared with others in the separate subworld the initiator is constructing. It may be directly expressed as a confidence exchanged with a close friend, family member, or children, or it may be that the sharing is indirect. Rather than being expressed in significant conversation, the definition of the marriage as troubled is created for others by a variety of mechanisms that relay

the message that the initiator is not happily married. The definition of the marriage as problematic becomes further objectivated as the secret, once held only by the initiator, then shared with the significant other, moves to a sphere beyond the couple themselves.

Other moves away occur that deeply threaten the coupled identity for the significant other and at the same time validate the autonomy of the initiator.

> I remember going to a party by myself and feeling comfortable. She never forgot that. I never realized the gravity of that to her.
>
> Graduate school became a symbolic issue. I was going to be a separate entity. That's probably the one thing I wanted to do that got the biggest negative emotional response from him.
>
> All that time I was developing more of a sense of being away from her. I didn't depend on her for any emotional feedback, companionship. I went to plays and movies with friends.

The friendship group, rather than focusing on the coupledness, relies on splintered sources that support separate identities. Though this situation can exist in relationships in which the coupled identity is validating for both participants, the distinction is that, in the process of uncoupling, there may not be shared conversation to link the separate subworld of the initiator with that of the significant other.

These movements away by the initiator heighten a sense of exclusion for the significant other. Deep commitment to other than the coupled identity—to a career, to a cause, to education, to a hobby, to another person—

reflects a lessened commitment to the marriage. The initiator's search for self-validation outside the marriage even may be demonstrated symbolically to the significant other by the removal of the wedding ring or by the desire, if the initiator is a woman, to revert to her maiden name. If the initiator's lessened commitment to the coupled identity is reflected in a lessened desire for sexual intimacy, the challenge to the identity of the significant other and the coupledness becomes undeniable. As the significant other recognizes the growing autonomy of the initiator, he, too, comes to accept the definition of the marriage as "troubled."

The roles assumed by each participant have implications for the impact of the uncoupling on each. Whereas the initiator has found other sources of self-realization outside the marriage, usually the significant other has not. The marriage still performs the major self-validating function. The significant other is committed to an ideology that supports the coupled identity. The secret of the "troubled" marriage has not been shared with others as it has by the initiator, meaning for the significant other the relationship in its changed construction remains unobjectivated. The challenge to the identity of the significant other and to the coupledness posed by the initiator may result in increased commitment to the coupled identity for the significant other. With the joint biography already separated in these ways, the couple enters into a period of "trying."

TRYING

Trying is a stage of intense definition negotiation by the partners. Now both share a definition of the marriage as troubled. However, each partner may seek to construct a new reality that is in opposition to that of the other. The significant other tries to negotiate a shared definition of the marriage as savable, whereas the initiator negotiates toward a shared definition that marks the marriage as unsavable.[2]

For the initiator, the uncoupling process is well underway. At some point the partner who originally perceived the coupled identity to be problematic and sought self-validation outside the coupled identity has experienced "psychological divorce." Sociologically, this can be defined as the point at which the individual's newly constructed separate subworld becomes the major nomos-building mechanism in his life space, replacing the nomos-building function of the coupled identity.

The initiator tries subtly to prepare the significant other to live alone. By encouraging the other to make new friends, find a job, get involved in outside activities, or seek additional education, the initiator hopes to decrease the other's commitment to and dependence upon the coupled identity for self-validation and move the other toward autonomy. This stage of preparation is not simply one of cold expediency for the benefit of the initiator, but is based on concern for the significant other and serves to mitigate the pain of the uncoupling process for both the initiator and the other.

For both, there is a hesitancy to sever the ties. In many cases, neither party is fully certain about the termination of the marriage. Mutual uncertainty may be more characteristic of the process. The relationship may weave back and forth between cycles of active trying and passive acceptance of the status quo due to the failure of each to pull the other to a common definition and the inability of either to make the break.

I didn't want to hurt him. I didn't want to be responsible for the demise of a marriage I no longer wanted. I could have forced him into being the one to achieve the breach, for I realized it was never going to happen by itself.

I didn't want to be the villain— the one to push her out into the big, bad world. I wanted to make sure she was at the same point I was.

I kept hoping some alternative would occur so that he would be willing to break. I kept wishing it would happen.

Frequently, in the trying stage, the partners turn to outside help for formal negotiation of the coupled identity. Counseling, though entered into with apparent common purpose, becomes another arena in which the partners attempt to negotiate a shared definition from their separately held definitions of the marriage as savable or unsavable. For the initiator, the counseling may serve as a step in the preparation of the significant other to live alone. Not only does it serve to bring the other to the definition of the marriage as unsavable, but also the counseling provides a resource for the significant other, in the person of the counselor. Often it happens that the other has turned to no one for comfort about the problem marriage. The initiator, sensitive to this need and unable to fill it himself, hopes the counselor will fill this role. The counseling has yet another function. It further objectivates the notion of the coupled identity as problematic.

At some point during this period of trying, the initiator may suggest separation. Yet, separation is not suggested as a formal leave-taking but as a *temporary* separation meant to clarify the relationship for both partners. Again, the concern on the part of the initiator for the significant other appears. Not wanting to hurt, yet recognizing the coupled identity as no longer valid, the temporary separation is encouraged as a further means of bringing the other to accept a definition of the marriage as unsavable, to increase

reliance of the other on outside resources of self-realization, and to initiate the physical breach gently.

Even at that point, at initial separation, I wasn't being honest. I knew fairly certainly that when we separated, it was for good, I let her believe that it was a means for us first finding out what was happening and then eventually possibly getting back together.

Should the initiator be hesitant to suggest a separation, the significant other may finally tire of the ambiguity of the relationship. No longer finding the coupling as it exists self-validating, the significant other may be the one to suggest a separation. The decision to separate may be the result of discussion and planning, or it may occur spontaneously, in a moment of anger. It may be mutually agreed upon, but more often it is not. However it emerges, the decision to separate is a difficult one for both partners.

OBJECTIVATION: RESTRUCTURING OF THE PRIVATE SPHERE

The separation is a transitional state in which everything needs definition, yet very little is capable of being defined. Economic status, friendship networks, personal habits, and sex life are all patterns of the past which need simultaneous reorganization. However, reorganization is hindered by the ambiguity of the relationship. The off-again, on-again wearing of the wedding rings is symbolic of the indecision in this stage. Each of the partners searches for new roles, without yet being free of the old.

For the initiator who has developed outside resources, the impact of this uncertainty is partially mitigated. For the significant other, who has not spent time in preparation for individual existence, the major self-validating function of the marriage is gone and nothing has emerged as a substitute.

> *I had lost my identity somewhere along the way. And I kept losing my identity. I kept letting him make all the decisions. I couldn't work. I wasn't able to be myself. I was letting someone else take over. I didn't have any control over it. I didn't know how to stop it. I was unsure that if anything really happened I could actually make it on my own or not.*

The separation precipitates a redefinition of self for the significant other. Without other resources for self-validation, and with the coupled identity now publicly challenged, the significant other begins a restructuring of the private sphere.

This restructuring occurs not only in the social realm but also entails a form of restructuring that is physical, tangible, and symbolic of the break in the coupled identity. For instance, if the initiator has been the one to leave, at some point the significant other begins reordering the residence they shared to suit the needs of one adult rather than two. Furniture is rearranged or thrown out. Closets and drawers are reorganized. A thorough house-cleaning may be undertaken. As the initiator has moved to a new location that reinforces his singularity, the significant other transforms the home that validated the coupling into one that likewise objectivates the new definition. Changes in the physical appearance of either or both partners may be a part of the symbolic restructuring of the private sphere. Weight losses, changes of hair style, or changes in clothing preferences further symbol-

ize the yielding of the mutual identity and the move toward autonomy.

Should the significant other be the one to leave, the move into a new location aids in the redefinition of self as an autonomous individual. For example, the necessity of surviving in a new environment, the eventual emergence of a new set of friends that define and relate to the significant other as a separate being instead of as half of a couple, and the creation of a new residence without the other person are all mechanisms which reinforce autonomy and a definition of singularity.

Though the initiator has long been involved in objectivating a separate reality, frequently for the significant other this stage is just beginning. Seldom does the secret of the troubled marriage become shared with others by this partner until it can no longer be deferred. Although the initiator actively has sought objectivation, the significant other has avoided it. Confronted with actual separation, however, the significant other responds by taking the subjectively experienced meanings and moving them to the objective level—by confiding in others, perhaps in writing, in letters or in diaries—any means that helps the other deal with the new reality.

There are some who must be told of the separation—children, parents, best friends. Not only are the two partners reconstructing their own reality, but they now must reconstruct the reality for others. Conversation provides the mechanism for reconstruction, simultaneously creating common definitions and working as a major objectivating apparatus. The longer the conversation goes on, the more massively real do the objectivations become to the partners. The result is a stabilization of the objectivated reality, as the new definition of uncoupledness continues to move outward.

Uncoupling precipitates a reordering of all other significant relationships. As in coupling, where all other relationships are reperceived and regrouped to account for and support the emergence of *the* significant other, in uncoupling the reordering supports the singularity of each partner. Significant relationships are lost, as former friends of the couple now align with one or the other or refuse to choose between the two. Ties with families of orientation, formerly somewhat attenuated because of the coupling, are frequently renewed. For each of the partners, pressure exists to stabilize characterizations of others and of self so that the world and self are brought toward consistency. Each partner approaches groups that strengthen the new definition each has created, and avoids those that weaken it. The groups with which each partner associates help co-define the new reality.

OBJECTIVATION: THE PUBLIC SPHERE

The uncoupling is further objectivated for the participants as the new definition is legitimized in the public sphere. Two separate households demand public identification as separate identities. New telephone listings, changes of mailing address, separate checking accounts, and charge accounts, for example, are all mechanisms by which the new reality becomes publicly reconstructed.

The decision to initiate legal proceedings confirms the uncoupling by the formal negotiation of a heretofore informally negotiated definition. The adversary process supporting separate identities, custody proceedings, the formal separation of the material base, the final removal of the rings all act as means of moving the new definition from the private to the public sphere. The uncoupling now becomes objectivated not only for the participants and their close intimates, but for casual acquaintances and strangers.

Objectivation acts as a constraint upon whatever social identity has been constructed. It can bind a couple together, or hinder their recoupling, once the uncoupling process has begun. Perhaps this can better be understood by considering the tenuous character of the extramarital affair. The very nature of the relationship is private. The coupling remains a secret shared by the two and seldom becomes objectivated in the public realm. Thus, the responsibility for the maintenance of that coupling usually rests solely with the two participants. When the relationship is no longer self-validating for one of the participants, the uncoupling does not involve a reconstruction of reality for others. The constraints imposed by the objectivation of a marital relationship which function to keep a couple in a marriage do not exist to the same extent in an affair. The fragility of the coupling is enhanced by its limited objectivation.

Berger and Kellner (1964, p. 6) note that the "degree of objectivation will depend on the number and intensity of the social relationships that are its carriers." As the uncoupling process has moved from a nonshared secret held within the initiator to the realm of public knowledge, the degree of objectivation has increased. The result is a continuing decline in the precariousness of the newly constructed reality over time.

DIVORCE: A STAGE IN THE PROCESS

Yet a decrease in precariousness is not synonymous with a completion of the uncoupling process. As marriage, or coupling, is a dramatic act of redefinition of self by two strangers as they move from autonomous identities to the construction of a joint biography, so uncoupling involves yet another redefinition of self as the participants move from mutual identity toward autonomy. It is this redefinition of self, for each participant, that completes the uncoupling. Divorce, then, may not be the final stage. In fact, divorce could be viewed as a nonstatus that is at some point on a continuum ranging from marriage (coupling) as an achieved status, to autonomy (uncoupling), likewise an achieved status. In other words, the uncoupling process might be viewed as a status transformation which is complete when the individual defines his salient status as "single" rather than "divorced." When the individual's newly constructed separate subworld becomes nomos-building—when it creates for the individual a sort of order in which he can experience his life as making sense—the uncoupling process is completed.

The completion of uncoupling does not occur at the same moment for each participant. For either or both of the participants, it may not occur until after the other has created a coupled identity with another person. With that step, the tentativeness is gone.

> When I learned of his intention to remarry, I did not realize how devastated I would be. It was just awful. I remember crying and crying. It was really a very bad thing that I did not know or expect. You really aren't divorced while that other person is still free. You still have a lot of your psychological marriage going—in fact, I'm still in that a little bit because I'm still single.

For some, the uncoupling may never be completed. One or both of the participants may never be able to construct a new and separate subworld that becomes self-validating. Witness, for example, the widow who continues to call herself "Mrs. John Doe," who associates with the same circle of friends, who continues to wear her wedding ring and observes wedding anniver-saries. For her, the coupled identity is still a major mechanism for self-validation, even though the partner is gone.

In fact, death as a form of uncoupling may be easier for the significant other to handle than divorce. There exist ritual techniques for dealing with it, and there is no ambiguity. The relationship is gone. There will be no further interaction between the partners. With divorce, or any uncoupling that occurs through the volition of one or both of the partners, the interaction may continue long after the relationship has been formally terminated. For the significant other—the one left behind, without resources for self-validation—the continuing interaction between the partners presents obstacles to autonomy.

> There's a point at which it's over. If your wife dies, you're a lot luckier, I think, because it's over. You either live with it, you kill yourself, or you make your own bed of misery. Unlike losing a wife through death, in divorce, she doesn't die. She keeps resurrecting it. I can't get over it, she won't die. I mean, she won't go away.

CONTINUITIES

Continuities are linkages between the partners that exist despite the formal termination of the coupled identity. Most important of these is the existence of shared loved ones—children, in-laws, and so on. Though in-laws may of necessity be excluded from the separately constructed subworlds, children can rarely be and, in their very existence, present continued substantiation of the coupled identity.

In many cases continuities are actively constructed by one or both of the participants after the formal termination of the relationship. These manufactured linkages speak to the difficulty of totally separating that common biography, by providing a continued mechanism for interaction. They may be constructed as a temporary bridge between the separated subworlds, or they may come to be a permanent interaction pattern. Symbolically, they seem to indicate caring on the part of either or both of the participants.

- The wife moves out. The husband spends his weekend helping her get settled—hanging pictures, moving furniture.
- The husband moves out, leaving his set of tools behind. Several years later, even after his remarriage, the tools are still there, and he comes to borrow them one at a time. The former wife is planning to move within the same city. The tools are boxed up, ready to be taken with her.
- The wife has moved out, but is slow to change her mailing address. Rather than marking her forwarding address on the envelopes and returning them by mail, the husband either delivers them once a week or the wife picks them up.
- The wife moves out. The husband resists dividing property with her that is obviously hers. The conflict necessitates many phone calls and visits.
- The husband moves out. Once a week he comes to the house to visit with the children on an evening when the wife is away. When she gets home, the two of them occasionally go out to dinner.
- A nice part of the marriage was shared shopping trips on Sunday afternoons. After the divorce, they still occasionally go shopping together.
- The holidays during the first year of separation were celebrated as they always had been—with the whole family together.

- During a particularly difficult divorce, the husband noted that he had finally succeeded in finding his wife a decent lawyer.

Continuities present unmeasurable variables in the uncoupling process. In this paper, uncoupling is defined as a reality socially constructed by the participants. The stages that mark the movement from a coupled identity to separate autonomous identities are characterized, using divorce for an ideal-type analysis. Yet, there is no intent to portray uncoupling as a compelling linear process from which there is no turning back. Such conceptualization would deny the human factor inherent in reality construction. Granted, as the original secret is moved from private to public, becoming increasingly objectivated, reconstructing the coupled identity becomes more and more difficult.

Each stage of objectivation acts as the closing of a door. Yet at any stage the process may be interrupted. The initiator may not find mechanisms of self-validation outside the coupling that reinforce his autonomy. Or the self-validation outside the coupling may be the very stuff that allows the initiator to stay *in* the relationship. Or continuities may intervene and reconstruction of the coupled identity may occur, despite the degree of objectivation, as in the following case.

Ellen met Jack in college. They fell in love and married. Jack had been blind since birth. He had pursued a college career in education and was also a musician. Both admired the independence of the other. In the marriage, she subordinated her career to his and helped him pursue a masters degree, as well as his musical interests. Her time was con-

sumed by his needs—for transportation and the taping and transcribing of music for the musicians in his group. He was teaching at a school for the blind by day and performing as a musician at night. They had a son, and her life, instead of turning outward, as his, revolved around family responsibilities. She gained weight. Jack, after twelve years of marriage, left Ellen for his high school sweetheart. Ellen grieved for a while, then began patching her life. She got a job, established her own credit, went back to college, and lost weight. She saw a lawyer, filed for divorce, joined Parents Without Partners, and began searching out singles groups. She dated. Throughout, Jack and Ellen saw each other occasionally and maintained a sexual relationship. The night before the divorce was final, they reconciled.

The uncoupling never was completed, though all stages of the process occurred, including the public objectivation that results from the initiation of the legal process, Ellen, in constructing an autonomous identity, became again the independent person Jack had first loved.[3] This, together with the continuities that existed between the two, created the basis for a common definition of the coupling as savable.

DISCUSSION

Berger and Kellner describe the process by which two individuals create a coupled identity for themselves. Here, we have started from the point of the coupled identity and examined the process by which people move out of such relationships. Using interview data, we have found that, although the renegotiation of separate realities is a complex web of subtle modifications, clear stages emerge which mark the uncoupling process. The emergent stages are like benchmarks which indicate the increasing objectivation of the changing definitions of reality, as these definitions move from the realm of the private to the public.

Beginning within the intimacy of the dyad, the initial objectivation occurs as the secret of the troubled marriage that the initiator has held is shared with the significant other. With this, the meaning has begun to move from the subjective to the objective. Definition negotiation begins. While attempting to negotiate a common definition, the initiator acts to increase the validation of his identity and place in the world by use of accompanying reconstructions of reality. The autonomy of the initiator increases as he finds self-validation outside the marriage and an ideology that supports the uncoupling. The increased autonomy of the initiator brings the significant other to accept a definition of the marriage as troubled, and they enter into the stage of "trying." The process continues, as counseling and separation further move the new definition into the public sphere.

The telling of others, the symbolic physical signs of the uncoupling, and the initiation of formal legal proceedings validate the increasing separation of the partners as they negotiate a new reality which is different from that constructed private sphere which validated their identity as a couple. Eventually, a redefinition of the mutual identity occurs in such a way that the joint biography is separated into two separate autonomous identities. As Berger and Kellner state that marriage is a dramatic act of redefinition of self by two individuals, so uncoupling is characterized by the same phenomenon. Self-realization, rather than coming from the coupledness, again comes from outside sources. Significant conversation again finds its source in nonoverlapping circles. The new definition of the relationship constructed by the participants has, in interaction with others, become common property.

Language is crucial to this process. Socially constructed worlds need validation. As conversation constantly reconfirms a coupled identity, so also does it act as the major validating mechanism for the move to singularity, not by specific articulation, but by the way in which it comes to revolve around the uncoupled identity as taken for granted.

The notion that the stages uncovered do broadly apply needs to be further confirmed. We need to know whether the process is invariant regardless of the heterosexuality, homosexuality, or social class of couples. Does it also apply for close friends? In what ways does the sex of the interviewer bias the data? Additionally, the stages in the process should be confirmed by interviews with both partners in a coupling. Due to the delicacy of the subject matter, this is difficult. In only one instance were both partners available to be interviewed for this study. Notwithstanding these limitations, the findings which emerge deserve consideration.

Most significant of these is the existence of an underlying order in a phenomenon generally regarded as a chaotic and disorderly process. Undoubtedly the discovery of order was encouraged by the methodology of the study. The information was gained by retrospective analysis on the part of the interviewees. Certainly the passage of time allowed events to be reconstructed in an orderly way that made sense. Nonetheless, as was previously noted, the interviewees were all at various stages in the uncoupling process—some at the "secret" stage and some five years hence. Yet, the stages which are discussed here

appeared without fail in every case and have been confirmed repeatedly by the other means described earlier.

In addition to this orderliness, the examination of the process of uncoupling discloses two other little-considered aspects of the process that need to be brought forth and questioned.

One is the caring. Generally, uncoupling is thought of as a conflict-ridden experience that ends as a bitter battle between two adversaries intent on doing each other in. Frequently, this is the case. Yet, the interviews for this study showed that in all cases, even the most emotion generating, again and again the concern of each of the participants for the other revealed itself. Apparently, the patterns of caring and responsibility that emerge between the partners in a coupling are not easily dispelled and in many cases persist throughout the uncoupling process and after, as suggested by the concept of continuities.

A second question that emerges from this examination of uncoupling is related to Berger and Kellner's thesis. They state that, for adults in our society, marriage is a significant validating relationship, one that is nomos-building. Marriage is, in fact, described as "a crucial nomic instrumentality" (1964, p. 4). Though Berger and Kellner at the outset do delimit the focus of their analysis to marriage as an ideal type, the question to be answered is, To what degree is this characterization of marriage appropriate today?

Recall, for example, the quote from one interviewee: "I was never psychologically married. I always felt strained by attempts that coupled me into a marital unit. I was just never comfortable as 'Mrs.'" The interviews for this study suggest that the nomos-building quality assumed to derive from marriage to the individual should be taken as problematic rather than as given. Gouldner (1959) suggests that the parts of a unit vary in the degree to which they are interdependent. His concept of functional autonomy may be extended to illuminate the variable forms that marriage, or coupling, may take and the accompanying degree of nomos. A relationship may exist in which the partners are highly interdependent, and the coupled identity does provide the major mechanism for self-validation, as Berger and Kellner suggest. Yet it is equally as likely that the participants are highly indepen-dent, or "loosely coupled" (Weick 1976; Corwin 1977), wherein mechanisms for self-validation originate *outside* the coupling rather than from the coupling itself. The connection between the form of the coupling, the degree to which it is or is not nomos-building, and the subsequent implications for uncoupling should be examined in future research.

Reading 34   Life-Span Adjustment of Children to Their Parents' Divorce*

PAUL R. AMATO

Children have always faced the threat of family disruption. In the past, death was more likely to disrupt families than was divorce. Around the turn of the century in the United States, about 25% of children experienced the death of a parent before age 15, compared with 7% or 8% who experienced parental divorce.[1] As a result of the increase in longevity, the proportion of dependent children who lost a parent through death decreased during this century; currently, only about 5% of children are so affected. But the divorce rate increased over this same period, and at current rates, between two-fifths and two-thirds of all recent first marriages will end in divorce or separation.[2] The high rate of marital dissolution means that about 40% of children will experience a parental divorce prior to the age of 16.[3] Although a substantial risk of family disruption has always been present, today it is much more likely to be caused by divorce than by death.

Americans traditionally have believed that a two-parent family is necessary for the successful socialization and development of children. Consequently, it was assumed that parental death leads to many problems for children, such as delinquency, depression, and even suicide in later life—assumptions that appeared to be confirmed by early research.[4]

More recent studies indicate that, although parental death disadvantages children, the long-term consequences are not as severe as people once believed.[5] Nevertheless, many social scientists assumed that children who "lost" a parent through divorce experienced serious problems similar to those experienced by children who lost a parent through death. Furthermore, whereas the death of a parent is usually unintended and unavoidable, marital dissolution is freely chosen by at least one parent. Consequently, the question of the impact of divorce on children took on moral overtones. These concerns, combined with the dramatic increase in the rate of divorce during the last few decades, resulted in a proliferation of studies on the effects of divorce on children.

This research literature does not always lead to firm conclusions. Many gaps exist in our knowledge, and weaknesses in study methodology mean that many findings are tentative at best. Nevertheless, a consensus is beginning to emerge among social scientists about the consequences of divorce for children. And, in spite of its limitations, this knowledge can help to

*Amato, Paul R. 1994. "Life-Span Adjustment of Children to Their Parents' Divorce." *The Future of Children,* Children and Divorce 4 (Spring): 143–157. Reprinted with permission of the Center for the Future of Children of the David and Lucile Packard Foundation.

inform policies designed to improve the well-being of children involved in parental marital dissolution.

HOW DO RESEARCHERS STUDY CHILDREN AND DIVORCE?

To understand how divorce affects children, social scientists predominately rely on two research designs: cross-sectional and longitudinal.[6] In a cross-sectional study,[7] researchers compare children from divorced and continuously intact two-parent families at a single point in time.[8] In a longitudinal study, researchers follow children over an extended period of time following marital dissolution.[8] Longitudinal studies usually include a comparison group of children from two-parent families as well. Although both types of research designs have methodological advantages and disadvantages, they provide useful information about adjustment.[6,8,9] Cross-sectional studies provide a "snapshot" that shows how children of divorce differ from other children, whereas longitudinal studies allow us to understand how children adjust to divorce over time.

In addition to studies of children, social scientists have studied the long-term consequences of divorce by comparing adults who experienced divorce as children with those who grew up in continuously intact families. Researchers also have carried out a small number of longitudinal studies in which children of divorce are followed into early adulthood.[10]

Three types of samples appear in the literature.[11] *Clinical samples* consist of children or adults who are in therapy or counseling. Clinical samples are useful in documenting the kinds of problems presented by offspring who adjust poorly to divorce, but these results cannot be generalized to the broad majority of people who never receive professional attention. Researchers obtain *convenience samples* of children or adults through community organizations (such as single-parent support groups) or other local sources. Convenience samples are relatively easy and inexpensive to obtain, but people in these groups may be atypical in unknown ways. Researchers select *random samples* of children or adults in a scientific manner such that the sample represents a clearly defined population within known limits.[12] These samples may be obtained from schools, court records, or households. Random samples allow us to make valid generalizations about the majority of children who experience divorce.[13] Unfortunately, these types of samples are also the most difficult and expensive to obtain.

Researchers match (or statistically equate) children or adults in the two samples (divorced and intact) on key variables known to be associated with both divorce and adjustment.[14] For example, parents of low socioeconomic status are more likely than other parents to divorce and to have children who exhibit behavioral and academic problems. Consequently, it is necessary to make sure that the socioeconomic backgrounds of parents in the two groups are comparable.

Researchers then select outcome measures that reflect children's and adults' functioning, or well-being. Common outcome measures for children include academic achievement, conduct, psychological adjustment, self-concept, social adjustment, and the quality of relations with parents. Common outcome measures for adults include psychological adjustment, conduct, use of mental health services, self-concept, social well-being, marital quality, separation or divorce, single parenthood, socioeconomic attainment, and physical health.

Social scientists gather information about children by interviewing one or both parents, questioning the child's teachers, administering tests to the child, or directly observing the child's behavior. Information is usually obtained from adults by interviewing them. Researchers then compare outcomes for those in the divorced and the continuously intact family groups. Statistical criteria are used to judge if differences in outcome measures are large enough to rule out the possibility of their being attributable to chance alone. Observed differences that are too large to be attributable to chance are assumed to be caused by divorce, or at least, by some factor(s) associated with divorce.

Unfortunately, because these studies are correlational, it is difficult to know for certain if divorce is responsible for observed differences between groups. It is always possible that groups might differ in ways that researchers cannot anticipate, measure, and control. For example, an unspecified parental personality characteristic might increase the risk of both divorce and child maladjustment. Firm conclusions about causation require experimentation; because we cannot randomly assign children to divorced and nondivorced families, our beliefs about the causal impact of divorce remain tentative.

HOW DO CHILDREN OF DIVORCE DIFFER FROM OTHER CHILDREN?

Those who delve into the published literature on this topic may experience some frustration, as the results vary a good deal from study to study. Many studies show that children of divorce have more problems than do children in continuously intact two-parent families.[15] But other studies show no difference,[16] and a few show that children in divorced families are better off in certain respects than children in two-parent families.[17] This inconsistency results from the fact that studies vary in their sampling strategies, choice of what outcomes to measure, methods of obtaining information, and techniques for analyzing data.

A technique known as *meta-analysis* was recently developed to deal with this very situa-

tion.[18] In a meta-analysis, the results of individual studies are expressed in terms of an "effect size" which summarizes the differences between children in divorced and intact groups on each outcome. Because these effect sizes are expressed in a common unit of measure, it is possible to combine them across all studies to determine whether significant effects exist for each topic being reviewed. It is also possible to examine how design features of studies, such as the nature of the sample, might affect the conclusions.[19]

In 1991, Amato and Keith pooled the results for 92 studies that involved more than 13,000 children ranging from pre-school to college age.[20] This meta-analysis confirmed that children in divorced families, on average, experience more problems and have a lower level of well-being than do children in continuously intact two-parent families.[21] These problems include lower academic achievement, more behavioral problems, poorer psychological adjustment, more negative self-concepts, more social difficulties, and more problematic relationships with both mothers and fathers.[22]

To determine if there are also differences in adjustment when children of divorce grow into adulthood, Amato and Keith carried out a second meta-analysis of 37 studies in which they examined adult children of divorce.[23] These results, based on pooled data from 80,000 adults, suggest that parental divorce has a detrimental impact on the life course.[24] Compared with those raised in intact two-parent families, adults who experienced a parental divorce had lower psychological well-being, more behavioral problems, less education, lower job status, a lower standard of living, lower marital satisfaction, a heightened risk of divorce, a heightened risk of being a single parent, and poorer physical health.[25]

The view that children adapt readily to divorce and show no lingering negative consequences is clearly inconsistent with the cumulative research in this area. However, several qualifications temper the seriousness of this conclusion. First, the average differences between children from divorced and continuously intact families are small rather than large. This fact suggests that divorce is not as severe a stressor for children as are other things that can go wrong during childhood. For example, a recent meta-analysis of studies dealing with childhood sexual abuse revealed average effect sizes three to four times larger than those based on studies of children of divorce.[26] Second, although children of divorce differ, on average, from children in continuously intact two-parent families, there is a great deal of overlap between the two groups.

To illustrate these points, the results of a hypothetical but typical study are shown in Figure 1. This figure shows the distribution of well-being scores (on a representative measure of well-being) for children in divorced and nondivorced families. The height of the curve represents the frequency with which children score at various levels of well-being. Lower scores on the left side of the figure indicate poorer outcomes, whereas higher scores on the right side of the figure indicate better outcomes.

The average for each group of children is represented by the highest point in each curve. Note that the average score of children in the divorced group is lower than the average score of children in the nondivorced group, indicating a lower level of well-being. At the same time, a large proportion of children in the divorced group score *higher* than the average score of children in the nondivorced group. Similarly, a large proportion of children in the nondivorced group score *lower* than the average score of children in the divorced group. This overlap reflects the diversity of outcomes for children in both groups. Although the figure is described in terms of children, the same conclusions apply to stud-

ies dealing with adults from divorced and intact families of origin.

This diversity helps us to understand why the *average* effects of divorce are relatively weak. Divorce may represent a severe stressor for some children, resulting in substantial impairment and decline in well-being. But for other children, divorce may be relatively inconsequential. And some children may show improvements following divorce. In other words, to inquire about the effects of divorce, as if all children were affected similarly, is to ask the wrong question. A better question would be, "Under what conditions is divorce harmful or beneficial to children?" This point is returned to below.

Variations by Gender of Child

Some researchers are interested in measuring differences in adjustment between children of divorce and children in intact families based on such variables as gender, ethnicity, age, and cohort membership in attempts to identify groups that may respond differently to divorce. Summarized below are the major findings with regard to the relationship between these variables and adjustment.

Several early influential studies found that boys in divorced families had more adjustment problems than did girls.[15] Because these studies have been widely cited, many have come to accept this finding as incontrovertible. Given that boys usually live with their mothers following family disruption, the loss of contact with the same-sex parent could account for such a difference. In addition, boys, compared with girls, may be exposed to more conflict, receive less support from parents and others (because they are believed to be tougher), and be picked on more by custodial mothers (because they resemble their fathers). Other observers have suggested that boys may be more psychologically vulnerable than girls to a range of stressors,

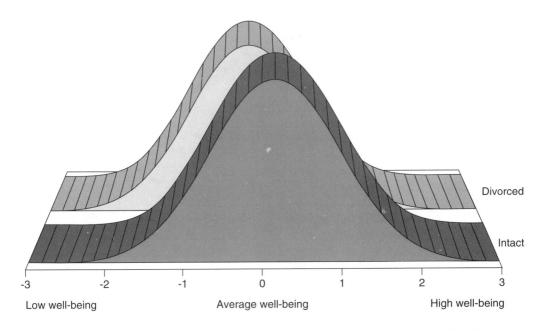

-3   -2   -1   0   1   2   3

Low well-being   Average well-being   High well-being

FIGURE 1   Typical Distribution of Well-Being Scores for Children in Divorced and Intact Families

including divorce.[27] However, a number of other studies have failed to find a gender difference in children's reactions to divorce,[17,28] and some studies have found that girls have more problems than do boys.[29]

Amato and Keith tried to clarify this issue in their meta-analytic studies by pooling the results from all studies that reported data for males and females separately.[20,23] For children, the literature reveals one major gender difference: the estimated negative effects of divorce on social adjustment are stronger for boys than for girls. Social adjustment includes measures of popularity, loneliness, and cooperativeness. In other areas, however, such as academic achievement, conduct, or psychological adjustment, no differences between boys and girls are apparent. Why a difference in social adjustment, in particular, should occur is unclear. Girls may be more socially skilled than boys, and this may make them less susceptible to any disruptive effects of divorce. Alternatively, the increased aggressiveness of boys from divorced families may make their social relationships especially problematic, at least in the short term.[30] Nevertheless, the meta-analysis suggests that boys do not always suffer more detrimental consequences of divorce than do girls.

The meta-analysis for adults also revealed minimal sex differences, with one exception: although both men and women from divorced families obtain less education than do those from continuously intact two-parent families, this difference is larger for women than for men. The reason for the greater vulnerability of women is somewhat unclear. One possibility is that noncustodial fathers are less likely to finance the higher education of daughters than sons.[31]

Variations by Ethnicity of Child

There is a scant amount of research on how divorce affects nonwhite children of divorce. For example, because relatively little research has focused on this population, Amato and Keith were unable to reach any conclusions about ethnic differences in children's reactions to divorce.[20] The lack of information on how divorce affects nonwhite children is a serious omission in this research literature.

With regard to African-American children, some research has suggested that academic deficits associated with living with a single mother are not as pronounced for black children as for white children.[32]

In relation to adults, Amato and Keith show that African Americans are affected less by parental divorce than are whites. For example, the gap in socioeconomic attainment between adults from divorced and nondivorced families of origin is greater among whites than among African Americans. This difference may have to do with the fact that divorce is more common, and perhaps more accepted, among African Americans than among whites. Also, because extended kin relations tend to be particularly strong among African Americans, single African-American mothers may receive more support from their extended families than do single white mothers.[33] Alternatively, given the large number of structural barriers that inhibit the attainment of African Americans, growing up in a divorced single-parent family may result in relatively little additional disadvantage.

We need additional research on divorce in different racial and ethnic groups, including African Americans, Asian Americans, Hispanics, and Native Americans. In addition to the adjustment of children of divorce, we need information on relationships between children and custodial and noncustodial parents, the role of extended kin in providing support, and, in general, how culture moderates the impact of marital dissolution on children.

Variations by Age of Child

Some of the best descriptions of how divorce affects children of different ages come from the work of Wallerstein and Kelly, who conducted detailed interviews with children and parents.[34] Although their sample appears to have overrepresented parents who had a difficult time adjusting to divorce, many of their conclusions about age differences have been supported by later studies. Observation of children during the first year after parental separation showed that preschool age children lack the cognitive sophistication to understand the meaning of divorce. Consequently, they react to the departure of one parent with a great deal of confusion. Because they do not understand what is happening, many become fearful. For example, a child may wonder, "Now that one parent is gone, what is to stop the other parent from leaving also?" Young children also tend to be egocentric, that is, they see themselves at the center of the world. This leads some children to blame themselves for their parents' divorce. For example, they may think, "Daddy left because I was bad." Regression to earlier stages of behavior is also common among very young children.

Children of primary school age have greater cognitive maturity and can more accurately grasp the meaning of divorce. However, their understanding of what divorce entails may lead them to grieve for the loss of the family as it was, and feelings of sadness and depression are common. Some children see the divorce as a personal rejection. However, because egocentrism decreases with age, many are able to place the blame elsewhere—usually on a parent.

Consequently, older children in this age group may feel a great deal of anger toward one, or sometimes both, parents.

Adolescents are more peer-oriented and less dependent on the family than are younger children. For this reason, they may be impacted less directly by the divorce. However, adolescents may still feel a considerable degree of anger toward one or both parents. In addition, adolescents are concerned about their own intimate relationships. The divorce of their parents may lead adolescents to question their own ability to maintain a long-term relationship with a partner.

The work of Wallerstein and Kelly suggests that children at every age are affected by divorce, although the nature of their reactions differs. But are these reactions more disturbing for one group than for another? Wallerstein and Kelly found that preschool children were the most distressed in the period following parental separation. However, 10 years later, the children of preschool age appeared to have adjusted better than children who were older at the time of family disruption.[35]

Many other studies have examined age at the time of divorce to see if it is associated with children's problems. However, these studies have yielded mixed and often inconsistent results, and the meta-analyses of children[20] and adults[23] were unable to cast much light on these issues.[36] A common problem in many data sets is that age at divorce and time since divorce are confounded. In other words, for a group of children of the same age, the younger they were at the time of divorce, the more time that has elapsed. But if we examine children whose parents all divorced at about the same time, then the more time that has passed, the older children are at the time of the study. Similarly, if we hold constant the age of the child at the time of divorce, then length of time and current age are perfectly correlated. In other words, it is impossible to separate the effects of age at divorce,

length of time since divorce, and current age. Given this problem, it is not surprising that research findings are unclear. Nevertheless, it is safe to say that divorce has the potential to impact negatively on children of all ages.

Year of Study

One additional noteworthy finding that emerged from the meta-analyses by Amato and Keith[20,23] concerns the year in which the study was conducted. These researchers found that older studies tended to yield larger differences between children from divorced and intact families than studies carried out more recently. This tendency was observed in studies of children (in relation to measures of academic achievement and conduct) and in studies of adults (in relation to measures of psychological adjustment, separation and divorce, material quality of life, and occupational quality).[23,37] The difference persisted when the fact that more recent studies are more methodologically sophisticated than earlier studies was taken into account.

This finding suggests that more recent cohorts of children are showing less severe effects of divorce than earlier cohorts. Two explanations are worth considering. First, as divorce has become more common, attitudes toward divorce have become more accepting, so children probably feel less stigmatized. Similarly, the increasing number of divorces makes it easier for children to obtain support from others in similar circumstances. Second, because the legal and social barriers to marital dissolution were stronger in the past, couples who obtained a divorce several decades ago probably had more serious problems and experienced more conflict prior to separation than do some divorcing couples today. Furthermore, divorces were probably more acrimonious before the introduction of no-fault divorce. Thus, children of divorce in the past may have been exposed to more dysfunctional family environments and higher levels of conflict than were more recent cohorts of children.

WHY DOES DIVORCE LOWER CHILDREN'S WELL-BEING?

Available research clearly shows an association between parental divorce and children's well-being. However, the causal mechanisms responsible for this association are just beginning to be understood. Most explanations refer to the absence of the noncustodial parent, the adjustment of the custodial parent, interparental conflict, economic hardship, and life stress. Variations in these factors may explain why divorce affects some children more adversely than others.

Parental Absence

According to this view, divorce affects children negatively to the extent that it results in a loss of time, assistance, and affection provided by the noncustodial parent. Mothers and fathers are both considered potentially important resources for children. Both can serve as sources of practical assistance, emotional support, protection, guidance, and supervision. Divorce usually brings about the departure of one parent— typically the father—from the child's household. Over time, the quantity and quality of contact between children and noncustodial parents often decreases, and this is believed to result in lower levels of adjustment for these children as compared with children from intact families.[38]

The parental absence explanation is supported by several lines of research. For example, some studies show that children who experience the death of a parent exhibit problems similar to those of children who "lose" a parent through divorce.[39] These findings are consistent with the notion that the absence of a parent *for any reason* is problematic for children. Also consistent with a parental absence perspective are studies showing that children who have another adult (such as

a grandparent or other relative) to fill some of the functions of the absent parent have fewer problems than do children who have no substitute for the absent parent.[40] In addition, although the results of studies in the area of access to the noncustodial parent and adjustment are mixed,[41] in general, studies show that a close relationship with both parents is associated with positive adjustment after divorce. One circumstance in which high levels of access may not produce positive adjustment in children is in high-conflict divorces. When conflict between parents is marked, frequent contact with the noncustodial parent may do more harm than good.[42]

Custodial Parental Adjustment and Parenting Skills

According to this view, divorce affects children negatively to the extent that it interferes with the custodial parents' psychological health and ability to parent effectively. Following divorce, custodial parents often exhibit symptoms of depression and anxiety. Lowered emotional well-being, in turn, is likely to impair single parents' child-rearing behaviors. Hetherington and colleagues found that, during the first year following separation, custodial parents were less affectionate toward their children, made fewer maturity demands, supervised them less, were more punitive, and were less consistent in dispensing discipline.[43]

Research provides clear support for this perspective. Almost all studies show that children are better adjusted when the custodial parent is in good mental health[44] and displays good child-rearing skills.[45] In particular, children are better off when custodial parents are affectionate, provide adequate supervision, exercise a moderate degree of control, provide explanations for rules, avoid harsh discipline, and are consistent in dispensing punishment. Also consistent with a parental adjustment perspective are studies showing that, when custodial parents have a good deal of social support, their children have fewer difficulties.[46]

Interparental Conflict

A third explanation for the effects of divorce on children focuses on the role of conflict between parents. A home marked by high levels of discord represents a problematic environment for children's socialization and development. Witnessing overt conflict is a direct stressor for children. Furthermore, parents who argue heatedly or resort to physical violence indirectly teach children that fighting is an appropriate method for resolving differences. As such, children in high-conflict families may not have opportunities to learn alternative ways to manage disagreements, such as negotiating and reaching compromises. Failure to acquire these social skills may interfere with children's ability to form and maintain friendships. Not surprisingly, numerous studies show that children living in high-conflict two-parent families are at increased risk for a variety of problems.[47] It seems likely, therefore, that many of the problems observed among children of divorce are actually caused by the conflict between parents that precedes and accompanies marital dissolution.

Studies show that children in high-conflict intact families are no better off—and often are worse off—than children in divorced single-parent families.[48] Indeed, children in single-parent families may show improvements in well-being following divorce if it represents an escape from an aversive and dysfunctional family environment. Furthermore, a study by Cherlin and colleagues shows that many, but not all, of the difficulties exhibited by children of divorce, such as behavioral problems and low academic test scores, are present *prior* to parental separation, especially for boys.[49] This finding is consistent with the notion that the lowered well-being of children is partly attributable to the conflict that precedes divorce. In addition,

conflict may increase around the time of the separation, and parents often continue to fight long after the divorce is final. Indeed, many studies show that children's adjustment is related to the level of conflict between parents following divorce.[50,51] It should be noted here that post-divorce adjustment may also be influenced by residual effects of conflict that occurred during the marriage.

Economic Hardship

Divorce typically results in a severe decline in standard of living for most custodial mothers and their children.[52] Economic hardship increases the risk of psychological and behavioral problems among children[53] and may negatively affect their nutrition and health.[54] Economic hardship also makes it difficult for custodial mothers to provide books, educational toys, home computers, and other resources that can facilitate children's academic attainment. Furthermore, economically pressed parents often move to neighborhoods where schools are poorly financed, crime rates are high, and services are inadequate.[55] Living under these circumstances may facilitate the entry of adolescents into delinquent subcultures. According to this view, divorce affects children negatively to the extent that it results in economic hardship.

Studies show that children's outcomes—especially measures of academic achievement—are related to the level of household income following divorce. For example, Guidubaldi and colleagues found that children in divorced families scored significantly lower than children in intact two-parent families on 27 out of 34 outcomes; taking income differences into account statistically reduced the number of significant differences to only 13.[56] Similarly, McLanahan found that income accounted for about half of the association between living in a single-parent family and high school completion for white students.[57] However, most studies show that, even when families are equated in terms of income, children of divorce continue to experience an increased risk of problems. This suggests that economic disadvantage, although important, is not the sole explanation for divorce effects.

Life Stress

Each of the factors noted above—loss of contact with the noncustodial parent, impaired child rearing by the custodial parent, conflict between parents, and a decline in standard of living—represents a stressor for children. In addition, divorce often sets into motion other events that may be stressful, such as moving, changing schools, and parental remarriage. And of course, parental remarriage brings about the possibility of additional divorces. Multiple instances of divorce expose children to repeated episodes of conflict, diminished parenting, and financial hardship.[58] For some children of divorce, stress accumulates throughout childhood.

Research generally supports a stress interpretation of children's adjustment following divorce. Divorces that are accompanied by a large number of other changes appear to have an especially negative impact on children.[59] Furthermore, parental remarriage sometimes exacerbates problems for children of divorce,[17,60] as does a second divorce.[61]

A General Perspective on How Divorce Affects Children

All five explanations for the effects of divorce on children appear to have merit, and a complete accounting for the effect of divorce on children must make reference to each. Because of variability in these five factors, the consequences of divorce differ considerably from one child to the next.

Consider a divorce in which a child loses contact with the father, the custodial mother is preoccupied and inattentive, the parents fight over child support and other issues, the house-

hold descends abruptly into poverty, and the separation is accompanied by a series of other uncontrollable changes. Under these circumstances, one would expect the divorce to have a substantial negative impact on the child. In contrast, consider a divorce in which the child continues to see the noncustodial father regularly, the custodial mother continues to be supportive and exercises appropriate discipline, the parents are able to cooperate without conflict, the child's standard of living changes little, and the transition is accompanied by no other major disruptions in the child's life. Under these circumstances, one would predict few negative consequences of divorce. Finally, consider a high-conflict marriage that ends in divorce. As the level of conflict subsides, the previously distant father grows closer to his child, and the previously distracted and stressed mother becomes warmer and more attentive. Assuming no major economic problems or additional disruptive changes, this divorce would probably have a positive impact on the child.

Overall, to understand how divorce affects children, it is necessary to assess how divorce changes the total configuration of resources and stressors in children's lives.[62] The five factors described above should also be considered when evaluating policy alternatives aimed at improving the well-being of children of divorce.

WHAT INTERVENTIONS MIGHT BENEFIT CHILDREN OF DIVORCE?

Concern for the well-being of children of divorce leads to a consideration of how various policies and interventions might reduce the risk of problems for them. The most commonly discussed interventions include lowering the incidence of divorce, joint custody, child support reform, enhancing the self-sufficiency of single mothers, and therapeutic programs for children and parents. Interventions suggested in this article are considered in the light of available research evidence.

Lowering the Incidence of Divorce

In the United States during the twentieth century, divorce became increasingly available as the result of a series of judicial decisions that widened the grounds for divorce. In 1970, no-fault divorce was introduced in California; presently it is available in all 50 states.[63] Under most forms of no-fault divorce, a divorce can be obtained without a restrictive waiting period if one partner wants it even if the other partner has done nothing to violate the marriage contract and wishes to keep the marriage together. This fact raises an interesting question: If the law were changed to make marital dissolution more difficult to obtain, and if doing so lowered the divorce rate, would we see a corresponding improvement in the well-being of children?

Several considerations suggest that this outcome is unlikely. First, although legal divorces occurred less often in the past, informal separations and desertions were not uncommon, especially among minorities and those of low socioeconomic status.[64] From a child's perspective, separation is no better than divorce. If the legal system were changed to make divorce more difficult, it would most likely increase the proportion of children living in separated but nondivorced families. It would also increase the proportion of people who spend their childhoods in high-conflict two-parent families. As noted above, high-conflict two-parent families present just as many problems for children as do divorced single-parent families, perhaps more so. Given that the legal system cannot stop married couples from living apart or fighting, changing the legal system to decrease the frequency of divorce is unlikely to improve the well-being of children.

Is it possible to lower the frequency of divorce by increasing marital happiness and stability? The government could enact certain changes toward this end, for example, by changing the tax code to benefit married parents. It is possible that such a policy would enhance the quality and stability of some marriages; however, providing these benefits to married-couple families would increase the relative disadvantage of single parents and their children, an undesirable outcome. Alternatively, the government could take steps to promote marriage preparation, enrichment, and counseling. Increasing the availability of such services would probably help to keep some marriages from ending in divorce. However, as Furstenberg and Cherlin suggest, the rise in divorce is the result of fundamental changes in American society, including shifts in personal values and the growing economic independence of women, factors that cannot be affected easily by government policies.[65] As such, any actions taken by government to strengthen marriage are likely to have only minor effects on the divorce rate.

Increasing the Incidence of Joint Physical Custody

The history of custody determination in the United States has changed over time primarily in response to societal influences. In the eighteenth century, fathers usually were awarded custody of their children as they were considered the dominant family figure and were most likely to have the financial means to care for them. In the nineteenth century, the preference for custody moved toward women. The reason for this shift was probably occasioned, in part, by the industrial revolution and the movement of men from the home to the workplace to earn a living. Women, in this circumstance, were needed to care for the children while men were at work and became the primary caretakers of children. At this time, child developmental theorists also focused on the importance of the mother-child relationship, and the assumption was that the children were usually better off under the custody of their mother. Recently, society has moved toward a dual-earner family, and child developmentalists have emphasized the importance of both parents to the child. These changes are currently reflected in the law which emphasizes the importance of maintaining relationships with both parents.[66] The result has been an increased interest in joint custody, which is now available as an option in most states.[59] *Joint physical custody* provides legal rights and responsibilities to both parents and is intended to grant children substantial portions of time with each parent. *Joint legal custody,* which is more common, provides legal rights and responsibilities to both parents, but the child lives with one parent.[66]

Joint legal custody may be beneficial to the extent that it keeps both parents involved in their children's lives. However, studies show few differences between joint legal and mother-custody families in the extent to which fathers pay child support, visit their children, and are involved in making decisions about their children, once parental income, education, and other predivorce parental characteristics are taken into account.[66,67] Although joint legal custody may have symbolic value in emphasizing the importance of both parents, it appears to make little difference in practice.

In contrast, joint physical custody is associated with greater father contact, involvement, and payment of child support.[68] Fathers also appear to be more satisfied with joint physical custody than with mother custody. For example, Shrier and colleagues found in 1991 that joint-custody fathers were significantly more satisfied than sole-maternal-custody fathers in two areas, including their legal rights and responsibilities as a parent and their current alimony and child

support financial arrangements.[66,69] Joint physical custody may be beneficial if it gives children frequent access to both parents. On the other hand, residential instability may be stressful for some children. Although few studies are available, some show that children in joint physical custody are better adjusted than are children with other custody arrangements,[70] and other studies show no difference.[71]

However, these results may present a picture that is too optimistic. Courts are most likely to grant joint physical custody to couples who request it. A large-scale study by Maccoby and Mnookin in California showed that couples with joint physical custody, compared with those who receive sole custody, are better educated and have higher incomes; furthermore, couples who request joint custody may be relatively less hostile, and fathers may be particularly committed to their children prior to divorce.[66,72] These findings suggest that some of the apparent positive "effect" of joint custody is a natural result of the type of people who request it in the first place.

It is unlikely that joint physical custody would work well if it were imposed on parents against their will. Under these conditions, joint custody may lead to more contact between fathers and their children but may also maintain and exacerbate conflict between parents.[73] Maccoby and Mnookin found that, although conflict over custody is relatively rare joint custody is sometimes used to resolve custody disputes. In their study, joint custody was awarded in about one-third of cases in which mothers and fathers had each initially sought sole custody; furthermore, the more legal conflict between parents, the more likely joint custody was to be awarded. Three and one-half years after separation, these couples were experiencing considerably more conflict and less cooperative parenting than couples in which both had wanted joint custody initially. This finding demonstrates that an award of joint custody does not improve the relationship between hostile parents.

As noted above, studies show that children's contact with noncustodial parents is harmful if postdivorce conflict between parents is high. To the extent that joint physical custody maintains contact between children and parents in an atmosphere of conflict, it may do as much (or more) harm than good.[74] Joint custody, therefore, would appear to be the best arrangement for children when parents are cooperative and request such an arrangement. But in cases where parents are unable to cooperate, or when one parent is violent or abusive, a more traditional custody arrangement would be preferable.

Does research suggest that children are better adjusted in mother- or father-custody households? From an economic perspective, one might expect children to be better off with fathers, given that men typically earn more money than do women. On the other hand, children may be cared for more competently by mothers than fathers, given that mothers usually have more child care experience. Studies that have compared the adjustment of children in mother- and father-custody households have yielded mixed results, with some favoring mother custody, some favoring father custody, and others favoring the placement of the child with the same-sex parent.[36]

A recent and thorough study by Downey and Powell,[75] based on a large national sample of children, found little evidence to support the notion that children are better off with the same-sex parent. On a few outcomes, children were better off in father-custody households. However, with household income controlled, children tended to be slightly better off with mothers. This finding suggests that the higher income of single-father households confers certain advantages on children, but if mothers earned as much as fathers, children would be better off with mothers. The overall finding of the study, however, is that the sex of the custodial parent has little to do with children's adjustment. In general then, it does not appear that either mother or father custody is inherently better for children, regardless of the sex of the child.

Child Support Reform

It is widely recognized that noncustodial fathers often fail to pay child support. In a 1987 study by the U.S. Bureau of the Census, about one-third of formerly married women with custody had no child support award. And among those with an award, one-fourth reported receiving no payments in the previous year.[76] In the past, it has been difficult for custodial mothers to seek compliance with awards because of the complications and expense involved. New provisions in the 1988 Family Support Act allow for states to recover child support payments through the taxation system.[77] Starting in 1994, all new payments will be subject to automatic withholding from parents' paychecks.

Child support payments represent only a fraction of most single mothers' income, usually no more than one-fifth.[78] As such, stricter enforcement of child support payments cannot be expected to have a dramatic impact on children's standard of living. Nevertheless, it is usually highly needed income. As noted above, economic hardship has negative consequences for children's health, academic achievement, and psychological adjustment. Consequently, any policy that reduces the economic hardship experienced by children of divorce would be helpful. Furthermore, the extra income derived from child support may decrease custodial mothers' stress and improve parental functioning, with beneficial consequences for children. Consistent with this view, two studies show that regular payment of child support by noncustodial fathers decreases children's behavior problems and increases academic test scores.[79] Furthermore, in these studies, the apparently beneficial effect of child support occurred in spite of the fact that contact between fathers and children was not related to children's well-being.

Research indicates that the majority of fathers are capable of paying the full amount of child support awarded; in fact, most are capable of paying more.[66] Based on these considerations, it would appear to be desirable to increase the economic support provided by non-custodial fathers to their children. This would include increasing the proportion of children with awards, increasing the level of awards, and enforcing child support awards more strictly. A guaranteed minimum child support benefit, in which the government sets a minimum benefit level and assures full payment when fathers are unable to comply, would also improve the standard of living of many children.[80]

Requiring fathers to increase their economic commitment to children may also lead them to increase visitation, if for no other reason than to make sure that their money is being spent wisely. A number of studies have shown that fathers who pay child support tend to visit their children more often and make more decisions about them than do fathers who fail to pay.[81] If increasing the level of compliance increases father visitation, it may increase conflict between some parents. On the other hand, some children may benefit from greater father involvement. Over-all, the benefits of increasing fathers' economic contribution to children would seem to outweigh any risks.

Economic Self-Sufficiency for Single Mothers

As noted above, stricter enforcement of child support awards will help to raise the standard of living of single mothers and their children. However, even if fathers comply fully with child support awards, the economic situation of many single mothers will remain precarious. To a large extent, the economic vulnerability of single

mothers reflects the larger inequality between men and women in American society. Not only do women earn less than men, but many married women sacrifice future earning potential to care for children by dropping out of the paid labor force, cutting back on the number of hours worked, taking jobs with more flexible hours, or taking jobs closer to home. Thus, divorcees are disadvantaged both by the lower wages paid to women and by their work histories. In the long run, single mothers and their children will achieve economic parity with single fathers only when women and men are equal in terms of earnings and time spent caring for children.

In the short term, however, certain steps can be taken to allow single mothers receiving public assistance to be economically self-sufficient. These steps would include the provision of job training and subsidized child care.[82] Although these programs operate at government expense, they are cost-effective to the extent that women and children become independent of further public assistance. Furthermore, many single mothers are "penalized" for working because they lose government benefits, such as health care and child care. Welfare reform that removes work disincentives by allowing women to earn a reasonable level of income without losing health care and child care benefits would be desirable. In fact, changes in these directions are being implemented as part of the Family Support Act of 1988.[83] Given that the employment of single mothers does not appear to be harmful to children and can provide a higher standard of living for children than does welfare, and given that economic self-sufficiency would probably improve the psychological well-being of single mothers, it seems likely that these changes will benefit children.

Therapeutic Interventions for Children

According to Cherlin, there are still no firm estimates on the proportion of children who experience harmful psychological effects from parental divorce.[2] Research suggests that, in many cases, children adjust well to divorce without the need for therapeutic intervention. However, our current understanding is that a minority of children do experience adjustment problems and are in need of therapeutic intervention. The type of therapeutic intervention suited for children varies according to the type and severity of the adjustment problems and the length of time they are expressed by the child. The major types of therapeutic interventions include child-oriented interventions and family-oriented interventions.[84]

Child-oriented interventions attempt to help children by alleviating the problems commonly experienced by them after divorce. Some intervention programs include private individual therapy. However, many single parents are unable to afford private therapy for their children and may enroll them in programs in which counselors work with groups of children.

Typically, in these sessions, children meet on a regular basis to share their experiences, learn about problem-solving strategies, and offer mutual support. Children may also view films, draw, or participate in role-playing exercises. Small groups are desirable for children of divorce for several reasons. Not only can they reach large numbers of children, but the group itself is therapeutic: children may find it easier to talk with other children than with adults about their experiences and feelings. Most group programs are located in schools; such programs have been introduced in thousands of school districts across the United States.

Evaluations of these programs have been attempted, and in spite of some methodological limitations, most are favorable: children from divorced families who participate, compared with those who do not, exhibit fewer maladaptive attitudes and beliefs about divorce, better classroom behavior, less anxiety and depression,

and improved self-concept.[85] Although much of the evidence is positive, it is not entirely clear which components of these programs are most effective. For example, improvement may be brought about by a better understanding of divorce, newly acquired communication skills, or the support of other students. Although more evaluation research is needed, the evidence is positive enough to warrant further development and introduction of therapeutic programs for children.

In addition to child-focused interventions, there are *family-focused interventions* including both educational and therapeutic programs. These programs are aimed at divorcing parents, with the intention of either improving parenting skills or reducing the level of conflict over children.[86] In principle, therapeutic interventions that improve parental child-rearing skills or decrease the level of conflict between parents should benefit children, although this effect has not yet been demonstrated.

WHAT DIRECTIONS SHOULD FUTURE RESEARCH TAKE?

All things being equal, existing research suggests that a well-functioning nuclear family with two caring parents may be a better environment for children's growth and development than a divorced single-parent family. Children of divorce, as a group, are at greater risk than children from intact families, as a group, for many psychological, academic, and social problems. And adults raised in divorced single-parent families, as a group, do not achieve the same level of psychological and material well-being as those raised in continuously intact two-parent families. However, we need to keep in mind that many children are better off living in single-parent households than in a two-parent families marked by conflict. Furthermore, we need to recognize that most single parents work hard to provide their children with a loving and structured family life. Many single-parent families function well, and most children raised in these settings develop into well-adjusted adults. Blaming single parents as a group for the problems experienced by children of divorce is a pointless exercise.

At this time, our knowledge about children and divorce needs to be expanded in certain directions. The long-term effect of divorce on children is the basic question that needs to be addressed. The answers to this question will inform social policy and the court system, shape models of intervention, and influence parental decision making. This type of information should be obtained from longitudinal and longitudinal-sequential designs. Needed are studies that begin prior to divorce, as well as studies that follow children of divorce through adolescence and into adulthood.[87]

Also needed are data on how a variety of factors—relations with parents, parental adjust-ment, economic well-being, conflict, and exposure to stressors—combine to affect children's response to divorce. This research should make it possible to determine which children lose the most through divorce, which children are relatively unaffected, and which children benefit.

Information on how divorce affects children in different racial and ethnic groups is another area of research that would be informative from the standpoint of both clinical and economic intervention.[33] And more evaluation of various interventions, both legal (joint custody, mediation, child support reform) and therapeutic, are also needed.

It is important to focus on establishing policies that will help narrow the gap in well-being between children of divorce and children from intact families. High divorce rates and single-parent families are facts of life in American society. If it is impossible to prevent children from experiencing parental divorce, steps must be taken to ease the transition.

Reading 35   Remarriage as an Incomplete Institution*

ANDREW CHERLIN

Sociologists believe that social institutions shape people's behavior in important ways. Gerth and Mills (1953, p. 173) wrote that institutions are organizations of social roles which "imprint their stamps upon the individual, modifying his external conduct as well as his inner life." More recently, Berger and Luckmann (1966) argued that institutions define not only acceptable behavior, as Gerth and Mills believed, but also objective reality itself. Social institutions range from political and economic systems to religion and language. And displayed prominently in any sociologist's catalogue of institutions is a fundamental form of social organization, the family.

The institution of the family provides social control of reproduction and child rearing. It also provides family members with guidelines for proper behavior in everyday family life, and, presumably, these guidelines contribute to the unity and stability of families. But in recent years, sociologists have de-emphasized the institutional basis of family unity in the United States. According to many scholars, contemporary families are held together more by consensus and mutual affection than by formal, institutional controls.

The main source of this viewpoint is an influential text by Ernest Burgess and Harvey Locke which appeared in 1945. They wrote:

The central thesis of this volume is that the family in historical times has been, and at present is, in transition from an institution to a companionship. In the past, the important factors unifying the family have been external, formal, and authoritarian, as the law, the mores, public opinion, tradition, the authority of the family head, rigid discipline, and elaborate ritual. At present, in the new emerging form of the companionship family, its unity inheres less and less in community pressures and more and more in such interpersonal relationships as the mutual affection, the sympathetic understanding, and the comradeship of its members. (p. vii)

In the institutional family, Burgess and Locke stated, unity derived from the unchallenged authority of the patriarch, which was supported by strong social pressure. But, they argued, with urbanization and the decline of patriarchal authority, a democratic family has emerged which creates its own unity from interpersonal relations.

Many subsequent studies have retained the idea of the companionship family in some form,

*Cherlin, Andrew. 1978. "Remarriage as an Incomplete Institution." *American Journal of Sociology* 84 (3):634–650. Published by The University of Chicago Press. © 1978 by The University of Chicago. All rights reserved.

such as the equalitarian family of Blood and Wolfe (1960) or the symmetrical family of Young and Wilmott (1973). Common to all is the notion that patriarchal authority has declined and sex roles have become less segregated. Historical studies of family life demonstrate that the authority of the husband was indeed stronger in the preindustrial West than it is now (see, e.g., Ariès 1962; Shorter 1975). As for today, numerous studies of "family power" have attempted to show that authority and power are shared more equally between spouses (see Blood and Wolfe 1960). Although these studies have been criticized (Safilios-Rothschild 1970), no one has claimed that patriarchal authority is as strong now as the historical record indicates it once was. Even if we believe that husbands still have more authority than wives, we can nevertheless agree that patriarchal authority seems to have declined in the United States in this century.

But it does not follow that institutional sources of family unity have declined also. Burgess and Locke reached this conclusion in part because of their assumption that the patriarch was the transmitter of social norms and values to his family. With the decline of the patriarch, so they believed, a vital institutional link between family and society was broken. This argument is similar to the perspective of Gerth and Mills, who wrote that a set of social roles becomes an institution when it is stabilized by a "head" who wields authority over the members. It follows from this premise that if the head loses his authority, the institutional nature of family life will become problematic.

Yet institutionalized patterns of behavior clearly persist in family life, despite the trend away from patriarchy and segregated sex roles. As others have noted (Dyer and Urban 1958; Nye and Berardo 1973), the equalitarian pattern may be as firmly institutionalized now as the traditional pattern was in the past. In the terms of Berger and Luckmann, most family behavior today is habitualized action which is accepted as typical by all members—that is, it is institutionalized behavior. In most everyday situations, parents and children base their behavior on social norms: parents know how harshly to discipline their children, and children learn from parents and friends which parental rules are fair and which to protest. These sources of institutionalization in the contemporary American family have received little attention from students of family unity, just as family members themselves pay little attention to them.

The presence of these habitualized patterns directly affects family unity. "Habitualization," Berger and Luckmann wrote, "carries with it the important psychological gain that choices are narrowed" (1966, p. 53). With choices narrowed, family members face fewer decisions which will cause disagreements and, correspondingly, have less difficulty maintaining family unity. Thus, institutional support for family unity exists through the routinization of everyday behavior even though the husband is no longer the unchallenged agent of social control.

Nowhere in contemporary family life is the psychological gain from habitualization more evident than in the families of remarried spouses and their children, where, paradoxically, habitualized behavior is often absent. We know that the unity of families of remarriages which follow a divorce is often precarious—as evidenced by the higher divorce rate for these families than for families of first marriages (U.S. Bureau of the Census 1976). And in the last few decades, remarriage after divorce—as opposed to remarriage after widowhood—has become the predominant form of remarriage. In this paper, I will argue that the higher divorce rate or remarriages after divorce is a consequence of the incomplete institutionalization of remarriage after divorce in our society. The institution of the family in the United States has developed in response to the needs of families of first marriages and families of remarriages after widowhood. But because of the complex structure, families of remarriages after divorce that include children from previous marriages must solve problems unknown to other types of families. For many of these problems, such as proper kinship terms, authority to discipline stepchildren, and legal relationships, no institutionalized solutions have emerged. As a result, there is more opportunity for disagreements and divisions among family members and more strain in many remarriages after divorce.

The incomplete institutionalization of remarriage after divorce reveals, by way of contrast, the high degree of institutionalization still present in first marriages. Family members, especially those in first marriages, rely on a wide range of habitualized behaviors to assist them in solving the common problems of family life. We take these behavioral patterns for granted until their absence forces us to create solutions on our own. Only then do we see the continuing importance of institutionalized patterns of family behavior for maintaining family unity.

I cannot provide definitive proof of the hypothesis linking the higher divorce rate for remarriages after divorce to incomplete institutionalization. There is very little quantitative information concerning remarriages. In fact, we do not even know how many stepparents and stepchildren there are in the United States. Nor has there ever been a large, random-sample survey designed with families of remarriages in mind. (Bernard's 1956 book on remarriage, for example, was based on information supplied nonrandomly by third parties.) There are, nevertheless, several studies which do provide valuable information, and there is much indirect evidence bearing on the plausibility of this hypothesis and of alternative explanations. I will review this evidence, and I will also refer occasionally to information I collected through personal interviews with a small, nonrandom sample of remarried couples and family counselors

in the northeast. Despite the lack of data, I believe that the problems of families of remarriages are worth examining, especially given the recent increases in divorce and remarriage rates. In the hope that this article will stimulate further investigations, I will also present suggestions for future research.

THE PROBLEM OF FAMILY UNITY

Remarriages have been common in the United States since its beginnings, but until this century almost all remarriages followed widowhood. In the Plymouth Colony, for instance, about one-third of all men and one-quarter of all women who lived full lifetimes remarried after the death of a spouse, but there was little divorce (Demos 1970). Even as late as the 1920s, more brides and grooms were remarrying after widowhood than after divorce, according to estimates by Jacobson (1959). Since then, however, a continued increase in divorce (Norton and Glick 1976) has altered this pattern. By 1975, 84 percent of all brides who were remarrying were previously divorced, and 16 percent were widowed. For grooms who were remarrying in 1975, 86 percent were previously divorced (U.S. National Center for Health Statistics 1977). Thus, it is only recently that remarriage after divorce has become the predominant form of remarriage.

And since the turn of the century, remarriages after divorce have increased as a proportion of all marriages. In 1900 only 3 percent of all brides—including both the single and previously married—were divorced (Jacobson 1959). In 1930, 9 percent of all brides were divorced (Jacobson 1959), and in 1975, 25 percent of all brides were divorced (U.S. National Center for Health Statistics 1977). As a result, in seven million families in 1970 one or both spouses had remarried after a divorce (U.S. Bureau of the Census 1973). Most of this increase is due to the rise in the divorce rate, but some part is due to the greater tendency of divorced and widowed adults to remarry. The remarriage rate for divorced and widowed women was about 50 percent higher in the mid-1970s than in 1940 (Norton and Glick 1976).

At the same time, the percentage of divorces which involved at least one child increased from 46 percent in 1950 to 60 percent in 1974 (U.S. National Center for Health Statistics 1953, 1977). The increase in the percentage of divorces which involve children means that more families of remarriages after divorce now have stepchildren. Although it is not possible with available data to calculate the exact number of families with stepchildren, we do know that in 1970 8.9 million children lived in two-parent families where one or both parents had been previously divorced (U.S. Bureau of the Census 1973). Some of these children—who constituted 15 percent of all children living in two-parent families—were from previous marriages, and others were from the remarriages.

Can these families of remarriages after divorce, many of which include children from previous marriages, maintain unity as well as do families of first marriages? Not according to the divorce rate. A number of studies have shown a greater risk of separation and divorce for remarriages after divorce (Becker, Landes, and Michael 1976; Bumpass and Sweet 1972; Cherlin 1977; Monahan 1958). Remarriages after widowhood appear, in contrast, to have a lower divorce rate than first marriages (Monahan 1958). A recent Bureau of the Census report (U.S. Bureau of the Census 1976) estimated that about 33 percent of all first marriages among people 25–35 may end in divorce, while about 40 percent of remarriages after divorce among people this age may end in divorce. The estimates are based on current rates of divorce, which could, of course, change greatly in the future.[1]

Conventional wisdom, however, seems to be that remarriages are more successful than first marriages. In a small, nonrandom sample of family counselors and remarried couples, I found most to be surprised at the news that divorce was more prevalent in remarriages. There are some plausible reasons for this popular misconception. Those who remarry are older, on the average, than those marrying for the first time and are presumably more mature. They have had more time to search the marriage market and to determine their own needs and preferences. In addition, divorced men may be in a better financial position and command greater work skills than younger, never-married men. (Divorced women who are supporting children, however, are often in a worse financial position—see Hoffman [1977].)

But despite these advantages, the divorce rate is higher in remarriages after divorce. The reported differences are often modest, but they appear consistently throughout 20 years of research. And the meaning of marital dissolution for family unity is clear: when a marriage dissolves, unity ends. The converse, though, is not necessarily true: a family may have a low degree of unity but remain nominally intact. Even with this limitation, I submit that the divorce rate is the best objective indicator of differences in family unity between remarriages and first marriages.

There are indicators of family unity other than divorce, but their meaning is less clear and their measurement is more difficult. There is the survey research tradition, for example, of asking people how happy or satisfied they are with their marriages. The invariable result is that almost everyone reports that they are very happy (see, e.g., Bradburn and Caplovitz 1965; Glenn 1975; Campbell, Converse, and Rodgers 1976). It may be that our high rate of divorce increases the general level of marital satisfaction by dissolving unsatisfactory marriages. But it is also possible that the satisfaction ratings are inflated by the reluctance of some respondents to admit that their marriages are less than fully satisfying. Marriage is an important part of life for most adults—the respondents in the Campbell et al. (1976) national sample rated it second only to health as the most important aspect of their lives—and people may be reluctant to admit publicly that their marriage is troubled.

Several recent studies, nevertheless, have shown that levels of satisfaction and happiness are lower among the remarried, although the differences typically are small. Besides the Campbell et al. study, these include Glenn and Weaver (1977), who found modest differences in marital happiness in the 1973, 1974, and 1975 General Social Surveys conducted by the National Opinion Research Center. They reported that for women, the difference between those who were remarried and those who were in a first marriage was statistically significant, while for men the difference was smaller and not significant. In addition, Renne (1971) reported that remarried, previously divorced persons were less happy with their marriages than those in first marriages in a probability sample of 4,452 Alameda County, California, households. Again, the differences were modest, but they were consistent within categories of age, sex, and race. No tests of significance were reported.

The higher divorce rate suggests that maintaining family unity is more difficult for families of remarriages after divorce. And the lower levels of marital satisfaction, which must be interpreted cautiously, also support this hypothesis. It is true, nevertheless, that many remarriages work well, and that the majority of remarriages will not end in divorce. And we must remember that the divorce rate is also at an all-time high for first marriages. But there is a difference of degree between remarriages and first marriages which appears consistently in research. We must ask why families of remarriages after divorce

seem to have more difficulty rehabilitating family unity than do families of first marriages. Several explanations have been proposed, and we will now assess the available evidence for each.

PREVIOUS EXPLANATIONS

One explanation, favored until recently by many psychiatrists, is that the problems of remarried people arise from personality disorders which preceded their marriages (see Bergler 1948). People in troubled marriages, according to this view, have unresolved personal conflicts which must be treated before a successful marriage can be achieved. Their problems lead them to marry second spouses who may be superficially quite different from their first spouse but are characterologically quite similar. As a result, this theory states, remarried people repeat the problems of their first marriages.

If this explanation were correct, one would expect that people in remarriages would show higher levels of psychiatric symptomatology than people in first marriages. But there is little evidence of this. On the contrary, Overall (1971) reported that in a sample of 2,000 clients seeking help for psychiatric problems, currently remarried people showed lower levels of psychopathology on a general rating scale than persons in first marriages and currently divorced persons. These findings, of course, apply only to people who sought psychiatric help. And it may be, as Overall noted, that the differences emerged because remarried people are more likely to seek help for less serious problems. The findings, nevertheless, weaken the psychoanalytic interpretation of the problems of remarried life.

On the other hand, Monahan (1958) and Cherlin (1977) reported that the divorce rate was considerably higher for people in their third marriages who had divorced twice than for people in their second marriages. Perhaps personality disorders among some of those who marry several times prevent them from achieving a successful marriage. But even with the currently high rates of divorce and remarriage, only a small proportion of all adults marry more than twice. About 10% of all adults in 1975 had married twice, but less than 2% had married three or more times (U.S. Bureau of the Census 1976).

Most remarried people, then, are in a second marriage. And the large number of people now divorcing and entering a second marriage also undercuts the psychoanalytic interpretation. If current rates hold, about one-third of all young married people will become divorced, and about four-fifths of these will remarry. It is hard to believe that the recent increases in divorce and remarriage are due to the sudden spread of marriage-threatening personality disorders to a large part of the young adult population. I conclude, instead, that the psychoanalytic explanation for the rise in divorce and the difficulties of remarried spouses and their children is at best incomplete.[2]

A second possible explanation is that once a person had divorced he or she is less hesitant to do so again. Having divorced once, a person knows how to get divorced and what to expect from family members, friends, and the courts. This explanation is plausible and probably accounts for some of the difference in divorce rates. But it does not account for all of the research findings on remarriage, such as the finding of Becker et al. (1976) that the presence of children from a previous marriage increased the probability of divorce for women in remarriages, while the presence of children from the new marriage reduced the probability of divorce. I will discuss the implications of this study below, but let me note here that a general decrease in the reluctance of remarried persons to divorce would not explain this finding. Moreover, the previously divorced may be more hesitant to divorce again because of the stigma attached to divorcing twice. Several remarried

people I interviewed expressed great reluctance to divorce a second time. They reasoned that friends and relatives excused one divorce but would judge them incompetent at marriage after two divorces.

Yet another explanation for the higher divorce rate is the belief that many remarried men are deficient at fulfilling their economic responsibilities. We know that divorce is more likely in families where the husband has low earnings (Goode 1956). Some remarried men, therefore, may be unable to earn a sufficient amount of money to support a family. It is conceivable that this inability to be a successful breadwinner could account for all of the divorce rate differential, but statistical studies of divorce suggest otherwise. Three recent multivariate analyses of survey data on divorce have shown that remarried persons still had a higher probability of divorce or separation, independent of controls for such socioeconomic variables as husband's earnings (Becker et al. 1976), husband's educational attainment (Bumpass and Sweet 1972), and husband's and wife's earnings, employment status, and savings (Cherlin 1977). These analyses show that controlling for low earnings can reduce the difference in divorce probabilities, but they also show that low earnings cannot fully explain the difference. It is possible, nevertheless, that a given amount of income must be spread thinner in many remarriages, because of child-support or alimony payments (although the remarried couple also may be receiving these payments). But this type of financial strain must be distinguished from the questionable notion that many remarried husbands are inherently unable to provide for a wife and children.

INSTITUTIONAL SUPPORT

The unsatisfactory nature of all these explanations leads us to consider one more interpretation.

I hypothesize that the difficulties of couples in remarriage after divorce stem from a lack of institutionalized guidelines for solving many common problems of their remarried life. The lack of institutional support is less serious when neither spouse has a child from from a previous marriage. In this case, the family of remarriage closely resembles families of first marriages, and most of the norms for first marriages apply. But when at least one spouse has children from a previous marriage, family life often differs sharply from first marriages. Frequently, as I will show, family members face problems quite unlike those in first marriages—problems for which institutionalized solutions do not exist. And without accepted solutions to their problems, families of remarriages must resolve difficult issues by themselves. As a result, solving everyday problems is sometimes impossible without engendering conflict and confusion among family members.

The complex structure of families of remarriages after divorce which include children from a previous marriage has been noted by others (Bernard 1956; Bohannan 1970; Duberman 1975). These families are expanded in the number of social roles and relationships they possess and also are expanded in space over more than one household. The additional social roles include stepparents, stepchildren, stepsiblings, and the new spouses of noncustodial parents, among others. And the links between the households are the children of previous marriages. These children are commonly in the custody of one parent—usually the mother—but they normally visit the noncustodial parent regularly. Thus they promote communication among the divorced parents, the new stepparent, and the noncustodial parent's new spouse.

Family relationships can be quite complex, because the new kin in a remarriage after divorce do not, in general, replace the kin from the first marriage as they do in a remarriage after widowhood. Rather, they add to the existing kin (Fast and Cain 1966). But this complexity alone does not necessarily imply that problems of family unity will develop. While families of remarriages may appear complicated to Americans, there are many societies in which complicated kinship rules and family patterns coexist with a functioning, stable family system (Bohannan 1963; Fox 1967).

In most of these societies, however, familial roles and relationships are well defined. Family life may seem complex to Westerners, but activity is regulated by established patterns of behavior. The central difference, then, between families of remarriages in the United States and complicated family situations in other societies is the lack of institutionalized social regulation of remarried life in this country. Our society, oriented toward first marriages, provides little guidance on problems peculiar to remarriages, especially remarriages after divorce.

In order to illustrate the incomplete institutionalization of remarriage and its consequences for family life, let us examine two of the major institutions in society: language and the law. "Language," Gerth and Mills (1953, p. 305) wrote, "is necessary to the operations of institutions. For the symbols used in institutions coordinate the roles that compose them, and justify the enactment of these roles by the members of the institution." Where no adequate terms exist for an important social role, the institutional support for this role is deficient, and general acceptance of the role as a legitimate pattern of activity is questionable.

Consider English terms for the roles peculiar to remarriage after divorce. The term "stepparent," as Bohannan (1970) has observed, originally meant a person who replaced a dead parent, not a person who was an additional parent. And the negative connotations of the "stepparent," especially the "stepmother," are well known (Bernard 1956; Smith 1953). Yet there are no other terms in use. In some situations, no term exists for a child to use in addressing a stepparent. If the child calls her mother "mom," for example, what should she call her stepmother? This lack of appropriate terms for parents in remarriages after divorce can have negative consequences for family functioning. In one family I interviewed, the wife's children wanted to call their stepfather "dad," but the stepfather's own children, who also lived in the household, refused to allow this usage. To them, sharing the term "dad" represented a threat to their claim on their father's attention and affection. The dispute caused bad feelings, and it impaired the father's ability to act as a parent to all the children in the household.

For more extended relationships, the lack of appropriate terms is even more acute. At least the word "stepparent," however inadequate, has a widely accepted meaning. But there is no term a child living with his mother can use to describe his relationship to the woman his father remarried after he divorced the child's mother. And, not surprisingly, the rights and duties of the child and this woman toward each other are unclear. Nor is the problem limited to kinship terms. Suppose a child's parents both remarry and he alternates between their households under a joint custody arrangement. Where, then, is his "home"? And who are the members of his "family"? These linguistic inadequacies correspond to the absence of widely accepted definitions for many of the roles and relationships in families of remarriage. The absence of proper terms is both a symptom and a cause of some of the problems of remarried life.

As for the law, it is both a means of social control and an indicator of accepted patterns of behavior. It was to the law, for instance, that Durkheim turned for evidence on the forms of social solidarity. When we examine family law, we find a set of traditional guidelines, based on precedent, which define the rights and duties of

family members. But as Weitzman (1974) has shown, implicit in the precedents is the assumption that the marriage in question is a first marriage. For example, Weitzman found no provisions for several problems of remarriage, such as balancing the financial obligations of husbands to their spouses and children from current and previous marriages, defining the wife's obligations to husbands and children from the new and the old marriages, and reconciling the competing claims of current and ex-spouses for shares of the estate of a deceased spouse.

Legal regulations concerning incest and consanguineal marriage are also inadequate for families of remarriages. In all states marriage and sexual relations are prohibited between persons closely related by blood, but in many states these restrictions do not cover sexual relations or marriage between other family members in a remarriage—between a stepmother and a stepson, for example, or between two stepchildren (Goldstein and Katz 1965). Mead (1970), among others, has argued that incest taboos serve the important function of allowing children to develop affection for and identification with other family members without the risk of sexual exploitation. She suggested that current beliefs about incest—as embodied in law and social norms—fail to provide adequate security and protection for children in households of remarriage.[3]

The law, then, ignores the special problems of families of remarriages after divorce. It assumes, for the most part, that remarriages are similar to first marriages. Families of remarriages after divorce, consequently, often must deal with problems such as financial obligations or sexual relations without legal regulations or clear legal precedent. The law, like the language, offers incomplete institutional support to families of remarriages.

In addition, other customs and conventions of family life are deficient when applied to remarriages after divorce. Stepparents, for example, have difficulty determining their proper disciplinary relationship to stepchildren. One woman I interviewed, determined not to show favoritism toward her own children, disciplined them more harshly than her stepchildren. Other couples who had children from the wife's previous marriage reported that the stepfather had difficulty establishing himself as a disciplinarian in the household. Fast and Cain (1966), in a study of about 50 case records from child-guidance settings, noted many uncertainties among stepparents about appropriate role behavior. They theorized that the uncertainties derived from the sharing of the role of parent between the stepparent and the noncustodial, biological parent. Years ago, when most remarriages took place after widowhood, this sharing did not exist. Now, even though most remarriages follow divorce, generally accepted guidelines for sharing parenthood still have not emerged.

There is other evidence consistent with the idea that the incomplete institutionalization of remarriage after divorce may underlie the difficulties of families of remarriages. Becker et al. (1976) analyzed the Survey of Economic Opportunity, a nationwide study of approximately 30,000 households. As I mentioned above, they found that the presence of children from a previous marriage increased the probability of divorce for women in remarriages, while the presence of children from the new marriage reduced the probability of divorce. This is as we would expect, since children from a previous marriage expand the family across households and complicate the structure of family roles and relationships. But children born into the new marriage bring none of these complications. Consequently, only children from a previous marriage should add to the special problems of families of remarriages.[4]

In addition, Goetting (1978a, 1978b) studies the attitudes of remarried people toward rela-tionships among adults who are associated by broken marital ties, such as ex-spouses and the people ex-spouses remarry. Bohannan (1970) has called these people "quasi-kin." Goetting presented hypothetical situations involving the behavior of quasi-kin to 90 remarried men and 90 remarried women who were white, previously divorced, and who had children from previous marriages. The subjects were asked to approve, disapprove, or express indifference about the behavior in each situation. Goetting then arbitrarily decided that the respondents reached "consensus" on a given situation if any of the three possible response categories received more than half of all responses. But even by this lenient definition, consensus was not reached on the proper behavior in most of the hypothetical situations. For example, in situations involving conversations between a person's present spouse and his or her ex-spouse, the only consensus of the respondents was that the pair should say "hello." Beyond that, there was no consensus on whether they should engage in polite conversation in public places or on the telephone or whether the ex-spouse should be invited into the new spouse's home while waiting to pick up his or her children. Since meetings of various quasi-kin must occur regularly in the lives of most respondents, their disagreement is indicative of their own confusion about how to act in common family situations.

Still, there are many aspects of remarried life which are similar to life in first marriages, and these are subject to established rules of behavior. Even some of the unique aspects of remarriage may be regulated by social norms—such as the norms concerning the size and nature of wedding ceremonies in remarriages (Hollingshead 1952). Furthermore, as Goode (1956) noted, remarriage is itself an institutional solution to the ambiguous status of the divorced (and not remarried) parent. But the day-to-day life of remarried adults and their children also includes many problems for which there are no institutionalized solutions. And since members of a household of remarriage often have competing or conflicting interests (Bernard 1956), the lack of consensual solutions can make these problems more serious than they otherwise would be. One anthropologist, noting the lack of relevant social norms, wrote, "the present situation approaches chaos, with each individual set of families having to work out its own destiny without any realistic guidelines" (Bohannan 1970, p. 137).

DISCUSSION AND SUGGESTIONS FOR RESEARCH

The lack of institutionalized support for remarriage after divorce from language, the law, and custom is apparent. But when institutional support for family life exists, we take it for granted. People in first marriages rarely stop to notice that a full set of kinship terms exists, that the law regulates their relationships, or that custom dictates much of their behavior toward spouses and children. Because they pay little attention to it, the institutional nature of everyday life in first marriages can be easily underestimated. But such support contributes to the unity of first marriages despite the decline of the patriarch, who was the agent of social control in past time. Institutional guidelines become manifest not only through the transmission of social pressure by a family head but also through the general acceptance of certain habitual behavior patterns as typical of family life. Since this latter process is an ongoing characteristic of social life, the pure "companionship" family—which, in fairness, Burgess and Locke defined only as an ideal type—will never emerge. We have seen this by examining the contrasting case of remarriage after divorce. In this type of marriage, institutional support is noticeably lacking in several respects, and this deficiency has direct consequences for proper family functioning. I have tried to show how the incomplete institutionalization of remarriage after divorce makes the maintenance of family unity more difficult.

One of the first tasks for future research on remarriage is to establish some basic social demographic facts: what proportion of remarried couples have children present from a previous marriage, what proportion have children present from the remarriage, how many children visit noncustodial parents, how frequent these visits are, and so on. As I mentioned, there is no reliable information on these questions now. The U.S. Bureau of the Census, for example, has not discriminated in most of its surveys between parents and stepparents or between children and stepchildren. Yet until figures are available, we can only guess at the number of families which face potential difficulties because of complex living arrangements.

And if we reinterviewed families of remarriage some time after obtaining this information from them, we could begin to test the importance of institutional support for family unity. It follows from the argument advanced here that the more complex the family's situation—the more quasi-kin who live nearby, the more frequently adults and children interact with quasi-kin, the more likely each remarried spouse is to have children from a previous marriage—the more serious becomes the lack of institutional guidelines. Thus, adults in remarriages with a more complex structure should be more likely to divorce or separate in the future, other things being equal. Also, a more complex structure might increase the financial strain on family members, so their earnings and financial obligations should be carefully assessed.

But beyond collecting this fundamental information, we need to discover, by a variety of means, what norms are emerging concerning remarriage and how they emerge. Content analyses of literature, for example, or close study of changes in the language and the law may be illuminating. Just in the past few years, discussion groups, adult education courses, newsletters, and self-help books for remarried parents have proliferated. Whether these developments are central to the institutionalization of remarriage remains to be seen, but they represent possible sources of information about institutionalization which should be monitored. In addition, detailed ethnographic studies could allow us to uncover emerging patterns of institutionalization among families of remarriages.

And in all these investigations of the institutionalization of remarried life, we must develop a perspective different from that of traditional family research. In much past research—starting with the work of Burgess and others—family sociologists have been concerned primarily with the interpersonal relations of family members, especially of husbands and wives (Lasch 1977). But sociologists' theories—and their research strategies—having assumed, for the most part, that interpersonal relations in families can be accounted for without many references to social institutions. Thus, Burgess and Locke (1945) popularized the notion of the companionship

family, whose stability depended largely on what went on within the household. And Locke (1951) measured marital adjustment through a questionnaire which focused largely on such personal characteristics as adaptability and sociability. Yet in order to understand family life—whether in first marriages or remarriages—we must explicitly consider the influences of social institutions on husbands and wives and on parents and children.

We need to know what the institutional links are between family and society which transmit social norms about everyday behavior. That is, we need to know exactly how patterns of family behavior come to be accepted and how proper solutions for family problems come to be taken for granted. And the recent rise in the number of remarriages after divorce may provide us with a natural laboratory for observing this process of institutionalization. As remarriage after divorce becomes more common, remarried parents and their children probably will generate standards of conduct in conjunction with the larger society. By observing these developments, we can improve our understanding of the sources of unity in married—and remarried—life.

Notes and References

NEW RULES: POSTWAR FAMILIES (1955–PRESENT)— STEVEN MINTZ

Notes

1. The quotation is from Joanmarie Kalter, "Television as Value Setter: Family," *TV Guide,* 23–29 July 1988, 6. On portrayals of the family on television during the 1950s, see Steven Mintz and Susan Kellogg, *Domestic Revolutions: A Social History of American Family Life* (New York: The Free Press, 1988), 190–94; James West Davidson and Mark Hamilton Lytle, "From Rosie to Lucy," in *After the Fact: The Art of Historical Detection* (2d ed.; New York: Alfred A. Knopf, 1986), 364–94.

2. Mintz and Kellogg, *Domestic Revolutions,* 203.

3. Kalter, "Television as Value Setter: Family," 6–11. Also see Alice Hoffman, "Move Over, Ozzie and Harriet," *New York Times,* 14 February 1988, 2:1.

4. Mintz and Kellogg, *Domestic Revolutions,* 203.

5. Peter N. Carroll, *It Seemed Like Nothing Happened: The Tragedy and Promise of America in the 1970's* (New York: Holt, Rinehart, and Winston, 1982), 278–79.

6. *New York Times,* 24 September 1988, 21.

7. Mintz and Kellogg, *Domestic Revolutions,* 203–4; Carroll, *It Seemed Like Nothing Happened,* 279.

8. Mintz and Kellogg, *Domestic Revolutions,* 204; Carroll, *It Seemed Like Nothing Happened,* 280–81.

9. Mintz and Kellogg, *Domestic Revolutions,* 204. On cohabitation, see *Houston Post* 23 April 1988, 14D.

10. Mintz and Kellogg, *Domestic Revolutions,* 204.

11. Stephen L. Klineberg discussed similar themes in a public lecture, "American Families in Transition: Challenges and Opportunities in a Revolutionary Time," delivered at Rice University, 15 February 1983.

12. Mary Jo Bane, *Here to Stay: American Families in the Twentieth Century* (New York: Basic Books, 1976), 12–13, 30; Sar A. Levitan and Richard S. Belous, *What's Happening to the American Family?* (Baltimore, Md.: Johns Hopkins University Press, 1981), 21, 63; Mary Jo Bane et al., "Child Care Settings in the United States," in *Child Care and Mediating Structures,* ed. Brigitte Berger and Sidney Callahan (Washington, D.C.: American Enterprise Institute for Public Policy Research, 1979), 19; Carol Tavris and Carole Offir, *The Longest War: Sex Differences in Perspective* (New York: Harcourt Brace Jovanovich, 1977); Stephen L. Klineberg, "Age of Vicarious Parenting Now Fading," *Houston Post* 25 June 1987, 3B.

13. Mintz and Kellogg, *Domestic Revolutions,* 177–82; Elaine Tyler May, *Homeward Bound: American Families in the Cold War*

(New York: Basic Books, 1988); Betty Friedan, *The Feminine Mystique* (New York: W. W. Norton & Company, 1963), 12, 41–42; Andrew J. Cherlin, "The 50's Family and Today's," *New York Times*, 18 November 1981, 1:31; idem., "Changing Family and Household: Contemporary Lessons from Historical Research," *Annual Review of Sociology* 9 (1983): 58–60; idem., *Marriage, Divorce, Remarriage* (Cambridge, Mass.: Harvard University Press, 1981); William H. Chafe, *The Unfinished Journey: America since World War II* (New York: Oxford University Press, 1986), 123–24; idem., *The American Woman: Her Changing Social, Economic, and Political Roles, 1920–1970* (New York: Oxford University Press, 1972), 177, 199–210; Godfrey Hodgson, *America in Our Time* (Garden City, N.Y.: Doubleday and Co., 1976), 50–51; Douglas T. Miller and Marion Nowak, *The Fifties: The Way We Really Were* (Garden City, N.Y.: Doubleday and Co., 1977), 147, 160.

14. See note 13.

15. Mintz and Kellogg, *Domestic Revolutions*, 178–79; Cherlin, "Changing Family and Household," 58–60; Cherlin, "The 50's Family," 1:31; Chafe, *Unfinished Journey*, 123; Hodgson, *America in Our Time*, 50–51.

16. Mintz and Kellogg, *Domestic Revolutions*, 198–99; Chafe, *Unfinished Journey*, 126–28; Jo Freeman, *The Politics of Women's Liberation* (New York: David McKay, 1975), 28–31; Friedan, *Feminine Mystique*, 17–20, 59.

17. Mintz and Kellogg, *Domestic Revolutions*, 199–200; Jeffrey Hart, *When the Going Was Good! American Life in the Fifties* (New York: Crown, 1982), 130–36; Kenneth Keniston, *The Uncommitted: Alienated Youth in American Society* (New York: Harcourt, Brace & World, 1965), 394–406.

18. Mintz and Kellogg, *Domestic Revolutions*, 205–6; Joseph Veroff, Elizabeth Douan, and Richard A. Kulka, *The Inner America: A Self Portrait from 1957 to 1976* (New York: Basic Books, 1981), 191–96; Daniel Yankelovich, *New Rules: Search for Self-Fulfillment in a World Turned Upside Down* (New York: Random House, 1981), 5, 68, 97, 99.

19. Mintz and Kellogg, *Domestic Revolutions*, 205–6; Veroff, Douan, and Kulka, *The Inner America*, 191–96; Yankelovich, *New Rules*, 5, 68, 97, 99.

20. Richard A. Easterlin, "The American Baby Boom in Historical Perspective," Occasional Paper no. 79 (Washington, D.C.: National Bureau of Economic Research, 1962); idem., "The Conflict between Aspirations and Resources," *Population and Development Review* 2 (September/December 1972), 417–26; idem., *Birth and Fortune: The Impact of Numbers on Personal Welfare* (New York: Basic Books, 1980); Arthur A. Campbell, "Baby Boom to Birth Dearth and Beyond," *Annals of the American Academy of Political and Social Science*, 435 (January 1978): 52–53.

21. Mintz and Kellogg, *Domestic Revolutions*, 206; Russell Jacoby, *Social Amnesia: A Critique of Conformist Psychology from Adler to Laing* (Boston: Beacon Press, 1975); Barbara Ehrenreich, *Hearts of Men: American Dreams and the Flight from Commitment* (Garden City, N.Y.: Doubleday and Co., 1983), 89–98, 122, 147, 164–65; Yankelovich, *New Rules*, 235.

22. Mintz and Kellogg, *Domestic Revolutions*, 204; Arlie Russell Hochschild, review of *Women and Love: A Cultural Revolution in Progress*, Shere Hite, *New York Times Book Review*, 15 November 1987, 34; Morton M. Hunt, *Sexual Behavior in the 1970s* (Chicago: Playboy Press, 1974), 235–40, 253–90; Philip Blumstein and Pepper Schwartz, *American Couples: Money, Work, Sex* (New York: William Morrow, 1983), 267–302.

23. Mintz and Kellogg, *Domestic Revolutions*, 208–9; William Manchester, *Glory and the Dream* (Boston: Little, Brown, and Company, 1974), 1035–36; Edward Sagarin, ed.,

"Sex and the Contemporary American Scene," *Annals of the American Academy of Political and Social Science* 376 (March 1968); Mintz and Kellogg, "Recent Trends in American Family History: Dimensions of Demographic and Cultural Change," *Houston Law Review* 21 (1984): 792–93.

24. Mintz and Kellogg, *Domestic Revolutions,* 208–9; Manchester, *Glory and the Dream,* 1035–36; Mintz and Kellogg, "Recent Trends in American Family History," 792–93.

25. Mintz and Kellogg, "Recent Trends in American Family History," 790–91.

26. Mintz and Kellogg, *Domestic Revolutions,* 223.

27. Ibid., 207–8.

28. Robert Bellah, et al. *Habits of the Heart: Individualism and Commitment in American Life* (Berkeley: University of California Press, 1985); Christopher Lasch, *Haven in a Heartless World: The Family Besieged* (New York: Basic Books, 1977); Yankelovich, *New Rules;* Brigitte and Peter Berger, *The War Over the Family: Capturing the Middle Ground* (Garden City, New York: Doubleday and Co., 1983).

29. Mintz and Kellogg, *Domestic Revolutions,* 228.

30. On shifting legal definitions of family, see Stephen J. Morse, "Family Law in Transition: From Traditional Families to Individual Liberty," in *Changing Images of the Family,* ed. Virginia Tufte and Barbara Myerhoff (New Haven, Conn.: Yale University Press, 1979), 322–25; Eva R. Rubin, *The Supreme Court and the American Family: Ideology and Issues* (Westport, Conn.: Greenwood Press, 1986), 143–61.

31. Mintz and Kellogg, *Domestic Revolutions,* 230–31.

32. Lee E. Teitelbaum, "Moral Discourse and Family Law," *Michigan Law Review* (1985): 430–34.

33. Lenore J. Weitzman and Ruth B. Dixon, "The Transformation of Legal Marriage through No-Fault Divorce: The Case of the United States," in *Marriage and Cohabitation in Contemporary Societies: Areas of Legal, Social, and Ethical Change,* ed. John M. Eckelaar and Sanford N. Katz (Toronto: Buttersworth, 1979), 143–53; Lynne Carol Halem, *Divorce Reform: Changing Legal and Social Perspectives* (New York: The Free Press, 1980), 233–83.

34. Weitzman and Dixon, "The Transformation of Legal Marriage through No-Fault Divorce," 143–53; Lenore J. Weitzman, *The Divorce Revolution: The Unexpected Social and Economic Consequences for Women and Children* (New York: The Free Press, 1985).

35. *New York Times,* 7 February 1983, A14; 18 April 1982, C1.

36. *New York Times,* 11 October 1980, 1:21; 3 May 1981, 4:9; 6 October 1980, 2:8; 15 January 1975, 1:71.

37. Mary Ann Glendon, *The New Family and the New Property* (Toronto: Buttersworth, 1981), 43.

38. Ibid., 11, 38, 49, 71–73.

39. Ibid., 61; *New York Times,* 7 February 1983, 1:4. As recently as 1956, thirty-eight states had filial responsibility statutes. See Carl E. Schneider, "Moral Discourse and the Transformation of American Family Law," *Michigan Law Review* (1985): 1813. Enforcement of such statutes was difficult because a child who was financially able to support a parent could claim that the parent's need had not been judicially determined, that the parent was unworthy of support, or that liability was shared by a number of children. See W. Walton Garrett, "Filial Responsibility Laws," *Journal of Family Law* 18 (1979–80): 804–8.

40. Schneider, "Moral Discourse and the Transformation of American Family Law," 1835–39.

41. Ibid., 1814–19.

42. On the changing legal treatment of children and adolescents, see Walter O. Weyrauch

and Sanford N. Katz, *American Family Law in Transition* (Washington, D.C.: Bureau of National Affairs, 1983), 496–98. On foster care, see Rubin, *Supreme Court and the American Family,* 156.

43. Mary Ann Glendon, *Abortion and Divorce in Western Law* (Cambridge, Mass.: Harvard University Press, 1987), 108–11. In the 1977 case of *Zablocki* v. *Redhail,* the Supreme Court struck down a Wisconsin statute that prohibited divorced parents from remarrying unless they provided proof that they were in compliance with child support orders, ruling that the law violated the individual's right to marry. See Morse, "Family Law in Transition," 333.

44. Glendon, *Abortion and Divorce in Western Law,* 86–104. Glendon maintains that European divorce laws, in sharp contrast to American no-fault divorce laws, require noncustodial fathers to maintain economic responsibility for their children. European governments have established strict formulas that realistically calculate the costs of raising children and have created bureaucratic mechanisms to compel fathers to pay support costs. When paternal support is inadequate, the state steps in to ensure adequate support.

45. Glendon, *Abortion and Divorce in Western Law,* 86–104.

46. Trends in the well-being of American youth are quantified in Office of Educational Research and Improvement, *Youth Indicators 1988* (Washington, D.C.: Government Printing Office, 1988). On youth employment, see Ellen Greenberger and Laurence Steinberg, *When Teenagers Work: The Psychological and Social Costs of Adolescent Employment* (New York: Basic Books, 1986), 3–46.

It is true that the suicide rate for white male adolescents increased 260 percent between 1950 and 1976, the illegitimacy rate among white adolescent females increased 143 percent over the same period, and the rate of death by homicide among white adolescent males increased 177 percent between 1959 and 1976. Yet, in spite of these percentage increases, the numbers remained at low levels. The white male adolescent homicide rate rose from 3 per 100,000 in 1959 to 8 per 100,000 in 1976; the white male adolescent suicide rate climbed from 4 per 100,000 in 1950 to 13 per 100,000 in 1976; and illegitimacy among white teenage women rose from 5.1 per 1,000 to 12.4 per 1,000. It is also easy to exaggerate drug use. Seventeen percent of all high school seniors have tried cocaine once in their lives; 54 percent have tried marijuana at least once. See Ira S. Steinberg, *The New Lost Generation: The Population Boom and Public Policy* (New York: St. Martin's Press, 1982), 7–19; Adam Paul Weisman, "I was a Drug-Hype Junkie," *New Republic,* 6 October 1986, 14–17.

47. Joan Beck, "Growing Up in America Is Tough," *Houston Chronicle,* 2 April 1986, A10; Marie Winn, *Children without Childhood* (New York: Pantheon, 1983); David Elkind, *The Hurried Child: Growing Up Too Soon* (Reading, Mass.: Addison-Wesley, 1981); Vance Packard, *Our Endangered Children: Growing Up in a Changing World* (Boston: Little, Brown and Company, 1983); Eda LeShan, *The Conspiracy against Childhood* (New York: Atheneum, 1967); Peter Uhlenberg and David Eggebeen, "The Declining Well-Being of American Adolescents," *Public Interest* 85 (Winter 1986): 25–38.

48. Mintz and Kellogg, *Domestic Revolutions,* 221; Victor R. Fuchs, *How We Live* (Cambridge, Mass.: Harvard University Press, 1983), 51, 55–56; 69–71; Bane, *Here to Stay,* 15; John P. Murray, *Television and Youth: 25 Years of Research and Controversy* (Stanford, Wash.: Boys Town Center, 1980), 67.

49. Mintz and Kellogg, *Domestic Revolutions,* 221; Marie Winn, *The Plug-In Drug* (New York: The Viking Press, 1977); Murray, *Television and Youth,* 18–57.

50. Mintz and Kellogg, *Domestic Revolutions,* 221; Murray, *Television and Youth,* 18–57.

51. Mintz and Kellogg, *Domestic Revolutions,* 221–22.

52. On the increasing numbers of working mothers, see Office of Educational Research and Improvement, *Youth Indicators 1988,* 38–41; Douglas J. Besharov, "Child Care Another Make-believe Crisis," *Houston Chronicle,* 28 August 1988, 1F.

53. U.S. Bureau of the Census, *Who's Minding the Kids?* (Washington, D.C.: Government Printing Office, 1987); *New York Times,* 11 May 1987, 18.

54. Mintz and Kellogg, *Domestic Revolutions,* 162; Claudia Wallis, "The Child Care Dilemma," *Time,* 22 June 1987, 63; Ellen Ruppel Shell, "Babes in Day Care," *Atlantic* (August 1988), 73–74.

55. See note 54.

56. See note 54.

57. Mintz and Kellogg, *Domestic Revolutions,* 225.

58. Ibid., 224–25.

59. Ann Milne, "Family Structure and the Achievement of Children," 5–41. Paper presented at the Conference on Education and the Family, Office of Educational Research and Improvement, U.S. Office of Education, Washington, D.C., 17–18 June 1988; *New York Times,* 7 April 1988, 24.

60. Milne, "Family Structure and the Achievement of Children," 6–7; *New York Times,* 7 April 1988, 24.

61. Mintz and Kellogg, *Domestic Revolutions,* 225–26; Levitan and Belous, *What's Happening to the American Family?,* 69–72; Halem, *Divorce Reform,* 191–93.

62. Packard, *Our Endangered Children,* 189–201; Halem, *Divorce Reform,* 174–81; Levitan and Belous, *What's Happening to the American Family?,* 69–72; Judith S. Wallerstein and Joan B. Kelley, *Surviving the Breakup: How Children and Parents Cope with Divorce* (New York: Basic Books, 1980); Cynthia Longfellow, "Divorce in Context: Its Impact on Children," in *Divorce and Separation: Conditions, Causes, and Consequences,* ed. George Levinger et al. (New York: Basic Books, 1979), 287–306.

63. See note 52.

64. Mintz and Kellogg, *Domestic Revolutions,* 226–27; *New York Times,* 7 April 1988, 24.

65. See note 64.

66. Mintz and Kellogg, *Domestic Revolutions,* 227; Fuchs, *How We Live,* 73–75, 149–50, 214; Levitan and Belous, *What's Happening to the American Family?,* 72–75; *New York Times,* 2 April 1974, 1:34; Weitzman, *Divorce Revolution.*

67. See note 66.

68. See note 66.

69. Maris A. Vinovskis, *An "Epidemic" of Adolescent Pregnancy?: Some Historical and Policy Considerations* (New York: Oxford University Press, 1988), 25–28.

70. Vinovskis, *An "Epidemic" of Adolescent Pregnancy?,* 28–31, 34–36.

71. Ibid., 29–31.

72. Frank Furstenberg et al., *Adolescent Mothers in Later Life* (New York: Cambridge University Press, 1987); *Houston Chronicle,* 7 September 1987, 1:7.

73. Vinovskis, *An "Epidemic" of Adolescent Pregnancy?,* 25–46.

74. *New York Times,* 14 November 1987, 14.

75. *Time,* 21 December 1987, 68.

76. *New York Times,* 15 November 1987, A17, E9; 14 November 1987, 14.

77. Elizabeth Pleck, *Domestic Tyranny: The Making of American Social Policy Against Family Violence from Colonial Times to the Present* (New York: Oxford University Press, 1987), 164–200.

78. Mintz and Kellogg, *Domestic Revolutions,* 210. Lee Rainwater and William L.

Yancey, *The Moynihan Report and the Politics of Controversy* (Cambridge, Mass.: MIT Press, 1967), includes the full text of *The Negro Family: The Case for National Action* as well as responses to the report by government policy makers, journalists, civil rights leaders, and academic social scientists.

79. Mintz and Kellogg, *Domestic Revolutions,* 210; Rainwater and Yancey, *Moynihan Report and the Politics of Controversy,* 51–60, 75–91.

80. Mintz and Kellogg, *Domestic Revolutions,* 210–11.

81. Ibid., 211–13; Yancey and Rainwater, *Moynihan Report and the Politics of Controversy,* 133–215; Andrew Billingsley, *Black Families in White America* (New York: Prentice-Hall, 1968); R. Farley and A. I. Hermalin, "Family Stability: A Comparison of Trends between Blacks and Whites," *American Sociological Review,* 36 (1971): 1–17; J. Heiss, "On the Transmission of Marital Instability in Black Families," *American Sociological Review* 37 (1972): 82–92; Robert B. Hill, *Strengths of Black Families* (New York: Emerson Hall, 1971); Joyce Ladner, *Tomorrow's Tomorrow* (Garden City, N.Y.: Doubleday and Co., 1972); R. Staples, "Toward a Sociology of the Black Family: A Theoretical and Methodological Assessment," *Journal of Marriage and the Family* 33 (1971): 119–38; Sar A. Levitan, William B. Johnston, and Robert Taggart, *Minorities in the United States: Problems, Progress, and Prospects* (Washington, D.C.: Public Affairs Press, 1975), 38; Carol B. Stack, *All Our Kin: Strategies for Survival in a Black Community* (New York: Harper and Row, 1974); Demitri B. Shimkin, Edith M. Shimkin, and Dennis A. Frate, eds., *The Extended Family in Black Societies* (Chicago: University of Chicago Press, 1978).

82. Mintz and Kellogg, *Domestic Revolutions,* 215; *New York Times* 29 February 1988, 1:13.

83. Charles Murray, *Losing Ground: American Social Policy, 1950–1980* (New York: Basic Books, 1984),129–33; idem., "No, Welfare Isn't Really the Problem," *Public Interest* no. 84 (Summer 1986): 5–6.

84. David Ellwood and Mary Jo Bane, "Household Composition and Poverty," in Sheldon H. Danziger and Daniel H. Weinberg, eds., *Fighting Poverty: What Works and What Doesn't* (Cambridge, Mass.: Harvard University Press, 1986), 209–31; Mintz and Kellogg, *Domestic Revolutions,* 215–16; Robert Greenstein, "Prisoners of the Economy," *New York Times Book Review,* 25 October 1987, 46; Sar A. Levitan and Clifford M. Johnson, *Beyond the Safety Net: Reviving the Promise of Opportunity in America* (Cambridge, Mass.: Ballinger, 1984), 64; Robert Lerman, "The Family, Poverty, and Welfare Programs: An Introductory Essay on Problems of Analysis and Policy," in U.S. Congress, Joint Economic Committee, *Studies in Public Welfare* (Washington, D.C.: Government Printing Office, 1974), 18–19; Marjorie Honig, "The Impact of Welfare Payment Levels on Family Stability," in U.S. Congress, *Studies in Pubic Welfare,* 37–53; Danziger and Weinberg, eds., *Fighting Poverty.*

85. William Julius Wilson, *The Truly Disadvantaged: The Inner City, the Underclass, and Public Policy* (Chicago: University of Chicago Press, 1987); *New York Times,* 16 November 1987, 18.

86. Christopher Jencks, "Deadly Neighborhoods," *New Republic,* 13 June 1988, 24–26.

87. Ibid., 28–30.

88. On new reproductive technologies, see E. Peter Volpe, *Test-Tube Conception: A Blend of Love and Science* (Macon, Ga.: Mercer University Press, 1987); Charles Krauthammer, "The Ethics of Human Manufacture," *New Republic,* 4 May 1987, 17–21; *New York Times,* 17 May 1987, 3:6; R. Snowden, G. D. Mitchell, and E. M. Snowden, *Artificial Reproduction: A*

Social Investigation (London: George Allen and Unwin, 1983).

89. On Lesley Brown see Volpe, *Test-Tube Conception,* 1–13.

90. On Mary Beth Whitehead, William Stern, and the Baby M. controversy, see *New York Times,* 4 February 1988, 1:1; 2 April 1987, 1:1; 1 April 1987, 1:1; 18 January 1987, 1:3; 15 February 1987, 4:22.

91. The ethical and moral challenges posed by new reproductive technologies are examined in Krauthammer, "The Ethics of Human Manufacture," 17–21; Snowden, Mitchell, and Snowden, *Artificial Reproduction,* 147–65; Leroy Walters, "Human in Vitro Fertilization: A Review of the Ethical Literature," *The Hastings Center Report* 9 (1979): 23–43; The Ethics Committee of the American Fertility Society, "Ethical Considerations of the New Reproductive Technologies," *Fertility and Sterility* 46, Supplement 1 (1986): 1–94; C. Grobstein, M. Flower, and J. Mendeloff, "Frozen Embryos: Policy Issues," *New England Journal of Medicine* 312 (1985): 1584–1588.

92. Mintz and Kellogg, *Domestic Revolutions,* 233–35, 240–41; Gilbert Y. Steiner, *The Futility of Family Policy* (Washington, D.C.: Brookings Institution, 1981); Kristin Luker, *Abortion and the Politics of Motherhood* (Berkeley: University of California Press, 1984).

93. Mintz and Kellogg, *Domestic Revolutions,* 237, 240–41; Kenneth Keniston and the Carnegie Council on Children, *All Our Children: The American Family under Pressure* (New York: Harcourt Brace Jovanovich, 1977), 216–21; Packard, *Our Endangered Children,* 343–63.

References

Bane, Mary Jo. *Here to Stay: American Families in the Twentieth Century.* New York: Basic Books, 1976.

Beck, Joan. "Growing Up in America Is Tough." *Houston Chronicle,* 2 April 1986: A10.

Bellah, Robert, et al. *Habits of the Heart: Individualism and Commitment in American Life.* Berkeley: University of California Press, 1985.

Berger, Brigitte, and Peter Berger. *The War Over the Family: Capturing the Middle Ground.* Garden City, N.Y.: Doubleday and Co., 1983.

Berger, Brigitte, and Sidney Callahan, eds. *Child Care and Mediating Structures.* Washington, D.C.: American Enterprise Institute for Public Policy Research, 1979.

Bernard, Jessie. *The Future of Marriage.* New York: Bantam Books, 1972.

———. *The Future of Motherhood.* New York: The Dial Press, 1974.

Besharov, Douglas J. "Child Care: Another Make-Believe Crisis," *Houston Chronicle,* 28 August 1988: 1F.

Billingsley, Andrew. *Black Families in White America.* Englewood Cliffs, N.J.: Prentice-Hall, 1968.

Blumstein, Philip, and Pepper Schwartz. *American Couples: Money, Work, Sex.* New York: William Morrow, 1983.

Bronfenbrenner, Urie. "Socialization and Social Class through Time and Space." In *Readings in Social Psychology,* ed. Eleanor Maccoby, Theodore Newcomb, and Eugene Hartley, 400–25. New York: Holt, Rinehart, and Winston, 1958,

Campbell, Arthur A. "Baby Boom to Birth Dearth and Beyond." *Annals of the American Academy of Political and Social Science* 435 (January 1978): 40–59.

Caplow, Theodore, et al. *Middletown Families: Fifty Years of Continuity and Change.* Minneapolis: University of Minnesota Press, 1982.

Carroll, Peter N. *It Seemed Like Nothing Happened: The Tragedy and Promise of America in the 1970's.* New York: Holt, Rinehart, and Winston, 1982.

Carter, Hugh, and Paul Glick. *Marriage and Divorce: A Social and Economic Study.* Cambridge, Mass.: Harvard University Press, 1976.

Castleman, Harry. *Watching TV—Four Decades of American Television.* New York: McGraw-Hill, 1982.

Chafe, William H. *The American Woman: Her Changing Social, Economic, and Political Roles, 1920–1970.* New York: Oxford University Press, 1972.

———. *The Unfinished Journey: America since World War II.* New York: Oxford University Press, 1986.

Cherlin, Andrew J. "Changing Family and Household: Contemporary Lessons from Historical Research." *Annual Review of Sociology* 9 (1983): 51–66.

———. "The 50's Family and Today's," *New York Times* 18 November 1981, 1:31.

———. *Marriage, Divorce, Remarriage.* Cambridge, Mass.: Harvard University Press, 1981.

Chilman, Catherine. *Adolescent Sexuality in a Changing American Society.* New York: John Wiley and Sons, 1983.

Danziger, Sheldon H., and Daniel H. Weinberg, eds. *Fighting Poverty: What Works and What Doesn't.* Cambridge, Mass.: Harvard University Press, 1986.

Davidson, James West, and Mark Hamilton Lytle, eds. "From Rosie to Lucy." In *After the Fact: The Art of Historical Detection.* 2d ed., 364–94. New York: Alfred A. Knopf, 1986.

Degler, Carl N. *At Odds: Women and the Family in America from the Revolution to the Present.* New York: Oxford University Press, 1980.

Easterlin, Richard A. "The American Baby Boom in Historical Perspective." Occasional Paper no. 79. Washington, D.C.: National Bureau of Economic Research, 1962.

———. *Birth and the Fortune: The Impact of Numbers on Personal Welfare.* New York: Basic Books, 1980.

———. "The Conflict between Aspirations and Resources." *Population and Development Review* 2 (September/December 1972): 417–26.

Ehrenreich, Barbara. *Hearts of Men: American Dreams and the Flight from Commitment.* Garden City, N.Y.: Doubleday and Co., 1983.

Elkind, David. *The Hurried Child: Growing Up Too Soon.* Reading, Mass.: Addison-Wesley, 1981.

The Ethics Committee of the American Fertility Society. "Ethical Considerations of the New Reproductive Technologies." *Fertility and Sterility* 46, Supplement 1 (1986): 1–94.

Farley, Reynolds, and Albert I. Hermalin. "Family Stability: A Comparison of Trends between Blacks and Whites." *American Sociological Review* 36 (1971): 1–17.

Freeman, Jo. *The Politics of Women's Liberation.* New York: David McKay, 1975.

Friedan, Betty. *The Feminine Mystique.* New York: W. W. Norton & Company, 1963.

Fuchs, Victor R. *How We Live.* Cambridge, Mass.: Harvard University Press, 1983.

Furstenberg, Frank, et al., *Adolescent Mothers in Later Life.* New York: Cambridge University Press, 1987.

Garrett, W. Walton. "Filial Responsibility Laws." *Journal of Family Law* 18 (1979-80): 804–8.

Glendon, Mary Ann. *Abortion and Divorce in Western Law.* Cambridge, Mass.: Harvard University Press, 1987.

———. *The New Family and the New Property.* Toronto: Butterworths, 1981.

Greenberger, Ellen, and Laurence Steinberg. *When Teenagers Work: The Psychological and Social Costs of Adolescent Employment.* New York: Basic Books, 1986.

Greenstein, Robert, "Prisoners of the Economy." *New York Times Book Review,* 25 October 1987, 46.

Grobstein, C., M. Flower, and J. Mendeloff. "Frozen Embryos: Policy Issues." *New England Journal of Medicine* 312 (1985): 1584–1588.

Halem, Lynne Carol. *Divorce Reform: Changing Legal and Social Perspectives.* New York: The Free Press, 1980.

Hart, Jeffrey. *When the Going Was Good! American Life in the Fifties.* New York: Crown, 1982.

Heiss, J. "On the Transmission of Marital Instability in Black Families." *American Sociological Review* 37 (1972): 82–92.

Hetherington, Mavis. "Effects of Father Absence on Personality Development in Adolescent Daughters." *Developmental Psychology* 7 (1972): 313–26.

Hill, Robert B. *Strengths of Black Families.* New York: Emerson Hall, 1971.

Hochschild, Arlie Russell. A review of *Women and Love: A Cultural Revolution in Progress* by Shere Hite. *New York Times Book Review,* 15 November 1987: 34.

Hodgson, Godfrey. *America in Our Time.* Garden City, N.Y.: Doubleday and Co., 1976.

Hoffman, Alice. "Move Over, Ozzie and Harriet." *New York Times,* 14 February 1988, 2:1.

Hunt, Morton M. *Sexual Behavior in the 1970s.* Chicago: Playboy Press, 1974.

Jacoby, Russell. *Social Amnesia: A Critique of Conformist Psychology from Adler to Laing.* Boston: Beacon Press, 1975.

Jencks, Christopher. "Deadly Neighbors." *New Republic,* 13 June 1988: 24–26.

Kalter, Joanmarie. "Television as Value Setter: Family," *TV Guide,* 23–29 July 1988, 5–15.

Keniston, Kenneth. *The Uncommitted: Alienated Youth in American Society.* New York: Harcourt, Brace & World, 1965.

Keniston, Kenneth, and the Carnegie Council on Children. *All Our Children: The American Family under Pressure.* New York: Harcourt Brace Jovanovich, 1977.

Klineberg, Stephen L. "Age of Vicarious Parenting Now Fading." *Houston Post,* 25 June 1987, 3B.

Klineberg, Stephen L. "American Families in Transition: Challenges and Opportunities in a Revolutionary Time." Public Lecture delivered at Rice University, 15 February 1983.

Kramer, Rita. *In Defense of the Family: Raising Children in America Today.* New York: Basic Books, 1983.

Krauthammer, Charles. "The Ethics of Human Manufacture." *New Republic,* 4 May 1987: 17–21.

Ladner, Joyce. *Tomorrow's Tomorrow: The Black Woman.* Garden City, N.Y.: Doubleday and Co., 1972.

Lasch, Christopher. *Haven in a Heartless World: The Family Besieged.* New York: Basic Books, 1977.

LeShan, Eda. *The Conspiracy against Childhood.* New York: Atheneum, 1967.

Levitan, Sar A., and Richard S. Belous. *What's Happening to the American Family?.* Baltimore, Md.: Johns Hopkins University Press, 1981.

Levitan, Sar A., and Clifford M. Johnson. *Beyond the Safety Net: Reviving the Promise of Opportunity in America.* Cambridge, Mass.: Ballinger, 1984.

Levitan, Sar A., William B. Johnston, and Robert Taggart. *Minorities in the United States: Problems, Progress, and Prospects.* Washington, D.C.: Public Affairs Press, 1975.

Longfellow, Cynthia. "Divorce in Context: Its Impact on Children." In *Divorce and Separation: Conditions, Causes, and Consequences,* ed. George Levinger, et al., 287–306. New York: Basic Books, 1979.

Luker, Kristin. *Abortion and the Politics of Motherhood.* Berkeley: University of California Press, 1994.

McAdoo, Harriette Pipes, ed. *Black Families.* Beverly Hills, Calif.: Sage Publications, 1981.

Manchester, William. *Glory and the Dream: A Narrative History of America, 1932–1972.* Boston: Little, Brown and Company, 1974.

May, Elaine Tyler. *Homeward Bound: American Families in the Cold War.* New York: Basic Books, 1988.

Miller, Douglas T., and Marion Nowak. *The Fifties: The Way We Really Were.* Garden City, N.Y.: Doubleday and Co., 1977.

Milne, Ann. "Family Structure and the Achievement of Children." Paper presented at the Conference on Education and the Family, Office of Educational Research and Improvement, U.S. Office of Education, Washington, D.C., 17–18 June 1988.

Mintz, Steven, and Susan Kellogg. *Domestic Revolutions: A Social History of American Family Life.* New York: The Free Press, 1988.

————. "Recent Trends in American Family History: Dimensions of Demographic and Cultural Change." *Houston Law Review* 21 (1984): 792–93.

Morse, Stephen J. "Family Law in Transition: From Traditional Families to Individual Liberty." In *Changing Images of the Family,* ed. Virginia Tufte and Barbara Myerhoff, 318–360. New Haven, Conn.: Yale University Press, 1979.

Murray, Charles. *Losing Ground: American Social Policy, 1950–1980.* New York: Basic Books 1984.

Murray, Charles. "No, Welfare Isn't Really the Problem." *Public Interest* 84 (Summer 1986): 3–11.

Murray, John P. *Television and Youth: 25 Years of Research and Controversy.* Stanford, Wash.: Boys Town Center, 1980.

Office of Educational Research and Improvement, U.S. Department of Education. *Youth Indicators 1988.* Washington, D.C.: Government Printing Office, 1988.

Packard, Vance. *Our Endangered Children: Growing Up in a Changing World.* Boston: Little, Brown and Company, 1983.

Pleck, Elizabeth. *Domestic Tyranny: The Making of American Social Policy against Family Violence from Colonial Times to the Present.* New York: Oxford University Press, 1987.

Rainwater, Lee, and William L. Yancey. *The Moynihan Report and the Politics of Controversy.* Cambridge, Mass.: MIT Press, 1967.

Rubin, Eva R. *The Supreme Court and the American Family: Ideology and Issues.* Westport, Conn.: Greenwood Press, 1986.

Sagarin, Edward, ed. "Sex and the Contemporary American Scene." *Annals of the American Academy of Political and Social Science* 376 (March 1968).

Schneider, Carl E. "Moral Discourse and the Transformation of American Family Law." *Michigan Law Review* (1985): 1803–79.

Shell, Ellen Ruppel. "Babes in Day Care." *Atlantic* (August 1988): 73–74.

Shimkin, Demitri B., Edith M. Shimkin, and Dennis A. Frate, eds. *The Extended Family in Black Societies.* Chicago: University of Chicago Press, 1978.

Snowden, R., G. D. Mitchell, and E. M. Snowden. *Artificial Reproduction: A Social Investigation.* London: George Allen and Unwin, 1983.

Stack, Carol B. *All Our Kin: Strategies for Survival in a Black Community.* New York: Harper and Row, 1974.

Staples, R. "Toward a Sociology of the Black Family: A Theoretical and Methodological Assessment." *Journal of Marriage and the Family* 33 (1971): 119-38.

Steinberg, Ira S. *The New Lost Generation: The Population Boom and Public Policy.* New York: St. Martin's Press, 1982.

Steiner, Gilbert Y. *The Futility of Family Policy.* Washington, D.C.: Brookings Institution, 1981.

Tavris, Carol, and Carole Offir. *The Longest War: Sex Differences in Perspective.* New York: Harcourt Brace Jovanovich, 1977.

Teitelbaum, Lee E. "Moral Discourse and Family Law." *Michigan Law Review* (1985): 430–34.

Uhlenberg, Peter, and David Eggebeen. "The Declining Well-Being of American Adolescents." *Public Interest* 85 (Winter 1986): 25–38.

U.S. Bureau of the Census. *Who's Minding the Kids?* Washington, D.C.: Government Printing Office, 1987.

U.S. Congress. Joint Economic Committee. *Studies in Public Welfare.* Washington, D.C.: Government Printing Office, 1974.

Veroff, Joseph, Elizabeth Douan, and Richard A. Kulka. *The Inner America: A Self Portrait from 1957 to 1976.* New York: Basic Books, 1981.

Vinovskis, Maris A. *An "Epidemic" of Adolescent Pregnancy?: Some Historical and Policy Considerations.* New York: Oxford University Press, 1988.

Volpe, E. Peter. *Test-Tube Conception: A Blend of Love and Science.* Macon, Ga.: Mercer University Press, 1987.

Wallerstein, Judith S., and Joan B. Kelley. *Surviving the Breakup: How Children and Parents Cope with Divorce.* New York: Basic Books, 1980.

Wallis, Claudia. "The Child Care Dilemma." *Time,* 22 June 1987: 54–63.

Walters, Leroy. "Human in Vitro Fertilization: A Review of the Ethical Literature." *The Hastings Center Report* 9 (1979): 23–43.

Weisman, Adam Paul. "I was a Drug-Hype Junkie." *New Republic,* 6 October 1986: 14–17.

Weiss, Robert. *Going It Alone: The Family Life and Social Situation of the Single Parent.* New York: Basic Books, 1979.

Weitzman, Lenore J. *The Divorce Revolution: The Unexpected Social and Economic Consequences of Women and Children.* New York: The Free Press, 1985.

Weitzman, Lenore J., and Ruth B. Dixon. "The Transformation of Legal Marriage through No-Fault Divorce: The Case of the United States." In *Marriage and Cohabitation in Contemporary Societies: Areas of Legal, Social, and Ethical Change,* ed. John M. Eekelaar and Sanford N. Katz, 143–53. Toronto: Butterworths, 1979.

Weyrauch, Walter O., and Sanford N. Katz. *American Family Law in Transition.* Washington, D.C.: Bureau of National Affairs, 1983.

Wilson, William Julius. *The Truly Disadvantaged: The Inner City, The Underclass, and Public Policy.* Chicago: University of Chicago Press, 1987.

Winn, Marie. *Children without Childhood.* New York: Pantheon Books, 1983.

———. *The Plug-In Drug.* New York: The Viking Press, 1977.

Yankelovich, Daniel. *New Rules: Search for Self-Fulfillment in a World Turned Upside Down.* New York: Random House, 1981.

THE WAR OVER THE FAMILY IS NOT OVER THE FAMILY— SUSAN COHEN AND MARY FAINSOD KATZENSTEIN

Notes

1. For a particularly helpful discussion of the New Right and neoconservatism, see Zillah Eisenstein (1982, Spring), "The Sexual Politics of the New Right: Understanding the 'Crisis of Liberalism' for the 1980s," *Signs,* 7(3). Her focus on the antifeminism of the Right adds an absolutely crucial dimension to existing analyses. Her description of neoconservatism as bent on conservatizing as opposed to dismantling the

welfare state (as the New Right intends) does however, raise the question of how neoconservatism can be distinguished from Carter liberalism, which also wanted to restrict the "excesses" of the welfare state.

2. Robert Coles' review of the Bergers' book questions whether the causal order might be the other way around: *New York Times Book Review,* May 15, 1983, p. 7.

3. The quotations in this paragraph are from a telephone interview Mary Katzenstein had with Mrs. Schlafly, Nov. 8, 1983.

4. The Bergers do not state this explicitly but the idea comes through clearly when they state that women, not men, should give priority to the family.

5. She discusses the liberating experience of living during a Vermont vacation without rules and without her husband, who was then in Europe, an experience liberating both for herself and her sons. But Rich does not generalize from this to children's needs in ordinary times.

6. This is similar but not identical to the 19th-century argument that women's entrance into the *public sphere* would enhance domestic and public life.

7. The laissez-faire view of the pro-life activists was described by the author to Mary Katzenstein in a separate conversation and does not appear in the book.

8. See Jessie Bernard's discussion of the difference that women's participation in the public sphere could make (1981, pp. 546–557).

References

Barber, B. R. 1983. "Beyond the Feminist Mystique." *The New Republic.* July 11: 26–32.

Berger, B., and P. L. Berger. 1983. *The War over the Family: Capturing the Middle Ground.* New York: Anchor Press/Doubleday.

Bernard, J. 1981. *The Female World.* New York: The Free Press.

Chodorow, N. 1978. *The Reproduction of Mothering: Psychoanalysis and the Sociology of Gender.* Berkeley: University of California Press.

Chodorow, N., and S. Contratto. 1982. "The Fantasy of the Perfect Mother." In *Rethinking the Family: Some Feminist Questions,* edited by B. Thorne and M. Yalom. New York: Longman.

Christensen, H. T. 1977. "Relationship between Differentiation and Equality in the Sex Role Structure." In *Beyond the Nuclear Family Model,* edited by L. Lenevo-Otevo. Beverly Hills: Sage.

Coles, R. 1983. "Honoring Fathers and Mothers." *New York Times Book Review.* May 15: 1.

Eisenstein, Z. 1982. "The Sexual Politics of the New Right: Understanding the Crisis of Liberalism for the 1980s." *Signs,* 7: 567–588.

Elshtain, J. B. 1981. *Public Man, Private Woman: Women in Social and Political Thought.* Princeton: Princeton University Press.

Elshtain, J. B. 1982. "Feminism, Family, and Community." *Dissent,* 29: 442–449.

Eishtain, J. B. 1983a. "Feminism, Community, Freedom." *Dissent,* 30: 247–255.

Elshtain, J. B. 1983b. "Feminism, Family, and Community." *Dissent,* 30: 103–109.

Falwell, J. 1980. *Listen America.* New York: Doubleday.

Firestone, S. (1970). *The Dialectic of Sex: The Case for Feminist Revolution.* New York: Bantam Books.

Freeman, J. 1975. *Politics of Women's Liberation.* New York: Longman.

Friedan, B. 1981. *The Second Stage.* New York: Summit Books.

Gilder, G. 1981. *Wealth and Poverty.* New York: Basic Books.

Gordon, L. 1982. "Why Nineteenth-Century Feminists Did Not Support 'Birth Control' and Twentieth-Century Feminists Do: Feminism, Reproduction, and the Family." In *Rethinking the Family: Some Feminist Questions,* edited by B. Thorne and M. Yalom. New York: Longman.

Katzenstein, M. 1983. Telephone interview with Mrs. Schlafly from the Schlaflys' home in Illinois. November 8.

Kramer, R. 1983. *In Defense of the Family: Raising Children in America Today.* New York: Basic Books.

Luker, K. 1983. *Abortion and the Politics of Motherhood.* Berkeley: University of California Press.

Mill, J. S. 1869/1970. "On Liberty." In *Essays on Sex Equality,* edited by A. S. Rossi. Chicago: University of Chicago Press.

Mill, J. S. 1869/1970. "The Subjection of Women." In *Essays on Sex Equality,* edited by A. S. Rossi. Chicago: University of Chicago Press.

Millet, K. 1970. *Sexual Politics.* New York: Avon Books. (*Sexual Politics* was revised a year after its original publication.)

Rich, A. 1976. *Of Women Born: Motherhood as Experience and Institution.* New York: W. W. Norton.

Rossi, A. 1977. "A Biosocial Perspective on Parenting." *Daedalus,* 106: 1–27.

Schlafly, P. 1978. *The Power of the Positive Woman.* New York: Jove Publications.

Schlafly, P. 1981. *The Power of the Christian Woman.* Cincinnati: Stanford Publications.

Stacey, J. 1986. Are Feminists Afraid to Leave Home? The Challenge of Conservative Pro-Family Feminism. In *What is Feminism?,* edited by J. Mitchell and A. Oakley. New York: Pantheon.

Thorne, B. 1987. "Re-Visioning Women and Social Change: Where Are the Children?" *Gender and Society,* 19: 85–109.

Thorne, B., and M. Yalom. (eds). 1982. *Rethinking the Family: Some Feminist Questions.* New York: Longman.

INTERPRETING THE AFRICAN HERITAGE IN AFRO-AMERICAN FAMILY ORGANIZATION— NIARA SUDARKASA

References

Agbasegbe, B. (1976) "The Role of Wife in the Black Extended Family: Perspectives from a Rural Community in Southern United States," pp. 124–138 in D. McGuigan (ed.) *New Research on Women and Sex Roles.* Ann Arbor: Center for Continuing Education of Women, University of Michigan.

———. (1981) "Some Aspects of Contemporary Rural Afroamerican Family Life in the Sea Islands of Southeastern United States." Presented at the Annual Meeting of the Association of Social and Behavioral Scientists, Atlanta, Georgia, March 1981.

Allen, W. R. (1978) "The search for Applicable Theories of Black Family Life." *Journal of Marriage and the Family* 40 (February): 117–129.

———. (1979) "Class, Culture, and Family Organization: The Effects of Class and Race on Family Structure in Urban America." *Journal of Comparative Family Studies* 10 (Autumn): 301–313.

Aschenbrenner, J. (1973) "Extended Families Among Black Americans." *Journal of Comparative Family Studies* 4: 257–268.

———. (1975) *Lifelines: Black Families in Chicago.* New York: Holt, Rinehart & Winston.

———. (1978) "Continuities and Variations in Black Family Structure," pp. 181–200 in D. B. Shimkin, E. M. Shimkin, and D. A. Frate (eds.) *The Extended Family in Black Societies.* The Hague: Mouton.

———. and C. H. Carr (1980) "Conjugal Relationships in the Context of the Black Extended Family." *Alternative Lifestyles* 3 (November): 463–484.

Bender, D. R. (1967) "A Refinement of the Concept of Household: Families, Co-residence, and Domestic Functions." *American Anthropologist* 69 (October): 493–504.

Billingsley, A. (1968) *Black Families in White America.* Englewood Cliffs, NJ: Prentice-Hall.

Blassingame, J. W. (1979) *The Slave Community.* New York: Oxford University Press.

Colson, E. (1962) "Family Change in Contemporary Africa." *Annals of the New York Academy of Sciences* 96 (January): 641–652.

DuBois, W. E. B. (1969) *The Negro American Family.* New York: New American Library. (Originally published, 1908).

Elkins, S. (1963) Slavery: A Problem in American Intellectual Life. New York: Grosset and Dunlap. (Originally published, 1959).

English, R. (1974) "Beyond Pathology: Research and Theoretical Perspectives on Black Families," pp. 39–52 in L. E. Gary (ed.) *Social Research and the Black Community: Selected Issues and Priorities.* Washington, DC: Institute for Urban Affairs and Research, Howard University.

Fortes, M. (1949) *The Web of Kinship among the Tallensi.* London: Oxford University Press.

———. (1950) "Kinship and Marriage Among the Ashanti," pp. 252–284 in A. R. Radcliffe-Brown and D. Forde (eds.) *African Systems of Kinship and Marriage.* London: Oxford University Press.

———. (1953) "The Structure of Unilineal Descent Groups." *American Anthropologist* 55 (January–March): 17–41.

Frazier, E. (1966) *The Negro Family in the United States.* Chicago: University of Chicago Press. (Originally published, 1939).

Furstenberg, F., T. Hershbert, and J. Modell (1975) "The Origins of the Female-headed Black Family: The Impact of the Urban Experience." *Journal of Interdisciplinary History* 6 (Autumn): 211–233.

Genovese, E. D. (1974) *Roll Jordan Roll: The World the Slaves Made.* New York: Random House.

Goody, J. (1976) *Production and Reproduction: A Comparative Study of the Domestic Domain.* Cambridge: Cambridge University Press.

Gutman, H. (1976) *The Black Family in Slavery and Freedom: 1750–1925.* New York: Random House.

Herskovits, M. J. (1958) *The Myth of the Negro Past.* Boston: Beacon. (Originally published, 1941).

Johnson, C. S. (1934) *Shadow of the Plantation.* Chicago: University of Chicago Press.

Kerri, J. N. (1979) "Understanding the African Family: Persistence, Continuity, and Change." *Western Journal of Black Studies* 3 (Spring): 14–17.

Landman, R. H. (1978) "Language Policies and Their Implications for Ethnic Relations in the Newly Sovereign States of Sub-Saharan Africa," pp. 69–90 in B. M. duToit (ed.) *Ethnicity in Modern Africa.* Boulder, CO: Westview Press.

Linton, R. (1936) *The Study of Man.* New York: Appleton-Century-Crofts.

Lloyd, P. C. (1968) "Divorce Among the Yoruba." *American Anthropologist* 70 (February): 67–81.

Maquet, J. (1972) *Civilizations of Black Africa.* London: Oxford University Press.

Marshall, G. A. [Niara Sudarkasa] (1968) "Marriage: Comparative Analysis," in *International Encyclopedia of the Social Sciences, Vol. 10.* New York: Macmillan/Free Press.

Murdock, G. P. (1949) *Social Structure.* New York: Macmillan.

Nobles, W. (1974a) "African Root and American Fruit: The Black Family." *Journal of Social and Behavioral Sciences* 20: 52–64.

———. (1974b) "Africanity: Its Role in Black Families." The Black Scholar 9 (June): 10–17.

———. (1978) "Toward an Empirical and Theoretical Framework for Defining Black Families." *Journal of Marriage and the Family* 40 (November): 679–688.

Okediji, P. A. (1975) "A Psychosocial Analysis of the Extended Family: The African Case." *African Urban Notes, Series B,* 1(3): 93–99. (African Studies Center, Michigan State University)

Onwuejeogwu, M. A. (1975) *The Social Anthropology of Africa: An Introduction.* London: Heinemann.

Oppong, C. (1974) *Marriage among a Matrilineal Elite: A Family Study of Ghanaian Senior Civil Servants.* Cambridge: Cambridge University Press.

Owens, L. H. (1976) *This Species of Property: Slave Life and Culture in the Old South.* New York: Oxford University Press.

Perdue, C. L., Jr., T. E. Barden, and R. K. Phillips [eds.] (1980) *Weevils in the Wheat: Interviews with Virginia Ex-Slaves.* Bloomington: Indiana University Press.

Powdermaker, H. (1939) *After Freedom: A Cultural Study in the Deep South.* New York: Viking.

Radcliffe-Brown, A. R. (1950) "Introduction," pp. 1–85 in A. R. Radcliffe-Brown and D. Forde (eds.) *African Systems of Kinship and Marriage.* London: Oxford University Press.

——— and D. Forde [eds.] (1950) *African Systems of Kinship and Marriage.* London: Oxford University Press.

Rivers, W. H. R. (1924) *Social Organization.* New York: Alfred Knopf.

Robertson, C. (1976) "Ga Women and Socioeconomic Change in Accra, Ghana," pp. 111–133 in N. J. Hafkin and E. G. Bay (eds.) *Women in Africa: Studies in Social and Eco-*

nomic Change. Stanford: Stanford University Press.

Shimkin, D. and V. Uchendu (1978) "Persistence, Borrowing, and Adaptive Changes in Black Kinship Systems: Some Issues and Their Significance," pp. 391–406 in D. Shimkin, E. M. Shimkin, and D. A. Frate (eds.) *The Extended Family in Black Societies.* The Hague: Mouton.

Shimkin, D., E. M. Shimkin, and D. A. Frate [eds.] (1978) *The Extended Family in Black Societies.* The Hague: Mouton.

Shorter, E. (1975) *The Making of the Modern Family.* New York: Basic Books.

Smith, R. T. (1973) "The Matrifocal Family," pp. 121–144 in J. Goody (ed.) *The Character of Kinship.* Cambridge: Cambridge University Press.

Stack, C. (1974) *All Our Kin.* New York: Harper & Row.

Staples, R. (1971) "Toward a Sociology of the Black Family: A Decade of Theory and Research." *Journal of Marriage and the Family* 33 (February): 19–38.

———. [ed.] (1978) *The Black Family: Essays and Studies.* Belmont, CA: Wadsworth

Stone, L. (1975) "The Rise of the Nuclear Family in Early Modern England: The Patriarchal Stage," pp. 13–57 in C. E. Rosenberg (ed.) *The Family in History.* Philadelphia: University of Pennsylvania Press.

Sudarkasa, N. (1973) Where Women Work: A Study of Yoruba Women in the Marketplace and in the Home. *Anthropological Papers* No. 53. Ann Arbor: Museum of Anthropology, University of Michigan.

———. (1975a) "An Exposition on the Value Premises Underlying Black Family Studies." *Journal of the National Medical Association* 19 (May): 235–239.

———. (1975b) "National Development Planning for the Promotion and Protection of the Family." *Proceedings of the Conference on*

Social Research and National Development, E. Akeredolu-Ale, ed. The Nigerian Institute of Social and Economic Research, lbadan, Nigeria.

———. (1976) "Female Employment and Family Organization in West Africa," pp. 48–63 in D. G. McGuigan (ed.) *New Research on Women and Sex Roles.* Ann Arbor: Center for Continuing Education of Women, University of Michigan.

———. (1980) "African and Afro-American Family Structure: A Comparison." *The Black Scholar* 11 (November–December): 37–60.

———. (1981) "Understanding the Dynamics of Consanguinity and Conjugality in Contemporary Black Family Organization." Presented at the Seventh Annual Third World Conference, Chicago, March 1981.

Tilly, L. A. and J. W. Scott (1978) *Women, Work, and Family.* New York: Holt, Rinehart & Winston.

Uchendu, V. (1965) *The Igbo of South-Eastern Nigeria.* New York: Holt, Rinehart & Winston.

Ware, H. (1979) "Polygyny: Women's Views in a Transitional Society, Nigeria 1975." *Journal of Marriage and the Family* 41 (February): 185–195.

Woodson, C. G. (1936) *The African Background Outlined.* Washington, DC: Association for the Study of Negro Life and History.

HOME, SWEET HOME: THE HOUSE AND THE YARD— KENNETH T. JACKSON

Notes

1. A careful study of the pre-Civil War suburban economy is Henry Claxton Binford, "The Suburban Enterprise: Jacksonian Towns and Boston Commuters, 1815–1860" (Ph.D. dissertation, Harvard University, 1973).

2. William Dean Howells, *Suburban Sketches* (New York, 1871), 11–12.

3. Philippe Ariès, *Centuries of Childhood* (New York, 1965), 8–12; Ariès, "The Family and the City," in Alice S. Rossi, ed., *The Family* (New York, 1978), 227–35; and Elizabeth Janeway, *Man's World, Woman's Place* (New York, 1971), 9–26.

4. One thrust of the recent work of French sociologists and cultural historians has been to deny that the family is the meeting ground for social and biological necessity. Instead, they have viewed it as an instrument of oppression and disaster. Jacques Donzelot, *The Policing of Families,* trans. Robert Harley (New York, 1979), 3–87. The notion of privacy and overcrowding, as Colin Duly has noted, is relative and in different cultures cannot simply be measured by counting the number of individuals sharing a house. Duly, *The Houses of Mankind* (London, 1979), 5–27.

5. Heinrich Engel, *The Japanese House: A Tradition for Contemporary Architecture* (Rutland, Vermont, 1964), 221–29; and Lewis Mumford, *The City in History; Its Origins, Its Transformations, and Its Prospects* (New York, 1961), passim.

6. For especially perceptive inquiries into these changes, see Kirk Jeffrey, "The Family as Utopian Retreat From the City: The Nineteenth Century Contribution," *Soundings,* LV (Spring 1972), 21–42; Philippe Ariès, "The Family and the City," *Daedalus,* CVI (Spring 1977), 227–35; and David P. Handlin, *The American Home: Architecture and Society, 1815–1915* (Boston 1979), passim.

7. William G. Eliot, Jr., *Lectures to Young Women* (Boston, 1880, first published in 1853), 55–56. Quoted in Jeffrey, "Family as Utopian Retreat," 21.

8. Gwendolyn Wright, *Building the Dream: A Social History of Housing in America* (New York, 1981), chapters 5 and 6.

9. Quoted in Wright, *Building the Dream,* chapter 5. On the other side of the issue, see Betty Friedan, *The Feminine Mystique* (New

York, 1963), 307, which called the home "a comfortable concentration camp."

10. *The American Builder,* September 1869, p. 180. Although faith in rising property values is traditional in the United States, housing prices have not kept pace with inflation over the past century. Matthew Edel, Elliott D. Sclar, and Daniel Luria, *Shaky Palaces: Homeownership and Social Mobility in Boston, 1870–1970* (New York: Columbia University Press, 1984).

11. Stephan A. Thernstorm and Peter R. Knights, "Men in Motion: Some Data and Speculation About Urban Population Mobility in Nineteenth Century America," *Journal of Interdisciplinary History,* I (Autumn 1970), 7–35. Theodore Caplow, et al., *Middletown Families: 50 Years of Change and Continuity* (Minneapolis, 1982), 104.

12. Quoted from Edel, *Shaky Palaces,* chapter 8.

13. Dolores Hayden, *The Grand Domestic Revolution: A History of Feminist Designs for American Homes, Neighborhoods, and Cities* (Cambridge, Mass., 1981), 34–38. Friedrich Engels, *The Origin of the Family, Private Property, and the State* (Moscow: Progress Publishers, 1977), 73–75. Jonathan Beecher and Richard Bienvenu, eds., *The Utopian Vision of Charles Fourier* (Boston, 1971).

14. Clare Cooper, "The House as Symbol of the Self," in Lan, Jen, et al., eds., *Designing for Human Behavior: Architecture and Behavioral Sciences* (Stroudsburg, Pa., 1974), 130–46.

THE FEMALE WORLD OF CARDS AND HOLIDAYS: WOMEN, FAMILIES, AND THE WORK OF KINSHIP— MICAELA di LEONARDO

Notes

1. Acknowledgment and gratitude to Carroll Smith-Rosenberg for my paraphrase of her title, "The Female World of Love and Ritual: Relations between Women in Nineteenth-Century America," *Signs: Journal of Women in Culture and Society* 1, no. 1 (August 1975): 1–29. [*Signs: Journal of Women in Culture and Society,* 1987, vol. 12, no. 3] © 1987 by The University of Chicago. All rights reserved 0097-9740/87/1203-0003$01.00.

2. Ann Landers letter printed in *Washington Post* (April 15, 1983); Carol Gilligan, *In a Different Voice* (Cambridge, Mass.: Harvard University Press, 1982), 17.

3. Heidi I. Hartmann, "The Family as the Locus of Gender, Class, and Political Struggle: The Example of Housework," *Signs* 6, no. 3 (Spring 1981): 366–94; and Christopher Lasch, *Haven in a Heartless World: The Family Besieged* (New York: Basic Books, 1977).

4. Representative examples of the first trend include Joann Vanek, "Time Spent on Housework," *Scientific American* 231 (November 1974): 116–20; Ruth Schwartz Cowan, "A Case Study of Technological and Social Change: The Washing Machine and the Working Wife," in *Clio's Consciousness Raised,* ed. Mary Hartmann and Lois Banner (New York: Harper & Row, 1974), 245–53; Ann Oakley, *Women's Work: The Housewife, Past and Present* (New York: Vintage, 1974); Hartmann; and Susan Strasser, *Never Done: A History of American Housework* (New York: Pantheon Books, 1982). Key contributions to the second trend include Louise Lamphere, "Strategies, Cooperation and Conflict among Women in Domestic Groups," in *Women, Culture and Society,* ed. Michelle Zimbalist Rosaldo and Louise Lamphere (Stanford, Calif.: Stanford University Press, 1974), 97–112; Mina Davis Caulfield, "Imperialism, the Family and the Cultures of Resistance," *Socialist Revolution* 20 (October 1974): 67–85; Smith-Rosenberg; Sylvia Junko Yanagisako, "Women-centered Kin Networks and Urban Bilateral Kinship," *American Ethnologist* 4, no. 2 (1977): 207–26; Jane Humphries, "The Working Class Family, Women's Liberation and

Class Struggle: The Case of Nineteenth Century British History," *Review of Radical Political Economics* 9 (Fall 1977): 25–41; Blanche Weisen Cook, "Female Support Networks and Political Activism: Lillian Wald, Crystal Eastman, Emma Goldman," in *A Heritage of Her Own,* ed. Nancy F. Cott and Elizabeth H. Pleck (New York: Simon & Schuster, 1979); Temma Kaplan, "Female Consciousness and Collective Action: The Case of Barcelona, 1910–1918," *Signs* 7, no. 3 (Spring 1982): 545–66.

5. On this debate, see Jon Weiner, "Women's History on Trial," *Nation* 241, no. 6 (September 7, 1985): 161, 176, 178–80; Karen J. Winkler, "Two Scholars' Conflict in Sears Sex-Bias Case Sets Off War in Women's History," *Chronicle of Higher Education* (February 5, 1986), 1, 8; Rosalind Rosenberg, "What Harms Women in the Workplace," *New York Times* (February 27, 1986); Alice Kessler-Harris, "Equal Employment Opportunity Commission vs. Sears Roebuck and Company: A Personal Account," *Radical History Review* 35 (April 1986): 57–79.

6. Portions of the following analysis are reported in Micaela di Leonardo, *The Varieties of Ethnic Experience: Kinship, Class and Gender among California Italian-Americans* (Ithaca, N.Y.: Cornell University Press, 1984), chap. 6.

7. Clearly, many women do, in fact, discuss their paid labor with willingness and clarity. The point here is that there are opposing gender tendencies in an identical interview situation, tendencies that are explicable in terms of both the material realities and current cultural constructions of gender.

8. Papanek has rightly focused on women's unacknowledged family status production, but what is conceived of as "family" shifts and varies (Hanna Papanek, "Family Status Production: The 'Work' and 'Non-Work' of Women," *Signs* 4, no. 4 ([Summer 1979]: 775–81).

9. Selma Greenberg, *Right from the Start: A Guide to Nonsexist Child Rearing* (Boston: Houghton Mifflin Co., 1978), 147. Another example of indirect support for kin work's gendered existence is a recent study of university math students, which found that a major reason for women's failure to pursue careers in mathematics was the pressure of family involvement. Compare David Maines et al., *Social Processes of Sex Differentiation in Mathematics* (Washington, D.C.: National Institute of Education, 1981).

10. Larissa Adler Lomnitz and Marisol Pérez Lizaur, "The History of a Mexican Urban Family," *Journal of Family History* 3, no. 4 (1978): 392–409, esp. 398; Matthews Hamabata, *For Love and Power: Family Business in Japan* (Chicago: University of Chicago Press, in press); Sylvia Junko Yanagisako, "Two Processes of Change in Japanese-American Kinship," *Journal of Anthropological Research* 31 (1975): 196–224; Maila Stivens, "Women and Their Kin: Kin, Class and Solidarity in a Middle-Class Suburb of Sydney, Australia," in *Women United, Women Divided,* ed. Patricia Caplan and Janet M. Bujra (Bloomington: Indiana University Press, 1979), 157–84.

11. Carol B. Stack, *All Our Kin: Strategies for Survival in a Black Community* (New York: Harper & Row, 1974). These cultural constructions may, however, vary within ethnic/racial populations as well.

12. Elizabeth Bott, *Family and Social Network,* 2d ed. (New York: Free Press, 1971); Michael Young and Peter Willmott, *Family and Kinship in East London* (London: Routledge & Kegan Paul, 1957); and idem, *Family and Class in a London Suburb* (London: Routledge & Kegan Paul, 1960). Classic studies that presume this class difference are Herbert Gans, *The Urban Villagers: Group and Class in the Life of Italian-Americans* (New York: Free Press, 1962), and Mirra Komarovsky, *Blue-Collar*

Marriage (New York: Random House, 1962). A recent example is Ilene Philipson, "Heterosexual Antagonisms and the Politics of Mothering," *Socialist Review* 12, no. 6 (November–December 1982): 55–77. Edward Shorter, *The Making of the Modern Family* (New York: Basic Books, 1975), epitomizes the pessimism of the "family sentiments" school. See also Mary Lyndon Shanley, "The History of the Family in Modern England: Review Essay," *Signs* 4, no. 4 (Summer 1979): 740–50.

13. Stack, *All Our Kin,* and Brett Williams, "The Trip Takes Us: Chicano Migrants to the Prairie" (Ph. D. diss., University of Illinois at Urbana-Champaign, 1975).

14. David Schneider and Raymond T. Smith, *Class Differences and Sex Roles in American Kinship and Family Structure* (Englewood Cliffs, N.J.: Prentice-Hall, Inc., 1973), esp. 27.

15. See Nelson Graburn, ed., *Readings in Kinship and Social Structure* (New York: Harper & Row, 1971), esp. 3–4.

16. The moral mother/cult of domesticity is analyzed in Barbara Welter, "The Cult of True Womanhood, 1820–1860," *American Quarterly* 18, no. 2 (Summer 1966): 151–74; Nancy Cott, *The Bonds of Womanhood: "Women's Sphere" in New England, 1780–1835* (New Haven, Conn.: Yale University Press, 1977); and Ruth Bloch, "American Feminine Ideals in Transition: The Rise of the Moral Mother, 1785–1815," *Feminist Studies* 4, no. 2 (June 1978): 101–26. The description of the general political-economic shift in the United States is based on Harry Braverman, *Labor and Monopoly Capital: The Degradation of Work in the Twentieth Century* (New York: Monthly Review Press, 1974); Peter Dobkin Hall, "Family Structure and Economic Organization: Massachusetts Merchants, 1700–1850," in *Family and Kin in Urban Communities, 1700–1950,* ed. Tamara K. Hareven (New York: New Viewpoints, 1977), 38–61; Michael Anderson, "Family Household

and the Industrial Revolution," in *The American Family in Social-Historical Perspective,* ed. Michael Gordon (New York: St. Martin's Press, 1978), 38–50; Tamara K. Hareven, *Amoskeag: Life and Work in an American Factory City* (New York: Pantheon Books, 1978); Richard Edwards, *Constested Terrain: The Transformation of the Workplace in the Twentieth Century* (New York: Basic Books, 1979); Mary Ryan, *The Cradle of the Middle Class: The Family in Oneida County, New York, 1790–1865* (Cambridge: Cambridge University Press, 1981); Alice Kessler-Harris, *Out to Work: A History of Wage-earning Women in the United States* (New York: Oxford University Press, 1982).

17. Ryan, *Cradle of the Middle Class,* 231–32.

18. Sylvia Junko Yanagisako, "Family and Household: The Analysis of Domestic Groups," *Annual Review of Anthropology* 8 (1979): 161–205.

19. See Donald J. Treiman and Heidi I. Hartmann, eds., *Women, Work and Wages: Equal Pay for Jobs of Equal Value* (Washington, D.C.: National Academy Press, 1981).

20. Lamphere (n. 4 above); Jane Fishburne Collier, "Women in Politics," in Rosaldo and Lamphere, eds. (n. 4 above), 89–96.

21. Nancy Folbre and Heidi I. Hartmann, "The Rhetoric of Self-Interest: Selfishness, Altruism, and Gender in Economic Theory," in *The Consequences of Economic Rhetoric,* ed. Arjo Klamer and Donald McCloskey (New York: Cambridge University Press, forthcoming).

MEXICAN AMERICAN WOMEN GRASSROOTS COMMUNITY ACTIVISTS: "MOTHERS OF EAST LOS ANGELES"—MARY PARDO

Notes

On September 15, 1989, another version of this paper was accepted for presentation at the 1990 International Sociological Association meetings to be held in Madrid, Spain, July 9, 1990.

1. See Vicky Randall, *Women and Politics, An International Perspective* (Chicago: University of Chicago Press, 1987), for a review of the central themes and debates in the literature. For two of the few books on Chicanas, work, and family, see Vicki L. Ruiz, *Cannery Women, Cannery Lives, Mexican Women, Unionization, and the California Food Processing Industry, 1930–1950* (Albuquerque: University of New Mexico Press, 1987), and Patricia Zavella, *Women's Work & Chicano Families* (Ithaca, N.Y.: Cornell University Press, 1987).

2. For recent exceptions to this approach, see Anne Witte Garland, *Women Activists: Challenging the Abuse of Power* (New York: The Feminist Press, 1988); Ann Bookman and Sandra Morgan, eds., *Women and the Politics of Empowerment* (Philadelphia: Temple University Press, 1987); Karen Sacks, *Caring by the Hour* (Chicago: University of Illinois Press, 1988). For a sociological analysis of community activism among Afro-American women see Cheryl Townsend Gilkes, "Holding Back the Ocean with a Broom," *The Black Woman* (Beverly Hills, Calif.: Sage Publications, 1980).

3. For two exceptions to this criticism, see Sara Evans, *Born for Liberty, A History of Women in America* (New York: The Free Press, 1989), and Bettina Aptheker, *Tapestries of Life, Women's Work, Women's Consciousness, and the Meaning of Daily Experience* (Amherst: The University of Massachusetts Press, 1989). For a critique, see Maxine Baca Zinn, Lynn Weber Cannon, Elizabeth Higginbotham, and Bonnie Thornton Dill, "The Costs of Exclusionary Practices in Women's Studies," *Signs* 11, no. 2 (Winter 1986).

4. For cases of grassroots activism among women in Latin America, see Sally W. Yudelman, *Hopeful Openings, A Study of Five Women's Development Organizations in Latin American and the Caribbean* (West Hartford, Conn.: Kumarian Press, 1987). For an excellent case analysis of how informal associations enlarge and empower women's world in Third World countries, see Kathryn S. March and Rachelle L. Taqqu, *Women's Informal Associations in Developing Countries, Catalysts for Change?* (Boulder, Colo.: Westview Press, 1986). Also, see Carmen Feijoó, "Women in Neighbourhoods: From Local Issues to Gender Problems," *Canadian Woman Studies* 6, no. 1 (Fall 1984) for a concise overview of the patterns of activism.

5. The relationship between Catholicism and political activism is varied and not unitary. In some Mexican American communities, grassroots activism relies on parish networks. See Isidro D. Ortiz, "Chicano Urban Politics and the Politics of Reform in the Seventies," *The Western Political Quarterly* 37, no. 4 (December 1984): 565–77. Also, see Joseph D. Sekul, "Communities Organized for Public Service: Citizen Power and Public Power in San Antonio," in *Latinos and the Political System,* edited by F. Chris Garcia (Notre Dame, Ind.: University of Notre Dame Press, 1988). Sekul tells how COPS members challenged prevailing patterns of power by working for the well-being of families and cites four former presidents who were Mexican American women, but he makes no special point of gender.

6. I also interviewed other members of the Coalition Against the Prison and local political office representatives. For a general reference, see James P. Spradley, *The Ethnographic Interview* (New York: Holt, Rinehart and Winston, 1979). For a review essay focused on the relevancy of the method for examining the diversity of women's experiences, see Susan N. G. Geiger, "Women's Life Histories: Method and Content," *Signs* 11, no. 2 (Winter 1982): 334–51.

7. During the last five years, over 300 newspaper articles have appeared on the issue. Frank

Villalobos generously shared his extensive newspaper archives with me. See Leo C. Wolinsky, "L.A. Prison Bill 'Locked Up' in New Clash," *Los Angeles Times,* 16 July 1987, sec. 1, p. 3; Rudy Acuña, "The Fate of East L.A.: One Big Jail," *Los Angeles Herald Examiner,* 28 April 1989, A15; Carolina Serna, "Eastside Residents Oppose Prison," *La Gente UCLA Student Newspaper* 17, no. 1 (October 1986): 5; Daniel M. Weintraub, "10,000 Fee Paid to Lawmaker Who Left Sickbed to Cast Vote," *Los Angeles Times,* 13 March 1988, sec. 1, p. 3.

8. Cerrell Associates, Inc., "Political Difficulties Facing Waste-to-Energy Conversion Plant Siting," Report Prepared for California Waste Management Board, State of California (Los Angeles, 1984): 43.

9. Jesus Sanchez, "The Environment: Whose Movement?" *California Tomorrow* 3, nos. 3 & 4 (Fall 1988): 13. Also see Rudy Acuña, *A Community Under Siege* (Los Angeles: Chicano Studies Research Center Publications, UCLA, 1984). The book and its title capture the sentiments and the history of a community that bears an unfair burden of city projects deemed undesirable by all residents.

10. James Vigil, Jr., field representative for Assemblywoman Gloria Molina, 1984–1996, Personal Interview, Whittier, Calif., 27 September 1989. Vigil stated that the Department of Corrections used a threefold strategy: political pressure in the legislature, the promise of jobs for residents, and contracts for local businesses.

11. Edward J. Boyer and Marita Hernandez, "Eastside Seethes over Prison Plan," *Los Angeles Times,* 13 August 1986, sec. 2, p. 1.

12. Martha Molina-Aviles, currently administrative assistant for Assemblywoman Lucille Roybal-Allard, 56th assembly district, and former field representative for Gloria Molina when she held this assembly seat, Personal Interview, Los Angeles, 5 June 1989. Molina-Aviles, who grew up in East Los Angeles, used her experiences and insights to help forge strong links among the women in MELA, other members of the coalition, and the assembly office.

13. MELA has also opposed the expansion of a county prison literally across the street from William Mead Housing Projects, home to 2,000 Latinos, Asians, and Afro-Americans, and a chemical treatment plant for toxic wastes.

14. The first of its kind in a metropolitan area, it would burn 125,000 pounds per day of hazardous wastes. For an excellent article that links recent struggles against hazardous waste dumps and incinerators in minority communities and features women in MELA, see Dick Russell, "Environmental Racism: Minority Communities and Their Battle against Toxics," *The Amicus Journal* 11, no. 2 (Spring 1989): 22–32.

15. Miguel G. Mendívil, field representative for Assemblywoman Lucille Roybal-Allard, 56th assembly district, Personal Interview, Los Angeles, 25 April 1989.

16. John Garcia and Rudolfo de la Garza, "Mobilizing the Mexican Immigrant: The Role of Mexican American Organizations," *The Western Political Quarterly* 38, no. 4 (December 1985): 551–64.

17. This concept is discussed in relation to Latino communities in David T. Abalos, *Latinos in the U.S., The Sacred and the Political* (Indiana: University of Notre Dame Press, 1986). The notion of transformation of traditional culture in struggles against oppression is certainly not a new one. For a brief essay on a longer work, see Frantz Fanon, "Algeria Unveiled," *The New Left Reader,* edited by Carl Oglesby (New York: Grove Press, Inc, 1969): 161–85.

18. Karen Sacks, *Caring by the Hour.*

19. Juana Gutiérrez, Personal Interview, Boyle Heights, East Los Angeles, 15 January 1988.

20. Erlinda Robles, Personal Interview, Boyle Heights, Los Angeles, 14 September 1989.

21. Mina Davis Caulfield, "Imperialism, the Family, and Cultures of Resistance," *Socialist Revolution* 29 (1974): 67–85.

22. Erlinda Robles, Personal Interview.

23. Ibid.

24. Juana Gutiérrez, Personal Interview.

25. Frank Villalobos, architect and urban planner, Personal Interview, Los Angeles, 2 May 1989.

26. The law student, Veronica Gutiérrez, is the daughter of Juana Gutiérrez, one of the cofounders of MELA. Martín Gutiérrez, one of her sons, was a field representative for Assemblywoman Lucille Roybal-Allard and also central to community mobilization. Ricardo Gutiérrez, Juana's husband, and almost all the other family members are community activists. They are a microcosm of the family networks that strengthened community mobilization and the Coalition Against the Prison. See Raymundo Reynoso, "Juana Beatrice Gutiérrez: La incansable lucha de una activista comunitaria," *La Opinion,* 6 Agosto de 1989, Acceso, p. 1, and Louis Sahagun, "The Mothers of East L.A. Transform Themselves and Their Community," *Los Angeles Times,* 13 August 1989, sec. 2, p. 1.

27. Frank Villalobos, Personal Interview.

28. Father John Moretta, Resurrection Parish, Personal Interview, Boyle Heights, Los Angeles, 24 May 1989.

29. The Plaza de Mayo mothers organized spontaneously to demand the return of their missing children, in open defiance of the Argentine military dictatorship. For a brief overview of the group and its relationship to other women's organizations in Argentina, and a synopsis of the criticism of the mothers that reveals ideological camps, see Gloria Bonder, "Women's Organizations in Argentina's Transition to Democracy," in *Women and Counter Power,* edited by Yolanda Cohen (New York: Black Rose Books, 1989): 65–85. There is no direct relationship between this group and MELA.

30. Aurora Castillo, Personal Interview, Boyle Heights, Los Angeles, 15 January 1988.

31. Aurora Castillo, Personal Interview.

32. Erlinda Robles, Personal Interview.

33. Ibid.

34. Reynoso, "Juana Beatriz Gutiérrez," p. 1.

35. For historical examples, see Chris Marín, "La Asociación Hispano-Americana de Madres Y Esposas: Tucson's Mexican American Women in World War II," *Renato Rosaldo Lecture Series 1: 1983–1984* (Tucson, Ariz.: Mexican American Studies Center, University of Arizona, Tucson, 1985) and Judy Aulette and Trudy Mills, "Something Old, Something New: Auxiliary Work in the 1983–1986 Copper Strike," *Feminist Studies* 14, no. 2 (Summer 1988): 251–69.

36. Mina Davis Caulfield, "Imperialism, the Family and Cultures of Resistance."

37. Aurora Castillo, Personal Interview.

38. As reconstructed by Juana Gutiérrez, Ricardo Gutiérrez, and Aurora Castillo.

39. Aurora Castillo, Personal Interview.

40. Juana Gutiérrez, Personal Interview.

41. Lucy Ramos, Personal Interview, Boyle Heights, Los Angeles, 3 May 1989.

42. Ibid.

43. For an overview of contemporary Third World struggles against environmental degradation, see Alan B. Durning, "Saving the Planet," *The Progressive* 53, no. 4 (April 1989): 35–59.

44. John Logan and Harvey Molotch, *Urban Fortunes* (Berkeley: University of California Press, 1988). Logan and Molotch use the term in reference to a coalition of business people, local politicians, and the media.

45. Mike Davis, "Chinatown, Part Two? The Internationalization of Downtown Los Angeles," *New Left Review,* no. 164 (July/August 1987): 64–86.

46. Paul Ong, *The Widening Divide, Income Inequality and Poverty in Los Angeles* (Los Angeles: The Research Group on the Los Angeles Economy, 1989). This UCLA-based study documents the growing gap between "haves" and "have nots" in the midst of the economic boom in Los Angeles. According to economists, the study mirrors a national trend in which rising employment levels are failing to lift the poor out of poverty or boost the middle class; see Jill Steward, "Two-Tiered Economy Feared as Dead End of Unskilled," *Los Angeles Times,* 25 June 1989, sec. 2, p. 1. At the same time, the California prison population will climb to more than twice its designed capacity by 1995. See Carl Ingram, "New Forecast Sees a Worse Jam in Prisons," *Los Angeles Times,* 27 June 1989, sec. 1, p. 23.

47. The point that urban land use policies are the products of class struggle—both cause and consequence—is made by Don Parson, "The Development of Redevelopment: Public Housing and Urban Renewal in Los Angeles," *International Journal of Urban and Regional Research* 6, no. 4 (December 1982): 392–413. Parson provides an excellent discussion of the working-class struggle for housing in the 1930s, the counterinitiative of urban renewal in the 1950s, and the inner city revolts of the 1960s.

48. Louise Tilly, "Paths of Proletarianization: Organization of Production, Sexual Division of Labor, and Women's Collective Action," *Signs* 7, no. 2 (1981): 400–17; Alice Kessler-Harris, "Women's Social Mission," *Women Have Always Worked* (Old Westbury, N.Y.: The Feminist Press, 1981): 102–35. For a literature review of women's activism during the Progressive Era, see Marilyn Gittell and Teresa Shtob, "Changing Women's Roles in Political Volunteerism and Reform of the City," in *Women and the American City,* edited by Catharine Stimpson et al. (Chicago: University of Chicago Press, 1981): 64–75.

49. Karen Sacks, *Caring by the Hour,* argues that often the significance of women's contributions is not "seen" because they take place in networks.

50. Aurora Castillo, Personal Interview.

IMMIGRANT FAMILIES IN THE CITY—MARK HUTTER

References

Anderson, Michael. 1971. *Family Structure in Nineteenth Century Lancashire.* Cambridge: Cambridge University Press.

Archdeacon, Thomas. 1983. *Becoming American: An Ethnic History.* New York: The Free Press.

Hareven, Tamara K. 1975. "Family Time and Industrial Time: Family and Work in a Planned Corporation Town, 1900–1924." *Journal of Urban History* 1 (May): 365–389.

Jones, Maldwyn Allen. 1960. *American Immigration.* Chicago, University of Chicago Press.

Metzker, Isaac (ed.) 1971. *A Bintel Brief.* New York: Ballatine Books.

Riis, Jacob A. 1957/1890. *How the Other Half Lives: Studies Among the Tenements of New York.* New York: Hill and Wang.

Seller, Maxine. 1977. *To Seek America: A History of Ethnic Life in the United States.* Englewood, New Jersey: Jerome S. Ozer, Publisher.

Yancey, William L., Eugene P. Ericksen, and Richard N. Juliani. 1976. "Emergent Ethnicity: A Review and Reformulation." *American Sociological Review* 4 (June): 391–402.

Yans-McLaughlin, Virginia. 1971. "Patterns of Work and Family Organization." Pp. 111–126 in *The Family in History: Interdisciplinary Essays,* edited by Theodore K. Rabb and Robert I. Rotberg. New York: Harper Torchbooks.

WHAT KIND OF IMMIGRANTS HAVE COME TO THE PHILADELPHIA AREA, WHERE DID THEY SETTLE, AND HOW ARE THEY DOING?— ROBERT J. YOUNG

Notes

1. In most areas of California and the Pacific Northwest the sizable Asian-Indian population virtually disappeared during the first half of the twentieth century due to restrictive immigration legislation, which denied resident males marriage partners of their own community. By the mid-1950s virtually the only legacy of that migration was an aged Asian-Indian community, centered in the Imperial Valley, intermarried with Mexican women.

2. In the Philadelphia area, the pattern often saw Chinese male populations remaining unmarried or producing children who were absorbed into the Afro-American community.

3. "Suburbs Absorb More Immigrants, Mostly the Educated and Affluent," *New York Times,* December 14, 1986.

4. The economic implications of the census data for 1980 showed the four largest Asian immigrant populations (Asian-Indian, Chinese, Filipino, and Korean) with family incomes above the national median. "We, the Asian and Pacific Islander Americans," U.S. Department of Commerce, Bureau of Census, 1988, p. 9.

5. Calculated on the basis of an estimated expenditure of $250,000 necessary to train a physician in the United States, the 2,000 plus annual flow of Asian Indian doctors in the early 1970s—to say nothing of the additional thousands of engineers—represented an "Aid Package" worth hundreds of millions. Address by Ambassador Nayar, Republic of India, in a speech to the Kerala Association, Philadelphia, PA, October 1984.

6. The Bicentennial celebrations acted as a catalyst for not only the first formal contacts between Philadelphia's administration and several newly established Asian-American organizations but also the beginning of several organizations locally and nationally began the process of political mobilization of immigrant populations. A notable example was the Association of Indians in America, which lobbied successfully for a new category in the 1980s Census—Asian-Indian.

7. "We, the Asian and Pacific Islander Americans," U.S. Department of Commerce, Bureau of Census, 1988, p. 6.

8. The reference is to a traditional business community, originally from Gujarat State in India and now widely represented in the motel business and in Seven-Eleven store franchises throughout the eastern and western United States. They are also a significant business community in East Africa and the Carribean.

9. These same four Asian nationalities also rank in the top four positions for Delaware Valley immigrants. *American Demographics,* cited in the *Philadelphia Inquirer.* August 4, 1988.

10. Through the 1980s the Philadelphia area, which ranks sixteenth in total number of arriving immigrants, ranks eight in terms of refugee resettlement. *Refugee Reports,* July 28, 1989.

11. The initial refugee flow in 1975 and 1976 was largely Vietnamese elites but included increasing percentages of Cambodians and Laotians by 1977. The elite nature of the Vietnamese flow is corroborated by the 1980 Census which noted that 75.1 percent of the adult population twenty-five years and older had a high school education or better. Unfortunately few had an education in English. See "We, the Asian and Pacific Islander Americans," U.S. Department of Commerce, Bureau of the Census, 1988, p. 11.

12. "Who are the Refugees, and Who's Going to Pay?" *The New York Times,* October 15, 1989.

13. The resettlement allowances that were provided by the federal government via resettlement agencies—usually not more that $500 per person—guaranteed poor housing conditions, since these funds barely covered the cost of a security deposit and the first month's rent, even in declining areas of Philadelphia. Many who settled in the suburbs initially had to move into the city.

14. Although in 1975 refugee resettlement was based on the availability of sponsors, it is equally apparent that political and economic considerations eventually resulted in a de facto policy that discouraged refugee concentrations and, in many cases, disallowed refugee movement to perceived islands of security such as California. This policy of "steering," ill-advised from the beginning, failed almost from its inception.

15. "Facing the Challenge of Asian Immigrants," *Catholic Standard and Times,* October 26, 1989.

16. Both personal interviews and demographic statistics note the substantial increase in the Korean-American community of the Delaware Valley, which community leaders estimate at 50,000 and growing. Interview with Mr. Yoan Kim cited above. Also see footnote 9.

17. If anything small business ownership may be higher in the Delaware Valley than on the West Coast where 30 percent to 40 percent of Korean immigrants are in business. See "The Koreans Big Entry Into Business," *New York Times,* September 24, 1989.

18. From a speech by Mr. Yoan Kim, President, Korean Businessmen's Association of Greater Philadelphia, Aug 10, 1989.

19. From an interview with Dr. Brotsky, Principal, Beverly Hills Middle School, September 15, 1989.

20. Beverly Hills Middle School interview.

21. There is also an interesting overlap with existing Protestant churches in the Delaware Valley, which results in dual congregations—one ethnic and one traditional—sharing facilities. There are at least five such Korean congregations and two Chinese in Delaware County alone. "Churches within Churches Now on the Local Scene," *Press Focus,* October 25, 1989.

22. The comprehensive organization of Korean business organizations, which includes seven subsets—from jewelers' to grocerymen's associations—makes possible communication throughout the Korean-American community via newsletters and publications.

23. Distribution of Asian Catholics throughout the region, however, presents problems of alienation for many new arrivals, especially those with language problems. Nationally and regionally this issue is being discussed. See "Facing the Challenge of Asian Immigrants," *Catholic Standard and Times,* October 26, 1989.

24. "Becoming a Second Generation," *India Abroad,* October 13, 1989.

25. S.E.A.M.A.A.C. Schools Outreach Program.

26. The recently initiated suit by the Asian-American Coalition, charging racism in the public schools of Philadelphia, whether correct or not, is an obvious sign of tensions.

27. "Dating, A Scary Cultural Gap," *India Abroad,* October 13, 1989.

28. From an interview with Mr. Samlien Nol, Executive Director, S.E.A.M.A.A.C. of Philadelphia, May 10, 1989.

29. "Who are the Refugees and Who's Going to Pay," *New York Times,* October 15, 1989.

30. "A New Wave from Vietnam: Out of the Prison Camps," *New York Times,* October 15, 1989.

31. See Appendix.

32. "Disorganized interpreter system hurts Asian-American, panel says," *The Philadelphia Inquirer,* November 1, 1989.

THE EXPANDED FAMILY AND FAMILY HONOR— RUTH HOROWITZ

Notes

1. A *quinceañera* is a young woman's fifteenth birthday celebration and is often referred to as a cotillion. It is a special birthday for a young girl in both Mexico and the United States and symbolizes her transition from childhood to adulthood. Traditionally, she then had to be chaperoned and guarded in her behavior. In the small villages of Mexico she is often given some new clothes, while on 32nd Street some of the girls have affairs for several hundred guests, such as the one described in the text.

2. See, for example, Diaz (1966), Foster (1967), Nelson (1971), and Romanucci-Ross (1973).

3. Several empirical studies support Bott's hypothesis. In England, Young and Willmot (1957) studied the problems of wives who moved from the Bethnal Green neighborhood where many of their kin lived and found that only forty years later networks of friends and kin developed again in Dagenham (Willmott 1963). Studies of the United States such as Handel and Rainwater (1964) and Rainwater and Handel (1964) found that geographic mobility brought an increase in homecenteredness and less sex role segregation between husband and wife in working class families.

Mobility has not affected familial sex roles in this way in the 32nd Street community, nor have lack of propinquity and urbanization affected the strength and importance of family ties. There is evidence that propinquity is not necessary to maintain the cohesion of extended kinship, and urbanization does not entirely destroy it (Coult and Habenstein 1962; Litwak 1960). Both studies found extended kinship among people who lived in different places and in urban areas.

4. For similar findings in other Chicano communities see Alvirez and Bean (1976),

Murillo (1971), Sena-Rivera (1979), Sotomayor (1972), and Temple-Trujillo (1974).

5. Mintz and Wolf (1950), in an historical analysis of *compadrazgo,* have documented its changes of function and content since the sixth century. According to Gibson (1966) *compadrazgo* was widely adopted in Mexico during the colonial period, when an epidemic caused significant depopulation and *compadres* became accepted as substitute parents.

Lomnitz (1977), in her study of a Mexico City shantytown, found that the function of the *compadre* relationship from the rural situation and from the "ideal model" had been strengthened and broadened in the shantytown. Rural *compadres* were never cited as necessary for emergency help and close friendship but were "respected" persons. However, through participant-observation, Lomnitz found in the shantytown that not only has the number of *compadre* relationships increased (for example, *compadres* are chosen for saint days, upon graduation from primary school, and so on), but *compadres* are frequently picked from neighbors and friends and are part of the reciprocal obligation network which is necessary for economic survival:

> The compadrazgo institution is being used in the shantytown to make preexisting reciprocity relations more solid and permanent. . . . I agree with Safa (1974, pp. 61–64) in that cooperation between equals is a result of necessity born of the social structure. If one lacks a powerful godfather one must make do with compadres (Lomnitz 1977, p. 162).

Compadrazgo is a way of legitimizing mutual assistance among neighbors and is judged in its "intensity and trustworthiness of reciprocal exchange" (Lomnitz 1977, p. 173).

6. Keefe, Padilla, and Carlos (1979) and Sena-Rivera (1979) argue that *compadrazgo* is

decreasing; however, Carlos (1973) has found that with urbanization ard modernization *compadres* still play an important role in Mexico and the relationship remains strong.

7. See Madsen (1964), Moore (1970), and Rubel (1966) for illustrations of its continued importance.

8. See Keefe, Padilla, and Carlos (1979), Murillo (1971), Rubel (1966), and Sena-Rivera (1979) for similar findings in other studies of Chicanos.

9. This "familism" in which individuals subordinate their needs to the collective can be traced back to Aztec culture (Mirandé and Enríquez 1979).

10. Alvirez and Bean (1976) argued that many Chicano families pool their resources, and Carlos (1973) has found that fictive kin help each other by finding jobs, lending money, and giving preferential treatment in business.

11. On some occasions, such as a fire or death, it might be permissible to accept emergency public aid, but it is still better if friends and family help out.

12. A fourteen-year-old girl explained:

> *I stay home until at least one o'clock in the summer every day to wash the kitchen and bathroom floors, otherwise they get dirty and sticky and the little kids crawl around on them all the time. In the winter during school, I do it before I go in the morning. Sometimes I'm late from school. We clean the whole house twice a week and my other sisters do the cooking and the washing.*

13. See Pitt-Rivers (1966) for an analysis of male honor in Spain.

14. See Hayner (1966) and Paz (1961), who argue that Aztec women were submissive to men. However, Mirandé and Enríquez (1979) argue that Aztec women had roles beyond wife and mother and that complete male domination occurred through external forces such as those imposed by colonialization (Baca Zinn 1975; Sosa Riddell 1974).

15. Similar patterns have been found in other Chicano communities (Flores 1971; Nieto-Gomez 1974; Vidal 1971).

16. Nelson (1971 p. 51) describes this phenomenon in her study of a Mexican village. In his analysis of psychological studies of the Mexican, Peñalosa (1968) found that they described the father-son relationship as distant and respectful and the father-daughter relationship as distant and conflict-free.

17. Diaz (1966), Fromm and Maccoby (1970), and Nelson (1971) so describe the fathers in the Mexican villages they studied. Rubel (1966) and Goodman and Beman (1971) describe similar findings in Chicano communities.

18. Diaz (1966) found that mothers expected their sons to become independent early in their lives in Tonalá, Mexico.

19. See Pitt-Rivers (1966) for an elaborate analysis of a similar situation in Spain.

20. A parent's problem in dealing with a son's or, for that matter, a daughter's education is exacerbated by problems in dealing with educational institutions and personnel. This is evident in the manner in which parents criticize their children's performances and in their fear of confronting school personnel, because the parents themselves lack education or feel unable to communicate in English. One teacher explained that he saw less than one half of the parents of his students and felt that these parents were immediately on the defensive when they came in. Typically a parent is called only if the teacher thinks there is something wrong with the student. Parents do not know that they can take the initiative, as many middle-class parents do, and demand things for their child, such as remedial aid or placement in a different class.

21. For a similar view of Mexican villages see Diaz (1966), Hayner (1966), and Nelson (1971).

22. The Virgin of Guadalupe symbolizes piety, virginity, and saintly submissiveness. She is the supreme good (Mirandé and Enríquez 1979). Peñalosa (1968) argues that "guadalupanismo," that is, the highly emotional, devout veneration of the Virgin of Guadalupe, is very strong in Mexican culture (see Bushell 1958; Madsen 1960).

23. See Fromm and Maccoby (1970) and Nelson (1971) for analyses of the Virgin Mother.

24. This traditional Mexican situation is similar to that of the Aztecs, who considered the mother the heart of the house, solely responsible for child rearing and cleaning, dedicated to her husband, and remaining respectable in the eyes of the community (Mirandé and Enríquez 1979, p. 14).

25. Gans (1962) describes a very similar situation among Italians living in the United States.

26. This has been documented in other Chicano communities (Murillo 1971).

27. In the modern media, concern for form and style is often linked to the violence of the cowboy in the movies.

> The gun tells us that he lives in a world of violence; and even that he "believes in violence." But the drama is one of self-restraint, the movement of violence must come in its own time and according to its special laws, or else it is valueless . . . it is not violence at all which is the "point" of the western movie, but a certain image of a man, a style, which expresses itself most clearly in violence (Warsow 1963, p. 239).

28. One rule of standard etiquette may place a man in a situation in which a claim to precedence is questioned, namely, apologizing profusely for an action already completed. An apology for an act committed is seen as an act of "gripping." If an individual attempts to place another in a demeaning situation, he must follow through on his claim. If a member of the Lions gang shouts "the Nobles suck" and there is by chance a Noble within hearing distance, the Noble will interpret the act as demeaning to his gang's honor and will follow through on the challenge. If the Lion apologizes, asking for forgiveness, he is "gripping," that is, placing himself in a subordinate position to the Noble, because only someone of higher status may grant forgiveness. Consequently, if the original challenger "grips," he loses his claim to precedence in that situation.

References

Alvirez, David and F. D. Bean. 1976. "The Mexican American Family." Pp. 271–292 in *Ethnic Families in America,* edited by C. H. Mindel and R. W. Habenstein. New York: Elsevier.

Baca Zinn, Maxine. 1975. "Political Familism: Toward Sex Role Equality in Chicano Families." *Aztlán: Chicano Journal of the Social Sciences and the Arts* 6:13–26.

Bushnell, John H. 1958. "La Virgen de Guadalupe as Surrogate Mother." *American Anthropologist* 60:261–265.

Carlos, Manuel L. 1973. "Fictive Kinship and Modernization in Mexico: A Comparative Analysis." *Anthropological Quarterly* 46: 75–91.

Coult, Allen and R. Habenstein. 1962. "The Study of Extended Kinship in Urban Society." *Sociological Quarterly* 3:141–145.

Diaz, May N. 1966. *Tonalá: Conservatism, Authority and Responsibility in a Mexican Town.* Berkeley: University of California Press.

Foster, George. 1967. *Tzintzunztán.* Boston: Little, Brown.

Fromm, Erich and Michael Maccoby. 1970. *Social Character in a Mexican Village.* Englewood Cliffs, NJ: Prentice-Hall.

Gans, Herbert. 1962. *The Urban Villagers.* New York: Free Press.

Gibson, Charles. 1966. *Spain in America.* New York: Harper and Row.

Handel, G. and L. Rainwater. 1964. "Persistence and Change in Working-Class Life-Styles." Pp. 36–41 in *Blue-Collar World,* edited by A. B. Shostak and W. Gomberg. Englewood Cliffs, NJ: Prentice-Hall.

Hayner, Norman. 1966. *New Patterns in Old Mexico.* New Haven: College and University Press.

Keefe, S. E., A. M. Padilla, and M. L. Carlos. 1979. "The Mexican-American Extended Family as an Emotional Support System." *Human Organization* 38:144–152.

Litwak, Eugene. 1960. "Geographic Mobility and Extended Family Cohesion." *American Sociological Review* 25:385–394.

Lomnitz, Larissa Adler. 1977. *Networks and Marginality.* Translated by Cinna Lomnitz. New York: Academic Press.

Madsen, William. 1960. *The Virgin's Children.* Austin: University of Texas Press.

Mintz, S. W. and E. R. Wolf. 1950. "An Analysis of Ritual Co-parenthood." *Southwestern Journal of Anthropology* 6:341–635.

Mirandé, A. and E. Enríquez. 1979. *La Chicana.* Chicago: University of Chicago Press.

Murillo, Nathan. 1971. "The Mexican-American Family." Pp. 97–108, *Chicanos: Social and Psychological Perspectives,* edited by N. N. Wagner and M. J. Haug. Saint Louis: C. V. Mosby.

Nelson, Cynthia. 1971. *The Waiting Village: Social Change in Rural Mexico.* Boston: Little, Brown.

Nieto-Gomez, Anna. 1974. "La Feminista." *Encuentro Feminil* 1:34–37.

Paz, Octavio. 1961. *The Labyrinth of Solitude.* Translated by Lysander Kemp. New York: Grove.

Peñalosa, Fernando. 1968. "Mexican Family Roles." *Journal of Marriage and the Family* 30:680–689.

Pitt-Rivers, Julian. 1966. *Honour and Social Status.* Pp. 19–78 in *Honour and Shame,* edited by J. Peristiany. Chicago: University of Chicago Press.

Rainwater, L. and G. Handel. 1964. "Changing Family Roles in the Working Class." Pp. 70–75 in *Blue-Collar World,* edited by A. W. Shostak and W. Gomberg. Englewood Cliffs, NJ: Prentice-Hall.

Romanucci-Ross, Lola. 1973. *Conflict, Violence and Morality in a Mexican Village.* Palo Alto: National Press Books.

Rubel, Arthur. 1966. *Across the Tracks.* Austin: University of Texas Press.

Seña-Rivera, Jaime. 1979. "The Extended Kinship of the United States: Competing Models and the Case of la Familia Chicana." *Journal of Marriage and the Family* 41:121–129.

Sosa Riddell, Adaljiza. 1974. "Chicanas and el Movimiento." *Aztlán: Chicano Journal of the Social Sciences and the Arts* 5:155–165.

Sotomayor, Marta. 1972. "Mexican American Interaction with Social Systems." *Social Casework* 52:316–322.

Temple-Trujillo, Rita E. 1974. "Conceptions of the Chicano Family." *Smith College Studies in Social Casework* 45:1–20.

Vidal, Mirta. 1971. *Women: New Voice of La Raza.* New York: Pathfinder.

Warsow, Robert. 1963. "The Gentleman with a Gun." In *An Anthology of Encounter Magazine,* edited by M. Lusky. New York: Basic Books.

Willmott, P. 1963. *The Evolution of a Community.* London: Routledge and Kegan Paul.

Young, M. and P. Willmott. 1957. *Family and Kinship in East London.* London: Routledge and Kegan Paul.

POVERTY AND FAMILY STRUCTURE: THE WIDENING GAP BETWEEN EVIDENCE AND PUBLIC POLICY ISSUES— WILLIAM JULIUS WILSON (WITH KATHRYN NECKERMAN)

Notes

1. Kenneth B. Clark, *Dark Ghetto: Dilemmas of Social Power* (New York: Harper and Row, 1965); Lee Rainwater, "Crucible of Identity: The Negro Lower-Class Family," *Daedalus* 95 (Winter 1966): 176–216; and Daniel R. Moynihan, *The Negro Family: The Case for National Action* (Washington, D.C.: Office of Policy Planning and Research, U.S. Department of Labor, 1965).

2. Moynihan, *Negro Family,* p. 48.

3. F. F. Furstenberg, Jr., T. Hershberg, and J. Modell, "The Origins of the Female-Headed Black Family: The Impact of the Urban Experience," *Journal of Interdisciplinary History,* 6 (1975): 211–33; E. H. Pleck, "The Two-Parent Household: Black Family Structure in Late Nineteenth-Century Boston," *Journal of Social History* 6 (Fall 1972): 3–31; Reynolds Farley, The Growth of the Black Population (Chicago: Markham, 1970); and R. Farley and A. I. Hermalin, "Family Stability: A Comparison of Trends between Blacks and Whites," American Sociological Review 36 (1971): 1–8.

4. E. Franklin Frazier, *The Negro Family in the United States* (Chicago: University of Chicago Press, 1939). Cf. A. H. Walker, "Racial Differences in Patterns of Marriage and Family Maintenance, 1890–1980," in *Feminism, Children, and New Families,* ed. S. M. Dornbush and M. H. Strober (New York: Guilford Press, 1985).

5. Herbert Gutman, *The Black Family in Slavery and Freedom, 1750–1925* (New York: Pantheon Books, 1976).

6. Furstenberg, Hershberg, and Modell, "Origins of Female-Headed Black Family"; C. A. Shifflett, "The Household Composition of Rural Black Families: Louisa, County, Virgina, 1880," *Journal of Interdisciplinary History* 6 (1975): 235–60; Pleck, "Two-Parent Household"; P. J. Lammermeir, "The Urban Black Family in the Nineteenth Century: A Study of Black Family Structure in the Ohio Valley, 1850–1880," *Journal of Marriage and the Family* 35 (August 1973): 440–56.

7. Pleck, "Two-Parent Household"; and Furstenberg, Hershberg, and Modell, "Origins of Female-Headed Black Family."

8. Furstenberg, Hershberg, and Modell, "Origins of Female-Headed Black Family."

9. Pleck, "Two-Parent Household."

10. Farley and Hermalin's "Family Stability" age-standardized figures show that between 1940 and 1960 the proportion of widows in the population dropped from 14 percent to 12 percent for white women, and from 24 percent to 17 percent for black women. During these two decades, however, the number of divorced women per 1,000 married women rose from 27.2 to 36.8 for whites, and from 29.1 to 71.3 for blacks. U.S. Bureau of the Census, *Census of the Population* (Washington, D.C.: Government Printing Office, 1943); and idem, *Current Population Reports,* Series P-20, "Marital Status and Family Status, March 1960" (Washington, D.C.: Government Printing Office, 1960).

11. U.S. Bureau of the Census, *Current Population Reports,* Series P-20, no. 388, "Household and Family Characteristics, March 1983" (Washington, D.C.: Government Printing Office, 1984).

12. National Office of Vital Statistics, *Vital Statistics of the United States,* vol. 1 (Washington, D.C.: U.S. Department of Health, Educa-

tion, and Welfare, 1957); and National Center for Health Statistics, "Advanced Report of Final Natality Statistics, 1980," in *Monthly Vital Statistics Report* (Washington, D.C.: U.S. Department of Health and Human Services, 1982); and U.S. Bureau of the Census, *Current Population Reports,* Series P-20, "Fertility of American Women, June 1981" (Washington, D.C.: Government Printing Office, 1983).

13. U.S. Bureau of the Census, "Marital Status, March 1960"; and idem, *Current Population Reports,* Series P-20, "Marital Status and Living Arrangements, March 1980" (Washington, D.C.: Government Printing Office, 1981).

14. M. O'Connell and M. J. Moore, "The Legitimacy Status of First Births to U.S. Women Aged 15–24, 1939–1978," *Family Planning Perspectives* 12 (1980): 16–25; and A. Cherlin, *Marriage, Divorce, Remarriage* (Cambridge, Mass.: Harvard University Press, 1981).

15. U.S. Bureau of the Census, *Current Population Reports,* Series P-20, "Characteristics of Single, Married, Widowed, and Divorced Persons in 1947" (Washington, D.C.: Government Printing Office, 1948); and idem, "Marital Status and Living Arrangements, March 1980."

16. Abundant evidence indicates that whites are more likely to remarry than blacks. For instance, a 1975 Current Population Survey showed that of women ages thirty-five to fifty-four who had been divorced or widowed, 53 percent of whites had remarried and were currently married and living with their husbands, as compared with only 38 percent of blacks (U.S. Bureau of the Census, *Current Population Reports,* Series P-20, "Marriage, Divorce, Widowhood, and Remarriage by Family Characteristics, June 1975" [Washington, D.C.: Government Printing Office, 1977]). In addition, National Center for Health Statistics data show that a higher proportion of white than black marriages are *remarriages,* despite the fact that blacks have higher rates of marital dissolution

(National Center for Health Statistics, "Marriage and Divorce," in *Vital Statistics of the United States,* 1978, vol. 3 [Washington, D.C.: U.S. Department of Health and Human Services, 1982]).

17. U.S. Bureau of the Census, "Marital Status and Living Arrangements."

18. U.S. Bureau of the Census, *Current Population Reports,* Series P-25, "Population Estimates" (Washington, D.C.: Government Printing Office, 1965); and idem, *Current Population Reports,* Series P-25, "Population Estimates" (Washington, D.C.: Government Printing Office, 1981).

19. Mary Jo Bane and David T. Ellwood, "The Dynamics of Children's Living Arrangements," working paper, supported by U.S. Department of Health and Human Services grant, contract no. HHS-100–82–0038, 1984.

20. P. Cutright, "Components of Change in the Number of Female Family Heads Aged 15–44: United States, 1940–1970," *Journal of Marriage and the Family* 36 (1974): 714–21.

21. Bane and Ellwood, "Dynamics of Children's Living Arrangements."

22. U.S. Bureau of the Census, *Current Population Reports,* Series P-23, "The Social and Economic Status of the Black Population in the United States: A Historical View, 1790–1978" (Washington, D.C.: Government Printing Office, 1979); and idem, *Current Population Reports,* Series P-20, "Marital Status and Family Status, March 1970" (Washington, D.C.: Government Printing Office, 1971); and idem, "Marital Status and Living Arrangements, March 1980."

23. Bane and Ellwood, "Dynamics of Children's Living Arrangements," p. 3.

24. Ibid., p. 23.

25. Mary Jo Bane and David T. Ellwood, "Single Mothers and Their Living Arrangements," working paper, supported by U.S. Department of Health and Human Services

grant, contract no. HHS-100–82–0038, 1984, quote on p. 27.

26. U.S. Bureau of the Census, *Current Population Reports,* Series P-60, no. 144, "Characteristics of the Population below Poverty Level, 1982" (Washington, D.C.: Government Printing Office, 1983).

27. Ibid.

28. G. J. Duncan, *Years of Poverty, Years of Plenty* (Ann Arbor: Institute for Social Research, University of Michigan, 1984).

29. U.S. Department of Health and Human Services, "Advance Report of Final Natality Statistics, 1980," in *Monthly Vital Statistics Report* (Washington, D.C.: Government Printing Office, 1982).

30. M. Zelnik and J. R. Kantner, "Sexual Activity, Contraceptive Use and Pregnancy among Metropolitan-Area Teenagers, 1971–1979," *Family Planning Perspectives* 12 (1980): 230–37.

31. Dennis P. Hogan, personal communication, 1984.

32. Clark, *Dark Ghetto,* p. 72.

33. Dennis P. Hogan, "Demographic Trends in Human Fertility and Parenting across the Life-Span," paper prepared for the Social Science Research Council Conference on Bio-Social Life-Span Approaches to Parental and Offspring Development, Elkridge, Md., May 1983; and idem, "Structural and Normative Factors in Single Parenthood among Black Adolescents," paper presented at the Annual Meeting of the American Sociological Association, San Antonio, Tex., August 1984.

34. Hogan, personal communication, 1984.

35. Hogan, "Structural and Normative Factors," p. 21.

36. Dennis P. Hogan and Evelyn M. Kitagawa, "The Impact of Social Status, Family Structure, and Neighborhood on the Fertility of Black Adolescents," *American Journal of Sociology* 90 (1985): 825–55.

37. Hogan, "Demographic Trends."

38. R. Easterlin, *Birth and Fortune: The Impact of Numbers on Personal Welfare* (New York: Basic Books, 1980); Dennis P. Hogan, *Transitions and Social Change: The Early Lives of American Men* (New York: Academic Press, 1981); and M. D. Evans, "Modernization, Economic Conditions and Family Formation: Evidence from Recent White and Nonwhite Cohorts," Ph.D. dissertation, University of Chicago, 1983. Cf. Hogan, "Demographic Trends."

39. Zelnik and Kantner, "Sexual Activity."

40. S. Hoffman and J. Holmes, "Husbands, Wives, and Divorce," in *Five Thousand American Families: Patterns of Economic Progress,* ed. J. N. Morgan, vol. 4 (Ann Arbor: Institute for Social Research, University of Michigan Press, 1976); S. Danziger, G. Jakubson, S. Schwartz, and E. Smolensky, "Work and Welfare as Determinants of Female Poverty and Household Headship," *Quarterly Journal of Economics* 97 (August 1982): 519–34; and H. I. Ross and I. Sawhill, *Time of Transition: The Growth of Families Headed by Women* (Washington, D.C.: Urban Institute, 1975).

41. U.S. Bureau of the Census, *Census of the Population,* 1980 (Washington, D.C.: Government Printing Office, 1984).

42. Ibid.

43. U.S. Bureau of the Census, "Characteristics of the Population below Poverty Level, 1982."

44. Charles Murray, *Losing Ground: American Social Policy, 1950–1980* (New York: Basic Books, 1984).

45. Cited in M. Feldstein, ed., *The American Economy in Transition* (Chicago: University of Chicago Press, 1980), p. 341.

46. P. Cutright, "Illegitimacy and Income Supplements," *Studies in Public Welfare,* paper no. 12 prepared for the use of the Subcommittee on Fiscal Policy of the Joint Economic Commit-

tee, Congress of the United States (Washington, D.C.: Government Printing Office, 1973); C. R. Winegarden, "The Fertility of AFDC Women: An Economic Analysis," *Journal of Economics and Business* 26 (1974): 159–66; A. Fechter and S. Greenfield, "Welfare and Illegitimacy: An Economic Model and Some Preliminary Results," working paper 963–1037 (Washington, D.C.: Urban Institute, 1973); Kristin Moore and Steven B. Caldwell, "Out-of-Wedlock Pregnancy and Childbearing," working paper no. 999–1002, Urban Institute, Washington, D.C., 1976; and D. R. Vining, Jr., "Illegitimacy and Public Policy," *Population and Development Review* 9 (1983): 105–10.

47. Vining, "Illegitimacy and Public Policy," p. 108.

48. Cutright, "Illegitimacy and Income Supplements"; David T. Ellwood and Mary Jo Bane, "The Impact of AFDC on Family Structure and Living Arrangements," prepared for the U.S. Department of Health and Human Services under grant no. 92A-82, 1984.

49. P. J. Placek and G. E. Hendershot, "Public Welfare and Family Planning: An Empirical Study of the 'Brood Sow' Myth," *Social Problems* 21(1974): 660–73; H. B. Presser and L. S. Salsberg, "Public Assistance and Early Family Formation: Is There a Pronatalist Effect?" *Social Problems* 23 (1975): 226–41; S. Polgar and V. Hiday, "The Effect of an Additional Birth on Low-Income Urban Families," *Population Studies* 28 (1974): 463–71; and Moore and Caldwell, "Out-of-Wedlock Pregnancy and Childbearing."

50. G. Cain, "The Effect of Income Maintenance Laws on Fertility in Results from the New Jersey-Pennsylvania Experiment," in *Final Report of the Graduated Work Incentive Experiment in New Jersey and Pennsylvania* (Madison, Wis., and Princeton, N.J.: Institute for Research on Poverty, University of Wisconsin, and Mathematica Policy Research, 1974).

51. M. C. Keeley, "The Effects of Negative Income Tax Programs on Fertility," *Journal of Human Resources* 9 (1980): 303–22.

52. Cutright and Madras, "AFDC and the Marital and Family Status of Ever-Married Women"; J. J. Minarik and R. S. Goldfarb, "AFDC Income, Recipient Rates, and Family Dissolution: A Comment," *Journal of Human Resources* 11 (Spring 1976): 243–50; M. Honig, "AFDC Income, Recipient Rates, and Family Dissolution," *Journal of Human Resources* 9 (Summer 1974): 303–22; and Ross and Sawhill, *Time of Transition*.

53. Honig, "AFDC Income, Recipient Rates, and Family Dissolution"; Minarik and Goldfarb, "AFDC Income, Recipient Rates, and Family Dissolution: A Comment"; Ross and Sawhill, *Time of Transition*; and Cutright and Madras, "AFDC and the Marital and Family Status of Ever-Married Women."

54. D. T. Ellwood and M. J. Bane, "Impact of AFDC on Family Structure and Living Arrangements," report prepared for the U.S. Department of Health and Human Services under grant no. 92A-82 (John F. Kennedy School of Government, Harvard University, 1984), p. 2.

55. In this connection, Ellwood and Bane state that "women in this group will tend to have married and had children at a very young age. Such marriages tend to be unstable, and thus it is plausible that welfare benefits might have an important impact on this group. Welfare may offer an alternative to an unhappy early marriage. . . . One should keep in mind, however, that even a sizable increase such as this one need not imply a very sizable increase in the number of single mothers. Among younger nonwhite women, divorced or separated mothers represent just 20% of all single mothers. A 50% increase in this group translates to only a 10% increase in the number of single mothers under 24. Thus even though welfare might have a significant impact on ever-married mothers, if welfare

does not influence births to nonmarried women, its overall impact on the fraction of all women who are single mothers would be small.... By contrast nearly 60% of all young white mothers report themselves as divorced or separated. A 50% increase here implies a much larger change in the number of single mothers. A large impact on divorce and separation then implies a much larger change in the number of women who are single mothers for whites than for nonwhites." Ellwood and Bane, "Impact of AFDC on Family Structure," p. 42.

56. Hoffman and Holmes, "Husbands, Wives, and Divorce"; Ross and Sawhill, *Time of Transition*; and Danziger et al., "Work and Welfare."

57. J. H. Bishop, "Jobs, Cash Transfers, and Marital Instability: A Review and Synthesis of the Evidence," *Journal of Human Resources* 15 (Summer 1980); 301–34; L. P. Groeneveld, M. Hannon, and N. Tuma, *Marital Stability: Final Report of the Seattle-Denver Income Maintenance Experiment,* vol. 1, Design and Result, pt. 5 (Menlo Park, Calif.: SRI International), p. 344; and L. P. Groeneveld, N. B. Tuma, and M. T. Hannon, "The Effects of Negative Income Tax Programs on Marital Dissolution," *Journal of Human Resources* 15 (1980): 654–74.

58. Hogan, "Demographic Trends"; and idem, "Structural and Normative Factors."

59. Ellwood and Bane, "Impact of AFDC on Family Structure," p. 8.

60. U.S. Bureau of the Census, *Census of the Population,* 1980.

61. Ibid.

62. Duncan, *Years of Poverty, Years of Plenty*; U.S. Bureau of the Census, "Social and Economic Status of the Black Population"; and U.S. Bureau of Labor Statistics, *Employment and Earnings* (Washington, D.C.: U.S. Department of Labor, January 1984).

63. W. E. Bakke, *Citizens without Work* (New Haven, Conn.: Yale University Press, 1940); M.

Komarovsky, *The Unemployed Man and His Family* (New York: Octagon Books, 1940); G. H. Elder, Jr., *Children of the Great Depression* (Chicago: University of Chicago Press, 1974); Honig, "AFDC Income, Recipient Rates, and Family Dissolution"; Ross and Sawhill, *Time of Transition*; I. Sawhill, G. E. Peabody, C. A. Jones, and S. B. Caldwell, *Income Transfers and Family Structure* (Washington, D.C.: Urban Institute, 1975); and Hoffman and Holmes, "Husbands, Wives, and Divorce"; Bishop, "Jobs, Cash Transfers, and Marital Instability"; P. Cutright, "Income and Family Events: Marital Instability," *Journal of Marriage and the Family* 33 (1971): 291–306; and A. Cohen, "Economic, Marital Instability and Race," Ph.D. dissertation, University of Wisconsin, Madison, 1979.

64. R. Farley, "Homicide Trends in the United States," *Demography* 17 (May 1980): 177–88; A. Blumstein, "On the Racial Disproportionality of United States' Prison Populations," *Journal of Criminal Law and Criminology* 73 (Fall 1982): 1259–81.

65. Several objections might be raised to these figures. First, it might be argued that the ratios are biased downward because of an undercount of young black men. This may be true, but it would seem that unenumerated men are not counted precisely because they do not have a stable attachment to labor force and family, and thus would be unlikely to be included in these figures even if they had been enumerated. Second, the employment figures are for the civilian labor force only and do not include men in the armed forces. Including men who are in the armed forces would smooth out the graph for men twenty to twenty-four years of age during the late 1960s, and would narrow the black-white gap a little because of slightly higher enlistment levels among blacks, but would not change the basic trends. The slight upturn in the index after 1954 for men twenty to twenty-four

is likely to represent the return of men in the armed forces to the civilian labor force following the Korean War. Finally, although some women may marry men other than employed men of their own age and race category, the figures are intended to convey the "marriage market" constraints facing most women.

66. While rising average incomes are likely to have enhanced family stability for black men who are employed, the more dramatic trends in unemployment and labor-force participation have outweighed increases in earnings to produce a net decline in family stability among blacks.

67. Ellwood and Bane, "Impact of AFDC on Family Structure."

68. Cutright and Madras, "AFDC and the Marital and Family Status of Ever-Married Women"; cf. G. S. Becker, E. M. Landes, and R. T. Michael, "An Economic Analysis of Marital Instability," *Journal of Political Economy* 85 (1977): 1141–87.

69. Center for the Study of Social Policy, "The 'Flip-Side' of Black Families Headed by Women: The Economic Status of Black Men," working paper, 1984; and Walker, "Racial Differences in Patterns of Marriage and Family Maintenance."

FAMILY DECLINE IN AMERICA—DAVID POPENOE

Notes

1. Norval Glenn, ed., "The State of the American Family," *Journal of Family Issues* 8 (No. 4, December 1987), Special Issue.

2. Sar A. Levitan and Richard S. Belous, *What's Happening to the American Family?* (Baltimore: Johns Hopkins, 1981), pp. 190, 15.

3. Sar A. Levitan, Richard S. Belous, and Frank Gallo, *What's Happening to the American Family?* (rev. ed.) (Baltimore: Johns Hopkins, 1988), pp. vi, viii.

4. Carl N. Degler, *At Odds: Women and the Family in America from the Revolution to the Present* (Oxford, England: Oxford University Press, 1980); Lawrence Stone, *The Family, Sex, and Marriage in England 1500–1800* (New York: Harper and Row, 1977); Steven Mintz and Susan Kellogg, *Domestic Revolutions: A Social History of the American Family* (New York: Free Press, 1988).

5. Andrew Cherlin and Frank F. Furstenberg, Jr., "The Changing European Family: Lessons for the American Reader," *Journal of Family Issues* 9 (No. 3, 1988), p. 294; John Modell, Frank F. Furstenberg, Jr., and Douglas Strong, "The Timing of Marriage in the Transition to Adulthood: Continuity and Change, 1860–1975," *American Journal of Sociology* 84 (1978), pp. S120–S150.

6. Susan Cotts Watkins, Jane A. Menken, and John Bongaarts, "Demographic Foundations of Family Change," *American Sociological Review* 52 (No. 3, 1987), pp. 346–358.

7. Andrew J. Cherlin, *Marriage, Divorce, Remarriage* (Cambridge, MA: Harvard University Press, 1981).

8. All data are from the U.S. Census Bureau, unless otherwise indicated.

9. Arthur G. Neal, Theodore Groat, and Jerry W. Wicks, "Attitudes about Having Children: A Study of 600 Couples in the Early Years of Marriage," *Journal of Marriage and the Family* 51 (No. 2, 1989), pp. 313–328; Joseph Veroff, Elizabeth Douvan, and Richard A. Kulka, *The Inner American: A Self-Portrait from 1957 to 1976* (New York: Basic Books, 1981); James A. Sweet and Larry L. Bumpass, *American Families and Households* (New York: Russell Sage Foundation, 1987), p. 400.

10. David E. Bloom and James Trussell, "What Are the Determinants of Delayed Childbearing and Permanent Childlessness in the United States?" *Demography* 21 (No. 4, 1984), pp. 591–611; Charles E. Westoff, "Perspective

on Nuptiality and Fertility," *Population and Development Review Supplement* (No. 12, 1986), pp. 155–170.

11. John D'Emilio and Estelle B. Freedman, *Intimate Matters: A History of Sexuality in America* (New York: Harper and Row, 1988).

12. From a 1987 study sponsored by the National Academy of Sciences, reported in *The New York Times,* February 27, 1989, p. B11.

13. Daniel Yankelovich, *New Rules: Searching for Self-Fulfillment in a World Turned Upside Down* (New York: Random House, 1981), p. 94.

14. Suzanne M. Bianchi and Daphne Spain, *American Women in Transition* (New York: Russell Sage Foundation, 1986); Victor R. Fuchs, *Women's Quest for Economic Equality* (Cambridge, MA: Harvard University Press, 1988).

15. Data assembled from U.S. Census reports by Maris A. Vinovskis, "The Unraveling of the Family Wage since World War II: Some Demographic, Economic, and Cultural Considerations," in Bryce Christensen, Allan Carlson, Maris Vinovskis, Richard Vedder, and Jean Bethke Elshtain, *The Family Wage: Work, Gender, and Children in the Modern Economy* (Rockford, IL: The Rockford Institute, 1988), pp. 33–58.

16. Lenore J. Weitzman, *The Divorce Revolution* (New York: Free Press, 1985).

17. Paul C. Glick, "Fifty Years of Family Demography; A Record of Social Change," *Journal of Marriage and the Family* 50 (No. 4, 1988), p. 868.

18. Robert Schoen, "The Continuing Retreat from Marriage: Figures from the 1983 U.S. Marital Status Life Tables," *Social Science Research* 71 (No. 2,1987), pp. 108–109; Teresa Castro Martin and Larry L. Bumpass, "Recent Trends in Marital Disruption," *Demography* 26 (No. 1, 1989), pp. 37–51.

19. Sanford M. Dornbusch and Myra H. Strober, *Feminism, Children, and the New Families* (New York: Guilford Press, 1988).

20. Sandra L. Hofferth, "Updating Children's Life Course," *Journal of Marriage and the Family* 47 (No. 1, 1985), pp. 93–115.

21. The 20-year downward spiral of family households came to a (temporary?) halt in the 1986–87 period, when the percentage of family households increased slightly, as documented in Judith Waldrop, "The Fashionable Family," *American Demographics* (March 1988).

22. Susan Cotts Watkins, Jane A. Menken, and John Bongaarts, op. cit., 1987.

23. Eugene Smolensky, Sheldon Danziger, and Peter Gottschalk, "The Declining Significance of Age in the United States: Trends in the Well-being of Children and the Elderly since 1939," in John L. Palmer, Timothy Smeeding, and Barbara Boyle Torrey, eds., *The Vulnerable* (Washington, DC: Urban Institute, 1988), pp. 29–54.

24. Report of House Select Committee on Children, Youth and Families, *The New York Times,* October 2, 1989, p. A12.

25. Kingsley Davis, ed., *Contemporary Marriage: Comparative Perspectives on a Changing Institution* (New York: Russell Sage Foundation, 1985).

26. Mary Ann Glendon, *The Transformation of Family Law* (Chicago: University of Chicago, 1989).

27. Robert N. Bellah, Richard Madsen, William M. Sullivan, Ann Swidler, and Steven M. Tipton, *Habits of the Heart: Individualism and Commitment in American Life* (Berkeley, CA: University of California Press, 1985).

28. Victor Fuchs, *How We Live* (Cambridge, MA: Harvard University Press, 1983).

29. Jean Bethke Elshtain, *Public Man, Private Wonwn: Women in Social and Political Thought* (Princeton, NJ: Princeton University Press, 1981).

30. Francesca M. Cancian, *Love in America: Gender and Self-Development* (Cambridge, England, and New York: Cambridge University Press, 1987).

31. *U.S. Children and Their Families: Current Conditions and Recent Trends, 1989* (Washington, DC: U.S. Government Printing Office). Nicholas Zill and Carolyn C. Rogers, "Recent Trends in the Well-being of Children in the United States and Their Implications for Public Policy," in Andrew Cherlin, ed., *The Changing American Family and Public Policy* (Washington, DC: Urban Institute, 1988), pp. 31–115; Peter Uhlenberg and David Eggebeen, "The Declining Well-being of American Adolescents," *The Public Interest* (No. 82, 1986), pp. 25–38.

32. Samuel H. Preston, "Children and the Elderly: Divergent Paths for America's Dependents," *Demography* 21 (No. 4, 1984), p. 443.

33. Frank F. Furstenberg, Jr., "Good Dads-Bad Dads: Two Faces of Fatherhood," in Andrew Cherlin, ed., *The Changing American Family and Public Policy* (Washington, DC: Urban Institute, 1988), pp. 193–218.

34. Barbara Ehrenreich, *The Hearts of Men: American Dreams and the Flight from Commitment* (New York: Anchor, 1983).

35. E. Mavis Hetherington and Josephine D. Arasteh, eds., *Impact of Divorce, Single Parenting, and Stepparenting on Children* (Hillsdale, NJ: Lawrence Erlbaum Associates, 1988); Sara McLanahan and Karen Booth, "Mother-Only Families: Problems, Prospects, and Politics," *Journal of Marriage and the Family* 51 (No. 3, 1989), pp. 557–580.

36. Urie Bronfenbrenner, *The Ecology of Human Development* (Cambridge, MA: Harvard University Press, 1979).

37. Alan Wolfe, *Whose Keeper? Social Science and Moral Obligation* (Berkeley, CA: University of California Press, 1989).

38. Peter L. Berger and Richard J. Neuhaus, *To Empower People: The Role of Mediating Structures in Public Policy* (Washington, DC: American Enterprise Institute, 1977).

39. Betty Friedan, *The Feminine Mystique* (New York: Laurel, 1983, 1963).

40. Sylvia Ann Hewlett, *A Lesser Life* (New York: William Morrow, 1986).

41. David Popenoe, *Disturbing the Nest: Family Change and Decline in Modern Societies* (New York: Aldine de Gruyter, 1988).

HISTORY AND CURRENT STATUS OF DIVORCE IN THE UNITED STATES— FRANK F. FURSTENBERG, JR.

Notes

1. Lichtenberger, J. P. *Divorce: A social interpretation.* New York: McGraw-Hill, 1931; Halem, L. C. *Divorce reform: Changing legal and social perspectives.* New York: Free Press, 1980.

2. O'Neill, W. L. *Divorce in the progressive era.* New Haven, CT: Yale University Press, 1973.

3. Weitzman, L. J. *The divorce revolution: The unexpected social and economic consequences for women and children in America.* New York: Free Press, 1985.

4. Goode, W. J. *World revolution and family patterns.* New York: Free Press, 1963; Davis, K., ed. *Contemporary marriage* New York: Russell Sage Foundation, 1985.

5. Hobbs, F., and Lippman, L. U.S. Bureau of the Census. *Children's well-being: An international comparison.* International Population Reports, Series P-95, No. 80. Washington, DC: U.S. Government Printing Office, 1990.

6. See note no. 1, Halem; Glendon, M.A. *Abortion and divorce in western law.* Cambridge, MA: Harvard University Press, 1987; Glendon, M.A. *The transformation of family law.* Chicago: University of Chicago Press, 1989.

7. Carter, H., and Glick, P. C. *Marriage and divorce: A social and economic study.* Cambridge, MA: Harvard University Press, 1976; Preston, S. H., and McDonald, J. The incidence of divorce within cohorts of American marriages

contracted since the Civil War. *Demography* (1979) 16:1–25; Weed, J. A. *National estimates of marriage dissolution and survivorships: United States.* Vital and Health Statistics, Series 3 (Analytic Statistics), No. 19. DHHS/PHS 81–1043. Hyattsville, MD: National Center for Health Statistics, 1980.

8. Stone, L. *Road to divorce: England 1530–1987.* Oxford: Oxford University Press, 1990.

9. Cherlin, A. J. *Marriage, divorce, remarriage.* Rev. ed. Cambridge, MA: Harvard University Press, 1992.

10. See note no. 7, Preston and McDonald.

11. National Center for Health Statistics. *Advance report of final divorce statistics, 1988.* Monthly Vital Statistics Report, Vol. 39, No. 12, Suppl. 2. Hyattsville, MD: Public Health Service, 1991.

12. Martin, T. C., and Bumpass, L. L. Recent trends in marital disruption. *Demography* (1989) 26:37–51.

13. Norton, A. J., and Miller, L. F. U.S. Bureau of the Census. *Marriage, divorce and remarriage in the 1990's.* Current Population Reports, Series P-23, No. 180. Washington, DC: U.S. Government Printing Office, 1992.

14. Saluter, A. F. U.S. Bureau of the Census. *Marital status and living arrangements: March 1991.* Current Population Reports, Series P-20, No. 461. Washington, DC: U.S. Government Printing Office, April 1992.

15. Bianchi, S. M., and Spain, D. *American women in transition.* New York: Russell Sage Foundation, 1986.

16. Saluter, A. F. U.S. Bureau of the Census. *Marital status and living arrangements: March 1992.* Current Population Reports, Series P-20, No. 468. Washington, DC: U.S. Government Printing Office, December 1992.

17. See note no. 7, Carter and Glick.

18. U.S. Bureau of the Census. *Households, families, and children: A 30-year perspective.* Current Population Reports, Series P-23, No. 181. Washington, DC: U.S. Government Printing Office, 1992, Figure 6.

19. See note no. 7, Weed. See also Bumpass, L. L., Martin, T. C., and Sweet, J. A. The impact of family background and early marital factors on marital disruption. *Journal of Family Issues* (1991) 12:22–42.

20. Bumpass, L. L., and Raley, R. K. Trends in the duration of single-parent families. National Survey of Families and Households, Working Paper No. 58. Madison: University of Wisconsin, 1993.

21. Bane, M. J. *Here to stay: American families in the twentieth century.* New York: Basic Books, 1976; Spanier, G. B., and Glick, P. C. Marital instability in the United States: Some correlates and recent changes. *Family Relations* (1981) 31:329–38.

22. Bumpass, L. L., Sweet, J. A., and Martin, T. C. Changing patterns of remarriage. *Journal of Marriage and the Family* (1990) 52:747–56.

23. Bumpass, L. L., Sweet, J. A., and Cherlin, A. The role of cohabitation in declining rates of marriage. *Journal of Marriage and the Family* (1991) 53:913–27.

24. Morgan, S. P., McDaniel, A., Miller, A. T., and Preston, S. Racial differences in household and family structure at the turn of the century. *American Journal of Sociology* (January 1993) 98:799–828; Ruggles, S., and Goeken, R. Race and multigenerational family structure, 1900–1980. In *The changing American family.* S. J. South and S. E. Tolnay, eds. Boulder, CO: Westview Press, 1992, pp. 15–42.

25. Cherlin offers a cogent summary of the debate. See note no. 9, Cherlin.

26. Gutman, H. G. *The Black family in slavery and freedom 1750–1925.* New York: Vintage Books, 1977; McAdoo, H. P. *Black families.* Beverly Hills, CA: Sage, 1981. See note no. 24, Morgan, McDaniel, Miller, and Preston.

27. Bennett, N. G., Bloom, D. E., and Craig, P. H. American marriage patterns in transition.

In *The changing American family*. S. J. South and S. E. Tolnay, eds. Boulder, CO: Westview Press, 1992, pp. 89–108.

28. Espenshade, T. J. *The recent decline of American marriage: Blacks and whites in comparative perspective*. Washington, DC: The Urban Institute, 1985.

29. Bean, F. D., and Tienda, M. *The Hispanic population in the United States*. New York: Russell Sage Foundation, 1988; U.S. Bureau of the Census. *Hispanic Americans today*. Current Population Reports, Series P-23, No. 183. Washington, DC: U.S. Government Printing Office, 1993.

30. U.S. Bureau of the Census. *Fertility of American women: June 1990*. Current Population Reports, Series P-20, No. 454. Washington, DC: U.S. Government Printing Office, 1991.

31. National Center for Health Statistics. *Advance report of final natality statistics, 1990*. Monthly Vital Statistics Report, Vol. 41, No. 9, Suppl. Hyattsville, MD: Public Health Service, 1993.

32. See note no. 4, Davis. See also Haskey, J. Formation and dissolution of unions in the different countries of Europe. In *European population*. Vol. 2. A. Blum and J. L. Rallu, eds. Paris: John Libbey Eurotext, 1993, pp. 211–29.

33. See note no. 32, Haskey.

34. Cherlin, A. J., and Furstenberg, Jr., F. F. The changing European family: Lessons for the American reader. *Journal of Family Issues* (1988) 9:291–97.

35. Kiernan, K., and Chase-Lansdale, P. L. Children and marital breakdown: Short- and long-term consequences. In *European population*. Vol. 2. A. Blum and J. L. Rallu, eds. Paris: John Libbey Eurotext, 1993, pp. 295–307.

36. See note no. 4, Davis.

37. Ross, H. L., and Sawhill, I. V. *Time of transition: The growth of families headed by women*. Washington, DC: The Urban Institute, 1975. Goode, W. J. *The family*. 2d ed. Engle-

wood Cliffs, NJ: Prentice-Hall, 1982. Levinger, G., and Moles, O. C. *Divorce and separation*. New York: Basic Books, 1979. Bernard, J. *Women, wives, mothers*. Chicago: Aldine, 1975. Nelson, R. R., and Skidmore, F. *American families and the economy: The high costs of living*. Washington, DC: National Academy Press, 1983. Becker, G. S. *A treatise on the family*. Cambridge, MA: Harvard University Press, 1981. Sweet, J. A., and Bumpass, L. L. *American families and households*. New York: Russell Sage Foundation, 1987.

38. Veroff, J., Douvan, E., and Kulka, R. A. The inner American: A self-portrait from 1957 to 1976. New York: Basic Books, 1981. Thornton, A., and Freedman, D. The changing American family. *Population Bulletin* (1983) 38:2–44. Bumpass, L. L. What's happening to the family: Interactions between demographic and institutional change. *Demography* (1990) 27:483–98.

39. Lesthaeghe, R., and Meekers, D. Value changes and the dimensions of families in the European community. *European Journal of Population* (1986) 2:225–68.

40. Wright, G. C., and Stetson, D. N. The impact of no-fault-divorce-law reform on divorce in American states. *Journal of Marriage and the Family* (1978) 40:575–80.

41. Thornton, A. Changing attitudes towards separation and divorce: Causes and consequences. *American Journal of Sociology* (1985) 90:856–72.

42. See note no. 38, Bumpass.

43. Furstenberg, Jr., F. F. Conjugal succession: Reentering marriage after divorce. In *Life span development and behavior*. Vol. 4. P. B. Baltes and O. G. Brim, eds. New York: Academic Press, 1982, pp. 107–46.

44. Blankenhorn, D., Bayme, S., and Elshtain, J. B., eds. *Rebuilding the nest: A new commitment to the American family*. Milwaukee, WI: Family Service America, 1990; Jost, Y. and Robinson, M. The CQ Researcher: Children and

divorce. *Congressional Quarterly Inc.* in conjunction with EBSCO Publishing (June 7, 1991) 1,5:349–68; Hewlett, S. A. *When the bough breaks: The cost of neglecting our children.* New York: Harper Perennial, 1991; Gill, R. T. For the sake of the children. *The Public Interest* (Summer 1992) 108:81–96.

45. Bumpass, L. L., and Sweet, J. A. Children's experience in single-parent families: Implications of cohabitation and marital transitions. *Family Planning Perspectives* (November/December 1989) 21:256–60; Furstenberg, Jr., F. F., and Cherlin, A. J. *Divided families: What happens to children when parents part.* Cambridge, MA: Harvard University Press, 1991.

46. Uhlenberg, P. Death and the family. In *The American family in social-historical perspective.* M. Gordon, ed. New York: St. Martin's Press, 1983, pp. 169–78.

47. See note no. 45, Furstenberg and Cherlin.

48. See note no. 23, Bumpass, Sweet, and Cherlin. See also Furstenberg, Jr., F. F., Nord, C. W., Peterson, J. L., and Zill, N. The life course of children of divorce: Marital disruption and parental conflict. *American Sociological Review* (1983) 48:656–68.

49. Hofferth, S. L. Updating children's life course. *Journal of Marriage and the Family* (1985) 47:93–115. See note no. 45, Bumpass and Sweet.

50. U.S. Bureau of the Census. *The Hispanic population in the United States: March 1989.* Current Population Reports, Series P-20, No. 444. Washington, DC: U.S. Government Printing Office, 1990.

51. Emery, R. E. *Marriage, divorce, and children's adjustment.* Newbury Park, CA: Sage, 1988; Wallerstein, J. S., and Blakeslee, S. *Second chances: Men, women, and children a decade after divorce.* New York: Ticknor and Fields, 1989; Chase-Lansdale, P. L., and Hetherington, M. The impact of divorce on life-span development: Short- and long-term effects. In

Life-span development and behavior. Vol. 10. P. B. Baltes, D. L. Featherman, and R. M. Lerner, eds. Hillsdale, NJ: Lawrence Erlbaum Associates, 1990, pp. 105–50.

52. Furstenberg, Jr., F. F., and Nord, C. W. Parenting apart: Patterns of childbearing after marital disruption. *Journal of Marriage and the Family* (1985) 47:898–904; Seltzer, J. A., and Bianchi, S. M. Children's contact with absent parents. *Journal of Marriage and the Family* (1988) 50:663–77; Teachman, J. D. Intergenerational resource transfers across disrupted households: Absent fathers' contributions to the well-being of their children. In *The changing American family.* S. J. South and S. E. Tolnay, eds. Boulder, CO: Westview Press, 1992, pp. 224–46.

53. See note no. 52, Furstenberg and Nord.

54. U.S. Bureau of the Census. *Child support and alimony: 1987.* Current Population Reports, Series P-23, No. 167. Washington, DC: U.S. Government Printing Office, 1990.

55. Furstenberg, Jr., F. F., and Harris, K. M. The disappearing American father? Divorce and the waning significance of biological parenthood. In *The changing American family.* S. J. South and S. E. Tolnay, eds. Boulder, CO: Westview Press, 1992, pp. 197–223; King, V. Nonresident father involvement and child well-being: Can dads make a difference? *Journal of Family Issues* (March 1994) 15:78–96.

56. Duncan, G. J., and Hoffman, S. D. A reconsideration of the economic consequences of marital dissolution. *Demography* (1985) 22:485–97.

57. Garfinkel, I. *Assuring child support: An extension of Social Security.* New York: Russell Sage Foundation, 1992.

58. Garfinkel, I., and McLanahan, S. S. *Single mothers and their children: A new American dilemma.* Washington, DC: Urban Institute Press, 1986.

59. Wallerstein, J. S., and Kelly, J. B. *Surviving the breakup: How children and parents cope with divorce.* New York: Basic Books, 1980.

60. Amato, P. R. Children's adjustment to divorce: Theories, hypotheses, and empirical support. *Journal of Marriage and the Family* (1993) 55:23–38.

61. Pasley, K., and Ihinger-Tallman, M., eds. *Remarriage and stepparenting: Current research and theory.* New York: Guilford Press, 1987; Ihinger-Tallman, M., and Pasley, K. *Remarriage.* Newbury Park, CA: Sage, 1987.

62. This conclusion is surprising, especially in view of the fact that most existing research relies on comparisons of children in single-parent and remarried families instead of carrying out longitudinal analyses of children making the transition from divorce to remarriage. Cross-sectional comparisons often fail to account for differences in families where remarriage does and does not occur. They also frequently ignore the experience of children whose parents have remarried and redivorced, counting them as continually divorced.

63. Cherlin, A. J. Remarriage as an incomplete institution. *American Journal of Sociology* (1978) 84:634–50.

64. Johnson, C. L. *Ex familia: Grandparents, parents, and children adjust to divorce.* New Brunswick, NJ: Rutgers University Press, 1988; Cooney, T. M., and Uhlenberg, P. Divorced men and their adult children after mid-life. *Journal of Marriage and the Family* (1990) 52:677–88.

65. Cherlin, A. J., and Furstenberg, Jr., F. F. *The new American grandparent.* New York: Basic Books, 1986.

66. Barber, B. L., and Eccles, J. S. Long-term influence of divorce and single parenting on adolescent family- and work-related values, behaviors, and aspirations. *Psychological Bulletin* (January 1992) 3:108–26.

67. Skolnick, A. *Embattled paradise: The American family in an age of uncertainty.* New York: Basic Books, 1991; Bellah, R. N. *Habits of the heart: Individualism and commitment in American life.* Berkeley: University of California Press, 1985.

68. Cherlin, A. J. Nostalgia as family policy. *The Public Interest* (Winter 1993) 110:77–91; Gill, R. T. Family breakdown as family policy. *The Public Interest* (Winter 1993) 110:84–91.

69. Whitehead, B. D. Dan Quayle was right. *The Atlantic* (April 1993) 271:47–84.

70. Hayes, C. D. *Risking the future: Adolescent sexuality, pregnancy, and childbearing.* Washington, DC: National Academy Press, 1987.

71. Chase-Lansdale, P. L., and Brooks-Gunn, J., eds. *Escape from poverty: What makes a difference for poor children?* New York: Cambridge University Press. In press.

72. Ellwood, D. T. *Poor support.* New York: Basic Books, 1988.

73. Furstenberg, Jr., F. F. Supporting fathers: Implications of the Family Support Act for men. Paper presented at the forum on the Family Support Act. Washington, D.C., November 1990.

74. Goode, W. J. Why men resist. In *Rethinking the family: Some feminist questions.* B. Thorne and M. Yalom, eds. New York: Longman, 1982, pp. 131–50; Thompson, L., and Walker, A. J. Women and men in marriage, work, and parenthood. *Journal of Marriage and the Family* (1989) 51:845–71; Hochschild, A. *The second shift: Working parents and the revolution at home.* New York: Viking Press, 1989; Gerson, K. *No man's land: Men's changing commitments to family and work.* New York: Basic Books, 1993.

75. National Commission on Children. *Beyond rhetoric: A new American agenda for children and families.* Washington, DC: National Commission on Children, 1991.

THE ECONOMY OF DATING— BETH L. BAILEY

Notes

1. Margaret Mead, *Male and Female* (New York: William Morrow, 1949; reprint ed., New York: Morrow Quill Paperbacks, 1967), p. 285. Mead first gave the substance of this book as the

Jacob Gimbel Lectures in Sex Psychology in 1946. The *Ladies' Home Journal* also ran much of Mead's discussion in 1949, including her description of dating as a "competitive game." (Margaret Mead, "Male and Female." *LHJ,* September 1949, p. 145.)

2. Willard Waller, "The Rating and Dating Complex," *American Sociological Review* 2 (1937): 727–34. Woman's popularity was described as associational—she received status as the object of man's choice. Undoubtedly, the right clothes, the right connections, and all the intangibles that come from the right background purchased male attention in the first place, but popular and scholarly accounts consistently slighted this angle.

3. Paula Fass, *The Damned and the Beautiful* (New York: Oxford University Press, 1977), p. 201.

4. IBID., p. 226.

5. Michael Gordon, "Was Waller Ever Right?" *Journal of Marriage and the Family* (*JMF*) 43 (February 1981): 67–75. Gordon questions the validity of Waller's model based on the atypicality of his sample. I do not insist that rating-dating actually governed individual acts and choices of either Penn State students or the population at large (although it may have), but it did provide a vocabulary for and a way of understanding the dating system for participants and observers alike. The language of rating-dating appears widespread in both college and noncollege sources, though with a significant time lag between colleges and the general population.

6. May Ellen Green, "Advice to Freshmen," *Mademoiselle,* August 1939, p. 88.

7. Fass, *Damned and Beautiful,* p. 200. Fass found the Northwestern arrangement reported in the *UCLA Daily* (13 November 1925). I found an apocryphal version of the story in "If Your Daughter Goes to College," *Better Homes and Gardens* (*BH&G*), May 1940.

8. Norton Hughes Jonathon, *Guidebook for the Young Man about Town* (Philadelphia: John C. Winston Co., 1949), pp. 129–31.

9. Betty Strickroot, "Damda Phi Data Sorority Rates BMOC's by Their Dating Value," *Michigan Daily,* 25 March 1936.

10. Editorial, "Where Do You Make Your Date?" *Massachusetts Collegian,* 10 October 1935, p. 2.

11. Elizabeth Eldridge, *Co-ediquette* (New York: E. P. Dutton & Co., 1936), p. 224. The author based her book on personal research and experience at several U.S. colleges and universities. This volume went through four printings in June–August 1936.

12. Anna Streese Richardson, "Dates in Christmas Socks," *Woman's Home Companion* (*WHC*), January 1940, p. 7.

13. Usage does change. The name Gay Head comes from the cliffs of Martha's Vineyard, where, as *Senior Scholastic* (*SS*) revealed in its teachers' supplement, Gay had been christened by a male editor with a bottle of raspberry soda (20 February 1937). In 1937 *Senior Scholastic* was used by 6,200 teachers in high school classrooms, and the teachers reported that "Boy Dates Girl" was extremely popular with students (Teachers' Supplement, 29 May 1937, p. A-3).

14. Gay Head, "Boy Dates Girl: The First Reel," *SS,* 19 September 1936, p. 18.

15. "Blind as a Bat," *LHJ,* December 1944, p. 8.

16. Gay Head, "Boy Dates Girl Jam Session," *SS* 22–27 February 1943, p. 29; "Should High School Students Go Steady?" *SS,* 20 October 1941, p. 38; "Jam Session," *SS,* 28 February–4 March 1944, p. 32. *Senior Scholastic* began its jam session polls in 1941; the first was on dutch dating.

TWO CAN MAKE A REVOLUTION—EGON MAYER

Notes

1. Francesco Alberoni, *Falling in Love* (New York: Random House, 1983), p. 6.

2. Ibid., p. 17.

3. John B. Halsted, *Romanticism: Definition, Explanation, and Evaluation* (Lexington, MA: D.C. Heath and Company, 1965).

4. Edward Shorter, *The Making of the Modern Family* (New York: Basic Books, Inc., 1975); Ellen K. Rothman, *Hands and Hearts: A History of Courtship in America* (New York: Basic Books, Inc., 1984).

5. Morton M. Hunt, *The Natural History of Love* (New York: Alfred A. Knopf, Inc./Minerva Press, 1959, 1967).

6. Ibid., p. 26.

7. Joseph Stein, *Fiddler on the Roof.* Broadway musical.

8. Hunt, *The Natural History of Love,* p. 25.

9. William M. Kephart, *The Family, Society, and the Individual,* 3d Ed. (New York: Houghton Mifflin Company, 1972), p. 137.

10. Shorter, *The Making of the Modern Family,* p. 148.

11. Selma Stern, *Court Jew* (Philadelphia, PA: Jewish Publication Society, 1951).

12. Rothman, *Hands and Hearts,* pp. 28–29.

13. Jan Lewis, *The Pursuit of Happiness: Family and Values in Jefferson's Virginia* (New York: Cambridge University Press, 1983).

14. Shorter, *The Making of the Modern Family,* pp. 121–122.

15. Ibid., p. 148.

16. J. Hector St. John Crevecoeur, *Letters of an American Farmer* (New York: Dolphin Books, n.d.), pp. 49–50.

17. Israel Zangwill, *The Melting Pot* (New York: Macmillan Company, 1908).

18. Arthur Mann, *The One and the Many* (Chicago: Chicago University Press, 1979), p. 100.

19. Ibid., p. 75–76.

20. Ibid., p. 111.

21. Ibid., p. 117.

22. Heinrich Graetz, *History of the Jews* (Philadelphia, PA: The Jewish Publication Society, 1956), v. 5, p. 697.

23. Malcolm H. Stern, "Jewish Marriage and Intermarriage in the Federal Period, 1776–1840," *American Jewish Archives* (November 1967), pp. 142–143.

24. Milton L. Barron, "The Incidence of Jewish Intermarriage in Europe and America," *American Sociological Review* 11:1 (February 1946), pp. 6–13.

25. Moshe Davis, "Mixed Marriage in Western Jewry," *Jewish Journal of Sociology* 10:2 (December 1968) pp. 177–210.

26. Ande Manners, *Poor Cousins* (Greenwich, CT: Fawcett Publications, 1972), p. 25.

27. Arthur Ruppin, *The Jews in the Modern World* (New York: Arno Press, 1973), pp. 318–321.

28. Chaim I. Waxman, *America's Jews in Transition* (Philadelphia, PA: Temple University Press, 1983), pp. 29–31.

29. National Jewish Population Study, "Intermarriage" (New York: Council of Jewish Federations, 1971). Mimeograph.

30. Isaac Metzker, *A Bintle Brief* (New York: Ballantine Books, 1971), pp. 76–77.

31. Ibid., pp. 91–92.

32. Julius Drachsler, *Democracy and Assimilation* (New York: Macmillan Company, 1920), p. 126.

33. Milton M. Gordon, *Assimilation in American Life* (New York: Oxford University Press, 1964), p. 80.

34. Elihu Bergman, "The American Jewish Population Erosion," *Midstream* 23:8 (October 1977).

35. Andrew M. Greeley, *Crisis in the Church* (Chicago: Thomas More Press, 1979), p. 150.

36. Richard D. Alba, "Social Assimilation among American Catholic National Origin Groups." *American Sociological Review* 41:6 (1976), pp. 1030–1046.

37. Konrad Bercovici, *Crimes of Charity* (1917).

38. Michael Novak, *The Rise of the Unmeltable Ethnics* (New York: Macmillan Publishing Company, 1971).

39. Herbert J. Gans, *The Levittowners* (New York: Vintage Books, 1969); Michael Parenti,

"Ethnic Politics and the Persistence of Ethnic Identification," *American Political Science Review* 61 (September 1967), pp. 717–726.

40. Bill R. Lindner, *How to Trace Your Family History* (New York: Dodd Mead Company, 1978); Arthur Kurzweil, *From Generation to Generation: How to Trace Your Jewish Genealogy* (New York: Morrow, 1980).

41. United Jewish Appeal, *Book of Songs and Blessings* (New York: United Jewish Appeal, 1980), p. 25.

42. Floyd J. Fowler, *1975 Community Survey: A Study of the Jewish Population of Greater Boston* (Boston: Combined Jewish Philanthropies, 1977); Albert Mayer, *The Jewish Population Study of the Greater Kansas City Area* (Kansas City: Jewish Federation, 1977); Bruce A. Phillips, *Denver Jewish Population Study* (Denver: Allied Jewish Federation, 1982).

43. David M. Eichhorn, *Conversion to Judaism* (New York; Ktav Publishing House, Inc., 1965), p. 213.

44. Slogan from a popular bill board advertisement in the New York area for Levy's Real Jewish Rye Bread.

ONE STYLE OF DOMINICAN BRIDAL SHOWER—ADELE BAHN AND ANGELA JAQUEZ

Notes

1. Arnold van Gennep, *The Rites of Passage* (Chicago: Univ. of Chicago Press, 1960), p. 67.

2. Of the seven showers observed, there was nudity or near-nudity of the bride-to-be in six cases. There was some discrepancy in the reports of the respondents about its occurrence at showers. Some respondents said that it was not typical and, in fact, violated strong norms of personal modesty.

3. The word "conventional" represents what the respondents say is more like an "*American shower*" (emphasis ours).

4. The respondents noted that some girls had attended sex education classes in school in New York City. Some said they had gotten information from friends and had attended other showers. Many made a point of saying that their mothers had told them nothing.

5. For a general discussion, see Manuel de Js. Guerrero, *El Machismo en Republica Dominica* (Santo Domingo, R.D.: Amigo del Hogar, 1975).

6. See Glenn Hendricks, *The Dominican Diaspora* (New York: Teachers College Press, 1974).

7. Comparative family structure, including Latin America, is described in Betty Yorburg, *Sexual Identity: Sex Roles and Social Change* (New York: John Wiley & Sons, 1974). See also Vivian Mota, "Politics and Feminism in the Dominican Republic: 1931–45 and 1966–74," in June Nash and Helen Icken Safa (eds.), *Sex and Class in Latin America* (Brooklyn: J. F. Bergin, 1980).

8. At the showers, alcoholic beverages are typically served only to the bride-to-be.

POLITICS AND POLITESSE: GENDER DEFERENCE AND FORMAL ETIQUETTE—PEARL W. BARTELT, MARK HUTTER, AND DAVID W. BARTELT

References

Arestz, Esther B. 1970. *The Best Behavior,* New York: Simon & Schuster.

Baldrige, Letitia. 1978. *The Amy Vanderbilt Complete Book of Etiquette: A Guide to Contemporary Living.* New York: Doubleday.

Bem, Sandra L. and Daryl J. Bem. 1979. "Training the Woman to Know her Place: the Power of a Nonconscious Ideology." Pp. 29–38 in *Social Interaction,* edited by Howard Robboy et al. New York: St. Martin's Press.

Berg, Barbara. 1978. *The Remembered Gate: Origins of American Feminism.* New York: Oxford University Press.

Bevans, Margaret. 1960. *McCalls Book of Everyday Etiquette.* New York: Golden Press.

Blood, Robert. 1972. *The Family.* New York: Free Press.

Blumer, Herbert R. 1958. "Race Prejudice as a Sense of Group Position." *Pacific Sociological Review* 1:3–7.

———. 1966. "Sociological Implications of the Thought of G. H. Mead." *American Journal of Sociology* 71(March):535–44.

Boykin, Eleanor. 1940. *This Way Please.* New York: Macmillan.

Braroe, Nels Winther. 1970. "Reciprocal Exploitation in an Indian-White Community." Pp. 240–250 in *Social Psychology Through Symbolic Interaction,* edited by Gregory P. Stone and Harvey A. Farberman. Waltham, MA: Ginn-Blaisdell.

Cavan, Sherri. 1970. "The Etiquette of Youth," Pp. 554–565 in *Social Psychology Through Symbolic Interaction,* edited by Gregory P. Stone and Harvey A. Farberman. Waltham, MA: Ginn-Blaisdell.

Collins, Randall. 1975. *Conflict Sociology.* New York: Academic Press.

Daniels, Arlene Kaplan. 1975. "Feminist Perspectives in Sociological Research." Pp. 340–380 in *Another Voice,* edited by Marcia Millman and Rosabeth Moss Kanter. New York: Anchor Books.

Davidoff, Lenore. 1975. *The Best Circles: Society Etiquette and the Season.* Totowa, NJ: Rowman & Littlefield.

De Beauvoir, Simone. 1953. *The Second Sex.* New York: Knopf.

Eichler, Lillian. 1922. *Book of Etiquette,* Vol. 2. Garden City, NY: Doubleday.

Engels, Friedrich. [1884] 1972. *The Origin of the Family, Private Property, and the State.* New York: Pathfinder Press.

Fenwick, Millicent. 1948. *Vogue's Book of Etiquette.* New York: Simon & Schuster.

Ford, Charlotte. 1980. *Book of Modern Manners.* New York: Simon & Schuster.

Gardner, Horace and Patrician Farren. 1937. *Courtesy Book.* Philadelphia: Lippincott.

Goffman, Erving. 1956. "The Nature of Deference and Demeanor." *American Anthropologist* 58: 473–502.

———. 1955. "On Facework: an Analysis of Ritual Elements in Social Interaction." *Psychiatry* 18(August):213–223.

———. 1977. "The Arrangement Between the Sexes." *Theory and Society* 4(Fall):301–331.

———. 1979. *Gender Advertisements.* Cambridge, MA: Harvard University Press.

Gordon, Michael and Penelope Shankweiler. 1971. "Different Equals Less: Female Sexuality in Recent Marriage Manuals." *Journal of Marriage and the Family* 33(August):459–466.

Green, W. C. 1922. *The Book of Good Manners.* New York: Social Mentor Publications.

Hale, Sara J. 1899. *Manners, Happy Home and Good Society.* Boston: Lee & Shepard.

Hardy, E. J. 1910. *How to Be Happy Though Civil: A Book on Manners.* New York: Scribner.

Hathaway, Helen. 1928. *Manners.* New York: Dutton.

Haupt, Enid. 1963. *The Seventeen Book of Etiquette and Entertaining.* New York: McKay.

Henley, Nancy M. 1977. *Body Politics.* Englewood Cliffs, NJ: Prentice-Hall.

Henley, Nancy and Jo Freeman. 1975. "The Sexual Politics of Interpersonal Behavior." Pp. 391–401 in *Women: A Feminist Perspective,* edited by Jo Freeman. Palo Alto, CA: Mayfield.

Hochschild, Arlie. 1983. *The Managed Heart: Commercialization of Human Feeling.* Berkeley: University of California Press.

Hubbard, Ruth. 1979, "Have Only Men Evolved?" Pp. 7–36 in *Women Look at Biology Looking at Women,* edited by Ruth Hubbard, Mary Sue Henifin, and Barbara Fried. Boston: Schenkman.

Hutter, Mark. 1981. *The Changing Family: Comparative Perspectives.* New York: Wiley.

———. 1983. "Urban Identification and the Rise of the Downtown Department Store." Presented at the annual meeting of the Society for the Study of Symbolic Interaction.

Lindesmith, Alfred, Anselm Strauss, and Norman Denzin. 1977. *Social Psychology,* 5th edition New York: Funk & Wagnalls.

Lofland, Lyn. 1973. *A World of Strangers.* New York: Basic Books.

MacKinnon, Catharine A. 1982. "Feminism, Marxism, Method and the State: An Agenda for Theory." *Signs* 7(3):515–544.

———. 1983. "Feminism, Marxism, Method and the State: Toward Feminist Jurisprudence." *Signs* 8(4):635–658.

Marks, Elaine and Isabelle de Courtivron (eds.). 1980. *New French Feminisms.* Amherst: University of Massachusetts Press.

Martin, Judith. 1982. *Miss Manners' Guide to Excruciatingly Correct Behavior.* New York: Antheneum.

Marx, Karl. [1869] 1959. *The Eighteenth Brumaire of Louis Bonaparte.* Pp. 314–338 in Lewis S. Feuer's *Marx and Engels: Basic Writings on Politics and Philosophy.* Garden City, NY: Doubleday Anchor.

Meltzer, Bernard N., John W. Petras, and Larry T. Reynolds, 1975. *Symbolic Interactionism: Genesis, Varieties, Criticisms.* London and Boston: Routledge & Kegan Paul.

Mills, C. Wright. 1940. "Situated Actions and Vocabularies of Motive." *American Sociological Review* 5(December):904–913.

———. 1959. *The Sociological Imagination.* New York: Grove.

Ortner, Sherry. 1974. "Is Female to Male as Nature is to Culture?" Pp. 67–87 in *Woman, Culture and Society,* edited by Michelle Zimbalist Rosaldo and Louise Lamphere. Stanford, CA: Stanford University Press.

Post, Elizabeth. 1975. *The New Emily Post's Etiquette.* New York: Funk & Wagnalls.

Ricouer, Paul. 1981. *Hermeneutics and the Human Sciences.* New York: Cambridge University Press.

Riesman, David, Nathan Glazer, and Reuz Denney. 1961. *The Lonely Crowd.* New Haven, CT. Yale University Press.

Rosaldo, Michelle Zimbalist. 1974. "Woman, Culture and Society: A Theoretical Overview." Pp. 17–42 in *Woman, Culture and Society,* edited by Michelle Zimbalist Rosaldo and Louise Lamphere. Stanford, CA: Stanford University Press.

Rothman, Sheila M. 1978, *Woman's Proper Place.* New York: Basic Books.

Said, Edward. 1983. *The World, the Text and the Critic.* Cambridge, MA: Harvard University Press.

Schlesinger, Arthur M. 1946. *Learning How to Behave.* New York: Macmillan.

Schwartzer, Alice. 1984. *After the Second Sex: Conversations with Simone de Beauvoir.* New York: Pantheon.

Siltanen, Janet and Michelle Stanworth (eds.). 1984. *Women and the Public Sphere: A Critique of Sociology and Politics.* New York: St. Martin's Press.

Stephens, William N. 1963. *The Family in Cross Cultural Perspective.* New York: Holt, Rinehart & Winston.

Stephenson, Margaret and Ruth Millett. 1936. *As Others Like You.* Bloomington, IL: McKnight & McKnight.

Stevens, Carilyn. 1934. *Etiquette in Daily Living.* Chicago: Associated Authors Service.

Stone, Gregory P. 1970. "The Circumstance and Situation of Social Status." Pp. 250–59 in

Social Psychology Through Symbolic Inter-action, edited by Gregory P. Stone and Harvey A. Farberman. Waltham, MA: Ginn-Blaisdell.

Vanderbilt, Amy. 1952. *New Complete Book of Etiquette.* Garden City, NY: Doubleday.

———. 1957. *Amy Vanderbilt's Complete Book of Etiquette.* Garden City, NY: Doubleday.

———. 1967. *New Complete Book of Etiquette: The Guide to Gracious Living.* Garden City, NY: Doubleday.

———. 1972. *Amy Vanderbilt's Etiquette.* Garden City. NY: Doubleday.

———. 1974. *Amy Vanderbilt's Everyday Etiquette.* Garden City, NY: Doubleday.

Winter, Irene. 1981. "Royal Rhetoric and the Development of Historical Narrative in Neo-Assyrian Reliefs." *Studies in Visual Communication* 7(2):2–38.

Wilson, Margery. 1940. *The New Etiquette.* New York: Stokes.

Yorburg, Betty. 1974. *Sexual Identity.* New York: Wiley.

THE FEMINIZATION OF LOVE— FRANCESCA M. CANCIAN

Notes

1. The term "feminization" of love is derived from Ann Douglas, *The Feminization of Culture* (New York: Alfred A. Knopf, 1977).

2. The term "androgyny" is problematic. It assumes rather than questions sex-role stereotypes (aggression is masculine, e.g.); it can lead to a utopian view that underestimates the social causes of sexism; and it suggests the complete absence of differences between men and women, which is biologically impossible. Nonetheless, I use the term because it best conveys my meaning: a combination of masculine and feminine styles of love. The negative and positive aspects of the concept "androgyny" are analyzed in a special issue of *Women's Studies*

(vol. 2, no. 2[1974]), edited by Cynthia Secor. Also see Sandra Bem, "Gender Schema Theory and Its Implications for Child Development: Raising Gender-aschematic Children in a Gender-schematic Society," *Signs: Journal of Women in Culture and Society* 8, no. 4 (1983): 598–616.

3. The quotations are from a study by Ann Swidler, "Ideologies of Love in Middle Class America" (paper presented at the annual meeting of the Pacific Sociological Association, San Diego, 1982). For useful reviews of the history of love, see Morton Hunt, *The Natural History of Love* (New York: Alfred A. Knopf, 1959); and Bernard Murstein, *Love, Sex and Marriage through the Ages* (New York: Springer, 1974).

4. See John Bowlby, *Attachment and Loss* (New York: Basic Books, 1969), on mother-infant attachment. The quotation is from Elaine Walster and G. William Walster, *A New Look at Love* (Reading, Mass.: Addison-Wesley Publishing Co., 1978), 9. Conceptions of love and adjustment used by family sociologists are reviewed in Robert Lewis and Graham Spanier, "Theorizing about the Quality and Stability of Marriage," in *Contemporary Theories about the Family,* ed. W. Burr, R. Hill, F. Nye, and I. Reiss (New York: Free Press, 1979), 268–94.

5. Mary Ryan, *Womanhood in America,* 2d ed. (New York: New Viewpoints, 1979), and *The Cradle of the Middle Class: The Family in Oneida County, N.Y, 1790–1865* (New York: Cambridge University Press, 1981); Barbara Ehrenreich and Deirdre English, *For Her Own Good: 150 Years of Experts' Advice to Women* (New York: Anchor Books, 1978); Barbara Welter, "The Cult of True Womanhood: 1820–1860," *American Quarterly* 18, no. 2(1966): 151–74; Carl N. Degler, *At Odds* (New York: Oxford University Press, 1980).

6. Alternative definitions of love are reviewed in Walster and Walster, Clyde Hendrick and Susan Hendrick, *Liking, Loving and*

Relating (Belmont, Calif.: Wadsworth Publishing Co., 1983); Ira Reiss, *Family Systems in America,* 3d ed. (New York: Holt, Rinehart & Winston, 1980), 113–41; Margaret Reedy, "Age and Sex Differences in Personal Needs and the Nature of Love" (Ph.D. diss., University of Southern California, 1977).

7. Abraham Maslow, *Motivation and Personality,* 2d ed. (New York: Harper & Row, 1970), 182–83.

8. Zick Rubin's scale is described in his article "Measurement of Romantic Love," *Journal of Personality and Social Psychology* 16, no. 2 (1970): 265–73; Lillian Rubin's book on marriage is *Intimate Strangers* (New York: Harper & Row, 1983), quote on 90.

9. The emphasis on mutual aid and instrumental love among poor people is described in Lillian Rubin, *Worlds of Pain* (New York: Basic Books, 1976); Rayna Rapp, "Family and Class in Contemporary America," in *Rethinking the Family,* ed. Barrie Thorne (New York: Longman, Inc., 1982), 168–87; S. M. Miller and F. Riessman, "The Working-Class Subculture," in *Blue-Collar World,* ed. A. Shostak and W. Greenberg (Englewood Cliffs, N.J.: Prentice-Hall, Inc., 1964), 24–36.

10. Francesca Cancian, Clynta Jackson, and Ann Wysocki, "A Survey of Close Relationships" (University of California, Irvine, School of Social Sciences, 1982, typescript).

11. Swidler.

12. *Webster's New Collegiate Dictionary* (Springfield, Mass.: G. C. Merriam Co., 1977).

13. Paul Rosencrantz, Helen Bee, Susan Vogel, Inge Broverman, and Donald Broverman, "Sex Role Stereotypes and Self-Concepts in College Students," *Journal of Consulting and Clinical Psychology* 32, no. 3 (1968): 287–95; Paul Rosencrantz, "Rosencrantz Discusses Changes in Stereotypes about Men and Women," *Second Century Radcliffe News* (Cambridge, Mass., June 1982), 5–6.

14. Nancy Chodorow, *The Reproduction of Mothering* (Berkeley: University of California Press, 1978), 169. Dorothy Dinnerstein presents a similar theory in *The Mermaid and the Minotaur: Sexual Arrangements and Human Malaise* (New York: Harper & Row, 1976). Freudian and biological dispositional theories about women's nurturance are surveyed in Jean Stockard and Miriam Johnson, *Sex Roles* (Englewood Cliffs, N.J.: Prentice-Hall, Inc., 1980).

15. Carol Gilligan, *In a Different Voice* (Cambridge, Mass: Harvard University Press, 1982), 32, 159–61; see also L. Rubin, *Intimate Strangers.*

16. Talcott Parsons and Robert F. Bales, *Family, Socialization and Interaction* (Glencoe, Ill., Free Press, 1955). For a critical review of family sociology from a feminist perspective, see Arlene Skolnick, *The Intimate Environment* (Boston: Little, Brown & Co., 1978). Radical feminist theories also support the feminized conception of love, but they have been less influential in social science, see, e.g., Mary Daly, *Gyn/Ecology; The Metaethics of Radical Feminism* (Boston: Beacon Press, 1979).

17. I have drawn most heavily on Ryan, *Womanhood,* (n. 5 above), Ryan, *Cradle* (n. 5 above), Ehrenreich and English (n. 5 above), Welter (n. 5 above).

18. Ryan, *Womanhood,* 24–25.

19. Similar changes occurred when culture and religion were feminized, according to Douglas (n. 1 above). Conceptions of God's love shifted toward an image of a sweet and tender parent, a "submissive, meek and forgiving" Christ (149).

20. On the persistence of women's wage inequality and responsibility for housework, see Stockard and Johnson (n. 14 above).

21. Jean Baker Miller, *Toward a New Psychology of Women* (Boston: Beacon Press, 1976). There are, of course, many exceptions to Miller's generalization, e.g., women who need

to be independent or who need an attachment with a woman.

22. In psychology, the work of Carl Jung, David Bakan, and Bem are especially relevant. See Carl Jung, "Anima and Animus," in *Two Essays on Analytical Psychology: Collected Works of C. G. Jung* (New York: Bollinger Foundation, 1953), 7:186–209; David Bakan, *The Duality of Human Existence* (Chicago: Rand McNally & Co., 1966). They are discussed in Bem's paper, "Beyond Androgyny," in *Family in Transition,* 2d ed., ed. A. Skolnick and J. Skolnick (Boston: Little, Brown & Co., 1977), 204–21. Carl Rogers exemplifies the human potential theme of self-development through the search for wholeness. See Carl Rogers, *On Becoming a Person* (Boston: Houghton Mifflin Co., 1961).

23. Chodorow (n. 14 above) refers to the effects of the division of labor and to power differences between men and women, and the special effects of women's being the primary parents are widely acknowledged among historians.

24. The data on Yale men are from Mirra Komarovsky, *Dilemma of Masculinity* (New York: W. W. Norton & Co., 1976). Angus Campbell reports that children are closer to their mothers than to their fathers, and daughters feel closer to their parents than do sons, on the basis of large national surveys, in *The Sense of Well-Being in America* (New York: McGraw-Hill Book Co., 1981), 96. However, the tendency of people to criticize their mothers more than their fathers seems to contradict these findings; e.g., see Donald Payne and Paul Mussen, "Parent-Child Relations and Father Identification among Adolescent Boys," *Journal of Abnormal and Social Psychology* 52 (1956): 358–62. Being "closer" to one's mother may refer mostly to spending more time together and knowing more about each other rather than to feeling more comfortable together.

25. Studies of differences in friendship by gender are reviewed in Wenda Dickens and

Daniel Perlman, "Friendship over the Life Cycle," in *Personal Relationships,* vol. 2, ed. Steve Duck and Robin Gilmour (London: Academic Press, 1981), 91–122, and Beth Hess, "Friendship and Gender Roles over the Life Course," in *Single Life,* ed. Peter Stein (New York: St. Martin's Press, 1981), 104–15. While almost all studies show that women have more close friends, Lionel Tiger argues that there is a unique bond between male friends in *Men in Groups* (London: Thomas Nelson, 1969).

26. Komarovsky, *Blue-Collar Marriage* (New York: Random House, 1962), 13.

27. Daniel Levinson, *The Seasons of a Man's Life* (New York: Alfred A. Knopf, 1978), 335.

28. The argument about the middle-aged switch was presented in the popular book *Passages,* by Gail Sheehy (New York: E. P. Dutton, 1976), and in more scholarly works, such as Levinson's. These studies are reviewed in Alice Rossi, "Life-Span Theories and Women's Lives," *Signs* 6, no. 1 (1980): 4–32. However, a survey by Claude Fischer and S. Oliker reports an increasing tendency for women to have more close friends than men beginning in middle age, in "Friendship, Gender and the Life Cycle," Working Paper no. 318 (Berkeley: University of California, Berkeley, Institute of Urban and Regional Development, 1980).

29. Studies on gender differences in self-disclosure are reviewed in Letitia Peplau and Steven Gordon, "Women and Men in Love: Sex Differences in Close Relationships," in *Women, Gender and Social Psychology,* ed. V. O'Leary, R. Unger, and B. Wallston (Hillsdale, N.J.: Lawrence Erlbaum Associates, 1985), 257–91. Also see Zick Rubin, Charles Hill, Letitia Peplau, and Christine Dunkel-Schetter, "Self-Disclosure in Dating Couples," *Journal of Marriage and the Family* 42, no. 2 (1980): 305–18.

30. Working-class patterns are described in Komarovsky, *Blue-Collar Marriage.* Middle-class patterns are reported by Lynne Davidson

and Lucille Duberman, "Friendship: Communication and Interactional Patterns in Same-Sex Dyads," *Sex Roles* 8, no. 8 (1982): 809–22. Similar findings are reported in Robert Lewis, "Emotional Intimacy among Men," *Journal of Social Issues* 34, no. 1 (1978): 108–21.

31. Rubin et al., "Self-Disclosure."

32. These studies, cited below, are based on the self-reports of men and women college students and may reflect norms more than behavior. The findings are that women feel and express affective and bodily emotional reactions more often than do men, except for hostile feelings. See also Jon Allen and Dorothy Haccoun, "Sex Differences in Emotionality," *Human Relations* 29, no. 8 (1976): 711–22; and Jack Balswick and Christine Avertt, "Gender, Interpersonal Orientation and Perceived Parental Expressiveness," *Journal of Marriage and the Family* 39, no. 1 (1977): 121–128. Gender differences in interaction styles are analyzed in Nancy Henley, *Body Politics: Power, Sex and Non-verbal Communication* (Englewood Cliffs, N.J.: Prentice-Hall, Inc., 1977). Also see Paula Fishman, "Interaction: The Work Women Do," *Social Problems* 25, no. 4 (1978): 397–406.

33. Gender differences in leisure are described in L. Rubin, *Worlds of Pain* (n. 9 above), 10. Also see Margaret Davis, "Sex Role Ideology as Portrayed in Men's and Women's Magazines" (Stanford University, typescript).

34. Bert Adams, *Kinship in an Urban Setting* (Chicago: Markham Publishing Co., 1968), 169.

35. Marjorie Lowenthal and Clayton Haven, "Interaction and Adaptation: Intimacy as a Critical Variable," *American Sociological Review* 33, no. 4 (1968): 20–30.

36. Joseph Pleck argues that family ties are the primary concern for many men, in *The Myth of Masculinity* (Cambridge, Mass.: MIT Press, 1981).

37. Gender-specific characteristics also are seen in same-sex relationships. See M. Caldwell and Letitia Peplau, "Sex Differences in Same Sex Friendship," *Sex Roles* 8, no. 7 (1982): 721–32; see also Davidson and Duberman (n. 30 above), 809–22. Part of the reason for the differences in friendship may be men's fear of homosexuality and of losing status with other men. An explanatory study found that men were most likely to express feelings of closeness if they were engaged in some activity such as sports that validated their masculinity (Scott Swain, "Male Intimacy in Same-Sex Friendships: The Impact of Gender-validating Activities" [paper presented at annual meeting of the American Sociological Association, August 1984]). For discussions of men's homophobia and fear of losing power, see Robert Brannon, "The Male Sex Role," in *The Forty-nine Percent Majority,* ed. Deborah David and Robert Brannon (Reading, Mass.: Addison-Wesley Publishing Co., 1976), 1–48. I am focusing on heterosexual relations, but similar gender-specific differences may characterize homosexual relations. Some studies find that, compared with homosexual men, lesbians place a higher value on tenderness and verbal self-disclosure and engage in sex less frequently. See e.g., Alan Bell and Martin Weinberg, *Homosexualities* (New York: Simon & Schuster, 1978).

38. Unlike most studies, Reedy (n. 6 above) did not find that women emphasized communication more than men. Her subjects were upper-middle-class couples who seemed to be very much in love.

39. Sara Allison Parelman, "Dimensions of Emotional Intimacy in Marriage" (Ph.D. diss., University of California, Los Angeles, 1980).

40. Both spouses thought their interaction was unpleasant if the other engaged in negative or displeasureable instrumental or affectional actions. Thomas Wills, Robert Weiss, and Gerald Patterson, "A Behavioral Analysis of the Determinants of Marital Satisfaction," *Journal of Consulting and Clinical Psychology* 42, no. 6 (1974): 802–11.

41. L. Rubin, *Worlds of Pain* (n. 9 above), 147.

42. See L. Rubin, *Worlds of Pain;* also see Richard Sennett and Jonathon Cobb, *Hidden Injuries of Class* (New York: Vintage, 1973).

43. For evidence on this point, see Morton Hunt, *Sexual Behavior in the 1970s* (Chicago: Playboy Press, 1974), 231; and Alexander Clark and Paul Wallin, "Women's Sexual Responsiveness and the Duration and Quality of Their Marriage," *American Journal of Sociology* 21, no. 2 (1965): 187–96.

44. Interview by Cynthia Garlich, "Interviews of Married Couples" (University of California, Irvine, School of Social Sciences, 1982).

45. For example, see Catharine MacKinnon, "Feminism, Marxism, Method, and the State: An Agenda for Theory," *Signs* 7, no. 3 (1982): 515–44. For a thoughtful discussion of this issue from a historical perspective, see Linda Gordon and Ellen Dubois, "Seeking Ecstacy on the Battlefield: Danger and Pleasure in Nineteenth Century Feminist Thought," *Feminist Review* 13, no. 1 (1983): 42–54.

46. Reedy (n. 6 above).

47. William Kephart, "Some Correlates of Romantic Love," *Journal of Marriage and the Family* 29, no. 3 (1967): 470–74. See Peplau and Gordon (n. 29 above) for an analysis of research on gender and romanticism.

48. Daniel Yankelovich, *The New Morality* (New York: McGraw-Hill Book Co., 1974), 98.

49. The link between love and power is explored in Francesca Cancian, "Gender Politics; Love and Power in the Private and Public Spheres," in *Gender and the Life Course,* ed. Alice S. Rossi (New York: Aldine Publishing Co., 1984), 253–64.

50. See Jane Flax, "The Family in Contemporary Feminist Thought," in *The Family in Political Thought,* ed. Jean B. Elshtain (Princeton, N.J.: Princeton University Press, 1981), 223–53.

51. Walter Gove, "Sex, Marital Status and Mortality," *American Journal of Sociology* 79, no. 1 (1973): 45–67.

52. This follows from the social exchange theory of power, which argues that person A will have a power advantage over B if A has more alternative sources for the gratifications she or he gets from B than B has for those from A. See Peter Blau, *Exchange and Power in Social Life* (New York: John Wiley & Sons, 1964), 117–18.

53. For a discussion of the devaluation of women's activities, see Michelle Rosaldo, "Woman, Culture and Society: A Theoretical Overview," in *Woman, Culture and Society,* ed. Michelle Rosaldo and Louise Lamphere (Stanford, Calif.: Stanford University Press, 1973), 17–42.

54. Gilligan (n. 15 above), 12–13.

55. Inge Broverman, Frank Clarkson, Paul Rosenkrantz, and Susan Vogel, "Sex-Role Stereotypes and Clinical Judgments of Mental Health," *Journal of Consulting Psychology* 34, no. 1 (1970): 1–7.

56. Welter (n. 5 above).

57. Levinson (n. 27 above).

58. L. Rubin, *Intimate Strangers* (n. 8 above); Harold Rausch, William Barry, Richard Hertel, and Mary Ann Swain, *Communication, Conflict and Marriage* (San Francisco: Jossey-Bass, Inc., 1974). This conflict is analyzed in Francesca Cancian, "Marital Conflict over Intimacy," in *The Psychosocial Interior of the Family,* 3d ed., ed. Gerald Handel (New York: Aldine Publishing Co., 1985), 277–92.

IS "STRAIGHT" TO "GAY" AS "FAMILY" IS TO "NO FAMILY"?—KATH WESTON

Notes

1. See Godwin (1983) and Hollibaugh (1979).

2. For an analysis that carefully distinguishes among the various senses of reproduction

and their equivocal usage in feminist and anthropological theory, see Yanagisako and Collier (1987).

3. On the distinction between family and household, see Rapp (1982) and Yanagisako (1979).

4. On relational definition and the arbitrariness of signs, see Saussure (1959).

5. For Lévi-Strauss (1963b:88), most symbolic contrasts are structured by a mediating third term. Apparently conflicting elements incorporate a hidden axis of commonality that allows the two to be brought into relationship with one another. Here sexual identity is the hidden term that links "straight" to "gay," while kinship mediates the oppositions further down in the chart. This sort of triadic relation lends dynamism to opposition, facilitating ideological transformations while ensuring a regulated, or structured, relationship between the old and the new.

My overall analysis departs from a Lévi-Straussian structuralism by historically situating these relations, discarding any presumption that they form a closed system, and avoiding the arbitrary isolation of categories for which structuralism has justly been criticized in the past (see Culler 1975; Fowler 1981; Jenkins 1979). The symbolic oppositions examined in this chapter incorporate indigenous categories in all their specificity (e.g., straight versus gay), rather than abstracting to universals of increasing generality and arguably decreasing utility (e.g., nature versus culture). Chronicled here is an ideological transformation faithful to history, process, and the perceptions of the lesbians and gay men who themselves identified each opposition included in the chart. For the deployment of these categories in everyday contexts, read on.

6. Notice how the contrasts in the chart map a relationship of difference (straight/gay) first onto a logical negation (family/no family, or A/NA), and then onto another relation of difference (biological [blood] family/families we choose [create], or A:B). On the generative potential of dichotomies that are constituted as A/B rather than A/NA, see N. Jay (1981:44).

References

Allen, Ronnie. 1987. "Times Have Changed at the *Herald. Gay Community News* (June 28–July 4).

Bourdieu, Pierre. 1977. *Outline of a Theory of Practice.* New York: Cambridge University Press.

Castells, Manuel and Karen Murphy. 1982. "Cultural Identity and Urban Structure: The Spatial Organization of San Francisco's Gay Community." In Norman I. Fainstein and Susan S. Fainstein (eds.), *Urban Policy Under Capitalism,* pp. 237–259. Beverly Hills, Calif.: Sage.

Cook, Blanche Wiesen. 1977. "Female Support Networks and Political Activism: Lillian Wald, Crystal Eastman, Emma Goldman." *Chrysalis* 3:44–61.

Culler, Jonathan. 1975. *Structuralist Poetics: Structuralism, Linguistics and the Study of Literature.* Ithaca, N.Y.: Cornell University Press.

FitzGerald, Frances. 1986. *Cities on a Hill: A Journal Through Contemporary American Cultures.* New York: Simon & Schuster.

Foucault, Michel. 1978. *The History of Sexuality.* Vol. 1. New York: Vintage.

Fowler, Roger. 1981. *Literature as Social Discourse: The Practice of Linguistic Criticism.* Bloomington: University of Indiana Press.

Godwin, Ronald S. 1983. "AIDS: A Moral and Political Timebomb." *Moral Majority Report* (July).

Hocquenghem, Guy. 1978. *Homosexual Desire.* London: Alison & Busby.

Hollibaugh, Amber. 1979. "Sexuality and the State: The Defeat of the Briggs Initiative and Beyond." *Socialist Review* 9(3):55–72.

Jay, Nancy. 1981. "Gender and Dichotomy." *Feminist Studies* 7(1):38–56.

Jenkins, Alan. 1979. *The Social Theory of Claude Levi-Strauss.* New York: St. Martin's Press.

Lazere, Arthur. 1986. "On the Job." *Coming Up!* (June).

Levi-Straus, Claude. 1963. *Totemism.* Boston: Beacon Hill.

Mendenhall, George. 1985. "Mickey Mouse Lawsuit Remains Despite Disney Dancing Decree." *Bay Area Report* (August 22).

Rapp, Rayna. 1982. "Family and Class in Contemporary America: Notes Toward an Understanding of Ideology." In Barrie Thorne with Marilyn Yalom, eds., *Rethinking the Family,* pp. 168–187. New York: Longman.

Saussure, Ferdinand de. 1959. *Course in General Linguistics.* New York: McGraw-Hill.

Silverstein, Charles. 1977. *A Family Matter: A Parents' Guide to Homosexuality.* New York: McGraw-Hill.

Smith, Barbara, ed. 1983. *Home Girls: A Black Feminist Anthology.* New York: Kitchen Table: Women of Color Press.

Watney, Simon. 1987. *Policing Desire: Pornography, AIDS, and the Media.* Minneapolis: University of Minnesota Press.

Yanagisako, Sylvia J. 1985. *Transforming the Past: Tradition and Kinship among Japanese Americans.* Stanford: Stanford University Press.

Yanagisako, Sylvia Junko and Jane Fishburne Collier. 1987. "Toward a Unified Analysis of Gender and Kinship." In Jane Fishburne Collier and Sylvia Junko Yanagisako, eds. *Gender and Kinship: Essays Toward a Unified Analysis,* pp. 14–50. Stanford: Stanford University Press.

THE ECONOMY OF GRATITUDE—ARLIE RUSSELL HOCHSCHILD

Notes

1. One of the few social analyses of gratitude comes from George Simmel (Wolff 1950, pp. 379–395) and Marcel Mauss (1967). In a very different tradition, largely based on experimental research, equity theory (though it does not treat gratitude per se) explores the circumstances that lead couples to feel that a social bond is satisfying or fair. (Elaine Walster 1976).

2. See *The Managed Heart: Commercialization of Human Feeling.* (Hochschild 1983, p. 76).

3. See Joel Davitz (1969, p. 60).

4. See William Ogburn, *Social Change* (New York: Viking Press, 1932) pp. 200–13. Ogburn argued that the material culture changed at a faster rate than the nonmaterial culture— e.g., the folk ways, social institutions—including the family. As Ogburn used the term, it obscures the role of power and interest; culture simply "lagged behind" economy, without serving the interests of any particular social group. In this analysis, the lag serves the interests of men who feel they have less than women to gain from the social changes which economic opportunity and need have now opened up.

5. In the nineteenth century, economic trends most directly affected men as industrialization drew them more than women into wage labor. This caused men to change their basic life ways more, and women to "culturally lag." Today, economic changes affect women more, causing women to change faster. Today the changing environment for women is the economy; the changing environment for men is women.

6. Thanks to Egbal Ahmad for the term "shock absorber."

7. I used three research methods. First, I mailed a short questionnaire on work and family life to every thirteenth name drawn from the personnel roster of the international headquarters of a large manufacturing company in San Francisco. Respondents who fit the research criteria (married, in a two-job family, caring for a child under six) were asked to volunteer for an in-depth follow-up interview. In this way I obtained families from the managerial, clerical, and production ranks. I then used a snowball sample to supplement the original sample, moving "sideways" at each occupational level. I also interviewed daycare workers and babysitters. Finally I did participant observation in selected homes. Data from this larger study will be reported in a forthcoming book, *The Second Shift: Inside The Two Job Marriage* (New York: Viking Press).

8. These and other personal names in this paper are fictitious.

9. The two couples differ in social class, ethnicity, and religion. Other research suggests a greater traditionalism among the working class, among the politically conservative, and among couples in which the wife and husband's mother is a homemaker. Differences in religious culture appear to make little difference: Jews are slightly more egalitarian, Catholics slightly less—but religious differences may also reflect class ones. (See Baruch and Barnett 1983; Pleck 1982; Kimball 1983; Hood 1983.)

10. When men endorsed the new gender rules (of status transfer) they could receive their wife's salary as a gift. Such wives did not have to "make up for" transgressing a rejected rule by a return of "extra" favors. One wife, a word processor, explained the response of her husband (a night watchman) to a recent promotion: "I really don't think it affects anything, because we look at it this way: If I make more than Will, or he makes more than me, we are both reaping the benefits of that. . . . " The gift was offered, and—culturally as well as materially—received.

Just as many men could not accept their wives' salaries if they were higher than their own, so many men could not accept their rises, after a point, in professional status. Men often reacted to a wife's period of occupational training differently from how women reacted to that of their husbands. When men were in training for a career, a working wife treated the training as a promissory note for a future gift. She often therefore took over housework and childcare to let him study. But men did not similarly take their wives' occupational training as the promissory note for a future gift. In one extreme example, a husband commented on his wife's writing of a Ph.D. thesis in political science: "I hate it, I can't tell you how I hate it. I feel I'm getting nothing out of it. It isn't a job. It isn't a cooked meal. It's nothing. I just hate it." At the time of the interview there was a glut on the academic market, but no man writing a dissertation in the study was greeted with such a response.

11. Seth was a mixed traditional—or "pseudo egalitarian"—in the sense that his rhetoric was more liberal than his economy of gratitude. This slippage between the surface and depth of an attitude is common adaptation to the pressure to change—which in this case, came from his wife.

12. There is considerable research evidence that women attribute more personal events (e.g., winning a game, doing well on an exam) to "luck" than men do. This finding has often been attributed to women's lower "locus of control." My field observations correspond to the laboratory evidence, and simply add both an explanation for the lower locus of control, and for their social management of it.

References

Baruch, Grace and Rosalind Barnett. 1980. "Correlates of Fathers' Participation in Family Work: A Technical Report." Working Paper 106. Wellesley, MA: Wellesley College Center for Research on Women.

Davitz, Joel. 1969. *The Language of Emotion.* New York/London: Academic Press.

Hochschild, Arlie. 1983. *The Managed Heart: The Commercialization of Human Feeling.* Berkeley/Los Angeles: University of California Press.

Hood, Jane. 1983. *Becoming a Two Job Family.* New York: Praeger.

Kimball, Gayle. 1983. *The 50–50 Marriage.* Boston: Beacon Press.

Lasch, Christopher. 1977. *Haven in a Heartless World.* New York: Basic Books.

Mauss, Marcel. 1967. *The Gift: Forms and Functions of Exchange in Archaic Societies.* New York: Norton.

O'Henry, William. 1961. "The Gift of the Magi." Pp. 323–328 in *What is the Short Story?,* edited by Eugene Current-Garcia and Walton R. Patrick. Glenview, IL: Scott, Foresman.

Pleck, Joseph. 1982. "Husbands' and Wives' Family Work: Paid Work and Adjustment." Working Paper 95. Wellesley, MA: Wellesley College Center for Research on Women.

Swidler, Ann. 1986. "Culture in Action: Symbols and Strategies." *American Sociological Review* 15 (April): 273–286.

Walster, Elaine. 1976. "New Directions in Equity Research." In *Advances in Experimental Social Psychology,* vol. 9, edited by L. Berkowitz and E. Walster. New York: Academic Press.

Wolff, Kurt H. 1950. *The Sociology of George Simmel.* New York: The Free Press.

THE GOOD-PROVIDER ROLE: ITS RISE AND FALL— JESSE BERNARD

Notes

1. Rainwater and Yancey (1967), critiquing current welfare policies, note that they "have robbed men of their manhood, women of their husbands, and children of their fathers. To create a stable monogamous family we need to provide men with the opportunity to be men, and that involves enabling them to perform occupationally" (p. 235).

2. Several years ago I presented a critique of what I called "extreme sex role specialization," including "work-intoxicated fathers." I noted that making success in the provider role the only test for real manliness was putting a lot of eggs into one basket. At both the blue-collar and the managerial levels, it was dysfunctional for families. I referred to the several attempts being made even then to correct the excesses of extreme sex role specialization: rural and urban communes, leaving jobs to take up small-scale enterprises that allowed more contact with families, and a rebellion against overtime in industry (Bernard 1975, pp. 217–239).

3. In one department of a South Carolina cotton mill early in the century, "every worker was a grass widow" (Smuts 1959, p. 54). Many women worked "because their husbands refused to provide for their families. There is no reason to think that husbands abandoned their duties more often than today, but the woman who was burdened by an irresponsible husband in 1890 usually had no recourse save taking on his responsibilities herself. If he deserted, the law-enforcement agencies of the time afforded little chance of finding and compelling him to provide support" (Smuts 1959, p. 54). The situation is not greatly improved today. In divorce child support is allotted in only a small number of cases and enforced in ever fewer. "Roughly half of all families with an absent parent don't have awards at all.... Where awards do exist they are usually for small amounts, typically ranging from $7 to $18 per child" (Jones 1976, abstract). A summary of all the studies available concludes that "approximately 20 percent of all divorced and separated mothers receive child support regularly, with an additional 7 percent receiving it 'sometimes': 8 percent of all divorced and separated women

receive alimony regularly or sometimes" (Jones 1976, p. 23).

4. Even though the annals of social work agencies are filled with cases of runaway husbands, in 1976 only 12.6% of all women were in the status of divorce and separation, and at least some of them were still being "provided for." Most men were at least trying to fulfill the good-provider role.

5. Although all the women in Lopata's (1971) sample saw breadwinning as important, fewer employed women (54%) than either non-employed urban (63%) or suburban (64%) women assigned it first place (p. 91).

6. Pleck and Lang (1979) found only one serious study contradicting their own conclusions: "Using data from the 1973 NORC (National Opinion Research Center) General Social Survey, Harry analyzed the bivariate relationship of job and family satisfaction to life happiness in men classified by family life cycle stage. In three of the five groups of husbands . . . job satisfaction had a stronger association than family satisfaction to life happiness" (pp. 5–6).

7. In 1978, a Yankelovich survey on "The New Work Psychology" suggested that leisure is now becoming a strict competitor for both family and work as a source of life satisfactions: "Family and work have grown less important than leisure: a majority of 60 percent say that although they enjoy their work, it is not their major source of satisfaction" (p. 46). A 1977 survey of Swedish men aged 18 to 35 found that the proportion saying the family was the main source of meaning in their lives declined from 45% in 1955 to 41% in 1977; the proportion indicating work as the main source of satisfaction dropped from 33% to 17%. The earlier tendency for men to identify themselves through their work is less marked these days. In the new value system, the individual says, in effect, "I am more than my role. I am myself" (Yankelovich, 1978). Is the increasing concern with leisure a

way to escape the dissatisfaction with both the alienating relations found on the work site and the demands for increased involvement with the family?

8. Men seem to be having problems with both work and family roles. Veroff (1978), for example, reports an increased "sense of dissatisfaction with the social relations in the work setting" and a "dissatisfaction with the affiliative nature of work" (p. 47). This dissatisfaction may be one of the factors that leads men to seek affiliative-need satisfaction in marriage, just as in the 19th century they looked to the home as shelter from the jungle of the outside world.

9. Among the indices of the waning of the good-provider role are the increasing number of married women in the labor force; the growth in the number of female-headed families; the growing trend toward egalitarian norms in marriage; the need for two earners in so many middle-class families; and the recognition of these trends in the abandonment of the identification of head of household as a male.

References

Babcock, B., A. E. Freedman, E. H. Norton, and S. C. Ross. 1975. *Sex Discrimination and the Law: Causes and Remedies.* Boston: Little, Brown.

Bernard, J. 1975. *Women, Wives, Mothers.* Chicago: Aldine.

———. 1976. "Homosociality and Female Depression." *Journal of Social Issues* 32:207–224.

Boulding, E. 1976. "Familial Constraints on Women's Work Roles." *SIGNS: Journal of Women in Culture and Society* 1:95–118.

Brenton, M. 1966. *The American Male.* New York: Coward-McCann.

Burke, R. and T. Weir. 1976. "Relationships of Wives Employment Status to Husband, Wife, and Pair Satisfaction and Performance." *Journal of Marriage and the Family* 38:279–287.

Chafe, W. 1978. "The Challenge of Sex Equality: A New Culture or Old Values Revisited?" Paper presented at the Radcliffe Pre-Centennial Conference, Cambridge, MA, April 2–4.

David, D. S. and R. Brannon (eds.). 1976. *The Forty-Nine Percent Majority: The Male Sex Role.* Reading, MA: Addison-Wesley.

Demos, J. 1974. "The American Family in Past Time." *American Scholar* 43:422–446.

Douvan, E. 1978. "Family Roles in a Twenty-Year Perspective." Paper presented at the Radcliffe Pre-Centennial Conference, Cambridge, MA, April 2–4.

Farrell, W. 1974. *The Liberated Man.* New York: Random House.

Fasteau, M. F. 1974. *The Male Machine.* New York: McGraw-Hill.

Fiedler, L. 1962. *Love and Death in the American Novel.* New York: Meredith.

Foner, P. S. 1979. *Women and the American Labor Movement.* New York: Free Press.

Freud, S. [1930] 1958. *Civilization and Its Discontents.* New York: Doubleday-Anchor.

Goldberg, H. 1976. *The Hazards of Being Male.* New York: New American Library.

Gould, R. E. 1974. "Measuring Masculinity by the Size of a Paycheck." In *Men and Masculinity,* edited by J. E. Pleck and J. Sawyer: Englewood Cliffs, NJ: Prentice-Hall. (Also published in *Ms.,* June 1973: 18ff.)

Hall, D. and F. Hall. 1979. *The Two-Career Couple.* Reading, MA: Addison-Wesley.

Hasselbart, S. 1978. *Some Underemphasized Issues About Men, Women, and Work.* Unpublished manuscript.

Jones, C. A. 1976. *A Review of Child Support Payment Performance.* Washington, DC. Urban Institute.

Keniston, K. 1965. *The Uncommitted: Alienated Youth in American Society.* New York: Harcourt, Brace & World.

Komarovsky, M. 1940. *The Unemployed Man and His Family.* New York: Dryden Press.

Lefkowitz, B. 1979. "Life Without Work." *Newsweek* (May 14): 31.

Lein, L. 1979. "Responsibility in the Allocation of Tasks." *Family Coordinator* 28: 489–496.

Liebow, E. 1966. *Tally's Corner.* Boston: Little, Brown.

Lopata, H. 1971. *Occupational Housewife.* New York: Oxford University Press.

Mainardi, P. 1970. "The Politics of Housework." In *Sisterhood Is Powerful,* edited by R. Morgan. New York: Vintage Books.

Pleck, J. H. and L. Lang. 1979. "Men's Family Work: Three Perspectives and Some New Data." *Family Coordinator* 28:481–488.

Pleck, J. H. and J. Sawyer (eds.). 1974. *Men and Masculinity.* Englewood Cliffs, NJ: Prentice-Hall.

Rainwater, L. and W. L. Yancey. 1967. *The Moynihan Report and the Politics of Controversy.* Cambridge, MA: M.I.T. Press.

Sarason, S. B. 1977. *Work, Aging, and Social Change.* New York: Free Press.

Scanzoni, J. H. 1975. *Sex Roles, Life Styles, and Childbearing: Changing Patterns in Marriage and the Family.* New York: Free Press.

———. 1979. "An Historical Perspective on Husband-Wife Bargaining Power and Marital Dissolution." In *Divorce and Separation in America,* edited by G. Levinger and O. Moles. New York: Basic Books.

Shostak, A. 1973. *Working Class Americans at Home.* Unpublished manuscript.

Smith, R. E. (ed.). 1979. *The Subtle Revolution.* Washington, DC: Urban Institute.

Smuts, R. W. 1959. *Women and Work in America.* New York: Columbia University Press.

Snyder, L. 1979. "The Deserting, Non-Supporting Father: Scapegoat of Family Non-Policy." *Family Coordinator* 38:594–598.

Tocqueville, A. de. 1840. *Democracy in America.* New York: J. & H. G. Langley.

Veroff, J. 1978. *Psychological Orientations to the Work Role: 1957–1976.* Unpublished manuscript.

Warner, W. L. and J. O. Ablegglen. 1955. *Big Business Leaders in America.* New York: Harper.

Yankelovich, D. 1978. "The New Psychological Contracts at Work." *Psychology Today* (May): 46–47, 49–50.

Zborowski, M. and E. Herzog. 1952. *Life Is With People.* New York: Schocken Books.

AFFLUENCE AND POVERTY— MARJORIE L. DeVAULT

Notes

1. According to USDA estimates, Americans spent about 12 percent of their disposable personal income on food in 1988. However, those in the 20 percent of households with the lowest incomes spent 42 percent of that income on food while those in the highest 20 percent spent only 9 percent on food (Blaylock, Elitzak, and Manchester 1989).

2. The USDA's Human Nutrition Information service computes the cost of providing the foods included in each of four menu plans, ranging from "thrifty" to "liberal," and uses the "thrifty" plan as the basis for setting food-stamp benefit levels. These cost estimates assume that food for all meals and snacks is prepared at home. See U.S. Department of Agriculture (1987a).

3. My approach conceives class as organized activity rather than simply in terms of social categories. For exemplary writing on class and family, see Rapp (1982), Smith (1985), Davidoff and Hall (1987), and Acker (1988).

4. In making these calculations, I relied on interviewees' commonsense understandings of the term "budget," and did not always probe to learn exactly what they meant. In most cases, I asked whether they had a budget, and their answer to this direct question provided the basis for assigning them to one of these categories or the other; in a few cases, I relied on spontaneous remarks about being "on a budget" or making decisions because of "my budget."

5. Generic products were first introduced in some stores in 1977, and were widely available in urban supermarkets by the time I conducted interviews. During the early 1980s, they were widely discussed in mainstream media, in features that typically presented their appearance as an industry response to consumer interest in lower prices (Hawes 1982). This media attention helps to explain why almost all those I talked with made some reference to generic products, whether they used them or not.

6. I have adopted the term used by the U.S. Census Bureau, which defines a "sub-family" as a married couple, or parent with one or more children, who live in a larger household and are related to the primary householder or spouse.

7. Congressional concern with the regulative aspects of food-stamp policy is evident in hearings on the program, as members of Congress debate issues such as whether recipients should be allowed to buy processed foods: in the early years of debate, some reasoned that "convenience foods" should be excluded because the government should not pay to substitute for poor people's labor.

8. I did not question informants in great detail about children's labor, and in any case, this study does not permit a definitive finding as to whether children in poor and working-class households help more than those in professional/managerial ones. However, my sense was that few of the wealthier parents relied on children for much actual assistance. Several reported that they believed in encouraging children's work, but found organizing and supervising it effectively

more burdensome than doing the work themselves. Many informants' children were still too young to provide real help with household chores.

9. The habit of cooking for others outside the family may be characteristic of black working-class communities as well. Bertie reported that she always included someone from the church in her family's Sunday dinner. And her comment suggests a special concern for men unattached to household groups: "We always have somebody in to eat. From church, some member who wants to stay for church in the evening... or some student who lives on campus. Or some young man who doesn't cook."

10. Professional economists, of course, develop more sophisticated theories that take account of such factors. Their theories also have an ideological cast, but a discussion of this issue goes beyond the scope of this book.

References

Abramovitz, Mimi. 1988. *Regulating the Lives of Women: Social Welfare Policy from Colonial Times to the Present.* Boston: South End Press.

Acker, Joan. 1988. Class, Gender and the Relations of Distribution. *Signs* 13: 473–97.

Blaylock, James, Howard Elitzak, and Alden Manchester. 1989. Food Expenditures. *National Food Review* (U.S. Department of Agriculture) 12(2):16–24.

Brown, Carol. 1981. Mothers, Fathers, and Children: From Private to Public Patriarchy. In Lydia Sargent, ed. *Women and Revolution,* 239–67. Boston, South End Press.

Caulfield, Minna Davis. 1974. Imperialism, the Family, and Cultures of Resistance. *Socialist Review* 42(2):676–85.

Charles, Nickie, and Marion Kerr. 1988. *Women, Food and Families.* Manchester: Manchester University Press.

Collins, Patricia Hill. 1990. *Black Feminist Thought: Knowledge, Consciousness, and the Politics of Empowerment.* Boston: Unwin Hyman.

Corrigan, Paul. 1977. The Welfare State as an Arena of Class Struggle. *Marxism Today,* March:87–93.

Davidoff, Leonore, and Catherine Hall. 1987. *Family Fortunes: Men and Women of the English Middle Class, 1780–1850.* Chicago: University of Chicago Press.

Davis, Angela Y. 1981. *Women, Race, and Class.* New York: Random House.

DeVault, Marjorie L., and James P. Pitts. 1984. Surplus and Scarcity: Hunger and the Origins of the Food Stamp Program. *Social Problems* 31:545–57.

Dickinson, James. 1986. From Poor Law to Social Insurance: The Periodization of State Intervention in the Reproduction Process. In James Dickinson and Bob Russell, eds. *Family, Economy, and State,* 113–49. New York: St. Martin's Press.

Evans, Sara. 1979. *Personal Politics: The Roots of Women's Liberation in the Civil Rights Movement and the New Left.* New York: Alfred A. Knopf.

Glenn, Evelyn Nakano. 1990. White Women/Women of Color: The Racial Division of Social Reproduction. Paper presented at the Henry A. Murray Research Center, Radcliffe College, April, Cambridge.

Gough, Ian. 1980. *The Political Economy of the Welfare State.* London: Macmillan.

Hawes, Jon M. 1982. *Retailing Strategies for Generic Brand Grocery Products.* Ann Arbor: UMI Research Press.

Hertz, Rosanna. 1986. *More Equal Than Others: Women and Men in Dual-Career Marriages.* Berkeley: University of California Press.

Jones, Jacqueline. 1985. *Labor of Love, Labor of Sorrow: Black Women, Work, and the Family from Slavery to the Present.* New York: Basic.

Joseph, Gloria I. 1981. Black Mothers and Daughters: Their Roles and Functions in American Society. In Gloria I. Joseph and Jill Lewis, *Comparative Differences: Conflicts in Black and White Feminist Perspectives,* 75–126. Boston: South End Press.

Kaplan, Jane Rachel, ed. 1980. *A Woman's Conflict: The Special Relationship Between Women and Food.* Englewood Cliffs, NJ: Prentice-Hall.

Luxton, Meg. 1980. *More Than a Labour of Love: Three Generations of Women's Work in the Home.* Toronto: The Women's Press.

Piven, Frances Fox, and Richard A. Cloward. 1979. *Poor People's Movements.* New York: Vintage.

Rapp, Rayna. 1982. Family and Class in Contemporary America: Notes Toward an Understanding of Ideology. In Barrie Thorne with Marilyn Yalom, eds. *Rethinking the Family,* 168–87. New York: Longman.

Riessman, Catherine Kohler. 1987. When Gender is Not Enough: Women Interviewing Women. *Gender and Society* 1:172–207.

Stack, Carol. 1974. *All Our Kin: Strategies for Survival in a Black Community.* New York: Harper and Row.

U.S. Bureau of the Census. 1989. *Statistical Abstract of the United States,* 109th ed. Washington, D.C.: U.S. Government Printing Office.

U.S. Department of Agriculture, Economic Research Service. 1987 Food Spending and Income. *National Food Review,* 1987 Yearbook, 24–33.

West, Guida. 1981. *The National Welfare Rights Movement: The Social Protest of Poor Women.* New York: Praeger.

"I NEVER DID ANY FIELDWORK, BUT I MILKED AN AWFUL LOT OF COWS!": USING RURAL WOMEN'S EXPERIENCE TO RECONCEPTUALIZE MODELS OF WORK—MAREENA McKINLEY WRIGHT

Notes

1. I use the term *labor option* to refer to the different kinds of work women did, although I am uncomfortable with using *option* to describe women's work when often circumstances kept that work from being optional. I do not intend to imply that this group of women always had an *option* whether to do a particular kind of work, especially normatively prescribed duties such as housekeeping and child care.

2. When I interviewed my informants, I promised them that everything they told me would be confidential and that they would not be identifiable in my research reports. I have changed names and details in the stories and quotes to protect the anonymity of my informants; however, the substance of their recollections remains unchanged.

3. While this explanation may be true for some women, we would commit an ecological fallacy to assume, based on aggregated data, that it is true for all women.

References

Abel, E. K. 1991. *Who cares for the elderly? Public policy and the experiences of adult daughters.* Philadelphia: Temple University Press.

Adams, J. 1991. "Individuality, efficiency, and domesticity: Ideological aspects of the exploitation of farm families and farm women." Paper presented to the annual meetings of the American Anthropological Association, Chicago, November.

Belsky, J., and J. Rovine. 1988. Nonmaternal care in the first year of life and the security of infant-parent attachment. *Child Development* 59: 157–67.

Beneria, L. 1991. "Accounting for women's work: Assessing the progress of two decades." Paper presented at UNRISD, Meeting on Social Development Indicators, Rabat, Morocco, April.

Boris, E., and C. R. Daniels, eds. 1989. *Homework: Historical and contemporary perspectives on paid labor at home.* Urbana: University of Illinois Press.

Bose, C. E. 1987. Dual spheres. In *Analyzing gender: A handbook of social science research,* edited by B. B. Hess and M. M. Ferree. Thousand Oaks, CA: Sage.

Buss, F. L. 1985. *Dignity: Lower income women tell of their lives and struggles.* Ann Arbor: University of Michigan Press.

Chaney, E., and M. G. Castro, eds. 1989. *Muchachas no more: Household workers in Latin America and the Caribbean.* Philadelphia: Temple University Press.

Collins, J. L., and M. Gimenez. 1990. *Work without wages: Comparative studies of domestic labor and self-employment.* Albany: State University of New York Press.

Collins, P. H. 1990. *Black feminist thought: Knowledge, consciousness, and the politics of empowerment.* New York: Routledge.

Conger, R. D., and G. H. Elder, Jr. 1994. *Rural families in a changing society.* New York: Aldine.

Cowan, R. S. 1983. *More work for mother.* New York: Basic Books,

Davis, K. 1984. Wives and work: The sex role revolution and its consequences. *Population and Development Review* 10:397–417.

Elder, G. H., Jr. 1974. *Children of the great depression.* Chicago: University of Chicago Press.

———. 1985. Perspectives on the life course. In *Life course dynamics,* edited by G. H. Elder, Jr. Ithaca, NY: Cornell University Press.

Elder, G. H., Jr., and R. Rockwell. 1976. The timing of marriage and women's life patterns. *Journal of Family History* 1(Autumn): 34–54.

Enloe, C. 1989. *Bananas, beaches, and bases.* Berkeley: University of California Press.

Fink, D. 1986. *Open country, Iowa: Rural women, tradition and change.* Albany: State University of New York Press.

Fink, D. 1992. *Agrarian women.* Chapel Hill: University of North Carolina Press.

Gerson, K. 1985. *Hard choices: How women decide about work, career, and motherhood.* Berkeley: University of California Press.

Glazer, N. 1990. Servants to capital: Unpaid domestic labor and paid work. In *Work without wages. Comparative studies of domestic labor and self-employment,* edited by J. L. Collins and M. Gimenez. Albany: State University of New York Press.

Hagestad, G. O. 1990. Social perspectives on the life course. In *Handbook of aging and the social sciences,* edited by R. H. Binstock and L. K. George. San Diego: Academic Press.

Haney, W. B., and J. B. Knowles, eds. 1988. *Women and farming: Changing roles, changing structures.* Boulder, CO: Westview.

Hertzog, A. R., R. L. Kahn, J. N. Morgan, J. S. Jackson, and T. C. Antonucci. 1989. Age differences in productive activities. *Journal of Gerontology* 44:129–38.

Hochschild, A. 1989. *The second shift.* New York: Avon Books.

Hossfeld, K. forthcoming. *Small, foreign, and female.* Berkeley: University of California Press.

Kreps, J., ed. 1976. *Women and the American economy: A look to the 1980s.* Englewood Cliffs, NJ: Prentice-Hall.

McLaughlin, S. D., B. D. Melber, J. O. G. Billy, D. M. Zimmerle, L. D. Winges, and T. R. Johnson, eds. 1988. *The changing lives of American women.* Chapel Hill: University of North Carolina Press.

Mies, M. 1986. *Patriarchy and accumulation on a world scale.* London: Zed Books.

Moen, P. 1992. *Women's two roles: A contemporary dilemma.* New York: Auburn House.

Oakley, A. 1974. *The sociology of housework.* London: Martin Robertson.

Osterud, N. G. 1991. *Bonds of community: The lives of farm women in nineteenth-century New York.* Ithaca, NY: Cornell University Press.

Pavalko, E. K., G. H. Elder, Jr., and E. C. Clipp. 1993. Worklives and longevity: Insights from a life course perspective. *Journal of Health and Social Behavior* 34:363–80.

Portes, A., and S. Sassen-Koob. 1987. Making it underground. *American Journal of Sociology* 93:30–61.

Romero, M. 1992. *Maid in America.* New York: Routledge.

Rosenfeld, R. A. 1985. *Farm women: Work, farm and family in the United States.* Chapel Hill: University of North Carolina Press.

Rothstein, F. A. 1994. Gender and multiple income strategies in rural Mexico: A twenty year perspective. In *Women in the Latin American development process,* edited by C. Bose and E. Acosta-Belen. Philadelphia: Temple University Press.

Strasser. S. 1982. *Never done: A history of American housework.* New York: Pantheon Books.

Strauss, A., and J. Corbin. 1990. *Basics of qualitative research: Grounded theory procedures and techniques.* Thousand Oaks, CA: Sage.

Truelove, C. 1990. Disguised industrial proletarians in rural Latin America: Women's informal-sector factory work and the social reproduction of coffee farm labor in Colombia. In *Women workers and global restructuring,* edited by K. Ward. Ithaca, NY: ILR Press.

Ward, K. 1990. Introduction and overview. In *Women workers and global restructuring,* edited by K. Ward. Ithaca, NY: ILR Press.

Ward, K., and J. L. Pyle. 1995. Gender, industrialization, and development. In *Women in the Latin American development process: From structural subordination to empowerment,* edited by C. Bose and E. Acosta-Belen. Philadelphia: Temple University Press.

OUR MOTHERS' GRIEF: RACIAL ETHNIC WOMEN AND THE MAINTENANCE OF FAMILIES— BONNIE THORNTON DILL

Notes

1. The term *reproductive labor* is used to refer to all of the work of women in the home. This includes but is not limited to: the buying and preparation of food and clothing, provision of emotional support and nurturance for all family members, bearing children, and planning, organizing, and carrying out a wide variety of tasks associated with their socialization. All of these activities are necessary for the growth of patriarchal capitalism because they maintain, sustain, stabilize, and *reproduce* (both biologically and socially) the labor force.

2. The term *white* is a global construct used to characterize peoples of European descent who migrated to and helped colonize America. In the seventeenth century, most of these immigrants were from the British Isles. However, during the time period covered by this article, European immigrants became increasingly diverse. It is a limitation of this article that time and space does not permit a fuller discussion of the variations in the white European immigrant experience. For the purposes of the argument made herein and of

the contrast it seeks to draw between the experiences of mainstream (European) cultural groups and that of racial/ethnic minorities, the differences among European settlers are joined and the broad similarities emphasized.

3. Cultural assaults, according to Caulfield (1974) are benign and systematic attacks on the institutions and forms of social organization that are fundamental to the maintenance and flourishing of a group's culture.

4. Recent research suggests that there were some tasks that were primarily assigned to males and some others to females. Whereas some gender-role distinctions with regard to work may have existed on some plantations, it is clear that slave women were not exempt from strenuous physical labor.

5. This term is used to refer to white Americans of European ancestry.

References

Aschenbrenner, Joyce. 1975. *Lifelines: Black Families in Change.* New York, NY: Holt, Rinehart, and Winston.

Barrera, Mario. 1979. *Race and Class in the Southwest.* Notre Dame, IN: Notre Dame University Press.

Blassingame, John. 1972. The *Slave Community: Plantation Life in the Antebellum South.* New York: Oxford University Press.

———. 1977. *Slave Testimony: Two Centuries of Letters, Speeches, Interviews, and Autobiographies.* Baton Rouge, LA: Louisiana State University Press.

Camarillo, Albert. 1979. *Chicanos in a Changing Society.* Cambridge, MA: Harvard University Press.

Caulfield, Mina Davis. 1974. "Imperialism, The Family, and Cultures of Resistance." *Socialist Review* 4(2)(October): 67–85.

Davis, Angela. 1971. "The Black Woman's Role in the Community of Slaves." *Black Scholar* 3(4)(December): 2–15.

———. 1981. *Women, Race and Class.* New York: Random House.

Degler, Carl. 1980. *At Odds.* New York: Oxford University Press.

Elasser, Nan Kyle MacKenzie, and Yvonne Tixier Y. Vigil. 1980. *Las Mujeres.* New York: The Feminist Press.

Garcia, Mario T. 1980. "The Chicano in American History: The Mexican Women of El Paso, 1880–1920—A Case Study." *Pacific Historical Review* 49(2)(May):315–358.

Genovese, Eugene D. and Elinor Miller, eds. 1974. *Plantation, Town, and County: Essays on the Local History of American Slave Society.* Urbana: University of Illinois Press.

Glenn, Evelyn Nakano. 1981. "Family Strategies of Chinese-Americans: An Institutional Analysis." Paper presented at the Society for the Study of Social Problems Annual Meetings.

Goldman, Marion S. 1981. *Gold Diggers and Silver Miners.* Ann Arbor: The University of Michigan Press.

Griswold del Castillo, Richard. 1979. *The Los Angeles Barrio: 1850–1890.* Los Angeles: The University of California Press.

Gutman, Herbert. 1976. *The Black Family in Slavery and Freedom: 1750–1925.* New York: Pantheon.

Hirata, Lucie Cheng. 1979. "Free, Indentured, Enslaved: Chinese Prostitutes in Nineteenth-Century America." *Signs* 5 (Autumn): 3–29.

Jones, Jacqueline. 1985. *Labor of Love, Labor of Sorrow.* New York: Basic Books.

Kennedy, Susan Estabrook. 1979. *If All We Did Was to Weep at Home: A History of White Working-Class Women in America.* Bloomington: Indiana University Press.

Kessler-Harris, Alice. 1981. *Women Have Always Worked.* Old Westbury: The Feminist Press.

———. 1982. *Out to Work.* New York: Oxford University Press.

Kingston, Maxine Hong. 1977. *The Woman Warrior.* Vintage Books.

Matthei, Julie. 1982. *An Economic History of Women in America.* New York: Schocken Books.

Nee, Victor G., and Brett de Bary Nee. 1973. *Long-time Californ'.* New York: Pantheon Books.

Saragoza, Alex M. 1983. "The Conceptualization of the History of the Chicano Family: Work, Family, and Migration in Chicanos." Research Proceedings of the Symposium on Chicano Research and Public Policy. Stanford, CA: Stanford University, Center for Chicano Research.

Shimkin, Demetri, E. M. Shimkin, and D. A. Frate, eds. 1978. *The Extended Family in Black Societies.* The Hague: Mouton.

Spruill, Julia Cherry. 1972. *Women's Life and Work in the Southern Colonies.* New York: W. W. Norton and Company (First published in 1938, University of North Carolina Press).

Stack, Carol S. 1974. *All our Kin: Strategies for Survival in a Black Community.* Harper and Row.

Sudarkasa, Niara. 1981. "Interpreting the African Heritage in Afro-American Family Organization." Pp. 37–53 in *Black Families,* edited by Harriette Pipes McAdoo. Beverly Hills, CA: Sage Publications.

White, Deborah Gray. 1985. *Aren't I a Woman: Female Slaves in the Plantation South.* New York: W. W. Norton.

Wright, Gwendolyn. 1981. *Building the Dream: A Social History of Housing in America.* New York: Pantheon Books.

Zaretsky, Eli. 1978. "The Effects of the Economic Crisis on the Family." Pp. 209–218 in *U.S. Capitalism in Crisis,* edited by Crisis Reader Editorial Collective. New York: Union of Radical Political Economists.

DUBIOUS CONCEPTIONS: THE CONTROVERSY OVER TEEN PREGNANCY—KRISTIN LUKER

Note

1. Teen pregnancy affects both young men and young women, but few data are gathered on young men. The availability of data leads me to speak of "teen mothers" throughout this article, but it is important to realize that this reflects an underlying, gendered definition of the situation.

OLDER PEOPLE AND THEIR FAMILIES: THE NEW PIONEERS—ETHEL SHANAS

References

Birren, J. E. and V. J. Renner. 1977. "Research on the Psychology of Aging: Principles and Experimentation." Pp. 3–38 in *Handbook of the Psychology of Aging,* edited by J. E. Birren and K. W. Schaie. New York: Van Nostrand-Reinhold.

Glick, P. G. 1979. "The Future Marital Status and Living Arrangements of the Elderly." *The Gerontologist* 19 (3): 301–309.

Neugarten, B. L. 1974. "Age Groups in American Society and the Rise of the Young-Old." *Annals of the American Academy* 415 (September): 187–198.

Plath, D. W. 1972. "Japan: The After Years." Pp. 133–150 in *Aging and Modernization,* edited by D. O. Cowgill and L. D. Holmes. New York: Appleton-Century-Crofts.

Rosow, I. 1976. "Status and Role Change Through the Life Span." Pp. 457–482 in *Handbook of Aging and the Social Sciences,* edited by R. H. Binstock and E. Shanas. New York: Van Nostrand-Reinhold.

Shanas, E. 1962. *The Health of Older People: A Social Survey.* Cambridge: Harvard University Press.

———— 1973. "Family-Kin Networks and Aging in Cross-Cultural Perspective." *Journal of Marriage and the Family* 35 (August): 505–511.

———— 1977. "The Elderly: Family, Bureaucracy and Family Help Patterns." Paper presented at a meeting of the Institut de la Vie, Vichy, France, April.

———— 1978. "A National Survey of the Aged." Final report to the Administration on Aging. Washington, D.C.: U.S. Department of Health, Education and Welfare.

———— 1979a. "The Family as a Social Support System in Old Age." *The Gerontologist* 19 (2): 169–174.

———— 1979b. "Social Myth as Hypothesis: The Case of the Family Relations of Old People." *The Gerontologist* 19 (1): 3–9.

Siegel, J. S. 1976. "Demographic Aspects of Aging and the Older Population of the United States." U.S. Bureau of the Census, Current Population Reports, Series P-23, No. 59. Washington, DC: U.S. Government Printing Office.

Sussman, M. B. and L. Burchinal. 1962. "Parental Aid to Married Children: Implications for Family Functioning." *Marriage and Family Living* 24: 320–332.

THE FUTURE OF GRANDPARENTHOOD— ANDREW CHERLIN AND FRANK FURSTENBERG, JR.

Notes

1. Joseph Veroff, Elizabeth Douvan, and Richard A. Kulka, *The Inner American: A Self Portrait from 1957 to 1976* (New York: Basic Books, 1981), 535. For a similar argument about the changing basis of self-identity in American society see Ralph H. Turner, "The Real Self: From Institution to Impulse," *American Journal of Sociology* 81 (March 1976): 989–1016.

2. Ronald Freedman, Ming-Cheng Chang, and Te-Hsiung Sun, "Household Composition, Extended Kinship, and Reproduction in Taiwan," *Population Studies* 36 (1980): 395–411.

3. Robert N. Bellah et al., *Habits of the Heart: Individualism and Commitment in American Life* (Berkeley: University of California Press, 1985), 90.

4. Arthur Kornhaber, "Grandparenthood and the 'New Social Contract'," in *Grandparenthood,* ed. Vern L. Bengtson and Joan F. Robertson (Beverly Hills, CA: Sage Publications, 1985), 159–71. Quoted at p. 159.

5. Arthur Kornhaber and Kenneth L. Woodward, *Grandparents/Grandchildren: The Vital Connection* (New York: Doubleday, Anchor Press, 1981), 147.

6. For an elaboration of the importance for marriage and fertility of "wealth flows" to and from the older generation, see John C. Caldwell, *Theory of Fertility Decline* (London: Academic Press, 1982).

7. Samuel H. Preston, "Children and the Elderly in the U.S.," *Scientific American* 251 (December 1984): 44–49.

8. Greg J. Duncan, Martha Hill, and Willard Rodgers, "The Changing Economic Status of the Young and Old," paper presented at the Workshop on Demographic Change and the Well-Being of Dependents, National Academy of Sciences, 5–7 September 1995.

9. Charles F. Westoff, "Marriage and Fertility in the Developed Countries," *Scientific American* 239 (December 1978): 51–57.

GRANDPARENTING STYLES: NATIVE AMERICAN PERSPECTIVES— JOAN WEIBEL-ORLANDO

Notes

This research was funded by grant 1R01 AGO 3794–2 from the National Institute on Aging.

1. There are, however, twenty-eight people in the sample. One woman is Caucasian and married to a Creek man. They lived in Los Angeles for eighteen years before returning, in 1976, to his hometown, a small city in south-central Oklahoma that is the administrative center of the Creek/Seminole Nation. One man is Mexican-American and married to a Sioux woman. They moved back to his wife's ancestral land on the Pine Ridge Reservation in South Dakota in 1981 after living for twenty-six years in Los Angeles.

2. In all cases fictitious names have been used to protect the privacy of those people who so generously shared their life stories, current activities, and views on grandparenthood with me.

Bibliography

Amoss, Pamela T. 1986. "Northwest Coast grandmother Myths." Unpublished paper presented at the 84th Annual Meeting of the American Anthropological Association, Philadelphia.

———. 1981. "Cultural Centrality and Prestige for the Elderly: The Coast Salish Case." In *Dimensions: Aging, Culture and Health.* C. Fry, ed. Brooklyn, N.Y.: J. F. Bergin.

Barnett, Homer. 1955. *The Coast Salish of British Columbia.* Eugene, Oreg.: University of Oregon.

Burton, Linda, and Vern Bengtson. 1985. "Black Grandmothers: Issues of Timing and Continuity in Roles." In *Grandparenthood.* Vern Bengtson and Joan Robinson, eds. Beverly Hills: Sage.

Cowgill, Donald, and Lowell Holmes, eds. 1972. *Aging and Modernization.* New York: Appleton-Century-Crofts.

Driver, Harold. 1969. *Indians of North America.* Chicago: University of Chicago Press.

Elmendorf, William W. and Alfred Kroeber. 1960. *The Structure of Twona Culture with Notes on Yurok Culture.* Pullman: Washington State University.

Erikson, Erik. 1963. *Childhood and Society.* New York: Norton.

Foreman, Grant. 1934. *The Five Civilized Tribes.* Norman: University of Oklahoma Press.

Holmes, Eleanor. 1986. "Aging in Modern and Traditional Societies." *The World and I,* No. 9. Baltimore: Washington Times.

Kroeber, Alfred. 1939. *Cultural and Natural Areas of Native North America.* vol. 38. University of California Publications in American Archaeology and Ethnology.

Myerhoff, Barbara G. 1978, "A Symbol Perfected in Death: Continuity and Ritual in the Life and Death of an Elderly Jew." In *Life's Career—Aging: Cultural Variations on Growing Old.* Barbara G. Myerhoff and Andrei Simic, eds. Beverly Hills: Sage.

Nahemow, Nina. 1987. "Grandparenthood among the Baganda: Role Option in Old Age." In *Growing Old in Different Societies.* Jay Sokolovsky, ed. Belmont, Calif.: Wadsworth.

Pettitt, George A. 1946. *Primitive Education in North America.* University of California Publications in American Archaeology and Ethnology 43:1–182.

Powers, William. 1977. *Oglala Religion.* Lincoln/London: University of Nebraska Press.

Schweitzer, Marjorie M. 1987. "The Elders: Cultural Dimensions of Aging in Two American Indian Communities. In *Growing*

Old in Different Societies. Jay Sokolovsky, ed. Acton, Mass.: Copley.

Shanas, Ethel, and Marvin Sussman. 1981. "The Family in Later Life: Social Structure and Social Policy." In *Aging: Social Change.* Sara Kifesler, James Morgan, and Valerie K. Oppenheimer, eds. New York: Academic.

Simic, Andrei. 1987. "Aging in the United States and Yugoslavia: Contrasting Models on Intergenerational Relationships." In *Growing Old in Different Societies.* Jay Sokolovsky, ed. Acton, Mass.: Copley.

Stack, Carol. 1974. *All Our Kin.* New York: Harper & Row.

Teftt, Stanton K. 1968. "Intergenerational Value Differentials and Family Structure Among the Wind River Shoshone." *American Anthropologist* 70:330–33.

Teski, Marea. 1987. "The Evolution of Aging, Ecology, and the Elderly in the Modern World." In *Growing Old in Different Societies.* Jay Sokolovsky, ed. Acton, Mass.: Copley.

Weibel, Joan. 1978. "Native Americans in Los Angeles: A Cross-Cultural Comparison of Assistance Patterns in an Urban Environment." *Anthropology UCLA* 2:81–98. Los Angeles: University of California Press.

THE VICTIMIZED SELF: THE CASE OF BATTERED WOMEN— JOHN M. JOHNSON AND KATHLEEN J. FERRARO

Notes

1. We owe a debt of gratitude to David Altheide, Paul Higgins, Mildred Daley Pagelow, and Carol A. B. Warren for comments on an earlier draft of this paper.

2. Data for our respective researches have been gained from direct field observations, depth interviewing, various kinds of official documents, and surveys. More details on the

data collection and analyses are to be found in Johnson (1975, 1981) and Ferraro (1979a, 1979b, 1981). An important resource for the research was the personal experience of the authors as cofounders and early leaders (1977–79) of an Arizona shelter for battered women.

References

Davidson, Terry. 1978. *Conjugal Crime.* New York: Hawthorn.

Ferraro, Kathleen J. 1979a. "Hard Love: Letting Go of an Abusive Husband." *Frontiers* 4(2):16–18.

———. 1979b. "Physical and Emotional Battering." *California Sociologist* 2(2):134–49.

———. 1981. "Battered Women and the Shelter Movement." Ph.D. dissertation, Department of Sociology, Arizona State University.

———. 1982. "Rationalizing Violence." Unpublished paper.

Gelles, Richard J. 1976. "Abused Wives: Why Do They Stay?" *Journal of Marriage and the Family* 38:659–68.

Hughes, Everett C. 1958. *Men and Their Work.* New York: Free Press.

Johnson, John M. 1975. *Doing Field Research.* New York: Free Press.

———. 1981. "Program Enterprise and Official Cooptation of the Battered Women's Shelter Movement." *American Behavioral Scientist* 24:827–42.

Martin, Del. 1976. *Battered Wives.* San Francisco, CA: Glide.

Pagelow, Mildred Daley. 1981. *Women-Battering.* Beverly Hills, CA: Sage.

Rasmussen, Paul K. and Kathleen J. Ferraro. 1979. "The Divorce Process." *Journal of Alternative Lifestyles* 2:443–60.

Roy, Maria (ed.). 1977. *Battered Women.* New York: Van Nostrand.

Walker, Lenore E. 1979. *The Battered Woman.* New York: Harper and Row.

THE CHANGING CONCEPT OF CHILD ABUSE AND ITS IMPACT ON THE INTEGRITY OF FAMILY LIFE—JOHN M. JOHNSON

Notes

1. Vincent de Francis, "Parents Who Abuse Children." *PTA Magazine* 58 (Nov. 1963): 16–18.

2. Lloyd de Mause, ed., *The History of Childhood* (New York: Psychohistory Press. 1974).

3. M. Harris, "Why Men Dominate Women." *New York Times Magazine,* 13 Nov. 1977. pp. 46ff.

4. Ibid., p. 120.

5. Samuel X. Radbill, "A History of Child Abuse and Infanticide," in R. Helfer and C. Kempe, eds., *The Battered Child* (Chicago: University of Chicago Press, 1968), p. 10.

6. Ibid., p. 12.

7. Ibid., p. 4.

8. Ibid.

9. T. Solomon, "History and Demography of Child Abuse." *Pediatrics* 51 (1963): 773–76.

10. John Caffey, "Multiple Fractures in the Long Bones of Infants Suffering from Chronic Subdural Hematoma." *American Journal of Roentgenology* 56 (Aug. 1946): 163–73.

11. Frederick N. Silverman, "Roentgen Manifestations of Unrecognized Skeletal Trauma in Infants." *American Journal of Roentgenology* 69 (March 1953): 413–26: Paul V. Wooley and W. A. Evans Jr., "Significance of Skeletal Lesions in Infants Resembling Those of Traumatic Origin." *Journal of the American Medical Association* 158 (June 1955):539–43.

12. C. Henry Kempe et al., "The Battered Child Syndrome." *Journal of the American Medical Association* 181 (July 1962): 17–24.

13. See Stephen J. Pfohl, "The 'Discovery' of Child Abuse." *Social Problems* 24 (Feb. 1977):

310–23: Peter Conrad and Joseph W. Schneider. *Deviance and Medicalization: From Badness to Sickness* (St. Louis: C. V. Mosby Co., 1980). pp. 161–71.

14. Pfohl, *n. 13.*

15. Knowledge of this meeting was gained from personal talks with Vincent de Francis.

16. Jack D. Douglas, *Defining America's Social Problems* (Englewood Cliffs, N.J.: Prentice-Hall, 1974).

17. M. G. Paulsen, "The Legal Framework for Child Protection." *Columbia Law Review* 67 (Jan. 1966): 1–49.

18. Vincent de Francis, *Child Abuse Legislation in the 1970s* (Denver: American Humane Association, 1970).

19. Vincent de Francis and C. I. Lucht, *Child Abuse and Legislation in the 1970s,* rev. ed. (Denver: American Humane Association, 1974).

20. Sanford Katz, "Child Neglect Laws in America." *Family Law Quarterly* 9 (Spring 1975): 295–331.

21. Saad Z. Nagi, *Child Maltreatment in the United States* (New York: Columbia University Press, 1977).

22. V. Cain, "Concern for Children in Placement." *Analysis of Child Abuse and Neglect* (Washington, D.C.: National Center on Child Abuse and Neglect, 1977).

23. Richard J. Gelles, *Family Violence* (Beverly Hills, Calif.: Sage Publications, 1979).

24. See Jeanne M. Giovannoni and Rosina M. Becerra, *Defining Child Abuse* (New York: Free Press, 1979); Gelles, *n.* 22; Alfred Kadushin and John A. Martin, *Child Abuse* (New York: Columbia University Press, 1981).

25. Leroy Pelton, "Child Abuse and Neglect: The Myth of Classlessness." *American Journal of Orthopsychiatry* 48 (Oct. 1978): 608–16.

26. Nagi, *n.* 21.

27. A "Type I Error" would be the labeling and processing of a caretaker as a child abuser who has not in fact abused a child.

28. Anthony M. Platt, *The Child Savers* (Chicago: University of Chicago Press, 1969).

29. Ellen Hoffman, "Policy and Politics: The Child Abuse Prevention and Treatment Act," in Richard Bourne and Eli H. Newberger, eds., *Critical Perspectives on Child Abuse* (Lexington, Mass.: Lexington Books, 1979), pp. 157–70.

30. A. Wolkenstein, "Hospital Acts on Child Abuse." *Journal of the American Hospital Association* 49 (March 1975): 103–6.

31. R. Polakow and D. Peabody, "Behavioral Treatment of Child Abuse." *International Journal of Offender Therapy and Comparative Criminology* 19 (1975): 100–108.

32. C. Hinton and J. Sterling, "Volunteers Serve as an Adjunct to Treatment for Child-Abusing Families." *Hospital and Community Psychiatry* 26 (March 1975): 136–37.

33. Jacobus Ten Broeck, "The Extended Family Center." *Children Today* 3 (April 1974): 2–6.

34. H. Lovens and J. Rako, "A Community Approach to the Prevention of Child Abuse." *Child Welfare* 54 (Feb 1975): 83–87.

35. Emilio Viano, "Attitudes Toward Child Abuse Among American Professionals." (Paper presented at the first meeting of the International Society for Research on Aggression, Toronto, Canada, 1974).

36. Giovannoni and Becerra, *n.* 24.

37. Gelles, *n.* 23, p. 61.

38. The research of Giovannoni and Becerra, *n.* 24, suggests that the traditional differences between the more supportive versus the more punitive professions are dissipating.

39. John M. Johnson, "Mass Media Reports and Deviance." (Paper presented at the annual meeting of the Society for the Study of Social Problems, San Francisco, 1982).

40. Harry D. Krause, *Family Law in a Nutshell* (St. Paul, Minn.: West Publishing Co., 1977), pp. 236–37.

41. Michael Wald, "State Intervention on Behalf of 'Neglected' Children: A Search for Realistic Standards." *Stanford Law Review* 27 (April 1975): 985–1040.

42. Gelles, *n.* 23.

43. Peter Conrad and Joseph W. Schneider, *Deviance and Medicalization: From Badness to Sickness* (St. Louis: C. V. Mosby Co., 1980).

44. Radbill, *n.* 5.

UNCOUPLING: THE SOCIAL CONSTRUCTION OF DIVORCE— DIANE VAUGHAN

Notes

1. For a sensitive and thought-provoking examination of these as integral components of divorce, see Willard Waller's beautiful qualitative study, *The Old Love and the New.*

2. This statement must be qualified. There are instances when the partners enter a stage of trying with shared definitions of the marriage as savable. The conditions under which the coupling can be preserved have to be negotiated. If they can arrive at a common definition of the coupling that is agreeable to both, the uncoupling process is terminated. But this analysis is of uncoupling, and there are two alternatives: (1) that they enter with common definitions of the marriage as savable but are not able to negotiate the conditions of the coupling so that the self-validation function is preserved or (2) that they enter the period of trying with opposing definitions, as stated here.

3. Waller interprets this phenomenon by using Jung's conceptualization of the container and the contained, analogous to the roles of initiator and significant other, respectively, in the present discussion. Notes Waller, "Or the contained, complicated by the process of divorcing, may develop those qualities whose lack the container previously deplored" (pp. 163–168).

References

Berger, Peter L. and Hansfried Kellner. 1964. "Marriage and the Construction of Reality." *Diogenes* 46:1–23,

Berger, Peter L. and Thomas Luckmann. 1966. *The Social Construction of Reality.* New York: Doubleday.

Bohannan, Paul. 1971. *Divorce and After.* Garden City, NY: Anchor.

Corwin, Ronald G. 1976. "Organizations at Loosely Coupled Systems: Evolution of a Perspective." Paper presented at the Seminar on Educational Organizations as Loosely Coupled Systems, Palo Alto, CA.

Davis, Murray S. 1973. *Intimate Relations.* New York: Free Press.

Epstein, Joseph E. 1975. *Divorce: The American Experience.* London: Jonathan Cape.

Goode, William J. 1956. *Women in Divorce.* New York: Free Press.

Gouldner, Alvin W. 1959. "Organizational Analysis." Pp. 400–428 in *Sociology Today,* edited by R. K. Merton, L. Bloom, and L. S. Cottrell, Jr. New York: Basic Books.

Krantzler, Mel. 1973. *Creative Divorce.* New York: New American Library.

Nichols, Jack. 1975. *Men's Liberation: A New Definition of Masculinity.* New York: Penguin.

Sullivan, Judy. 1974. *Mama Doesn't Live Here Anymore.* New York: Pyramid.

Waller, Willard. 1930. *The Old Love and the New.* Carbondale, IL: Southern Illinois University Press.

Walum, Laurel Richardson. 1977. *The Dynamics of Sex and Gender: A Sociological Perspective.* Chicago: Rand McNally.

Weber, Max. 1930. *The Protestant Ethic and the Spirit of Capitalism.* Translated by Talcott Parsons. New York: Charles Scribner's Sons.

Weick, Karl E. 1976. "Educational Organizations as Loosely Coupled Systems." *Administrative Science Quarterly,* 21:1–19.

Weiss, Robert. 1975. *Marital Separation.* New York: Basic Books.

LIFE-SPAN ADJUSTMENT OF CHILDREN TO THEIR PARENTS' DIVORCE—PAUL R. AMATO

Notes

1. Furstenberg, Jr., F. F. and Cherlin, A. J. *Divided families: What happens to children when parents part.* Cambridge, MA: Harvard University Press, 1991, pp. 1–15; Uhlenberg, P. Death and the family. *Journal of Family History* (1980) 5:313–20.

2. Cherlin, A. *Marriage, divorce, remarriage.* Rev. ed. Cambridge, MA: Harvard University Press, 1992.

3. Bumpass, L. Children and marital disruption: A replication and update. *Demography* (1984) 21:71–82.

4. For examples, see the articles in *The child in his family: The impact of disease and death.* E. J. Anthony, ed. New York: Wiley, 1973.

5. Crook, T., and Eliot, J. Parental death during childhood and adult depression: A critical review of the literature. *Psychological Bulletin* (1980) 87:252–59.

6. The cross-sectional and longitudinal designs are used widely in adjustment research and other developmental research because they are suited for studies in which there are one or more nonmanipulable independent variables. In this instance, the researcher must select subjects who already possess different levels of a particular characteristic. Examples of nonmanipulable independent variables include age, sex, marital status of parents, and socioeconomic status. The use of nonmanipulable independent variables in a study usually precludes the use of true experimental designs which involve the random assignment of subjects to groups. Subjects are randomly assigned to eliminate the influence of extraneous variables. If the influence of extrane-

ous variables has been accomplished in a study and there are significant differences found between groups on a dependent variable, then the researcher may state with confidence that the independent variable caused the results to differ between groups. In studies without random assignment of subjects, including those using cross-sectional and longitudinal designs, statements about cause and effect relationships cannot be made. Researchers are unable to determine which variable caused which or if some other extraneous variable(s) could be responsible for an observed relationship between the variables. It should be noted that this difficulty is inherent in the literature on adjustment to divorce. Although cause and effect relationships may not be known, what is known is that there is a correlation between parental marital status and children's adjustment, and the knowledge that this correlation exists helps to assist the process of policymaking in this area. For a further discussion of the differences between experimental and nonexperimental designs, see Miller, S. A. *Developmental research methods.* Englewood Cliffs, NJ: Prentice-Hall, 1987; Cozby, P. C., Worden, P. E., and Kee, D. W. *Research methods in human development.* Mountain View, CA: Mayfield, 1989.

7. The optimal comparison group would be families that would potentially divorce, but stay together for the sake of the children. However, this population of families would be very difficult to sample. Another available comparison group would be continuously intact two-parent families. However, this comparison group is not consistently used by researchers. Many classifications in cross-sectional research are based on the current marital status of parents. The intact group is heterogeneous as to marital history, and the divorced group is not similar as to the time of divorce or the age of the children when it took place. Some of the most prominent longitudinal studies have no comparison group of intact fam-

ilies. See, for example, Wallerstein, J. S., and Corbin, S. B. Father-child relationships after divorce: Child support and educational opportunity. *Family Law Quarterly* (1986) 20:109–28; Maccoby, E. E., and Mnookin, R. H. *Dividing the child: Social and legal dilemmas of custody.* Cambridge, MA: Harvard University Press, 1992.

8. For example, a researcher using a cross-sectional design might study four different groups of children, grouped by age (for example, 3, 6, 9, and 12) and parental marital status (married or divorced) to see if children from divorced families exhibit significantly more aggression than children from intact families. If the researcher finds that aggressive behavior is, indeed, significantly more likely in children from divorced families, the researcher cannot determine the direction of the relationship, that is, whether the divorce increased aggression in these children or high levels of aggression in the children caused the divorce. In addition, the researcher is unable to determine if some extraneous variable caused both high aggression and divorce, for example, low socioeconomic status.

For the developmental researcher, there are advantages and disadvantages to using this type of research design. The cross-sectional design is relatively inexpensive and timely, which makes it a popular choice for many researchers. However, a number of difficulties may threaten the validity and reliability of the results. These difficulties include the following: there is no direct measure of age changes; the issue of individual stability over time cannot be addressed; there is a possibility of selection bias; there may be difficulty establishing measurement equivalence; and there is an inevitable confounding of age and time of birth. Some of these problems are avoidable with adequate planning and control; however, the problem of the confounding of age and time of birth (cohort) is intrinsic in the cross-sectional design, and it is impossible to avoid.

Another design that is available to researchers but is seldom used is called the cross-sectional-sequential design. A cross-sectional-sequential study tests separate cross-sectional samples at two or more times of measurement. In comparison to a standard cross-sectional design, this sequential design has the advantage of at least partly unconfounding age and year of birth (because there are at least two different cohorts for each age tested), and it also provides a comparison of the same age group at different times of testing (called a time-lag comparison). It would be advantageous to use this research design in the future for some types of adjustment research.

9. There are major advantages and disadvantages to this type of design. The advantages include the following: a researcher can observe actual changes occurring in subjects over time; irrelevant sources of variability are not of concern; there are no cohort effects because the same cohort is being studied over time and there is no selection bias. Disadvantages that may influence reliability and validity include the following: an expensive and time-consuming design; subject attrition; selective dropout; possible obsolescence of tests and instruments; a potentially biased sample; measurement of only a single cohort; effects of repeated testing; reactivity; difficulty of establishing equivalent measures; and the inevitable confounding of the age of subjects and the historical time of testing. As with the cross-sectional design, some of these problems are avoidable. However, it is impossible to avoid the confounding of age with time of measurement in the longitudinal approach. This confounding follows from the fact that the age comparisons are all within subject. Therefore, if we want to test subjects of different ages, we must test at different times. For an in-depth discussion of longitudinal designs, see Menard, S. *Longitudinal research.* Series: Quantitative App-

lications in the Social Sciences, No. 07-076. Newbury Park, CA: Sage, 1991.

A design that is available to developmental researchers and is more complicated but should assist in disentangling the contributions of age, generation, and time of measurement is called the longitudinal-sequential design. In this design, the samples are selected from different cohorts (that is, years of birth), and they are tested repeatedly across the same time span. This design offers at least three advantages over a standard longitudinal design. The longitudinal comparisons are not limited to a single generation or cohort because samples are drawn from different birth years. In addition, there is a cross-sectional component to the design because different age groups are tested at each time of measurement. Finally, the same age group is represented at different times of measurement. More information is provided than in a standard longitudinal design, and there is greater opportunity to disentangle causative factors. See Baltes, P. B., Reese, H. W., and Nesselroade, J. R. *Life-span developmental psychology: Introduction to research methods.* Monterey, CA: Brooks/Cole, 1977.

10. Wallerstein, J. S. Children of divorce: Preliminary report of a ten-year follow-up of young children. *American Journal of Orthopsychiatry* (1984) 54:444–58; Wallerstein, J. S. Children of divorce: Preliminary report of a ten-year follow-up of older children and adolescents. *Journal of the American Academy of Child Psychiatry* (1985) 24:545–53; Wallerstein, J. S. Women after divorce: Preliminary report from a ten-year follow-up. *American Journal of Orthopsychiatry* (1986) 56:65–77; Wallerstein, J. S. Children of divorce: Report of a ten-year follow-up of early latency-age children. *American Journal of Orthopsychiatry* (1987) 57:199–211; Wallerstein, J. S., and Blakeslee, S. *Second chances: Men, women, and*

children a decade after divorce. New York: Ticknor and Fields, 1989; Wallerstein, J. S., and Corbin, S. B. Daughters of divorce: Report from a ten-year follow-up. *American Journal of Orthopsychiatry* (October 1989) 59:593–604; Wallerstein, J. S., and Kelly, J. B. *Surviving the breakup: How children and parents cope with divorce.* New York: Basic Books, 1980.

11. For a discussion of sampling, see Kerlinger, F. N. *Foundations of behavioral research.* New York: Holt, Rinehart and Winston, 1973.

12. It should be noted that there are no perfect random samples on this subject. The national studies select ever-divorced families, who are limited by geography, the choice of schools included (rarely private schools, which is a problem in places where a large segment of children, often those with the best advantages, are not enrolled in public schools), or use the court sampling frame, which offers insufficient address data to draw a comprehensive sample.

13. This type of random selection of samples should not be confused with random assignment of subjects to groups.

14. For a discussion of matching, see note no. 6, Miller.

15. See, for example, Guidubaldi, J., Cleminshaw, H. K., Perry, J. D., and McLoughlin, C. S. The impact of parental divorce on children: Report of the nationwide NASP study. *School Psychology Review* (1983) 12:300–23; Hetherington, E. M., Cox, M., and Cox, R. Effects of divorce on parents and children. In *Nontraditional families.* M. E. Lamb, ed. Hillsdale, NJ: Lawrence Erlbaum Associates, 1982, pp. 223–88; see note no. 10, Wallerstein and Kelly.

16. See, for example, Baydar, N. Effects of parental separation and reentry into union on the emotional well-being of children. *Journal of Marriage and the Family* (1988) 50:967–81; Enos, D. M., and Handal, P. J. Relation of paren-

tal marital status and perceived family conflict to adjustment in white adolescents. *Journal of Consulting and Clinical Psychology* (1986) 54:820–24; Mechanic, D., and Hansell, S. Divorce, family conflict, and adolescents' well-being. *Journal of Health and Social Behavior* (1989) 30:105–16.

17. Amato, P. R., and Ochiltree, G. Child and adolescent competence in intact, one-parent, and stepfamilies. *Journal of Divorce* (1987) 10:75–96.

18. See Glass, G. V., McGaw, B., and Smith, M. L. An evaluation of meta-analysis. In *Meta-analysis in social research.* Newbury Park, CA: Sage, 1981.

19. The term *meta-analysis* refers to the quantitative combinations of data from independent studies. The procedure is valuable when the result is a descriptive summary of the weight of the available evidence. Summaries are necessary primarily because there are conflicting results in the literature and, at some point, it is valuable to know where the weight of the evidence falls. The primary goals of meta-analysis include determining whether significant effects exist for the topic being reviewed, estimating the magnitude of effects, and relating the existence and magnitude of effects of variations in design and procedure across studies. Proponents of meta-analysis argue that meta-analysis can achieve a greater precision and generalizability of findings than single studies. They then have the potential to provide more definitive evidence for policymaking than can be realized by other means. However, there are logical and methodological difficulties with the technique that need to be understood when interpreting the results of any meta-analysis. First, there is the problem of the selection of studies, that is, how to determine which studies should be included in the meta-analysis. Oakes contends that any rule establishment in this area presents impossible difficul-

ties. A second problem is that, if a researcher includes only published studies in the meta-analysis, there is the danger of overestimating differences between groups. This danger arises because journal articles are not a representative sample of work addressed in any particular research area. Significant research findings are more likely to be published than nonsignificant research findings. To control for this problem, the researcher must trace unpublished research and incorporate it into the analysis. A third problem is that the use of meta-analysis may overinflate differences between groups because a high proportion of reported statistically significant results are spurious. Finally, because of the diversity of the types of samples that are included in the meta-analysis, it is difficult—if not impossible—to know what population the results are applicable to. For more in-depth discussions of the technique, its advantages, and its disadvantages, see note no. 18, Glass, McGaw, and Smith; Oakes, M. The logic and role of meta-analysis in clinical research. *Statistical Methods in Medical Research* (1993) 2:146–60; note no. 6, Miller; Thompson, S. G., and Pocock, S. J. Can meta-analyses be trusted? *The Lancet* (November 2, 1991) 338:1127–30; Wolf, F. M. *Meta-analysis: Quantitative methods for research synthesis.* Series: Quantitative Applications in Social Sciences, No. 07-059. Beverly Hills, CA: Sage, 1986.

20. Amato, P. R., and Keith, B. Parental divorce and the well-being of children: A meta analysis. *Psychological Bulletin* (1991) 100:26–46. Studies were included if they met the following criteria: (1) were published in an academic journal or book, (2) included a sample of children of divorce as well as a sample of children from continuously intact two-parent families, (3) involved quantitative measures of any of the outcomes listed below in note no. 21, and (4) provided sufficient information to calculate an effect size.

21. In the meta-analysis for children, measures of well-being were coded into the following eight categories: academic achievement (standardized achievement tests, grades, teachers' ratings, or intelligence); conduct (misbehavior, aggression, or delinquency); psychological adjustment (depression, anxiety, or happiness); self-concept (self-esteem, perceived competence, or internal locus of control); social adjustment (popularity, loneliness, or cooperativeness); mother-child and father-child relations (affection, help, or quality of interaction), and other.

22. Mean effect sizes ranged from .06 for the "other" category (not significant) to −.23 for conduct (p .001), with an overall effect size of −.17 across all outcomes. Effect sizes reflect the difference between groups in standard deviation units. A negative effect size indicates that children of divorce exhibit lower well-being than do children in intact two-parent families. With the exception of the "other" category, all mean effect sizes were statistically significant (p .001).

23. Amato, P. R., and Keith, B. Parental divorce and adult well-being: A meta-analysis. *Journal of Marriage and the Family* (1991) 53:43–58.

24. In the meta-analysis for adults, outcomes were coded into the following 15 categories: psychological well-being (emotional adjustment, depression, anxiety, life-satisfaction); behavior/conduct (criminal behavior, drug use, alcoholism, suicide, teenage pregnancy, teenage marriage); use of mental health services; self-concept (self-esteem, self-efficacy, sense of power, internal locus of control); social well-being (number of friends, social participation, social support, contact with parents and extended family); marital quality (marital satisfaction, marital disagreements, marital instability); separation or divorce; one-parent family status; quality of relations with one's children;

quality of general family relations (over-all ratings of family life); educational attainment (high school graduation; years of education); occupational quality (occupational prestige, job autonomy, job satisfaction); material quality of life (income, assets held, housing quality, welfare dependency, perceived economic strain); physical health (chronic problems, disability), and other.

25. Mean effect sizes ranged from −.02 for relations with children (not significant) to −.36 for becoming a single parent (p .001), with an effect size of −.20 across all outcomes. All mean effect sizes were significant (at least p .01) except for relations with children and self-concept.

26. Kendall-Tackett, K. A., Williams, L. M., and Finkelhor, D. Impact of sexual abuse on children: A review and synthesis of recent empirical studies. *Psychological Bulletin* (1993) 113:164–80. Effect sizes in this meta-analysis ranged from .39 to .66, indicating poorer adjustment for sexually abused children than for non-abused children.

27. Rutter, M. Sex differences in children's responses to family stress. In *The child in his family*. Vol. 1. E. J. Anthony and C. Koupernik, eds. New York: Wiley, 1970.

28. See, for example, Booth, A., Brinkerhoff, D. B., and White, L. K. The impact of parental divorce on courtship. *Journal of Marriage and the Family* (1984) 46:85–94; Smith, T. E. Parental separation and adolescents' academic self-concepts: An effort to solve the puzzle of separation effects. *Journal of Marriage and the Family* (1990) 52:107–18.

29. Slater, E., Steward, K. J., and Linn, M. W. The effects of family disruption on adolescent males and females. *Adolescence* (1983) 18:931–42.

30. See Peterson, J. L., and Zill, N. Marital disruption, parent-child relationships, and behavior problems in children. *Journal of Mar-*

riage and the Family (1986) 48:295–307; Hetherington, E. M., and Chase-Lansdale, P. L. The impact of divorce on life-span development: Short and long term effects. In *Life-span development and behavior.* P. B. Baltes, D. L. Featherman, and R. M. Lerner, eds. Hillsdale, NJ: Lawrence Erlbaum Associates, 1990.

31. See note no. 7, Wallerstein and Corbin.

32. Hetherington, E. M., Camara, K. A., and Featherman, D. L. Achievement and intellectual functioning of children in one-parent households. In *Achievement and achievement motives.* J. T. Spence, ed. San Francisco: W. H. Freeman, 1983.

33. Del Carmen, R., and Virgo, G. N. Marital disruption and nonresidential parenting: A multicultural perspective. In *Nonresidential parenting: New vistas in family living.* C. Depner and J. Bray, eds. Newbury Park, CA: Sage, 1993, pp. 13–36.

34. See note no. 10, Wallerstein and Kelly.

35. See note no. 10, Wallerstein and Blakeslee.

36. For a summary of these studies, see Amato, P. R. Children's adjustment to divorce: Theories, hypotheses, and empirical support. *Journal of Marriage and the Family* (1993) 55:23–38.

37. See note no. 20, Amato and Keith.

38. Furstenberg, Jr., F. F., and Nord, C. W. Parenting apart: Patterns of child-rearing after marital disruption. *Journal of Marriage and the Family* (1985) 47:893–904; Seltzer, J. A. Relationships between fathers and children who live apart: The father's role after separation. *Journal of Marriage and the Family* (1991) 53:79–101.

39. This trend was confirmed in the meta-analysis by Amato and Keith; see note no. 23. For examples of studies, see Amato P. R. Parental absence during childhood and depression in later life. *Sociological Quarterly* (1991) 32:543–56; Gregory, I. Introspective data following childhood loss of a parent: Delinquency and high school dropout. *Archives of General*

Psychiatry (1965) 13:99–109; Saucier, J., and Ambert, A. Parental marital status and adolescents' optimism about their future. *Journal of Youth and Adolescence* (1982) 11:345–53. Our meta-analysis also showed that, although children who experience parental death are worse off than those in intact two-parent families, they have higher levels of well-being than do children of divorce.

40. Cochran, M., Larner, M., Riley, D., et al. *Extending families: The social networks of parents and their children.* Cambridge, MA: Cambridge University Press, 1990; Dornbusch, S., Carlsmith, J. M., Bushwall, S. J., et al. Single parents, extended households, and the control of adolescents. *Child Development* (1985) 56:326–41.

41. Kelly, J. B. Current research on children's postdivorce adjustment: No simple answers. *Family and Conciliation Courts Review* (1993) 31:29–49.

42. Amato, P. R., and Rezac, S. J. Contact with nonresident parents, interparental conflict, and children's behavior. Paper presented at the Annual Meeting of the Midwest Sociological Society. Chicago, IL, 1993; Healy, Jr., J., Malley, J., and Stewart, A. Children and their fathers after parental separation. *American Journal of Orthopsychiatry* (1990) 60:531–43; see note no. 15, Hetherington, Cox, and Cox.

43. See note no. 15, Hetherington, Cox, and Cox. See also Simons, R. L., Beaman, J., Conger, R. D., and Chao, W. Stress, support, and antisocial behavior traits as determinants of emotional well-being and parenting practices among single mothers. *Journal of Marriage and the Family* (1993) 55:385–98.

44. Kline, M., Tschann, J. M., Johnston, J. R., and Wallerstein, J. S. Children's adjustment in joint and sole physical custody families. *Developmental Psychology* (1989) 25:430–38. Guidubaldi, J., and Perry, J. D. Divorce and mental health sequelae for children: A two year follow-up of a nationwide sample. *Journal of the*

American Academy of Child Psychiatry (1985) 24:531–37; and Kalter, N., Kloner, A., Schreiser, S., and Olka, K. Predictors of children's postdivorce adjustment. *American Journal of Orthopsychiatry* (1989) 59:605–18.

45. Guidubaldi, J., Cleminshaw, H. K., Perry, J. D., et al. The role of selected family environment factors in children's post-divorce adjustment. *Family Relations* (1986) 35:141–51; see note no. 15, Hetherington, Cox, and Cox. See note no. 10, Wallerstein and Kelly; note no. 44, Kalter, Kloner, Schreiser, and Olka; note no. 30, Peterson and Zill.

46. Of course, it is also likely that well-behaved children allow parents to behave in a positive and competent manner, whereas ill-behaved children stimulate problematic parental behaviors. Undoubtedly, children influence parents just as parents influence children. However, this does not invalidate the notion that divorce-induced stress can interfere with a person's ability to function effectively as a parent and that a parent's failure to function effectively might have negative consequences for children.

47. Emery, R. Interparental conflict and the children of discord and divorce. *Psychological Bulletin* (1982) 92:310–30; Grych, J. H., and Fincham, F. D. Marital conflict and children's adjustment: A cognitive-contextual framework. *Psychological Bulletin* (1990) 108:267–90.

48. See note no. 28, Booth, Brinkerhoff, and White. See note no. 16, Enos and Handal; and Mechanic and Hansell; Long, N., Forehand, R., Fauber, R., and Brody, G. H. Self-perceived and independently observed competence of young adolescents as a function of parental marital conflict and recent divorce. *Journal of Abnormal Child Psychology* (1987) 15:15–27; see note no. 30, Peterson and Zill.

49. Cherlin, A. J., Furstenberg, Jr., F. F., Chase-Lansdale, P. L., et al. Longitudinal studies of effects of divorce on children in Great Britain and the United States. *Science* (1991) 252:1386–89. Similar findings were reported by

Block, J. H., Block, J., and Gjerde, P. R. The personality of children prior to divorce. *Child Development* (1986) 57:827–40.

50. Johnston, J. R., Kline, M., and Tschann, J. M. Ongoing postdivorce conflict: Effects on children of joint custody and frequent access. *American Journal of Orthopsychiatry* (1999) 59:576–92; Kurdek, L. A., and Berg, B. Correlates of children's adjustment to their parents' divorces. In *Children and divorce.* L. A. Kurdek, ed. San Francisco: Jossey-Bass, 1983; Shaw, D. S., and Emery, R. E. Parental conflict and other correlates of the adjustment of school-age children whose parents have separated. *Journal of Abnormal Child Psychology* (1987) 15:269–81.

51. It is also probable that children's problems, to a certain extent, exacerbate conflict between parents.

52. Duncan, G. J., and Hoffman, S. D. Economic consequences of marital instability. In *Horizontal equity, uncertainty, and economic well-being.* M. David and T. Smeeding, eds. Chicago: University of Chicago Press, 1985; Weitzman, L. J. *The divorce revolution: The unexpected social and economic consequences for women and children in America.* New York: Free Press, 1985.

53. McLeod, J. D., and Shanahan, M. J. Poverty, parenting, and children's mental health. *American Sociological Review* (1993) 58:351–66.

54. Williams, D. R. Socioeconomic differentials in health: A review and redirection. *Social Psychology Quarterly* (1990) 52:81–99.

55. McLanahan, S., and Booth, K. Mother-only families: Problems, prospects, and politics. *Journal of Marriage and the Family* (1989) 51:557–80.

56. See note no. 15, Guidubaldi, Cleminshaw, Perry, and McLoughlin.

57. McLanahan, S. Family structure and the reproduction of poverty. *American Journal of Sociology* (1985) 90:873–901.

58. For a review of the effects of serial marriages (involving three or more marriages) and divorces on child adjustment, see Brody, G. H., Neubaum, E., and Forehand, R. Serial marriage: A heuristic analysis of an emerging family form. *Psychological Bulletin* (1988) 103:211–22.

59. Hodges, W. F., Tierney, C. W., and Buchsbaum, H. K. The cumulative effect of stress on preschool children of divorced and intact families. *Journal of Marriage and the Family* (1984) 46:611–19; Stolberg, A. L., and Anker, J. M. Cognitive and behavioral changes in children resulting from parental divorce and consequent environmental changes. *Journal of Divorce* (1983) 7:23–37.

60. See note no. 16, Baydar. Hetherington and her colleagues found that the remarriage of the custodial mother was associated with increased problems for girls but decreased problems for boys. Hetherington, E. M., Cox, M., and Cox, R. Long-term effects of divorce and remarriage on the adjustment of children. *Journal of the American Academy of Child Psychiatry* (1985) 24:518–30.

61. Amato, P. R., and Booth, A. The consequences of parental divorce and marital unhappiness for adult well-being. *Social Forces* (1991) 69:895–914.

62. For similar perspectives, see Hetherington, E. M. Coping with family transitions: Winners, losers, and survivors. *Child Development* (1989) 60:1–14; Kurdek, L. A. An integrative perspective on children's divorce adjustment. *American Psychologist* 36:856–66.

63. Glendon, M. A. *The transformation of family law: State, law, and family in the United States and Western Europe.* Chicago: University of Chicago Press, 1989. See note no. 52, Weitzman.

64. See note no. 63, Glendon; Sweet, J. A., and Bumpass, L. L. *American families and households.* New York: Russell Sage Foundation, 1990.

65. See note no. 1, Furstenberg and Cherlin.

66. See note no. 7, Maccoby and Mnookin.

67. Seltzer, J. Legal custody arrangements and children's economic welfare. *American Journal of Sociology* (1991) 96:895–929.

68. Arditti, J. A. Differences between fathers with joint custody and noncustodial fathers. *American Journal of Orthopsychiatry* (1992) 62:186–95; Bowman, M., and Ahrons, C. R. Impact of legal custody status on fathers' parenting postdivorce. *Journal of Marriage and the Family* (1985) 47:481–88; Dudley, J. R. Exploring ways to get divorced fathers to comply willingly with child support agreements. *Journal of Divorce* (1991) 14:121–33; Leupnitz, D. A comparison of maternal, paternal, and joint custody: Understanding the varieties of postdivorce family life. *Journal of Divorce* (1986) 9:1–12.

69. See note no. 68, Arditti; Little, M. A. The impact of the custody plan on the family: A five year follow up. *Family and Conciliation Courts Review* (1992) 30:243–51; Shrier, D. K., Simring, S. K., Shapiro, E. T., and Greif, J. B. Level of satisfaction of fathers and mothers with joint or sole custody arrangements. *Journal of Divorce and Remarriage* (1991) 16:163–69.

70. Buchanan, C. M., Maccoby, E. E., and Dornbusch, S. M. Adolescents and their families after divorce: Three residential arrangements compared. *Journal of Research on Adolescents* (1992) 2:261–91; Glover, R. J., and Steele, C. Comparing the effects on the child of postdivorce parenting arrangements. *Journal of Divorce* (1989) 12:185–201; Wolchik, S. A., Braver, S. L., and Sandler, I. N. Maternal versus joint custody: Children's postseparation experiences and adjustment. *Journal of Clinical Child Psychology* (1985) 14:5–10.

71. Kline, M., Tschann, J. M., Johnston, J. R., and Wallerstein, J. S. Children's adjustment in joint and sole physical custody families. *Developmental Psychology* (1988) 25:430–38; Leupnitz, D. *Child custody.* Lexington, MA: D. C. Heath, 1982; Pearson, J., and Thoennes, N. Cus-

tody after divorce: Demographic and attitudinal patterns. *American Journal of Orthopsychiatry* (1990) 60:233–49.

72. See note no. 68, Arditti; note no. 71, Pearson and Thoennes; Steinman, S. The experience of children in a joint custody arrangement: A report of a study. *American Journal of Orthopsychiatry* (1981) 24:554–62.

73. Nelson, R. Parental hostility, conflict, and communication in joint and sole custody families. *Journal of Divorce* (1989) 13:145–57.

74. Buchanan, C. M., Maccoby, E. E., and Dornbusch, S. M. Caught between parents: Adolescents' experience in divorced homes. *Child Development* (1991) 62:1008–29; Johnston, J. R., Kline, M., and Tschann, J. M. Ongoing postdivorce conflict: Effects on children of joint custody and frequent access. *American Journal of Orthopsychiatry* (1989) 59:576–92.

75. Downey, D., and Powell, B. Do children in single-parent households fare better living with same-sex parents? *Journal of Marriage and the Family* (1993) 55:55–71.

76. U.S. Bureau of the Census. *Child support and alimony: 1987.* Current Population Reports, Series P-23, No. 167. Washington, DC: U.S. Government Printing Office, 1990.

77. Public Law No. 100-485, reprinted in *1988 U.S. Code Cong. & Admin. News,* 102 Stat. 2343.

78. See note no. 52, Duncan and Hoffman.

79. Furstenberg, Jr., F. F., Morgan, S. P., and Allison, P. D. Paternal participation and children's well-being after marital dissolution. *American Sociological Review* (1987) 52:695–701; King, V. Nonresidential father involvement and child well-being: Can dads make a difference? Paper presented at the annual meeting of the Population Association of America. Cincinnati, OH, 1993.

80. For a discussion of child support reform, see Garfinkel, I. *Assuring child support: An*

extension of Social Security. New York: Russell Sage Foundation, 1992; Garfinkel, I., and McLanahan, S. S. *Single mothers and their children: A new American dilemma.* Washington, DC: Urban Institute Press, 1986.

81. Seltzer, J. A., and Bianchi, S. M. Children's contact with absent parents. *Journal of Marriage and the Family* (1988) 50:663–77; Seltzer, J., Schaeffer, N. C., and Charng, H. Family ties after divorce: The relationship between visiting and paying child support. *Journal of Marriage and the Family* (1989) 51:1013–32.

82. Britto, K. The Family Support Act of 1988 Welfare Reform (Public Law 100-485). Vol. 2, No. 3. National Conference of State Legislatures. Denver, CO, 1989.

83. Aldous, J. Family policy in the 1980s: Controversy and consensus. *Journal of Marriage and the Family* (1990) 52:1136–51.

84. Grych, J., and Fincham, F. D. Interventions for children of divorce: Toward greater integration of research and action. *Psychological Bulletin* (1992) 111:434–54.

85. Anderson, R. F., Kinney, J., and Gerler, E. R. The effects of divorce groups on children's classroom behavior and attitudes toward divorce. *Elementary School Guidance and Counseling* (1984) 19:70–76; Crosbie-Burnett, M., and Newcomer, L. L. Group counseling children of divorce: The effects of a multimodel intervention. *Journal of Divorce* (1989) 13:69–78. Pedro-Carroll, J., and Cowan, E. L. The children of divorce intervention program: An investigation of the efficacy of a school based intervention program. *Journal of Consulting and Clinical Psychology* (1985) 53:603–11; Stolberg, A. J., and Garrison, K. M. Evaluating a primary prevention program for children of divorce. *American Journal of Community Psychology* (1985) 13:111–24.

86. Bloom, B. L., Hodges, W. F., and Caldwell, R. A. A preventive program for the newly separated: Initial evaluation. *American Journal of Community Psychology* (1982) 10:251–64; Bloom, B. L., Hodges, W. F., Kern, M. B., and McFaddin, S. C. A preventive intervention program for the newly separated: Final evaluations. *American Journal of Orthopsychiatry* (1985) 55:9–26; Zibbell, R. A. A short-term, small-group education and counseling program for separated and divorced parents in conflict. *Journal of Divorce and Remarriage* (1992) 18:189–203.

87. Wallerstein, J. S. The long-term effects of divorce on children: A review. *Journal of the American Academy of Child Adolescent Psychiatry* (1991) 30:349–60.

REMARRIAGE AS AN INCOMPLETE INSTITUTION— ANDREW CHERLIN

Notes

1. A study by McCarthy (1977), however, suggests that remarriages may be more stable than first marriages for blacks. Using life-table techniques on data from 10,000 women under age 45 collected in the 1973 Survey of Family Growth, McCarthy reported that the probability of separation and divorce during the first 15 years of marriage is lower for blacks in remarriages than in first marriages, but is about 50 percent higher for whites in remarriages than for whites in first marriages.

2. Despite the lack of convincing evidence, I am reluctant to discount this explanation completely. Clinical psychologists and psychiatrists with whom I have talked insist that many troubled married persons they have treated had made the same mistakes twice and were in need of therapy to resolve long-standing problems. Their clinical experience should not be ignored, but this "divorce-proness" syndrome seems inadequate as a complete explanation for the greater problems of remarried people.

3. Bernard (1956) noted this problem in the preface to the reprinted edition of her book on remarriage. "Institutional patterns," she wrote, "are needed to help remarried parents establish relationships with one another conducive to the protection of their children."

4. In an earlier paper (Cherlin 1977), I found that children affected the probability that a woman in a first marriage or remarriage would divorce only when the children were of pre-school age. But the National Longitudinal Surveys of Mature Women, from which this analysis was drawn, contained no information about whether the children of remarried wives were from the woman's previous or current marriage. Since the Becker et al. (1976) results showed that his distinction is crucial, we cannot draw any relevant inferences about children and remarriage from my earlier study.

References

Ariès, Philippe. 1962. *Centuries of Childhood.* New York: Knopf.

Becker, G., E. Landes, and R. Michael. 1976. "Economics of Marital Instability." Working Paper No. 153. Stanford, CA: National Bureau of Economic Research.

Berger, Peter L. and Thomas Luckmann. 1966. *The Social Construction of Reality.* New York: Doubleday.

Bergler, Edmund. 1948. *Divorce Won't Help.* New York: Harper & Bros.

Bernard, Jessie. 1956. *Remarriage.* New York: Dryden.

Blood, Robert O. and Donald M. Wolfe. 1960. *Husbands and Wives.* New York: Free Press,

Bohannan, Paul. 1963. *Social Anthropology.* New York: Holt, Rinehart & Winston.

———. 1970. "Divorce Chains, Households of Remarriage, and Multiple Divorces." Pp. 127–39 in *Divorce and After,* edited by Paul Bohannan. New York: Doubleday.

Bradburn, Norman, and David Caplovitz. 1965. *Reports on Happiness.* Chicago: Aldine.

Bumpass, L. L. and A. Sweet. 1972. "Differentials in Marital Instability: 1970." *American Sociological Review* 37 (December): 754–66.

Burgess, Ernest W. and Harvey J. Locke. 1945. *The Family: From Institution to Companionship.* New York: American.

Campbell, Angus, Philip E. Converse, and Willard L. Rodgers. 1976. *The Quality of American Life.* New York: Russell Sage.

Cherlin, A. 1977. "The Effects of Children on Marital Dissolution." *Demography* 14 (August): 265–72.

Demos, John. 1970. *A Little Commonwealth: Family Life in Plymouth Colony.* New York: Oxford University Press.

Duberman, Lucile. 1975. *The Reconstructed Family.* Chicago: Nelson-Hall.

Dyer, W. G. and D. Urban. 1958. "The Institutionalization of Equalitarian Family Norms." *Journal of Marriage and Family Living* 20 (February): 53–58.

Fast, I. and A. C. Cain. 1966. "The Stepparent Role: Potential for Disturbances in Family Functioning." *American Journal of Orthopsychiatry* 36 (April): 485–91.

Fox, Robin. 1967. *Kinship and Marriage.* Baltimore: Penguin.

Gerth, Hans and C. Wright Mills. 1953. *Character and Social Structure.* New York: Harcourt, Brace & Co.

Glenn, N. 1975. "The Contribution of Marriage to the Psychological Well-Being of Males and Females." *Journal of Marriage and the Family* 37 (August): 594–601.

Glenn, N. and C. Weaver. 1977. "The Marital Happiness of Remarried Divorced Persons." *Journal of Marriage and the Family* 39 (May): 331–37.

Goetting, Ann. 1978a. "The Normative Integration of the Former Spouse Relationship."

Paper presented at the annual meeting of the American Sociological Association. San Francisco, September 4–8.

———. 1978b. "The Normative Integration of Two Divorce Chain Relationships." Paper presented at the annual meeting of the Southwestern Sociological Association, Houston, April 12–15.

Goldstein, Joseph, and Jay Katz. 1965. *The Family and the Law.* New York: Free Press.

Goode, William J. 1956. *Women in Divorce.* New York: Free Press.

Hoffman, S. 1977. "Marital Instability and the Economic Status of Women." *Demography* 14 (February): 67–76.

Hollingshead, A. B. 1952. "Marital Status and Wedding Behavior." *Marriage and Family Living* (November): 308–11.

Jacobson, Paul H. 1959. *American Marriage and Divorce.* New York: Rinehart.

Lasch, Christopher. 1977. *Haven in a Heartless World: The Family Besieged.* New York: Basic.

Locke, Harvey, J. 1951. *Predicting Adjustment in Marriage: A Comparison of a Divorced and a Happily Married Group.* New York: Holt.

McCarthy, J. F. 1977. "A Comparison of Dissolution of First and Second Marriages." Paper presented at the 1977 annual meeting of the Population Association of America, St. Louis, April 21–23.

Mead, M. 1970. "Anomalies in American Postdivorce Relationships." Pp. 107–25 in *Divorce and After,* edited by Paul Bohannan. New York: Doubleday.

Monahan, T. P. 1958. "The Changing Nature and Instability of Remarriages." *Eugenics Quarterly* 5:73–85.

Norton, A. J and P. C. Glick. 1976. "Marital Instability: Past, Present, and Future." *Journal of Social Issues* 32 (Winter): 5–20.

Nye, F. Ivan and Felix M. Berardo. 1973. *The Family: Its Structure and Interaction.* New York: Macmillan.

Overall, J. E. 1971. "Associations between Marital History and the Nature of Manifest Psychopathology." *Journal of Abnormal Psychology* 78 (2): 213–21.

Renne, K. S. 1971. "Health and Marital Experience in an Urban Population." *Journal of Marriage and the Family* 33 (May): 338–50.

Safilios-Rothschild, Constantina. 1970. "The Study of Family Power Structure: A Review 1960–1969." *Journal of Marriage and the Family* 32 (November): 539–52.

Shorter, Edward. 1975. *The Making of the Modern Family.* New York: Basic.

Smith, William C. 1953. *The Stepchild.* Chicago: University of Chicago Press.

U.S. Bureau of the Census. 1973. *U.S. Census of the Population: 1970. Persons by Family Characteristics.* Final Report PC(2)-4B. Washington, DC: Government Printing Office

———. 1976. *Number, Timing, and Duration of Marriages and Divorces in the United States: June 1975.* Current Population Reports, Series P-20, No, 297. Washington DC: Government Printing Office.

U.S. National Center for Health Statistics. 1953. *Vital Statistics of the United States, 1950. Vol. 2. Marriage, Divorce, Natality, Fetal Mortality, and Infant Mortality Data.* Washington DC: Government Printing Office.

———. 1977. *Visual Statistic Report. Advance Report. Final Marriage Statistics, 1975.* Washington, DC: Government Printing Office.

Weitzman, L. J. 1974. "Legal Regulation of Marriage: Tradition and Change." *California Law Review* 62: 1169–1288.

Young, Michael and Peter Wilmott. 1973. *The Symmetrical Family.* New York: Pantheon.